THE Encyclopedia of Baby and Child Care

THE Encyclopedia of Baby and Child Care

by
LENDON H. SMITH, M.D.

A Warner Communications Company

Warner Books Edition

This Warner Books Edition is published by arrangement with Prentice-Hall, Inc.

Warner Books, Inc., 666 Fifth Avenue, New York, N. Y. 10103.

A Warner Communications Company

Cover design by New Studio, Inc.

Book design by Helen Roberts

First Warner Books Printing: November 1980

10 9 8 7 6 5 4

Printed in the United States of America

Library of Congress Cataloging in Publication Data

Smith, Lendon H 1921—
The encyclopedia of baby and child care.

Reprint of the ed. published by Prentice-Hall, Englewood Cliffs, N. J.
Bibliography: p.
Includes index.
1. Children—Care and hygiene. 2. Children—
Diseases. I. Title. [DNLM: 1. Child care—Encyclopedia—Popular works. 2. Infant care—Encyclopedias—Popular works. WS13 S654e 1972a]
RJ61.S662 1980 618.92 80-16846
ISBN 0-446-38336-8 (U.S.A.)
ISBN 0-446-38337-6 (Canada)

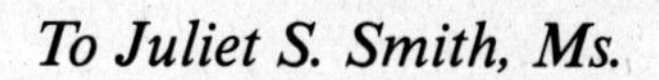

To Juliet S. Smith, Ms.

Acknowledgments

My thanks to my consultants, specialists, and bright practical leaders in their fields who reviewed various sections of this book.

S. Gorham Babson, M.D., Professor of Pediatrics, University of Oregon Medical School, Portland, Oregon

Jack E. Battalia, M.D., Clinical Instructor in Surgery, University of Oregon Medical School, Portland, Oregon

John W. Bussman, M.D., Associate Clinical Professor of Pediatrics, University of Oregon Medical School, Portland, Oregon

Clyde H. DuVall, Jr., M.D., Portland, Oregon

Peggy Copple Ferry, M.D., Assistant Professor of Pediatrics and Neurology; Assistant Professor, Crippled Children's Division, University of Oregon Medical School, Portland, Oregon

Herbert Wayne Goodman, D.D.S., Portland, Oregon

Marvin Greenbaum, Ph.D., Adjunct Professor of Psychology, University of Oregon, Eugene, Oregon

Frederick A. J. Kingery, M.D., Clinical Professor of Dermatology, University of Oregon Medical School, Portland, Oregon

Harvey D. Klevit, M.D., Permanente Hospital, Portland, Oregon; Associate Clinical Professor of Pediatrics, University of Oregon Medical School, Portland, Oregon

Paul B. Myers, M.D., Assistant Clinical Professor of Otolaryngology, University of Oregon Medical School, Portland, Oregon

Richard W. Olmstead, M.D., Professor and Head, Department of Pediatrics, University of Oregon Medical School, Portland, Oregon

Robert M. Rankin, M.D., Clinical Instructor in Orthopedics, University of Oregon Medical School, Portland, Oregon

Ivan L. Sandoz, M.D., Assistant Clinical Professor of Urology, University of Oregon Medical School, Portland, Oregon, and

Arthur J. Seaman, M.D., Head, Division of Hematology; Professor of Medicine, University of Oregon Medical School, Portland, Oregon

Where disagreement occurred, it was resolved with compromise or deletion. If any errors have remained, however, I am to blame, and the publisher will allow changes and additions in future printings.

My thanks also go to the following ladies for some tedious nitpicking hours: Jackie Fisk, Virginia Wrightson, Sally Judd, Mazie Sakai, Mary DesCamp.

Nancy Elsner looked at every letter and prevented things like the "public bone" from distracting the reader.

Peggy Moss is the glue that has held this whole thing (and me) together until it was bound.

—God bless you all!

Contents

Introduction: How to Use This Book

This encyclopedia is not intended to replace your family doctor or your pediatrician, just to help you know when you need his help—and when you don't. Also, it should help you gain some insight into how your child's body operates, how he grows and develops, and how your care and feeding affect his health and behavior.

There may seem to be a fearsome array of diseases and dangers in the following pages, but you shouldn't feel that they are all out there, threatening, waiting to grab you. It's just that because the human being is such a fantastically complex organism, there are many things that can go wrong with it. I have tried to give you a representative picture of what we doctors *do* see, because a working knowledge of how the body goes wrong helps you remember how to keep it running *right.* (There are all sorts of tests, vitamins, and simple hygienic procedures that parents often overlook because they're unaware of the consequences.)

Also, parents often wonder if "the doctor's telling me everything." When he's seen hundreds of cases of chickenpox, the doctor may not think it's necessary to go into the difference between this common disease and smallpox, but a parent may want to know nonetheless. This book, then, should take some of the job of explanation off your pediatrician's shoulders. When your child comes down with a cough, you can eliminate the more frightening possibilities to your own satisfaction. You should let the doctor make the diagnosis, of course, but in the meantime, you can rest assured that that cough isn't nearly as serious as you first worried it *might* be. So, short of some conditions which are so rare as to be almost irrelevant, I have tried to give you as complete a picture as possible of what can conceivably be amiss. I hope to dispel some old wives' tales and permit the troubled parent to assume her role of the interpreter of her child's behavior for the doctor. Parents might be able to correct a condition with home remedies and not need to call for more professional advice.

This book can be used in any of three ways:

1. If you want to find out quickly about a specific topic—let's say, mumps—look it up in the index in the back of the book for page reference.

2. If your child has certain symptoms—say, fever—and you wonder what might be causing them, look up the *main* symptom either in the index or in the outlines at the beginning of each section. By checking the various entries associated with those symptoms you may be able to narrow down the possibilities. You may find it is something you can treat at home (using Section 4). You may, of course, be unable to rule out something frightening, in which case your doctor must be consulted.

3. If you are just interested in understanding the interrelationship between discipline and guilt, for instance, you can just browse. Each entry is cross-referenced so that you can travel easily from "Anemia" to such related topics as "Diet" and "Blood cells." Just by dipping in wherever you like, and following the cross-reference trail as far as you like, you can build up a thorough understanding of your child's "inner ecology." As you will notice, no one topic is isolated unto itself; each depends on, develops into, or stems from something else, and the book is designed with this in mind.

The outlines that precede each section list some very rare, serious possibilities, but equal listing does not imply equal frequency. (When first confronted with a patient with a headache, we think "allergy" and not "brain tumor.")

Occasionally symptoms are listed in the outlines, where you might find them easily. In general, Roman (plain) type means a **bold-face** entry in the text following the outline. A cross reference—for example, "(Section 9)"—in the outline means the entry is discussed in another section, but is relevant to the symptoms being considered. *Italicized* entries are usually subheads discussed under the bold-face entries. An *italicized* word in the text means that the item is discussed elsewhere. For the page number, look in the index in the back.

I found it difficult to justify the inclusion of some diseases in some sections. We think of tuberculosis as a respiratory infection (Section 9), but a child may not cough when ill with TB. Weakness and paralysis must involve both nerves (Section 15) and muscles (Section 7), so redundancy will be common. A rare disease, "porphyria," may first appear as a skin problem (Section 6) or as a behavior problem (Section 16), but the first sign may be red urine, so the disease is in the Urinary section (Section 13). My attempts to make the body "neat" may only serve to show how beautifully complicated the human is.

You may not find all the subentries as **bold-face** entries in the text, but referring to a closely related time should get some answer. For example, read all of "Behavior disorders" (Section 16) before looking for a specific item; read all of "Gait" (Section 7) if your child has a limp.

Again, the doctor likes to (and should) make the diagnosis. The wise parent can help him do this by listing for him the various observed phenomena that permit but one conclusion; for example, "My child has an itchy anus, wakes up at night, complains of stomachaches, and grinds his teeth when he is asleep." The doctor can answer that with but one diagnosis: "Pinworms."

If this book helps you get along better with your child's doctor, helps you worry less, and helps you understand the complex interrelationships of your child's mind and body, then we'll have achieved what we set out to do. The publishers intend to revise it periodically to keep it all up-to-date, so if you have suggestions or comments, please let me know. Many of the observations and insights in this book came through the courtesy of parents like yourself.

LENDON H. SMITH, M.D.

THE Encyclopedia of Baby and Child Care

PART ONE

WHEN YOU WANT TO KNOW QUICKLY

SECTION 1

Emergencies, First Aid, and Poisonings *

A. Accidents

B. Battered child

C. Skin

Abrasions
Angioedema (Hypersensitivity, Section 3)
Bites
Bleeding (Section 8)
Burns
Chemical
Cuts
Cyanosis (Sections 5, 8, 9)
Fingernail or toenail injury (Subungual hematoma)
Fish hook
Frostbite
Gangrene
Genital lacerations
Hemorrhage (Cuts, also Sections 5, 8)
Hives (Section 6)
Puncture wounds
Stings (see Bites)
Sunburn

D. Bones and joints

Ankle (also Section 7)
Baseball finger (also Section 7)
Broken bones
Clavicle (also Birth injury, Section 5)
Elbow (Subluxation of radial head)
March fracture (Section 7)
Rib fracture
Wrist bone

E. Head injuries

Ear
Foreign bodies (also Section 14)
Eye
Abrasion
Chemical burn
Foreign body (also Section 14)
Mouth
Electric burn
Frenulum tear (Section 14)
Puncture
Nose
Epistaxis (Nosebleed)
Foreign body
Injury (also Section 5)

*Read **Accidents** first.

Skull Fracture
(also Head injuries)
Teeth (Section 14)
Avulsion (Section 14)
Displaced (Section 14)
Tongue bites and trauma

F. Neck

Spinal cord injuries (Section 15)
Wry neck (Section 7)

G. Chest (also Section 9)

Sudden cough, wheeze, cyanosis, pain
Asthma (Section 9)
Congestive heart failure (Section 8)
Croup (Section 9)
Epiglottitis (Section 9)
Foreign body in larynx or trachea (Section 9)
Foreign body in bronchus (Section 9)
Inhaled objects
Pericarditis (Section 8)
Pneumothorax (Section 8)
Pulmonary embolism (Section 8)
Pulmonary hypertension (Section 8)
Rib fracture

H. Abdomen

Bleeding into intestinal tract (Section 12)
Intraabdominal bleeding (also Infectious mononucleosis, Section 9)
Pain (Section 12)
Swallowed foreign body (also Esophagus, Foreign bodies, Section 12)

I. Genitals

Female
Cuts
Genital lacerations
Sexual molestation
Male
Foreskin stuck (Paraphinosis, Section 13)
Hernia (Section 12)
Painful testicle (Torsion, Section 13)

J. Loss of consciousness

Coma (Section 15)
Convulsions (Section 15)
Diabetes mellitus (Section 10)
Drowning
Electric shock
Fainting (also Syncope, Section 15)
Heat exhaustion
Heat stroke
Hypoglycemia (Section 10)
Poisoning
Shock

K. Poisons

Acrodynia
Drugs
Food poisoning (Section 12)
Heavy metal
Arsenic
Lead
Mercury (also *Acrodynia*)
Zinc

Household
Plants
Remedies
Exchange transfusion (Section 18)
Peritoneal dialysis (Section 12)
Syrup of Ipecac

L. First aid

Artificial respiration
Broken bones
Burns
Cardiac massage
Cuts
Drowning
Spinal injuries (Section 15)

M. Airborne

Carbon monoxide
Gasoline fume inhalation
Nitrogen dioxide
Radiation
Radioactive fallout
Strontium 90

N. Miscellaneous

Batteries
Firearms

Abdominal pain—see Section 12.

Abrasion is the loss of the superficial skin layers due to friction (e.g., skinned knee or elbow after a fall on cement sidewalk). It appears as a raw area with oozing of serum and blood.

Cleansing with water is essential. Several quarts of lukewarm water should be poured over the raw area despite the child's objections. Soap is not essential and may even irritate. A special effort should be made to remove dirt, grime, and sand as foreign objects preclude healing. Bits of asphalt may have to be teased (or scrubbed) out; if allowed to remain, they will be incorporated in the new skin and produce a dark cast in the area, like a tattoo.

The area is patted dry and a large, thick, dry, sterile nonadherent dressing is placed over the wound to prevent bacteria from being introduced, but also to permit some aeration of the raw surface. Newer bandages are nonsticking, but still porous. (Some prefer a thin layer of an antibiotic ointment like Neosporin®, Spectrocin®, Garamycin® on the raw surface first to preclude chance of infection and allow some mobility to the area, but the ointments may macerate the wound and interfere with healing; there is also a risk of sensitizing the skin to these medicines.)

This initial dressing must be kept dry for about four to six days, at which time it may be changed. If a nonadherent dressing is used, it will not have to be soaked off. If the abrasion is not covered with new skin, another dressing is reapplied.

Dressings provide a clean covering to prevent the introduction of bacteria, absorb serum and blood from the raw surface and immobilize the area as motion impedes healing.

Do not use waxed paper or plastic over a burn or abrasion. It may be easier to remove, but the occlusive dressing, serum, and blood provide an ideal culture medium for bacterial growth despite antibiotic ointments. Do not use iodine, alcohol, mercury tinctures, and such; these irritate more than help. If after two or three days no signs of healing are present or if the area becomes *more* tender, *more* red, and an increase of yellow or green exudate appears, medical attention is necessary, and possibly hot packs and internal antibiotics. Lack of attention may lead to *impetigo,* absorption of toxins, and *glomerulonephritis.*

Corneal abrasion (involving the area of the eyeball in front of the pupil) is usually painful and requires medical attention.

Accidents are the major cause of death and deformity from childhood through adolescence, now that infections are under better control. Most are preventable. Each age has its favorite: the one- to four-year-old is more susceptible to poisonings, burns, aspiration (breathing poisonous fumes or inhaling foreign objects), and falls. The adolescent is more likely to be hurt in motor-vehicle accidents, shot by an "un-loaded" gun, or drown.

Car accidents kill more than 50,000 people a year; the number with permanent scarring or disfigurement is several times that. Better highways and safer cars will improve the statistics, but fewer drunks on the road might cut the toll in half.

The toddler should be protected from his own curiosity. What seems an obvious "no-no" to us is an attractive adventure to him.

Throw old medicines away. *Boric acid* is no longer considered a worthwhile medicine and is a poison. Baby *aspirin* should be purchased in small bottles (thirty or so tablets per bottle) or on paper strips. All purses should be up on a shelf or out of sight. *Gasoline, kerosene, paint thinner, furniture polish,* and other indigestibles should be stored in their own containers—*not* in pop bottles—and out of reach. *Lead* paint should not be used indoors or on children's furniture. Laundry products have to be stored out of reach. Have *syrup of ipecac* on hand to induce vomiting. (See *Poisons.*)

Protective play areas, indoors and out, should seal the toddler away from cars, steps, and sudden voids. Special car seats and seat belts are a must in cars. Everyone should strap his child into the seat of a car when traveling; in an automobile collision, a child's light body frequently ricochets through the interior of the car like a Ping-Pong ball.

Some families—and children—are more accident-prone than others. Awkward, *hyperactive,* and *brain-damaged* children are more likely to fall, stumble, blunder through a glass door or impulsively pull hot soup off the stove. (See *Teeth,* Section 14; *Cerebral dysfunction,* Section 15.)

You are supposed to teach your child the dangers of the world, but don't overdo your admonishments ("Don't stick beans up your nose") lest they act as inducements to experiment.

The wise mother might get down on her hands and knees at the level of her accident-prone, one- to three-year-old child and scoot around the floor. See what attractive, low-down nuisances there are in the house, such as detergents under the sink, bottles of kerosene and gasoline, various sharp objects. Make sure your baby cannot climb onto high furniture or cabinets. Remove doors from unused refrigerators, and have suitable locks or combinations on the medicine closet. Electric wall sockets should be covered. Always, always disconnect appliances from the wall socket; terrible mouth burns result when a toddler puts the "hot" end of an appliance cord in his mouth.

Acrodynia is a complex of symptoms due to *mercury poisoning* and/or sensitivity. Medical students learned the diagnostic giveaways by memorizing the five *P*'s: pain, perspiration, photophobia (the victim is hypersensitive to light), pigmentation, and pyorrhea. Although other heavy metal salt poisonings will give similar symptoms and signs, the syndrome has largely died out because mercury teething powders are no longer manufactured, but adults working with mercury salts should be adequately protected from this poison. Treatment is getting this poison out of the way and the avoidance of further contact. (See *Batteries.*)

Ankle is subject to many stresses. Sprained ankles are so common that it is surprising there is no uniform treatment. Some broken ankles will heal completely with no care, while a bad sprain (torn ligaments plus bleeding) may never heal exactly right even under constant orthopedic management. The doctor should be consulted in either case. (See *Ankle,* Section 7.)

A few basic rules for sprains: rest, do not let the ankle bear weight, ice for eight to twelve hours, and elevation for the first day are important first-aid measures. The brave adolescent who plays ball on an injured ankle so he won't be a quitter or sissy may wreck his future athletic career. If, on the third day, cautious weight bearing with the ankle supported with tape or Ace® bandage is painful, the foot should not be used. Mother Nature is telling the victim that healing has not yet taken place. X rays may or may not be necessary; a cast may hold things together to speed healing.

Artificial respiration is the mechanical or manual art of breathing for a victim who has ceased breathing due to drowning, heart attack, electrical shock, or injury.

It is obvious that an airway must be cleared from mouth to lungs by removing water, food, or vomit from the victim's mouth, pulling the tongue forward and arching the head backward. When air is blown in with mouth-to-mouth contact maintained (and the victim's nose pinched), the ribs or chest wall should move, showing

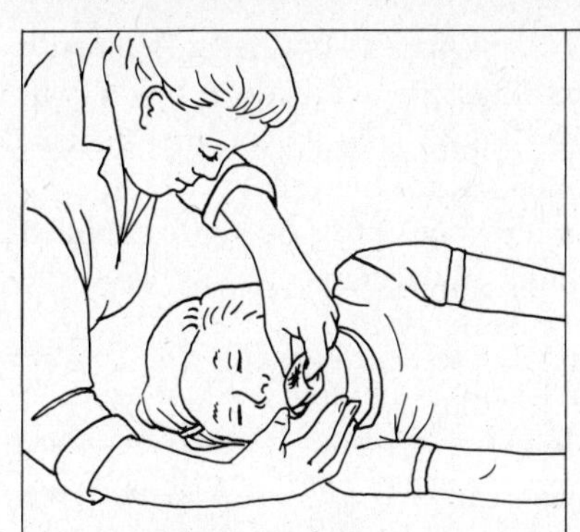

(a) With fingers, search the mouth for obstructions.

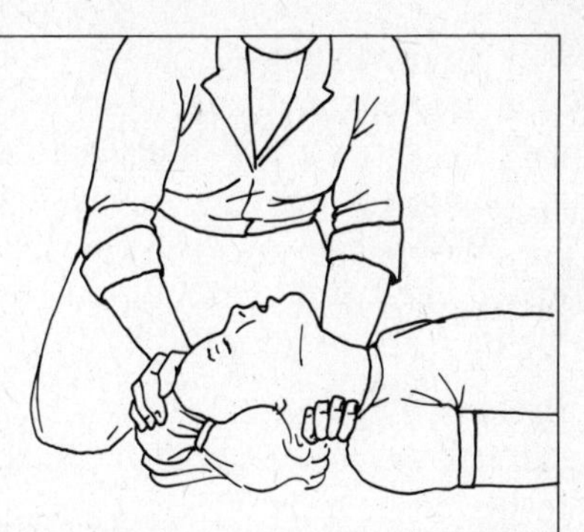

(b) Place child on back and tilt back head to keep tongue out of airway.

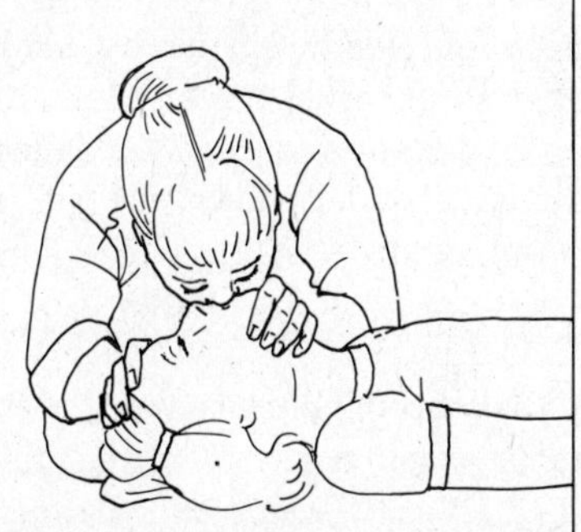

(c) With your mouth, force air into child's lungs by breathing into mouth and nose if baby or small child or...

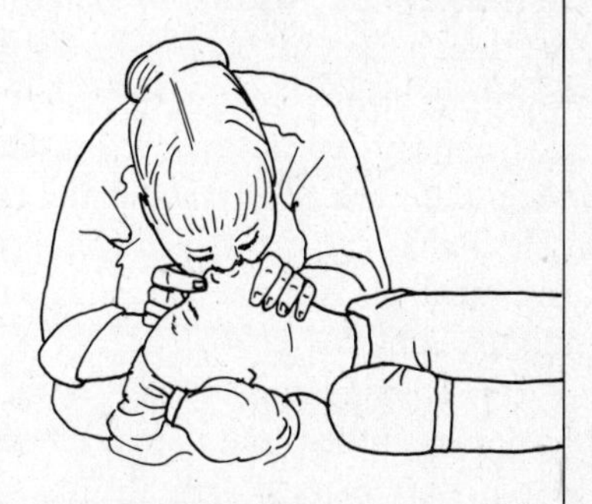

(d) ...breathing into mouth and pinching nose of larger child.

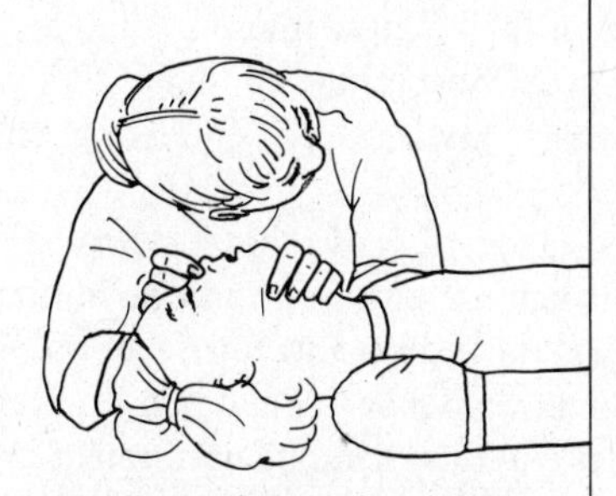

(e) Listen for deflation of lungs. Repeat every 3 seconds for infant, every 5 seconds for child, until breathing resumes.

ARTIFICIAL RESPIRATION
(mouth-to-mouth)

that air is getting to the lungs. This is repeated fifteen to twenty times a minute. If the heart is beating, the circulating blood will pick up oxygen from the lungs and deliver this important nutrient to the brain which cannot long function without oxygen.

With a baby or small child, some manual pressure can be applied to the chest wall to simulate breathing movements. In any case, the victim needs oxygen, and help should be obtained.

Baseball finger is a common chip fracture children sustain when a ball hits the end of an outstretched finger. The tendon, tightly attached to the bone, pulls off a small fragment at that point. Swelling, pain, and bruising are noted immediately. Splinting for three or four weeks is the usual requirement for normal healing. (See Section 7.)

Battered child is the new name given to a child, usually under two or three years of age, who has been physically beaten by adults. Multiple bruises, black eyes, fractured skull, broken arms, legs, and ribs appear repeatedly. The location and appearance of the injuries belie the history given by the parents: "He fell down the stairs," "He rolled off the table," "He fell out of bed." X rays reveal new and healing fractures at sites rarely hurt when a toddler falls or bumps himself.

It is small consolation to know that throughout history, children have been killed, mutilated, or beaten by their parents and that these parents are usually sick, drunk, or psychotic. It seems odd that some acceptable way has not been developed for parents to easily transfer their unwanted children to couples who are childless.

Most normal parents become exasperated, frustrated, and occasionally screaming mad because of their children's behavior. Most will—if normal—admit, with some guilt feelings, that "I could wring his neck." But normal parents don't. Most children sense this ambivalent love-hate feeling and display just enough endearing traits to balance the aggravating ones.

Because we are our brothers' keepers, laws have been passed to protect plaintiffs in suits brought against adults who beat, mutilate, or abuse children. Court action can be brought against parents and their children removed when medical evidence indicates a child has been battered. Placing a child back in this harsh environment only puts him at risk for another physical attack which might end fatally.

It sounds odd for a mother to abuse her child and then bring him to the doctor, but it happens just often enough to suggest that she *wants* someone to find out and put a stop to it. Somehow, through the fog of her disturbed psyche, she is signaling for help. (See *Cruelty to children,* Section 16.)

Batteries contain mercury. The dry cell used for flashlights has an insignificant amount of mercury, but the small mercury cell battery used for transistor radios and hearing aids has a lethal dose. If a child swallows the latter, he may be in danger if the casing is broken. These batteries will occasionally explode, so they should never be discarded in stove or fireplace; in addition to the explosion, there is the danger of mercury fumes.

Bites

Animal bites range from the barely noted blue bruises of the tooth marks of the playful family dog to flesh ripped off by the savage bear. Most are harmless puncture wounds and contiguous abrasions which require only regular cleansing plus a *tetanus* booster (usually given as a DT, or *diphtheria-tetanus,* if it has been more than five years since the last booster), but some bites will raise the fear of the dread *rabies* (see Section 2). Animal bites are usually less likely to cause a skin infection than human bites, simply because animal teeth, spaced further apart, do not harbor as much bacteria. If a bite becomes infected, it usually becomes red, swollen, tender, and exudes some purulent material. Treatment as outlined under *Abscess* (Section 6) would be appropriate.

Many surgeons feel more secure giving the DT shots if it is a puncture wound. A tear, scratch, or abrasion would be less likely to need protection from tetanus. If the doctor can be reassured that the patient has had three or four DT shots and the most recent one was five years before, he can safely omit it. Most booster shots can be given within a day or two of the bite. However, each wound must be evaluated individually by the treating physician.

Chiggers, fleas, mosquitoes, and *nits* produce very irritating local reactions in susceptible people.

Insect bites are common in children playing outdoors in the summer. The danger of disease transmission is minimal in our country, but *malaria, encephalitis, typhus, Rocky Mountain spotted fever, yellow fever,* and *tularemia* are occasionally reported.

The bite itself is usually very pruritic to children, who will scratch the top layer of skin off and introduce an infection. (See *Impetigo,*

Section 6.) The location of the itchy papules is usually where clothing ends—ankles, neck, wrists, beltline. The lesions are frequently lined up in a triad with one-fourth inch separating spaces, as if to represent breakfast, lunch, and dinner for the biter. The bitee may overreact with a large, hivelike wheal due to an allergic histamine release. Daily *antihistamine* ingestion may abort this uncomfortable reaction. *Cortisone* ointments may ease the local inflammation. Some have been able to prevent the bite by the oral intake of vitamin B or brewers' yeast tablets every four hours. This gets to the skin and so nauseates the insect that he moves on. Obviously, perfumed soaps and hair sprays will attract the bugs.

Bee stings in this country cause more deaths than snake bites. People can be severely allergic to bee venom, and for some reason, adolescent males react more severely than anyone else. *Antihistamines* should be given immediately after the bite of any stinging insect. This sometimes reduces the swelling, itching, and pain that develop anywhere from a few hours to a whole day later. But the person who has violent reaction such as generalized *hives,* swelling in the throat, or fainting, requires an *epinephrine* injection, and/or oxygen from a doctor. If a person has had such a generalized reaction, he should get immunizing shots to protect himself.

An emergency kit should be carried by those who have had a generalized reaction. It includes a torniquet, antihistamine, disposable syringe and needle, with *epinephrine* and *isoproterenol* tablets which should be allowed to dissolve under the tongue.

Scorpion bite usually causes only a local pain and swelling, but some scorpion poisons have an affinity for the nervous system, causing a motor paralysis and convulsions. As death may occur in young children, a specific antivenin should be given. Intravenous fluids with *glucose* and ingestion of *phenobarbital* will usually control the symptoms.

Snake bites are common. The garter snakes, or those without fangs (they just have even teeth), are harmless; no treatment is necessary. The poisonous ones, rattlesnakes, copperheads, and coral snakes, cause about fifteen deaths per year in the United States out of about 6,000 reported bites. Early spring is the most lethal time as the poison sacs are full of venom after the winter hibernation.

Identifying the snake is important for diagnosis and treatment. The paired fang punctures in the skin give away the rattlesnakes and copperhead varieties, but the coral snake may give but a slight wound. The latter snake, however, can be identified by the black snout and adjacent red and yellow stripes. ("Red next to yellow, kill the fellow; red next to black, venom lack.") The colorful, innocuous king snake has a red snout and the red and black areas are adjacent.

Symptoms usually occur within a few minutes of the bite. A burning pain and local swelling soon involve the whole limb. Hemorrhages occur. Vomiting of blood, shock, and respiratory paralysis suggest a fatal outcome. A hemorrhagic toxin and a neurotoxin are found in snake venom.

The victim must be *carried* to the hospital, as activity speeds the venom spread. A tourniquet should be applied only snugly—not with enough pressure to occlude arterial flow. Ice may be helpful. Cutting open the skin at the fang-hole sites and sucking out some of the venom is helpful if there is considerable swelling. Some advocate surgical excision of the whole area (two-inch plug) if it can be done within two hours.

The above measures should be taken but they must not delay getting the patient to a facility where antivenin therapy is available.

Spider bites are painful but rarely fatal. The black widow spider's venom produces immediate local pain, weakness, and severe muscle and abdominal cramps. Specific antivenin and calcium given intravenously will slow down the action. The hairy brown spider (found in the southern part of the Midwest in the United States) produces an ugly sore that takes weeks to heal. Early surgical removal of the bite area would speed healing.

Tarantula bites are painful, produce local redness and swelling. Generalized reactions have not been reported.

Tick paralysis is due to the injection of the saliva of the wood tick. If a patient in tick country develops muscle weakness, he should be inspected thoroughly for a tick. Rapid recovery of function usually follows its removal.

The Rocky Mountain wood tick may carry *spotted fever.* (See Section 2.)

Travelers in tick country should protect themselves with high boots and adequate clothing that has been treated with repellents (Benzyl benzoate). They should inspect themselves thoroughly twice a day for ticks, especially in the groin, armpits, nape of neck, and scalp.

The tick can be asphyxiated by coating it with heavy ointment. After about twenty minutes, it can be removed more easily. It is best to remove the tick *in toto* as infection may follow retention of parts. Some protection of local skin at the bite site and of the tick remover must be afforded as the tick feces may carry infection.

Broken bones are often quite obvious when they occur in an arm or leg, but hairline fractures can appear merely with pain and swelling. They all need professional care. The patient should be transported with suitable splinting to a hospital or doctor's office. The obvious bone deformities should be splinted without any attempt to manipulate them. "Splint them where they lie." If a fracture is suspected, careful X rays should be taken because of the need for proper positioning of the bones while healing. Perhaps the most effective "splinting" method that can be done at home is to use a rolled-up newspaper, blanket, or even a pillow to softly support the break. Careful splinting prevents a simple fracture from becoming compound—that is, having the bone end push through the skin. This latter condition may result in infection, which complicates healing. (See *Ankle, Baseball finger, March fracture,* Section 7, *Clavicle.*)

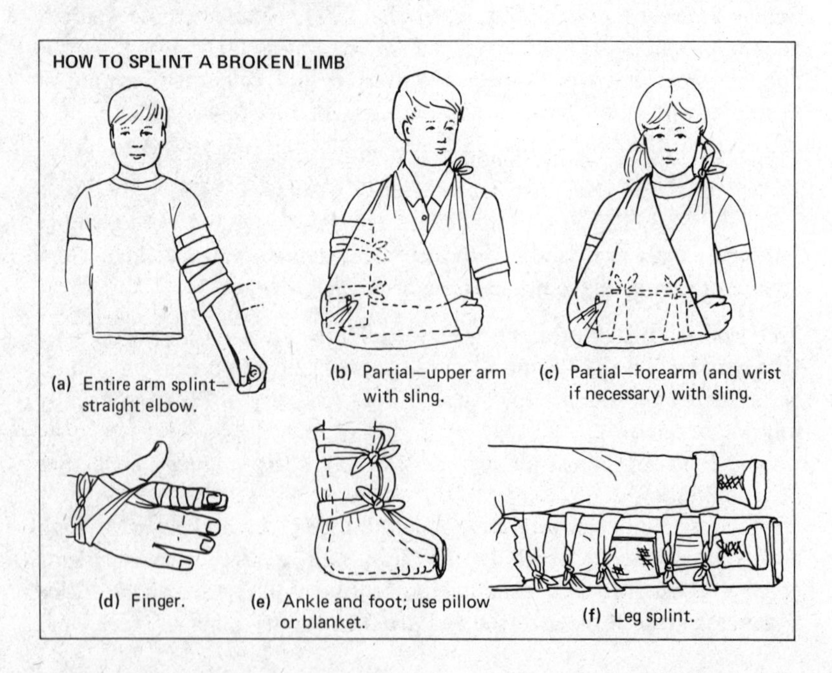
HOW TO SPLINT A BROKEN LIMB

(a) Entire arm splint—straight elbow.

(b) Partial—upper arm with sling.

(c) Partial—forearm (and wrist if necessary) with sling.

(d) Finger.

(e) Ankle and foot; use pillow or blanket.

(f) Leg splint.

Burns should be treated immediately, even before the doctor is summoned, by immersing the affected part in ice water—not just cold water but ice water. If it is a hand or a foot, some ice in a bucket of water will do. If the extremity is kept immersed from one to four hours, the cold may keep a first-degree burn from becoming a second or a second from becoming a third. If the burned area is on the body, an icepack can be made from a wet washcloth with ice in it, perhaps covered with some sort of plastic, and a big towel on top to hold it in place. Again, leave it on from one to four hours. Make sure the frigid water reaches the skin. This usually soothes the pain and somehow interferes with the formation of poison or toxin produced by burned tissue. A sterile dry dressing is next applied (see *Abrasion*). Never use butter, lard, grease, or ointments on a burn—only the ice or cleansing water or the sterile dressing. With large burns requiring hospital attention, a clean sheet is best to wrap up the burn during transport. Any gunk on the skin must be cleaned off which adds further trauma.

Chemical burns must be washed with running water immediately. This diluting and neutralizing effect must be continued for at least thirty minutes. Neutralizing an acid with an alkali (or alkali with an acid) may cause further injury from the heat of the chemical reaction, and the delay caused by looking for the suitable antidote allows for continued tissue destruction. Flood it with water!

Carbon monoxide is a poisonous gas formed by the incomplete burning of carbon (carbon dioxide is completely oxidized), commonly found in auto exhaust. Carbon monoxide competes with oxygen in the blood's red cells, and thus the body cells become starved for oxygen. Inhalation symptoms are related to the amount inhaled, varying from headache, weakness, and giddiness, to coma and respiratory cessation. A peculiar cherry-red color may be noted on the lips of a victim. Treatment is removal from the gas and inhalation of oxygen.

Cardiac massage is the emergency effort to compress the pulseless heart so as to eject blood into the aorta. In the infant, intermittent finger pressure on the lower third of the sternum at the rate of one hundred per minute may keep the circulation going until the heart begins its automatic beat. In the older child, both hands (the heel of one hand on top of the other) are required to press on the breast bone at the rate of sixty to eighty times per minute.

Chest pain—see Section 8, Part I, and Section 9

Clavicles, or collarbones, are located between the shoulder and the top of the breastbone. They are the easiest bones to break and the easiest to heal with little orthopedic assistance. The bone may be broken during the birth of a large baby through a small or contracted pelvis. This injury usually results from a fall in which the patient strikes his shoulder. The collarbone cracks or splinters, and the bone ends override. The victim may have few symptoms except a tender discolored knob at the site for a few days. Healing takes place with no residual deformity. The callus of hard calcium may be detectable a few days after the injury and remain for four to eight weeks.

Cuts are tears in the skin, most frequent in the two-year-old child who stumbles, falls, and opens a gash on his forehead. The opening gapes apart due to the elastic nature of the skin; blood flows freely and often alarmingly. Head lacerations bleed especially vigorously because of the abundant blood supply, but for the same reason they heal rapidly.

Basic steps are to clean the area with running water and apply a compression dressing to squash the blood vessels flat, thus controlling the bleeding. The next step is to determine whether the cut needs to be sutured. Surgeons like to suture things, so they will if you ask them; but doctors are finding that many cuts can be efficiently pulled together by taping. This is a satisfactory compromise, because cuts on the head heal rapidly. Besides, taping can be done with less physical and emotional trauma for the young child. In any event, some decision has to be made before six or eight hours have elapsed. If the wound is left open after that time, infection can set in, and sometimes the wound *has* to be left open—which can mean scarring. It is routine to give a tetanus booster for any break in the skin, if the child has not received a booster within the previous five years.

When bleeding occurs, do not panic. Clean the wound; control bleeding with pressure and not a tourniquet; and make arrangements for medical help, whether it is suturing or taping.

Genital lacerations in the female usually result from sitting down suddenly on the edge of a box, a chair, or bike bar. Contusions, abrasions, and cuts may all be present. Suturing may be indicated if a large gap is present, although these tissues fall together and heal easily. If penetration is suspected (picket fence injury), a urologist may have to evaluate the integrity of the urethra.

Salty urine passing over the open sore is painful. A protective gob of an antibiotic ointment may ease the passage. Urination while sitting in a sitz bath will be more comfortable.

Drowning is death from asphyxia due to laryngeal spasm and/or water in the lungs and/or *ventricular fibrillation.* Once the near-drowned victim has been brought to shore, no time should be wasted with postural drainage. Every effort should be made to get oxygen to the brain. If the pupils are dilated and fixed, death probably has already occurred. If the patient is pulseless, cardiac massage is to be carried out simultaneously with mouth-to-mouth breathing. (See *Artificial respiration, Cardiac massage.*)

Ears, foreign bodies—see *Foreign bodies*

Elbow—see *Subluxation of the radial head*

Electric shock effects are related to the current flowing through the body rather than the voltage. Alternating current is more dangerous than direct current of the same voltage.

Death is assumed to be from *ventricular fibrillation* or respiratory paralysis. (See *Artificial respiration.*) Electrical burns are treated as in *Burns.*

Epistaxis is a nosebleed. It is sometimes difficult to stop. Nosebleeds are common in children during cold, dry weather, during the hot summer, or after slight trauma. Old tricks like placing a cold knife on the back of the neck or putting ice on the lip or gums are of doubtful value. Almost all nosebleeds originate from eroded capillaries on the first one inch of the nasal septum. Pressure must be applied *there* to flatten the capillaries. Make a tampon by wetting a piece of tissue or part of a cotton ball; it should be big enough just to slide into the nostril. Sometimes a lubricant will help; some favor putting a few drops of a nose-drop solution on the surface of the wad to act as a vasoconstrictor. Push this into the nose and then pinch the wings of the nose together snugly for ten to fifteen minutes. This should stop the bleeding. The patient should bend forward, not lie down; if blood drips out, increase the pressure. Leave the tampon in place for another ten minutes and then s-l-o-w-l-y withdraw it. This should leave a clear, open passageway free of clot. If a clot is allowed to form in the nose, it dries, cracks, and opens the vessels again. Some lubricant should be applied to the raw area for a week until healing is complete. If hemorrhage is frequent, cauterizing with a silver-nitrate stick may help.

Eye injuries—(See also *Eyes, Foreign bodies,* Section 14.) Traumatic abrasions to sclera usually leave a bright red area. Patching the eye after a suitable antibiotic ointment is applied is usually all that is necessary. The ophthalmologist should be consulted to prevent corneal scarring.

Chemicals in the eye should be washed out immediately to dilute the possible corrosive action on the conjunctiva. The running tap water should be maintained with forcible retraction of the lids for a full twenty minutes. Immediate action is important; then call the ophthalmologist. Foreign objects such as sand and cinders in the eye should be washed out. Continued irritation suggests an object stuck on the inside of the upper lid. The lid can be everted by having the patient look down; the upper lashes are grasped, and using a thin stick, roll the margin of the lid back over it, exposing the tarsal plate. The cinder can be teased off with a bit of cotton.

Penetrating eyeball injuries (BB shot) must be treated by an ophthalmologist.

Blows about the eye usually cause only *palpebral hematomata.* If double vision occurs, an orbital blowout fracture may have occurred. Surgery is indicated.

Fainting spells. The very young faint because of organic problems—*anemia,* disease, *epilepsy,* or *breath holding.* The adolescent is more likely to faint from *hysteria* or hyperventilation.

Fainting spells are fairly common in some children with an unstable neurovascular system. Fright, pain, or deep breathing will allow the blood vessels in the abdomen to dilate, effectively reducing the blood and oxygen supply to the brain. The child who cries when stuck for a blood sample or when given a shot will rarely faint. On the other hand, the stoical child who sits quietly during the procedure may turn pale and keel over on the floor two minutes later.

If no reasonable stimulus can be blamed for the episode, the victim should at least be checked for anemia. If fainting occurs on an empty stomach, a fasting blood sugar might be obtained. An *electroencephalogram* should be considered next if attacks are periodic and without an emotional inciting agent. (See *Syncope,* Section 15.)

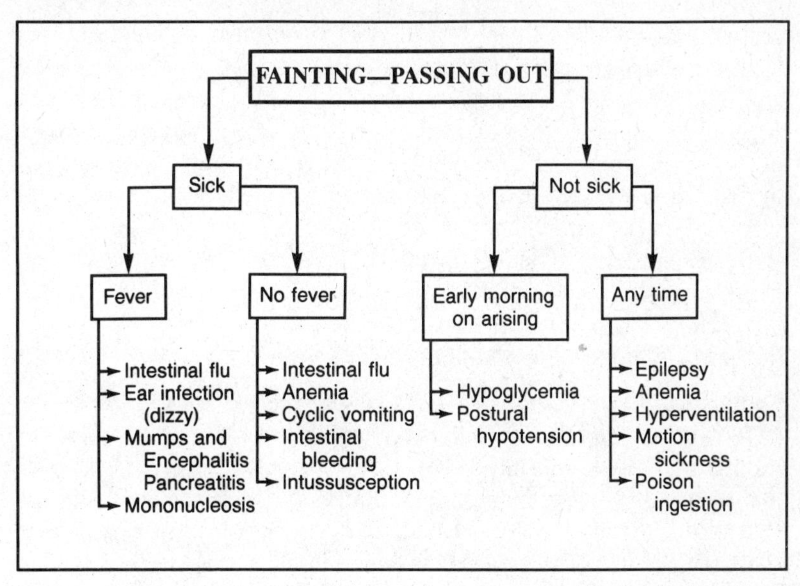

Firearms and "unloaded" guns are the cause of too many deaths and wounds. If they are in the house, no matter how securely locked up, the child, youth, or adolescent will eventually get his hands on them.

Farmers who need a handy weapon for animal predators must devise some method of separating ammunition and weapon that still allows for ready use to protect livestock. City folk should rely on police protection.

Fish hook, when stuck in the skin, must be pushed through until the barb is exposed. This is then cut off and the remainder is pulled back through from whence it came.

Foreign bodies—see location of foreign body: *Bronchi, Ear, Esophagus, Eye* in appropriate sections.

Foreign body in the nose is frequently found in an allergic child with an itchy nose; he has been warned not to pick his nose. He cannot ignore the sensation, so he gets around the admonishment by shoving something handy into his nose. Beans, beads, candy, nuts, thumbtacks, bits of paper, pills, buttons have all been used. The child refuses to admit his act or has forgotten it. After a few days an infection occurs, and a foul-smelling (fetid), bloody, purulent discharge occurs from the involved nostril (usually only one).

The messy glob can defy extraction. An old doctor in the South suggested "blowing" the child's nose for him. Have the child lie down on his back, cover his nose with a tissue, occluding the uninvolved nostril, then with close mouth-to-mouth contact, blow sharply and vigorously. The air column turns about the palate and pushes out the mess into the tissue—hopefully. Tweezers might next be tried. If unsuccessful, the ear, nose, and throat doctor should be called. Anesthesia may be necessary.

Some allergy control would be advisable to prevent a recurrence.

Swallowed foreign object. If a child has swallowed his foreign object, it is worth remembering that the narrowest passage is between the mouth and the stomach. If he is able to eat a piece of bread or a teaspoon of applesauce on top of his marble or keychain, it implies that the shiny little thing has at least reached his stomach. From there on, the rest of the journey is fairly simple. Occasionally a foreign object will get hung up at the anal sphincter, and sometimes has to be teased out with a lubricated finger. Pennies and dimes seem to travel through easily. A nickel possibly could get hung up, and a quarter almost always does. For some reason, sharp objects such as thumbtacks and pins almost never penetrate the intestinal wall en route through the body. It seems to recoil from the sharp object, which will tumble on through, possibly to get stuck at the anal opening. (See *Foreign bodies, Esophagus,* Section 12.)

Foreign objects in the ears sometimes have to be washed out with a syringe, and occasionally a nose-and-throat doctor has to use specially devised forceps to retrieve them. Washing out vegetable matter (seeds) with water may allow the object to swell, making removal more difficult. (See *Ears,* Section 14.)

Objects that are inhaled are a special problem for the doctor who, under suitable anesthesia, has to go down into the bronchial tubing. Sudden onset of wheezing, coughing, turning blue, and gasping would usually give away the aspiration of a foreign object into the lung. (See *Larynx, Bronchi, Trachea,* Section 9.)

Frostbite is the formation of ice crystals in the skin cells and blood vessels due to exposure to low temperature. Redness, then pallor, occurs. Immediate immersion in hot water (103° to 105°) is the best treatment. Comfortably hot bath water is 95° to 97°. Twenty minutes are usually required to pink up the nail beds. The more rapid rewarming, the better the results. The ice must be melted, and oxygen must reenter the tissues. The frozen tissues must *not* be rubbed; they are already damaged enough.

Gangrene is death of tissue. It usually follows *burns, frostbite,* bacteremia (bacteria lodge in a capillary, plug it, destroy it, and prevent nourishment to the tissue supplied by that capillary), and infections due to contaminated wounds. *Antibiotics* may destroy bacteria responsible for the infection, and the new hyperbaric treatment (subjecting the patient to high oxygen pressure) may revitalize near-dead tissue and preclude amputation of the affected part.

Gasoline fume inhalation may cause sudden loss of consciousness or even death. Moderate inhalation produces euphoria, drunkenness, *ataxia,* and confusion. (See *Glue sniffing,* Section 16.) Chronic exposure may cause *anemia, polyneuritis,* memory loss, *headache,* and muscular weakness.

Fresh air and psychological intervention are required.

Genital lacerations—see *Cuts*

Head injuries usually cause some concussion. Concussion is a swelling of the brain, the symptoms of which are headache, drowsiness, and vomiting. The skull may or may not be cracked; X rays of the skull are not as important as the symptoms. The pupils may or may not be dilated, constricted, or unequal. Concussion in most cases lasts six to ten hours, after which the victim's symptoms improve. If after twelve to twenty-four hours the headache, drowsiness, and vomiting become worse, then bleeding into or over the surface of the brain must be considered. It is not necessary to keep the patient awake in the first few hours to observe symptoms; it is probably better to allow him to sleep, but to arouse him every twenty to thirty minutes to evaluate his level of consciousness. (See *Skull fracture.*)

Heat exhaustion reveals itself by falling blood pressure due to intense dilation of the blood vessels of the skin. Decreased blood supply to the brain causes convulsion and coma. Treatment is total immersion in ice water and fluids given orally or intravenously.

Heat stroke. An average active boy must produce and evaporate over a pint of sweat an hour to keep his temperature down. If the day is humid or he is fully clothed, he cannot vaporize the sweat. Heat stroke is the result of increasing heat production (exercise) and decreasing heat loss (high environmental temperature and humidity, plus insulating clothing). All this plus inadequate water and salt replacement leads to collapse and death if treatment is not provided.

If temperature is above 70° or so, football practice, for instance, should be postponed or conducted in shorts so that the skin can be exposed to the air for vaporization of sweat. Usually the body has enough salt stored so that only water need be provided and encouraged during play.

Heimlich manuever—see illustration opposite

Hemorrhage is the egress of blood out of the containing vessels. (See *Bleeding,* Section 8, also *Cuts.*)

Intraabdominal bleeding is usually the result of a severe blow to this unprotected area (car, sledding, or skiing accident). The "wind" is knocked out of the victim, but after an hour of rest he fails to perk up. Rapid pulse, falling blood pressure, pallor, lead to shock in minutes or hours (arterial hemorrhage or slow venous leak). An enlarged spleen from *infectious mononucleosis* or *leukemia* are most vulnerable, but a cracked floating rib could lacerate a kidney. Intestines could be lacerated.

Hospitalization is mandatory to monitor the blood pressure, pulse, and blood count. Surgery is indicated when shock is corrected.

Mouth electric burns occur when the child places a "live" extension cord plug in his mouth. The ice treatment for burns should be tried, but is of little benefit. Plastic surgery is usually necessary later.

Mouth puncture wounds usually gush with blood immediately, but are treated symptomatically unless bleeding does not subside to a slight ooze in thirty minutes. No local treatment is necessary. On the third day a white clot is seen at the site; this is not pus but a normal clot with the red cells washed away.

A tetanus booster is indicated if none has been given for five years.

Nitrogen dioxide causes silo-filler's disease. Nitric oxide in fresh silage forms this gas when it comes in contact with oxygen in the air. It is heavier than air so it settles on the surface of the crop in

HEIMLICH MANEUVER

Stand behind the child, extend your arms under child's arms.

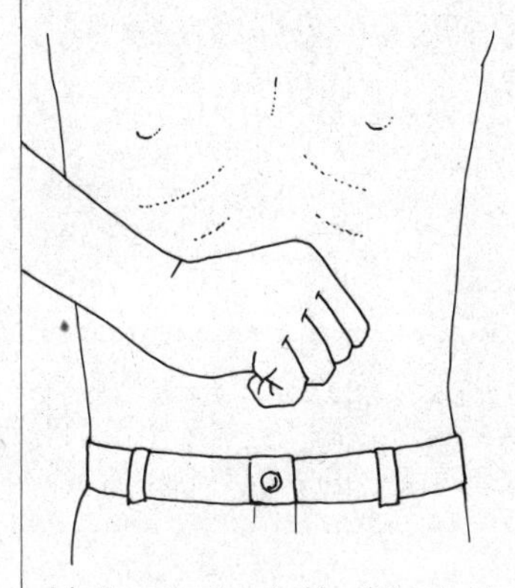

(a) Place the thumb side of the clenched fist between the rib cage and the navel.

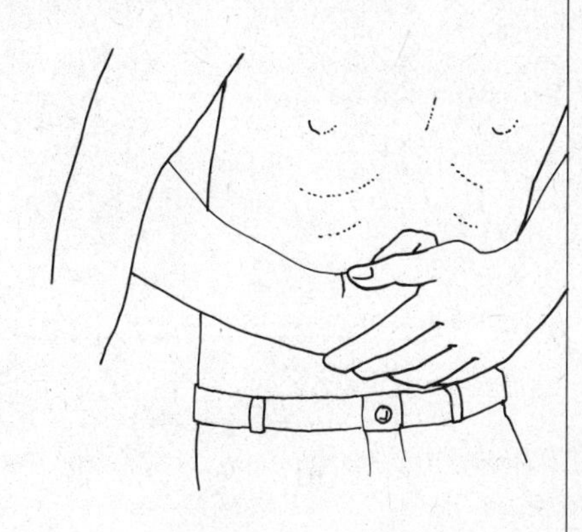

(b) Grasp the fist with the other hand.

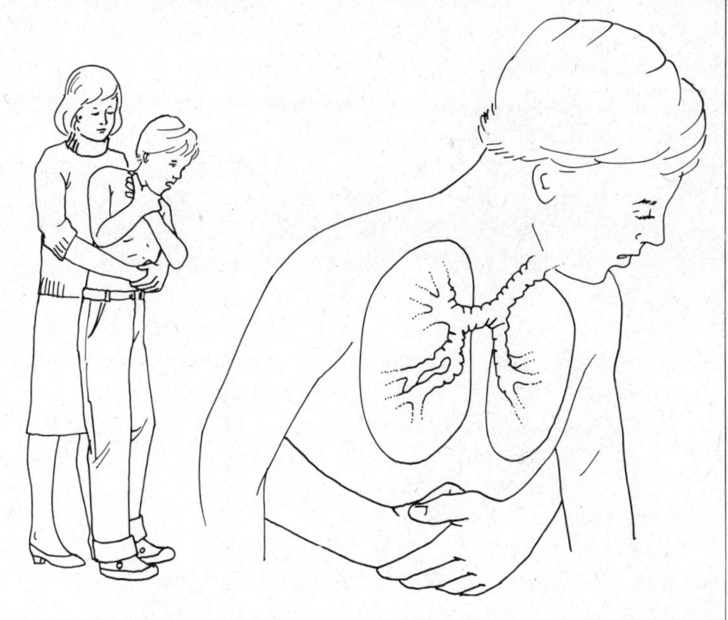

(c) Push fist upward into body quickly 4 times to force air out of lungs and dislodge object from airway.

Too-vigorous thrusting can crack a rib or injure the liver.

the silo. Pulmonary edema and cyanosis may lead to death. Proper air circulation in barns and silos is the obvious preventative.

Nosebleed—see *Epistaxis*

Nose, foreign bodies—see *Foreign bodies*

Nose injury is common after falling face down or not catching a ball. It is actually difficult to break a small child's nose because of the large amount of cartilage that constitutes his nasal structure. If the nose has been struck and bleeds from the inside, it implies that the cartilage or bone has broken through the mucous membranes. Whether the bones are still in good alignment or not is difficult to tell. X rays may be necessary to determine this. In general, if the tip of the nose is centered between the pupils of the eyes when the patient is evaluated from the front view, then his nose may not be broken. Also, if the bridge of the nose is not depressed, it may not be broken. However, many septal injuries cause a collection of blood on one side. This interferes with healing; one side of the nose may grow faster than the other or destruction of the septum may lead to a saddle nose. The patient may develop a deviated septum later in life, even though he might not have actually broken his nose.

It is difficult to know exactly what to do with a nose injury. If there is doubt, careful X rays will determine if bone (but not cartilage) segments are out of place. In the first three or four days, these bones can be moved back to the proper position for healing. Otherwise—if they heal in incorrect positions—remedial surgery will be necessary later in life.

Poisons require an immediate call to the doctor or your local Poison Control Board. Have the numbers handy—then read on.

Doctors are called at least daily about a toddler getting into something that was left about: detergents, polish, lye, and solvents that were stored under the sink or in a handy cupboard. Forty percent of poison cases occur in the kitchen.

The two- to four-year-old is likely to get into the unlocked medicine cabinet or mother's purse. *Aspirin* is still the favorite because it is so handy; the incidence is much less now because the number of pills of baby aspirin is limited to thirty-six per bottle. (This amount still might kill the child, but not so frequently or rapidly.) Seventy percent of poison cases involve substances that are visible to the child.

Every home with small children should have a bottle of *Syrup of Ipecac* handy. Three teaspoons of this emetic should be given while you are placing the call to your doctor—and the local poison-control center. Make the child drink six ounces of water. Vomiting should occur in about fifteen to thirty minutes. Vomiting empties the stomach more efficiently than lavage (passing a stomach tube, injecting water, aspirating the stomach contents until the return is clear). Some doctors will inject apomorphine, which irritates the vomiting center of the brain and always causes vomiting (unless the ingested poison is an antiemetic, like Thorazine®). But apomorphine has a late sedative effect that might obscure some important symptoms. *Vomiting may be dangerous if kerosene or petroleum distillates have been ingested.*

Emptying the stomach *as soon as possible* after poison ingestion may be lifesaving.

Some specific symptoms and usual causative agents:

(a) Vomiting, cramps, diarrhea: acids, alkali, metals.

(b) Convulsions: stimulants, strychnine, amphetamines, ephedrine, ergot, DDT.

(c) Coma, stupor: Alcohol, atropine, morphine, barbiturates.

(d) Dilated pupils: atropine, amphetamines, ephedrine, cocaine.

(e) Pinpoint pupils: morphine, muscarine, nicotine.

(f) Cherry red lips: carbon monoxide.

(g) Cyanosis: cyanide, strychnine, aniline dyes.

The empty bottle or list of ingredients *must* be brought along to the doctor's office or emergency room.

Activated charcoal will absorb large amounts of some drugs (a teaspoonful in a glass of water). A mixture of milk and egg white will subdue toxic effects of metals. Strong tea counteracts some alkaloids.

An *exchange transfusion* is valuable if the blood level of the poison is directly related to the severity of the symptoms.

This book cannot possibly even touch on the majority of all known poisons. You can get sick from excess water ingestion! A few of the more common poisons on the shelf and in the kitchen will be mentioned:

Acetanilid (phenacetin) and its metabolic end product, acetaminophen, may cause *methemoglobinemia* with its characteristic muddy cyanosis. Dyspnea and weakness are associated.

Syrup of ipecac is used for large doses. Withdrawal of the drug is indicated if symptoms are due to long term but low dosage use.

Acetone is widely used as fingernail polish remover. Inhalation will cause cough, drowsiness, headache and fatigue. The victim should be moved to fresh air.

Acids (sulfuric, nitric, hydrochloric) immediately burn holes in the membranes they touch. Massive amounts of water must be given immediately. If the patient survives the shock and bloody diarrhea, he will surely have esophageal strictures.

Alcohol (Ethyl)—or the one found in the liquor cabinet. Intoxication, coma, and death result if enough is consumed. Intoxication is defined as a blood alcohol level about 0.1 percent; in some states this provides grounds for license revocation for drunken driving. Some infants have been made very drunk by inhalation of alcohol during alcohol sponge for fever.

Alcohol, isopropyl (rubbing), is usually vomited before a toxic dose can be consumed. Effects are similar to ethyl alcohol.

Treatment consists of keeping the patient from hurting himself, emptying his stomach if he has not vomited, offering sodium bicarbonate (one teaspoon to a tumbler of water every hour), and ingestion of coffee or tea.

Methyl or *wood alcohol* (denatured alcohol has methyl in it) may be fatal if more than one ounce has been consumed. Blindness may be permanent if the victim recovers. The stomach should be washed out as soon as possible.

Alkalis such as sodium and potassium hydroxide are used to clean drains and are highly corrosive to human tissue. If these are ingested, ulcerations in the mouth and esophagus form which lead to scarring and secondary stenosis. Rinsing with copious amounts of water, followed by mineral or olive oil may prevent some of the damage. (See *Lye.*)

Amphetamines will cause irritability, restlessness, hallucinations, fear, panic, paranoid states, exhaustion, *convulsions,* and coma. Syrup of ipecac should be given.

Aniline and nitrobenzene are dyes found in laundry marks and some shoe polishes. Cyanosis (methemoglobinemia) is the result; syrup of ipecac should be given if ingested.

Arsenic is used in insecticides, ant poison, wallpaper, and paints.

Massive ingestion is followed by severe vomiting and violent bloody diarrhea; shock and convulsions lead to an early demise.

Slow or chronic ingestion or inhalation may cause erythema, alopecia, scaliness, neuritis, paralyses, anemia.

BAL (British AntiLewisite) is an effective antidote.

Aspirin—see *Salicylates*

Atropine (present in Jimson weed, deadly nightshade, henbane, Jerusalem cherry, eyedrops, and stomach-relaxing medicines) will cause dilated pupils, hot, dry, flushed skin, fever above 104°, dry mouth, and delirium. Syrup of ipecac should be given.

Barbiturates are common poisons, and five sleeping pills are enough to worry about. Syrup of ipecac should be given first. The comatose patient may need a respirator and repeated injections of stimulants.

Barium salts are contained in depilatories. Muscle tightness and tremors may end with coma.

Benzene causes weakness, nausea, then staggering, blurred vision, delirium, and coma. (See *Hydrocarbons.*)

Bleaches are commonly ingested by children but rarely cause more than local irritation. Milk ingestion is probably the best antidote.

Boric acid is a chemical formerly used for eye care and as a diaper-rinse chemical. Tears are about as effective as boric acid for eyes; if an infection exists, more efficient antibiotic solutions or ointments are available. Boric acid is actually a lethal substance and should not be in the house; it serves no purpose medically. At one time boric acid crystals were sprinkled in the diaper to counteract the ammonia formed. Some babies with open sores on their buttocks absorbed the chemical and died of *acidosis.*

Borax, sodium tetraborate, can be as lethal as *boric acid.*

Vomiting and bloody diarrhea will kill the baby. An *exchange transfusion* is necessary. Vinegar as a diaper rinse will accomplish the neutralization of ammonia almost as well as boric acid.

Bromide poisoning is rare now and usually takes a chronic form: the cause is prolonged self-medication with nerve tonics or headache remedies. Agitation and tremors or sluggishness with weakness may be seen in a variety of patterns. An acne-like rash is common. After use is discontinued, the kidneys will excrete the bromide over a few weeks' time.

Cadmium-plated pitchers may lose some of the metal if an acid juice is stored in them. Intestinal symptoms may be severe.

Caffeine is found in a number of drinks: an average cup of coffee contains up to twenty milligrams per ounce, tea a little less. The cola drinks have but three to five milligrams per ounce. Excitement, insomnia, and delirium would require about thirty cups of coffee (one gram of caffeine) to develop. Rapid heart beat, muscle twitches, ringing in the ears may progress to convulsions. Syrup of ipecac should be given to induce vomiting if large amounts have been ingested. Barbiturates will make the patient quiet until the caffeine is out of the system.

Calamine lotion causes cramps and vomiting when ingested. Syrup of ipecac is worthwhile if the patient has not already vomited.

Camphor in some mothballs and camphorated oil is highly toxic. One teaspoon of the latter will kill a child. Immediate giving of syrup of ipecac and gastric lavage is the early treatment.

Carbon tetrachloride (in floor waxes and fire extinguishers) will poison by inhalation, skin absorption, or ingestion. Dizziness, confusion, and collapse occur first; liver and kidney damage may follow. Treatment: see *Hydrocarbons.*

Cathartics and laxatives may be taken by children especially if attractively disguised as candy. Give syrup of ipecac to induce vomiting; follow with milk. Paregoric and/or atropine might counteract the cramps.

For magnesium salts overingestion, calcium gluconate is a specific antidote.

Catnip is a poison and must not be made into a tea or used as a colic medicine.

Chlorinated insecticides (DDT, chlordane, aldrin, endrin, etc.) are highly toxic. Skin absorption may be fatal. One-half teaspoonful taken internally may be lethal. Symptoms are hyperexcitability followed by coma and respiratory arrest. Ipecac indicated. (See *Insecticides.*)

Christmas tree decorations are consumed frequently by children. The thin bulbs seem to pass easily with only a minimum of throat scratching. If a bit of food can pass to the stomach, the chips will move on through.

Bubbling lights contain hydrocarbon but of only mild toxicity. Lethargy or excitement may occur. If more than two are consumed the stomach should be emptied.

Tinsel, lead and tin, if consumed may cause mechanical problems (choking), but is not poisonous in itself.

Angel hair, spun glass, may scratch the gullet but healing is prompt. Passage is easy.

Cocaine (butacaine, benzocaine, nupercaine) is a local anesthetic. Ingestion causes hyperexcitability, confusion, delirium, and dilated pupils. Small doses of sedatives can be used to calm a patient without producing coma.

Codeine is an analgesic similar to morphine, but has little of the euphoria inducing quality of the latter so is not considered addicting. The lethal dose is about 0.5 gram. It is a common ingredient in cough syrups (Cheracol® has 0.06 gram in an ounce). Moderate doses may cause excitement and ataxia. If there is any doubt about the ingested amount, use syrup of ipecac.

Contraceptives, oral, are frequently left at the bedside for the mother's convenience. No harm comes to the child by an occasional dose; it just throws the mother's schedule off a little. The child's stomach probably should be emptied if he takes more than five or ten pills.

Crayons usually contain harmless vegetable dyes (supposed to be marked with AP, CP or CS 130-146). Some have *aniline* dyes but the small amount incorporated in the wax of the crayon is not sufficient to cause harm.

Creosote—see *Phenols*

Cyanide rapidly causes giddiness, headache, then cyanosis. Death may occur in seconds. The odor of bitter almonds may be on the breath. Amylnitrite inhalation may be lifesaving.

Detergents are not soaps; their action in cleaning is to lower the surface tension of water and emulsify the dirt. The phosphates they contain and the alkalinity of the solution may cause esophageal burning if swallowed, but rarely as severe as with alkalis. Stomach pain, diarrhea, and distention usually respond to milk and fluids.

Electric dishwashing detergents are very toxic and may cause a corrosion of the esophagus. (See *Alkali.*)

If a cleanser contains pine oil or hydrocarbons, the toxicity is much increased because of the danger of aspiration into the lungs and the subsequent chemical pneumonia. (See *Hydrocarbons.*)

Digitalis and its various derivatives are valuable heart stimulants. Children may ingest these if grandmother's purse is left within reach. Nausea, vomiting, and cardiac arrhythmia may occur.

Syrup of ipecac is the early treatment. Specialized hospital monitoring of the ECG and intravenous fluids may be necessary in severe poisonings.

Ergot (Cafergot®) is a widely used migraine headache control medication. An overdose causes intestinal symptoms, disturbances of speech and vision. Numbness and tingling might suggest the early onset of gangrene because ergot has a vasoconstricting effect. Syrup of ipecac is indicated for an overdose. It has been used to induce a miscarriage, but the dose that works on the uterus will cause severe abdominal cramps and coma, and is usually enough to kill the patient.

Epoxy resin glues may cause skin and mucous membrane irritation. Cleansing with *acetone* may prevent a dermatitis or conjunctivitis.

Fluoride in excess will inhibit cellular enzyme systems. (The tablets prescribed for the unlucky children who do not have fluoride added to their water supply contain only 1 milligram of the fluoride ion. A poisonous ingestion would have to be above a hundred pills at one sitting.) Severe diarrhea and cramps occur, followed by collapse and cyanosis. Calcium chloride in the lavage solution precipitates the fluoride. Milk also is helpful.

Golf balls used to contain irritating substances. Children may crack them open and get some of this material in their eyes. Washing with water is usually the only treatment.

Hexachlorophene is a bacteriostatic chemical frequently recommended for skin and wound cleansing. If it is not thoroughly rinsed off from denuded areas (burns, large wounds) enough may be absorbed to cause convulsions.

Ingestion is usually followed by severe intestinal irritation and convulsions.

Hydrocarbons include petroleum distillates, benzene, turpentine, gasoline, and kerosene. Following ingestion the patient develops lethargy or coma, and if some of the material gets to the lungs, severe cough, dyspnea, and cyanosis (a chemical pneumonia) follow.

Some authorities believe that the material is absorbed from the intestines, and when it arrives in the lungs, it causes this chemical pneumonia. Others feel that it only gets to the lungs during ingestion or lavage when some is aspirated into the trachea. Both may be right, but more than two or three teaspoonfuls ingested require treating. A *careful* lavage with the patient's head dependent may empty the stomach if the hydrocarbon is not absorbed and also preclude aspiration. Olive oil is thought to be a safer solvent to place in the stomach than mineral oil. A saline purge may urge the material out of the bowels before much absorption can take place. Oxygen and antibiotics are the treatment for the lung inflammation.

Iodine may corrode the intestinal lining. Quantities of starch solution or egg white will neutralize it.

Insecticides include a large group of chemicals designed to control crop destroying insects and diseases.

DDT may be slowly absorbed from ingested sprayed foods or through the skin. It is stored in body fat for long periods of time. The general population has accumulated a significant amount (higher in the Untied States than elsewhere) but apparently not enough to be toxic.

Toxic doses cause vomiting, abdominal pain, blurred vision, and cough. Chronic poisoning affects the nervous system: fatigue, headache and ataxia develop. Lindane and benzene hexachloride have similar toxic properties.

Treatment is stomach lavage for ingestion and thorough bathing for skin contact.

Iron (tonic, blood builders) is very irritating to the stomach and intestines. Just a few pills will cause bloody emesis and diarrhea. Pallor and drowsiness precede coma. A chelating agent will bind the iron into a harmless complex which is excreted in the urine.

Kerosene (see *Hydrocarbons*) is a common household agent often swallowed by the curious toddler because it was left in an accessible location in a handy container—often in pop bottle. If more than two or three teaspoonsful have been ingested, the child may develop cramps, vomiting, drowsiness, and a severe cough with wheeze and cyanosis.

Lead poisoning is not uncommon in children living in old, crowded, paint-peeling ghetto areas. Old paint on the crib and walls is the most common source, but it may come from lead pipes, lead in fruit sprays, lead in toys, or lead in the air—if storage batteries are burned.

If the daily lead intake is greater than the body's ability to excrete it or deposit it in the bones, signs of poisoning develop slowly. Irritability, *headache,* stomachache, anemia, and pallor are signs of many diseases, but when confusion, poor coordination, weakness—all signs of brain involvement—progress to *convulsions* and coma, lead poisoning should be considered.

The first step in diagnosing lead poisoning is to think of it. Many a "peculiar" child, written off as a neurotic, has later been found to have lead in his brain and bones. A pale child with headaches who eats dirt or plaster should have a urine test for lead, a blood test for anemia (lead causes stippling in the red cells), X rays for lead lines in the bones. Spinal fluid is under extra pressure because of the swollen brain. Urine shows albumin and blood.

The treatment is the removal of environmental lead so that it cannot get to the patient, plus the mobilization of lead from the tissues and its excretion. Some chemicals are capable of forming nontoxic compounds with lead, which are then safely eliminated in the urine.

Even with careful removal of lead from the body, the brain may be irreversibly damaged. Mental retardation is the most common residual defect.

Lye (sodium and potassium hydroxide) causes corrosion of the mouth and esophagus. If lavage with water and vinegar is done rapidly, the esophagus may not become too scarred. If a stricture occurs, prolonged surgery may be the only way to fashion a new esophagus.

Mercury poisoning is usually due to the inadvertent ingestion of bichloride of mercury. Intestinal hemorrhages and profuse diarrhea may cause shock, coma, and death. If the patient survives this, he may succumb because of the kidney damage due to uremia. The sooner he vomits after ingestion, the better the chance of recovery. Ipecac would be helpful, followed by lavage of the stomach with milk. Frequent injections of BAL may detoxify the chemical. Chronic ingestion of mercury is less common now since it is a known poison and not used as formerly in teething powders. (It is also found in calomel, mercury ointments, and paint.) (See *Acrodynia.*)

The pure metal, quicksilver, in toys and thermometers provides little danger although stomach acids could convert some to the dangerous salt form.

Tuna fish from some areas have been found to be contaminated with mercury salts. A Texas family was poisoned when they ate a pig which had eaten mercury-treated grain that was intended for use as seed.

Mescal, or peyote, is produced from a cactus that grows along the Rio Grande River. Hallucinations of bright and vivid lights and colors plus muscle twitching are a few of the effects of this hallucinogen. The patient will recover without treatment.

Moth balls—see *Naphthalene*

Nail polish remover—see *Acetone*

Naphthalene (moth balls) poisoning should be treated immediately with an emetic (ipecac syrup). Absorption causes destruction of red cells, blood in the urine, and anemia. Liver damage may occur; convulsions suggest brain involvement.

Narcotic addiction is rare in children, but larger numbers of adolescents are becoming addicted to heroin. (See *Morphine,* Section 4.) A baby born to an addict will have withdrawal symptoms, as his body, too, has become physically dependent upon the drug.

The baby might show a variety of symptoms: cramps, crying, irritability, vomiting, pallor, sneezing, convulsions. He would need a sedative or tranquilizer. A severe case requires continuation of the same narcotic. Each day the baby is given a reduced dose so he can be weaned away from the drug. This initial experience with a narcotic would not make him more susceptible in later life; only his environment would determine that.

Nicotine in tobacco (when eaten—although a child can become nauseated smoking a cigar) can cause frightening symptoms of diarrhea, perspiration, shock, and confusion. Syrup of ipecac should be given immediately to empty the stomach; this is followed by tea or coffee.

Nutmeg may cause excitement or delirium followed by collapse and coma. Syrup of ipecac early is standard.

Opiates (e.g., *Morphine*) cause drowsiness, coma, and pinpoint pupils. Respiratory depression—two to four breaths a minute—might require a respiratory. Specific antagonists for morphine are Lorfan® and Nalline®.

Pencil lead is graphite and has no toxic effect. Indelible pencils contain a harmless dye.

Phenols (creosote, carbolic acid, Lysol®) cause rapid respiratory failure. Lavage is done with olive oil, as these chemicals are soluble in it.

Phenolphthalein is widely used in candy-flavored cathartics (like Exlax®). Violent cramps and severe diarrhea occur minutes or hours after ingestion. If emesis does not occur immediately and symptoms have already begun—because the child let no one know what he had done—paregoric is a proper antidote. Rash, high fever, dehydration, and kidney and liver damage might ensue.

Phosphorus is found in rodent poisons, fertilizers, and fireworks. (The phosphorus in present day match heads is red phosphorus and nontoxic.) Rapid onset of intestinal symptoms is followed by coma, liver injury, jaundice, and hemorrhages. Syrup of ipecac should be given and followed by lavage.

Phosphate esters (chlorothion, malathion, parathion) may be inhaled, ingested, or absorbed through the skin. A metabolite of these highly toxic substances inhibits the action of cholinesterase which metabolizes acetyl choline. Functions of the body depending upon the latter chemical for action are overstimulated: cramps, diarrhea, cough, increased sweating, pinpoint pupils, slow heart rate follow. (See *Mushroom poisoning.*) Atropine is the antidote.

Plant foods and *fertilizers* are usually safe to ingest, but some contain nitrates. Bacteria in the intestine may convert these to nitrites which may cause *methemoglobinemia.*

Polishes and *waxes* for furniture and floor are basically *hydrocarbons.*

Salicylates (*aspirin,* some liniments) are the most common poisons. One grain of aspirin per 10 pounds of body weight is the usual therapeutic dose; but one grain per pound may cause ringing in the ears and stomach distress in some people. These symptoms should be cause for administering syrup of ipecac even two to four hours after ingestion, as some is usually still in the stomach.

Hyperventilation (air hunger) is the first clue. The body compensates for the *acidosis* by exhaling carbon dioxide (an acid). This respiratory alkalosis urges the kidneys to secrete base alkaline substances, and metabolic acidosis occurs. This mixture of problems is aggravated by ketosis. Intravenous fluids with monitoring of the salicylate blood level and pH (acidity) becomes complicated. Bleeding problems, coma, and cyanosis may warrant an *exchange transfusion.*

Scouring powder is usually composed of inert abrasives and has no effect on the ingester. An occasional one contains sodium perborate but it takes a tablespoon or more to be lethal. Induce vomiting and call the doctor.

Shampoos and hair care preparations are usually safe unless large amounts are consumed. Hair sprays will cause intense eye irritation. Wash with running water for fifteen to twenty minutes.

Strontium 90 is a radioactive mineral present in cow's milk and assumed to be due to radioactive fallout from nuclear testing. When cows graze in a contaminated pasture, the undersirable material is incorporated into their milk. This is of minor importance, but is just one more problem added to our environmental difficulties.

Strychnine causes central-nervous-system stimulation. Tense muscles proceed to twitching and convulsions. The contraction of the muscles may impair breathing and result in cyanosis. The patient alternates between severe, painful convulsions and coma. *Barbiturates* may control the convulsions.

Talc is dangerous when inhaled as it produces a violent (depending on amount) pulmonary reaction that is almost impossible to treat. Talcum powders for use in armpits and groin should be used sparingly; do not allow a cloud of this silicate to settle down on the baby. Sprinkle a little in your hand and transfer this to his skin.

Thallium content in pesticides has been limited by law but cases of poisoning occasionally occur. Children ingesting rodent or ant bait with thallium develop pain, fever, diarrhea, and the give-away sign, hair loss (*alopecia*). BAL is not very effective. Call the doctor immediately.

Warfarin is a rat poison that interferes with blood coagulation. The effect is slow but may last several days. *Hemorrhages* occur from nose, mouth, and intestines. Blood transfusions and vitamin K are necessary.

Zinc poisoning may be caused by ingestion of acid foods or liquids stored or cooked in galvanized containers. Severe vomiting, diarrhea, shock, and collapse are clues. Survivors may have esophageal strictures and kidney damage. Doctor should be called if any of these symptoms occur.

Poisonous plants are ubiquitous. *It would be best to induce vomiting after the ingestion of any unknown substance.* Where specific treatment is not given, the doctor should be called.

House plants

Castor bean—whole plant, especially the bean. If swallowed whole, there is no absorption; if chewed, severe cramps and convulsions. Give syrup of ipecac.

Dumbcane, elephant's ear, calla lily, philodendron, dracunculus, caladium—whole plant. Severe swelling of lips, mouth, tongue, and throat results. Wash with water and milk. Systemic symptoms are rare.

Poinsettia—leaves and petals cause vomiting, cramps, and diarrhea.

Lantana—especially the berries—causes intestinal irritation, muscular weakness.

Mistletoe—especially the berries—causes intestinal cramps and circulatory collapse.

Vegetables

Mango skin causes intestinal upset and rashes.

Potato—green tubers and new sprouts—causes intestinal symptoms and circulatory collapse.

Rhubarb—leaves only—causes intestinal symptoms, hemorrhages, severe burning and ulcers in the mouth.

Garden plants

Bleeding heart—foliage—causes trembling, ataxia, convulsions.

Buttercup—entire plant—causes intestinal irritation and blisters.

Christmas rose—entire plant—causes intestinal symptoms, circulatory collapse, neuritis, and convulsions.

Crocus—entire plant—causes intestinal symptoms and circulatory collapse.

Daffodil—bulb—causes intestinal cramps.

Daphne—entire plant—causes intestinal symptoms.

Deadly nightshade—entire plant—see *Atropine.*

Foxglove—leaves—see *Digitalis.*

Hemlock—entire plant—causes intestinal symptoms and weakness.

Iris—root—causes intestinal symptoms.

Jessamine—entire plant—causes profuse sweating, weakness, and convulsions.

Jimson weed—entire plant—acts like *atropine.*

Larkspur and delphinium—entire plant—cause intestinal upset and coma.

Lily of the valley—entire plant—see *Digitalis.*

Monkshood—entire plant—causes symptoms like those of Christmas rose.

Morning glory—seeds—see *LSD,* Section 16.

Mountain laurel—entire plant—causes salivation, lacrimation, cardiac collapse, convulsions.

Narcissus and jonquil—see *Daffodil.*

Oleander—entire plant—see *Digitalis.*

Pokeweed—root—causes burning in the mouth, vomiting, cramps, blindness, weakness, and convulsions.

Rhododendron—entire plant—see *Mountain laurel.*

Star of Bethlehem—entire plant—causes intestinal symptoms and has the effect of *digitalis.*

Sweet pea—seeds—causes paralysis and weak pulse.

Wisteria—pods and seeds—causes severe intestinal symptoms.

Yew—entire plant—causes intestinal symptoms and muscular weakness.

Shrubs and trees

Black locust—bark, leaves, seeds—causes intestinal symptoms, weakness, and coma.

Box—entire plant—causes intestinal symptoms and convulsions.

Cherry—entire plant *except fruit*—causes coma, convulsions, as in *cyanide* poisoning, especially if seeds are chewed.

Elderberry—entire plant *except berries*—see *Cyanide.*

Holly—berries—causes intestinal symptoms and coma.

Horse chestnut—nuts—causes vomiting, weakness, and coma.

Oak—leaves and acorns—causes intestinal symptoms and kidney damage.

Privet—leaves and berries—see *Mountain laurel.*

Wild plants

Jack-in-the-pulpit—entire plant, especially the root—see *Rhubarb leaves.*

Mushroom poisoning is caused by muscarine which produces abdominal cramps, perspiration, convulsions, coma, and death. *Atropine* counteracts this chemical, and large doses may have to be given frequently until the chemical is metabolized.

(I know people who pick their own mushrooms in the woods. If they are unsure of their toxic effect, they will have one small slice of one. If no symptoms occur within the hour, they assume that they are of a nonpoisonous variety and include them in the dinner. A dangerous practice—buy your mushrooms from your friendly, reliable grocer.)

Skunk cabbage—leaves—see *Rhubarb leaves.*

Water hemlock—entire plant, especially the roots—causes rapid collapse, intestinal cramps, convulsions, coma.

Puncture wounds require no more than gentle washing with running water to flush out superficial dirt. Vigorous scrubbing with soap and brush or use of alcohol or medicines other than topical antibiotic ointments will only cause further damage to injured skin. A *tetanus* booster (preferably a diphtheria-tetanus) should be administered within the next forty-eight hours if there has been no booster within five years. (See *Bites.*)

Puncture wounds of the foot require special handling by a surgeon. Because of the anatomy of the foot and the fact that bits of shoe, sock, sand, and dirt have been pushed into deep, inaccessible regions, many surgeons now feel obliged to remove a small cone of tissue including the puncture tract to prevent infection.

Radiation by X rays is essential in making diagnosis of many body ills, but it must be remembered that X rays are destructive. Excessive X-ray radiation is more harmful to growing tissues and cells than to adult organs, because of the higher rate of cell division in the younger age groups.

The government has set guidelines for radiation exposure for atomic-energy workers, with the recommendation that the general population receive much less. Cosmic rays and certain trace radioactive elements bombard us all the time. Diagnostic X rays may increase the amount of radiation to a person comparable to the increase he would receive if he moved to the mountains (more cosmic rays).

Some defective color-television sets may emit some harmful X rays, although this seems to be a minor hazard. But enough minors can add up to a major, so if possible, X rays are to be respected and avoided unless a diagnosis cannot be made without them.

Some statistics suggest a higher-than-normal rate of thyroid cancer in those who were X rayed for thymus enlargement as infants. Some feel that, if a pregnant woman receives X rays, her baby has a greater chance of developing leukemia. Those receiving X-ray therapy for acne may develop a skin cancer in later life.

The radiologists are aware of these hazards, and procedures and equipment are now designed to reduce excessive exposure. Most doctors feel that X rays should be limited to real diagnostic problems or trauma cases; X rays, however, are less injurious than the fluoroscope. A dentist who X rays teeth too frequently (once a year is plenty) or a doctor who X rays every bruise might be censured.

Evidence of growth distortion, especially of the spine, may occur some years after X radiation for cancer. Some authorities now feel that X radiation should be limited to those cancerous growths that demonstrate local invasion at the time of surgery. If the cancer is well contained, postoperative radiation may not be necessary and may, in fact, do harm; scoliosis of the spine is common years later in those who survive the original cancer.

X radiation of a hemangioma in a small child with a lot of growing to do should be done only if the blood-vessel tumor is interfering with some vital function (vision, breathing).

Radioactive fallout is composed of the small bits of dust made radioactive by above-ground nuclear bomb explosions. They are sucked up into the mushroom cloud, drift through the sky and settle on the ground, or are washed out of the sky by rain. This extra environment radiation is an added danger to germ cells that are already being bombarded by cosmic rays. Radioactivity is only destructive.

Rib fracture is common after a direct blow to the chest (falls on objects, car accidents). X rays are usually not indicated in the simple cases. Although taping the chest has long been the standard treatment, a few patients have developed pneumonia because of inadequate aeration of lungs. Rest and analgesics (codeine) are now advised. An elastic bandage could be used for broken ribs which lie below the lungs.

Sexual molestation is the genital fondling or forcing of sexual attention on a child by an adult (usually a male). Occasionally penile penetration and ejaculation occur. Obviously, something is wrong with the perpetrator; a normal male should pick on someone his own size. He needs help. So does the mother, for this is a frightening, anger-provoking, hysteria-producing situation for parents. The police should be notified. The child should be examined—usually nothing is found. Most children survive these perverse acts with a minimum of physical and psychic trauma. (Children are more frightened by their angry mothers.) They assume that, if an adult wants to do this, it is acceptable (they may even feel flattered by the attention). They suffer no guilt unless the mother overreacts and somehow gets the message to the child that any pleasurable sensation derived from this area is wicked. The kind doctor is supposed to probe about with questions to elicit the child's attitudes and feelings. Ventilation of thoughts is a healthy way to resolve suppressed, harmful notions about what happened. Follow-up studies on girls who have been molested as children reveal surprisingly little distortion of psychosexual development.

The myth that the fondled boy turns into a homosexual has also been debunked.

Shock is the condition of low blood pressure sufficient to prevent oxygenation of body tissues, notably the brain. *Syncope* would be a mild form of shock but easily treated by the recumbent position. More severe forms are due to circulatory collapse because of acute blood or serum loss (ruptured spleen, severe *epistaxis,* arterial bleeding, diabetes, extensive burns).

Prolonged vomiting and diarrhea will eventually deplete the serum of its fluid necessary to maintain adequate volume. *Septicemia* and *anaphylaxis* will cause a circulatory collapse.

The treatment is to correct the cause if possible; hospitalization is mandatory.

The patient is to be kept flat. Control of bleeding by pressure is safer than a tourniquet. Comfort is provided, but extra warmth is not indicated. Reassurance is important. Intravenous therapy is indicated.

Skull fracture is common in children but may go undetected since an X ray is not taken every time a child falls down the steps and bumps his head. Doctors see many children with head injuries, but their only symptoms are due to concussion. Recovery is not affected by an X ray, although it may reveal a crack or line without any depression of bone fragments into the brain.

The fracture or the X-ray findings are of little significance by themselves since intervention is dictated by the persistence and/or severity of the symptoms. (see *Head injuries.*)

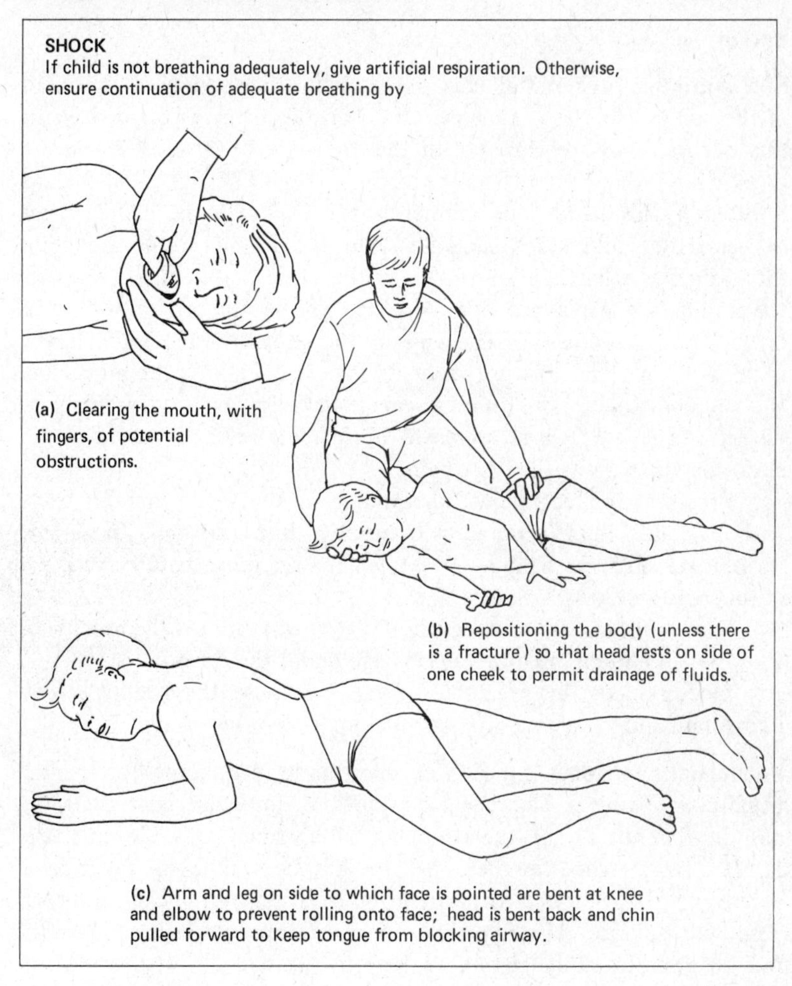

Each of the following should be tested periodically (every hour, perhaps): (a) *response to pain* (none, withdrawal, or retaliation), (b) *response to verbal contact* (none, nonspecific, or inappropriate), (c) *amnesia* (last remembered event—with time, if events closer to the injury are remembered, the patient is improving), (d) *recent memory* (if events since the injury are remembered and recall of random digits is correct, the patient is recovering, because with brain damage, the ability to recall events is one of the first functions to go).

Sprain—see *Ankle,* also Section 7

Subluxation of the radial head is a partial dislocation of the head of the radius bone at the elbow. Often mistaken for a sprained wrist, this occurs almost exclusively in the under-four-year-old. The cause is a tug on the hand when the child's arm is straight. (The child is lifted by his hands; the mother is walking with the child's hand in hers, the child stops suddenly, and the mother pulls the child forward. Or, a friendly adult swings the child about in a circle; or, the infant in the playpen doesn't let go of the playpen railing when he sits down suddenly.) The end of the radius bone at the elbow is pulled down and forward from its usual position at the joint. The sudden pain makes the child scream and hold his arm uselessly at his side. The whole arm seems to hurt from wrist to shoulder, but elbow bending elicits the most pain.

Pressure applied against the radius at the elbow simultaneous with forceful elbow bending will usually drop the bone back into its normal position with a "pop" and cause immediate restoration of function and loss of pain.

Some children are prone to this, but growth reduces the proclivity. Children should be lifted by the rib cage under their arms.

Doctors like this treatable problem because the results are so immediate and gratifying.

Subungual hematoma is a blob of blood under a fingernail or toenail, usually following a hammer blow (to the fingernail instead of the nail in the board), or the dropping of a stone on a shoeless toe. If there is no escape for the blood, the pressure builds up and creates severe pain. If the affected part can be held high up above the heart, pain will subside. Heating the end of an opened paper clip until red hot and carefully piercing a hole in the nail (only the nail, not the skin beneath) will allow the trapped blood to escape, and the pain will stop. A new nail usually grows out within six months.

Sunburn can be treated like burns, if one can get the ice on the struggling victim. Usually the treatment is delayed beyond the time of benefit. Vinegar rinses and tomato juice have their advocates. When the blisters break, treat as an *abrasion.*

Toenail—see *Subungual hematoma*

Tongue bites or trauma from sticks or toys shoved in the mouth are common. Bleeding is brisk and alarming at first, but because of the good blood supply, these wounds heal rapidly. A tetanus booster is appropriate if the foreign object has been on the ground. Surgery is rarely needed; a widely gaping wound will heal spontaneously in a week with no care. The scarring is minimal. Suturing may be necessary for a wide wound from which bleeding has not slowed to an ooze by an hour or so. Many parents are alarmed by the white material that fills the defect on the second or third day. It is not pus but the normal fibrin clot from which the saliva has washed the red blood cells. Mouth rinses are not necessary; saliva takes care of the problem. Pain may be assuaged with aspirin or local anesthetic troches—something with a "caine" drug in it (see *Anesthesia,* Section 4).

Wrist bone. A fall on the outstretched hand may result in a fracture of the wrist bone and give a characteristic "silver fork" deformity. This may not be too obvious, but in a child it may involve the growth center of the bone. (See *Broken bones.*)

SECTION 2
Fevers *

A. Bacterial infections

Bacteria causing infections
- *Escherichia coli*
- *Gram negative bacteria*
- *Listeria monocytogenes* ,
- *Meningococcus (Septicemia)*
- *Pneumococcus* (Pneumonia, Section 9)
- *Pseudomonas aeruginosa*
- *Salmonella* (Food poisoning, Section 12)
- *Shigella* (Section 12)
- *Staphylococcus*
- *Streptococcus*

Diseases
- *Bang's disease*
- *Brucellosis*
- *Bubonic plague*
- *Cavernous sinus thrombosis*
- *Diphtheria*
- *Gonorrhea*
- *Meningitis*
- *Peritonitis*
- *Peritonsillar abscess*
- *Pharyngitis*
- *Pneumonia* (Section 9)
- *Pott's disease*
- *Pyelonephritis* (Section 13)
- *Retropharyngeal abscess*
- *Scarlet fever*
- *Septicemia*
- *Tetanus*
- *Tonsillitis*
- *Tuberculosis* (Section 9)
- *Tularemia*
- *Typhoid fever*
- *Undulant fever*

B. Viral infections (see also Interferon)

Viruses causing infections
- *Adenovirus* (Neck, Section 14)
- *Coxsackie*
- *Enterovirus and ECHO*
- *Herpes*
- *Influenza* (Section 9)
- *Rhinovirus* (Nose, Section 14)

Diseases
- *Cat-scratch disease*
- *Chickenpox*
  - *Chickenpox myocarditis*
- *Cold, common* (Section 14)
- *Cytomegalic inclusion disease*
- *Encephalitis* (Section 15)
- *Fifth disease* (Erythema infectiosum)
- *Gingivostomatitis*
- *Hand, foot, and mouth disease*
- *Hemolytic-uremic syndrome*
- *Herpangina*
- *Herpes progenitalis*
- *Herpes simplex*

*Read **Temperature** first.

Herpes zoster (Shingles) (Section 6)
Herpetic stomatitis
Infectious hepatitis (Section 12)
Infectious lymphocytosis
Infectious mononucleosis
Infectious neuronitis (Section 15)
Influenza (Section 9)
Lymphogranuloma inguinale
Measles
Mumps
Myositis (Section 7)
Poliomyelitis (Section 15)
Rabies
Reye's syndrome (Section 15)
Roseola infantum
Rubella
Rubeola
Smallpox
Yellow fever

C. Fungal, mycotic infections

Actinomycosis (Section 6)
Blastomycosis (Section 9)
Coccidioidomycosis (San Joaquin Fever) (Section 9)
Cryptococcosis (Section 9)
Histoplasmosis (Section 9)
Nocardiosis (Section 9)

D. Worms

Parasites (Section 12)
Trichinosis

E. Protozoan diseases

Malaria
Toxoplasmosis

F. Spirochete infections

Leptospirosis
Weil's disease
Rat-bite fever
Syphilis

G. Tests

Antistreptolysin titre (See Streptococcus)
Culture and sensitivity studies (Antibacterials, Section 4)
Heterophil
Throat culture (See Streptococcus)

H. Autoimmune diseases

Glomerulonephritis (Section 13)
Lupus erythematosus
Polyarteritis nodosa
Rheumatic fever
Chorea
Thyroiditis (Section 10)

I. Rickettsial diseases

Q fever
Rocky Mountain spotted fever
Scrub typhus
Typhus

COMMON CAUSES OF FEVER & SORE THROAT
Chickenpox
Coxsackie virus
Enterovirus
Gingivostomatitis
Herpes simplex
Herpangina
Infectious mononucleosis
Influenza
Scarlet fever
Tonsillitis

RARE CAUSES OF FEVER & SORE THROAT
Diphtheria
Hand, foot & mouth disease
Infectious lymphocytosis
Peritonsillar abscess
Retropharyngeal abscess

COMMON CAUSES OF FEVER & RASH
Chickenpox
Enterovirus
Erythema infectiosum
Exanthems chart
Infectious mononucleosis
Measles
Roseola
Rubella
Rubeola
Scarlet fever (Scarlatina)

RARE CAUSES OF FEVER & RASH
Erythema nodosum (Section 6)
Leptospirosis
Listeria monocytogenes
Lupus erythematosus
Polyarteritis nodosa
Rat-bite fever
Rickettsial diseases
Septicemia
  Meningococcocemia
Smallpox
Syphilis
Toxoplasmosis
Typhoid fever

FEVER & SKIN SORES
Cat-scratch disease
Mycotic infection
Polyarteritis nodosa
Rat-bite fever

RARE CAUSES OF FEVER
Brucellosis (Bang's disease)
Bubonic plague
Hemolytic-uremic syndrome
Kawasaki disease
Malaria
Mycotic infection
Tuberculosis
Typhoid fever

CAUSES OF FEVER & SEVERE HEADACHE
Cavernous sinus thrombosis
Encephalitis (Section 14)
  Viral, Herpes,
  Mumps, Mononucleosis
Ethmoiditis (Section 14)
Meningitis
Poliomyelitis (Section 15)
Reye's disease (Section 15)

FEVER & JOINT PAIN
(see Bones, Section 7)

FEVER & COUGH
(See Respiratory, Section 9)

FEVER & ABDOMINAL PAIN
(See Abdomen, Section 12)

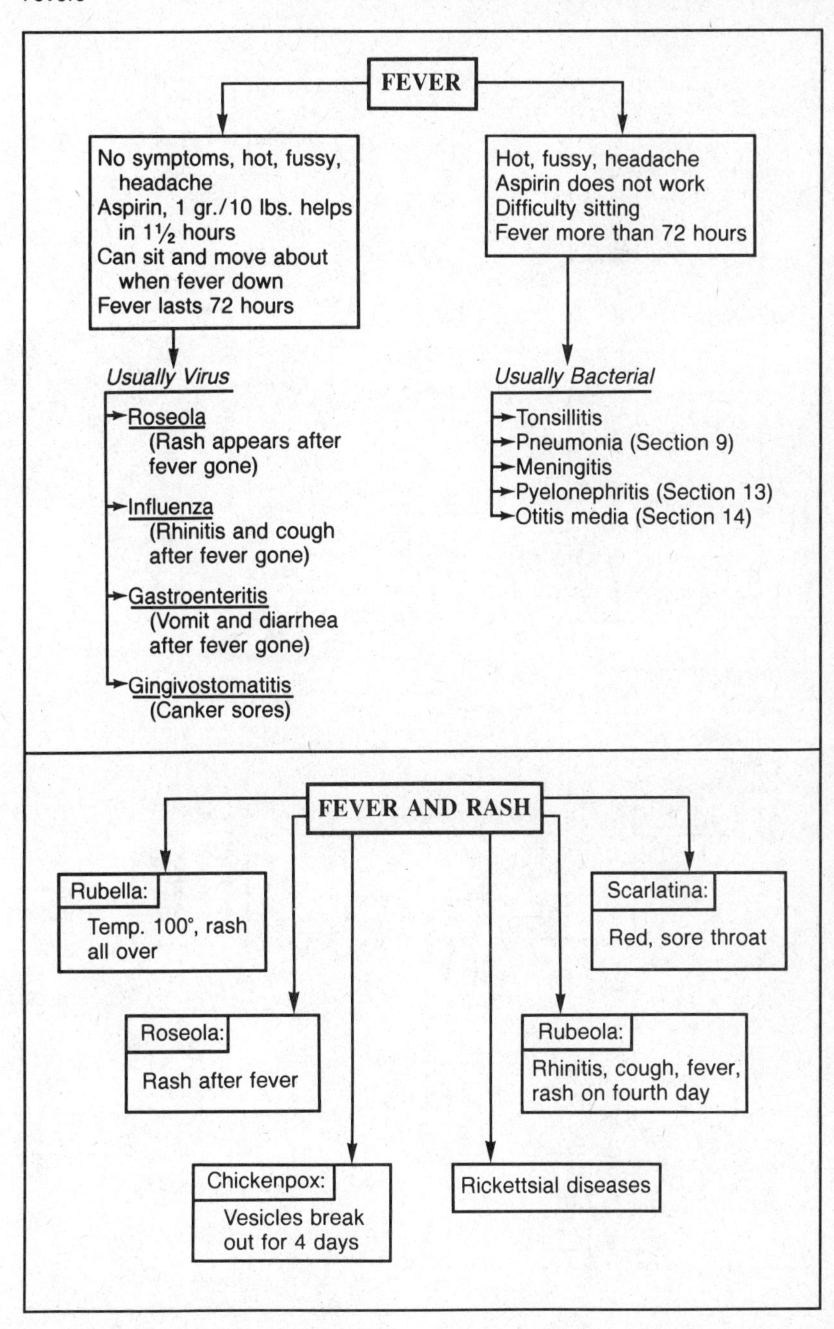
FEVER
No symptoms, hot, fussy, headache
Aspirin, 1 gr./10 lbs. helps in 1½ hours
Can sit and move about when fever down
Fever lasts 72 hours
Usually Virus
Roseola
(Rash appears after fever gone)
Influenza
(Rhinitis and cough after fever gone)
Gastroenteritis
(Vomit and diarrhea after fever gone)
Gingivostomatitis
(Canker sores)
Hot, fussy, headache
Aspirin does not work
Difficulty sitting
Fever more than 72 hours
Usually Bacterial
Tonsillitis
Pneumonia (Section 9)
Meningitis
Pyelonephritis (Section 13)
Otitis media (Section 14)
FEVER AND RASH
Rubella:
Temp. 100°, rash all over
Roseola:
Rash after fever
Chickenpox:
Vesicles break out for 4 days
Rickettsial diseases
Rubeola:
Rhinitis, cough, fever, rash on fourth day
Scarlatina:
Red, sore throat

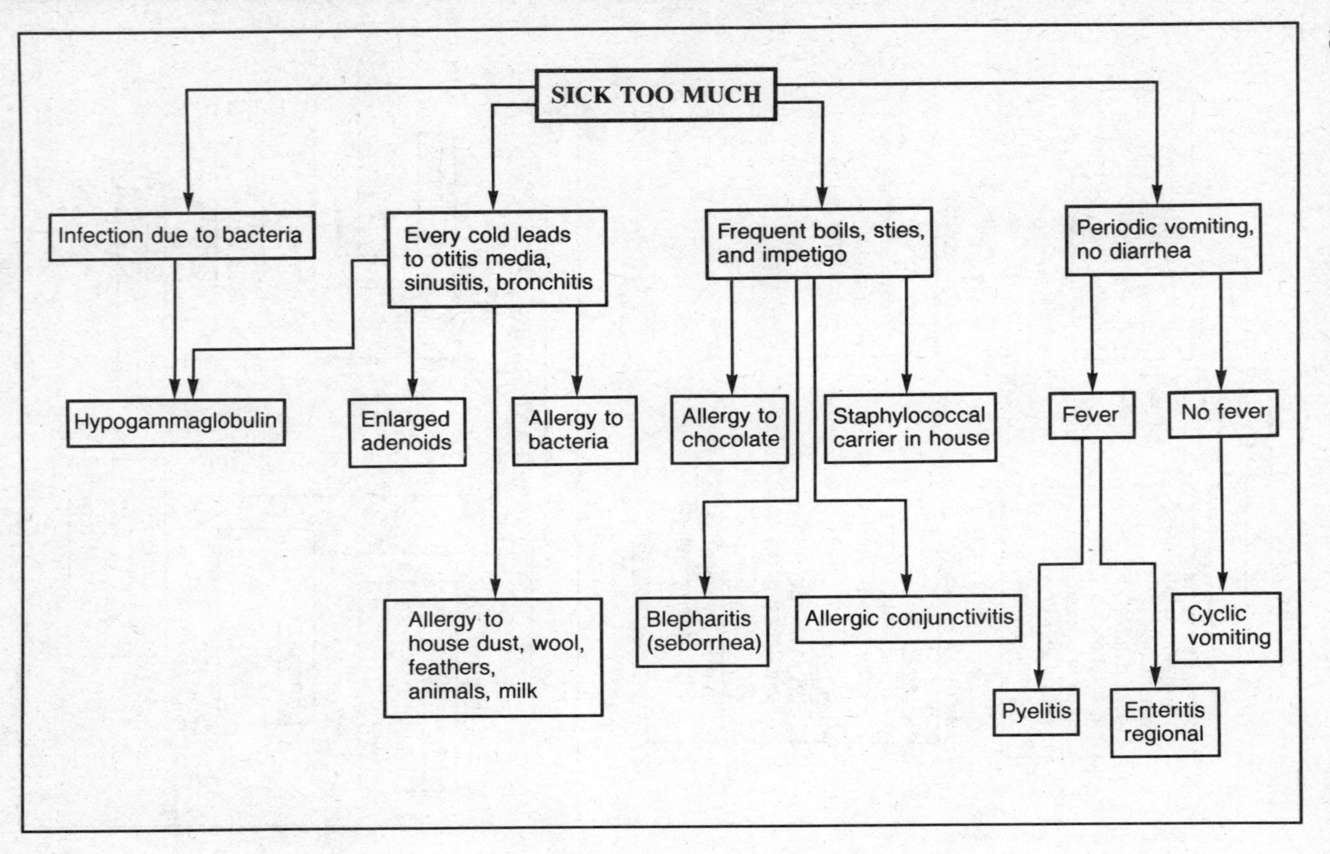
SICK TOO MUCH
Infection due to bacteria
Every cold leads to otitis media, sinusitis, bronchitis
Frequent boils, sties, and impetigo
Periodic vomiting, no diarrhea
Hypogammaglobulin
Enlarged adenoids
Allergy to bacteria
Allergy to chocolate
Staphylococcal carrier in house
Fever
No fever
Allergy to house dust, wool, feathers, animals, milk
Blepharitis (seborrhea)
Allergic conjunctivitis
Cyclic vomiting
Pyelitis
Enteritis regional

Bacterial infections, as opposed to *virus* infections, are germ infections of the body and are usually characterized by the formation of pus (skin *abscesses, sties, pyelonephritis, tonsillitis, sinusitis,* etc.). Bacterial infections respond to *antibiotics* (*penicillin, sulfa, mycin drugs*), while viral infections do not. If the patient is not too sick or feverish, a day or two of rest, fluids, and aspirin might be tried first to test the body's ability to fight the infection. If these measures do not allow the patient to improve, antibiotics would be appropriate.

A green or yellow mucus draining from the nose or noted in the sputum after coughing means that bacteria are present and could be treated. The decision to treat a rather mild infection may be difficult to make, depending on the presence of fever, discomfort, proposed trip or vacation, presence of infants or elderly people in the home, and other factors.

More severe infections—*tonsillitis, pyelitis, pneumonia*—might best be treated on recognition, and the patient may be ambulatory the next day. For overwhelming infections—*meningitis, endocarditis, septicemia, liver abscess*—hospitalization seems mandatory. Repeated serious bacterial infections suggest the need to test *immune globulins* (see Section 8).

Doctors try *not* to use antibiotics on nonlife-threatening diseases, because the patient may develop an allergy to the medicine, thus preventing its use for a possible future and more serious infection. A further drawback is that the use of antibiotics has allowed some bacteria such as staphylococcus to become resistant to treatment. (See *E. coli, gram-negative bacteria, pseudomonas, staphylococcus, streptococcus, listeria.*)

Bang's disease—see *Brucellosis*

Brucellosis, or undulant fever or Bang's disease, is transmitted to man from domestic animals, most notably the cow and the pig. The symptoms may be sudden—with chills, fever, malaise, cough—or slow with only lassitude suggesting a neurosis. As the disease becomes less frequent due to elimination of infected animals and pasteurization of milk, it is rarely thought of by the doctor, who may never have seen a case. Skin and blood tests may confirm the diagnosis; treatment with mycin drugs is fairly standard.

Bubonic plague, rarely reported in the United States, occurs when infected fleas bite humans. A bacterium, Pasteurella pestis, invades the broken skin, sets up an infection in the nearby lymph node. (Bubonic plague is so-called because the nodes are called buboes.)

Fever, prostration, and severe pain in the node suggest the disease. A pneumonic form is rapidly fatal if treatment has been delayed.

Cat-scratch disease is considered a *virus* infection resulting from a minor scratch from a cat who harbors the infectious material in his claws. After two or three weeks the nearby *lymph nodes* swell, become tender, and the victim may feel sick with a low-grade fever. If the hand is scratched, the armpit glands swell; if the leg, the groin glands may enlarge to one-inch size. A *skin test* may suggest the diagnosis. The treatment is time, since the virus is untreatable. If the gland is needled, fluid may be obtained for diagnosis.

Cavernous sinus thrombosis is the occlusion of veins deep inside the head, usually due to an infected clot which has spread from the nose, eyes, and upper lip. A pimple in the nose may release bacteria into the veins inside the skull. This infected, thrombosed clot causes fever, chills, *headaches,* swollen lids, and *blindness.* Immediate *antibiotic* treatment is necessary. Care should be taken in the management of innocuous-looking infections of lip and nose.

Chickenpox, or varicella, is the second most contagious disease in the world, the first being *smallpox.* Accordingly, it is usually contracted by a child before he is five or six. This is fortunate, because chickenpox is a very severe illness in an adult, and complications are much more frequent. Also, the second case of chickenpox in a home is usually more violent than the first. Most doctors now believe that, if an older child brings this disease home when there is a baby in the house, an injection of *gamma globulin* for the baby will make the disease lighter and the complications—such as high fever, *pneumonia,* or *encephalitis*—less likely. A significant number of victims get distressing sores in the mouth and down the throat. This symptom is usually associated with a high fever and general misery. Baking-soda baths and various lotions to pat on the skin are worth trying. At present, there are specific *antihistaminics* that help cut down on some of the itching (Section 4).

Obviously, the more the child digs at his sores, the more likely he is to scar. However, I have seen some children who did not touch their skin and still had permanent pits, and others who scratched their skin unmercifully but did not develop scars.

Doctors are trying to get the schools to change the laws about chickenpox, so that a child who is not too sick can come to school and expose the whole class. Then the majority of the population would be able to get it while they are still young. A child with uncomplicated chickenpox does not need to be confined to his bed and may be up and around the house—even outside. However, he is still contagious. Some doctors feel the possibility of contagion exists as long as there are sores on the skin, but most now feel that this is not true, and that probably no one is contagious once his pox (the water blisters) have dried up.

This virus disease is usually mild. A severe case may be confused with smallpox (now extinct); a mild case may present only the appearance of flea bites. Chickenpox sores begin as small papules—like bites—which in a day become water blisters (vesicles), which in another day become pustules, which in another day scab over. The victim breaks out for four or five days; the rash begins on the trunk and spreads out to arms and legs and face; thus after three days one area of the body will display lesions in different stages of development from the others. If the scalp has lesions, this confirms the diagnosis, as the human rarely gets bitten there. Regional lymph nodes will swell; glands on the back of the head (just above where the neck muscles attach to the skull) are characteristically enlarged and tender in chickenpox. Vitamin C in big doses (5–10 grams a day) will speed recovery.

An adult may acquire *herpes zoster* from a child with chickenpox, and vice versa. (See Section 6.)

Chickenpox myocarditis is a rare complication. Abdominal pain, shortness of breath, and listlessness draw attention to this problem. Oxygen, *diuretics,* and *digitalis* usually control the symptoms.

Chorea (Sydenham's). Along with the bizarre, purposeless movements, the victim may have personality and behavior changes including mania, suspiciousness, temporary lowering of general intellectual function, confusion, and disorientation. The *EEG* may become diffusely abnormal but return to prechorea patterns in a few weeks or months. (See Section 15, also *Rheumatic fever.*)

Coxsackie virus infections are responsible for a number of isolated and epidemic illnesses with a wide variety of symptoms. Some will cause *encephalitis* and *myocarditis,* occasionally ending fatally. One variety causes *herpangina;* another pleurodynia or the *devil's grip.* Most are accompanied by *headache* and sore throat; if associated with a rash, they may be mistaken for one of the *measles.* (See *Virus.*)

Treatment is *aspirin,* fluids, and rest. Children under five years seem to have a great number of these "viruses that are going around," but one attack renders immunity to that particular strain. There are, however, about thirty strains.

Cytomegalic-inclusion disease is a *viral* infection creating severe symptoms if acquired before birth. The affected baby may have *jaundice,* enlarged *liver* and *spleen, hemorrhages* because of low *platelet* count, and *calcium* deposits in the *brain.* If the baby survives, he may be left with a variety of nervous-system defects (*hydrocephalus, blindness, retardation, brain dysfunction,* etc.).

Diphtheria is a rare but severe bacterial infection, usually manifest as a severe sore throat and extreme prostration. Since the routine baby shots (DPT) have been given almost universally to infants, the disease is rarely seen or considered in children. Apparently a few carriers (who harbor germs in their throats but are not themselves sick) are responsible for the few cases seen each year—largely in adults who may not have maintained their childhood immunity. (Some years ago a half dozen cases in Oregon were traced to a dance instructor who was a carrier. Her mother had not believed in the shots so she had little immunity; her students on whom she breathed had lost their immunity and developed the disease. Her son was unaffected because he had been recently boosted with DPT.)

The bacteria in the throat stimulate the production of a thick, dirty membrane that may grow into the windpipe causing obstruction to breathing (black diphtheria). The powerful poison will damage the heart muscle (*congestive heart failure*) or the nerves (*paralysis*).

Penicillin is usually used along with antitoxin to kill the germs and neutralize the poison, but despite modern care and an early diagnosis, the death rate is about 10 percent.

If a carrier is identified, the germs can usually be eliminated with penicillin, but tonsil and adenoid removal may also be required.

Obviously the use of preventive DPT shots is the best way to avoid this horrible infection.

Diphtheria bacteria in skin lesions may be discovered in people associated with victims of pharyngeal diphtheria. It can be a mode of the spread of this disease.

Enterovirus infections include a wide variety of virus-caused human infections. The *viruses* that live in the intestinal tract include *polio, Coxsackie* and *ECHO,* and cause *paralysis, canker sores, hepatitis,* rashes, *respiratory infections, diarrhea, pharyngitis,* muscle inflammation (*myositis*), and *encephalitis.*

ECHO virus infections were discovered after culture techniques were perfected. A large number of separate viruses were isolated from the intestinal tract. At first it was thought they were "orphan" viruses and were not responsible for any specific disease; hence the name Enteric Cytopathogenic Human Orphan. At least thirty have been associated with and presumed to be responsible for a number of virus illnesses—usually called a "flu" or "that virus that is going around." Fever is usually present for two or three days, then resolves, terminating with a sore throat, cold symptoms, cough, *diarrhea, measles-like* rash or severe *headache,* muscle weakness, and *poliolike* symptoms (stiff neck and back with muscle pain and weakness). *Antibiotics* are valueless; *aspirin* and rest are the main treatment. If there is doubt about the etiology in a specific case, a *white blood count* will be helpful; a low or normal count with a predominance of *lymphocytes* suggests a virus or untreatable disease, and antibiotics are *not* given. Vitamin C in large doses (5–30 grams per day) is a potent antiviral agent. It helps the body make *interferon.*

Epidemic parotitis—see *Mumps*

Erythema infectiosum, or fifth disease (the fifth form of measles), is a mild *virus* infection sometimes confused with sunburn, *allergy,* or German *measles.* There is little or no fever. Red, apparently sunburned cheeks appear suddenly, and a mottled, pink, reticular or laceworklike rash soon follows on forearms, and lower legs. Less rash is noted on the trunk. Incubation period is about ten days. No treatment is necessary. The rash may last for a week or more, but the child need not be kept home from school or away from other children.

Adults with this disease frequently have wrist- and knee-joint swelling and pain, but recover without residual *arthritis.* A recent study indicated that this disease, occasionally confused with *rubella,* does not affect the baby if a pregnant woman is afflicted with it. (See *Exanthems.*)

Escherichia coli is the most common bacterium in the intestinal tract. It is not considered harmful if it stays in the lumen of the gut, but if the appendix ruptures, these bacteria will cause an *abscess*

EXANTHEMS

Disease	*Symptoms and signs*	*Characteristics of rash*
Erythema infectiosum	Low grade fever, headache, pharyngitis	Flushed cheeks; reticulated erythema on extremities (often itchy) exacerberated by sunlight, pressure, heat. Lasts two to five weeks.
Rubella	Low grade fever, eye and throat inflammation, sensitive lymph nodes behind ears	Pink-red macules around mouth spreading to trunk. Lasts less than five days.
Scarlet fever	Temperature 101° to 103° F. for 3 to 4 days; headache, sore throat, vomiting, exudative tonsillitis	Rash appears one to two days after onset, beginning on neck, chest, axillae, rapidly becoming generalized. Streptococci in throat culture. Duration five to seven days. Skin on hands and feet peels.
Enteroviral exanthems	Temperature 101° to 103° F., pharyngitis, gastrointestinal symptoms	Rash with fever or after fever drops; nonitchy macules on face and chest, possibly palms and soles. Lasts one to five days.
Rubeola (measles)	Temperature 103° to 104° F., inflammation, cough, conjunctivitis, Koplik's spots	On fourth day, at height of fever and cough, macules develop on forehead, spread to face, neck, arms, and trunk, reach feet by third day. Rash becomes confluent and brownish.
Roseola	High fever for three to four days resolving by crisis; febrile convulsions may occur	When fever drops, rose-pink macules appear on trunk, spread to neck and behind ears, often not on face or extremities. Duration three days or less. (95% in children under 3 years.) Swollen occipital lymph nodes.
Infectious mononucleosis	Temperature to 101° F., malaise, sore throat, pharyngitis, prominent lymph nodes, enlarged spleen	Rash in only five to fifteen percent of cases. Small pink macules or papules on trunk and upper arms last one to two days. Tonsillitis, enlarged spleen; heterophile antibody reaction.

or *peritonitis.* An infection in the buttocks can result if a rectal split or sore allows a fistula to burrow through the rectal wall into adjacent tissue and point out to the skin.

If a newborn becomes ill with *septicemia, pneumonia,* or *meningitis, E. coli* is the usual causative agent. Formerly these infections were always fatal, but new drugs have been synthesized which are curative if the disease is recognized in time.

Fever is a rise in body *temperature* due to invasion by infectious organisms or toxins. Some *allergies* may occasionally elevate the temperature; so may eating meat. Exhausting exercise, increased environmental temperature, or lesions in the temperature-regulating center of the brain may also produce fever.

A common cause of rectal temperature of 100° to 103° on the second to fifth day of life is *dehydration,* especially in the breast-fed baby receiving little fluid while awaiting his mother's milk to "come in." His *kidneys* are unable to concentrate urine well at this age, so when he excretes large amounts of dilute urine, he loses weight, and his blood becomes concentrated. If a few ounces of water by mouth do not reduce the fever and irritability in an hour, other more serious reasons for the fever must be investigated.

A baby born in the winter might be overbundled by conscientious parents, although the room temperature is normal, and heavy covering is not needed. A low, even heat in the immediate crib area of 65° to 70° should be ideal. Fairly pale urine passed two or three times a day would be a minimal amount to preclude dehydration fever.

Fevers in children are most often due to *virus* infections that are self-limited, not serious, and untreatable by present-day medicine. For a child with fever, here are two rules of thumb:

1. Give the child *aspirin*—one grain for every ten pounds of body weight, given every four hours. It takes an hour and a half for a dose to be effective. If the fever is reduced by a degree or two, an hour and a half after administration, it implies the disease causing the fever is not serious.

2. The fever should not last for more than seventy-two hours. If it can be controlled with aspirin, and the child can take some nourishment and move about during the three days of fever, it implies that the child is controlling the infection and/or it is not serious and/or it is a virus. Vitamin C does help the immune systems work better, so adding 500 milligrams of vitamin C per hour (for a child)

and 1,000 milligrams per hour (for an adult) is a safe and often effective way to combat an infection.

Rubbing alcohol mixed with an equal quantity of water is a good fever reducer when spread all over the body and allowed to evaporate. Vaporization removes heat from the body surface; therefore the skin must be hot to the touch for this treatment to be effective. A comfortably hot bath (96° F.) might be used first to bring the feverish patient's hot blood to the surface. Then the alcohol-water mixture can be applied. Alcohol alone may evaporate fast enough to produce uncomfortable coldness, so it is usually cut with water. (See *Bacterial infections, Virus.*) (Inhaling too much alcohol can cause coma.)

Fifth disease—see *Erythema infectiosum*

Gingivostomatitis is an acute *viral* infection of the mouth, almost exclusively seen in the one- to three-year-old child during the summer months. The onset is sudden with fever, drooling (the throat is too sore to swallow), *headache,* and much crying. The fever lasts two to five days; at this time the child *feels* better, but the pain in the mouth gets worse because vesicles (or blisters) in the mouth open up and become raw ulcers. The child of this age refuses to allow anyone to put painkilling medicine in his mouth. The picture is one of a miserable child, refusing all help, crying, and drooling. He may sleep for an hour at night, then awaken suddenly because he swallowed in his sleep. The pain is as sharp as a knife stuck in his throat. (See *Mouth,* Section 14.)

No medicine is effective; only *aspirin* is of value. An older co-operative child might get some relief by sucking on a local anesthetic lozenge which would numb his nerve endings. (A teaspoonful of an *antihistamine syrup* held in the mouth helps.) The sores heal in a week.

Gonorrhea is a venereal disease (spread by sexual contact) of epidemic proportions in adolescents and young, sexually active adults. Some authorities feel that it is spreading because of the increased use of contraceptive pills and the abandonment of the condom, which offers local contact protection.

A few days after contact with an infected female, the male usually develops an exquisitely painful, profuse, yellow urethral discharge. The acute symptoms usually drive him to the doctor rapidly for relief.

The female may be severely infected and contagious but have no symptoms to suggest medical attention. In the last few years this gonococcus germ has become more resistant to therapy, and the old-time, one-shot-of-*penicillin* cure is rapidly becoming ineffective. *Tetracycline* is effective in many cases and should be used if the disease is suspected. Most doctors have found that the diagnosis is made on suspicion of contact, because the classical smear and culture may be unrewarding. (Tetracycline is also good for treatment of acne.)

Gram-negative bacteria is the name given to certain bacteria which do not stain with the gram dye (pseudomonas, E. coli, klebsiella, proteus, are examples). These germs are usually more resistant to *antibiotic* therapy than the germs that stain with the gram stain (gram-positive germs are streptococcus, pneumococcus, and some others).

Hand, foot, and mouth disease is an acute virus infection (*Coxsackie*) which causes fever, vesicles on the hands and feet, and ulcers in the mouth. No treatment is available; it lasts a week or so.

Hemolytic-uremic syndrome is a violent disease that begins as an ordinary *respiratory infection* plus *intestinal flu.* Instead of recovering in a few days, the patient becomes feverish, develops *kidney* failure with associated lack of urine, *hypertension, convulsions,* and *coma.* It may be due to a virus that produces clotting in the kidney capillaries. The red cells will hemolyze also, so pallor and *jaundice* will occur.

Treatment is directed to maintaining fluid, glucose, and *electrolyte* balance and controlling the elevated *blood pressure* and abnormal clotting while awaiting the kidney pathology to resolve. Mortality is high.

Herpangina is an acute *viral* infection with *headache,* violent sore throat, and high fever (105° in infants). Vesicles on a red base appear on the soft palate and sides of the throat. After three days of fever, the temperature returns to normal, and the patient feels better, but the throat becomes more sore as the vesicles become ulcers. Shooting pains to ears may suggest an ear infection. These heal spontaneously after a week of whining and drooling.

Doctors are frequently tricked into treating this, as the redness of the throat and violence of the fever onset suggest a *streptococcal* infection. The *white cell count* is low, however, which is typical of a virus, and a throat culture grows no hemolytic streptococcus.

Treatment is aspirin and fluids. If the child is cooperative enough, he may be soothed by sucking on a local anesthetic lozenge that numbs the raw nerves in the ulcers.

Herpes progenitalis is a herpetic infection creating vesicles and ulcers on the lips of the *vagina.* Fever and painful urination are the main symptoms. A *bladder* infection due to bacteria must be ruled out. Cleanliness and *aspirin* are the treatment.

If a pregnant woman with a herpetic vaginal infection delivers her baby while the infection is active, the baby may develop a severe systemic herpetic infection that resembles *septicemia:* fever, *jaundice, vomiting,* lethargy. Secondary *bacterial* infections may cause a fatal termination.

Herpes simplex is a *virus* which causes a wide variety of skin, eye, mucous-membrane, and nervous-system diseases. Almost every child has had a herpetic infection by the time he is five or six years old, probably associated with teething, which allows the virus to invade the host. After this, recurrences are common after trauma, a cold, exposure to sunshine, stress, menses, or bacterial infections (*canker sores*). Once the primary infection has been subdued, the host harbors the virus and can be a source of infection to other nonimmune people. (Parents frequently infect their children.) The primary infection is usually seen in the six-month- to three-year-old child as *herpangina* or *gingivostomatitis.* If a baby with *eczema* acquires herpes, he develops *eczema herpeticum* which, with a high fever and prostration, may be fatal. (It must be distinguished from *eczema vaccinatum.*)

Herpetic meningoencephalitis will occur if this *virus* invades the brain. Fever, *headache, vomiting, convulsions* could be fatal. Treatment can only be supportive, with I-V fluids and perhaps neurosurgical decompression.

Herpetic stomatitis—see *Gengivostomatitis*

Heterophil test, or Paul-Bunnell agglutination test, is usually positive in the blood of *infectious-mononucleosis* patients. Antibodies in the patient's blood will agglutinate sheep cells under certain circumstances. (See *Infectious mononucleosis.*)

Infectious lymphocytosis is assumed to be a *virus* infection which, like most *respiratory infections,* begins with fever, sore throat, abdominal pain, and *headache.* A *white blood count* may be taken by the doctor in an effort to make a definite diagnosis. (A low count—under 12,000 cells per cubic millimeter—suggests a virus.) This disease gives high white counts (20,000 and above) which suggests a bacterial infection (treatable with antibiotics), but the high percentage of *lymphocytes* argues for a virus—and untreatable—disease. The patient should rest and be given aspirin and fluids.

Infectious mononucleosis is an acute, probably viral disease found predominately in adolescents. This illness with some medical embarrassment was formerly called the interns-nurses' disease. This "kissing disease" is not strictly confined to lovers, but the young adult seems to be very susceptible. At least close proximity is required for passage.

It sneaks up on the victim. A few days of malaise and *anorexia* pass before the characteristic swollen neck glands, sore throat, and chills begin. Fever is at its peak (100° to 103°) by the eighth to tenth day, and lethargy, weakness, and *headache* are common. *Jaundice* from *liver* involvement occurs in 10 percent of cases and may cause a misdiagnosis of *hepatitis.* The *spleen* is enlarged in 75 percent of victims and is prone to rupture if injured. The exquisite headache may suggest *encephalitis,* and, indeed, a spinal test may reveal increased cell count.

By the second week a blood test (*heterophil* or Paul-Bunnell test) is positive in most patients. Usually by this time the doctor has tried some *penicillin* on the patient because of the swollen tonsils, sore throat, swollen glands, and small *hemorrhages* on the soft palate, all suggesting a strep infection. Lack of response to penicillin rules out a strep infection, so mononucleosis is about all that's left.

No specific treatment is indicated except *aspirin,* fluids, *codeine* for pain, and rest while the spleen is enlarged. Complete rest serves only to weaken the muscles and prolongs convalescence. Vitamin C in big doses (5–20 grams a day) early will shorten the course of the illness.

By the third week the fever and malaise are considerably reduced, and except for some lethargy, the patient is well by the end of the fourth week.

"Chronic" mono is not a recognized disease. Complications—for example, secondary bacterial infections—are the only things that prolong the symptoms.

An occasional patient will develop a generalized macular rash (see *Exanthems*) and a positive (false) blood test for *syphilis* that could frighten an unwary adolescent who thought he only kissed his date goodnight.

Infectious neuronitis—see *Guillain-Barré,* Section 15

Interferon is a naturally occurring antiviral *protein.* It blocks *virus* replication within the cells, but it is active for only a short period of time, and it is in short supply. New methods of manufacture or methods of stimulating the body to produce its own interferon will soon provide a valuable weapon against viruses. Vitamin C helps the body make interferon.

Kawasaki disease was first described in Japan and originally called "mucocutaneous lymph-node syndrome." It strikes young children with fever, enlarged neck nodes, redness and swelling of the eyes, and redness and peeling of the skin of the hands and feet. In Japan the death rate is less than 2 percent. In the United States the disease is uncommon. The most serious complications affect the coronary arteries and the heart muscle. Kawasaki disease remains a mystery in terms of cause, and using aspirin is the mainstay of therapy.

Leptospirosis is a *spirochetal* disease (caused by an organism similar to the *syphilis* organism) carried by rodents who pass the organism in their urine. Many other animals, wild and domestic, become carriers; therefore, farmers, shepherds, veterinarians are more frequently at risk.

The disease may be mild or severe. It may act as a mild flu with headache, fever, malaise, or it may cause overwhelming collapse with symptoms of encephalitis. Some patients have more liver and kidney involvement with *jaundice, albumin,* and *blood in the urine,* and *hemorrhages* in the skin.

The average doctor would not see many cases (fewer than a hundred are reported in the United States each year), so when confronted with a patient with these symptoms, he often assumes that it's a bad case of flu. Urine and blood cultures would reveal its presence if the doctor thought to ask the laboratory to look for it.

Penicillin is the remedy, but the response is slow.

Listeria monocytogenes is an uncommon organism that may cause *meningitis.* A rare baby may be born with this infection causing *pneumonia, diarrhea,* and rashes. It is difficult to identify, but responds well to *penicillin.*

Lupus erythematosus is a disease of connective tissue, and since connective tissue is widespread throughout the body, many organs and tissues are involved. The body's immune mechanisms are active (elevated *gamma globulin*) and many antibodies can be detected, as if the body had developed a reaction against itself. It can be confused with *arthritis, rheumatic fever, Stevens-Johnson syndrome, vasculitis,* and *nephritis,* as the joints, heart, skin, blood vessels, and kidneys are involved to varying degrees.

It may be sudden or insidious in onset; it may be mild or severe in involvement. It may follow some obvious infection or drug ingestion. Females are the more likely victims; late childhood or early adolescence is a common age.

Fever, malaise, joint pain, and rash are common early symptoms. A red, papular, and scaly rash over the bridge of the nose and onto the cheeks (butterfly-shaped) is supposed to be diagnostic. *Pleurisy, pericarditis,* and *peritonitis* confirm the disease if associated with the above skin rash and *arthritis.* The presence of the *L. erythematosus* cell in the blood is the final step in the diagnosis.

Treatment is suppressive, not curative. *Cortisone, antibiotics, aspirin* are helpful. The kidney involvement is most likely to progress to failure. The death rate is high, although some have survived years with the disease smoldering unrecognized.

Lymphogranuloma inguinale (venereum) is considered to be a venereal infection and hence is rare in children unless they are in contact with an infected—and most likely disturbed—adult. It is a *virus* infection that produces large, tender *lymph nodes,* usually inguinal. These may coalesce and drain.

Tetracycline is usually effective.

Malaria, a rare *parasitic* infection in the United States, is now being reported more frequently because of the rapidity and extent of foreign travel. The bite of the infected Anopheles mosquito passes this parasite from one person to another. These invade and multiply in red cells, which rupture. The spiking fever is due to the release of these parasites and red-cell debris into the bloodstream. The released parasites invade new red cells, and the cycle is repeated every two to three days, depending on the malaria type. Fever, *anemia, blood in the urine* (black water fever), and enlarged *spleen* are characteristic features. A blood smear reveals the parasites.

People in malarial areas should take antimalarial drugs, as the disease is serious and occasionally fatal. A variety of medicines is available (for example, chloroquine and quinine), but the organisms are developing resistance to some.

Worldwide mosquito control is reducing the vectors, but the chemicals used to eradicate the pests disturb local ecology.

Malta fever—see *Brucellosis*

Measles is the name usually applied to the hard, coughing, black, or two-week measles, best referred to as *rubeola. Roseola, rubella, fifth disease* (erythema infectiosum), and Boston measles are all measles but have definite manifestations to distinguish them clearly one from another. They are all viruses with rashes, but many other virus diseases will display rashes due to the viremia (*virus* floating in the bloodstream and irritating the capillaries which will dilate and produce transient flushing); if doctors are unsure, they say "toxic rash." (See *Exanthems.*)

At present a live vaccine is available which produces active immunity against *rubeola* and *rubella.* Rubeola vaccine is usually given at fifteen months of age. The maternal immune *globulins* may inactivate the live virus if it is introduced before this time. It is about 96 percent effective. Most of us are now seeing a few cases of hard measles (rubeola) for the first time since 1965 as not all children are being routinely immunized.

Meningitis is a severe, rapidly progressive, frequently fatal infection of the meninges. It is a bacterial infection of the surface lining of the brain, usually considered to be blood-borne. Bacteria are carried from the nose or throat to the brain, where they create a usually characteristic set of symptoms—high fever, *coma,* and a stiff neck and back. Upon examination, pus is found in the spinal fluid. *Antibiotics,* if given early enough, are usually curative, and if the infection is not too overwhelming, the patient can usually be saved. One type, due to the meningococcus, is considered to be contagious; the others, because the infection is quite well locked up inside the brain, are not.

The meningococcus type is often found in school dormitories or army or navy barracks where many people live together. It used to respond very nicely to *sulfa* drugs, but some strains are now becoming quite resistant. It is rapidly overwhelming, sudden in onset, and sometimes fatal before diagnosis can be made and treatment instituted.

The classical symptoms of *headache,* fever, stiff neck, and stupor are usually absent or difficult to determine in the newborn. The infant may only vomit, become irritable, and change his sleeping habits.

He may have no fever. He may be limp instead of stiff. His fontanel (soft spot) is frequently full or tense. (A mother might wisely palpate this area occasionally to become familiar with the normal tenseness. It will become sunken with *dehydration* and full and tense with meningitis.) Irritability when handled may be the only clue to this infection in a small baby.

In the older child with fever and headache, two reliable tests may suggest meningitis: (a) Kernig's sign: the supine child resists having his leg raised to close to a 90° angle with the horizontal; (b) Brudzinski's: the supine child will flex his knees when his head is flexed forward onto his chest.

When the disease is suspected, a spinal-fluid tap (see *Lumbar puncture,* Section 15) is done to establish the diagnosis. If the cell count is in the thousands and consists mainly of polymorphonuclear *white cells,* the diagnosis of bacterial meningitis is assured. Some of this fluid is cultured in the incubator so that some of the bacteria will grow to a number allowing identification. While the lab is tagging the germs, the patient is usually treated with antibiotics appropriate for the majority of invaders. In the newborn, *E. coli* is more common. In the toddler, *H. influenza* is the usual germ. *Pneumococcus, streptococcus, staphylococcus* are less common invaders.

It takes twelve to twenty-four hours for the antibiotic to be absorbed, arrive at the meninges, and kill enough bacteria to make a difference. Nursing care, intravenous fluid, oxygen are all directed toward holding the patient together until the antibiotic becomes effective. The laboratory sends the results of the culture and sensitivity studies; when the particular germ is identified, the most effective antibiotics are continued and the inappropriate ones stopped.

Although the patient may respond to the treatment, the severity of the damage to the brain may leave defects in learning, motor control, and attention span.

If the spinal tap produces fluid with cell count in the hundreds and consisting mainly of *lymphocytes,* it suggests a *virus* infection. (*Mumps* and *infectious mononucleosis* might produce this same severe group of symptoms.) There is no treatment, as viruses do not respond to antibiotics. Although the patient is gravely ill with fever and *headache,* he usually recovers completely with no residual neurological defects. This disease is usually called meningoencephalitis.

Subdural effusion (see *Intracranial bleeding,* Section 15) is a thick fluid that may accumulate in the subdural space during the course of meningitis. It must be suspected if the victim fails to respond after a few days of adequate treatment. The fluid must be drained by needle tapping, easily performed in an infant through the skull suture lines.

The tubercle bacillus may break away from the lung and seed into the brain. This *tuberculous meningitis* is difficult to diagnose, because it may begin innocuously with headache and malaise (Thomas Wolfe died of this disease). The findings in the spinal fluid may suggest a virus. Every doubtful case of meningitis, in which an obvious bacterium is not manifest, should have some screening testing done for tuberculosis. (It may be a virus, but a TB tine test would be the minimum workup.)

Tuberculous *meningitis* is a severe and crippling inflammation of the brain. The patient develops stiffness of the back, fever, coma, severe *constipation,* and *dermatographia* (pressure on the skin produces welts). Antituberculosis drugs may save the patient's life, but the already damaged nervous system may not return to complete normal function. Spasticity of arms or legs, *deafness, impulsivity,* and *hyperactivity* are but a few of the residual defects.

A few endocrine syndromes have been reported after recovery from TB meningitis if the bacteria have invaded and presumably impaired the function of the *pituitary* gland and/or the *hypothalamus. Sexual precocity, hypogonadism, growth retardation, diabetes insipidus,* or severe *obesity* may be present. X rays frequently show calcium deposits in the pituitary or hypothalamic areas.

Mumps, or epidemic parotitis, is a *virus* inflammation of the salivary glands. The victim is usually five to eight years old and acquires it from his classmates. Characteristically, he has swollen cheeks that fill out the pocket below the ear lobe—not to be confused with the swollen glands from tonsillitis, which are high in the neck under the corner of the jawbone. Before the swelling occurs, the pain may suggest an ear infection. In general, this is not a serious infection unless it (a) leads to *encephalitis,* in which case the patient may be severely incapacitated with a high fever and an exquisite headache, or (b) goes to the *pancreas* and produces a severe stomachache, fever, and *vomiting.* (See *Pancreatitis,* Section 12.)

There is now a live mumps vaccine that seems to give permanent protection from this disease. There is no medical reason why a patient with mumps cannot be ambulatory if he feels well enough for it.

He may select his own diet, but it is true that sour foods such as pickles and lemons may give him some jaw spasm.

The incubation period is about three weeks from the time of exposure. A patient is probably contagious for a day before and for the five days after the swelling becomes obvious. Once the swelling is down enough so that the glands are not visible (but still palpable), the patient is probably not contagious.

The parotid glands (curving about the earlobe and extending into the cheeks) are the most likely glands involved, but the submandibular glands (directly under the molars) and the sublingual glands (swelling makes a double chin) may all swell together, creating a grotesque moon face.

The virus floating in the bloodstream may lodge in and produce inflammation of *brain, kidneys, pancreas, testes* (*Orchitis,* Section 13), *ovaries,* and *thyroid.* The virus in the auditory nerve may cause *deafness,* usually only unilateral.

Recurrent parotitis is probably due to a different virus (*Coxsackie*).

A mumps hyperimmune *gamma globulin* has not been effective. (A couple I know, exposed to mumps by their children, got the expensive shot, went to Hawaii on their long-planned trip, spent ten days staring at the ceiling with severe mumps, recovered, got leied, said "Aloha," and came home.)

The live mumps vaccine will not protect a person if it is given after exposure. The body produces active immunity in about four to six weeks after the vaccine; this is not enough time to beat the three-week incubation period.

Myositis is inflammation or infection of muscles, usually due to *Coxsackie virus.* It lasts about a week; hot packs, rest, and *aspirin* are indicated.

Osteomyelitis—see Section 7

Parotitis—see *Mumps*

Peritonitis may be secondary to a rupture of the *appendix* or other intestinal area (see *Anal fistula,* Section 12). The germs that leak out from the burst organ set up an intense reaction as the peritoneal area tries to wall it off. Prostration, chills, and high fever, tense, exquisitely tender abdomen, sunken eyes, and *dehydration* suggest that an emergency is present. Although surgery is necessary, the patient first must be hydrated intravenously, his stomach aspirated, and antibiotic treatment begun. (see *Peritonitis,* Section 12.)

Peritonitis may be a complication of *nephrosis.*

Peritonitis due to *tuberculosis* is rare now but indicates that the bacteria have invaded the entire body. Evidence is found in the lungs primarily, but also in the meninges and bones. An abdominal (mesenteric) *lymph node* breaks down and spews the organism into the peritoneal space. The germs colonize and reveal themselves as small bumps (tubercles) spread diffusely over the surface of the abdominal organs. Symptoms evolve slowly with lethargy, low-grade fever, and a vague abdominal discomfiture. Because it is so rarely seen nowadays, it is near the bottom of the list of diseases to be considered when a patient complains of the above symptoms.

Routine *tuberculosis skin testing* is important as this insidious, persistent disease still crops up.

Peritonsillar abscess, quinsy, is a sequel of *tonsillitis.* It is rarely seen now because most severe, *streptococcal* tonsillitis victims receive *antibiotics* before the bacteria have a chance to invade the tissues behind the tonsils.

After a few days of a sore throat, the patient becomes worse with chills, fever, throbbing throat pain, spasm of jaw muscles to the extent of refusal to swallow or speak. If the mouth can be pried open sufficiently, the affected side of the throat can be seen as a cherry red mass pushed over to the midline.

If the spasm (or trismus) of the jaw muscles does not permit the mouth to open, an abscess between the tonsillar capsule and the jaw muscle is surely present and surgical drainage is required. (The anesthesia used will allow the mouth to be opened sufficiently to permit incision and aspiration of the pus.)

If the patient can open his mouth enough to allow the doctor to visualize the swelling, the condition may be a cellulitis and will respond to massive penicillin therapy.

Most doctors recommend tonsillectomy when the condition subsides as quinsy is frequently recurrent.

Pharyngitis is an inflammation of the pharynx. Most of these are due to viruses (*Adenovirus, Neck,* Section 14) and are not treatable. The general principles of care and treatment are outlined under *tonsillitis.*

Polyarteritis nodosa is a generalized small blood-vessel inflammation; the disease is widespread, and each organ system produces characteristic symptoms. The cause is unknown but is assumed to be some type of *allergy* to oneself. It is rare in childhood. Fever, generalized aches and pains, weakness, and weight loss would fit any generalized infection like *vasculitis, rheumatic fever,* and rheumatoid *arthritis.*

The inflammation in the *lungs* produces cough, wheeze, and *bronchitis;* in the *brain, delirium, paralysis,* and coma; in the *kidney,* a *nephritis* picture with *albuminuria, hematuria,* and *hypertension.* The skin shows *hemorrhages,* rashes, and nodules. The heart shows *myocarditis.*

Cortisone drugs may suppress the symptoms; the response to this drug suggests that the disease is an overwhelming allergy. Death is the usual outcome if *heart* and *renal failure* coexist.

Protozoan diseases are due to parasites which invade the host through bites (*malaria*), ingestion (*amebiasis*), or the placenta (*toxoplasmosis*). They are destructive, chronic, and difficult to eradicate completely.

Pseudomonas aeruginosa is a bacterium found widely in the soil. It causes severe infections (usually sepsis, in the lung or in burns) in malnourished or debilitated victims. Its hardiness makes it difficult to treat with the usual antibiotics, and the strong medicines effective against it may be just as toxic to the patient. Due to immaturity of immune mechanisms, the newborn—especially the premature—and the aged are more susceptible; despite early recognition and vigorous treatment, the death rate of infected patients is high.

Skin infection will exude green or bluish colored pus and cause local slough of gangrenous skin. Scrupulous care of incubators and oxygen equipment may not be sufficient to eradicate the germ from the premie's environment, and he may inhale the germ into his lungs. Patients with *cystic fibrosis* seem prone to lung involvement with it, as do surgical patients, or those with urinary-tract obstruction and infection.

This bacterium is a common contaminant of third-degree burns, but surgical cleansing plus local application of silver nitrate prophylactically will often prevent its invasion.

Polymycin, gentamycin, and carbenicillin are effective antibiotics against pseudomonas.

Q fever is a *rickettsial disease* seen in people who care for cows, sheep, or goats, or work with hides or animal hair. The organism is inhaled or carried by ticks.

High fever, *headache,* pain on eye movement, and respiratory symptoms may last a week or two. *Tetracycline* is an effective suppressant and will shorten the course of the disease.

Rabbit fever—see *Tularemia*

Rabies, hydrophobia, is an almost uniformly fatal *viral* disease of the nervous system. The virus is inoculated into the victim by a rabid cat, dog, bat, fox, skunk, or other wild animal (apparently *not* by members of the rodent family). The virus travels by way of the nerves to the brain, where an *encephalitis* is produced. This causes extreme excitement, anxiety, hyperactivity, pain, and finally exhaustion, coma, and death. The spasm of the throat muscles gives it the name "hydrophobia" (fear of water).

The incubation period from bite to first symptoms depends on the distance between the injury and the brain. If the foot is bitten, symptoms might be delayed one or two months, but a bite on the face would shorten the time to seven to ten days. Numbness, tingling, or crawling sensations are noted along the nerve pathway. Soon restlessness, excitability, and then terror overcome the patient.

Because of the fatal outcome, people bitten by rabid animals should receive the hyperimmune serum followed by rabies vaccine. The committee of the World Health Organization has established basic rules for treatment. Surveillance of the suspected animal is most important. A dog who has bitten a human must be quarantined; if the animal dies and the characteristic negri bodies are found in its brain at autopsy, the bitten person must be given the vaccine. Bats are known to harbor the virus in their saliva but be unaffected themselves (they are carriers). Bat bites demand treatment without delay, as waiting for the demise of the bat is fruitless. Domestic animals are an unlikely source of the disease because of the inoculation most states now require.

The wound must be washed thoroughly with soap and water. Nitric acid kills the virus but causes scar tissue. A doctor should be consulted so a plan can be made. Usually a booster tetanus shot is all that is recommended. If the dog or cat is known to the neighborhood, its behavior has not changed, and it does not die within the week or so after the bite, nothing need be done. The animal should *not* be destroyed because of the attack; it is important that it be kept alive so that behavior may be observed.

Apparently chipmunks, rats, mice, and gerbils are unable to carry the virus, so their bites need only local treatment.

(A rabies death occurred in our town a few years ago in a boy who had been bitten by a dog in Spain. Before the diagnosis was established, he had, of course, spread the virus about the hospital. Twenty-two hospital personnel ended up receiving the vaccine as a precaution.)

Rat-bite fever is uncommon, considering the number of children who are bitten by rats. Fever, joint pain, and a rash one to three weeks after a rat bite suggest the disease. One form is due to a spiral-formed organism; the other is due to bacteria. In the spiral form the original bite becomes a painful ulcer. Fortunately, both types respond to *penicillin.*

Retropharyngeal abscess (see *Peritonsillar abscess*) is a pus pocket in the *lymph nodes* in the space between the back wall of the pharynx and the neck bones (vertebrae) and may accompany throat infections in the small child. Germs in these glands may grow sufficiently to rupture the glands, and pus forms in this space, pushing the back wall of the pharynx forward. Inability to swallow, gurgling throat sounds, high fever, head arched back, and an obvious red bulge in the throat suggest the diagnosis. The condition is uncommon now because most severe sore throats are treated before a pus pocket can form.

Abscesses in this area should be drained surgically; if they burst, the pus may be aspirated into the lungs. Penicillin is important to prevent the spread of the infection.

Rheumatic fever is an inflammation of a variety of body tissues: joints *(arthritis),* skin (rashes), brain *(chorea),* and, of most importance, the *heart* and its valves. It is always preceded by a *streptococcal* infection—usually a strep throat—of the group A beta hemolytic streptococcus. The patient recovers from the initial sore throat, but within two to four weeks he begins to run a fever, develop migratory joint aches (ankles, wrists, knees, elbows with or without redness and swelling), develops a rapid *heart rate* disproportionate to the *temperature* elevation, and less frequently begins to make involuntary, purposeless movements (*chorea* or St. Vitus' dance). Nodules form about his joints or in his scalp, and he may blossom with a rash (erythema marginatum) of irregularly curved lines over the trunk.

Heart murmurs are heard, the blood shows some *anemia,* the *sedimentation rate* is elevated as are the streptococcal antibodies. The chest X ray usually shows some enlargement, and the *electrocardiogram* may show changes. The throat culture is usually positive for the beta hemolytic (blood on the culture plate is hemolysed by the bacteria, leaving a clear space) if the triggering strep throat was fairly recent and/or untreated.

Not all of the above findings need be present to establish the diagnosis, but some combination of physical findings and laboratory evidence must be present.

It is estimated that about 3 to 5 percent of untreated strep throats will lead to rheumatic fever, but only one tenth of that number will do so if adequately treated (with ten full days of *penicillin*).

Treatment must be individualized, as some cases are mild with only a few joint aches and little heart involvement, while others may have a malignant, rapidly fatal, overwhelming *carditis* unresponsive to all care.

Controversy still exists about the use of *cortisonelike* drugs that suppress many of the inflammatory joint and heart manifestations. Some doctors feel that only the severe heart patients should receive cortisone and that all others will do well on aspirin alone. Penicillin is usually given to be sure the strep has been eradicated from the throat. Bed rest until the sedimentation rate is normal seems sensible, but most bored children cheat on this when they begin to feel better. Oxygen, heart stimulants *(digitalis)* may be required in severe cases, especially if *pericarditis* is present.

The exact etiology of this disease is obscure; the most plausible theory is that the streptococcal infection stimulates the body to manufacture antistrep antibodies, which then attack some antigen in the heart, joints, and skin.

A first attack usually leaves the heart relatively free of permanent sequelae, but subsequent attacks of strep will almost surely produce scarring of the heart valves. (See *Heart,* Section 8.) For this reason, the child is placed on prophylactic penicillin at least until he is through high school. A monthly injection of a long-acting penicillin seems to be the most reliable prophylaxis available. The oral medication is unintentionally but frequently skipped in the best of homes.

Rickettsial diseases are those illnesses due to organisms smaller than bacteria and larger than *viruses.* Like viruses they require the living cell for growth. They are transmitted by the bite of a louse, mite, or tick. *Antibiotics* are helpful in suppressing the growth of the organism. (See *Rocky Mountain spotted fever, Q fever, Typhus,* and *Scrub typhus.*)

Rocky Mountain spotted fever is a febrile illness with rash due to a rickettsia, an organism somewhere between a *virus* and a bacterium. It is transmitted to man from wild animals or the family dog by the bite of a tick. Although first discovered in Montana, it is not uncommon in other parts of the country where the family dog may harbor ticks infected from the wild animal reservoir (rabbits, squirrels, chipmunks). Two to three hundred cases are reported yearly in the United States, most of them in the South Atlantic states.

The disease begins with fever, *headache,* malaise, chills, and muscle aches. In a few days a macular rash appears, usually on the wrists and ankles, and spreads to the body; it soon becomes *hemorrhagic* (*purpura* and *petechiae*). *Conjunctivitis,* swollen lids, enlarged *liver* and *spleen, delirium, coma,* and *convulsions* may all be present in all grades of severity. *Myocarditis,* renal involvement, and *lung* inflammation may be severe enough to prove fatal. A blood agglutinin test may help establish the diagnosis, since not all patients recall the tick bite. The *white cell count* is low (3,000 to 12,000). *Tetracycline* drugs will help the body control the infection but are not considered dramatically curative.

Roseola infantum is an acute, febrile, viral illness most commonly seen in the six- to eighteen-month age group. It is second only to influenza as a cause of fever in babies. It is sometimes called teething fever or teething rash, because its onset is frequently associated with tooth eruption. Apparently the baby harbors the virus (possibly in the mouth), and it invades the system when the crown of a tooth breaks through the gum. Its contagious nature is not obvious.

A sudden high fever (104° to 106°) may be accompanied by a frightening convulsion. The eyelids may be red-rimmed, but few other symptoms occur; the baby is just hot and fussy. He may clutch the side of his head as if he has an earache; he probably does have a headache. *Aspirin* and a bath usually bring the fever down temporarily, but it recurs in three hours. When the fever responds, the baby acts almost normal and can be made to smile and eat. (This is in contrast to a bacterial infection which usually does not respond to *aspirin,* and if it does, the child does not feel better. The bacterial toxins keep him feeling punk.)

The fever usually lasts seventy-two hours—almost on the nose—then disappears rapidly to be replaced with a macular rash predominantly on the trunk and face and only slightly on the arms and legs. Swollen *glands* in the back of the head just above the attachment of the neck muscles help to diagnose roseola. It is the only disease that has a rash *after* the fever falls. Many babies will be fussy and irritable after the fever drops until the rash blossoms; then with a sigh of relief, they smile and relax.

Examination during the fever reveals no good pathology. The throat is usually a vermilion color—not the blood red of a streptococcal infection. The white blood count is almost always low, even down to 3,000 to 5,000 cells per cubic millimeter with a predominance of lymphocytes; this is a giveaway for a virus.

An occasional, unsure doctor will treat the feverish baby with a *penicillin* shot at hour sixty. The fever falls at hour seventy-two. When the rash appears at hour eighty, everyone assumes that the rash is due to a penicillin allergy.

No treatment is available because it is a viral disease; reassurance and *aspirin* are all that is necessary.

Rubella, or German measles, mild, or three-day measles, may be hardly noticed in a child because there is little or no fever (100° or less), few symptoms except a slight *headache* and a macular rash which rarely itches. A sudden appearing, generalized macular rash is often the first clue that the disease is present. No spots are bigger than a quarter of an inch, except on the face, where they frequently coalesce so that the cheeks appear flushed. The giveaway (if an epidemic does not make one suspicious) is the presence of enlarged *lymph nodes* on the mastoid bone directly behind the ears. These feel like rubbery peanuts between the skin and the bone, bobbling back and forth when massaged. Eighty percent of children have had the disease by age twelve. Adults are usually more toxic when infected; joint aches and 101° temperature are common.

The only real problem with this disease is the damage it will induce in a prenatal baby during the mother's illness. Infection in the first three months of the pregnancy is the most dangerous time for the baby; organs are being formed, and the *virus* invades the cells, disrupting normal completion of important tissues. *Cataracts, deafness, heart anomalies,* and *mental deficiency* may occur singly or in combination, but anomalies of almost every organ may appear.

Some 10,000 babies were born with the congenital rubella syndrome after the 1964 epidemic. The virus could be isolated from them after birth. If a woman contracts rubella in her pregnancy, she should be aware of the risks of bearing a malformed child. Most women elect to have an abortion performed if they are so afflicted in the first three months.

Since 1969 a rubella vaccine (live) has been available; it appears to be effective in protecting the susceptible. If widely used, it should eliminate the disease and at least one cause of congenital anomalies.

So many viral illnesses produce a rash easily confused with rubella that it is better to immunize all children with or without a history of possible rubella.

Rubeola, or hard measles, two-week measles, coughing measles, or black measles, has largely disappeared in the last ten years because almost all children are now immunized against it at age fifteen months. (See *Measles.*)

It begins about ten days after exposure with a fever (the *virus* is invading). The fever drops, but a dry cough develops, then watery, red-rimmed eyes become increasingly bothersome. The fever recurs and rises daily until the fourth day when it may reach 103° to 105°. The cough is especially persistent but still dry. The watery nose (often bloody), red eyes (light-sensitive), and redness inside the mouth make the patient uncomfortable. Swollen *glands* are noted on the back of the head. A few white spots (Koplik's spots) may be seen inside the cheeks. Finally at the height of the fever the cough becomes worse and the rash appears. Pink macules about one-fourth inch in size begin at the hairline, spread to the face—where they become confluent—and sweep down over the body. This takes about twenty-four hours. Symptoms do not abate until after the rash has arrived at the toes (in contrast to roseola in which the rash appears *after* the fever falls). The next day the fever is down, the cough loosens, and the rash begins to fade. Four days of getting worse, then four days of getting better is the pattern in an uncomplicated case. The patient is contagious throughout this time.

Because it is a *respiratory infection,* the incidence of *bronchitis, pneumonia, otitis,* and *adenitis* is high. Appropriate *antibiotics* are indicated only when these secondary infections arise. Not infrequently the virus invades the nervous system, and *encephalitis* symptoms predominate. The viremia may depress the *platelets* and *hemorrhages* appear in the rash (black measles). *Cortisone* may be indicated for this complication.

Treatment consists of *aspirin,* warm baths (not to "bring out the rash" but only to make the patient more comfortable), *antihis-*

taminics for the itch and to encourage rest. The eyes are light sensitive (photophobia) so a darkened room is common sense, but light does not damage the eyes.

Since most adults have had this disease by age six or seven years and have developed immunity, a baby will be immune by passive transfer of the mother's *immune globulins* via the placenta. After age four months he becomes susceptible. The live measles vaccine is routinely given at age fifteen months. If an unimmunized child is exposed to measles, he should be given a dose of *gamma globulin* just sufficient to allow him to have a modified case. He gets the disease, but in a mild form; the immunity he develops is enough to protect him. It is pointless to give him the vaccine after exposure as he will be unable to develop enough immunity within ten days to prevent a full-blown case. Many inadequately immunized adolescents are getting a measleslike illness. If there is doubt about measles immunizations done in the 1960s, revaccination should be done.

San Joaquin Valley fever—See *Coccidioidomycosis,* Section 9

Scarlet fever is a *streptococcal* sore throat or tonsillitis or pharyngitis (if tonsils are absent) which is accompanied by a red, generalized rash resembling sunburn. If the rash is fine, small, nonconfluent, and more obvious in the armpits, groin, and cheeks, the name "scarlatina" is often used. There is usually a pallor around the lips. Any one of several types of group A beta hemolytic streptococci may be responsible. A person may become immune to the toxin that causes the rash, but not to reinfection by the streptococcus. (See *Dick skin test,* Section 6.)

The incubation period is short, taking but two to four days for transmission from one person to another. Fever, *headache, vomiting,* and weakness are followed in a day or two by the rash. *Aspirin* may reduce the fever somewhat, but the toxins floating about in the bloodstream make the patient feel miserable in spite of the reduced temperature.

The throat and tonsils are red and swollen. The inflammation is usually a deep, blood red. *Hemorrhages* may occur. (With a viral infection, the throat is usually more vermilion or pink.) The glands in the neck just under the curve of the jawbone become swollen and tender. Hyponasal speech is common, in contrast to the hoarseness of *croup* or the sore *trachea* accompanying the *flu.*

A strawberry tongue is associated with a streptococcal sore throat (with or without the rash). At first, it is white-coated and the papillae protrude through; in a few days the coat sloughs off, leaving the red tongue. This color, with the tongue papillae lying on top, is reminiscent of a ripe strawberry.

The *white blood count* is elevated, suggesting a bacterial infection (20,000 with a high percentage of polymorphonuclear leukocytes). The urine usually has increased amounts of albumin. *Anemia* is common.

A week after the fever subsides, the skin about the fingers and toes will peel off as if sunburned.

In a typical case, a throat culture is usually not necessary, but if there is doubt, a positive throat culture for beta hemolytic streptococcus will confirm the diagnosis.

The standard treatment is ten days of penicillin; if the patient is allergic to penicillin, *erythromycin* is satisfactory. *Tetracyclines* or *sulfa* drugs are not to be used. With this regimen the chance of *glomerulonephritis* (Section 13) or *rheumatic fever* is diminished.

The fever falls rapidly within ten to twelve hours after treatment is begun, and the rash fades soon after. The treatment, however, must go on for the full ten days because of the risk of recurrence and the danger of complications in an inadequately treated case.

After forty-eight hours of treatment and twenty-four hours of no fever, the patient is considered well enough to resume full activity and noncontagious enough to return to school.

No one is sure if prophylactic penicillin is worth giving to family and school contacts. It seems wise to culture the throats of family members and treat those with positive cultures. It may be best to observe other casual contacts and treat them with the full ten days of penicillin, if they develop the strep sore throat. A couple of days of inadequate penicillin may mask a contact's symptoms; he might be better off getting the infection and being treated adequately. Some doctors feel more secure if they take a culture at the end of treatment to ascertain strep-free throat.

(I recall a boy who was scalded with hot coffee and subsequently developed scarlet fever. His mother had a minor sore throat which proved to be a strep; when she changed his dressings, she exhaled her bacteria into his wound.)

Scrub typhus, or tsutsugamushi fever, is a rickettsial disease found all over Southeast Asia. Rodents harbor the disease, and a mite or chigger carries it to man. About two weeks after the bite a fever and *headache* appear. Within a week a macular rash blossoms. Death may occur if the lungs or heart are involved. *Tetracyclines* speed recovery.

Septicemia, or sepsis, is a bacterial bloodstream infection. The defense mechanisms of the blood *(white blood cells* and *immune globulins)* are usually able to pick off the stray bacterium that manages to sneak through mucus membranes or skin and float about in the bloodstream. If these invading organisms are too numerous or multiply faster than the defense can destroy them, septicemia occurs.

It is not uncommon in the weak premature whose mother's membrane (sac about the baby in utero) ruptured a few days before delivery. The infection may enter through the vessels in the contaminated cord stump.

Poor feeding, *cyanosis, jaundice,* fever, and coma and death may occur so rapidly in the susceptible newborn that by the time the diagnosis is suspected, remedial *antibiotics* are too late.

Meningococcemia is a septicemia due to the meningococcus. Bacterial *endocarditis* will allow bacteria to float about in the bloodstream (bacteremia).

Waterhouse-Friderichsen syndrome is a frequently fatal complication of septicemia (especially of the meningococcus). It is assumed that massive *hemorrhages* into the cortex of the adrenal glands act as the final blow to the already exhausted body. The shock due to the lack of circulating cortisone hormones may occur so rapidly that restorative measures cannot be initiated in time to prevent fatal circulatory collapse. (See *Meningitis.*)

Smallpox is a severe, occasionally fatal *virus* disease, considered to be the most contagious disease in the world. It is credited with wiping out more Indians during the white man's conquest of North America than did the colonists' and pioneers' bullets.

It is considered air borne; the virus may remain viable for months in the blankets or books of a victim. The incubation period is about two weeks. The patient rapidly develops a fever (up to 106°), *headache,* backache (a professor in medical school said he made the diagnosis in a doubtful case before the characteristic rash appeared because the feverish patient he was called to see had such a severe backache), *convulsions,* and *coma.* Within a couple of days papules appear which become vesicles. In a week these are pustules. This sequence of events takes place in all the lesions simultaneously (in contrast to *chickenpox,* in which new lesions break out in crops daily for five days); the face, palms, and soles show the greatest density of lesions (in contrast to chickenpox in which the lesions are predominately on the trunk). The lesions crust over by the end of the second week, and these scabs fall off in the third week. Permanent scars are common on the face (this is infrequent in chickenpox). If hemorrhages appear early in the course of the disease, a fatal outcome is usual.

The last big epidemic in the United States was in 1924 when three Canadian hoboes brought the disease to Connecticut; 74,000 cases were traced to this source. In 1979 the World Health Organization declared smallpox a nondisease; the last reported case was in Ethiopia.

Sodoku—see *Rat-bite fever*

Spirochete infections include *Syphilis,* Yaws, *Leptospirosis,* and *Rat-bite fever.*

Spotted fever—see *Rocky Mountain spotted fever*

Staphylococcus is a smart, tough, ubiquitous germ that has become resistant to many *antibiotics.* It is a common cause of newborn infections (breast *abscess, pneumonia, impetigo, Ritter's disease*), childhood skin infection (boils, *impetigo, absess*), and fatal *pneumonia* in the debilitated elderly. It is usually responsible for the lung infections in the patient with *cystic fibrosis*—especially after frequent courses of antibiotics.

Cultures of the nasal secretions of hospital personnel reveal a high incidence of staphylococcal germs. The newborn baby's umbilical cord stump is a convenient place for germs to grow. In a few days or weeks after going home, the baby may develop pustules or impetigo. Scrupulous hand washing and use of antibacterial soap (hexachlorophene followed by careful rinsing) usually precludes the spread of the menace.

Many strains of staphylococcus produce an enzyme, penicillinase, which destroys penicillin, so the administration of the latter drug is of no benefit. Oxacillin is a synthetic penicillin widely used when the staphylococcus is suspected. (See *Antibacterials,* Section 4.)

Streptococcus (See *Erysipelas,* Section 6, *Scarlet fever, Rheumatic fever,* and *Glomerulonephritis,* Section 13) is a common germ that the pediatrician fears and respects but is almost ecstatic to discover, because this naïve germ has not yet learned to become resistant to antibiotics. We know that we can guarantee a dramatic improvement in fever and malaise in only eight to twelve hours with *penicillin* or erythromycin. We are so discouraged with "flu" because this *virus* responds to nothing except rest and big doses of Vitamin C early.

(The strep is not as malignant as it used to be; my father tells of wild strep infections in the thirties when children ran 105° temperatures for days without letup, had huge swollen *glands,* and *abcessed* ears.)

The streptococcus group of bacteria can be divided into a large number of subspecies. The ones that cause disease in man are more likely to be hemolytic (dissolve red cells); this property is used to identify a strep throat. A cotton swab is touched on the victim's *tonsils* and then placed on a culture plate containing red (sheep) cells. If a clear area appears after a night in the incubator, it suggests that a strep infection is the cause of the patient's tonsillitis, and ten days of penicillin are in order.

Most streptococcal infections promote the development of certain antibodies that attest to a recent strep infection. (Antistreptolysin titer is high after scarlet fever and at the onset of rheumatic fever.)

Infants less than a year old rarely have clinically recognizable strep infections. School and military bases have near epidemics. Direct contact is the main source of infection; contaminated milk, water, or food is infrequently the cause. Carriers of the strep are common, but not necessarily the source of an epidemic spread.

Not every strep throat should be treated on the first day of symptoms. Some evidence indicates that one to three days of infection may provide the development of some immunity to future attacks. One attack of *scarlet fever* will permit the formation of immunity to the toxin that causes the rash, but does not preclude the development of immunity to another strep infection.

Syphilis is a communicable disease spread by intimate contact, usually genital. It is caused by a *spirochete* that is clever enough to eat away only slowly at its host without destroying him, but at the same time provides enough discomfiture and stigmata to remind him of his past indiscretions.

Congenital syphilis is often overlooked, because it is so unexpected in this age of *penicillin* and the compulsory premarital blood test

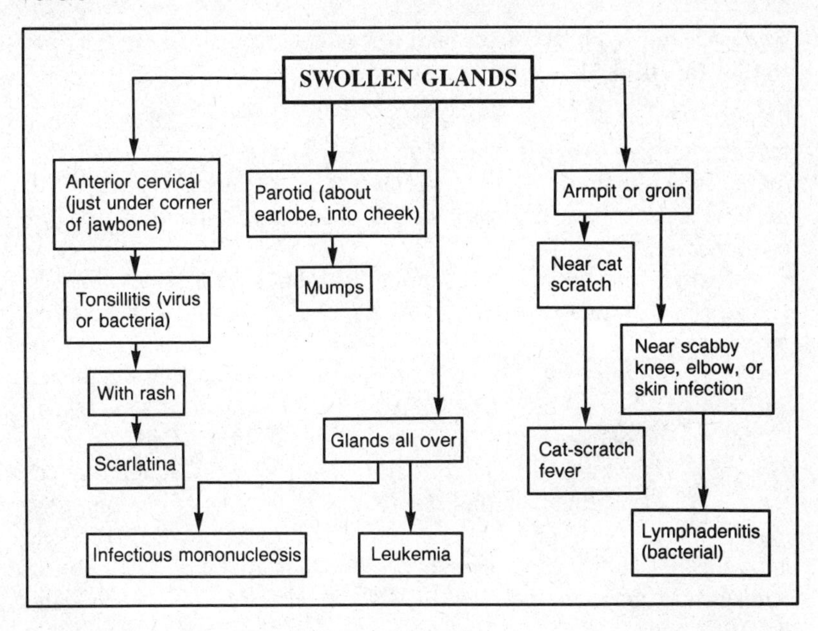

for syphilis. It seems wise for the obstetrician to repeat this test during the pregnancy as early treatment may prevent the birth of a syphilitic baby. Although the baby is infected before birth, the evidence may not be manifest for weeks or months, or not until age ten years when peg teeth, nerve deafness, eye inflammation, saber shins, and perforation of the palate give away what has happened.

The early signs in a baby with congenital syphilis include fever, *anemia, failure to gain,* generalized rash, profuse runny nose, enlarged *liver* and *spleen.* The organism may be found in scrapings from the lesions, and blood tests are positive. It is easy to diagnose if it is thought of.

Penicillin is the standard treatment and is usually successful in eliminating all the signs of the disease if accomplished in infancy. If treatment is delayed until childhood, the stigmata are usually not eliminated.

Acquired syphilis is being seen increasingly in the younger adolescent. The chancre, the herald for the portal of entry, is painless, so medical assistance is not sought until the generalized rash appears in the secondary stage, a couple of weeks after exposure. Frequently *gonorrhea* and syphilis coexist, and fortunately the spirochete responds to the same penicillin given for gonorrhea.

Temperature of most normal human bodies is around 98.6° F. when taken rectally. A lower reading of 96° to 97° suggest shock, *dehydration,* or excessive cooling (as in a premature in a faulty incubator). It may be a sign that the temperature is about to shoot up to 103° or more.

A high temperature is common in infants with *virus* illnesses. (I observed 107° in a two-year-old with the "flu"; recovery was prompt without obvious neurological sequelae.) The highest recorded temperature with survival I have heard about was in an Oriental man with malaria; he had 110° for a while.

It is not necessary to subtract a degree from the reading when reporting a fever to the doctor, although 105° *does* sound "safer" than 106°. Depending on the extent of skin capillary dilation, oral, axillary (armpit), or rectal temperature may be the same (if the skin is totally red and hot) or unequal (rectum hot and skin cool). Rectal temperature may be 105°, oral 104°, and axillary 103°. Rectal and oral thermometers can be used interchangeably in these orifices; only esthetics and hygiene dictate use as labeled. Because of a few scary reports of broken rectal thermometers and perforated recta, it seems wise to use the axillary method (retain four minutes) until the child is five or six years old, and is cooperatively nonbiting enough to try the oral (under the tongue for three minutes with mouth closed) method.

The doctor may have the mother evaluate her child's condition by keeping a temperature chart for a few days. A normal child might have 98° in the morning on arising and 99° in the evening. A two-degree swing usually is worth investigating (98° to 100°, or even 97° to 99°) with other tests (*blood count, sedimentation rate,* X ray, *urinalysis*). Doctors usually recommend full activity the day following an evening temperature of less than 100°, although more than 99.5° suggests that a disease is still active. The child's level of interest in food and activity may be more important in evaluating sickness and health than the temperature.

We are trying to switch to centigrade readings, and worldwide science uses this more than Fahrenheit. Try reporting the next fever in centigrade and see how sharp your doctor is.

Fahrenheit	Centigrade
98.6°	37°
100.0°	38°
102.2°	39°
104.0°	40°
105.8°	41°

Tetanus, or lockjaw, is a severe, painful, frequently fatal disease (60 percent mortality rate), due to a toxin produced by a germ, *Clostridium tetani,* that enters the body through a break in the skin. A minor cut may allow the germ to enter, but a rusty nail or a crushing wound is a more likely portal of entry. The germ does better in deep wounds, as it grows in the absence of oxygen.

Within a week or so after the invasion of the germ, the patient notices muscle stiffness, especially of the neck and back. His jaw can be opened only with difficulty. *Headache,* chills, and sweating are followed by *convulsions* triggered by slight stimuli. The mouth is drawn into a fixed grin, the head is pulled back and the back arched. The patient becomes fearful. He may die of respiratory complications or uncontrolled seizures.

Newborn babies may develop tetanus through the contaminated umbilical stump. (In some rural areas, the home delivery is climaxed by using a shoelace to tie off the umbilical cord.) Tetanus antitoxin neutralizes the toxin. *Penicillin* occasionally kills the tetanus germs but does not neutralize the toxin. For those not adequately immunized by DPT or DT shots, a human antitetanus *globulin* is available for passive protection.

Prevention by active immunity takes the worry out of contaminated wounds. The DPT shots given in infancy may give lasting immunity, but most doctors give the two-year-old and the five-year-old a booster. A routine booster of DT every ten years is more than adequate. More frequent boosters cause needless reactions. If a few years have gone by since the last booster and the patient receives a significant wound, he should have a DT booster within twenty-four to forty-eight hours. The wound should be washed thoroughly with soap, water, and a brush, despite the child's objections.

That so few cases of tetanus have developed in our army is a miracle, considering the number of soldiers and the number of dirty wounds.

Tonsillitis is an inflammation of the tonsils—either *viral* or bacterial, the latter usually due to the *streptococcus.* Many viral throat infections superficially resemble a strep throat and are treated; the response may be coincidental to the *penicillin* administration, and so the drug gets the credit, but the condition was going to clear anyway, as viruses do.

When a child becomes ill with a fever and a sore throat or tonsillitis, he has usually become ill with a virus (80 percent or more have been found to be viral) even though the tonsils and adjacent tissues are reddened. The mother may elect to do either of the following:

1. She may treat him with *aspirin,* hot baths, bed rest, and fluids for seventy-two hours and see what course the disease takes. If hoarseness, a watery, runny nose, and a cough develop after the seventy-two hours of fever, she may call it "that virus that's going around." When a child is asked where his throat hurts, and he points to his larynx, chances are that it's the virus. If he points up high into his open mouth and sounds hyponasal, or if his palate is immobile, he is more likely to have a bacterial tonsillitis and, therefore, need treatment.

2. She may request an examination and a throat culture and a white blood count. If the throat culture grows a pathogenic streptococcus and the white count is elevated, a full ten days of penicillin is mandatory.

Some evidence seems to justify home care with aspirin, rest, and fluids for three days. If a cold and cough develop, it must be a virus. If fever persists and glands enlarge in the neck, treatment should be requested. This latter case is probably a strep, but three days of supportive care seems to allow the body enough time to develop some strep antibodies for the next invasion. Penicillin used *too* early in the disease may preclude any antibody development.

Toxoplasmosis is a protozoan-caused disease that may be acquired *in utero* from the infected mother, or acquired at any time during life from some animal host—either by ingestion of infected meat or inhalation of the organism in dust.

The congenital variety, when fully manifest, may cause fever, *jaundice,* rash, *chorioretinitis* (inflammation of the retina lining), and *encephalitis* with subsequent calcium deposits and *hydrocephalus.* Death from convulsions and respiratory failure may be a better outcome than the vegetable life of severe retardation associated with the hydrocephalus. The disease may also resemble *erythroblastosis, syphilis,* or *cytomegalic-inclusion disease.*

The acquired variety may suggest itself with only some generalized swollen lymph glands, or it may be severe and overwhelming with fever, enlarged *liver* and *spleen,* rash, *encephalitis,* and *lung* and *heart disease.* It may resemble *infectious mononucleosis,* or *Hodgkin's disease.*

The few blood and skin tests available may reveal the presence of the disease, but since the illness is not common, the doctor rarely thinks of it until other illnesses are ruled out. Toxoplasmosis is a strange and unpredictable disease. By the time it is diagnosed, the patient may have recovered. *Sulfa,* in combination with another drug, may speed recovery or at least aid the body in its attempt to wall off the invader.

Trichinosis (see *Nematode infections,* Section 12) is a worm infestation usually acquired by eating infected, poorly cooked pork. The larval worms in the muscle of the meat hatch after ingestion, become adults, attach to the bowel wall, and produce larvae that migrate via the bloodstream to the muscles of the human. If the infected meat contained only a few organisms, few symptoms will be noted; but if many of the larvae have been consumed, a violent intestinal reaction with cramps and diarrhea may occur.

Fever, muscle pain, stiffness, and pain on breathing may drag on for the several weeks which the larvae migrate through the body. The *eosinophiles* in the blood count are elevated; a biopsy of a muscle may reveal the larvae; a skin test for trichinosis becomes positive after the first three or four weeks.

Treatment is mainly preventive. Adequate cooking of pork will kill the larvae. (One recent report described a family who were all afflicted when they ate their family pig without cooking it adequately. The pig got *his* trichinosis from a bear the father had killed and used as hog fodder. It might be wise to cook your pig's food also.)

Storing of pork for a period of thirty days at a temperature of 5° F. (as required by the U.S. Department of Agriculture) will destroy *Trichinella* organisms. If home-slaughtered animals are to be consumed, the meat should be cooked until all of the pink color has disappeared and a temperature of 185° F. has been reached throughout. Baking the meat uncovered in a 350° oven for thirty-five minutes per pound will achieve this. Pickling or smoking alone does not destroy the organisms.

Tsutsugamushi fever—see *Scrub typhus*

Tularemia or rabbit fever is a bacterial disease transmitted from animals to man by ticks, fleas, or lice. Hunters, sheep shearers, or animal handlers are more likely to acquire this infection.

A small sore develops at the skin site where the bacteria have entered; the local *lymph nodes* enlarge and may become abscessed. Fever, chills, rashes, and, if the bacteria have been inhaled or ingested, symptoms of *pneumonia* or intestinal infection predominate.

Some patients are extremely ill for long periods of time; most are only mildly out of sorts. *Antibiotics* are effective as treatment.

Typhoid fever is a bacterial infection whose predominant symptoms are intestinal. Adequate sanitation has suppressed its spread, but isolated, explosive epidemics still appear. A not uncommon combination of inadequately controlled water supply, overtaxed sewage facilities in "health" resorts in late summer can allow one carrier to infect scores of innocent vacationers. Obviously, the health department must continue constant surveillance of public water supplies and known carriers who must not be cooks or food handlers (Typhoid Mary left a string of victims in her wake.) The newer *antibiotics* are usually successful in eliminating the bacteria from the carrier.

The ingested bacteria invade the bloodstream through the intestinal wall and multiply in the liver, spleen, and lymph tissue. The toxin released causes fever, *headache,* prostration, and suppression of *white-cell* response in the bone marrow. (A white blood count may be low during this phase of the disease and hence suggests "flu" or a *virus* condition.) Rose spots on the trunk appear in half the patients. Foul *diarrhea* is usual but may be absent; the fever and enlarged spleen may suggest a number of other diseases—*septicemia, meningitis, miliary tuberculosis, rheumatic fever, infectious mononucleosis.*

If the victim does have typhoid fever, a blood culture should grow the causative bacillus in the first week of fever, when a blood agglutination test is usually positive. *Hemorrhage* from the bowel, shock, *kidney* infection, *peritonitis, meningitis,* and *arthritis* have all been reported.

A small percentage of clinically well patients will become carriers. The gall bladder and the kidney are the usual organs harboring the germ.

Chloramphenicol or *ampicillin* is an effective antibiotic. Strict isolation, intravenous fluids, and/or blood may be necessary. A cure is recorded if three negative urine and stool cultures have been obtained.

Typhoid immunization shots are available for those who must travel in areas where the disease is endemic. (I remember a patient, age eight years, who seemed to have the "flu." He had a couple of loose stools accompanied by a high fever and seemed more knocked out than usual, but his white count was only 5,000. After about five days of this, we ordered agglutination tests for everything the lab could do. The lab technician was so excited when she called, she stammered: "Has he—he—he had any typhoid shots recently? Well, his t—t—titer is still positive when diluted 4,000 times!"

Chloramphenicol cured him, and we subsequently found typhoid germs in the well at his grandmother's house where he had visited two weeks prior to his fever.)

Typhus, a *rickettsial disease,* was first described in ancient Greece. It has been associated with most of the wars since, and probably did more damage than the actual fighting.

A louse acquires the organism by feeding on an infected victim, then passes its typhus-contaminated feces on to its next host. The new patient succumbs when the organism invades through a crack in the skin or is inhaled. Fever, prostration, delirium, and headache are followed in a few days by a rose-colored rash on the trunk. The fever continues for yet another week, and if the patient does not succumb to *pneumonia, kidney* failure, or severe *brain* involvement, he recovers—usually completely.

Agglutination tests will clinch the diagnosis, and the tetracycline drugs provide consistent cure. Obviously, good personal sanitation is the best preventive. DDT has been the best louse killer, but it is now considered a "dirty" chemical because it is not biodegradable.

Undulant fever—see *Brucellosis*

Variola—see *Smallpox*

Virus is the term given to an ultramicroscopic particle which multiplies inside the body cells and produces various disease states: *measles, flu, mumps, chickenpox, colds, canker sores, polio,* etc. Specific antiviral agents have not yet proved as effective as have *antibiotics* against bacterial infections. A specific virus is responsible for a specific disease, although infection by one may produce immunity against another:

previous infection by the cowpox virus (vaccination) will protect the body from *smallpox* (and sometimes the *canker-sore* virus). Most children have about forty to sixty different virus infections before age seven, at which time they normally have only one or two a year (one or two bad colds a year, one attack of *vomiting* and *diarrhea* every year or so, one attack of fever and laryngeal cough every two or three years). Eighty percent of children's infections are "the virus that is going around." (See *Coxsackie, Enterovirus, Herpes, Interferon.*)

The fever of a virus infection may serve a therapeutic function. As an example, polio virus grows well in tissue culture at 95° F., but poorly at 103° to 104°. Controlling the fever too well may prolong the infection. Vitamin C enhances the production of interferon and if given early in large doses (500–1,000 milligrams hourly), it will shorten the course of the "flu."

Weil's syndrome is a severe form of *leptospirosis.* (See *Coxsackie, Enterovirus.*)

Yellow fever is a viral disease seen mainly in the tropics. It spreads chiefly via the mosquito which harbors the virus after biting a victim of the disease.

It is usually a mild disease and after a week of prostration, the patient recovers. But a small percent (about five percent) of patients exhibit severe jaundice, hemorrhages in the skin and from the nose and intestinal tract, accompanied by high fever. Of these five percent severely affected, some epidemics have resulted in fifty percent casualties.

After yellow fever, cirrhosis of the liver is surprisingly rare. There is no antibiotic for this disease, as it is a virus. An effective yellow-fever vaccine should be administered to those planning to visit an area where the disease is endemic.

SECTION 3

Allergies and Immunizations

Allergies

Antibodies
(also Immunity, Section 8)
Antigens
Atopy
Asthma (Section 9)
Eczema (Section 6)
Hay fever (Section 14)
Delayed hypersensitivity
(also Skin tests, Section 6)
Desensitization
Hypersensitivity
Anaphylaxis
(also Shock, Section 1)
Angioedema
Autoimmunity (also
Section 2)
Hives
Chronic
Cold
Mediators
Serum sickness
(also DPT immunization)

See also:
Allergy Checklist, under
Asthma (Section 9)
Bedwetting (Section 13)
Colic (Section 11)
Gastrointestinal allergy
(Section 12)
Tension-fatigue syndrome
(Section 15)

Allergic Manifestations in Children

Gastrointestinal

Abdominal distension
Abdominal pain
Allergic parotitis
Aphthous stomatitis
Bloody stools
Cheilitis
Diarrhea
Geographical tongue
Malabsorption syndrome
Mucous colitis
Pruritis ani
Ulcerative colitis
Vomiting

Genitourinary

Dysuria
Enuresis
Frequency
Hematuria
Suprapubic pain
Vulvovaginitis

Respiratory

Allergic bronchitis
Allergic rhinitis
Allergic tracheitis
Asthma
Nasal polyps
Serous otitis media

Skin

Allergic purpura
Angioedema (see Hypersensitivity)
Atopic eczema
Contact dermatitis
Drug rashes
Urticaria

Miscellaneous

Allergic conjunctivitis
Allergic convulsions
Allergic fever
Allergic headache
Allergic myalgia and arthralgia
Pseudomononucleosis
Tension-fatigue syndrome

Allergy is a broad term, loosely applied to any body reaction that cannot be explained by infection or injury or tumor growth. If a patient has gas after drinking milk, he has what we call an allergy, although a lack of the lactase enzyme may be at fault. The term "allergy" should really be limited to *eczema,* allergic *rhinitis* (*hay fever*), bronchial *asthma* (see also Allergy Checklist, under *Asthma,* Section 9), drug reactions, *serum sickness,* and *contact dermatitis.*

Allergies or sensitivities or reactions are so common in infants and children that the pediatrician must deal with these frustrating irritations every day. Avoidance of the usual offending agents makes common sense; cautious, delayed introduction of the more likely allergenic foods may prevent a permanent problem. (A patient of mine was fed egg at three months to increase her iron intake; she promptly developed hives. When egg was reintroduced at nine months, she reacted with angioedema, cramps, and diarrhea. Egg at eighteen months caused an anaphylactic shock with pallor and collapse on the floor. I am convinced if the egg had not been served until after one year of age, she would not have developed the allergy at all.)

Clinical allergy is the condition of altered immunological response to ingested, injected, inhaled, or absorbed substances called antigens.

When inhalants, contactants, and ingestants have been eliminated and the child is still ailing, a doctor and/or allergist must be consulted to plot the course. Allergy therapy is slow and frustrating because benefits are not immediate or dramatic. An honest doctor will restrain his optimism with "Give me two or three years; I think we can help." A large number of *antihistamine* drugs have been manufactured to block the histamine's irritating effects. Some work beautifully; others have side effects (dry mouth and drowsiness) that are more irritating than the original allergic reaction. *Epinephrine* will counteract histamine; *ephedrine* and propanolamin act similarly. *Corticosteroids* are also useful in controlling allergy, but work by a different mechanism than histamine blockage. In most allergies the assumption can be made that the adrenal glands are not producing enough cortisol, a hormone. Extra vitamins (C, A, B_6, pantothenic acid), calcium, and zinc will help nourish the adrenals to produce sufficient cortisol to interrupt the antigen-antibody response. (See *Hypersensitivity: Anaphylaxis, Atopy, Serum sickness.*)

Antibodies are synthesized by the body in response to an antigen. They respond specifically to that antigen when it is reintroduced into the body. This combination of antibody and antigen then initiates a further host reaction: the release of mediators. Histamine is one. These mediators acting on local tissues and blood vessels are responsible for the observed symptoms (*hay fever, asthma,* etc.). In this way generally harmless things become a menace to the host.

These protein antibodies are called *immunoglobulins:* IgA, IgM, IgG and a recently studied IgE—thought to be the carrier of human atopic reaginic activity.

Antigens are protein substances which stimulate the body to produce antibodies against them. They are usually foreign substances (proteins, carbohydrates, lipids, etc.) with large molecules. Their surface regions have antigenic properties, called allergens (liver extract, horse serum). Penicillin is a hapten, a simpler compound; it combines with host protein to become an allergen. The antigens in the body at the time of measles excite the body to manufacture substances that counteract this virus. This protein antibody produced will remain in the system and effectively repel a new invasion of measles virus if there is a later exposure. (See *Immunity,* Section 8.)

Atopy is the constitutional and familial susceptibility to immediate allergic reactions. This type of sensitivity is seen in 10 percent of the population. These individuals carry the skin-sensitizing or atopic antibody called reagin. They do not have any other type of immunological deficiency and are no more susceptible to auto-immune diseases than the normal population.

Atopic reactions include *asthma, hives, hay fever,* and *eczema.* In most cases a combination of inciting agents is present before the victim has symptoms. These include susceptibility (positive family history), exposure to sensitizing agents (egg ingestion, grass pollen inhalation), infection (virus or bacterial), emotional trauma, and physical trauma (weather change, injury, teething). Atopic patients' reagin is chiefly carried by immunoglobulin E. The other immunoglobulins, however, also serve the carrier function.

When atopic individuals are desensitized, a new antibody, called blocking antibody, is formed. Relief from disturbing allergic symptoms is not directly related to the level of this blocking antibody, but the blocking antibody seems to increase the threshold of tolerance to injected allergens.

Patients with serum sickness develop reagins to the offending drug or serum (for example, horse serum). Reagins can be demonstrated in the serum of patients with the alarming *anaphylaxis* after drug ingestion or bee stings.

Antibody response to the initial injection of an antigen is usually not detectable until an interval of several days. IgM and IgG are the usual immunoglobulins affected. The response to a repeated exposure of the same antigen is more rapid, greater, and remains higher than after the initial one. (Thus the use of three DPT baby shots in the first few months of a baby's life; the timing of the interval is not so important as the number.)

This antibody response takes place in the lymph tissues of the body (spleen and lymph nodes). (See Section 8.)

Antibody proteins are synthesized by the same cellular biochemical process that is used to manufacture other of the body's proteins (hemoglobin, insulin). Somehow the antigen affects the antibody manufacturing cell to alter its aminoacid chain sequence so that antibody protein is produced that will be specific against that antigen. Each daughter cell is equipped to manufacture a similar altered protein; herein lies the memory of the host resistance to foreign substances, whether the fighting of disease or remembering to react to a drug.

Cold hives is the unique sensitivity to cold only, usually from the sudden change rather than the degree of coldness. Occasionally drowning occurs if a susceptible person swims in cold water (massive *histamine* release). The chilled skin becomes swollen and red. (I knew a girl who drank her cola at room temperature to prevent her hand from swelling to ugly proportions.) Periactin® (see *Antihistaminics*) is helpful in controlling this common condition.

Delayed hypersensitivity is the general name for the positive response to skin testing of a variety of bacterial, viral, fungal, and parasitic diseases. If the tested person has had the disease for which he is being tested, his skin will develop a red, itchy swelling in forty-eight to seventy-two hours—for example, the reaction to a *tuberculosis skin test.* This delayed sensitivity reaction is based on the fact that the body becomes sensitized to the complex proteins of the invading organism. (A positive reaction to the TB skin test means previous exposure to the tuberculosis germ, but tells nothing of the current disease state). As a result, when derivatives of these infected agents are injected into the skin, the local tissue responds with edema and capillary dilation.

Delayed hypersensitivity is a cellular immunity. Circulating antibody is not involved in delayed hypersensitivity; histamine and the other mediators are not present in this reaction. Some drugs and metals will cause this reaction. It is a reliable diagnostic aid to detect previous infection of *tuberculosis, histoplasmosis, cat-scratch fever, brucellosis, coccidioidomycosis, trichinosis,* and *mumps* (although the latter test is unreliable). Patch tests for contact allergies like cosmetics, formalin (in Perma-press® clothing), chemicals in shoe leather, and poison oak all employ the principles of delayed hypersensitivity. (See *Skin tests,* Section 6.)

The allergic patient's symptoms are highly individual, and characteristically change with time from one organ system to another. The baby who has had eczema will frequently develop hay fever when playing ball in the grass in May at age seven. Asthma may supervene when he gets a dog or cat at age twelve. Other factors are usually related to the allergic symptoms and may even be blamed because they seem to be the inciting agent: infection, emotional factors, temperature changes, and chemical irritants. The history of the patient's allergic background is the most important part of the diagnostic detective work. The family background is important too, since about 60 percent of allergic people have a positive family history.

Desensitization is the reduction of a patient's response to a foreign substance and is generally used in relation to allergic reactions. Desensitizing someone to grass pollens or house dust is usually accomplished by injections of the offending material. Aqueous injections of grass pollens are given once or twice a week in increasing doses just short of local and systemic reactions. Successful desensitization is measured by decrease in symptoms (*hay fever* or *asthma* in the grass season). It may take two or three years. Treatment in the meantime consists of *antihistaminics,* antiwheeze medicines, and/or *cortisone* during the height of the season. Desensitization during the season is difficult as the injected allergens stir up more reactions because the patient is inhaling the pollens as well.

Desensitization to severe *bee sting* reaction is usually easily and effectively carried out by repeated injection of bee vaccine. Dosage is increased depending on local reaction and lifetime maintenance is suggested.

Injections of a stock solution of the usual respiratory bacteria (dead, of course) will significantly cut down on secondary infections.

(See *Sinusitis,* Section 14.) The allergist prefers to make his own vaccine from the patient's bacteria (autogenous vaccine).

Food allergy is a fairly common condition in infancy, and probably everyone is sensitive to at least one food. About one baby in fifteen will develop a cow's milk allergy (he may get cow's milk protein when breast fed—if his mother is drinking milk) during his first month, partially because of the relatively large amounts he has to drink to satisfy his fantastic hunger. Milk allergy may manifest itself as nasal congestion, cough, or wheeze, but intestinal symptoms are more common. Soy-bean, goat, or meat milks usually relieve the symptoms within forty-eight hours.

Cookies and teething biscuits—containing wheat—may produce distressing gas and diarrhea. Allergy may be the cause, but an inborn error of metabolism (gluten-enzyme lack) may produce similar symptoms. Some foods, including corn, pork, and nuts, may produce lethargy, headaches, bedwetting, asthma, fever, or may be masked as various psychosomatic illnesses. Some will only produce symptoms if ingested together or if the patient is sick or fatigued. Intestinal flu, for instance, may trigger an intestinal food allergy.

If an infant is allergic to one food, he seems to be more likely to develop other food sensitivities. For this reason, egg, wheat, chocolate, fish, citrus, tomato, peaches, green vegetables, and pork are best introduced to the diet only after the first year. Diet elimination is more helpful in determining a food allergy than skin testing.

In general, respiratory symptoms are more likely to be due to inhalants—grass, fur, feathers, wool, ragweed pollen. Intestinal symptoms are more likely to be due to foods.

Many behavior problems in children (and adults) have been laid directly to allergies. Many surly, crabby children have become cheerful and pleasant after desensitization and/or food eliminations.

Even children with *electroencephalographic* abnormalities may be improved by withdrawal of offending foods. *Grand* and *petit mal* attacks have been relieved in some. Hyperkinetic behavior, insomnia, restlessness, irritability, oversensitiveness, crossness, fatigue, salivation, chilliness, hypotension, tearing, negativism, unreasonableness, shyness, quickness to anger, suspiciousness, numbness, tingling, and tremors are but a few of the conditions that have improved after the allergenic food has been eliminated. A rule: if a symptom doesn't make sense, think of allergies.

Histamine is the most important chemical thought to be released by cells in the immediate allergic response, producing the characteristic flare and wheal in the skin—also known as hives. Swollen tissue (puffy eyelids, swollen fingers) may be allergic reactions (angioedema). Spasms of smooth muscles (bronchial-muscle spasm causes asthma, intestinal-muscle spasm causes cramps) and increased secretion of cells *(allergic rhinitis)* are all manifestations of allergic response.

Hypersensitivity is the response of the body to the antibody-antigen reaction.

1. *Autoimmunity* is a form of hypersensitivity in which the antigen is native to the host (*rheumatic fever, thyroiditis*).

2. *Anaphylaxis* or immediate hypersensitivity occurs within minutes of a repeated antigen exposure. It is a violent allergic response to a substance, usually following ingestion (nuts, seafood, certain drugs) or injection (*penicillin,* horse serum, *bee sting*). The victim goes into shock, the blood pressure falls, pulse is rapid and weak, and pallor and cyanosis appear. Treatment is epinephrine injection, oxygen, intravenous fluids, *antihistamines,* and *cortisone* under medical supervision.

3. *Serum sickness* is a hypersensitivity, a milder form of the *anaphylactic* reaction. It usually appears a week or two following ingestion of some sensitizing substance (drug, serum, chemical, food); if the level of sensitivity is great, it shows up in minutes or hours (hives while receiving a blood transfusion).

Hives (urticaria) and *angioedema* are usually the hallmark of serum sickness. Eyelids, lips, and tongue are swollen and itchy. Hives appear at pressure areas (on the feet where shoes rub and at the belt line). Swollen tender joints are typical. (See *Arthritis,* Section 7.)

Angioedema is the sudden swelling usually of eyelids, lips, or ears, most often assumed to be an allergic response to a drug, food or insect *bite.* Cold or emotion may be the triggering agent. The swelling is only slightly pink and is not tender; it may only itch or tingle. It is often associated with *hives.* In only about half of the cases is the causative agent clearly recognized. (Common ones are milk, tomato, chocolate, horse serum.) The swelling is gone in one or two days, and although *antihistaminics* are usually given, their benefit is doubtful.

The sudden, alarming swelling may suggest an infection (*abscess* or *cellulitis*), but the absence of pain will rule out a bacterial etiology.

The avoidance of the offender, if known, is the obvious cure. *Epinephrine* (adrenalin), followed by daily use of *ephedrine* and antihistaminics, provides comfort while the body is dealing with the antibody-antigen reaction. *Cortisone* drugs are helpful if severe headaches and arthralgia are disabling. Chronic hives seem to go on for weeks or months and are apparently due to some long-lasting mediator of the antibody-antigen response.

Serum sickness is triggered by the antibody-antigen response: the immunoglobulin G carries the antibody. Horse serum injections were formerly the most common cause of this disease.

Most people have had the DPT injection, and only a DT booster is necessary. (See *Puncture wounds,* Section 1.) Human antitetanus serum which is less sensitizing is now available. Serum sickness following *penicillin* is fairly common; the reaction is less severe if oral penicillin is used instead of injections. Stinging bees, wasps, hornets, and yellow jackets cause serum sickness in the sensitized. A vaccine is available for desensitization.

Treatment is symptomatic depending on the location and severity of the problem. *Epinephrine, ephedrine, antihistaminics* are standard. *ACTH* or *cortisone* is to be used for severe involvement such as breathing distress or nervous system symptoms (*cerebral edema*).

Mediators of sensitivity reactions are formed after the antibody meets the antigen. These react on local blood vessels and tissues (bee sting) or are carried to distant parts of the body by the circulation where a variety of observable reactions may occur (*hives, asthma, shock*).

Kinins are formed in response to enzyme splitting of proteins following the antibody-antigen response. Tissue responses are similar to the effects seen with *histamine.* It may be important in *angioedema.*

A slow-reacting substance is a mediator that acts like histamine, but has a more prolonged action and is not neutralized by antihistamine.

Serotonin is considered a mediator, but its role in allergic disease is unclear.

Immunization is the artificial development of disease resistance by making the body respond to inoculation with dead or attenuated germs, viruses, and toxins. The body responds with its immune mechanisms, producing "memory" antibodies. (See *Allergy.*) When the system is next challenged with the actual disease germs or viruses, the already alert *white cells* and *immune globulins* are able to resist immediately without having to go through the "learning" process. In the unimmunized child the delay in the initial sensitizing process required to mobilize these defenses may be lethal, so the baby shots are usually begun in the first two or three months of life before some friendly neighborhood carrier breathes on the susceptible infant.

BCG is a vaccine against *tuberculosis.* It produces some immunity in the body by sensitizing the tissues to react if the body is invaded. If a mother is an open tuberculosis case, her baby should be given the BCG vaccine and removed from her environment until she is no longer contagious. The BCG prevents the rapid spread of TB so often seen in infants. *All those given BCG will react positively to the tine test.*

Diphtheria/whooping cough/tetanus (DPT, where P stands for "pertussis") is the standard three-in-one shot given intramuscularly at monthly intervals (three shots). We still see these diseases occasionally, but only in the unimmunized. One shot will give protection to 80 percent or so of infants; two shots protect 90 percent, and three shots 95 percent. Many mothers (and some doctors) are afraid that a delay in the schedule will vitiate the protection. Not so. The same protection will obtain if the interval between shots is six months; the two-month interval times three is just a convenience. Do not start over; just get the three shots completed as soon as possible. Extra vitamin C (200–500 milligrams), B_6 (50–100 milligrams), and calcium (500–1,000 milligrams) given the day before and the day of the shots will cut down the reaction. A minor cold without fever is *not* a contraindication.

Some research evidence indicates that these three baby shots offer protection until age *thirty,* but most of us give a booster at eighteen months or two years and again at school time (five years). The P is dropped at this age, because whooping cough is not a killer after infancy, but the whooping-cough germs in the vaccine give alarming reactions.

Just the DT is used every ten years as a routine, or given within forty-eight hours after a significant puncture wound if more than five years has elapsed since the last DT. The practice of a yearly booster of DT prior to summer camp is to be deplored as unnecessary and potentially dangerous (see *Hypersensitivity*). If a booster is necessary, it should be the DT and not just tetanus.

Live measles (rubeola) *vaccine* (not the dead or killed vaccine) has virtually wiped out this serious childhood disease. It is best given at the fifteen-month checkup; if given earlier, the retained immune protein from the mother may vitiate an effective response. Some reaction (fever, rash) can be expected six to eight days later, but is not serious. There are reported cases of *measles* in previously vaccinated children, but the protection rate is above 95 percent.

Live poliomyelitis vaccine (Sabin) combining all three *polio* viruses is usually given orally with the infant *DPT* shots. It is an attenuated virus and provides a mild or subliminal (unrecognized) disease in the intestinal-tract lining. If the "real thing" comes along later, the cells of the intestine are able to recognize it as an enemy and destroy it before it invades the system. This offers superior protection to that of the *killed polio vaccine.* (See *Salk vaccine.*)

The standard course is a set of trivalent drops given orally, followed by another set at least two months later (conveniently given at the time of the first and third DPT inoculations). Booster doses are recommended at age two and five years.

Salk vaccine is the killed *poliomyelitis virus.* When injected it does not produce the disease but stimulates the body to produce immunity. It has been largely supplanted by *Sabin vaccine.*

Immunizations

Bacterial vaccines (also *Sinusitis,* Section 14)
BCG
Diphtheria
Influenza
Measles
Mumps
Pertussis
Poliomyelitis
Rubella
Smallpox
Tetanus

Smallpox vaccination was the standard method of immunizing against *smallpox.* Two centuries ago it was observed that dairy maids who had developed cowpox (a virus disease of cattle) were immune to smallpox. The fluid from the pox of the cow or calf was transferred to the patient. On the tenth day, he developed a vesicle in the skin at the site of inoculation; it eventually dried up, leaving a small scar (no scar, no take).

Vaccination has wiped out the disease, so no one needs to be vaccinated anymore. Actually the vaccination can be fatal. Not even travelers need vaccinations now.

Vaccines. Some protection against *hepatitis* and *chickenpox* is offered by the prophylactic use of *gamma globulin* soon after exposure. This is only a passive and temporary method to protect the body.

Influenza vaccines are available and have some use in protecting elderly or sickly people. The difficulties have been twofold: (a) the shot frequently gives a reaction almost as distressing as the disease itself, and (b) the patient may be immunized against influenza B, but it's influenza A that happens to be "that virus that's going around."

Rubella vaccine (for protection against German or three-day measles) and mumps vaccine are safe, effective, and inexpensive. Their use is suggested.

Vaccines for other diseases (influenza, *mononucleosis, syphillis,* tooth decay) will soon be available if the promise of present research is fulfilled.

(See also *Immunizations* [*Diphtheria/whooping cough/tetanus, Live poliomyelitis vaccine, Live measles vaccine, Salk vaccine, Smallpox vaccination*].)

SECTION 4

Drugs and Medicines

A wide variety of drugs is available for many human diseases. The potent and dangerous ones usually require a prescription from your doctor; directions should be read and complied with.

Only a few of the common drugs used in practice are listed in the outline below.

Drug dosage for children is better calculated by surface area percent than by weight. It works out that a thirteen-pound three-month-old should get approximately 20 percent of the adult dose of most medicines. The fifty-pound seven-year-old should be taking about half the adult dose.

Metric measures are becoming more widely used and allow for better scientific and industrial communication throughout the world. Following are a few of the more common equivalents:

Apothecary	*Metric*		
1 grain	60 milligrams *or*	0.06	grams
5 grains	300 milligrams *or*	0.3	grams
60 grains (1 dram)		4.0	grams
1 ounce		30.0	grams
1 pound		480.0	grams
10 pounds		4.8	kilograms
1 minim (1 drop)		0.06	milliliters
15 minim		1.0	milliliters
60 minim (one teaspoon)		4.0	milliliters
1 fluid ounce		30.0	milliliters
16 fluid ounces (1 pint)		500.0	milliliters
32 fluid ounces (1 quart)		1,000.0	milliliters

(The above equivalents are approximate. To be strictly accurate, 1,000 milliliters, or one liter, is equal to 1.0567 quarts.)

A. Allergy and hay fever

Antihistaminics:
These include Actidil®, Ambodryl®, Benadryl®, Chlor-trimeton®, Clistin®, Decapryn®, Dimetane®, Disomer®, Forhistal®, Histadyl®, Phenergan®, Polaramine®, Trimeton®.
Corticosteroids

B. Anemia

Ferrous sulfate
Vitamin B_{12}

C. Antiseptics

D. Asthma

Bronchodilators
Cromolyn
Epinephrine
Norepinephrine
Pseudoephedrine

E. Behavior disorders

Anxiety relieving medicines include:
Barbiturates
Benadryl®
Haldol®
Mellaril®
Tofranil®
Tranquilizers
Valium®
(Every doctor has his favorites: Compazine®, Sparine®, Stelazine®, Thorazine®, are but a few.)
Depression relieving medicines include dextroamphetamine sulfate. (Some other drugs that might help: Aventyl®, Elavil®, Ritalin®, Tofranil®.)
Hyperactivity is usually controlled with dextroamphetamine sulfate. (See this entry for use of Benzedrine®, Biphetamine®, Desoxyn® and Ritalin®.)

F. Caries

Fluoride

G. Cold (watery, runny nose)

(See *Nose,* Section 14)
(Some feel that if an *antihistaminic* is combined with a *decongestant* greater relief is obtained. Examples: Actifed®, Contac®, Co-Pyronil®, Demazin®, Dimetapp®, Naldecon®, Novahistine®, Ornade®, Triaminic®.)
Nasal decongestants (Nose drops and sprays include Afrin®, Benzedrex® inhaler, Otrivin®, Neosynephrine®, Privine®, Tyzine®.)
Oral decongestants (see Pseudoephedrine)

H. Constipation

Laxatives

I. Convulsions

Anticonvulsant drugs
Dilantin®
Ketogenic diet
Valium®

J. Cough

Allergic cough (most cough syrups contain an antihistamine. Examples: Ambenyl expectorant®, Dimetane expectorant®, Novahistine expectorant®, Phenergan expectorant®, Triaminic expectorant®).

Croupy cough (may be helped with an antihistamine, but alcohol seems to give good results: Nyquil®—25% alcohol). Alcohol cough mixture, *Syrup of Ipecac* (Section 1). Frequent, irritating cough (may respond to cough syrups containing alcohol, iodides, chloroform, ammonium chloride and glyceryl guaiacolate). Ipsatol® smells like an oldfashioned cough syrup. Spell it backwards plus T.

Cough with wheeze or asthma (may be helped with Actified C expectorant®, Asbron Elixir®, Quadrinal Suspension®, Tedrol Suspension®).Bronchodilators

K. Diarrhea

Antidiarrheal medicines
Paregoric

L. Ear

(Preparations for Otitis externa [swimmer's ear], Otitis media. See also Antibacterials and Section 14)

M. Eye drops and ointments

(Ammoniated mercury and boric acid [a poison] are of no value for eye problems. Neosporin® topical ointment can be used for purulent conjunctivitis if handy. Allergic conjunctivitis is soothed with Antistine®, Collyrium with Ephedrine®, or Isohist eye drops®. See Cortisone.)

N. Fever (Section 2)

Acetaminophen
Aspirin

(APC, Anacin and Empirin compound all have caffeine so are not recommended for fever. Salicylamine as in Liquiprin® and Saltin® is not worthwhile for fever; occasionally tripling the dose does some good.)

O. Heart failure

Digitalis
Diuretics

(Digitoxin, digoxin, lantoside-C increases the strength of the heart muscle contraction and alters the electrical conductivity.)

P. Hormones

Corticosteroids (see Sections 2 and 4; see also Allergy, Section 3; Autoimmune disease, Sections 2 and 8)

Estrogens

Insulin (Section 10)

Pitressin
Progesterone
Testosterone
Thyroid

Q. Infections

(See Sections 2, 9, 12, 13)
Penicillin
Tetracyclines
New *antibacterials* are being introduced frequently. A few antibiotics like ampicillin and erythromycin are discussed.
(See also Chloramphenicol, Sulfonamides.)
Antifungal medicines:
Amphotericin B
Grisofulvin
Nystatin
Antituberculosis medicines:
Isoniazid
Para-aminosalicylic acid
Streptomycin

R. Insommia

Antihistaminics
Barbiturates
Chloral hydrate (*Noctec®*)
Paraldehyde
Tranquilizers

S. Pain

Acetaminophen
Anesthesia
Atropine
Scopolamine
Aspirin
Cafergot®
Cocaine
Codeine phosphate
Darvon®
Demerol®
Heroin
Methadone
Morphine sulfate
Salicylamide

T. Skin Diseases

(Ammoniated mercury and potassium permanganate are not recommended. Boric acid should not be in the house; it is very poisonous.)
Acne
Lotions
Sulfur ointments
Ammoniacal diaper
Methionine
Ointments
Sunshine on diapers (Section 13)
Vinegar in diapers (Section 13)
Anti-itch effect
Periactin®
Tacaryl®
Temaril®
Chafed skin
Powders
Dandruff
Shampoos
Dry skin
Oils
Eczema, neurodermatitis
Antihistamines (effective for anti-itch properties) include Periactin®, Tacaryl® and Temaril®.
Coal tar preparations
Cortisone drugs

Ointments
Soaps

Fungus or yeast infections
Amphotericin B
Griseofulvin
Nystatin
Tinactin® (new and effective)
Undecylenic acid
Whitfield's ointment

Impetigo
Hydrogen peroxide
Neomycin
Ointments combining antibiotics

Infected skin
Abscess (Section 6)
Ammoniacal diaper (Section 13)

Inflamed skin
Lotions
Oatmeal
Open wet dressings
Burow's solution

Scabies
Kwell®

Sunburn protection
A-fil
Ointments
Uval®

U. Worms

Gentian-violet tablets
Pyrvinium pamoate (Povan®)
Hookworms are usually treated with bephenium or tetrachlorethylene; pinworms and roundworms with piperazine citrate (Antepar®) or pyrvinium, also Vermox®; threadworms with thiabendazole; whipworms with hexylresorcinol.

V. Vomiting

Antiemetics
Antihistaminics (With antimotion sickness effect include Benadryl®, Dramamine® and Marezine®.)
Ipecac syrup

W. Miscellaneous

Elective surgery
Histamine
Quinidine
Radioisotopes
Reserpine

Acetaminophen, or Tempra®, Tylenol® (no prescription needed) is a safe pain and fever reducer, but inform your doctor if your child has impaired liver or kidney function. About one grain (60 milligrams) for each ten pounds of body weight every three to four hours is about right. It does not cause the stomach upset or possible gastric bleeding occasionally seen with *aspirin,* but it is questionable if it is as effective.

Alcohol cough mixture. For the dry, irritating, or croupy, barky, brassy cough that gets worse at night, the following mixture may help:

1 part gin, vodka, or bourbon
1 part lemon juice
1 part honey (or brown sugar)

For the twenty-five- to thirty-five-pound child, a teaspoonful of this given every hour or so at night, along with steam, will frequently allow everyone to get some sleep.

Amphotericin B (Fungisone®) is a toxic drug. It is used internally only if nothing else is effective for mycotic infections. Externally as an ointment it is an effective remedy for *Moniliasis.*

Anesthesia is the state of loss of sensation, purposely produced in a person so he will not feel pain. The type and amount of anesthetic is best determined by the surgeon and/or anesthetist.

Most lacerations are sutured after the use of a local anesthetic (the -caine drugs are used, for example, Novocain®). Even after complete numbing of the injured area, the most stable, relaxed child may have to be held down when faced with the strange environment of the operating room.

Some -caine drugs have been incorporated in lozenges and provide some relief to victims of sores in the mouth. Benadryl® syrup held in the mouth causes numbing. Local anesthetic ointments are not to be used for *atopic eczema;* the risk of sensitization is great.

General anesthetics (inhalation, such as ether, or intravenous, such as pentothal) are necessary for deep surgery because of the need for muscle relaxation.

Antibacterials are medicines able to destroy bacteria. *Penicillin* was the first to be recognized and produced. Other mycin drugs are being discovered and synthesized, and almost every bacterial and *rickettsial* *disease* now has a medicine to treat it. (Sulfa drugs are considered bacteriostatic—prohibiting further bacterial multiplication.)

Antibacterials should be used only for specific bacterial infections. Indiscriminate use may sensitize the patient to the drug or help promote the development of resistant strains of bacteria. At one time it was thought smart to treat a cold with an antibacterial to preclude the arrival of a secondary bacterial invasion. Some high-risk patients need this special treatment, but on the whole, time has indicated this to be a poor policy.

The use of cold and cough remedies that include antibacterials is not recommended. The amount of the antibiotic is usually not sufficient to be therapeutic and the patient runs the risk of becoming sensitive to the drug or his bacteria may become resistant to the antibiotic.

For serious infections—usually treated in the hospital—the victim's infecting organism is identified, and tests (both test tube and agar plate) run against a variety of antibiotics to determine the susceptibility or sensitivity of the organism.

Some diseases are best treated with drugs which experience has shown to be specific:

Penicillin and erythromycin work best on *streptococcal* sore throat and scarlet fever, and on pneumococcal or classical lobar pneumonia. If an allergy to penicillin is suspected, the injection is best given in the lower part of the upper arm so a tourniquet may be applied to slow absorption if a reaction occurs.

It is usually best to administer penicillin orally one half hour before mealtime and/or two hours after. Two or three big doses a day are probably just as effective as four doses scattered through the twenty-four hours; it is certainly more convenient for the mother to give the drug when the child awakens and then at bedtime, two hours after supper. Because of its occasional destruction by stomach acids, oral use is usually restricted to less serious infections.

Phenoxymethyl penicillin is more resistant to the activity of stomach acid and absorption may be more reliable.

Penicillin is widely used as a prophylactic agent to prevent a streptococcal infection in a child who has previously suffered *rheumatic fever.* One attack of rheumatic fever may not be damaging to the heart valves, but recurrent attacks triggered by a strep infection almost always scar them. It is probably better to inject a long-acting penicillin once a month, as even the best of well-motivated families forget to give the medicine daily.

A patient waiting for his *tonsillectomy* day may be best served with daily penicillin to preclude the possibility of fever and sore throat on the day of scheduled surgery. However, it is supposed to be cheating to give penicillin to an ear-infection-prone patient to prevent secondary bacterial invasion just because he has a cold.

Penicillin is definitely *not* the best antibiotic for use in eyes or on skin, as this frequently leads to sensitivity. Other antibiotics not ordinarily used internally would be best to apply to infected skin or eyes.

If a child is labeled penicillin-sensitive but is suffering from some serious disease requiring the drug, a skin test using minute amounts of penicillin may indicate whether this sensitivity is in fact present.

Mixtures of sulfa and penicillin have fallen into disfavor chiefly because of the confusion over the cause if an allergic reaction develops. (See *Sulfonamides.*)

Erythromycin is effective against the organism causing virus pneumonia (*Mycoplasma pneumoniae*). Erythromycin is usually used if the patient is allergic to penicillin as it has the same range of effectiveness.

Methicillin, cloxacillin, nafcillin, and oxacillin are penicillins usually used for staphylococcal infections resistant to regular penicillin.

Ampicillin, another penicillin, is a popular drug for many of the respiratory and urinary-tract infections of childhood, although a number of patients develop diarrhea from its use. It is the drug of choice for *salmonella* infections and *typhoid fever.* The most common form of meningitis in children (that due to *H. influenza*) is usually treated with this drug.

Ampicillin or *sulfa* is used for ear infections under age two years, for hemophilus *meningitis,* and children's kidney and bladder infections.

Tetracyclines are effective against the agents causing gonorrhea, acne, respiratory infections, virus *pneumonia, rickettsial* diseases, as well as trachoma and *psittacosis.*

Tetracycline and related drugs will stain the permanent unerupted teeth of the child under six years old. If possible, other drugs should be used for this age group. Use of aluminum hydroxide will prevent absorption. Outdated tetracycline may cause kidney damage, so be sure to check the date on the prescription bottle.

Cephaloloridine, cephalothin, colistin, kanamycin, polymyxin are valuable for severe infections usually due to gram-negative types of bacteria. If all else fails, colistin might be used against bacillary dysentery if the tests show it to be the best drug. Carbenicillin is useful for kidney infections.

Nitrofurans are valuable drugs for infections but are usually not the primary ones used. Because excretion takes place predominantly in the urine, they are used for urinary infections responding poorly to sulfa or ampicillin. Reactions are not uncommon. A Furacin-urethral insert® may be useful for vaginitis in a small girl.

Lincomycin is a rapidly acting drug with indications similar to penicillin. It is rarely used orally because of the frequency of cramps and diarrhea. It is valuable in *osteomyelitis* because of its ability to penetrate bone to get at the bacteria.

Neomycin is an effective intestinal antibacterial agent. Heavy use may cause hearing deficits or kidney damage.

Anticonvulsant drugs are those used to control the seizures of *epilepsy. Phenobarbital* is the oldest, most effective, cheapest, and safest. Dilantin®, Mysoline®, Celontin®, Zarontin® are other drugs sometimes used in combinations. Some are almost specific for certain types of seizures, but it is routine to begin with phenobarbital for almost all seizures. Others are added if control is poor.

The above or Mesantoin®, Gemonil®, Milontin®, and bromides all may be tried in various combinations and amounts.

Ideally the drug should control the seizures without disturbing the patient (drowsiness, irritability, stomachaches, blurred vision, skin rashes). Insufficient dosage or failure to use combinations are the chief causes of poor control.

Phenobarbital is usually tried first and increased until control is achieved or unfavorable symptoms occur. If tolerance is obtained but control is incomplete, another drug is added. If no reduction in seizures is effected, another drug is substituted. Valproic acid, a new drug, shows promise.

Grand mal seizures are traditionally treated with phenobarbital and/or Dilantin®. (Alternates: Gemonil®, Mebaral® for phenobarbital. Mesantoin® is second after Dilantin®.) Psychomotor epilepsy may respond best to Celontin®. Petit mal is treated with Zarontin®, but Milontin®, Tridione®, and Paradione® may be used as alternates. Diamox® is rarely used. Although phenobarbital infrequently controls petit mal it is often used first because of cost and safety.

Antidiarrheal medicines are difficult to evaluate because most cases of diarrhea are self limited. If a child has the usual intestinal flu (lasts seven days) and he is given Kaopectate® on the sixth day, the drug is credited with the cure.

Gantanol®, Diodoquin® and Entero-Vioform® have been used for *chronic, nonspecific diarrhea.*

Opium tincture is recommended for the severe cramps of diarrhea rather than *paregoric.* It acts directly on the muscle of the intestines and deadens the severity of the cramping. Five drops three times a day is about the proper dose for a child.

Antispasmodics (Robinul®, Pamine®, Darbid®, Pro-Banthine®) are used to counteract the severe cramping of intestinal muscles. Their main indication is for peptic ulcer, but intestinal cramping of diarrhea and irritable bowel may be reduced also. The beneficial dose for the intestines frequently produces side effects elsewhere (drowsiness, dry mouth, large pupils with blurred vision, rapid heart, and difficulty in urinating).

Flagyl® and Atabrine® have been used against Giardia. Lomotil® decreases intestinal motility and will reduce the frequency of the stools. Drowsiness and dizziness are not uncommon.

Antiemetics or vomiting control medicines have been helpful in precluding the need for intravenous fluids in *dehydration* (section 10) which frequently occurs with *gastroenteritis* or *cyclic vomiting* (Section 12).

The following are commonly used: Thorazine®, prochlorperazine (Compazine®), Tigan®, Phenergan®.

Most of these cause drowsiness. Some susceptible patients may develop a frightening rigidity with even therapeutic doses: head drawn back, stiffness of body in a position resembling the *tonic neck reflex* of the infant (Section 5).

Antihistaminics are chemicals that counteract histamine, the chief chemical released by cells when an allergy manifests itself. (See *Allergy,* Section 3; *Allergic rhinitis,* Section 14; *Hives,* Section 6.) Many of these can be purchased without a prescription and are the chief ingredients of "cold tablets," along with *aspirin* and often a decongestant. *Caffeine* is usually included as well, because as a side effect most antihistaminics tend to make the patient drowsy. Indeed, because of the soporific effect of many antihistaminics, they are frequently used to "suggest" sleep to the resistant two-year-old or "help settle" a child in a new situation or "quiet" a wild toddler on a trip.

At best, antihistaminics only control the allergic symptoms, and an effort should be made to find the offending allergen and eliminate it. If avoiding contact is impossible (as in the case of airborne pollens) and the distress is debilitating, skin tests and possibly desensitizing shots should be sought.

Doctors are given a great number of antihistaminic drugs to give to their patients as samples. The drug companies, of course, hope that the patient will like the effect and buy their drug. Ask your doctor for a few if you suspect allergic problems.

Phenergan® is frequently used as a colic medicine when mixed with Nembutal® in an elixir. Many parents take this (or some antihistaminic) along on a trip. It may be given while traveling to subdue the restless child bouncing in the back seat, or used for bee sting or to settle a child for the night in a strange bed.

Antihistaminics are combined with decongestants and cough suppressants to soothe the tickle and bark of the common cold.

Antihistaminics are often available in time-release forms. If little beads are enclosed in a capsule, about half of them may be shaken into a teaspoon of jam. This might settle the restless three- to five-year-old with a cold or hay fever for the whole night.

Most antihistaminics may be purchased without a prescription. A teaspoonful is about right for most thirty- to forty-pound children. This obviously would be decreased for smaller and increased for larger children.

If asthma is associated with hay fever, it is suggested that antihistaminics be used with caution as the drying effect of the drug may cause mucus to be trapped in the narrow bronchial tubes.

Antihypertensive drugs are rarely used in children.

Antiseptics (alcohol, mercurials, iodine, silver nitrate, phenols) are useful to kill skin bacteria, but their use in open wounds usually causes more harm to the tissues already damaged by the original trauma. (See *Abrasions,* Section 1; *Hydrogen peroxide.*)

Recent findings indicate that when giving injections, the skin does not have to be cleansed with the traditional alcohol-soaked cotton ball. If the needle is sterile, the skin may be entered without any preparation. This is helpful in giving the necessary booster to the apprehensive two- to ten-year-old. If he can be distracted and stuck simultaneously, he may not even notice the injection.

Antiworm medicines. Gentian-violet tablets may be used for pinworms, but they are irritating, may cause purple emeses, and are not as effective as the ones below, but they may be purchased over the counter.

Piperazine citrate (Antepar®) is a safe and effective remedy for pinworms and roundworms.

Pyrvinium pamoate (Povan®) is a reliable, safe, and effective worm remedy. The drug is a strong red dye and nauseates many people; it is best given outdoors after supper. Vermox® is safe and effective; one tablet is usually enough.

Aspirin is the doctor's friend: "Take two aspirin and come in tomorrow." This remedy for fever and pain was discovered almost a hundred years ago. A few people are sensitive to the drug, but there are now some aspirin substitutes that work almost as well. A good rule to remember: one grain of aspirin for every ten pounds of body weight; this amount can be safely given every four hours. Each dosage takes about an hour and a half to work. If the fever is reduced or the headache is better within an hour and a half, then the condition is probably not too serious.

It is wise not to have too much baby aspirin in the house. A dose of one grain for every pound could be dangerous. If a child has eaten more than this amount, you should make him vomit by giving him syrup of ipecac. Failing this, his stomach should be pumped. Aspirin is an acid, and an overdose may sometimes put the body into a state of irreversible *acidosis.* (See *Salicylate poisoning,* Section 1.)

It is now well documented that many people become severely *anemic* due to the small but constant internal blood loss which may accompany repeated aspirin ingestion. The acidity of aspirin irritates the lining of the stomach, producing tiny bleeding points which take a while to heal. A few sensitive people will wheeze if given aspirin. Aspirin (the acetyl side chain) will reduce the effectiveness of platelets in bleeding control (see *Purpura,* Section 8). Patients with *coagulation* defects should use some other medicine besides aspirin for pain. *APC,* or aspirin, phenacetin and caffeine, is a somewhat irrational combination. Phenacetin has similar effects on fever and pain to those of aspirin. The *caffeine* in this mixture may be beneficial if a vascular or migraine headache is being treated, but its stimulating effect makes it a poor drug for a child with a fever.

Atropine suppresses mucous secretion; it is valuable when administered before surgery. It also relaxes the colicky cramping of the intestines, and so may be used for babies who vomit or are subject to gas and cramps. Dosage must be accurate, as an overdose can cause fever. There are a number of atropinelike drugs used as *antispasmodics.*

Barbiturates are sedatives and anticonvulsant drugs. They are cheap and usually safe. They are used for the control of *colic,* as a bedtime relaxer or daytime tension reducer, but their chief use is in epilepsy where their safety record urges their use as first choice in almost all types. Frequently the dopy side effect that accompanies the beneficial effect precludes heavy use, and other drugs must be substituted. Children frequently respond in a paradoxical way to them, acting as if stimulated and drunk. Some recent research indicates that barbiturates diminish the sleeper's ability to dream, which in turn might lead to irritability. Many people develop a tolerance to these drugs and find they have to take increasing amounts to achieve the desired results. A doctor, obviously, should be monitoring the prescription refills to ward off accidental—or purposeful—overdoses.

Phenobarbital is long-acting. Small, spaced doses might allay anxiety. It is the safest and cheapest. Insomnia may be controlled with Butisol®, Amytal®, Nembutal®, and Seconal®. The latter two are quick-acting and often used as a preanesthetic sedative. Pentothal® is a rapid-acting barbiturate used as an intravenous anesthetic. Some parents find it wise to have a few Nembutal® capsules on hand to insert rectally for their febrile-seizure-prone child.

Benadryl®, diphenhydramine, is an *antihistaminic* drug that has some sedative effect, or at least a quieting action on the brain. It is used effectively for calming a *hyperactive* child or soothing a wildly aggressive child, as well as for *allergic* problems.

Bronchodilators are used for asthma and bronchitis. *Epinephrine,* ephedrine, *pseudoephedrine* (Sudafed®), phenylephrine, and isoproterenol (Isuprel®) are the commonly used ones. Aminophylline is used less in children because of the ease of toxicity. Side effects of an overdose may be frightening and include palpitation, elevated blood pressure, headache, sleeplessness, and excitability.

Burow's solution is the standard solution for wetting dressings used for weepy, inflamed skin. It cleanses, soothes, maintains drainage, and controls the skin temperature. A cotton dressing over the weepy area is saturated with the solution. It is changed every two hours and removed every four hours for fifteen minutes to prevent maceration.

Cafergot® contains *caffeine* and ergotamine. Both drugs constrict the blood vessels in the scalp and on the surface of the brain. It is used for migraine and vascular headaches. (See Section 15.)

Caffeine is a widely used stimulant found in coffee and tea. Because of its effect on blood vessels, it is incorporated in headache remedies with *aspirin* (with brand names such as Anacin, Empirin Compound®). If aspirin plus caffeine relieves a *headache* more effectively than aspirin alone, it suggests the victim is suffering from vascular headaches or a migraine-related condition.

Chloral hydrate, Noctec®, is usually a safe and rapid-acting sedative for children. It is less likely to cause excitement than the *barbiturates.* It is the power behind the Mickey Finn.

Chloramphenicol, or Chloromycetin®, is a powerful *antibiotic* widely used against *gram-negative bacteria* and the *Staphylococcus.* Its well-known toxic effects in lowering the white blood count and depressing the activity of the bone marrow have given it a bad reputation. It is suggested that its use be confined to life-threatening infections (*meningitis,* staphylococcal *pneumonia*) when other antibiotics are ineffective.

Chlorpheniramine, or Chlortrimeton®, etc. (some available without a prescription) is a safe *antihistaminic* and the usual one found in advertised cold and cough remedies. Drowsiness is common. One-half teaspoon every four hours is the dose for a fifteen- to twenty-pound child. It sometimes helps to double this at bedtime if an occasional dose is skipped. One teaspoon every four hours can be given if weight is thirty to forty-five pounds; if fifty to eighty pounds, half of adult dose; eighty pounds and over, adult dose.

Coal-tar preparations (Cor-tar-Quin®, Pragma-tar®) are time-honored for the treatment of chronic eczema and neurodermatitis. They are usually now combined with cortisone drugs to help inflammation and reduce itch.

Cocaine is less used now because of the development of other potent, less toxic local anesthetics. Overdose or excessive absorption from an area being anesthetized causes confusion, tremors, tachycardia, abdominal pain.

Codeine phosphate is a pain-killing, cough-suppressing, constipating, possibly addicting drug. It is commonly used in cough syrups and is ideal for earaches and toothaches.

Most cough syrups contain about 10 milligrams per teaspoon which is about the right dose for a thirty- to thirty-five-pound three- to four-year-old.

While awaiting the relief of pain of an earache from the antibiotic, a mother might give her child codeine (Cheracol®) along with the *aspirin.* (Something to try for an earache: boil a Bermuda onion. Remove the soft, warm core and slide it into the ear canal; the pain may disappear immediately. The doctor may raise his eyebrows when he does the posttreatment ear check.)

Doses of codeine of about 30 to 65 milligrams (½ to 1 grain) are about equivalent to 650 milligrams (10 grains) of aspirin. The more common combination is codeine (30 milligrams), aspirin (230 milligrams or 2 grains), phenacetin (150 milligrams), and caffeine (30 milligrams) called Empirin Compound® with codeine #3. The simple combination of codeine and aspirin makes more sense (codeine, 30 milligrams, with aspirin, 325 milligrams).

Corticosteroids are used as a replacement if a deficiency exists, but they are useful for inflammatory diseases, for rheumatic fever, nephritis, and severe allergic problems.

Cortisone drugs are incorporated into ointments which clear many inflamed, itchy skins (atopic eczema) and eyes. They suppress the scaliness of *psoriasis.*

Cromolyn is an antiasthma medicine in powder form, delivered by a jet of air into the bronchial tree. It is of value only as a preventive.

Darvon® is used for the relief of painful conditions although it is not quite as effective as codeine. Some drug dependency may be associated with its abuse.

Demerol® (Meperidine) differs chemically from morphine but has similar action. It is widely used for obstetrical pain relief, but does have some depressant effect on the infant's respiratory rate.

Dextroamphetamine sulfate, Dexedrine®, is a stimulant to most people, but has a paradoxical calming effect on hyperactive children as it prolongs the attention span. (See *Cerebral dysfunction,* Section 15.) It has been widely used and abused by the obese and many alienated youths seeking escape or thrills.

It stimulates an inhibitory center so the hyperactive child may disregard unimportant stimuli. Tolerance develops in 10 percent, and the dose has to be increased to notice the initial effects again. It has been useful in narcolepsy and some forms of epilepsy.

In the treatment of the hyperactive child, dextroamphetamine sulfate is the drug of first choice. It is begun at breakfast with one half a tablet (2½ milligrams). In one hour, the teacher and/or the parent should notice a decrease in activity and a lengthening of the span of attention. Usually a reduction in the appetite for lunch is noted if the proper dose has been given. If nothing happens, the dose is increased to three-fourths of one tablet the next morning. This increase of one-fourth tablet is repeated daily until the desired effect is produced. If a reduction in lunch appetite is achieved, but neither activity nor concentration is affected, the medicine is changed to Ritalin® or Benzedrine® and the same procedure is repeated. Doubt about the diagnosis must be considered if no improvement in behavior accompanies an appetite loss. Increasing the dose when the appetite is reduced by at least half is not usually indicated. If possible, the medicine should be discontinued on weekends to preclude the establishment of tolerance. It is not unusual for a child to be controlled on 5 milligrams in September, but to need 10 milligrams in January and 20 milligrams by May.

A repeat noon dose of about half the breakfast dose is usually necessary. Occasionally, one-fourth or one-half of the morning dose is again used at 4 or 5 P.M. Some hyperactive children can fall asleep *more* easily with a late evening dose.

Eleven-year-olds and older may do better with a single time release tablet or capsule at breakfast; most are very embarrassed to take medicine in the presence of their peer group at school. (Biphetamine®, 7½, 12½, and 20 milligram capsules; Desoxyn® gradumets, 5, 10, and 15 milligrams; Dexedrine sulfate® spansules, 5, 10, and 15 milligrams.)

Some children do even better with a combination of a short action (dextroamphetamine) and a long action (spansule) medicine, both given at breakfast. The former gets the child going and the latter keeps him going.

Digitalis is a chemical found in a plant leaf (foxglove) that acts as a heart-muscle stimulant, especially valuable in cases of *heart failure* and abnormal rhythm disturbances.

Dilantin®, or diphenylhydantoin sodium, DPH, is a widely used drug for *grand mal epilepsy.* It seems to have a calming effect on the "irritable focus" of the brain from which radiates the electrical activity responsible for a seizure. Although widely used and in large doses, it has a few toxic side effects that must be monitored: swollen gums, rashes, hairiness, and suppression of *white blood cells.* Overdoses may lead to a drunken, wide-based *gait,* or behavior anomalies.

DPH has some success in controlling many nonepileptic phenomena such as abdominal *migraine,* weak or "neurasthenic" states, *hyperactivity* (if dextroamphetamine fails), impulsive or temper outbursts, some night terrors, sleep walking, and runaway "habits."

Good follow-up care requires periodic blood counts and dosage adjustments.

Diuretics act by preventing sodium reabsorption in the tubules of the kidneys. The excess sodium requires water for solubility; thus both the salt and the water are passed out in the urine. These drugs are most helpful in reducing the accumulated edema fluid of heart failure. They are less effective for the fluid accumulation of nephritis, nephrosis, cirrhosis, pregnancy, and premenstrual tension.

Mercurial diuretics must be injected; thiazides (Diuril® and many others) may be taken orally.

Ear preparations are only effective if the ear canal is clean and free of debris. (One does not paint a board covered with old paint, dirt, and grease.) The canals must be syringed out with water. Wax may be broken up with *hydrogen peroxide* or Debrox® first. *Swimmer's ear* (otitis externa) can be prevented by keeping the canal dry and free of debris; alcohol (a drying agent) is used in the canal after contact with water. If infection is present, the canals are cleansed, then an antibiotic otic solution is instilled four times a day, occasionally accompanied by a cotton wick saturated with the same material (Aerosporin®, Chloromycetin®, Furacin®, Neopolycin®, Cortisporin®).

Vosol® has acetic acid (somewhat antibacterial) and its use may prevent a recurrence. Burow's solution can be used in the ear for acute inflammation.

Auralgan® or Otodyne® are the traditional drops for the pain of otitis media, but the core of a boiled, warm Bermuda onion works as well. When the pain is gone, however, the patient may foolishly avoid definitive treatment, thus allowing complications to occur. (See *Codeine.*)

Elective surgery (repair of congenital anomalies)—as opposed to emergency surgery (*appendectomy*)—is best delayed until age five or six years. The child under three or four usually does not comprehend that parents, doctors, nurses, and hospital are trying to help; he thinks he is being punished for something and reacts with anxiety, fear, or panic. He may revert to a more infantile level of reacting for a long period after the surgery has been consciously forgotten.

If possible, a child should visit the hospital before his entrance for surgery, so he may see for himself that the place is not a torture chamber. A favorite toy should accompany him, and his parents should be with him before the surgery and upon recovery.

Some tranquilizer may allay anxiety even better than the standard *barbiturate, atropine,* and *morphine* preanesthetic mixtures; frequently, all are necessary for the wilder ones. Indeed, many children have a paradoxical reaction to drugs, and instead of calming the child, a barbiturate may make him climb the wall.

Epinephrine, or adrenalin, is a chemical secreted by the adrenal glands which prepare the body for fight or flight. When injected, it stimulates the heart to beat faster, but it is mainly used for the relief of asthma. It may be lifesaving in severe *allergic* reactions, such as bee stings or laryngeal spasm due to food allergies.

Estrogens are secreted by the mature ovary; they may be given orally for a variety of female complaints. The hormone (along with *progesterone*) produces secondary female characteristics in delayed maturation associated with *amenhorrhea;* here the *pituitary* did not produce the *gonadotrophic* hormone or, if it did, the ovary was unresponsive. (See Section 10.)

The use of estrogens in the treatment of acne has proven helpful many times. The hormone serves to counteract the androgens (adrenal hormone) which encourage oily, sebaceous skin.

The height of an adult female can sometimes be controlled by the use of estrogens before puberty. It is a tricky business and side effects are not uncommon.

Expectorants to increase the flow of mucus and "loosen the phlegm" are of doubtful value, but are traditional in cough mixtures.

Ammonium chloride is acidifying. Potassium iodide may cause fever, parotid swelling, or rashes, Its use many confuse thyroid function testing. Glyceryl guaiacolate is of doubtful benefit; it is supposed to soothe the throat. Syrup of ipecac increases the flow of phelgm but is an emetic, causing nausea and vomiting in high doses.

Eye drops and ointments. For conjuctivitis (yellow or green matter coming from the eye) some antibiotic ointment or drop is the treatment of choice. Sulfa, penicillin, erythromycin, and tetracycline drugs should be avoided in ophthalmic preparations because of the risk of sensitization. Best to use gentamicin or sulfacetamide.

It is difficult to get the medicine next to the eyeball in a squirmy child; the lower lid must be pulled down and the ointment squirted into the pocket between the inside of the lid and the eyeball. It is best not to drop the liquid directly onto the naked eyeball; with the child on his back and his eyes shut, two or three drops may be placed at the hollow next to the bridge of his nose. When he opens his eyes, the fluid will run into the eyeball area with a minimum of fright.

Ferrous sulfate, gluconate, lactate, are iron salts traditionally used to treat iron-deficiency anemia. Some intestinal tracts are very sensitive to iron, and stomachaches and *diarrhea* may preclude giving usual doses. One available form is in a time-release capsule (Feosol Spansule®) that is slowly dissolved as it travels through the bowel; this provides a sufficient dose with fewer side effects.

However, iron absorption is maximal in the duodenum, the few inches just beyond the stomach, so coated tablets may cause less irritation, but also result in less than optimum absorption. Gastrointestinal irritation is less if the iron is administered after meals, three times a day. Iron liquid temporarily stains the teeth, so it might best be mixed with food or drink or dropped on the back of the tongue and quickly washed down with juice. Two to four milligrams of elemental iron per day is the prophylactic dose for a baby on a milk diet until solid foods with iron can be started at age 5 to 8 months. Injectable iron (Imferon®) is only used if some intestinal disease precludes the oral route. Iron must be given without other hematologic agents (B_{12}, folic acid, copper) as the diagnosis of other forms of anemia will be obscured. Some feel large doses of vitamin C will facilitate the absorption of iron. To produce optimum storage of iron in the body, iron should be continued for several months or a year. Children may need extra iron while growing; menstruating and pregnant women could use a little extra, but a grown man on an adequate diet may overload his storage depots if he takes extra iron. Some people cannot absorb adequate iron if consuming dairy products.

Fluoride in the form of sodium salt is usually combined with vitamins for the infant living in a fluoride deficient area. After age eighteen months or two years when enough molars have erupted, the child can chew up the small soluble tablet. A prescription is necessary; bottles of 1,000 tablets are available and should retail for about five dollars or less. Some busy mothers forget the daily dose and give two tablets every other day or three tablets every three days, but daily ingestion is best.

If a baby is getting milk with vitamins already added, it is accurate, but a little time-consuming, to dissolve one fluoride tablet in one feeding a day. Some authorities feel it is too risky to give more than once a week and then only with dolomite.

Griseofulvin (Fulvisen®) is the standard therapy for *ringworm* of the scalp. It migrates to the dermis; the new hairs growing out are thus free of the fungus.

Haldol®, haloperidol, is a useful drug to calm an aggressive, hyperactive child if amphetamines or Ritalin® are inappropriate.

Heroin is a morphine derivative.

Histamine is a chemical released from certain cells of the body in response to foreign substances (bee-sting venom), drugs, trauma, and immune reactions in the body. It is responsible for the hive, the plugged, swollen nasal passages during the hay-fever season, the red itchy area of the insect bite. (See *Allergy,* Section 3.)

Antihistaminics are widely used to control *allergies,* but once the target cell has been triggered by the histamine, the antihistaminic does little good. It is best to give the antihistaminic at the time of the bee sting (or a little before, if a bite can be anticipated) before the histamine is released.

Once the target cell has been stimulated to react, epinephrine would be more effective in counteracting the effects. (Epinephrine helps allergic asthma while an antihistaminic might make it worse because it might dry out the tissues.)

Hydrogen peroxide solution releases nascent oxygen when applied to open wounds. Some slight antibacterial effect is less important than the mechanical loosening of debris. This may facilitate the more important water washing which should be accomplished with every wound. A few drops of this in the ear canal may ease the removal of hard wax by irrigation.

Ipecac syrup is an emetic and worth having in a house where small children live. If a child ingests poisons or medicines, the mother should call the doctor and with his counsel administer three teaspoonsful. A six-ounce glass of water will facilitate the emesis. If no vomiting has occurred within twenty minutes, the dose can be readministered. If the child still does not vomit, the stomach should be pumped. If Thorazine®, Compazine®, Phenergan® have been swallowed (they are antiemetics), the ipecac might not be effective. Vomiting should not be induced if petroleum products (kerosene, gasoline, turpentine) have been ingested; they might be aspirated on the way out of the stomach, and the resultant violent chemical *pneumonia* would be worse than the intestinal irritation from the retained hydrocarbon. (See *Hydrocarbon,* Section 2.)

Isoniazid is a well tolerated and effective medicine against the less serious forms of *tuberculosis.* Resistant forms have developed since its discovery, so in the more severe forms of TB other drugs such as *streptomycin* must be added.

Its use as the sole agent is usually confined to children who have a positive reaction to the skin test for tuberculosis when previous tests have been negative. (The tine test is positive, and a chest X ray reveals only a primary complex with no fever and no sedimentation-rate increase.)

Ketogenic diet has been useful in the control of *grand* and *petit mal seizures,* but the difficulties inherent in maintaining this diet limit its use. It involves restricting fluids to the point of mild dehydration and the administration of acid-producing drinks along with asparagus, butter, and other foods that yield acids when metabolized.

Kwell® (gamma benzene hexachloride) is the treatment of choice for scabies and may also be effective (as a powder) against lice (*pediculosis*). It discourages ticks and kills chiggers. The cream is applied to involved areas and not washed off for 24 hours. It may be necessary to repeat the application to stubborn areas a week later.

Lasix® is a diuretic used to help the body get rid of excess fluid.

Laxatives (see also Section 12). Castor oil on an empty stomach will usually produce a few watery, large stools in two to four hours after ingestion. The patient may have nothing to pass for the next two to four days.

Cascara usually produces a generous stool in several hours.

Phenolphthalein will reward the ingester with a large, sloppy stool in several hours.

Bulk laxatives contain cellulose, bran, or plantago or psyllium seed. These produce a more natural stool than the cramping agents. They absorb and hold moisture so are best taken with much fluid. (Bu-lax®, Metamucil®, Mucilose® and L-A® formula are examples.)

Glycerin rectal suppositories are often used for infants to soften the oncoming stool and lubricate the lining to promote easier passage. It would be better to change the diet or give an oral preparation to soften the stools. A parent can do as much good to stimulate the passage of a reluctant stool by gently inserting a well lubricated little finger about one half inch into the rectum. This gives the baby the bearing down urge and if a stool is there he usually pushes it out. The method is cheap and convenient.

Mineral oil may be used on a short-term basis, but is not recommended because of the chance of oil deposits in the lungs, production of thin stools that do not stimulate adequately the rectal and anal areas, and the possibility that oil-soluble vitamins may be lost in the mineral oil and not absorbed.

Lotions are powders suspended in water. These cool, dry, and protect inflamed, intact skin. These shake solutions will improve acne (sulfur, resorcinol, salicylic acid). (Vleminckx solution smells terrible.) The druggist know which ones are working; ask for their recommendations.

Acne preparations: The parent might ask the druggist for these items or preparations similar to them. If after a month of use the condition is not under control, the doctor's advice must be sought. Early treatment may prevent permanent scarring.

1. Lotio alba or white lotion
   Zinc sulfate—8%
   Sulfurated potash—8%
   In rose water
2. One to three percent salicylic acid in 70% rubbing alcohol helps the skin to peel.

3. 20% sulfur
   10% benzoyl peroxide in polyethylene glycol
4. Degreasing the skin
   5% acetone in 70% ethyl alcohol
5. Degreasing and cleaning the skin
   Sodium borate—4.0 grams
   Precipitated sulfur—4.0 grams
   Acetone—30.0 cc.
   Camphor spirit—enough to make 100 cc. total.
   Apply morning and evening.

Mellaril®, thioridazine, is a tranquilizer especially helpful for anxious and/or hyperactive children. The amphetamines do not work well before age five years; Mellaril® may help control the overly busy child until then. This quiets down the restless, disruptive child enough to give the mother a chance to practice some behavior-modification techniques.

Methadone is a narcotic now widely publicized as a heroin blocking agent. Most methods of treatment for heroin addiction have failed. It has been suggested that the addiction has altered the addict's metabolism, and his cells have become dependent on heroin for enzymatic function, as a diabetic might be considered to be "addicted" to insulin. Methadone satisfies this cellular need and at the same time prevents the high that the addict usually experiences when he gets his heroin fix. This controlled program has succeeded in reducing crime (addicts need ten to fifty dollars a day for heroin), and allowing many to be self-respecting job holders. Group and individual psychotherapy is usually performed concomitantly.

Methionine is a valuable, safe chemical used to acidify the urine. A prescribed dose at suppertime will counteract the ammoniacal diaper.

Morphine sulfate is a narcotic with pain-reducing and euphoriant properties. Addiction is common. Many people became severely addicted to it before the Harrison Narcotic Act of 1914, because it had been used in many remedies that could be purchased over the counter, such as tonics, cough syrups, sedatives, rejuvenators, snakebite remedies. It has limited pediatric use, but is helpful for cancer pain, preoperative medication, the anxiety of heart failure.

Nasal decongestants are valuable agents to constrict the surface blood vessels in the nasal mucous membranes. Easier breathing and occasional relief of sinus congestion headache are the benefits. Prolonged use may make the medication ineffective or cause a rebound phenomenon in which the membranes swell up more than originally.

The chief disadvantage is the difficulty of getting the nose drops into the reluctant child. An under-eight-month-old baby can be held on the mother's lap, two drops put in each nostril, and then his mouth held clamped shut. He has to sniff them up on his next inhalation.

The decongestants act on colds, hay fever stuffiness, and are helpful in relieving the obstruction in the eustachian tubes in ear infections. Locally administered by drop or spray, there is usually immediate relief. Orally ingested, the effect is slower but may be more prolonged. Treatment interruption is suggested; use for two or three days, then discontinue for a day or two. Bacterial contamination may occur unless the dropper is rinsed in hot water after use; a fresh, clean bottle should be obtained at time of refill at the drug store.

Neomycin is an antibiotic widely used in antibacterial ointments. It is effective against a variety of skin bacteria and is valuable for the treatment of *impetigo.* Because it is used so commonly, many people have become sensitive to it. Instead of a minor skin infection healing, the treated area develops an allergy and burns, stings, itches, and becomes more reddened.

Norepinephrine is a hormone excreted by the medulla (central area) or the adrenal glands. It will increase blood pressure when discharged into the circulation. It is related to epinephrine and is used to treat some types of shock.

Norgesic® is used to reduce pain of muscle and bone origin. It is a chemical combined with aspirin and caffeine.

Nystatin combined with cortisone in an ointment is rapidly effective against skin candidiasis (monilia).

Nystatin is the standard treatment for oral and intestinal thrush. Given orally, it usually clears the lesions in a few days. The old treatment with *gentian violet* was unsightly and irritating. Boroglycerine and zephiran are too slow.

Oatmeal can be cooked, placed in cheesecloth, and the soggy mess applied to inflamed skin. Neater commercial packages are available (Aveeno®).

Oils are standard for the dry skin of those in low humidity areas or with neurodermatitis. Emulsified oil (Alpha-Keri®, Avenol®, Domol®) in the bath will be retained on the skin to hold the moisture in; the usual soap and water bath dries the skin as the natural oils are washed away with the dirt.

Ointments (usually with petrolatum, lanolin, or mineral oil as the base) are used for chronic, thick, dry, scaly skin to soften and hold moisture (cold cream, Lubriderm®, Acid Mantle®). Chronic eczema and neurodermatitis are aided because these ointments will prevent moisture from leaving the skin. Some powders (zinc oxide, titanium dioxide, talc) are incorporated in petrolatum as sun-screening or wet diaper protection.

Ointments combining antibiotics are widely used on children's skin as they protect *abrasions* from becoming secondarily infected (*impetigo*), are not painful, and allow the healing skin to bend without cracking. They can be purchased over the counter and are a must in a first aid kit. Sensitization with burning, itching, and redness is possible—and fairly common with *neomycin*—but less so than with penicillin or sulfa ointments. Some are safe to use for purulent conjunctivitis, but eye ointments are preferable. Neosporin®, Neo-Polycin®, Polysporin®, Bacimycin®, Spectrocin®, all contain two or three of the following: Bacitracin, gramicidin, neomycin, polymyxin. Furacin® is a valuable antibiotic when applied as an ointment but is frequently sensitizing.

Ointments containing antihistaminics are of no benefit to the skin. They may cause sensitization, and a rash will appear when other antihistaminics are taken orally.

Open wet dressings (usually water based) cool the skin and thus soothe red, inflamed areas. Closed, wet dressings increase the heat produced by skin capillaries and allow the skin to soften; infection may be promoted. Burns and abrasions should not be treated with occlusive dressings. However, hot, wet dressings are effective in the local treatment of abscesses, furuncles, boils, as they allow the pus to localize and drain.

Para-aminosalicylic acid is valuable as it enhances the effect of other anti-tuberculosis drugs, although it, by itself, does not kill germs. It frequently causes gastric (stomach) irritation, however.

Paraldehyde is a safe sedative, but little used because of the offensive odor produced by the excretion of the drug via the lungs.

Paregoric is an opium *(morphine)* derivative widely used for the relief of abdominal cramps. The dose is a drop per pound three or four times a day. If he can be induced to take it, a thirty-pound child should get about half a teaspoonful.

Penicillin is a valuable, safe, effective antibiotic widely used for *streptococcal* and *pneumococcal* infections. Because of the rather frequent development of allergy to it and the formation of resistant bacteria, its use is not indicated for colds and other virus infections. It is better withheld for a time of necessity.

Frequently a child will be treated with penicillin for *roseola* because the fever is high and the throat looks pink. After three days the fever returns to normal and the parents thank the penicillin. But the response would have been the same without the use of penicillin because the fever associated with roseola subsides in three days.

Pitressin, vasopressin, is the drug used for the treatment of *diabetes insipidus.* A powder of this can be insufflated into the nose once control has been obtained by use of the injectable form.

Powders (zinc oxide, stearate, talc, corn starch) allow skin to slide over skin without friction. Some cooling and anti-itch effect may be provided. They are occasionally used in a baby's groin, armpits, or under the chin to prevent frictional irritation. They must never be used if the skin is broken open. (See *Talc,* Section 1.)

Progesterone is useful in prolonged uterine bleeding that may occur at the *menarche;* ovulation fails to occur and the normal progesterone is not produced by the *corpus luteum.* The continued estrogen stimulation makes the uterine lining overgrow. Constant sloughing of this endometrium produces the protracted menstrual flow.

Propranolol is a beta-adrenergic blocking agent useful in reducing high blood pressure. Rarely used in children.

Pseudoephedrine, Sudafed®, is a safe and widely used bronchial tube dilator (in asthma) and a decongestant (internal nose drop). It is incorporated in syrups (often with *antihistaminics*) to shrink the nasopharyngeal membranes and prevent or treat plugged eustachian tubes, a condition usually associated with upper *respiratory infections* and *otitis media.* It is safer, more effective, more easily administered, and less likely to produce local membrane irritation than nose drops or nasal sprays. (No prescription needed.)

Pyridium® is a safe drug used to relieve the pain of urinary-tract inflammation.

Quinidine is a cardiac depressant used to control rapid heart rate.

Radioisotopes are chemicals converted to radioactive substances to be used for diagnostic tests. As an example, radioactive iodine is taken by the patient, and his thyroid gland is tested with a Geiger counter to estimate how fast the iodine is taken up.

Reserpine is a valuable drug used to reduce blood pressure. It is most frequently used for the hypertension associated with glomerulonephritis.

Scopolamine acts as does *atropine.* Its use as a preoperative medication tends to reduce the amount of saliva and bronchial secretions produced by the anesthetic. It also has some calming effect on the anxious child.

Shampoos containing sulfur and salicylic acid are usually best for the dandruff and oily scalp of those with seborrheic dermatitis. Tar preparations might work better for psoriasis.

For seborrhea of the scalp:

Coal tar—2%
Precipitated sulfur—2%
Salicylic acid—2%
In hydrophilic ointment
Applied at night

Hexachlorophene is widely used to kill surface germs but must be rinsed well. It is the standard (pHisohex®) for handwashing for nurses and doctors prior to surgery but is no longer used on the skin of newborns or infants. It may be combined with sulfur and salicylic acid in anti-dandruff and anti-seborrheic shampoos (pHisodan®, Fostex®, Sebulex®).

Soaps are usually alkaline and will irritate already inflamed skin.

Acid soaps are usually recommended for use on eczematous skin (Lowila®, pHisoderm®, Nutrogena®). Do not use hexachlorophene on open wounds or large abrasions.

Streptomycin is an antibacterial drug widely used against the *tuberculosis* germ. It may save the patient from the ravages of a severe tuberculous infection, but the risk of deafness and kidney damage is high. The TB germ frequently develops resistance to streptomycin, so other antituberculosis medicines are usually employed simultaneously.

Sulfonamides make up the general group of "sulfa" drugs used to treat infections.

Sulfonamides are bacteriostatic and interfere with the metabolism of the bacteria. Since penicillin acts only on metabolizing bacteria, sulfa drugs might prevent the penicillin from exerting its optimal effect. Resistance to sulfa has been reported frequently (see *Gonorrhea* and *Meningococcemia,* Section 2). Sulfa ointments and powders are rarely used on wounds because pus and debris make them ineffective bacteriostatic agents. The risk of sensitization is enhanced by topical use; it would be wise to avoid sulfa eye ointments and drops because of this risk.

Sulfa drugs are used for bacterial upper *respiratory infections, sinusitis, otitis media, cystitis, pyelitis,* susceptible strains of *meningococcus, nocardiosis* and *toxoplasmosis.* Their widest use is for urinary infections. Trachoma is usually responsive to sulfa. Many *shigella* infections (bacillary dysentery) are cured by sulfa, but resistant bacteria are common. (Actinomycosis and nocardiosis are now thought to be bacterial and respond to penicillin and sulfa, respectively.)

Sulfa is not as effective as a prophylactic drug against a recurrence of *streptococcal* infection for a *rheumatic-fever* victim, but it is the next best drug if the patient is allergic to *penicillin.* Although it has been used as a prophylactic drug to ward off *otitis media* or *bronchitis* when a susceptible patient develops a cold or *influenza,* the danger of producing a resistant bacteria is high. The chance of triggering an allergic response is increased. Some patients may have to take the drug daily because of kidney or bladder infections that have refused to clear with surgery, dilations, or diet.

Sulfa should not be used if the patient is dehydrated as it may crystallize in the urine with associated obstruction or bleeding. Liver damage is another contraindication. It has been causally related to the development of the *Stevens-Johnson syndrome.* An occasional patient, usually a young child, is stimulated or made "high," or is wakeful and has bad dreams when on sulfa.

Sulfur ointments are principally used for acne and seborrheic dermatitis. Salicylic acid is usually incorporated to help flake off superficial skin so the oil may escape from the sebaceous glands.

Sunburn prevention

Best: Uval® or A-fil; or
Red veterinary petrolatum with
15% p-aminobenzoic acid.

Testosterone is a hormone secreted by the Leydig cells in the testes (other cells produce spermatozoa). This hormone is androgenic; it produces secondary sexual characteristics: body hair, deep voice, increased muscle mass. The adrenal glands produce another androgenic hormone, but in very small amounts. The hormone may be given in *Klinefelter's syndrome* or for Leydig cell failure due to *mumps orchitis* or post-testicular injury.

Rarely would testosterone (like steroids—having a positive effect on protein metabolism) be used on children with growth failure or malnutrition. Some beneficial influences on growth and nutrition might be negated by an early puberty side-effect and an ultimate shorter-than-expected height.

Tetracyclines are antibiotics valuable in the treatment of *respiratory infections, gonorrhea, mycoplasma, acne,* and *pneumonia.* The hazards of their use are tooth discoloration, development of *thrush, diarrhea, headache* from increased intracranial pressure, and skin rashes when exposed to the sun.

Thyroid is made from the powdered glands of animals. *Hypothyroidism* and *cretinism* are the conditions obviously needing this hormone replacement; the treatment is continued for life. Nontoxic goiter is reduced in size by thyroid as it suppresses the secretion of the pituitary thyrotrophic hormone. It is beneficial for *thyroiditis* (Hashimoto's).

Thyroid hormone is used for a variety of conditions suggesting hypothyroidism (sluggishness, constipation, fatigue, delayed growth, and obesity) but without clearcut evidence of deficient thyroid production, its use is condemned.

Tofranil®, or imipramine, is a *tranquilizer* that has proved of value in the control of enuresis. Its twofold action of elevating mood (the child doesn't sleep so soundly or is more aware of a full bladder) and increasing the tone of the sphincter (pursestring) muscle at the outlet of the *bladder* seems to be responsible for the dry bed. The drug helps the victim establish new pathways of response (staying dry) that continue after the drug is discontinued.

Tranquilizers are drugs with a relaxing or *anxiety*-reducing effect on the nervous system. The ideal drug should allow the patient normal activity and freedom from "nervousness" without undue drowsiness, the usual side effect. In children it is common to find side effects of somnolence and/or apparent drunkenness present when the dose is sufficient to relieve the anxiety.

Some psychiatrically oriented doctors decry the use of tranquilizers for children on the ground that they "cover" the anxiety symptoms in patients who should really be having psychotherapy. Most doctors feel that the medicine allows enough return to normal behavior so that some attention may *then* be paid to any family imbalance that may be present.

To calm the overly active youngster for a car ride, to settle him for bedtime, or to help keep him out of mischief when visiting relatives, we have found some *antihistaminics* to be safe and usually effective. Benadryl® and Phenergan® are the most widely used; motion sickness remedies are the next best.

Undecylenic acid is the usual over-the-counter ointment for *ringworm* of the skin or *athlete's foot.*

Valium®, diazepam, is a valuable *tranquilizer* and has some success in the treatment of convulsive disorders, especially *status epilepticus.*

Vitamin B_{12} (cyanocobalamin) is injected into the muscle of victims of pernicious anemia and some forms of megaloblastic anemia. (Old-time "liver shots" are still helpful.) If this form of anemia has been diagnosed, the injections must continue—usually monthly—for life. Daily shots of B_{12} will help an attack of shingles.

Whitfield's ointment (benzoic and salicylic acids) is another antifungal over-the-counter agent.

If this or undecylenic acid fails, a very effective, safe, topical antifungal agent (Tinactin®) is then prescribed by the doctor.

PART TWO

ANATOMY AND DEVELOPMENT

SECTION 5
The Newborn Baby

The newborn (or neonatal) period is the first month after *birth.* It must be the most difficult time of adjustment in life, because two thirds of all the deaths during the first year occur at this time. *Congenital anomalies* of *heart, nervous system, lungs* account for some of the mortality; up until now, the placenta circulation has supported the baby's oxygen and nutritional needs in the uterus.

Establishing adequate respiration is the neonate's chief job. (Read *Birth* first.) The *premature* baby, the Caesarian section baby, the second of a pair of twins, and the baby of a diabetic mother are especially prone to *respiratory distress. Cyanosis* is frequently seen transiently, but prolonged severe blueness may lead to neurological problems in the older child. (See *Hyperactivity,* Section 15; *Apgar score.*) Excess *bilirubin* is the baby's next hurdle (see *Erythroblastosis fetalis*), then adequate nutrition (see *Diet,* Section 11).

A. Newborn

Amniocentesis
Apgar score
Birth
Birth injury
- *Bump on head (Caput succedaneum, Cephalohematoma)*
- *Cerebral palsy* (Section 15)
- *Facial nerve palsy*
- *Nose injury*
- *Weak arm (Brachial palsy, broken clavicle)*
- *Wry neck (Torticollis)*

Body temperature
Death
Dehydration fever (see Fever, Section 2)
Dwarfism (Section 10)
- *Primordial dwarfs*

Low birth weight
Mortality
Multiple births
Postmaturity
Premature infant
Reflexes
- *Moro response*
- *Sucking reflex*
- *Tonic neck reflex*

Weak muscles
- *Floppy infant syndrome* (Section 15)
- *Myasthenia neonatorum*

B. Respiratory problems

Acidosis
Anoxia
Asphyxia
Atelectasis (Section 9)
Big tongue (see Macroglossia, Section 14)
Diaphragmatic hernia
Fetal distress syndrome
Posterior choanal obstruction
Respiratory distress syndrome
Stridor
Tracheo-esophageal fistula

C. Jaundice

Bilirubin, Kernicterus
Cytomegalic-inclusion disease (Section 2)
Erythroblastosis fetalis
Exchange transfusion (Section 8)
Hemolytic disease of newborn
Septicemia (Section 2)
Stillborn due to Rh disease, Hydrops fetalis
Test for Rh disease (Amniocentesis)
Toxoplasmosis (Section 2)

D. Bleeding tendency

Coagulation disorders (Section 8)
Hemorrhagic disease of newborn
Purpura (Section 8)

E. Seizures in the neonate

Hypoparathyroidism (Section 10)
Intracranial bleeding (Section 15)
Low blood sugar (Hypoglycemia, Section 10)
Tetany or Hypocalcemia (also Calcium, Section 10; Tetany, Section 15)

F. Vomiting, abdominal distension, intestinal obstruction

Anal atresia
Anal ring
Anal stenosis
Excess amniotic fluid in mother (Polyhydramnios)
First stool (Meconium)
Intestinal obstruction (Section 12)
Megacolon (Section 12)
Stool, absence of
Tracheo-esophageal fistula

G. Diarrhea

H. Navel and umbilical cord

Care of
Hernia (Section 12)
Omphalocele
Umbilical granuloma

I. Urinary and genital organs

Circumcision
Extrophy of bladder
Hermaphroditism
Inguinal hernia (Section 12)
Penis (also Section 13)
Swollen scrotum (Hydrocele)
Urethral opening misplaced (Hypospadias)
Vulva

J. Skin

Albinism
Bathing
Mongolian spots (Section 6)
Bruises (Ecchymoses)
Breasts
Cradle cap (also Seborrhea, Section 6)
Eczema (Section 6)
Flea bite dermatitis (Erythema toxicum)
Impetigo, pustules (Pemphigus)
Marble skin (cutis marmorata)
Pilonidal dimple
Red diaper area (Moniliasis)
Stork bites; strawberry mark (Hemangioma)
Whiteheads on face (Milia)

K. Eyes

Blood spot on eye (Subconjunctival hemorrhage, Section 14)
Care of (Eye care)
Coloboma (Iris defect)
Glaucoma
Plugged tear duct (Section 14)
Pus (Ophthalmia neonatorum)
Retrolental fibroplasia

L. Mouth

Cleft lip and palate
Drooling
Epstein's pearls
Natal teeth
Tongue-tie
Weak chin (Pierre Robin syndrome; Treacher-Collins syndrome)
White spots (Oral moniliasis)

M. Congenital abnormalities

Absent arms (Phocomelia)
Absent skull and brain (Anencephaly)
Back defect (Meningomyelocele)
Cleidocranial dyostosis (Section 7)
Clubfoot
Congenital heart defects
- *Associated with cyanosis*
  - *Eisenmenger syndrome*
  - *Pulmonary atresia*
  - *Tetralogy of Fallot*
  - *Transposition of the great vessels*
  - *Tricuspid atresia*
  - *Ventricular septal defects (if large)*
- *Producing no cyanosis*
  - *Aortic stenosis*
  - *Atrial septal defect*
  - *Coarctation of aorta*
  - *Ductus arteriosus*
  - *Foramen ovale*
  - *Mitral insufficiency* (Section 8)
  - *Pulmonic stenosis*

Dislocation of hips
Extra fingers or toes (Polydactyly)
Floppy infant syndrome (Section 15)
Fused fingers or toes (Syndactyly)
Hydranencephaly (Section 15)

Acidosis is an overly acid state of the blood due to asphyxia with insufficient oxygen reaching the infant's tissues. When present at birth, there is an increased chance of depression (low *Apgar score*), hyaline membrane disease *(respiratory distress syndrome),* and damage to the brain. Asphyxia is the impairment of the gas exchange to the fetus via the placenta (placental separation or disease, cord prolapse, toxemia, prolonged labor). Uncorrected asphyxia leads to acidosis.

Mothers over thirty-five years of age or with *diabetes* or uterine bleeding are more likely to have babies showing asphyxia/acidosis. *Postmature* and *low birth weight* babies may have asphyxia/acidosis if placental insufficiency is extreme.

Signs of developing acidosis before delivery are slow heart rate (*bradycardia*—less than 100 beats per minute) or a rapid heart rate (*tachycardia*—more than 180 beats per minute) and *meconium* staining of the amniotic fluid. Some obstetrical centers test the baby's blood during delivery by taking a sample of blood from the scalp (if the head is the presenting part). If acidosis is detected, remedial measures can be implemented more rapidly after delivery (resuscitation, oxygen, and intravenous alkali).

Albinism may be generalized (in which case the patient is termed an albino) or localized to the skin, hair, or eyes (see Waardenberg syndrome, Section 6). This genetic trait is due to an enzyme lack (tyrosinase), and no melanin or pigment is produced. Photophobia, *nystagmus, strabismus* are commonly associated symptoms. Because of their lack of protective pigment in the skin and eyes, albinos are exquisitely sensitive to sunlight.

Amniocentesis is the withdrawal of fluid by needle from the bag of waters which surrounds the fetus in the uterine cavity. Analyses of this fluid as early as the twelfth week of gestation can give much information regarding the health of the fetus; for example, severity of erythroblastosis, maturity of fetus, meconium passage. Examination of fetal cells after appropriate culture allows determination of certain hereditary (inborn errors of metabolism) or genetic defects (Down's syndrome). If pathology is present a decision can then be made as to the benefits of a therapeutic abortion.

Anal atresia, or imperforate anus, is the absence of any passageway from the rectum to the outside. Prior to surgery, a piece of metal is taped to the skin where the anus should be; an X ray is taken with the baby held upside down. The gas in the rectum rises so the X ray will show the distance between the air and the metal. The surgeon will then be able to see how extensive the operation must be to form the necessary passageway.

Anal ring is a membranous tissue found in one quarter of all babies at birth. Its location, about half an inch inside the anal opening, serves as a partial obstruction to the easy passage of the stool and is a cause of *colic.* The gentle insertion of a lubricated little finger will diagnose as well as treat this problem.

Anal stenosis is the severe narrowing of the anal opening requiring surgical intervention.

Anencephaly is a rare condition of incomplete brain and head formation. The top and back of the head are missing, giving the face a grotesque, froglike appearance. Babies with this condition are born dead or die soon after birth.

Anoxia is a term often used to describe the lack of oxygen some children suffer either before, during, or after delivery; during a high fever and convulsion, or during a severe attack of *pneumonia* or *bronchitis* (Section 9). The condition is usually manifested by *cyanosis* or blueness. Not all anoxia is permanently harmful, but it can lead to specific injuries to the nervous system. In general, the earlier in life and the longer the anoxia, the more likely is the danger of damage.

Apgar score is named after Virginia Apgar, who developed a point system to evaluate more accurately the condition of the newborn. A depressed score often indicates asphysia and has some predictive value relative to anoxia. The higher the score, the better the baby's condition. A score of 10 is perfect.

	0	1	2
Heart Rate	Absent	Under 100	100+
Respiratory Effort	Absent	Slow, irregular	Good, cries
Muscle Tone	Limp	Some flexion	Active
Reflex irritability (Slap to soles of feet)	No response	Grimace	Cry
Color	Blue, pale	Pink body, blue extremities	Pink

Asphyxia—see *Acidosis*

Bathing, as people have learned over the centuries, not only makes the individual socially acceptable, but prevents a number of skin infections. Bathing usually discourages the growth of various small chiggers, mites, and lice that some of our not-so-remote ancestors were prone to harbor on their persons. Most odors people have are due to the growth of bacteria and fungi, and putting on clean clothing after a bath seems to discourage them.

Most mothers are baffled when they are faced with bathing a new baby. They feel that this must be done only by an expert. Most hospitals have a nurse who demonstrates the procedure as if it were almost a religious rite. As a matter of fact, a baby's bath should be quick, simple, and pleasant for everyone.

For a new baby, it is usually not necessary to do more than go over his dirty, sweaty areas with a wet washcloth. When he starts to sleep through the night, a full bath is necessary, or a somewhat disagreeable odor will develop. Neither is it necessary to postpone the whole immersion bath until the *navel* is completely healed. Actually, it might be better to bathe this raw area so that it will be cleaner and less likely to support dangerous bacteria.

Most soaps are alkaline and tend to dry and crack the skin so acidic soaps (pH below 6 or 7) are best. Hexachlorophene, a bacteriostatic chemical, has been standard, but recent studies indicate it may be absorbed through the skin and cause irritation of the nervous system. If a doctor recommends it, use sparingly and rinse off thoroughly. Most newborn nurseries will continue to use hexachlorophene soaps but sparingly and with adequate rinsing. Bathing your baby in a plastic dishpan is probably preferable to the hard sink. Make sure the water is pleasantly warm, and use as little soap as possible. If your baby has a great deal of *cradle cap* or scaly scalp, it is worthwhile to rub in some mineral oil before the bath to soften the scales. Then soap and a soft brush may remove the scaliness effectively. Some oily material naturally found in the *genitalia* is protective, and vigorous effort to remove it is unwise. Dry thoroughly in the armpits and between the fingers and toes. Some doctors recommend using alcohol to clean the navel, but it is too drying; the navel often cracks and bleeds. It might be better to use petroleum jelly or antibiotic ointment in this area. Powders are not necessary, and, moreover, powder is a severe irritant. If a baby gets a sprinkling of this in his eyes or inhales some, he will be quite unhappy. Baby oils can produce a pleasant, perfumed odor on the baby—and often make him break out with a contact rash! If his skin is dry and oil is necessary, a very small amount of mineral oil is the safest thing to put on the scaly areas. Bathtime is a pleasant time to stimulate, cuddle, tickle, and sing to your baby—an opportunity to offer love and warmth.

Bilirubin is a chemical pigment derived chiefly from old red cells and is manifested as jaundice when the level in the infant becomes excessive. If the amount of bilirubin rises rapidly in the newborn, it usually reflects increased *hemolysis* (destruction of red cells) due to Rh or ABO incompatibility which is magnified by an immature enzyme system; the baby becomes yellow or orange-tinged. The exchange transfusion serves to remove the bilirubin-laden blood, which can be toxic to the immature brain. This *jaundice* appears in the first forty-eight hours. A rapidly rising bilirubin level on the first or second day of life usually requires the *exchange transfusion,* since the light treatment is a little slow.

Transient hyperbilirubinemia of the newborn usually appears after the third day, and the level is usually not high enough to be dangerous. A mother may note the yellow sclerae and skin when she unwraps the baby on her first day home from the hospital. It would be wise to monitor the serum bilirubin level for a day or so, although this late-appearing jaundice rarely affects the nervous system. Light treatment (exposing the jaundiced baby's skin to strong light) has been found to lower significantly the bilirubin in the blood more rapidly than time alone. Most babies with detectable jaundice should be provided with this therapy.

Excess bilirubin in the newborn can cause permanent damage to the nervous system. Nerve *deafness, mental retardation, athetosis,* and *learning disorders* have been reported as late results of hyperbilirubinemia.

Birth, the first crisis you and your child have to face, should be as nontraumatic as possible. We now know that women under eighteen and women over thirty-five have a much greater chance of both birth and pregnancy anomalies. An obstetrician can control many of the factors of abnormal birth, but a certain amount of chance is, of course, involved on that day. You should have complete reliance and trust in your obstetrician, because he can help you better than anyone else.

The biggest problem to avoid is *anoxia-hypoxia,* or a lack of oxygen to your baby's nervous system; when extreme or prolonged it may cause brain damage. Doctors usually do not administer too much anesthesia to the mother, so that her baby will be able to initiate respiration himself. If the doctor is delayed, the nurses will usually allow delivery to proceed. In some cases, it is better for the mother to deliver spontaneously in the taxicab than to go to a less-than-adequate hospital and have her baby held back by overwhelming sedatives or mechanical means.

If the obstetrician suspects *Rh problems,* maternal *diabetes,* need for a Caesarean section, or likelihood of a *premature* birth, a pediatrician should be in attendance in the delivery room.

The baby at birth is covered with a vernix which helps to prevent intrauterine maceration of the skin. Only the excess on face, armpits, and groin needs to be removed; the remainder disappears spontaneously. If this vernix and the nails are bile-stained, intrauterine oxygen lack is suggested, as the baby passes stool into the amniotic fluid if anoxia has occurred.

If the baby's heart and lungs are normal, vigorous crying will increase the oxygenation of the red cells, and the skin pinks up. If *cyanosis* is increased with crying and struggling, *heart anomalies* or *lung* pathology are surely present.

The skin of a normal, full-term baby has a soft velvety texture. Dry, cracked skin suggests *postmaturity.*

Every baby should have the benefit of a complete physical examination by someone trained and experienced in newborn care. Examination of the infant in front of the mother is a useful method for reassuring her that all is well. Deviations from the normal can be explained at that time, right in the hospital.

Home examination of the baby in the first week is a valuable way for a mother to find out if her baby is connected up properly. The doctor may not be able to perform some of these tests because of poor patient cooperation.

Satisfactory general tone of the baby may be difficult to determine for the mother with limited experience, but the nursery nurse should apprise her of this. (See *Apgar score.*) The baby should be alert and responsive when awake, suck well, blink his eyes when a bright light is flashed into them or a loud sound is made nearby. He cries and withdraws his foot when pinched. Yawning, sneezing, and coughing are observed. *Moro* and *tonic neck response* (see *Reflexes*) should be present. A baby should fight to rid his face of a cloth; movements of right and left side should be equally vigorous. When the baby is held prone (face down) in the examiner's hand and his spine is massaged, he should arch his back, lift his head, arms, and legs to form an arc. When he relaxes his head, arms and legs should all droop down with gravity. A normal newborn will make alternating stepping movements when held upright with his soles allowed to touch a smooth surface. If the top of his foot touches the edge of a table, he will lift it up and step onto the table top.

If the baby seems to perform these actions well, it can be assumed that his *nervous system* is adequate.

Birth injury is any physical damage the baby experiences due to the birth process. Fractured skull, excessive molding of skull bones, forceps marks, *Bell's palsy, broken arm, leg,* or *collarbone,* ruptured spleen and liver are all examples. Modern obstetrical techniques, including the cutting of the birth-canal opening (episiotomy), and Caesarian section, are all designed to deliver the baby with as little trauma as possible. Part of the miracle of birth is that so few babies are damaged during this giant squeeze. Obviously the skull with its enclosed vulnerable brain is the most precious part of the baby and must be eased along. The baby must not be delivered too fast or too slowly (too fast: cerebral blood vessels torn; too slowly: oxygen supply reduced). Attention must be paid to the oxygen supply from the still-attached placenta and cord until the new infant is breathing on his own. Birth injury from oxygen deprivation may be more detrimental to ultimate cerebral function than a skull injury. As little anesthetic and pain-relieving drugs as possible are to be given to the mother; these same drugs can slow lung and heart response in the baby. (See *Anoxia;* also *Brain damage, Intracranial bleeding,* Section 15.)

Birth injuries are less frequent now because of better obstetrical care, but the absolute irreducible minimum has not been reached. Broken bones from a tumultuous delivery or the passage of a big baby through a small pelvis can heal, but the damage to the nervous system from excessive head molding, *intracranial bleeding, anoxia,* or untreated *bilirubinemia* is permanent.

Cephalohematoma, caput succedaneum, and *subconjunctival hemorrhages* (Section 14) are fairly obvious indicators of some difficulty in the delivery process, but do not necessarily indicate any hurt to deeper, more vital structures. A skull fracture may not be suspected because the baby acts and sucks well; a knobbiness on the side of the head noted after a week might be the first clue that something has happened.

The clavicle (*collarbone*) is easily broken because of its position between the shoulder and midchest. A large baby passing through a small birth canal might snap his clavicle. He will be fussy when moved during the first week, but his hunger pains are more compelling than the shoulder pain. Some doctors prefer to strap the arm to the chest for a few days. In a week a large knob of calcium appears at the fracture site.

Body temperature of newborn is obviously the same as the mother's at birth, but may drop rapidly in the first few minutes if the infant is not covered. The *premature,* with little fat to insulate him, is especially susceptible to chilling, and increased oxygen is necessary if environmental temperature is low relative to body temperature. Overheating also requires extra oxygen, so the trick is to produce a crib temperature that neither overheats nor chills the newborn. Fever in a healthy baby on the third day is usually due to dehydration. (See *Fever,* Section 2.)

Bowel movement—see *Meconium*

Brachial palsy is the weakness or paralysis of some or all of the muscles of one arm due to nerve injury at birth. When the head of the baby has been delivered, but the shoulder is reluctant, the stretched nerves deep in the neck may be torn. In the more common type of injury the affected arm is held close to the body with the hand clenched. If recovery occurs in a few months, it was only a bruise; if function does not return, the original trauma must have severed the nerves. Neurosurgery may help; the alternative is a useless, shriveled arm.

Breasts of the newborn baby are usually enlarged as a result of the mother's hormones which passed through the placenta. Even some milk (witch's milk) may be expressed from them. (Don't do it, though; infection may follow.)

Caput succedaneum is the swollen scalp resulting from the pressures of the birth process on this presenting part. This waterlogged skin recedes to normal within two days after birth.

Cephalohematoma is a collection of blood between a skull bone and its outer periosteal lining. It commonly appears after childbirth because of the pressure of the mother's pelvic bones on the baby's head. A few of these will be associated with a linear fracture, but healing is routine without special care. The periosteum, because it has been irritated, will produce a thin layer of bone about the outer edge of this squishy lump, suggesting a depressed skull fracture to the unwary mother. It all calcifies in a few weeks, but some children are left with a knobby prominence for years.

Circumcision is the removal of some or all of the foreskin which covers the glans or head of the *penis.* This is usually done in the first few days of life when the infant cannot localize his pain sensations.

Most urologists are in favor of circumcision of the newborn for the following reasons: a) Cancer of the penis, though rare, develops almost exclusively in men that were not circumcised in infancy; b) the painful and serious complication of *paraphymosis* cannot develop if circumcision is done in infancy; c) balanitis (superficial inflammation of the glans of the penis and the inside of the foreskin) is common in adult males who have not been circumcised, due to the chronic irritating effects of urine and smegma caught in the warm moist folds between the foreskin and the glans (circumcision—a much more complicated procedure in the adult—often has to be done in such men); d) a circumcised penis is easier to keep clean; e) recent research reports indicate that cancer of the cervix in the female is more common in the wives of uncircumcised men.

Detractors feel it is barbaric and a needless, ritualistic, surgical habit. The foreskin provides some protection against diaper rash. Frequently an ulcer will develop just inside the meatal opening in the circumcised; when this heals, some stenosis of the urethra may develop, which could create bladder and kidney pressure. Also, the ring or bell devices used during the operation occasionally constrict the blood supply, causing loss of penile tissue.

A fantastic amount of emotional thinking is involved on both sides of the controversy. The exhausted mother, already confused by old wives' tales and what her mother-in-law did to her husband, usually leaves the decision up to the obstetrician, who may be influenced by his own mother's choice.

The mother has heard that uncircumcised males masturbate more, her uncircumcised son may be laughed at in the locker room, or there is "trouble" in general if the operation is not done.

Cleft lip, or harelip, may appear as a slight indentation of the upper lip or may occur inside the *nose* and be associated with cleft gum, missing teeth, and *cleft palate.* Bilateral cleft lip is a double fissure with the nares leaving a nub of upper lip in the center. Feeding is difficult because suction is impossible, so large nipple holes are used with the baby in a half upright position. The surgeon usually closes this defect before two months of age for cosmetic and feeding reasons.

The risk of afflicted siblings is higher if a parent had the same defect.

Cleft palate is often associated with a *cleft lip,* is more difficult to repair because of the absence of tissue available to close the defect, and is almost always coupled with some deafness. Repair is usually attempted before meaningful speech at age two, but the size of the opening will largely dictate the optimum surgical timing.

When the palate has been surgically constructed, it is often too short, resulting in hypernasal speech. Further surgical revision may be necessary. Chronic *ear* infections suggest that the *adenoids* should be removed. This may help the eardrum but may increase the airflow about the already short palate, thus aggravating the hypernasality of the speech. Because of the multifaceted problem, a team consisting of the plastic surgeon, otolaryngologist, pediatrician, dentist, and speech therapist would be ideal for such victims.

Clubfoot is any deviation of the foot (in, out, up, or down) that cannot be manipulated to the normal position without painful force. At birth most babies' feet are turned in, in what is called a "position of comfort"; this is due to the fetal position in the cramped uterus. These feet can be easily manipulated to the physiological position without pain to the baby. The clubfoot, however, is fixed by short tendons and bone position and can only be manipulated a few degrees toward the normal. The treatment is plaster casts, which are revised every two weeks or so to allow for growth; each revision of the cast applies more deliberate but gentle pressure to return the bent foot to the normal position. Usually overcorrection is attempted, because the elastic tendons will swing the foot back to the original malformation. Correction is begun in the nursery and usually continues with casts for three to six months; then stiff shoes are needed well beyond walking age. Tendon-lengthening surgery may be necessary.

A search for *Spina bifida* (see Section 15) should be made when clubfoot is present; dislocated hips are frequently associated with clubfeet.

Coloboma is a defect in the *eye* due to the failure of formation of tissue in the embryo. It is usually a cleft in the iris but may extend back to involve the optic nerve.

Congenital abnormalities include all the defects and deficiencies and anomalies a baby might have at birth. The cause of these problems may lie in defective egg or sperm, defective genes from either parent, *chromosomal abnormalities* (see Section 10), or intrauterine factors (mechanical, chemical, nutritional, infectious or X ray). Oxygen lack accounts for the largest group of problems found at birth; genetic or inherited anomalies are next, while other prebirth environmental influences are found less commonly.

Some malformations are incompatible with life *in utero* and account for about one fifth of fetal deaths. After birth, some defective babies die because of surgically uncorrectable deformities.

Many babies appear normal in structure and function but have a congenital problem that appears only at times of stress (*diabetes*), or the anomaly may make the host more susceptible to infection (inherited *allergy* tendencies and immune globulin deficiencies, see Section 8). Some *psychoses* are considered inherited, but would not become manifest unless the environment were faulty.

(See *Clubfoot, Congenital heart defects,* etc.—the part of the body where anomaly may be suspected; also Section 10.)

Congenital heart defects—see also Section 8

Aortic stenosis is a narrowing of the *aorta* at its attachment to the heart. This congenital lesion is usually mild and may cause no symptoms. A rather loud *murmur* heard to the right of the upper end of the sternum (aortic area) and transmitted to the neck vessels suggests this anomaly. If signs of left heart strain are found by X ray, *electrocardiogram* or *catheter* studies, surgery should be considered. Sudden exertion in sports may precipitate ventricular fibrillation if the stenosis is severe enough to compromise emptying of the left ventricle.

Aortic stenosis due to *rheumatic* valvular disease is rare, but if associated with regurgitation would produce a strain on the left ventricle and possibly left heart failure.

Stenosis of the aorta just above the valves has been seen in children whose mothers received large doses of vitamin D during pregnancy.

Wide-set eyes (*hypertelorism*), flattened, short nose, and mental retardation have been associated with the *hypercalcemia.*

Atrial septal defect is any opening between the atrial chambers of the heart. The right atrium receives blue, unoxygenated blood from the body; the left receives freshly oxygenated red blood from the *lungs.* Usually the pressure in the left atrium, which contains bright red, oxygen-rich blood, is higher than that in the right atrium, which receives the blue or unoxygenated blood from the body. Thus, blood from the left atrium returns through the abnormal opening into the right atrium and is returned to the lungs another time. This unnecessary recycling increases the work of the heart, which is, in essence, "spinning its wheels." Patients with sizeable atrial septal defects have a decreased ability to exercise, slowed growth and more respiratory infections than the average child. If the pressure in the right side is greater, some blue blood will be forced through the hiatus to the left side. The victim will be *cyanotic* to the extent of the percentage of blue-red mixture. If the opening is small, growth is adequate, heart size normal to X ray, cyanosis is absent, and activity is not compromised, a period of expectant observation should be allowed. Open-heart surgery should be considered for those children with shortness of breath or growth failure. Usually this is done in later childhood before the rapid growth of adolescence.

A very few atrial septal defects close spontaneously.

Coarctation of aorta is the narrowing of the large blood vessel just beyond the area that sends branches to the head and arms. The effect is elevated *blood pressure* in the arms and head and decreased blood pressure in the legs. The increased pressure puts a strain on the heart (which may go into failure), and creates increased pressure in the vessels in the brain (which may cause *nosebleeds, headaches,* and cerebral hemorrhages). The reduced blood flow to the legs may cause weakness, coldness, and cramps. The quality of the *pulse* in the groin should be felt in every newborn examination so that the condition can be diagnosed early.

Surgery is recommended in the first ten years or so, depending on the severity of symptoms. The narrowed segment is removed and the normal-sized ends are sutured together.

Ductus arteriosus is the vessel connecting the aorta and pulmonary artery before birth. It allows blood to bypass the lungs which are not expanded before birth. After birth, the lungs expand and accept the full flow of blood from the right side of the heart. The ductus should close within the first day of life and scar shut permanently in a few months. When the ductus fails to close, blood from the aorta flows into the lower-pressure pulmonary artery, congesting the lungs and forcing the heart to work harder. Patients with patent (open) ductus have bounding pulses and a continuous "machinery-like" murmur over the upper chest. If the ductus causes congestive failure it should be closed surgically at any age. If there are no symptoms, the ductus should be closed by surgery after the patient reaches his first birthday (a few children will have the ductus close spontaneously as late as one year).

Eisenmenger syndrome is a combination of congenital heart lesions consisting of pulmonary hypertension and a septal defect. The victim is usually short of breath, *cyanotic,* fatigued, and subject to *lung infection.* Surgery is not indicated.

Foramen ovale (the oval hole) is an opening between the heart atria before birth, which allows venous blood from the body to flow to the left side of the heart, bypassing the lungs. During intrauterine life, the fetus gets oxygen from the mother's bloodstream; the lungs are not inhaling any air, so there is little point for the blood to flow through them. At birth the lungs expand, and blood flows from right heart to the lungs for the new source of oxygen. The pressure of the blood on the left side of the heart forces a valve to close this foramen ovale. If pressure on the right side of the heart increases due to other anomalies, unoxygenated blood may force the valve open; this blue blood will cause *cyanosis.* If this foramen is patent as an isolated lesion, no corrective surgery is necessary. If it is patent and cyanosis is present, other lesions causing increased right atrial pressure must be corrected.

Pulmonary atresia is the absence of a functional pulmonary artery. The blood from the right ventricle passes through a defect in the septum or through a patent ductus to the aorta. As this blood is not oxygenated, the patient is severely cyanotic. Surgery is difficult, but partial correction is possible.

Pulmonic stenosis is a narrowing of the pulmonary outflow from the right ventricle. This may occur at the valve or in a thickening of muscle below the valve, interfering with passage of blood into the lungs and requiring the right ventricle to increase its pressure in order to force the blood through the narrow area. This obstruction to blood flow causes a loud murmur, but often surprisingly few symptoms. Children with pulmonic stenosis may, however, tire before the normal child.

Tetralogy of Fallot, the most common cause of cyanotic heart disease in infants, consists of pulmonary stenosis, ventricular septal defect, an aorta which receives blood from right and left ventricles, and enlargement of the right ventricle. Obviously, the blood does not get oxygenated properly and what does get oxygenated becomes mixed with blue, unoxygenated blood. The fingers become clubbed; shortness of breath and squatting are characteristic. Growth is slowed. Surgery has been perfected to the point that risks are small.

Transposition of the great vessels produces severe cyanosis early as the aorta arises from the right ventricle and the pulmonary artery from the left ventricle. Two independent circulations operate: blue, unoxygenated blood coming to the right side of the heart is pumped right back into the body without oxygen; red oxygenated blood is pumped back through the lungs again. If the ductus remains open or a septal defect is present, the blood will become mixed and life is possible. If a communication between the two sides of the heart is not present, the newborn rapidly deteriorates with cyanosis and heart failure. A surgical bypass would be lifesaving. Later, a more definitive operation would be attempted to divert the blue blood to the lungs and the oxygenated blood to the circulation.

Tricuspid atresia means that there is no opening between the right atrium and ventricle, thus no way for blood to get oxygenated in the lungs. The blood usually flows through a septal defect so this unoxygenated blood gets to the systemic side, causing severe cyanosis. Prognosis is poor, but surgery has improved the outlook.

Ventricular septal defects are openings in the common wall between the two ventricles. Large openings may allow mixing; they sometimes close spontaneously with time and growth of adjacent tissue. If the defect is large enough to allow significant mixing, the infant may feed poorly, have shortness of breath, rapid pulse, and slow growth. A respiratory infection may increase the pressure on the right ventricle, forcing blue blood to the left ventricle, thus causing cyanosis.

These fairly common defects account for most of the organic

murmurs heard in children. Open-heart surgery is best done for the patient after age two, when risks are less. Surgery is not recommended for patients with no symptoms, normal heart size, or normal ECG, and if pressures in the various chambers (determined by *cardiac catheterization*) are normal.

Cradle cap is the crusty, scaly patches of adherent, yellow skin found on some babies' scalps. The tendency is hereditary and is one of the manifestations of seborrheic *dematitis.* These people often have red scaly areas behind their ears, in their groins, and on eyelid edges. Their acne in adolescence is usually more severe than average because of their oily skin.

Mild cases can be cleared up by softening the scales with mineral oil, then shampooing with soap and a soft brush. Severe cases respond to a *cortisone* cream. These areas are susceptible to secondary bacterial and yeast infection. Preparations containing *sulfur, salicylic acid,* and/or *coal tar* may have to be used frequently for control. Most cases respond in a few days to oral pyridoxine.

Cutis marmorata is an alarming-looking but innocuous, transient dilation of skin capillaries in a large lace-work or reticular pattern. Normal one-inch areas of skin are bordered by blue streaks. This "marble skin" affects only the trunk and legs. The blue color is derived from the unoxygenated blood slowly moving through these dilated capillaries.

Death of a newborn child due to an infection is so uncommon now that it usually results from neglect or misdiagnosis. Proper vaccination precludes a number of diseases; proper sanitation and public-health measures have reduced the incidence of others. Antibiotics, if given in time, cure *pneumonia* and *meningitis,* both killers in the old days. If a child does die today, the parents feel guilt that they may have called the wrong doctor plus the basic shock of their loss.

Sudden unexpected death (SUD) or crib death, which strikes down two out of every one thousand babies at age two-to-six months, seems to mock the mother who thought she was doing a good job. When the baby is found dead in his crib in the morning, the distraught parents can only blame themselves. The doctors can find no reason for the death, which is frustrating to a man of science. Overwhelming milk *allergy,* sudden *pneumonia, septicemia* (Section 2), *intracranial bleeding* (Section 15), heart failure, low *gamma globulin* (Section 8), calcium metabolism derangement all have been proposed as causes, but repeated postmortem examinations show no consistent pattern.

Some faulty neuro-chemical-muscular reflex may explain some cases. The infant "forgets" to breathe in response to the high CO_2 and low O_2 levels in the blood. An apnea monitor has helped those with this tendency.

Research may someday uncover the reason and lead to control. In the meantime the parents must realize that there was nothing that they could have done; even if they had had a *suspicion* that trouble was coming and had seen a doctor the day before, no warning, symptom, or test would have predicted the tragedy.

Diaphragmatic hernia is the upward movement of abdominal organs into the chest cavity through an opening in the diaphragm. It may be congenital, and the chest can be almost completely filled with liver, stomach, and intestines. The lungs cannot expand to support life; emergency surgery may replace the abdominal contents, close the defect, and allow the lungs to expand.

Diarrhea in the newborn nursery in epidemic proportions is less common now because the babies are frequently sent home in three days. The cause is usually traced to a carrier state in a nurse, attendant, or service personnel. (See Section 12.)

Dislocation of the hips is usually congenital and is more accurately described as *subluxation.* The top end of the thigh bone (femur) is not well seated in the pelvis bone, as the space is not adequate or the joint ligaments are too relaxed. Early diagnosis is essential, for treatment by splints or casts in the first year is usually successful. If diagnosis is delayed until walking is established (duck-waddle *gait*), surgery may be necessary, and results may be poor.

Every infant, therefore, must have his hips tested in the first few weeks for this not uncommon condition. If resistance is met when thighs are abducted or if a clicking is noted on hip manipulation, X rays are advised, and orthopedic consultation is suggested. (See also *Gait,* Section 7.)

Drooling of saliva in the newborn raises the possibility of an esophageal obstruction. If a swallow of sugar water is returned immediately without stomach juices, the diagnosis would be almost assured.

Ecchymoses are bruises. These are common in the newborn because of the trauma of delivery and appear on the presenting part (back of head for normal delivery, buttocks for breech, and face if this area was at the opening of the womb at delivery time). These superficial collections of blood from broken blood vessels clear rapidly in a few days, but because of the inability of the liver to handle this extra amount of blood pigment, the skin may become jaundiced on about the third day. The immature infant is especially susceptible to ecchymoses.

Epstein's pearls are small, white, hard collections of cells frequently seen near the midline in the roof of the mouth of the newborn. They usually disappear in a few weeks and mean nothing.

Erythema toxicum is a skin condition common in newborns, now thought to be due to an *allergy* to some food the mother ingested just prior to delivery. There are red maculopapules resembling flea bites that are occasionally confused with early staphylococcal pustules. No treatment is indicated, as they disappear in a few days.

Erythroblastosis fetalis, or Rh disease, when translated means the newborn baby is manufacturing a large number of "blast" (early forms of red blood) cells. When red blood cells are destroyed, the bone marrow is stimulated to manufacture a large number of new ones. When the baby's blood type is different from his mother's, she becomes literally "inoculated" against it. A few of a baby's cells can leak into the mother's circulation (usually during the turbulence of uterine contractions at childbirth). Her defense mechanism manufactures antibodies against these invaders. That first baby will be born normally, of course, but if enough of her antibodies then get into a second or third baby's circulation, they may destroy sufficient of the infant's red cells (of the Rh+ variety) to cause death in utero, or if born alive, anemia and increasing jaundice with the threat of *brain damage.*

Usually the disease becomes manifest shortly after birth, so there is time to exchange the baby's blood after a normal, full-term delivery. The *exchange transfustion* (see Section 8) replaces about three quarters of the baby's blood with its accompanying maternal antibodies and much bilirubin. Some afflicted babies develop *anemia, jaundice,* and *edema in utero,* so it is necessary to deliver them prematurely in order that they may benefit from the transfusion. A hazardous intrauterine transfusion technique has been used to maintain life in some babies too small to live on their own. All mothers who might have erythroblastotic babies can now be identified and given anti Rh-D gamma globulin soon after their first pregnancy to neutralize the Rh *antigens.* These antigens are present in the baby's red cells. If they enter the mother's circulation, she will manufacture anti-Rh antibodies. The injection neutralizes these antigens before she manufactures the antibodies.

Rh is an antigen found in the red cells of about 85 percent of Caucasians. If an Rh negative (no Rh antigen in red cells) woman becomes pregnant with a baby who is Rh positive, she might have a baby with erythroblastosis. All pregnant women should be tested for the Rh factor and the presence of antibodies. Not all women develop the antibodies (if the baby's red cells did not enter her circulation), nor do all babies with erythroblastosis need the transfusion. If the baby is not too sick at birth, monitoring the bilirubin level in the blood will be sufficient to determine if the transfusion is necessary. If an excessive amount of bilirubin develops in the circulation, it may be deposited in the brain and cause brain damage. (See *Bilirubin, Kernicterus.*)

In the absence of Rh factors, a form of erythroblastosis may occur if the mother is blood group O and the baby is type A, B, or AB. This is usually not a severe condition.

Extra fingers or toes—see *Polydactyly*

Extrophy of the bladder is a rare congenital lesion in which all or part of the bladder wall is exposed on the outside of the lower abdomen. The *ureters* constantly drip urine onto the surface of this red, raw area. Infection may ascend into the *kidneys.* Plastic surgery to reconstruct a functioning hollow organ is the goal; occasionally loops of intestine are used. (See Section 13.)

Eye care. Routine care of infants' and children's *eyes* should be limited to a gentle wipe with a wet washcloth (no soap) over the closed lids. Tears do the rest. Constant red veins, crusting, matter, blinking, tearing are signs of trouble.

Photo-flash pictures do not injure the eyes.

Facial nerve palsy seen in the newborn is thought to be due to pressure from the baby's hand or foot or obstetrical forceps against the nerve which activates the muscles that depress the corner of the mouth. It only appears on crying, as the mouth is pulled down toward the unaffected side. It usually disappears after some months when innervation is restored by nerve regrowth. (See also Section 15.)

Fetal distress syndrome is usually the result of the baby's trying to breathe while still in the womb. Because his mother's placenta is providing him with a lowered oxygen supply, he reflexively tries to breathe, but only inhales the amniotic fluid plus cellular debris and meconium. This material may get far down in the bronchial tubes where it cannot be sucked out when he is delivered. Obstruction to breathing follows with cyanosis, sternal retraction, and superimposed pneumonia.

Fused fingers or toes—see *Syndactyly*

Glaucoma, or increased intraocular pressure, is common in people over forty, but rare in children. It is obvious by three months of age and is usually associated with other eye or congenital nervous-system diseases. The mother may first note constant tearing, extreme avoidance of lights, and a misty cornea. An enlarged, hard eyeball is a late sign. The doctor—and the mother—should routinely palpate the eyeball (with lids closed) in the first few weeks of life. Two fingers are placed on the lids and gently rotated as if massaging the eyeball. The tension felt should be equal to that of a normal adult eyeball. Babies with glaucoma have very hard eyeballs.

Immediate surgery may be curative. A new channel has to be made at the edge of the iris to allow eyeball fluid to drain properly. Surgical results may not be perfect, even with reoperation, but the alternative is blindness.

Hemangioma is a blood-vessel tumor. The flat, port-wine stain (*nevus flammeus*) remains like a red dye; if unsightly, it may be obliterated by tattooing, but most people apply a covering cosmetic and try to forget it. The strawberry mark is usually a pale spot on the neck, trunk, or arms at birth which by one or two months has become a slightly raised, very red area whose color is due to the blood in the dilated capillaries. These usually enlarge until about one year of age, at which time fibrosis of the capillaries occurs, and the color bleaches out. By age four they are barely detectable as flat, thin-skinned areas which do not tan well. (They are *not* caused by the mother eating strawberries during the pregnancy.) Masterful inattention seems to be the best treatment, since dry ice, radiation, and surgery leave more scarring than does natural involution. The cavernous hemangioma lies under slightly bluish skin. It may involute by itself, but if in eyelids, wing of nose, lips, or ears, destruction of tissue might be avoided by surgery or X ray.

Hemangiomata may appear in bones, kidney, larynx, salivary glands, etc., and give rise to symptoms relative to the involved tissue.

A large facial hemangioma may be associated with a vascular invasion of underlying skull and meninges. Victims may have *convulsions* and *mental retardation.* (See *Sturge-Weber syndrome,* Section 15.)

Stork bites are areas of dilated capillaries (pink skin) on eyelids, center of forehead, and back of neck. They fade by age one or two, but will recur with excitement or crying. (If your five-year-old denies lifting the quarter from your purse, look at the back of his neck; if the red splotch has returned, chances are good that he is lying to you.)

Hemolytic disease of the newborn is usually due to Rh incompatibility. The baby inherited Rh-positive blood from the father, and the mother is Rh-negative. Her system makes antibodies against Rh-positive blood causing the baby's blood to hemolyze. (See *Erythroblastosis fetalis.*)

Hemorrhagic disease of the newborn may appear on the second day of life due to a deficiency of *vitamin K.* To prevent this, babies are usually given an injection of this vitamin at birth to maintain an adequate level until the vitamin is synthesized by the bacteria in their intestines. Bleeding from the bowel (melena, or black, tarry stools) and the cord stump is rapidly controlled by such an injection. Severe *liver* disease may prevent the synthesis of these factors, although vitamin K is present. Occasionally, prolonged use of intestinal antibiotics may destroy the bacteria which manufacture the vitamins, and bleeding occurs.

Hermaphroditism is bisexuality. This rare form of sex-gland misadventure is diagnosed by finding (usually in a biopsy) both ovarian and testicular tissue. The external genitalia may be ambiguous (an organ bigger than a clitoris but smaller than a *penis, hypospadias,* rudimentary *vagina*). In the condition called intersex, the gonads are *ovaries* or *testes,* but the external genitalia are of the opposite sex.

A female pseudohermaphroditism patient will have ovaries but masculine external genitalia (or sometimes indeterminate). This may occur if the mother received steroids during the first few months of her pregnancy; these have masculinizing effects on the growing embryo. X rays after injected dye would reveal a uterus. Children with this condition are to be reared as females. Corrective surgery should be done by age four or five.

A male pseudohermaphrodite would have testes, usually undescended or rudimentary, and a variety of female or ambiguous sexual organs.

X rays using dye to outline the vagina and/or uterus, study of cells to ascertain chromosomal sex, and biopsy to differentiate testes from ovaries may have to be done before a decision can be made as to which sex the patient should be assigned. Plastic surgery can be remarkably helpful in allowing these mixtures to develop a reasonably healthy psychosexual attitude.

Hydranencephaly—see Section 15

Hydrocele is a watery (serum-like) fluid jacket surrounding a *testicle.* It is common in the newborn, for the lining of the testis is formed by a membrane contiguous with the peritoneum. This congenital condition usually is self-correcting by one year of age. *Inguinal hernias* are often associated with hydroceles, and may appear simultaneously or appear months or years after the hydrocele disappears.

It is observed as an oval, tense sac with the testis on the inner wall. It is translucent and is not tender. No treatment is worthwhile. If the mother notes the sac enlarging after activity and diminishing after quiet sleep, a hernia is surely associated, and surgery should be considered.

Hypospadias is the appearance of the urethral opening on the underside of the *penis* instead of at the end. The penis is usually bowed down also. If the penis is small, the opening is near the scrotum, and the *testes* have not descended, some form of *hermaphroditism* might be suspected and searched for. Other urinary anomalies may be associated with this condition. A urologist usually can reconstruct a well-functioning penis, beginning surgery at about age two or three. A number of operations are often required, but the goal of standing to urinate by school age can usually be achieved.

Jaundice is most commonly "physiologic" but exaggerated in the premature because the excreting mechanism of the liver is temporarily overwhelmed by the normally produced bilirubin from expected red cell destruction (one percent a day). Bilirubin excretion is handled by the placenta through the mother during fetal life—thus the infant's enzyme system is delayed in performing this function. It may also be due to hemolytic disease (as in *erythroblastosis,* ABO incompatibility, or excess synthetic vitamin K). If the liver enzymes are not active, jaundice may result (as in *anoxia, dehydration, septicemia, cytomegalic-inclusion disease, syphilis, toxoplasmosis, herpes,* infant of diabetic mother, *cretinism,* drug inhibition, or Crigler-Najjar syndrome, a rare genetic enzyme defect). If a *biliary obstruction* is present, bile cannot flow into the intestine, and jaundice occurs (due to *hepatitis, biliary atresia* [Section 12], *lipidoses, galactosemia, neoplasm*).

Various blood and liver tests usually indicate the first two groups. Biliary atresia may be diagnosed by liver biopsy and/or a radioactive dye uptake test.

A breast-fed baby may remain jaundiced because of the presence of a hormone in the milk which depresses the activity of an enzyme.

Kernicterus is the yellow staining seen in areas of the brain after a baby has had excessive *hyperbilirubinemia.* The baby with *erythroblastosis* may develop this condition if treatment with *exchange transfusions* and artificial light have not kept his bilirubin level down to safe levels. These bile stains in the brain may be permanent and cause *athetosis, spasticity,* and/or *brain damage.*

Prematurity increases susceptibility to the neurological damage of bilirubinemia. Albumin in the blood will bind bilirubin to it, and thus less bilirubin is available to pass into the brain to cause damage. The premature infant may have albumin with poor binding capacities. Excess vitamin K has been known to bind albumin, thus permitting more free bilirubin to attack the brain. Sulfa drugs and some antibiotics as well as oxygen lack (*hypoxia*) may permit bilirubin passage into the brain.

Low birth weight in a baby is defined as less than five and one half pounds (2,500 grams) at birth. For predictive purposes it is now best to divide small babies into two groups: (a) the *premature* whose date of conception is accurately known and whose weight is commensurate with his stage of development; and (b) the small-for-his-age baby whose small size suggests some noxious intrauterine influence. Actually, prematurity suggests a time factor, and those babies born less than thirty-seven weeks after the first day of the mother's last menstrual period should be considered premature. However, some women have poor memories and/or irregular periods so the 2,500 gram weight is an easier standard for statistical purposes. However, up to 40 percent of infants of low birth-weight are mature and many premature infants may be over 2,500 grams.

Meconium is the first stool the newborn baby passes. The first part is usually dry, sticky, spinach-green (from bile), and contains swallowed cells but, of course, no bacteria. An infant suffering intrauterine anoxia may pass meconium in utero. A dysmature infant (sometimes post-mature) who suffers fetal malnutrition and often anoxia frequently has stained nails and skin at birth from this event. (A post-mature infant is not necessarily dysmature nor is a dysmature necessarily over-mature.) A breech baby (born buttocks first) may pass this stool during labor.

If the meconium is especially dry and forms such a hard plug that chemical and mechanical means are necessary to remove it, the baby may have *megacolon* or *cystic fibrosis* (lack of pancreatic enzyme). If the meconium is dry and generalized throughout the small bowel causing symptoms of obstruction, cystic fibrosis is surely present, and surgical removal of the plugs is usually necessary. It is called meconium ileus.

Meningomyelocele is a severe form of *spina bifida* (Section 15) in which the lower spinal cord nerves protrude out through the vertebral defect in a sac of spinal fluid or a raw open defect. This obvious congenital condition is frequently associated with absence of motor and sensory function to the legs. The neurosurgeon tries to close this in the first day of life so an ascending infection will not cause a fatal meningitis. *Hydrocephalus* (see Section 15), frequently complicates the crippling paralysis of legs and sphincter muscles (bladder and rectum).

Milia are the white or yellow, one-millimeter-sized pimples frequently seen over the nose, forehead, and chin of the newborn. They are plugs of skin debris and disappear in a few weeks.

Moniliasis of the genital area, or candidiasis, is a common diaper area rash. If a mother says there is no ammonia smell and she has "tried everything," it usually means this yeast infection is present. The mother may have the same yeast present as a vaginal infection, which must be cleared up simultaneously with the infant's treatment.

The rash covers the pubic area and genitalia and is solidly red. At the junction of the rash with normal skin small vesicles may be noted.

Treatment is slow but worthwhile. Recurrences are common. *Nystatin* or Amphotericin B are the best remedies.

Mortality rates for children have been reduced over the past several years in all categories except accidents.

Rates for the first few days are higher than those for any other time. Immature and/or *low birth weight* babies are more prone to *respiratory-distress syndrome, intracranial bleeding,* and infection. *Congenital abnormalities* and birth injuries are the next most common killers of the newborn. Seventy percent of the babies who die are in the low-birth-weight group (two to three out of one hundred live births, 80,000 deaths out of 4 million annual births). The remainder are due to infection, accidents, and malignancies.

From age one year on through *adolescence,* accidents account for about one third of the deaths. Congenital anomalies, *pneumonia,* and malignancies follow in close order. (See *Death.*)

Multiple births. Twins occur naturally about once in every eighty-eight births, but multiple births are more common following the use of fertility drugs. Obviously twins of different sexes must be the result of the fertilization of two separate ova (polyovular pregnancy). About one third of all twins born are monovular—that is, only one ovum was fertilized. These twins are identical: same sex, same color eyes and hair, same configuration of nose, face, ears, hands, and feet. Skin and organ transplants are compatible and blood types indentical. Examination of the placenta at birth helps to determine whether twins are identical or fraternal.

Most twins are born prematurely, since the large size of the uterus stimulates labor pains two to four weeks before the nine months are up. The second born of the pair is more likely to suffer some *anoxia* because its circulation may be impaired during the birth of the first. It is not unusual for a mother to note that, although her twins may *look* exactly alike, one is more restless or hyperactive or talkative than the other.

Twins are cute when dressed alike, but it must be remembered that they are separate individuals, and every attempt should be made to help them emphasize their difference. They should be dressed differently and, if possible, sent to separate schools, and engage in different sports and hobbies as one is usually a little smarter, more agile or clever than the other. Mothers of twins find the book *Twins and Supertwins* by Amram Scheinfeld (Lippincott, 1967) very helpful.

Myasthenia neonatorum is the temporary weakness of muscles of babies born to mothers with *myasthenia gravis.* Eyelids droop, the mouth hangs open, sucking is weak, swallowing and respiration are labored, and the general tone of the body is diminished (the infant is "floppy"). Neostigmine given intramuscularly controls this in a few minutes. This medicine is given every few hours for several days until the baby can function without it. (See Section 15.)

Natal teeth are those teeth that have erupted at birth. They may be enclosed in an eruption cyst. Neonatal teeth are those that erupt in the first month of life. As these teeth may be the primary ones, they should not be extracted because the jaw arch length may become foreshortened.

Navel, or umbilicus, is the small pit in the center of the abdomen through which the baby received nourishment and oxygen during uterine life. The umbilical cord from the placenta (the afterbirth—a large vascular organ attached to the inside of the uterus) contains a vein bringing blood and oxygen to the baby, and two arteries through which waste products and carbon dioxide are returned to the placenta and hence to the mother for removal. Directly after birth, the arteries constrict, and blood rarely leaks from them, although a clamp or umbilical tie is usually applied as a precaution. The cord dries up and sloughs off in seven to ten days, leaving a bit of raw stump like a third-degree burn. If alcohol is used on this area for cleansing, it frequently dries, cracks, and bleeds or becomes infected. A bit of antibiotic ointment is best rubbed into this area, to kill any bacterial growth and keep it soft and pliable. Soaps containing hexachlorophene are worthwhile to cut down the chance of bacterial infection if used sparingly and rinsed adequately.

Some babies have extra skin extending up the cord for one half to one inch. It takes several months or a year for this fingerlike protrusion to shrink and flatten down evenly with the surrounding skin. It has nothing to do with the way the obstetrician clamped the cord.

(For hernia see *Hernia, umbilical,* Section 12.)

Nose injuries. One authority states that 5 percent of infants have significant injury to the nose from the birth process. Obstetricians, pediatricians, and mothers should be aware of this, as many dislodged noses can be lifted back to the normal midline position.

Omphalocele is the protrusion of intestinal contents through the umbilical hiatus with no overlying skin (a hernia is a protrusion but is covered with skin). It is considered a surgical emergency to replace the contents back in the abdominal cavity before infection and adhesions foul it. The difficulty lies mainly in the fact that the abdominal cavity is too small to hold all the intestines, for the growth of the cavity depends to a large extent on the presence of the bowel all during uterine growth. Surgery may be performed in stages, the intestines being inserted over the weeks as the cavity expands.

Ophthalmia neonatorum is newborn *conjunctivitis* and is acquired during passage through the birth canal. Swollen eyelids and yellow matter are diagnostic. If *gonorrhea* is suspected, systemic *penicillin* usually clears it up. The mother should be treated also. After the newborn period this green or yellow conjunctivitis is usually due to an obstruction to the *tear duct.* (See Section 14.) As the tears cannot flow freely into the nose because of an obstruction of this passageway from the inner corner of the lids into the nasal passage, bacteria grow (as in stagnant water). Almost any *sulfa* or antibiotic ointment placed in the eyes three times a day for three days will clear this up temporarily. The purulent matter will return until the obstruction is relieved.

Oral moniliasis, or thrush, is easily diagnosed by noting the small milk-curd-like spots on the gums, tongue, and cheek areas of the infant. This yeast infection may be associated with genital *candidiasis.* The mother may have suffered from an itchy vaginal discharge during pregnancy. (See *Moniliasis,* Section 14.)

It frequently disappears spontaneously and causes little discomfort. It may be treated with *nystatin*.

Pemphigus of newborn is another name for *impetigo.* It begins at about one week of age as rapidly developing blisters near the navel or in the diaper area. Blisters break open, the raw surface beneath forms a crust, and new lesions develop nearby.

Because the newborn has little resistance to infection, it spreads and may lead to *septicemia.* The *staphylococcus* is the usual offender, and the source may be nursery personnel or the mother, who may carry the bacteria in their noses or on their hands. The raw navel stump is a good place for germs to grow, and nurses must wash their hands properly when moving from one infant to another.

Antibiotic ointment plus hexachlorophene soap (used very sparingly) is prophylactic as well as curative. A sick baby must be treated with internal antibiotics.

If antibacterial soaps are not used in the first few weeks of life, newborn babies easily develop impetigo near the navel. The open umbilical stump is a good culture medium for the growth and dissemination of bacteria, often the resistant staphylococcus. The sores about the navel start as two-millimeter water blisters, which enlarge to one-centimeter pustules and break open, leaving a raw wound and spewing infectious material to begin more sores nearby. Doctors occasionally see a breast *abscess* in a baby that has developed from an infected navel. The condition may spread rapidly and involve a major amount of the skin; *septicemia* and death may follow. Systemic antibiotics are usually indicated if the disease is advancing rapidly, as the baby has little immunity to this nasty bacterial infection.

If impetigo attacks are repetitious, use of the antibiotic ointment in the nose of *all* family members twice a day for a week or two might cut down the spread, as these germs are usually carried there. If sores begin at the corners of the mouth, a food allergy must be suspected as the inciting event (citrus, tomato, and chocolate); the infection is the secondary invader.

Children with eczema are especially prone to impetigo because their skin is usually excoriated.

Penis is the male sex organ. If the meatus (urinary orifice) is not obvious at the end, *hypospadias* is present, but the rare possibility of the infant being a female with a large clitoris must be considered. If the infant cannot be assigned definitely to one sex or the other by examination of the genitalia, then urine, blood, and chromosome studies may be helpful.

The foreskin at birth usually covers the entire glans (head), but retraction is to be avoided. (See *Circumcision.*) Between the foreskin and the glans is a cheesy material (smegma) that acts as a protective coating and should not be removed. The foreskin usually becomes retractable by age three when the lining of this area is complete.

The male foreskin may stick to the head of the penis, but time will disengage it. The more forceful the efforts to separate the tissues, the more likely new, tougher adhesions will appear. If urine flows freely and the foreskin can be retracted at least halfway back, leave it alone. An anxious parent may encourage the doctor to take action, and because he *does* do something, the parents then assume there was something wrong in the first place. A chain of events can be initiated which makes the child abnormally conscious of a basically insignificant problem.

A normal urinary stream from a baby boy should arch in the air at least a foot high and splash down at least as far away as his feet. Report to your physician a dribbling stream or a fine stream associated with abdominal straining. Both testicles should be in the scrotum at birth; cold, wet diapers may encourage the scrotal muscles to contract, pushing the testicles up into the fat over the pubic bone where casual observation may miss them. A warm bath should allow them to drop back into position in the scrotum.

Phocomelia has come to our attention recently because of the *thalidomide* tragedy in Germany. Some mothers who took this effective, "safe" drug for sleep in their early pregnancy delivered children with hands or fingers that seemed to be attached directly to the shoulders, with little or no intervening arm. The condition may appear sporadically with no history of drug ingestion, trauma, X ray, or infectious insult to blame. Orthopedic appliances are helpful in allowing more normal function. It is amazing how cheerful these children can be despite their severe handicap.

Pierre Robin syndrome, or hypoplasia of the mandible, is essentially an underdeveloped lower jaw. The normal-sized tongue falls back into the pharynx, causing airway obstruction and difficult feeding. If the baby is kept prone, the tongue falls forward, and breathing, though noisy, is possible. Occasionally the tongue must be temporarily sutured to the lower lip to hold it forward. A few months of growth usually allow enough oral room to accommodate the tongue. Orthodontic work is usually necessary in childhood, although the child's profile at age six may reveal only a weak chin. Eye anomalies may be associated. (See *Treacher-Collins syndrome.*)

Pilonidal dimple is a common depression at the lower end of the sacrum. It represents the lower end of the neural tube of the embryo. A sinus tract may extend to or into the underlying bone. As the child grows, it may become shallow or disappear. A cyst or sinus in this area may become infected, usually after adolescence. (See *Pilonidal cyst,* Section 6.)

Polydactyly is an excess of fingers or toes, which may be of no importance except as a conversation piece. Surgery may be worthwhile if foot pain is prominent. Extra fingers loosely attached may be ligated in the newborn nursery. Other anomalies may be associated (*congenital heart lesions* and *chondrodysplasia*).

Polyhydramnios is the excess accumulation of amniotic fluid in the pregnant woman. It suggests that the baby has a high intestinal obstruction (esophageal, duodenal, or jejunal stenosis). The amniotic fluid and urine of the baby cannot be swallowed, absorbed, and transferred to the placenta and mother.

The mother's abdomen is huge; the baby vomits because of the obstruction.

Posterior choanal obstruction is a not uncommon congenital defect. A membrane or thin plate of bone lies over the nasal passage at its junction with the throat. The newborn has difficulty breathing while feeding, but he seems pink and fit when he cries, as he is breathing through his open mouth. A catheter will not pass easily if the obstruction is due to a membrane, and won't pass at all if the wall is bony.

Surgery is indicated for the latter type of problem. The membranous type is usually cured by passing the tube that makes the diagnosis.

Postmaturity is the condition of longer than the usual intrauterine life—forty-two weeks of completed gestation as measured from the first day of the LMP.* It is most often found in the first pregnancy of a woman over thirty. The baby is not necessarily larger, but is lacking in vernix, so his skin is dry and cracked and may have loose folds as if he had *lost* weight. He seems alert, has long nails, and has lost the fine hair seen on the usual term baby. His skin is usually white in contrast to the pink, velvety skin of the forty-week newborn.

Any advantages of a long intrauterine life are negated by the risks of *anoxia* due to placental aging. A week or so past the due date is compatible with health, but beyond forty-two or forty-three weeks, the baby becomes anoxic, and skin and nails are meconium stained—a sure sign of *fetal distress.*

The obstetrician has a real dilemma when confronted with a woman who cannot remember the date of her last menstrual period. The baby seems large enough, but he would hate to perform a Caesarian section to preclude the delivery of a postmature baby and find that he has interrupted the gestation of a thirty-five-week-old, 4½-pound premature. An X ray of the intrauterine bones may provide guidelines. (If the distal femoral *epiphysis* [Section 7] is present, the baby is near term. Distal tibial epiphysis is a more certain indication of term

*Last menstrual period.

when dealing with post-maturity. Unfortunately intrauterine growth retardation delays ossification. The new techniques for determining maturity and size are: amniocentesis and sonar for establishing body-size from the diameter of the head.)

Premature infant is a baby born before thirty-seven weeks have elapsed from the first day of its mother's last menstrual period. His skin is thin and shiny, his hair short, his nails have not extended beyond the nail bed, the absence of ear cartilage allows his ears to fold easily, he has but two creases on his soles, and his nipple nodule is less than one-fourth inch in diameter.

He is subject to *bruises* into his skin and *intracranial bleeding* because of capillary fragility. Amounts of *bilirubin* which would be innocuous to the full-term baby will be harmful to his nervous system. He is very susceptible to infection and *septicemia.* Low blood sugar (*hypoglycemia,* Section 10) may cause convulsions and brain damage. Due to immaturity and metabolic defects, he frequently suffers from *respiratory-distress syndrome.*

Prematurity (less than thirty-seven weeks gestation) is more likely to be seen when the uterus is mechanically unable to carry the baby to term, or if the placenta separates early. Small-for-age babies are usually the result of maternal malnutrition, infection, maternal age (greater than thirty-five years), or uterine exhaustion (a womb that has borne more than four children). These conditions frequently operate together; they are not mutually exclusive.

The United States has a high rate of neonatal deaths (babies who die in the first month). Since infections have been put under control with antibiotics, small babies comprise the bulk of these fatalities.

Statistical analysis of the mothers who produce the largest number of these risky babies reveals (a) the mothers' ages at conception are seventeen years or less, (b) their diets are generally lacking in protein, iron, calcium, vitamin C, and calories, (c) they receive little prenatal care, (d) they smoke, (e) they are short, and (f) they have some chronic disease. Also, if the mother is unwed, the rate is 50 percent higher than the rate in general.

Low-birth-weight babies not only have a lower survival rate but a much greater chance of having a variety of neurological disorders (*hyperactivity, impulsivity,* short attention span, *mental retardation*).

The premature needs oxygen, warmth, and food. Techniques in

large centers are quite sophisticated and have monitoring devices (with buzzers) to signal breathing and heart-rate change. Feeding is accomplished by gavage by small catheters (tube feeding) with amounts of a teaspoon only at first, gradually increased. When the baby is mature enough to suck on the tube, he may be tried on the bottle. The most important factor in his care is a nurse, who must be intelligent, quick, alert, and well-trained. Her attention will determine the survival statistics of the nursery.

If the baby survives all the above onslaughts, he is faced with a lifetime struggle with a variety of subtle neurological defects. Prematures are more likely to be afflicted with the *hyperactive* syndrome. The long-lasting effects of lying for weeks in a quiet environment (the incubator) are just being assessed. The uterus is a noisy, active place, and the sensory deprivation the baby suffers without human stimulation may permanently impair sensory perception. New techniques of incubator care include more touch and movement and involvement of the mother in the early care.

Much could be done to solve the basic problems which seem to combine to produce a vicious cycle. A girl born in poverty, ignorance, or under the influence of old wives' tales may not have eaten properly and may have suffered an absolute reduction in number of brain cells. This girl's retardation would prevent her from competing adequately in school; she drops out and engages in something that, for her, represents some success—sex. The last thing in her mind during her pregnancy is adequate nutrition for her baby. Her doomed, small baby repeats the same pattern.

The double frustration of this circumstance lies in the fact that, even if the expectant mother *did* become motivated to do something about her baby, it is already too late to undeprive the child. The mother's body will not arrive at full womanhood until she is seventeen or eighteen years old; her nutritional deficiencies preclude a healthy beginning for the baby; her poverty or ignorance of minimum food requirements would not provide sufficient nourishment for the baby, and her short stature adds another risk at delivery time. It appears that two or three generations of proper diet and education will be necessary to break this self-perpetuating, socio-psycho-neuro-maladaptation.

Good evidence indicates that protein deprivation *in utero* cuts down the *number* of cells; no new cells will appear even if the diet is corrected. The body and its organs (especially the brain) will never achieve their full potential. Malnutrition after the baby is six months or a year old is reversible because then only the cell *size* is involved.

But in some centers retardation of the girl or poverty are minor factors in the mothers of "premies." The major factor, regardless of age and health, is an unwelcome and often rejected pregnancy. Diet may be a factor, but stress is much more important. Therefore, education in pregnancy control is far more applicable in prevention of prematurity.

New rules for pregnant women: gain an average of twenty-four pounds during the nine-month period, eat good animal protein daily, don't curb calories (if calories are deficient, protein is burned for fuel and is not available for cell growth), iron and other vitamins and minerals are worthwhile, some salt is safe—as is eating what you like as long as your diet is balanced.

Primordial dwarfs are small at birth and remain so. *Anomalies,* single or multiple, are usually associated. (See Section 10.)

Reflexes

Moro response is a normal reflex the newborn baby shows when lying on his back. If his support is moved or his head allowed to drop back, he should throw his arms out (extend) and then curve and pull them in (flex) as if he were reaching for his mother because of fear of falling (as if his mother were swinging from branch to branch). If the reflex cannot be elicited in the first two or three weeks, some defect in the nervous system is suggested (*anoxia, septicemia, hypoglycemia, bleeding*). Normal babies will lose this response after the first month or so.

Sucking reflex is well developed before birth in the normal baby. Touching the lips will initiate sucking movements. A related reflex (rooting) is the turning of the baby's head to a touch stimulus on the cheek.

Tonic neck reflex is the response the baby makes when lying on his back with his head turned to one side; if his head is turned to the right, his right arm and leg straighten and his left elbow and knee flex (also called fencing position reflex). This reflex suggests that the baby is hooked up properly, but it is not always elicited in a normal baby. Its persistent absence may be associated with *intracerebral bleeding, kernicterus,* or other nervous-system pathology.

Respiratory distress syndrome, or hyaline membrane disease, is the end result of a number of factors operating on the circulation in the lungs at birth. It is the most common cause of death in the premature; the survivors frequently suffer from the *hyperactive* syndrome later in life.

At birth the premature frequently does not cry and breathe immediately or spontaneously. Carbon dioxide builds up in the blood, causing acidosis and increasing the resistance to blood flow through the pulmonary arterioles. The blood is not oxygenated, and cyanosis develops. Chilling of the baby while resuscitating him increases his oxygen needs and intensifies the cyanosis. Fluid leaking from capillaries into the alveolar air sacs further interferes with oxygen-carbon dioxide exchange. Carbon dioxide increases, resulting in more acidosis and further increased pulmonary-vessel blood-flow resistance. The vicious cycle continues until the lungs fill up with a gelatinous fluid—the hyaline membrane seen at autopsy.

Prematures, babies of diabetic mothers, or those born by Caesarian section are vulnerable to this. Once the grunting respiration and retraction of the chest wall occur with cyanosis, the process is well established; treatment, when tardy, is less successful than if prophylactic measures are taken at the moment of birth.

The routine is to incubate the baby, pass a fine catheter into an umbilical vessel and begin an infusion of water, sugar, and bicarbonate which serves to give energy and an alkali to counteract the acidosis. The blood is monitored for carbon dioxide, acidity, and bicarbonate; adjustments are made in the minerals in the intravenous infusion. Oxygen and warmth are provided in the incubator, which is also provided with electronic devices to signal the nurse if heartbeat or respiration fall below a critical level.

If the baby survives the first forty-eight hours and is improving, he will probably continue to improve unless a superimposed infection takes him. An infection might be introduced via the umbilical catheter, but he is more likely to develop a *pneumonia.* Some intensive-care centers use antibiotics routinely for babies with *respiratory distress.*

Retrolental fibroplasia is scar tissue formation behind the lens in the eye. The condition appears to be due to the toxic effects of excessive oxygen administration to the premature in the incubator. Oxygen now is rarely given above a concentration of 30 to 40 percent (air is 20 percent), and only for short periods in amounts just sufficient to prevent cyanosis. Sufficient oxygen to barely relieve cyanosis depends on expert clinical observation and longitudinal laboratory measurements in gauging oxygen requirements. Thirty units of vitamin E daily, given for a few days, seem to prevent this problem.

Seizures in the neonate are serious, since the involved infants have a high mortality rate (20 percent), and many of the survivors are permanently crippled (*mental retardation, brain damage, cerebral palsy, convulsions*).

Hypocalcemia is the most common cause of seizures, and such cases have the best outlook. Intracranial birth injuries, *anoxia, hypoglycemia,* infection (*rubella, cytomegalic-inclusion disease, toxoplasmosis, syphilis*), and congenital anomalies account for the others. The outlook is grim for many of these patients. *Hypoglycemia* in newborns is associated with maternal toxemia, maternal diabetes, and severe fetal undergrowth commonly enough to suggest giving prophylactic intravenous glucose to these babies.

The convulsing newborn should have blood studies for calcium, sugar, a urinalysis, and a spinal-fluid examination for blood and bacteria. A brain-wave test (EEG) has been helpful for diagnosis as well as for prognosis.

Causes: infection (*septicemia, meningitis, rubella, toxoplasmosis, syphilis*), metabolic (low sugar, calcium, magnesium, or pyridoxine, *bilirubin* excess), defective development (*hydrocephalus, tuberous sclerosis, heart anomalies* with *cyanosis*).

Stool, absence of—nonpassage of stool from birth (for more than 24 hours) suggests a congenital obstruction of the intestines (atresia, stenosis, volvulus) or a meconium ileus. (See *Cystic fibrosis,* Section 9.)

Difficult passage from birth on suggests an *anal ring* (easily diagnosed and treated at birth by insertion of finger), or congenital *megacolon* (defect of innervation of rectal segment of bowel—see Section 12). The latter victims have a growth failure associated with distended abdomen and usually require enemata to have a partial movement. Surgery is required.

Stridor, or noisy inbreathing, is common in the small infant, and is felt to be due to "floppy" vocal cords which vibrate excessively, especially on inspiration. With age the cords stiffen, and the noise disappears. The baby is usually comfortable, sucks and gains well, but tends to keep the worried parents up because each breath sounds to them as if it may be his last. *Colds* and allergic phlegm aggravate the noise. If chest muscles must be used to suck in the air, or *cyanosis* is present, a view of the area with a laryngoscope is warranted. Occasionally a web or cyst which increases wind resistance is found.

Syndactyly is fusion of fingers or toes. It may be just a skin fusion, but occasionally the bones are involved. Other anomalies are often associated. The second and third toes are commonly fused as a hereditary trait. Function is not affected, but surgery is appropriate for the child with fused fingers.

Tetany of the newborn may occur from *parathyroid-gland* imbalance and/or excess phosphate in the formula. (See Section 15.) The low birth weight baby is more likely to develop this in the first few days of life. If the mother has *hyperparathyroidism,* her baby is very susceptible to tetany. Of course, if the baby is born without parathyroid glands—rare, he will soon show tetany.

Thalidomide—see *Phocomelia*

Tongue-tie in the old days (before 1965) was thought to be responsible for lisping or stuttering—or even not talking at all. Nobody in the medical profession believes this now, but just in case there might be some truth to this old wives' tale, doctors still clip the frenum, if it is short. The frenum is a web of tough tissue that is attached to the underside of the tip of the tongue and to the floor of the mouth just behind the lower gum. If it is short, the tongue will form a *V* with the apex of the angle of the tongue held down to the gum level. It seems sensible to nip the membrane to allow the tongue greater mobility, but there are just enough horror stories about babies developing uncontrollable hemorrhages into the tongue muscle to warrant caution. The frenum is stretchable; time and use permit more freedom of motion. After all, none of the sounds used in speech require the tongue to reach farther forward than the teeth.

(I knew an attractive, speech-perfect nurse with a tongue-tie; her only complaint was that licking stamps caused a small ulcer on her frenum.)

Torticollis (wry neck) is the tilting of the head to one side, and is most usually due to intrauterine or delivery forces. No matter what the cause, the result is a lump in the muscle which runs from the mastoid bone to the top of the sternum (sternocleidomastoid muscle). This lump causes a muscle contraction forcing the head to tip down, with the chin pointing *away* from the affected muscle. Usually the muscle relaxes and stretches by age six months; this "cure" is aided by daily, passive exercises consisting of turning the head to the other side. It is of some benefit to put the baby in his bed on his back with the unaffected side nearest a blank wall. Attention-getting devices are placed on the affected side, so that, to make visual contact, he must turn his head out to the room, thus stretching the muscle.

If manipulation and time are not solving the problem, surgery is to be done before the infant grows into childhood, or the whole face and head may become misshapen—like a parallelogram instead of a square.

Tracheo-esophageal fistula partially describes a congenital defect that becomes manifest only after birth when the newborn tries to breathe and swallow. The esophagus ends in a blind pouch just an inch or two from the throat, so any milk or water is immediately regurgitated. The trachea is connected to a pouch of esophagus extending up from the stomach, so each breath bloats the stomach with air, and small amounts of stomach acid reflux up this tube and drop into the lungs.

There are many variants, but the treatment is surgical. The fistula is disconnected, and if the two blind pouches of esophagus are close enough, they may be connected. If not, a segment of bowel may be used to bridge the defect.

The condition may be suspected before birth if the mother suffers from excess amniotic fluid (*polyhydramnios*). Normally during pregnancy the fetus continually swallows amniotic fluid which is absorbed into his bloodstream and is passed via the placenta to the mother's circulation for reuse or excretion. If the baby has a bowel atresia or stenosis, he is unable to cycle the fluid, and it continues to collect *in utero*.

Treacher-Collins syndrome is a defective formation of the jaw and facial bones characterized by an underdeveloped lower jaw, sunken cheek bones, deformed ears, large mouth, and eyelids that slant downward at the outer corners—the opposite of the Oriental upward slanting. Much dental work is required for this congenital condition.

Umbilical granuloma is a tuft of blood vessels that is frequently left after the cord dries up and falls off. It is red, and secretes a purulent fluid mixed with blood. Touching it with silver nitrate will shrink the tumor by scarring the capillaries. When it is flat enough, the skin can grow over the raw area.

Rarely will an umbilical fistula tract remain attached to the intestine; a fecal odor plus persistent ooze from the navel will alert the mother to a problem. Urine leak will indicate a persistent urachus, a tubal remnant connected to the bladder.

Vulva is the female sexual area. Usually little examination of this area is done in infancy except to spread the labia and ascertain that everything, including the vaginal opening, is present. Usually some white exudate is found in the creases when this is done, and zealous removal will cause irritation as the material provides some natural protection from burning urine. The newborn female may pass some stringy mucous, sometimes blood tinged, from the vagina. This is the secretion sloughed away as the baby's internal organs shrink to normal infant size as they recover from the effects of her mother's hormones.

Wry neck—see Torticollis and also Section 7.

SECTION 6

The Skin *

A. Red, tender areas

Boil (Abscess)
Burn (first-degree) (Section 1)
Carbuncle
Cellulitis
Epidermolysis bullosa
Erysipelas
Erythema nodosum
Folliculitis
Furuncle
Phlebitis (Section 8)
Red streaks (Lymphangitis)
Runaround infection of nail (Paronychia)
Sore breast (Mastitis)
Sore finger pad (Felon)
Stings—see Bites (Section 1)

B. Itchy, pruritic

Allergy (Section 3)
Angioedema (Section 3)
Bites (Section 1)
Chickenpox (Section 2)
Contact dermatitis
Creeping eruption
Eczema
Hives
Lice (Pediculosis)
Neurodermatitis
Nummular eczema
Papular urticaria
Poison oak or ivy
Seven year itch (Scabies)
Sunlight reactions
Swimmer's itch (Cercarial dermatitis)

C. Scaly

Cradle cap (Seborrheic dermatitis)
Dandruff (Seborrheic dermatitis)
Fish skin (Ichthyosis)
Fungus infection (mycotic)
Athlete's foot
Ringworm
Tinea versicolor
Pityriasis alba
Pityriasis rosea
Psoriasis

D. Red areas or spots (exanthems)

Dermatitis
No fever
Acrodynia (Section 1)
Blood spots (petechia, purpura), (Section 8)
Fifth disease (erythema infectiosum), (Section 2)
Prickly heat (*Miliaria*)

*Read **Skin** first.

Syphilis (Section 2)
Tuberous sclerosis (Section 15)
With fever (also Section 2)
Dermatomyositis
Eczema herpeticum
Erythema multiforme exudativum
Erythema nodosum
Lupus erythematosus (Section 2)
Polyarteritis nodosa (Section 2)
Rheumatic fever (Section 2)

E. Vesicles, blisters, bullae

Acrodermatitis chronica enteropathica
Burn (second degree) (Section 1)
Chickenpox (Section 2)
Cold sore (Herpes simplex) (Section 2)
Diaper rash (Ammoniacal diaper, Section 13)
Ecthyma
Epidermolysis bullosa
Impetigo
Incontinentia pigmenti
Poison oak dermatitis
Shingles (Herpes zoster)

F. Swollen, waterlogged, thickened

Angioedema (Section 3)
Edema
Filariasis
Heart failure (Section 8)
Leprosy
Lymphedema
Nephrosis (Section 13)
Sodium retention (Hypernatremia, (Section .10)

G. Skin color

Blue (Cyanosis) (also Section 5 and Section 8)
Methemoglobinemia (Section 8)
Mongolian spots (Nevus)
Brown (mole)
Incontinentia pigmenti
Neurofibromatosis
Xeroderma pigmentosum
Red
Exanthems
Hemangioma (Section 5)
Port wine stain
Stork bite
Strawberry mark
Spider angioma
White
Albinism (Section 5)
Pityriasis alba
Vitiligo
Yellow
Carotenemia
Jaundice (Sections 5 and 8)
Ascariasis (Section 12)
Bile ducts (Section 12)
Hemolytic anemia (Section 8)
Hepatitis (Section 12)

H. Hair and scalp

Dandruff (Seborrheic dermatitis)
Hair loss
Alopecia
Ringworm of scalp
Trichotillomania (Section 16)
Wen (Epidermoid cyst)

I. Bumps, growths, cysts

Cyst
Epidermoid

Pilonidal
Keloid
Lymph nodes
Molluscum contagiosum
Neurofibromatosis
Warts
Plantar
Xanthoma

J. Acne

K. Miscellaneous

Creeping eruption
Dermatoglyphics
Dermatographia
Ectodermal dysplasia
Elastic skin (Cutis laxa)
Fistula
Sandpaper skin (Keratosis pilaris)
Skin tests
Sunlight reactions
Sweaty skin (Hyperhydrosis) (also Acrodynia, Section 1)

L. Diaper dermatitis (rash)

Ammoniacal diaper (Section 13)
Anal area (food, usually peaches)
All over (fluid, usually citrus, tomato)
Creases
Seborrheic dermatitis
Intertrigo (chafing)
Edges of diaper (Contact dermatitis from plastic or rubber liner)
Genital area (Moniliasis) (Section 5)

M. Draining sores

Actinomycosis
Blastomycosis (Section 9)
Branchial cleft cyst (Section 14)
Fistula
Lymphogranuloma (Section 2)
Sporotrichosis

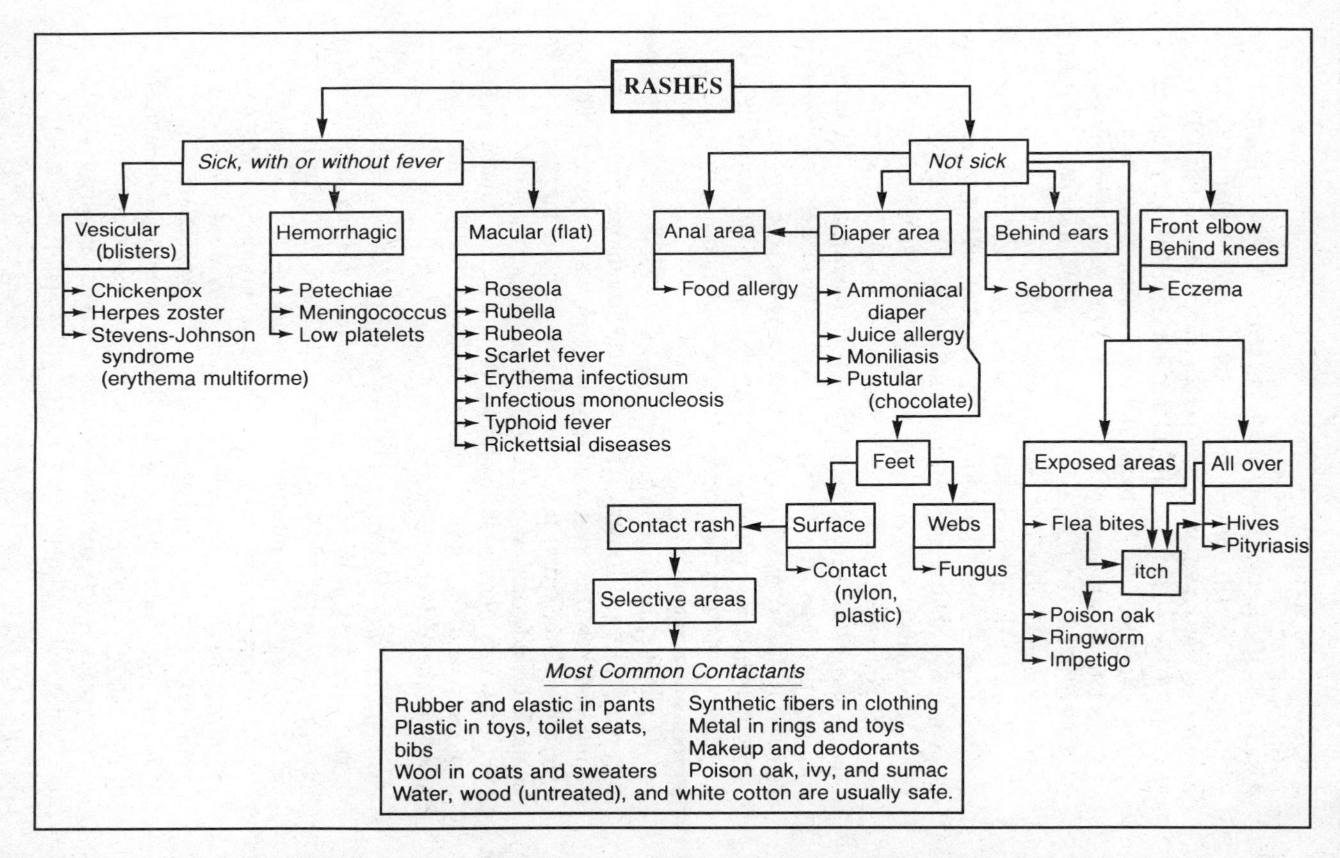

RASHES
Sick, with or without fever
Vesicular (blisters)
Chickenpox
Herpes zoster
Stevens-Johnson syndrome (erythema multiforme)
Hemorrhagic
Petechiae
Meningococcus
Low platelets
Macular (flat)
Roseola
Rubella
Rubeola
Scarlet fever
Erythema infectiosum
Infectious mononucleosis
Typhoid fever
Rickettsial diseases
Not sick
Anal area
Food allergy
Diaper area
Ammoniacal diaper
Juice allergy
Moniliasis
Pustular (chocolate)
Behind ears
Seborrhea
Front elbow
Behind knees
Eczema
Feet
Surface
Contact (nylon, plastic)
Webs
Fungus
Contact rash
Selective areas
Exposed areas
All over
Flea bites
itch
Hives
Pityriasis
Poison oak
Ringworm
Impetigo
Most Common Contactants
Rubber and elastic in pants
Plastic in toys, toilet seats, bibs
Wool in coats and sweaters
Synthetic fibers in clothing
Metal in rings and toys
Makeup and deodorants
Poison oak, ivy, and sumac
Water, wood (untreated), and white cotton are usually safe.

Abrasions—see Section 1

Abscess is a nice name for a boil. It hurts, is red, hot, and turgid with pus. It usually results from a break in the skin with the simultaneous introduction of contaminated material. Possible causes could be a bite—from an insect or another child—a cat scratch, or a sliver. Boils on the buttocks, however, often follow the ingestion of chocolate. Continuous hot packs help the body defenses wall off the infection, kill the trapped bacteria, and allow absorption of debris, or rupture and discharge of retained pus.

Three layers are essential for an effective hot pack. First, add one teaspoon of table or epsom salt to one quart of hot water. Saturate a small towel or washcloth in this solution and place it over abscess. Cover completely with a plastic sheet to keep out all air and retain heat. (If convenient, add a hot-water bottle next.) Over all this place a large, dry bath towel or beach towel, and secure it to the adjacent area. Let this remain for twenty-four hours; the redness and tenderness should then have decreased. A dry dressing may be put on the area between hot-pack treatments. If improvement is not noted in a day or so, your doctor may advise internal antibiotics and/or surgical incision and drainage.

If pimples, boils, sties, or pustules persist or recur, they suggest that *staphylococcal* bacteria are being carried in the victim or in a family member (the victim may also have an allergy to chocolate ingestion and the irritated skin becomes secondarily infected). Control methods include daily showers with hexachlorophene soap (rinse well after use), inserting an antibiotic ointment in every family member's nose daily, and the possible use of staphylococcal vaccine injections to bolster the patient's immunity.

Acne is the curse of adolescence. At an age when a youth is having problems enough with his image, his grades, his budding sexuality, his parents, and his rebellion, he is saddled with pimples, blackheads, and greasy skin in the most conspicuous places.

Fifteen percent of adolescents have no problem at all. Another 15 percent have deep pustules and cysts; they need specialized care to minimize scarring. The remaining majority must content themselves with soap and water used vigorously on a washcloth, sunlamp treatments, various drying and peeling ointments recommended by friends and druggists, and occasionally intermittent ingestion of *vitamin A.* The aim of all treatment is to allow the oil glands to discharge their secretions before they dry and plug up (resulting in blackheads) or become infected (pimples to pustules to abscesses to scars).

Rubbing alcohol will act as a grease dissolver and cleanser for the oily adolescent skin. Its drying effect may allow the oil glands to discharge their secretions more easily, thus precluding blackhead and pimple formation. After a washcloth and soap-and-water washing of face, shoulders, and chest, an alcohol-saturated cotton ball should be rubbed vigorously over the acne-bearing skin to cleanse and dry it further.

If soap and water plus alcohol cleansing are ineffective in the control, exposure to sunlight or ultraviolet light therapy (just enough to produce a pink flush and slight peeling) is the next step.

Most authorities feel chocolate and cola drinks are taboo and that greasy foods should be restricted. Whole milk and high butterfat ingestion are important inciting agents. If the elimination of dairy products for a month does not improve the skin, milk may be re-introduced. Skim milk is preferable, in any case.

Tetracycline in the lowest dose possible to effect control seems to be safe. (See Section 4.) Zinc, about 30 to 60 milligrams, as in zinc sulphate or gluconate, helps reduce acne.

If these modalities are ineffective, a dermatologist might want to try cryotherapy (cold treatment) or intracystic injection of cortisone drugs. X-ray therapy is not the ideal approach but many dermatologists, skilled in its use, consider it not unsafe.

Oral contraceptives will frequently control acne, but if the girl is still growing there is some danger of early closure of the epiphyses.

Acrodermatitis chronica enteropathica is a rare, sometimes fatal, familial disease of infants characterized by vesicles and bulla about the mouth, anus, arms, and legs. Hair and nails are lost. Diarrhea is associated. It is now found that most cases are due to a zinc deficiency.

Actinomycosis is a fungus infection which shows itself as a draining abscess about the jaw, but can cause a lung infection resembling tuberculosis. Massive doses of antibiotic may slow the spread of infection.

Alopecia is baldness. Total hair loss may follow severe illness like typhoid fever or poison ingestion. If the baldness is patchy, *ringworm of the scalp* must be ruled out. Some hairstyles (pigtails or pony tails) may pull sufficiently on the roots of the hair to separate the shaft. Tight curlers may loosen hairs. Alopecia areata is patchy baldness leaving smooth, denuded skin. No known cause has been found, and hair usually returns eventually. Compulsive hair pulling of *trichotillomania* (Section 16) may be mistaken for this condition. Some neuropsychiatric problem is usually present with trichotillomania. (See *Thallium poisoning,* Section 1.) If stress initiated hair loss, large amounts of vitamins C, B complex, and A and calcium and zinc may help the hair regrow.

Athlete's foot is a fungus infection, most common in adolescents where it is perhaps related to sweating and insufficient foot hygiene. The webs between the toes become cracked, white, and thickened, and the areas itch and burn. Redness and scaling on the ball of the foot may be related (or may be due to contact with plastic shoe inserts or nylon). Newer antifungal preparations are effective but may cause local irritation. Most victims first try some ointment with undecylenic acid; these are slower, but may irritate less. (See Skin diseases, Section 4.)

Carbuncle is the abscesslike infection due to the extension of furunculosis to deeper tissues. A minor *staphylococcal* infection in a hair follicle may spread to adjacent follicles and then invade tissue under the skin. Antistaph antibiotics sometimes are required for extended periods. Surgery may be necessary. Reinfection suggests susceptibility to staphylococcal infections, and a regimen of careful bathing, search for carrier, and antistaph-bacteria vaccine injections may be worthwhile. A patient with recurrent skin infections might have diabetes or low *immune globulins* (See *Abscess.*)

Carotenemia is the appearance of the pigment carotene in the blood to a level that allows staining of the skin. It is only noticed in the thick layers (palms, soles, and nose) and is never seen in the whites of the eyes (in contrast to *jaundice,* where bile pigment is the coloring agent). This harmless condition appears after the large ingestion of carrots, squash, and sweet potato, the usual safe vegetables offered babies in infancy. The pigment is dissipated after age two unless these yellow foods are given in abundance. It may be seen in *hypothyroidism.*

Cellulitis is any inflamation of cells. The term is usually used in reference to red, tender, hot skin adjacent to an infected, oozing, or nonhealing wound. When the skin is inflamed, the streptococcus or staphylococcus is more likely involved. If hot packs and antibiotic ointments are locally ineffective, systemic antibiotics are employed. *Abscesses, pustules,* and *lymphangitis* might accompany cellulitis.

Cercarial dermatitis (swimmer's itch) is due to the skin invasion of bird flukes (a bird parasite). An intense itch is noted after swimming in lakes or oceans. This schistosome disease is worldwide. (See *Schistosomiasis,* Section 12.)

Contact dermatitis is a skin rash due to a sensitivity to some substance. The rash is usually red, itchy, slightly raised but may become papular, vesicular, and/or scaly. Secondary infection (pustules, *impetigo*) may develop if scratching of the surface has occurred.

Poison oak or *ivy* is the most common cause, but plastic, hair sprays, soap (especially bubble bath), earrings, nylon clothing or socks, permanent-press clothing, rubber diaper liners, safety pins, tape, toilet seats, metal rings, or eyeglass frames are all frequent causes of the condition.

Rubberized or plastic mattress covers can cause an extensive rash on a baby despite intervening cotton sheeting. A red neck rash usually is due to a plastic bib, but the nylon thread in the label or piping of his shirt may be the cause. Most baby oils have perfumes which can irritate a baby's skin. Neomycin in antibiotic ointments may sensitize the skin and make a treated sore look more inflamed than before treatment. Pacifiers may cause a mouth rash; teething powders may make the gums red. Colored toilet paper may create a red perianal rash. Retained laundry soap may produce a diaper rash, and so forth.

The detective work that the dermatologist must perform in determining the cause of some of these rashes is prodigious.

Rule of thumb: if a skin rash appears in an odd place, an allergy must be considered.

Creeping eruption or larva migrans is common in the South where children play on the ground contaminated by the larvae of dog and cat worms. These larvae burrow through the skin and slowly migrate in a serpentine path. Cryotherapy (cold) may be enough to eliminate these worms if not too numerous. (See *Toxacara canis,* Section 12.)

A new oral medication has been used effectively.

Cutis laxa is an inherited skin disorder in which the skin hangs in loose folds—as it does in the aged—because of a defect of the elastic fibers.

Cuts are tears in the skin. For treatment, see Section 1.

Cyanosis, or blue skin discoloration, is produced when at least 5 grams of *hemoglobin* per 100 cubic centimeters of blood are not oxygenated. (If a child is very anemic—less than 5 grams per 100 cubic centimeters of hemoglobin—he will be pale but not cyanotic.) Frequently a newborn has 18 to 20 gram of hemoglobin and appears blue-tinged, as it is difficult to oxygenate all his hemoglobin When he is quiet, breathing shallowly, and with a stomach full of food, he may appear plethoric and/or cyanotic. A few lusty cries, and he pinks up immediately because he has oxygenated all his hemoglobin.

Cyanosis is produced by (a) the presence of abnormal hemoglobin unable to transport oxygen, b) inadequate ventilation due to central-nervous-system depression or airway obstruction, or (c) mixing of unoxygenated blood into the arterial blood because of a heart anomaly. Some causes are:

a. *Methemoglobinemia,* an abnormal hemoglobin (see Section 8)

b. *Central nervous system—intracranial bleeding*—(see *Newborn,* Section 5)

c. *Pulmonary—posterior choanal astresia, vascular ring,* Laryngeal web, or cyst, *Pierre-Robin syndrome,* and "floppy" trachea. In the lungs, *respiratory-distress syndrome, atelectasis* (Section 9), *diaphragmatic hernia.* (See Section 5)

d. *Cardiac* (see *Heart,* Sections 5 and 8)

Cyst is a saclike growth usually tightly distended with a fluid secretion. Symptoms referable to these benign swellings would be correlated with their size and nearness to vital structures. Some effort should be made to rule out the possibility of a malignancy. (See *Bone, Ganglion,* Section 7; *Thyroglossal duct cyst,* Section 9; *Epidermoid cyst, Pilonidal cyst*.)

Dermatitis is an inflammation of the skin, usually due to bacterial infection (*impetigo*), fungal infection (*athlete's foot, ringworm*), *allergy* (*hives,* drug reaction, *eczema*), contact (*poison oak,* plastic, soap, ammonia), *seborrheic dermatitis,* hormone imbalance (*acne*), viremia (*measles, pityriasis rosea, roseola, rubella, chickenpox,* etc.).

Any rash could be called dermatitis. The red inflammation often seen between the buttocks about the anal opening is usually due to a food or medicine reaction. If a mysterious rash appears on the body and is accompanied by this perianal rash, it suggests that some food (citrus, peaches, apricots, pineapple, chocolate, egg) or a drug consumed in the previous twenty-four hours is responsible.

Dermatoglyphics are the patterns of loops, whorls, and arches on fingers. These lines and the creases on the palms and soles have patterns that are determined genetically; they give some clue as to commonly associated anomalies. *Down's syndrome* has a characteristic pattern, but in other chromosomal defects the correlation is less consistent. There is growing evidence that certain wildly violent, impulsive, antisocial types may have fewer dermal lines; whether this is predictive or not remains to be seen.

Dermatographia is a condition in which mild pressure to the skin evokes a wheal or hive—a type of physical allergy. The patient's serum contains abnormal amounts of antibodies which react with an antigen released by trauma, albeit slight. Histamine is next released which is the *sine qua non* of the hive.

Antihistaminics are helpful, but daily calcium, vitamin C, and pantothenic acid should suppress the problem more permanently.

When the atopic skin is stroked, a white dermatographism usually appears—not the usual red lines.

Dermatomyositis is a rare disease of unknown cause, manifested by inflammation of the muscles and skin rashes over cheeks, elbows, and knees. The muscles become weak or sore. Lymph nodes, liver, spleen, heart, and kidneys may become inflamed. After a few months or years of this smoldering activity, contractures and atrophy of muscles lead to extreme debility. Physiotherapy and *cortisone* drugs are the mainstays of therapy; the outlook is dim without this care.

Diaper dermatitis is any rash in the diaper area and can be considered a contact rash usually caused by the breakdown products of the urine, notably ammonia. Ammonia usually causes blisters and ulcers. (See *Ammoniacal diaper,* Section 13, *Dermatitis.*)

Ammoniacal diaper usually occurs in the morning. The strong ammonia smell is due to bacterial action that changes the urea in the urine to ammonia. Some babies are terribly sensitive to ammonia and develop redness, blisters, and ulcers. Boiling and bleaching the diapers are of no benefit. Some attempt must be made to (1) destroy the bacteria that live in the diaper and (2) counteract the ammonia. The diapers can be soaked in various bacteriocidal solutions, or they can be put out in the sunshine. When the bacteria are eliminated, no ammonia will form. Pouring an ounce of vinegar in the second of two double nighttime diapers (so that the vinegar doesn't actually touch the baby's skin) will acidify the urine and neutralize the ammonia. Adding extra water to the child's diet will not wash the ammonia out and only serves to make the condition worse: The more urine produced, the more ammonia will form. An effort should be made to cut down the child's fluid intake. In general, if he is urinating two or three times a day, he is probably getting a sufficient amount of fluid.

Fluid components in the diet to which the baby is sensitive (citrus, tomato, etc.) might cause redness and scaling on areas where the urine contacts the skin. Solids in the diet (peaches, eggs, apricots, chocolate, etc.) more likely irritate the skin near the anal opening *between* the buttocks where the diaper does *not* touch. Poorly rinsed diapers containing soap remnants would cause red, rough skin everywhere the diapers touch. A rash at the belt line and about upper thighs would come from contact with the edge of the rubber or plastic diaper liner. A wild red rash common in the first few weeks is caused by a yeast, monilia, and would grow well in this area because it is dark and wet there. (See *Moniliasis,* Section 5.)

Ecthyma is a bacterial skin infection caused by the *streptococcus* or *staphylococcus* (like *impetigo*), but the involvement is deeper into the skin, since scarring usually occurs upon healing. If the crusted scab is removed, an ulcer is found with attendant blood and pus. Some authorities now feel that local antibiotic ointments are not enough, so systemic antistrep or antistaph medicine is added to ward off possible kidney or rheumatic complications.

Ectodermal dysplasia is a general term for ectodermal defects genetically transmitted, in which the skin glands, hair, tooth enamel, or nails are absent or deficient. One type of patient has no sweat glands and will develop a high fever in response to elevated environmental temperature. Peg-shaped teeth, deafness, and thickened palm skin may be associated.

Eczema is a word that means itchy, scaly, weeping dermatitis. Most infants with eczema (three percent of all children) have the *atopic* variety, which mean an hereditary allergic background. (See *Allergy,* Section 3.)

The familial tendency to develop asthma, hayfever and/or atopic dermatitis affects twenty percent of the population (inherited as a simple dominant gene). These atopic people form increased amounts of immune proteins including immunoglobulin E (see Section 3) in response to ingested and inhaled antigens. Atopic disorders are disorders of immune and tissue response aggravated by the environment and ingested and inhaled allergens.

The dermatitis is usually found on the cheeks and the flexor surfaces of the knees and elbows. These areas periodically become eroded, weepy, and secondarily infected.

Psychological factors are important triggering agents in the older child or adult. Ingestion of certain foods may aggravate the basic condition. (Milk, wheat, egg, citrus, tomato most usually are responsible.)

Atopic skin is inherently itchy and the itch-scratch-itch cycle is readily established. These people are very intolerant to wool or rough textured fabrics.

Atopic skin is basically dry and the horny layer is thicker than normal. Retained sweat is irritating; atopics are worse in a hot, humid environment.

Skin blood vessels of atopics respond abnormally. Skin of flexor areas of elbows and knees retains greater than normal warmth; skin temperature at night is warmer; atopic victims more often dig at their skin during the night.

Rules:

1. Infrequent bathing with a minimum of soap. Water cleansing after a messy bowel movement, and soap and water cleansing of the hands if they are filthy are allowed. Bathing with an acid soap may be safe if the water is treated with an oil and emulsifier. This oily film may encourage the retention of water in the dry skin. Soap and water shampoo is allowed if the body is protected.

2. The entire skin surface is cleansed at least twice a day with Cetaphil® or Wibi® lotion. It is rubbed in until it foams and then gently wiped off with a soft cloth, leaving a lotion film. It may be reapplied to particularly dry or itchy areas several times a day.

3. Some dermatologists feel that oily or greasy lubricants are taboo, but they may soften the skin by preventing the escape of moisture.

4. Inflamed or pruritic areas of the eczema are treated with a steroid preparation (cortisone ointment) several times daily. The par-

ents should begin to apply it sparingly but frequently (three or four times a day) to a new lesion as soon as it is noticed. Early treatment shortens the duration.

5. If any evidence of secondary infection is present a course of seven to ten days of systemic antibiotic therapy is given (usually erythromycin). Potential allergic sensitizers such as topical antihistamines and anesthetics should not be used on atopic skin. The routine use of topical antibiotics in atopic dermatitis is not necessary. Since topical antibiotics are potential allergens, they should be used infrequently for short periods of time.

Early effective therapy of active lesions is essential. The parents must be educated in how to handle flareups as soon as they begin.

6. Elixir of Benadryl® is prescribed for nighttime sedation and for its antipruritic effect, since much scratching is done at night.

Only soft cotton clothing should be worn next to the skin; it should be well rinsed and free of starch. No wool, fur, or other napped or scratchy fabric should come in direct contact with the skin. Atopic children should be under-clothed. Graduated exposure to sunlight is beneficial, as is swimming, if precautions are taken to prevent over-drying.

These children usually outgrow the worst of their eczema at eighteen to twenty months, but just as the mother is beginning to relax about skin care and diet, the problem may move to the nose and lungs; hay fever and asthma frequently follow. Half of children who have atopic eczema will develop some respiratory allergy in later childhood and they usually have strongly positive skin test responses. (It is suggested that atopic eczema is *not* a true allergy in the sense that when a sensitizing food is given to a child with eczema, he may develop a hive rather than a flareup of his eczema.)

Desensitizing vaccine shots are helpful at this time, although they seem to be almost worthless for eczema. If some infectious trigger mechanism seems to play a role in causation (i.e., each bacterial upper respiratory infection makes the eczema worse), the use of a bacterial vaccine may be beneficial.

Children with agammaglobulinemia frequently have eczematous lesions, but gamma globulin injections are *not* to be given to atopics unless their IgG level is low. Extra vitamins (C, B complex, A) and zinc may promote healing.

Eczema herpeticum is the widespread vesicular eruption occurring in eczematous patients infected with the virus, herpes simplex. It resembles the eczema vaccination and is serious. Eczematous patients will acquire this if exposed to a person with herpes (cold sore).

Edema is fluid accumulation in body tissues due to heart failure, low protein in the blood (hypoproteinemia), vascular injury, trauma, or *allergy.*

If the heart is failing due to *myocarditis* or scarred valves from *rheumatic fever,* the sluggishly flowing blood through the lungs will force water into the alveolar air sacs—*pulmonary edema.* The liver may be similarly involved with edema fluid from back pressure. (The edema fluid in the ankles seen in the elderly with heart failure is rare in children.)

Nephrosis causes edema of eyelids and the body in general, because of the loss of protein through the urine. The lowered osmotic pressure of the blood will thus allow the water to leak out of the capillaries into the tissues.

Edema developing suddenly without sickness or trauma is usually allergic angioneurotic edema—especially if the eyelids, lips, or tongue are affected. The giveaway would be the concomitant appearance of hives. (Chocolate, citrus, tomato, fish, etc., are the common offenders.)

Ehlers-Danlos syndrome—see *Cutis laxa*

Epidermoid cysts are firm, round nodules in skin of scalp, face, or neck. They move with the skin when palpated (in contrast to lymph glands which always slide about *under* the skin), and are not tender unless infected. It appears as if the secretions of a sebaceous gland were unable to escape to the surface. If it is unsightly, tender, or subject to irritation, removal is worthwhile. A surgeon must remove it *in toto,* or the lining glands will secrete more fluid and the cyst will recur.

Epidermolysis bullosa is a rare hereditary skin disease in which the top layer of skin blisters off after slight trauma. It leaves large raw areas like a second-degree burn.

Erysipelas is a *streptococcal infection* of the skin rarely seen nowadays. The skin is very tender, red, and produces a raised border at the junction with normal skin. Newborns are more likely to acquire this near the nipples or navel. *Penicillin* is curative.

Erythema multiforme exudativum, or Stevens-Johnson syndrome, is a wild skin disease due to a supersensitivity to an antigenic stimulus, most commonly to drug ingestion (usually *phenobarbital* or *sulfa*). A measleslike rash, fever, malaise are followed by vesicles about the openings of mouth, nose, eyes, urethra, and anus. Supportive measures—fluid, massive cortisone therapy, ointments, and antibiotics for secondary infection—are all that can be offered.

Erythema nodosum is characterized by painful, red papules scattered over the shins and legs. These one or two centimeter bumps rise and change color for two weeks, then recede for two more. It is more common in the adolescent or older female.

It is assumed to be a reaction or sensitivity to the presence of some disease process elsewhere in the body. A throat culture for *streptococci,* a *sedimentation rate,* a *tuberculosis skin test,* an X ray of the chest and bowels should be a part of a minimum investigation. This is a signal that something is wrong elsewhere in the body.

Exanthems (see chart in Section 2) are infections which produce rashes. *Chickenpox* develops blisters over the four days of development. *Roseola* has a rash *after* two or three days of fever. *Rubella* (German, or three-day, measles) produces a rash on the first day, usually with little or no fever. *Rubeola* (hard measles) develops a rash at the height of the fever and cough. *Erythema infectiosum* shows red cheeks and lacework rash on arms and legs. But almost all of the Coxsackie or ECHO (see Section 2 under *Enterovirus*) viruses can produce a rash; the viremia (virus in bloodstream) must irritate the capillaries and make them dilate. These are virus infections. *Scarlatina* is an exanthematous disease because a rash appears, but the toxin which produces the rash is formed from the bacteria growing in the throat. *Meningococcemia* rash is formed from the bacteria themselves that are floating about in the bloodstream, then lodge in a capillary, destroy the wall, and cause a minute hemorrhage into the skin. *Rocky Mountain spotted fever* (see Section 2) is a rickettsial disease with a generalized rash.

Felon is a painful *cellulitis* in the finger tip. This red, hot, tender, swollen ball of finger may require surgery if hot packs and antibiotics do not bring relief within twenty-four hours.

Filariasis, rare in our country, is a worm infestation passed to humans by flies, mosquitoes, or gnats. These larvae then invade the tissues, migrate to local *lymph nodes,* grow to adulthood, mate, and produce young. The result may be the blocking of lymph drainage. The grotesque leg, arm, or skin swelling and thickening is the end result of their obstruction (elephantiasis). Some of the worms may migrate to the eye, causing blindness. Surgical removal of involved nodes plus medicines provide a holding action to further extension of the invader.

Fistula is an abnormal communication between organs. The most common is from the rectum to the skin of the buttocks and produces a draining sore. (See *Anal fistula,* Section 12.)

Folliculitis is a discrete, *staphylococcal infection* of the hair follicle. It begins as a red, tender papule which soon forms a pustule or pimple. If scratched, the top is torn off and the bacteria spread to other follicles. Hot soaks or packs may help them resolve. An antibacterial soap (hexachlorophene) and ointment will not cure it, but may preclude its spread. Adolescents will have these infections on their faces, but when they appear on the buttocks, it usually means that the victim has consumed chocolate.

The itchy bumps from an *allergy* to chocolate soon become infected. This condition is commonly seen a few days after Halloween, Easter, and birthday parties when large amounts of chocolate have been consumed.

Fungus infections are usually confined to the skin or hair in children, but some fungi will invade the body (*actinomycosis, blastomycosis, cryptococcosis, sporotrichosis, histoplasmosis, coccidioidomycosis*). (See *Athlete's foot, Ringworm, Ringworm of scalp,* this section.)

Furuncle is a staphylococcal infection somewhere between the size of a pimple and a boil. In three days pus develops which can be pushed out when the skin covering the pus is thin enough. Hot packs (see *Abscess*) help localize the infection. Antibiotic soaps and ointments will not treat the already developed furuncle but may slow its surface spread to adjacent follicles. Athletes are prone to this infection because of breaks in the skin. Clean skin and equipment is a must.

Hair (see *Alopecia*) may be lost for a variety of reasons. When *ringworm of the scalp* has been ruled out, congenital conditions (rare) may be considered. Alopecia areata must be distinguished from hair loss from fever, X-ray radiation, *syphilis, vitamin A,* and thallium poisoning. *Hypothyroid* patients may lose hair. A frustrated, angry, impulsive child with hair loss may be pulling out his hair. (See *Trichotillomania,* Section 16.)

Herpes zoster, or shingles, is an infection of the skin caused by the chickenpox virus. First papules, then vesicles and ulcers appear in a pattern that corresponds to local nerve distribution. (They may appear on one side of forehead or an area down the arm or following a rib from spine in back to breastbone in front.) It itches, burns, tingles, and hurts like *neuritis.* It may become secondarily infected.

Fever is often associated. The lesions continue to break out for a week along the course of the nerve; they finally dry up after two to three weeks.

It is unusual for shingles to occur in children; it is more common in the elderly. Since the disease is caused by the *chickenpox* virus, the father of a child with *chickenpox* may become infected with herpes zoster two weeks after the start of his child's illness. The father, in turn, may give chickenpox to another child in two weeks.

Aspirin and *codeine* are standard treatment. A zoster *gamma globulin* is available to attenuate either chickenpox or herpes in susceptible exposees. Injections of vitamin B_{12} (1,000 micrograms per day) for a few days will speed recovery.

Hives, or welts, are the signal that the body has taken in some allergen, usually a food. The skin rash is red, swollen, and itchy; the eruptions are of an irregular size and shape, and occasionally have a bleached center. Flare and wheal are characteristic. In only about twenty percent of the cases is an obvious food the inciting agent. Hives are assumed to be the result of histamine release from certain cells in the body. Hives, therefore, may follow any inciting agent—cold, heat, fever, emotion, virus infections—whenever histamine is released. (See *Allergy, Angioedema,* Section 3.)

Frequently a mother reports that her child has hives, and she can think of nothing new in the diet to explain it. Careful questioning may reveal a dollop of catsup on last night's meat loaf or one chocolate-chip cookie. It is possible that the cow who gave the milk the child drank might have eaten something unusual (like thistles) or have been given penicillin for mastitis, and the child happens to be sensitive to it.

The child is usually not sick, only fussy, irritable, and scratching himself, often to the point of bleeding. Antihistaminics are indicated but are not curative, as the hives constantly move from one area to another usually for a week. It seems to take that long for the irritant to be excreted.

If the victim is especially irritable or suffering from breathing obstruction (asthma or croup), immediate attention by a doctor is required. *Epinephrine, ephedrine,* and/or *cortisone* might be needed.

Hyperhydrosis is excessive sweating. It is normal with high environmental temperature and physical exertion. Excess palm sweat does not *have* to mean nervous instability. Aluminum chloride applications may control the problem. It is occasionally seen in heavy metal poisoning (see *Acrodynia,* Section 1). Night sweats are a possible sign of *tuberculosis* or *rickets.*

Ichthyosis, or fish skin, is an inherited tendency to thick, scaly skin. In some forms there is increased redness; some victims develop blisters. Thick, dry skin is shed and becomes unsightly and uncomfortable.

Soaking in a bath twice a day may restore some of the absent moisture to the scales. Lanolin or petrolatum may be used afterward to help hold the moisture.

Impetigo is a skin infection manifested by oozy, crusty sores, usually following a break in the skin from a bite, scrape, burn or scratched hive. Children usually pick at anything on their skin; this habit, combined with a purulent nasal discharge, is a good way to seed germs into any break in the skin. Germs grow well in the bloody serum and produce more pus, which inhibits growth of the normal skin over the defect. Skin infections in or on the nose and upper lip are especially dangerous because venous drainage ends in the deep veins near the brain. (See *Cavernous sinus thrombosis,* Section 2.)

Streptococcus and *staphylococcus* are the usual inhabitants of these sores. If they are small and few, they are easily controlled with an antibiotic ointment, rubbed on after a bath, or soaking that removes the scab. An antibacterial soap containing hexachlorophene is the best kind to use, followed by the ointment; then a nonsticky dressing is applied. To avoid sensitivity, an antibiotic ointment, containing medicines not usually used internally, is best. (*Neomycin,* polymycin, bacitracin, are better than *sulfa* or *penicillin* ointments.)

If sores are extensive and thought to be streptococcal, an internal antibiotic penicillin, erythromycin, might heal them from inside faster and preclude development of *rheumatic fever, scarlatina,* or *glomerulonephritis.*

I recall one patient with a second-degree coffee burn on his arm who later developed *scarlet fever.* His mother had a strep throat and breathed some germs on his open wound when changing the dressing.

Incontinentia pigmenti is a bizarre skin disease found only in the female. The vesicles on arms and legs progress to patches of thick skin and finally to swirls of brown pigment as if they were painted on. It may be associated with *seizures* and *retardation.*

Intertrigo is chafing, common in fat babies. The groin and armpits are red. Some talc allows the skin to slide without irritation, but powder must be used on intact skin only. Breaks in the skin are best treated with an antibiotic ointment.

Keloid is a dense fibrous tumor usually developing during the healing of a wound. Negroes are more susceptible. X-ray therapy and cortisone treatment may be helpful in suppressing this tendency. Vitamin E rubbed on wounds may suppress the keloid formation.

Keratosis pilaris (sandpaper skin) is a common condition that makes the outer sides of upper arms and thighs feel like a nutmeg grater. Papules develop at the hair follicles. No symptoms except cosmetic are noted. In the summer when the sun stimulates the skin to peel off the lesions disappear. High doses of vitamin A or other *keratolytic agents* (see *Sulfur ointments,* Section 4) are helpful.

Leprosy (Hansen's disease) is a rare disease in the United States. The leprosy bacteria responsible is related to the *tuberculosis* germ. It is only slightly contagious; after exposure, signs of the disease may take years to develop.

It reveals itself by patches or nodules of thickened skin on face or hands, or by areas of anesthesia (no feeling). As sensation is reduced in these areas, the patient does not withdraw from pain, and a variety of scars and deformities develop.

New drugs are reasonably effective, but control is difficult to evaluate because of the long latent period between recognition and improvement in appearance. Patients are sometimes confined in special leprosy centers while awaiting "cures."

Lymphangitis is the name for the tender, red streaks adjacent to an area of infection, usually impetigo. It represents infection in the lymph vessels draining the wound; it is *not* blood poisoning. The nearby lymph nodes are swollen and tender also. If hot packs (see

Abscess) do not clear this overnight, internal antibiotics are indicated (usually *penicillin*).

Lymphedema usually involves an arm or leg, following an infectious or traumatic obstruction to lymph flow. The limb becomes swollen and thick with lymph fluid. Elephantiasis is lymphedema due to the obstruction of lymph flow caused by the filaria larvae. (See *Filariasis.*)

Lymph nodes in the axillae (armpits) enlarge following hand or arm infection. These glands trap poisons, germs, and viruses infecting the areas distal to them. *Cat-scratch disease* is characterized by swelling of the glands that drain the area of the scratch. A scabbed-over, infected abrasion of the knee will send bacteria to the lymph nodes in the groin, sometimes causing alarming swelling. An enlarged gland may be confused with an early hernia.

Lymph glands swollen all over the body may be seen in *infectious mononucleosis, tularemia,* and *roseola.* A persistent gland swelling which does not respond to time (this rules out *virus*) or antibiotics (rules out bacteria) should be biopsied or removed *in toto* for microscopic examination. *Tuberculosis* of lymph glands is rarely seen but possible.

Mastitis is inflammaion or infection of the breast. Lactating women may acquire this in the early days of nursing and may have to terminate *breast feeding* before it subsides. The breast becomes red, warm, and tender; antibiotics may be necessary. Most babies have swollen breasts at birth which, if manipulated, will exhibit some milk escaping from the nipple (witches' milk). Fooling with the baby's breast may encourage a mastitis requiring hotpacks and antibiotics. A baby acquires infection more easily because of limited defenses and the proximity of the oozy umbilical-cord stump.

Miliaria, or prickly heat, is a skin inflammation due to plugged sweat glands, usually associated with elevated environmental temperature. Lesions are more obvious in the warm areas of the body. Small red papules which may blister are characteristic. Treatment is cooling off the skin with bathing and dressing in as little clothing as possible.

The fortuitous discovery that *vitamin C* will clear up this persistent rash does not mean that it is due to vitamin C deficiency. It only means that vitamin C is curative in some occult way.

Mole, or **pigmented nevus,** is the common brown spot on most of us. These spots appear sometime before adolescence. The average adult has some thirty to forty moles scattered over his body. Several types are described: the flat (macular) mole, the slightly elevated (papular) mole, the halo nevus (mole surrounded by a ring of depigmented skin), pedunculated mole (attached to the skin by a neck of tissue) the giant nevus (brown pigment covering much of the trunk, like a bathing suit), and hairy moles.

A malignant melanoma, the cancerous mole, is rare in children and can appear spontaneously without arising from a previous benign brown mole. The giant nevus and moles on genitalia or under the nails are more prone to develop malignant changes.

Surgery is recommended if the diagnosis is doubtful (microscopic examination usually reveals malignant changes), for cosmetic reasons, or if any of the following occur:

a. Change of size, shape, color
b. Appearance of bleeding or ulceration
c. Pain or inflammation in or around the mole

Molluscum contagiosum, a virus infection, appears on the skin as a rounded, shiny papule with a central depression. A dozen or so may be found in one area. They may be skewered and pried out with a pointed scalpel after proper cleansing with soap and water. An antibiotic ointment should be applied to the raw areas after this surgery. Some advocate their removal with tweezers: grab, pinch, pull. Perhaps a child might prefer the least traumatic of all therapies: diddling the lesion with a pointed wooden stick and applying a drop of phenol (carbolic acid).

The virus causing these lesions is spread from person to person by contact, especially if warmth and moisture are present, as in summer swimming pools.

Mycotic infections are those due to fungi and would properly include *ringworm* and *athlete's foot.* The term is usually reserved for systemic fungus diseases. (See *Blastomycosis,* Section 9.)

Neurodermatitis, as the name implies, is a chronically inflamed patch of skin that is perpetuated by the itch-scratch cycle. The skin becomes thickened, dried, and hence susceptible to a renewed cycle of itch-scratch when the next frustrating event in the victim's life causes local blood-vessel dilation. Many children with *eczema* outgrow that diagnostic term only to be relabeled as victims of neurodermatitis.

Elbows, knees, ankles, abdomen are the common sites. Anger, frustration, dry weather, house dust, too much alkaline soap in the bath, wool are all trigger mechanisms that alert the patient to the need to scratch; the finger nails change the sensation from a burning itch to a more tolerable pain.

Cortisone creams or coal-tar ointments provide control. (See *Eczema.*)

Neurofibromatosis, or Recklinghausen's disease, is an inherited condition characterized by generalized brown patches (café-au-lait spots) and tumors in and under the skin arising from nerves. Bone cysts and a variety of brain lesions are associated. Surgical removal of neurofibromata causing pressure symptoms is the only treatment available.

Nevus is the general name for blood-vessel or cell anomalies of the skin. A pigmented nevus is a *mole.* A vascular nevus obviously contains blood-vessels that impart the red or blue color to them. (See *Hemangioma,* Section 5.)

Mongolian spot is a blue discoloration of the skin of the lower back and buttocks characteristically seen on Oriental babies and also on Indian and Mediterranean types. This resembles a bruise and fades with age.

Nummular eczema is a patch of red, papular, scaly skin that is intensely pruritic (itchy). Inhalants, foods, and contact irritants may be at least inciting agents. The victims are probably atopic. (See *Eczema.*) *Cortisone* creams are rapid in effecting control, but the condition is chronic.

Papular urticaria describes itchy bumps on the skin and is a common condition in children. Papules appear on arms, legs, neck, belt line, and ankles. The child cannot restrain himself from scratching and soon erodes the surface; impetigo may develop. It is reminiscent of an insect bite but is more persistent and recurrent. It is thought to be due to a hypersensitivity to the saliva of mosquitoes, nits, bedbugs, lice, fleas, gnats, mites, and chiggers. If spraying the bed and room with a safe-for-humans insect spray (*not* DDT) and defleaing the cat and dog are of no benefit, a professional fumigator may be needed. In the old days a herd of sheep would be run through the house, and the fleas would leap to their new hosts.

Paronychia is an infection of the skin about the nail. It is most frequently seen about the large toenail in people who wear tight socks or shoes and/or in those who have clipped their nails in a curve instead of straight across. The skin rolls over the growing corners of the nail. The nail pushes into the skin and, like a sliver, sets up an infection, unfortunately due to the resistant *staphylococcus.* (See *Ingrown toenail,* Section 7.) A baby may acquire this if he sleeps on his stomach with his feet turned out. The pressure of his feet against the sheet pushes the skin against the nail and the infection invades the broken skin. If the infection is treated early—while it is just red cellulitis—a hot pack may halt the infection (see *Abscess,* this section) while the nail is growing out to a normal, nonirritating length. Wearing shoes to bed might ease this foot-sheet pressure.

Hot packs, antibiotic ointments, elevating the nail by pushing cotton under the leading edge, and internal antibiotics may control the condition while the nail is growing out beyond the skin fold. Granulation tissue, abscess formation, and pus under the nail may require surgical repair.

A *yeast* (Candida) may cause a smoldering infection about the nail. Little pus forms, but the nail breaks off and becomes misshapen. The child with this condition is usually a thumb or finger sucker and acquires it from an insignificant mouth infection (*thrush*).

Pediculosis, or lice infestation, is a parasitic disease usually of the scalp (less commonly of the body or pubic area). The louse must feed daily on the blood of the scalp, setting up an unignorable itch. The broken skin frequently gets infected. Baby lice become glued to the hair shaft as tiny grayish blobs.

Antilouse shampoos (Kwell® is standard) are now very effective; all family members should be suspected (and *in*spected). Lice on the eyelashes are often associated with mysterious blue spots on the body.

Pilonidal cyst (see *Pilonidal dimple,* Section 5) is the collection of cellular debris in and under the skin at the lower end of the sacrum or tailbone. About one out of twenty babies is born with a dimple in this area that is of no significance if the bottom of the depression is visible; normal cleanliness will preclude infection. But if this dimple leads to a tunnel or sinus tract lined with oil and sweat glands, a cyst may form, and easily becomes infected if bacteria invade and grow. This rarely occurs before adolescence. It was called jeep's disease during World War II, since the trauma of riding on unpadded seats was felt to be causative. If infected, wide surgical excision is recommended.

Pityriasis alba means white, scaly spots and is a common, chronic skin condition usually affecting the face. Slightly scaly, white one-quarter to one-half inch circles devoid of pigment are all that appear. It is more obvious in the summer because of the contrast with the surrounding tanned skin. It is considered a very mild type of eczema. The reaction of the skin is so slight that only the scaling and de-pigmentation are noted. *Cortisone* cream will rapidly control the lesions.

Pityriasis rosea is a skin eruption occasionally associated with a *respiratory infection* and hence is assumed to be a *virus.* A circular, slightly pinkish, slightly fawn-colored slightly scaly patch appears on the trunk, shoulder, or thigh. It looks so much like *ringworm* that almost everyone treats it with an antifungal cream. Of course, it doesn't go away. Within two weeks after the appearance of this herald spot, the trunk blossoms with many oval-shaped patches of similar appearance. The long axes of the ovals are parallel to the ribs, so the patient's trunk resembles a Christmas tree. Lesions are rare on arms, face, or legs. They last a month. Treatment on the twenty-ninth day may speed recovery. *Cortisone* will effectively quiet the condition if the patient is uncomfortable.

Plantar warts are ordinary warts partially covered by the thick skin on the plantar surface of the foot. They feel as if one is walking on a stone. The skin beneath the wart is stimulated to produce more protective skin, and thus the problem is perpetuated. Scraping, picking, clipping have no effect, as the wart root must be removed. Surgery, X ray, and electrocautery all have their supporters. A slower, but less painful method uses a drop of acid or a solution of ground-up June bugs (Cantharone®). These latter act as vesicants (blister producers) and slowly eat through the growth and separate it from the normal skin underneath. New skin fills in the hole without scarring. Repeated applications may be necessary.

Poison ivy or **oak** is a contact rash due to exposure to the oil on the leaf of the *Rhus toxicodendron* plant. It begins as reddened, itchy, burning patches of skin on exposed areas after contact with the plant. It appears for five days in new areas as the skin progresses to *edema* and blister formation.

The sting, itch, and burn is intolerable to some and scratching may lead to *impetigo.* Lotions with local anesthetics and internal anti-histamines are of limited value. If the patient cannot sleep, systemic (oral or intramuscular) *cortisone* is very effective; it works better if given before blisters form.

It is important that the susceptible, exposed person rip off his clothes and bathe himself with much soap and water as soon as possible. All his clothes must be cleaned; he must wear only fresh clothing. Some people break out from the smoke of ivy burning miles away. (A patient, nine months old, developed generalized rash when she crawled on the carpet where her father had walked after tramping through the vines.) Once the victim has bathed, he is no longer contagious. The serum or ooze from his blisters will not affect another person, only his unwashed clothing will.

Desensitizing oral or injectable vaccines may be helpful for those who are sensitive and cannot avoid the plant. They must be given well ahead of the next exposure to allow the body time to build up an immunity.

Port wine stain—see *Hemangioma,* Section 5

Prickly heat—see *Miliaria*

Psoriasis is a chronic hereditary skin condition formerly thought to afflict only adults. The indolent, scaly, well-circumscribed patches on the scalp, back, knees (front), and elbows (back) usually seen in adults may be mistaken for chronic *eczema,* dandruff, or *seborrhea.* Some children will develop a sudden papular rash that becomes scaly in two weeks and then clears, only to recur with the typical silver scales. Sometimes the nails become pitted and deformed, reminiscent of a fungus invasion.

No known cause has been found, but there is a family trait. The soft, warm areas of skin when involved will respond easily to *cortisone* ointments applied as needed. Thicker areas may do better with coal-tar and salicylic-acid ointments. A lifetime of ointment dabbing can be anticipated. Vitamins C, B complex, and A are helpful.

Rashes—see diagram at beginning of section

Ringworm of the body is called tinea corporis (see *Fungus infection, Athlete's foot*). It is caused by a fungus, is very common in children, and is spread by close contact with animals or humans. It is usually found on the exposed surfaces—face, neck, forearms, and lower legs.

It is round or oval, scaly, slightly pink with a raised border as it grows peripherally. Tiny vesicles may dot this leading edge. The center may be almost clear once the lesion is well developed.

Whitfield's ointment, or any ointment with undecylenic acid usually clears this up in a few days. Tinactin® drops are rapidly curative. A stubborn case may need griseofulvin orally for ten days.

Ringworm of the scalp, or tinea capitis, is caused by a fungus which invades the hair shaft, producing a brittleness that allows the hair to break, leaving a well-circumscribed area of stubble. Rarely is there any skin inflammation or itch associated. Some types produce only a scaly patch; others invade the skin, producing a violently sensitive, swollen sore, or multiple crusts.

The vast majority are spread by human contact; a few cases may be related to animal exposure. The typical area affected is on the back of the head, where contact has been made with infected hairs left on a theater, bus, or school seat by a previously infected child. The condition is rare in adults.

Most patients with this circular area of stubble are easily diagnosed by shining a Wood's light in the area. The special ultraviolet light will cause the diseased hairs to emit a light green fluorescence. If the fluorescence is absent but fungus must be ruled out the hairs may be treated with an alkali and examined under the microscope for the characteristic plant. A culture medium is available for the dermatological purists.

Until recently, shaving, X-ray treatments, mechanical depilation, and *antifungal* ointments were the only available treatments for this stubborn problem. Now a two-week course of an internal and relatively safe drug is sufficient to stop the fungus growth in the shaft while the hair continues to grow out. The fungostatic medicine griseofulvin, deposits itself in the skin layer, allowing uninvolved hair to emerge. A re-examination with the light about six weeks after therapy usually reveals no fluorescence.

It is permissible to allow the child to return to school as long as he is under treatment and a gob of *Whitfield's ointment* is rubbed into the patch of stubble.

Scabies, or seven-year itch, is due to the burrowing into the skin by a mite. The mother mite lays her eggs in these tunnels. A sensitivity develops, followed by an unignorable itch. These linear, pink areas are most likely to be found in the warm places of the body: webs of fingers, inner side of wrists, groin, folds in front of armpits, and the penis.

Scrapings will reveal the mites and eggs. Treatment offers relief in a day or two; a lotion with benzyl benzoate applied after a hot bath will quiet this infestation. Repetition may be necessary. *Impetigo* is a common secondary infection.

Seborrheic dermatitis is a chronic skin problem manifesting itself as yellow, greasy scales in the scalp (cradle cap), reddened, weepy areas where the skin creases (groin, behind ears), reddened, thick eyelids (granulating lids), and excessively oily skin, blackheads, and pimples in the adolescent.

A variety of environmental, dietary, and infectious influences will distort the basic condition. *Monilia* (or Candida), a yeast, loves to grow in the seborrheic skin. Frequently a secondary bacterial infection contaminates the weepy rawness behind the ears. (See *Impetigo.*) Certain foods often make more crusts form on the scalp; changing the fat in the milk to polyunsaturated types or switching to skimmed milk may lessen the tendency to cradle cap (one mother called it "crib crust"). The child with chronic red-rimmed eyelids may be helped by a no-milk, no-chocolate diet, inhalation-allergy control and cortisone eye ointment. The adolescent with much acne may or may not profit by diet restriction, but soaps that have a keratolytic (skin peeling) effect are worthwhile.

Keratolytic ointments (see *Sulfur ointments,* Section 4) are helpful where the skin is thick (scalp); daily shampoos may be all that is necessary, but lotions with *sulfur, salicylic acid,* and/or coal tar will effectively peel off the crusts. If there is much redness, *candidiasis* may be superimposed.

The weepy ooze behind the ears should first be treated with an antibiotic ointment, and if redness remains, *cortisone* ointment will quiet it down. For the groin and diaper area, a cortisone and anticandida cream is the best; the persistent diaper rash usually means that seborrhea and thrush are coexisting. Vitamin B_6 (50 to 100 milligrams per day for two to three weeks) often helps eliminate it.

Sinus (congenital dermal) is a tiny, skin-lined tube from the skin surface into the spinal canal. It can allow infection to work into the spinal fluid, causing *meningitis.* If infection recurs in the tube, it must be surgically removed. (See *Pilonidal cyst.*)

Skin is a conglomerant organ consisting mainly of epithelial covering and connective tissue to hold it in place. It relates to the body through nerves and capillaries and serves as a physical and immune protection.

Temperature regulation and sense perception are important functions.

In the following description of skin diseases, terms are used which may be unfamiliar to the reader. The dermatologist has to see most skin lesions because of the difficulty of describing lesions over the phone.

Macule is flat, small, not palpable change of color. (Freckles, *vitiligo,* first-degree burn, *roseola, stork bites.*)

Patch is a large macule. (*Mongolian spots,* sunburn, nevus flammeus.)

Papule is an elevation the size of a pea or less; color may or may not be changed. It is visible and palpable. (Most *moles.*)

Nodule is a large papule. (Some drug eruptions.)

Plaque is a flat nodule.

Vesicle is an elevation the size of a pea or less but containing clear fluid. (*Chickenpox, herpes simplex* and *herpes zoster, contact dermatitis.*)

Bulla is a large vesicle. (*Poison oak,* second-degree burn.)

Blister is a term used for both vesicle and bulla.

Pustule is a pus-filled elevation smaller than a pea. (*Acne,* iodide drug reacton, *smallpox, folliculitis,* chocolate dermatitis.)

Furuncle is a large pustule.

Abscess and *carbuncle* are big furuncles.

Wheal or *hive* is a solid elevation as small as a match head or as big as a palm. (Insect bites, angioedema.)

Oozing is seen when serum exudes from broken skin. (Broken second-degree bulla, *atopic eczema, impetigo, abrasion.*)

Crusting or *scabbing* is the coagulation of blood and serum on the surface of denuded skin. (Healing chickenpox, abraded skin.)

Scaling is the visible exfoliation of the skin. (Pityriasis.)

Ulceration is a deep loss of skin.

Pigmentation refers to an increase in melanin. (Suntan, *moles.*)

Scarring is the replacement of lost tissue by connective tissue.

Skin tests used by the doctors for the confirmation of disease are fairly accurate and frequently highly specific. Most are mentioned in the sections dealing with the disease for which the test is specific. (See *Hypersensitivity,* in *Allergy,* Section 3.)

Dick test is not much used now, but is a skin test to see if a person is immune to the rash toxin of *scarlet fever.* A standard dose of *strep* toxin is injected into the skin; if no redness of at least a centimeter is present the next day, it is assumed that the patient is immune to that strep toxin (he can still get other strep infections).

Frei test is of diagnostic aid in *lymphogranuloma venereum* (see Section 2). The killed *virus* is injected into the skin, and if the patient has had the disease, a red papule will appear in two days.

Shick test is a skin test used to determine a person's immunity to *diphtheria* toxin. If a patient is immune to diphtheria, no local skin reaction will be present seventy-two hours after the infection of the toxin from this bacterium. If a red area develops, it means that he is susceptible and should be immunized. After three DPT shots, the infant almost always shows the immune reaction. Although the test is little used at present, it has some value in ascertaining a patient's immune response.

Other skin tests available:

Blastomycin for *blastomycosis* (see Section 9)
Brucella for *brucellosis* (see Section 2)
Coccidioidin for *coccidioidomycosis* (see Section 9)
Echinococcus for *echinococcal* disease (see Section 12)
Histoplasmin for *histoplasmosis* (see Section 9)
Toxoplasma for *toxoplasmosis* (see Section 2)
Trichinella for *trichinosis* (see Section 2)
Tularemia for *tularemia* (see Section 2)

Tuberculin skin test is the most widely used test for disease. If the tubercle bacillus has been inhaled into the *lungs* and the body reacts to this invasion, it becomes hypersensitive (see *Hypersensitivity,* Section 3) or allergic to the protein of the germ. This response takes about six weeks to develop after initial exposure to the bacteria and remains positive for years or life. When a small amount of this protein is injected into the skin by needle or tine test, the local cells react, and within 48 to 72 hours a red papule is easily noted. A chest X ray is taken to determine the extent of the initial lesion.

The most efficient testing method is to mass-screen a whole class or school with the tine (or multiple puncture) test. The positive reactors are X rayed to determine the extent of the disease, and all the child's contacts are X rayed. Someone has an open case; that is, usually an adult with a cavity in his lungs is exhaling tuberculosis germs onto contacts.

If the patient has been exposed to other bacilli related to tuberculosis, false positive reactions are occasionally obtained.

Spider angioma is a loop of a dilated blood vessel found in the skin from which radiate capillaries (like the legs of a spider). With pressure, the vessels bleach, and the angioma disappears. These vessel tufts usually form as a response to some long-forgotten, minor, penetrating trauma. When the child is old enough to hold still and/or wants it removed for cosmetic reasons (usually around age thirteen), an electric needle can be used to scar the central vessel which feeds blood to the "legs."

Sporotrichosis is a fungal disease usually manifest by nodules and skin ulcers. The fungus enters the skin through small breaks or abrasions, and the nodules occur along the lymph channels that drain the area. Lung involvement may resemble that of tuberculosis.

Response to treatment with iodides and/or amphotericin B is slow.

Stevens-Johnson syndrome—see *Erythema multiforme exudativum*

Stork bite—see *Hemangioma,* Section 5

Strawberry mark—see *Hemangioma,* Section 5

Sunlight reactions other than the usual red sunburn followed by tan pigmentation in several days are common:

a. Fair-skinned people with few pigment-producing cells just peel and stay white (no melanogenesis).

b. Exposure to sunlight while under treatment with *tetracycline* and some *tranquilizers* (see Section 4) may cause hives, eczematous lesions or itchy papules. The following drugs may also provoke skin eruptions when the ingester is exposed to sunlight: barbiturates, Benadryl®, Declomycin®, griseofulvin, oral contraceptives, Phenergan®, salicylates, and sulfa drugs.

c. Some susceptible people will overrespond to the first sunlight exposure in March or April with burning and itching soon followed by itchy red papules on cheeks, arms, and hands. Occasionally vesicles form suggesting poison oak dermatitis. Tanning eventually follows. The skin is normal all winter.

d. *Lupus erythematosus* may have to be considered and the rare Hartnup disease may express itself by the same solar eruption. *Por-*

phyria, a rare pigment metabolism disorder, may be first diagnosed after solar exposure because of the erythema and vesicles that occur. (See Section 13.)

Swimmer's itch is due to the penetration of the immature blood fluke. (See *Cercarial dermatitis.*)

Tinea capitis—see *Ringworm of the scalp*

Tinea corporis—see *Ringworm*

Tinea pedis—see *Athlete's foot*

Tinea versicolor is a mild but frequently chronic and recurrent fungus infection characterized by small or large, discrete or confluent, pigmented or hypopigmented areas of minimally scaling skin. The trunk is usually involved, but face, neck or shoulders may show this moth-eaten rash. The mother thinks her child hasn't bathed and he thinks it is flaking off sunburn.

A family search should be made for other cases. Sodium thiosulfate is the standard treatment, but a recurrence is expected.

Urticaria—see *Hives*

Vitiligo is the patchy loss of pigment from the skin. The moth-eaten appearance is more obvious in the summer as the normal skin surrounding the white areas responds to the sun with excess pigment. The only treatment is the use of cosmetic applications.

Warts are localized growths of skin due to a virus, not to dirt or to handling frogs. After months or years the usual ones on the hands may disappear spontaneously. When they appear on the bottom of the feet (the plantar area), they are called *plantar warts.* Because of the discomfort they produce, they are usually removed by surgery or chemical applications. X ray is now used less frequently.

Albeit innocuous, warts can be very persistent and a challenge to the dermatologist. Despite surgery, liquid nitrogen treatment, hypnosis, bismuth injections, and X ray, they can continue to recur.

Occasionally they all disappear as if the patient developed some sort of wart immunity.

Application of an ether extract of ground-up June bugs (Cantharone®) produces a vesiculation (blistering) which is often sufficient to separate the growth from the underlying dermis. This treatment is safe, leaves no scar, and its application is painless to the apprehensive child—bloodless surgery at its best. Recurrences in a family may be traced to a neglected wart on mother, father, or sibling. Vitamin A will help the skin shuck off warts.

Xanthomas are yellow tumors easily seen on the skin of eyelids, scalp, knuckles, or knees of victims with cholesterol metabolism anomalies. If the serum cholesterol is increased over a period of time, xanthomas may become multiple and obvious. *Cirrhosis* or biliary obstruction, uncontrolled *diabetes,* von Gierke's disease, and the lipoproteinemia syndromes may be associated with multiple xanthomata.

If the xanthomas are obvious and the blood cholesterol is normal, the patient must be evaluated for *lipidoses* or *white blood cell* abnormalities. They can occur, however, in normal people.

Xeroderma pigmentosum is a rare, hereditary, usually fatal skin disorder in which large freckles develop into skin cancers. Sunlight rapidly triggers photophobia, conjunctivitis, and freckling.

SECTION 7
Bones and Muscles

A. Bones

Epiphyses
Orthopedics
Ossification centers
Posture

B. Congenital deformities

Cervical rib
Club foot (Section 5)
Dislocated hips (Section 5)
Missing clavicles (Cleidocranial dysostosis)
Short neck (Klippel-Feil syndrome)
Wry neck (Torticollis) (also Section 5)

C. Bone pain

Bone spur (*Exostosis, Osteochondroma*)
Caffey's disease
Chondrosarcoma
Eosinophilic granuloma (also Neoplasms, Section 10)
Epiphysitis
- *Heel (Sever's disease)*
- *Hip (Coxa plana or Perthes' disease)*
- *Shin (Osgood-Schlatter's disease)*
- *Spine (Scheuermann's disease)*

Exostosis
Fracture (Section 1)
Ganglion
Giant cell tumor
Hand-Schuller-Christian disease
Hypervitaminosis A (Section 11)
Osteoma
Rib syndrome
Tennis elbow

D. Bone pain with fever

Caffey's disease
Ewing's sarcoma
Osteomyelitis
Tuberculosis (Pott's disease)

E. Bones break easily

Albers-Schönberg disease
Cyst of bone
Eosinophilic granuloma
Osteogenesis imperfecta

F. Joint pain or stiffness

Ankle strain
Arthritis
- *Allergic*
- *Hemophilic*
- *Juvenile rheumatoid*
- *Traumatic*

Arthrogryposis
Synovitis, traumatic (Hip)

G. Joint pain with fever

Arthritis
- *Juvenile rheumatoid (Still's disease)*
- *Lupus erythematosus* (Section 2)
- *Polyarteritis nodosa* (Section 2)
- *Septic*

Rheumatic fever (also Section 2)

H. Back pain, weakness or stiffness

Disk, ruptured intervertebral
Posture
Pott's disease
Scheuermann's disease
Scoliosis
Spondylitis, ankylosing
Spondylolisthesis
Vertebrae

I. Gait disorders

a. Drunken gait
- *Ataxia, cerebellar* (also Section 15)
- *Drugs* (also Section 4)

b. Foot drop
- *Hypotonia*
- *Lead poisoning* (Section 1)
- *Paralysis*
- *Poliomyelitis* (Sections 25, 15)

c. Stiff gait
- *Fracture of fibula*
- *Knee or ankle strain*
- *March fracture*
- *Muscular dystrophy*
- *Posture*
- *Shoes*
- *Spastic diplegia* (Section 15)
- *Synovitis*—see Hip

d. Rolling, lurching
- *Congenital subluxation* (see Hip)
- *Encephalitis* (Section 15)
- *Knock knees* (Genu valgum)
- *Vertigo* (Section 14)

J. Muscle pain

Back pain
- *Disk, ruptured intervertebral*

Cramps
Dermatomyositis (Section 6)
Glycogen storage disease
Myositis
- *Ossificans*
- *Traumatic*

Trichinosis (Section 2)
Wry neck (Torticollis)

K. Muscle weakness

Atrophy
Cervical rib
Glycogen storage disease
Hypotonia
Muscular dystrophy
Myasthenia (Section 15)
Paralysis
- *Periodic familial*

Poliomyelitis (Sections 2, 15)

L. Feet

Bunion
Clubfoot (Section 5)
Flat feet
- *Congenital*
- *Pronated ankles*
- *Rocker foot*

Hammer toe
Ingrown toenail
March fracture

Nails, toe
Pigeon toe
Shoes
Toe, overlapping little

M. Legs

Bowlegs (Genu varum)
Cyst behind knee (Baker's cyst)
Knee cap (Patella)
Knock knees (Genu valgum)
Tibial torsion
Weak knees (Genu recurvatum)

N. Hips

Arthritis
  Septic
Congenital subluxation
Coxa plana or Perthes' disease
Dislocated (Section 5)
Slipped epiphysis
Synovitis

O. Athletics

Boxing
  Cauliflower ear (Section 14)
Diet
Epilepsy and sports
Furuncle (Section 6)
Pulse rate (Section 8)
Rules

P. Injuries (also Section 1)

Ankle
Baseball finger
Knee
March fracture
Myositis
Pulled elbow (subluxation of head of radius—Section 1)
Tennis elbow

Albers-Schönberg disease, or osteosclerosis fragilis or osteopetrosis, is a generalized hardening of the bones that increases their susceptibility to fractures. No evidence of this genetic trait is obvious until an X ray is taken, at which time the increased amount of calcium and density of the bones is noted. *Cataracts, blindness, deafness, anemia,* enlargement of *liver* and *spleen* may occur. Some healthy adults may have a mild form of this disease.

Alkaline phosphatase, an *enzyme* detected by a blood test, is elevated during active bone formation. Lack or excess is related to various bone diseases. Growing children have a higher level than adults. It is eliminated by the liver; patients with liver disease may have high levels.

Ankle strain usually occurs when the weight of the body is imposed on the turned-in, flexed foot. The ligaments extending from the outer ankle bone to the side of the foot are torn. Pain, swelling and, after a few days, a bruise are noted. If most of the fibers are intact, a few days of rest are sufficient to restore painless, normal function. If most of the fibers are torn, pain and swelling persist and a permanently weak ankle, prone to repeated sprains is the result. X rays, plaster immobilization, and possible tendon surgery may be necessary. Improper mobilization or too early ambulation are the chief causes of an unstable, weak ankle. Occasionally a hairline fracture occurs in one of the supporting foot bones; without proper immobilization it may undergo degeneration.

Progressive exercises against resistance give strength to the supporting muscles and are the best way to insure a strong joint. The low shoes now worn by football players have not been associated with an increase in ankle injuries.

Arthritis is joint inflammation.

Allergic arthritis, or at least joint aches related to certain food ingestion, is fairly common but should not lead to permanent disability. I assume an internal "hive" or some type of tissue swelling in the joint lining accounts for the symptoms which might last a day or two. Citrus, tomato, chocolate, milk, pork, nuts, fish, or seasonings are the likely offending agents.

Hemophilic arthritis is a common complication of hemophilia. After a trivial injury a joint—usually the knee—becomes acutely and painfully distended with blood. Reabsorption leaves the joint tender and swollen. With each recurrence recovery is less complete. The adjacent muscles atrophy because of disease and the joint becomes stiff, resembling rheumatoid arthritis. Rest and elevation are important, but the only treatment is antihemophiliac globulin. (See Section 8.)

Juvenile rheumatoid arthritis (Still's disease) is a severe, progressive, crippling disease somewhat related to rheumatic fever. It appears to be one of the diseases in which the body's immune mechanisms overreact. The joints swell and become painfully stiff. Because of disuse, the adjacent muscles atrophy, thus exaggerating the problem. Modern drugs (cortisone, ACTH) and physiotherapy are instilling motion and hope into these victims. Much can be accomplished if treatment is begun early. Many cases are controlled with big doses of vitamins C and B complex, calcium, and zinc.

The chief problem is making an accurate diagnosis, for the onset of the disease (more frequent in girls at age four or five years) may be sneaky—with vague joint aches and irritability—or it may come as a violent 106° temperature that rages for days or weeks without any other clues.

The joint inflammation (knee, wrist, and cervical spine most frequently) comes and goes for many years. About half the treated patients recover completely at puberty with no residual deformity. Some develop permanent deformities before the disease quiets down. About one third go on to adult rheumatoid arthritis.

Septic arthritis, or bacterial arthritis is most often due to the *staphylococcus* and is usually dramatic with sudden onset of chills, high fever, and severe pain—usually about the hip.

The knee and shoulder joints are the next most common sites, but this suppurative arthritis can occur in any joint and have an insidious onset with only low grade fever, stiffness, and pain. Infection in some other organ (teeth, tonsils, lungs) plus some forgotten minor trauma may be inciting factors. *Tuberculosis, brucellosis,* and *gonorrhea* are occasionally joint invaders. After suitable blood tests and X rays for diagnosis, huge intravenous doses of anti-staphylococcus antibiotics are given in the hospital. Traction to counteract the spasm of the muscles about the joint is necessary to keep the joint surfaces from further damage as pus in the joint space is very destructive. Authorities recommend needle-tapping and drainage of the joint space. Although the infection may be cured, the scar tissue remaining may preclude perfect joint function.

Traumatic arthritis, as the name suggests, is the pain and swelling in a joint that follows an injury—most commonly in the *knee.*

If a joint is injured to the point of swelling, pain, and limitation of motion, then rest and support are indicated. Cold applications in the first twelve hours are worthwhile to control swelling. Thereafter heat, gentle and intermittent, may encourage the swelling to resolve itself more quickly. Excessive, constant, and deep heat (diathermy and ultra sound) may be dangerous if used early as it may *increase* the swelling. Deep heat is more beneficial for old injuries. Use of the joint prior to healing only causes further injury and may produce more internal scarring. No one seems to have any guidelines to indicate whether the victim needs orthopedic attendance for a sprain on the first day, or whether he should wait until seven days go by and face the usual, "You should have called last week." However, persistent, severe pain on weight bearing or with motion of the joint usually brings the normally alert patient to the doctor in the first three days.

Arthrogryposis is the congenital stiffness of a number of joints because of thickness and inelasticity of the joint capsules. It may be mild or severe; the adjacent muscles are usually thin, weak, and replaced with fibrous tissue. Clubfeet may be associated. Partial correction may be accomplished by a combined approach using bracing, exercises, and surgery.

Athletics includes any organized program to improve physical fitness, either as a team effort or by individual activity. Competition is the usual motivating force.

The toddler loves to use his big muscles for running, jumping, and climbing, and needs little encouragement to exercise—just room to do it in.

Suitable sports for children before maturity are running, swimming, and non-contact games. Strengthening the muscles about the knee by running should help to support the knee. (See *Knee.*)

Most schools have physical-education programs in which all children must participate to some degree. Athletic ability and strength are almost completely dependent on genetically determined traits. The active, agile child with straight legs finds he can run well. He does so and is rewarded for running well. This encourages him to run more, which soon makes him even better at it. The fat, *knock-kneed* boy hates to run because he always loses. He runs less because he hates to be ridiculed; any skill he had is lost from disuse. He might, however, do well in swimming. Parents who want their children to do well athletically must first stand back and get a good look at their child's type, then decide in which endeavor he would be most likely to succeed. (Motivation and family interest—or pressure—provide the final push.)

All sizes: wrestling, because contestants are matched for weight
Small, thin, wiry: track, baseball, gymnastics, tennis
Long, thin: sprinting, cross-country, basketball
Heavy, weak ligaments: swimming, billiards

Orthopedic surgeons see so many injuries that they suggest that no contact sports be allowed at least until the adolescent is fully grown with fused *epiphyses* (after the cartilage between shaft and growing ends of bones is completely calcified). Sports-minded children will not heed this warning, of course. Supplied with proper equipment and opportunity at school, pressure from the coach (who recognizes potential), and support from parents, the young athlete may find his real place in a life in which academic or hobby interests play only minor roles.

The following are a few minimum requirements for a school-based athletic program in which contact sports are featured:

1. A well-trained coach or trainer
2. An M.D., preferably an orthopedic surgeon, on call and in attendance at games
3. Up-to-date protective equipment that fits
4. Fluids and minerals supplied freely before, during, and after exertion
5. No head spearing (butting opponent with the head). (Traumatized neck vertebrae may result)
6. Preseason training to increase muscle strength and endurance
7. Some knowledge of knee mechanics applied to equipment and practice:

(a) Heel cleats should not be used. If the foot is flatly fixed on turf and the leg is hit, the knee will give way. If the heel can slide away at impact, the knee may not be injured.

(b) Deep knee bends do strengthen thigh muscles, but tend to put severe strain on the cartilaginous inner surface of the patella (knee cap). The cartilage may degenerate; a painful grating may follow. Half-squats or running serves to strengthen muscles just as well.

(c) Runners who might be blocked or tackled should run on their toes and take short, quick strides.

(d) The tall, rapidly growing adolescent who is flatfooted, knock-kneed, and whose knees can bend backward slightly, is a greater risk in contact sports than the mature youth who is slightly bowlegged. The former is usually not anxious to be active in sports anyway; his wishes should be respected, or he should be encouraged to run, swim, or at least avoid contact sports until he is older.

8. Careful grouping according to sex, weight, size, skill, and physical maturation

9. A pitcher should be a physically mature adolescent before he is allowed to throw a curved or screw ball. (The rotational torque on his elbow may cause permanent damage.)

10. A pitcher under thirteen or fourteen years of age should pitch only two or three innings per game

11. Taping ankles prior to a game may prevent the more serious ligamentous tears but probably does not preclude minor strains

Society applauds the aggressive male, but sports appear to be the only area where he may be hostile and still socially acceptable.

Athletics for epileptics. In no way should a controlled epileptic be forced to abandon sports. A variety of long-term studies does not provide any valid evidence that contact sports increase susceptibility or increase frequency or severity of seizures.

Boxing apparently leads to the *brain damage* that many of us expected. A British study indicated that the longer the career and the more fights the boxer had, the more likely was there to be evidence of brain damage, *retinal* detachment, double vision, slurred speech, defective memory, shuffling *gait,* and tremors. (See *Cauliflower ear,* Section 14).

A young man determined to embark on a boxing career should be aware of the risks. Close medical supervision is mandatory.

Diet for athletes. The myth of lots of protein, mineral, and vitamin supplements has been exploded by recent studies. Adequate nutrition is important, but for sustained physical effort (cycling, long-distance running, or cross-country skiing), the inclusion of extra carbohydrates and liquids along with the hard work of physical training seems to be of consistent benefit.

Atrophy is the reduction of size of a tissue or organ, usually from disuse.

Calf (gastrocnemius) muscle atrophy and front of shin bone (anterior tibial) muscle atrophy are common following polio and force the victim to lift his foot high and slap it down to walk.

Usually muscles atrophy from lack of use because of nerve injury, *muscular dystrophy,* or pain (*arthritis*). The most common cause of atrophy is the disuse of muscles from bed rest.

Quadriceps atrophy is the decrease in size and strength of the large thigh muscles always seen during prolonged bed rest. A forced program of simple straight-leg raising will help maintain the tone of these important antigravity muscles so that convalescent ambulation will not be so difficult.

Back pain is unusual in children. Persistent pain unassociated with some obvious trauma suggests a congenital weakness of the spine (*spina bifida,* lumbosacral asymmetry, *spondylolisthesis.*) Acquired lesions (*scoliosis,* lordosis, and *epiphysial* disorders) often sneak up on an adolescent. X rays are required for diagnosis. Disk protrusion as a cause of pain is unusual in children. *Tuberculosis, ankylosing spondylitis,* and *rheumatoid* disease are uncommon, but cause pain and limitation of spine flexibility.

Ill-advised exercises once thought to strengthen and increase the flexibility of the back are now known to be dangerous. Touching the toes with the knees straight creates a leverage on the bodies of the vertebrae many times the weight of the exerciser. The intervertebral disks may suffer if the exercise is vigorous and prolonged.

Baker's cyst is a tense, nontender, fluid-filled sac appearing just behind the knee joint. Repeated friction of muscles and tendons due to stooping and squatting allow this to form. Surgical removal is suggested if symptoms develop.

Baseball finger results when the end of a finger or thumb is suddenly flexed by a blow. The tendon that extends the end of the finger may be torn loose, occasionally pulling a piece of bone with it. A splint or plaster holding the middle joint flexed and the last joint extended for a month may be sufficient to allow a firm, usable reattachment. Surgery is necessary for a nonunion.

Bones (see *Broken bones,* Section 1) are the girders of the body, giving it shape, protecting vital areas (such as the brain and heart), and allowing motion.

Maturation of the bones can be evaluated by X rays of the growth centers. As these centers mature, calcium is deposited in the cartilage, and these denser areas can be seen in the films. Standard age tables for the appearance of these ossification centers indicate whether bone age is advanced or retarded. (See *Epiphyses.*)

Bone spur—see *Exostosis, Osteochondroma*

Bunion is a deformity of the large toe causing it to deviate laterally (to the other toes) while the head of the metatarsal bone deviates medially. Hereditary predisposition and tight, pointed shoes are contributory.

Caffey's disease, or infantile cortical hyperostosis, is the increased thickening of one or several of the bones. The jaw bone (mandible) and collarbones (clavicles) are most commonly involved. The infant may run a fever, become fretful, and refuse to move the affected part. It may appear as an abscess or be misdiagnosed as a bone infection, *hypervitaminosis A, scurvy,* or trauma. The disease lasts weeks or months. The cause is unknown, but all cases clear without residual defect.

Cervical rib is an extra rib arising from the last (7th) cervical vertebra. It is usually bilateral and impinges upon or narrows the space through which the nerve plexus and subclavian artery must pass from the upper chest area to the arm. Pain and tingling of the little and ring fingers and of the hand on that side may progress to weakness, numbness, and absence of pulse. Similar symptoms occur in the absence of a cervical rib if the scalene muscles (from vertebrae to first rib) are thick and pinch the nerves and arteries between them (scalenus anticus syndrome). Surgery is indicated in either case.

Chondrosarcoma is a malignant bone tumor usually appearing at knee, shoulder, or in the pelvic bones. Increase in size and pain necessitate removal. As X-ray therapy is ineffective, amputation is the treatment of choice.

Cleidocranial dysostosis is a genetic defect in which the collarbones (clavicles) are partially or completely absent, sometimes to the degree that the shoulders can be apposed in front of the chest. The skull bones are not properly ossified and the head may bulge out at front and sides. No treatment is available, but patients usually lead normal lives.

Clubfoot—see *Newborn, Congenital abnormalities,* Section 5

Cortical hyperostosis—see *Caffey's disease*

Coxa plana—see *Hip*

Cramps, or charleyhorse, muscle spasm, or growing pains, are usually nocturnal. They may be confused with *rheumatic fever* arthralgia, but are not migratory. They typically appear in a healthy, active boy who, after a day of heavy exercise, falls exhausted into bed. In about an hour he awakens with a scream and clutches his shin, calf, instep, or behind his knee. Heat, massage, and aspirin allow him to sleep again in about an hour.

Local accumulation of lactic acid following exercise, plus a temporary reduction of *calcium,* seems to be the underlying factor in producing the painful muscle spasm. There is a familial tendency. We all need about 1,000 milligrams of calcium a day. Dolomite or bone meal should help.

Vitamin D in doses of 1,000 units per day for a week should prevent the attacks for several weeks when treatment might be necessary again if the pain recurs.

Vitamin E (tocopherol) may be curative also because it improves glycogen storage in the muscles.

If pain is present during the day, then organic disease must be ruled out. In *rheumatic fever* the pain moves from joint to joint; in rheumatoid arthritis morning stiffness of joints is usually present; in hip disease, the pain is worse during the day—*coxa plana, tuberculosis* of the hip, slipped *epiphysis;* in knee disease (or hip or ankle) a limp is present— *Osgood-Schlatter's disease;* in *osteoid osteoma* or cancer of the bone the pain is present day and night. (See *Sedimentation rate,* Section 8.)

Cyst (see *Baker's cyst, Ganglion*) of the bone usually appears during the period of rapid growth (nine to fourteen years) in the upper end of humerus or femur. It may reveal itself as a dull ache or may be fractured by a mild trauma because the overlying bone has been thinned. The fracture may initiate new bone growth which obliterates the cavity. Scraping out the cyst and inserting bone chips is usually curative.

Disk, ruptured intervertebral. This is rare before adulthood, but might occur after lifting, a fall on the buttocks or a blow to the back—anything that might allow this disk pad (between the bodies of the vertebrae) to push through the confining ligaments of the spine and compress nerve fibers near the spinal cord.

Severe low back pain first occurs. As time passes the backache comes on with little inciting stimulus (cough, sneeze). Finally the pain in the back is largely replaced by buttocks, calf, ankle, and foot pain. Numbness is usually associated.

Dystrophy, muscular—see *Muscular dystrophy*

Eosinophilic granuloma is usually a solitary lesion in a rib, the skull, or a vertebra. Local bone pain and slight swelling or a fracture draw attention to the area. X ray reveals a punched-out area. X-ray treatment, curettage, and insertion of bone chips are usually restorative. It may progress to *Hand-Schuller-Christian disease* months or years later (see *Neoplasms,* Section 10).

Epiphyses are the ossification (or bone-growth) centers of the long bones. They are seen in X rays as areas of *calcium,* separated from the ends of the bone shafts by an area of cartilage (which appears clear in the X ray). Their appearance in the X rays is helpful in determining the age of the fetus. If the epiphyses at the lower end of the femora are present in the X ray of a woman's abdomen near the end of her pregnancy, it suggests that the baby is full-term.

If ossification centers of at least two wrist bones and epiphysis of the radius are not seen by four to five months of age, *thyroid* deficiency (*hypothyroidism*) is a strong possibility. Wrist X rays are taken in evaluating growth failure. The epiphyses have a characteristic appearance in *rickets, scurvy, lead poisoning,* and in epiphysitis. (*Sever's disease, Osgood-Schlatter's disease.*) *Coxa plana* is a necrosis of the epiphysis of the femur at the hip joint.

Epiphysitis (see *Scheuermann's disease, Osgood-Schlatter's disease, Sever's disease*) is an inflammation of the growing end of some bones and appears at specific ages depending on the bone involved.

Ewing's sarcoma develops from the marrow of a long bone causing pain and fever. Surgery and X ray offer little hope of cure.

Exostosis is a bone spur, usually multiple, hereditary, and appearing at the ends of long bones. It is not malignant, but surgery is necessary if it interferes with function or causes pain. Periodic evaluation is necessary as a small percent may become malignant.

Flat foot is the normal appearance of children's feet; they should not be judged by adult standards. They are short, wide, and thick in infancy and do not begin to look like "feet" until about five or six years of age. Children's feet look especially flat from age two to four; this is accentuated by the knock-kneed appearance at the same age. The arch of the standing five-year-old should be high enough to insert a finger underneath. About 70 to 80 percent of children have flat feet despite stiff shoes or bare feet or lifts or supports. Genetic factors are more responsible than shoes for the ultimate arch.

If there is a normal range of motion of ankle and foot joints, and if the child has no pain on walking, the feet probably require no special shoes. People who walk with feet everted (externally rotated, opposite of *pigeon toed*) will exaggerate a flat-footed tendency, and pain and tenderness will develop in the tendons just above the ankle bone on the inside of the shin. Learning to walk with feet slightly turned in will relieve this.

Shoe salesmen will often insist that parents purchase high-laced stiff shoes with a built-in Thomas heel (part of the heel extends forward under the arch). After a few years of wearing these shoes, the child develops an arch and the assumption is that the shoes have done it. We know, however, that the arch was going to develop anyway. High-laced shoes stay on the feet better, since children are prone to pull shoes off, but soft-soled shoes, moccasins, or tennis shoes are better for growing feet, as they allow greater use of foot muscles. Shoes are only needed for protection from sharp objects on floor or ground. Foot and ankle support is a matter of inborn ligamentous integrity and some muscle education, not stiff shoes.

Pronated ankles are usually a family trait, associated with flat feet. The ankles and arches roll inward, and shoes often wear out rapidly on the inside. If pain in arches and calves is associated with this, some arch support in the shoe will help the symptoms, but will not correct the pronation. The support lifts up the arch only while in position; the foot usually slides away from the correction. Some effort to strengthen the foot and calf muscles may provide relief. Running barefoot on wet sand at the beach seems appropriate; or a systematic program of foot exercises using a sponge-rubber-covered board may ease the cramps. (Vimulator by Vitaped Co. is one such device.) (See *Knock-knees.*)

Congenital flat foot (or rocker foot) is a pathological condition in which some bones of the foot are out of alignment pushing down where the arch should be. The heel is also everted; the victim walks on the inner border of his heel. (When the patient is viewed from behind, the Achilles tendon lies more to the medial side.) No permanent cure is possible with splints, lifts, braces, or built-up shoes. A specially molded plastic shoe insert may control the condition as weight bearing during growth with the arch in this abnormal position tends to aggravate the deformity. Definite improvement *can* occur but it takes years. Surgery on the bones and ligaments is recommended near the end of full growth.

Foot—see *Clubfoot,* Section 5; *Flat foot; Pigeon toe; Shoes*

Gait in the normal child varies with age, but once the broadbased, halting steps of early toddling have been mastered, each child develops a painless rhythmical gait of his own. Many first steps suggest a neurological defect: an infant may advance one foot and slide the other one into position near it as if he had had a stroke or had been in a chain gang. Apparently the nerves to the muscles of the legs develop faster on one side than on the other. This equalizes in three or four weeks.

Ataxia or drunken, unsteady, broadbased gait is seen in cerebellar conditions or drug overdose (*alcohol, phenobarbital, antihistamines, Dilantin®, tranquilizers,* etc.).

In cerebellar *ataxia* (see Section 15) the patient drifts to the affected side; a tumor in the cerebellum must be ruled out.

Ear infections may cause unsteady gait (see *Vertigo,* Section 14).

The child who has suffered a severe encephalitis walks with short steps with hips and knees slightly flexed. He throws his hips from side to side in a lurch.

Genu valgum or knock-knees, if severe enough, may force the child to swing his legs out in a curve to avoid rubbing his knees together.

Some limps are due to ill-fitting shoes. The diagnosis can be made by watching the child walk while barefoot and noting if the limp disappears.

The most common limp is that due to an injury or pulled muscle. It usually takes ten days to recover normal function.

Inflammation such as synovitis (see *Hip*) or *rheumatic fever* will usually allow walking with a limp, but *osteomyelitis* and *septic arthritis* are usually too painful to permit weight bearing. If the child can bear some weight and limps less after the first four days, watchful waiting is in order. If the limp is worse after five days or continues after ten days, it should be investigated. Some children sleep soundly in a position which pinches the nerve that passes over the outside of the knee. Paralysis of the lower leg seems obvious for about an hour after arising. It should be temporary.

One unusual case of leg paralysis due to pressure on the sciatic nerve was reported two years ago in a ten-year-old girl who sat on a cement step reading comics for thirty minutes. She could not stand immediately afterward and noted numbness and tingling below the knee. Complete recovery required nine months.

Muscular dystrophy forces the patient to walk on his toes because his calf muscles are contracted.

Spastic diplegia or tenseness of muscles would preclude an easy, lithe gait. All variations of this are possible—from slight awkwardness to inability to put one foot in front of another.

Weak muscles, such as might occur after *poliomyelitis,* would affect the gait, depending on which muscles were involved. The muscles on the front of the calf raise the foot; if these are weak, a loose, flapping foot would result. If the calf muscle is weak, the patient cannot push off, as he is unable to lift his heel.

Foot drop in a child is a common sign of *lead poisoning.* He has to throw his foot out (like a swimmer in flippers) so his toes clear the floor. The toe hits the floor first, then the heel.

Trauma to calf or thigh or foot will force the child to limp. Muscle bruising or myositis usually permit ambulation but with a limp. A broken bone is usually too painful to allow ambulation. An incomplete fracture might allow a few days of weight bearing.

Ganglion is a cyst containing a clear gelatin material usually found connected to a tendon sheath in the wrist. If the cyst is tender and interferes with motion, surgical removal is advised. (Rupturing the so-called Bible bump by a sharp blow with the Good Book was once practiced, but recurrence was common.)

Genu recurvatum is the condition of hyperextensibility of the knee joint. (Knee can be bent backward beyond the vertical.) If the trait continues into adolescence, the youth should not be allowed to participate in contact sports, as this unstable knee joint is susceptible to injury. Severe forms due to injury must be corrected surgically.

Genu valgum (knock-knees) is the normal look of almost all two- to four-year-old children when standing up. At age three the trait is at its peak. When this child stands straight with the knees barely touching, a gap of two to three inches will be noted between the ankle bones, and the arch is virtually nonexistent. *Without special shoes* this distance will diminish until age six or seven, when the child usually assumes the leg proportions he will retain his whole life. About 60 percent of adults have about one to two inches of space between their ankle bones when standing erect with knees just touching. About 20 percent of adults have "perfect" legs—knees and ankles touching easily when at attention. All others are bow-legged. Skilled runners and agile athletes are in these last two groups.

Separation of more than four inches if associated with pain and pronation of ankles might suggest the use of a Thomas heel or arch (metatarsal) support to invert the foot, drive the knees apart, and thus provide freer ambulation. The severely knock-kneed child may have to run by swinging his legs in a grotesque arc to avoid banging his knees together. A vertical bar the length of the leg with a tight strap about the knee may encourage the growing leg to straighten.

Genu varum (bowlegs). Most children look a little bowlegged when they start to walk. It does not represent *rickets,* which is rarely seen these days, but is rather a natural curving of the legs. Usually, after the child walks and grows—or by the time he gets beyond two years of age—his legs become more knock-kneed, and he looks flat-footed. It may be associated with or aggravated by pigeon-toed feet, which should be corrected. Persistence of bowed legs into adulthood is usually a genetic feature and, if not severe, is compatible with increased athletic skills.

Grandmother's admonition not to let a baby walk too early is based on her fear of rickets, or soft bones. Nowadays, almost all milk (except skimmed) contains vitamin D, and babies receive supplements of vitamin D along with other vitamins. If a baby has been taking adequate doses of vitamin D, his mild bow-legged appearance is normal. It is frustrating to the baby to be restricted from walking. If he wants to walk early, he should. If his back and legs bother him, he will stop walking and sit down. (See *Rickets,* Section 11.)

It is difficult to determine when an exaggerated bowleg tendency becomes a pathological condition. X rays might be worthwhile for the doubtful case; an abnormal *epiphysis* (growing end of tibia) may be revealed. Surgery is suggested if bracing is ineffective for these rare cases.

Giant cell tumor is a benign tumor found at the end of long bones after age 5 years. Swelling, nocturnal pain suggest an X ray. The X ray shows an expanding, calcium-deficient area with thin overlying bone, resembling a cyst. Scooping out the tumor followed by insertion of bone chips may be enough treatment.

Glycogen storage disease. In one type of this disease, glycogen is stored normally in the muscles, but it cannot be broken down to glucose due to a deficiency of the enzyme, glucose-6-phosphatase. The patient may do well unless he overexerts, when severe cramps and weakness force him to slow down. (See *Glycogen* in Sections 8, 10, and 12.)

Hammer toe is assumed to be a genetic defect as it is often bilateral and familial. The second toe is usually involved. The first toe joint is sharply flexed downward so the tip of the toe (instead of the ball) strikes the floor. A callus overlies the flexed joint; another callus forms at the tip. Tight shoes or socks aggravate the problem. When noticed in infancy a piece of tape might be placed over the flexed joint and anchored under the adjacent toes. Daily extending the toe might reduce the defect. Failing in this, surgery is the definitive treatment.

Hand-Schuller-Christian disease is a condition of unknown cause (enzyme defect?) in which cells (usually *eosinophils,* see *Blood cells,* Section 8) invade the bone (usually skull) but also cause skin eruptions, mouth lesions and, if the hypothalamic area of the brain is involved, *diabetes insipidus* (see Section 10). It usually begins in the preschooler with growth failure, anemia, irritability, and tender bones.

No known treatment exists, but anticancer therapy shows promise. X-ray radiation may involute the bone lesions. (See *eosinophilic granuloma,* this section, and also Section 10.)

Hip is the ball-in-socket joint between the femur and the pelvic bone. It is a stable joint because it is nestled in this socket and is surrounded with a capsule of tough fibrous tissue and big muscles.

Congenital subluxation of the hip joint is usually diagnosable at birth, but may not be obvious until one year of age when the child takes a few steps. As the head of the femur is not securely locked in the socket, it slides up the side of the pelvic bone. To balance this weakness, the child bends his trunk over to the affected side in order to lift up the opposite foot to step.

Every baby should be tested for this weakness at birth and again at the six-week checkup. If the thigh bone seems to click when manipulated or the distance from the groin to the knee seems shortened or the leg cannot be easily abducted (turned outward), X rays should be taken to evaluate the problem. Special braces are used to hold the femur in proper position; this is often enough to encourage a good joint formation.

In subluxation, the head of the femur is partially unseated from its usual position. Dislocation means that the head is completely out of the socket. Subluxation may go undetected until the child starts to walk; then dislocaton occurs because the faulty hip joint is unable to support the weight of the body.

Treatment is much easier if the diagnosis is made early; sometimes just bulky diapers are sufficient to force abduction. In countries where mothers constantly carry their babies about on their backs with their legs separated, this condition is almost unknown. Late treatment would require a body cast or operative reduction, but normal function is frequently not obtained.

Coxa plana or *Perthes' disease* mainly affects males between five and ten years of age. A limp that persists for two or more weeks brings the child to the doctor who can find nothing but muscle spasm. Pain is usually vague—an ache in the groin, inside of thigh or knee. X rays reveal that the *epiphysis* at the head of the femur is undergoing destruction (aseptic neurosis); the *calcium* fragments and finally reossifies. This takes two years or more to run the cycle.

No cause has been found. Extra vitamin C, calcium, magnesium, and vitamin D will encourage healing.

Standard treatment is no weight bearing until reossification has taken place. This is no easy task for a mother with a lively five- to ten-year-old boy!

Portions of the epiphysis die over several weeks time. The regenerating bone is slow to calcify and is unable to withstand the stress of weight bearing. If the child is ambulatory, it will heal, but with a permanent deformity. Non-weight-bearing is essential until evidence of complete reossification of the epiphysis appears in the X ray (two to three years). Failure to adhere to this no-weight-bearing rule will usually result in a permanent limp, shorter leg, muscle atrophy, limitations of hip motion, and arthritic changes.

Septic arthritis (see *Arthritis*) shows itself with high fever, severe pain, and spasm of hip muscles.

Slipped epiphysis is more likely seen in the heavy child, so weight bearing has been assumed to cause this slipping of the growing head of the femur.

The rapidly growing boy (age ten to seventeen) is the most susceptible. He might have suffered an almost forgotten injury a few weeks before he develops symptoms. A dull ache in the groin and/or pain and stiffness in the inner side of the thigh and knee are relieved by rest. A limp soon develops. As the epiphysis slips off the neck of the femur (thigh bone) due to the shearing force of the body weight, the pain and limp increase. Surgery using nails or pins to hold the epiphysis in place during growth is the recommended treatment.

Synovitis is a traumatic inflammation of the hip joint and the most common cause of a limp in a child. Pain may be about the hip, thigh or knee. The inciting injury may have been ignored in the excitement of play. Occasionally a tonsil infection is associated. It is difficult to abduct (turn out) the thigh at the hip because of the painful spasm. Some avoidance of weight bearing is worthwhile, albeit impossible with some age groups. Traction may be necessary. The limp should be almost gone in seven to ten days; if not, *Coxa plana* must be considered.

Hyperostosis—see *Caffey's disease*

Hypotonia, or lack of muscle tone, may be the result of a number of conditions. Birth trauma to the brain may cause hypotonia instead of spasticity. *Myasthenia gravis, kernicterus, poliomyelitis, muscular dystrophy, rickets, scurvy, malnutrition,* and *hypopotassemia* will have accompanying hypotonia.

A congenital type of hypotonia prevents the child from walking at the usual age, but he may catch up by late childhood and appear almost normal, in contrast to the usual myopathies which cause progressive weakness and deformity. (See *Floppy infant syndrome,* Section 15.)

Ingrown toenail usually follows cutting the nails too short or too curved so that the nail grows into the skin. Tight shoes (or socks) or pressure from sleeping prone in the spread eagle (or frog position) will force the skin against the nail. Like a sliver in the skin, an infection follows (*paronychia*). Nightly packs (alcohol and glycerin, equal parts, on a cotton ball) placed over the area and then covered with plastic, and elevating the corners of the nail with bits of cotton while awaiting the nail to grow out beyond the skin may be enough. This treatment takes three weeks; if unsuccessful, surgery may be the next step. Internal antibiotics may be necessary for cellulitis or lymphangitis. Occasionally pus undermines the nail; when it sloughs off, the skin heals and a new nail will grow normally. Always cut the toenail off *square* and *beyond* the skin edge.

Klippel-Feil syndrome describes the presence of fewer than the normal number of cervical vertebrae. The neck is short, the hairline low and neck motion may be limited.

Knee is a joint with a complicated gliding and rotating motion rather than a simple hinge-like action. Running and half squats are the best exercises to maintain its stability. Injuries to the supportive structures (ligaments, cartilage, or menisci) are frequently encountered in sports. Sudden twisting with knees flexed or sudden standing with foot turned out or turning with foot firmly fixed to the ground are the usual actions causing injury or tearing of the two semilunar cartilages (menisci)—crescent-shaped shock absorbers between femur and tibia. The above forces will split them or tear them away from the ligaments on the sides of the knees.

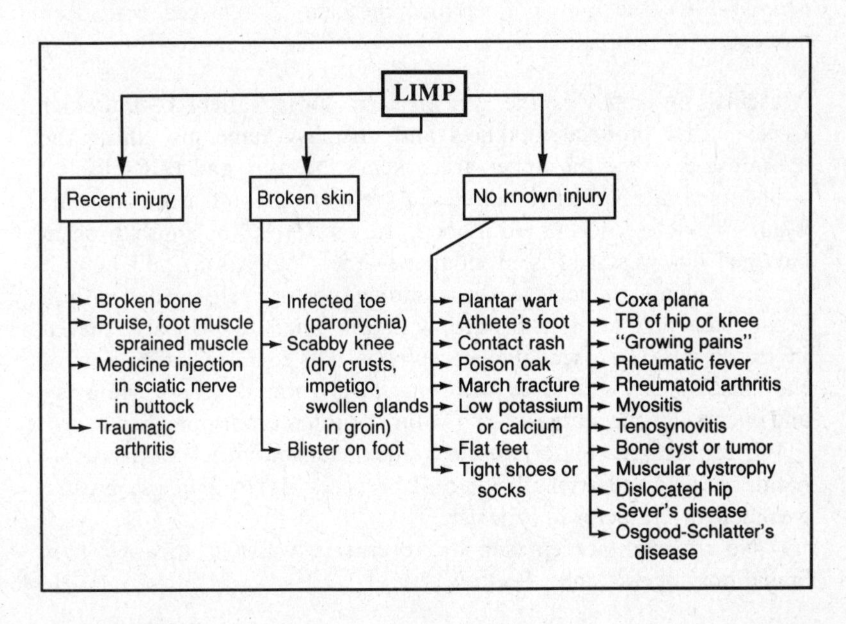

Knee injuries require careful diagnostic study before appropriate treatment can be outlined intelligently. Permanent damage to ligaments can lead to arthritic changes due to excessive instability. Various combinations of disability result; effusion, giving-away, locking, clicking, tenderness and atrophy of the thigh muscles. A torn meniscus is removed surgically (see *Patella*).

Marble bones—see *Albers-Schönberg disease*

March fracture occurs after vigorous exercise or a prolonged hike. The mid shaft of the second metatarsal gives way from this stress. Pain, tenderness, and some swelling are noticed in the mid-arch. The thin fracture line usually does not show in the X ray until a callus forms at the site in the third week. No weight bearing with crutches is sufficient, but casting for three weeks may allow the bone to heal with less discomfort.

Muscles are protein contractile cells varying in length from a few millimeters (inner ear) to almost a yard long (thigh). Each muscle fiber receives one motor end plate, a branch of a nerve. Sensory nerve endings send messages to the brain to tell the owner where his muscle is or what it is doing. If the nerve is cut or dies (after *poliomyelitis*), the muscle fiber atrophies and is replaced with scar tissue.

Muscular dystrophy is the general term for a variety of muscular diseases that produce weakness and atrophy. Some just affect the eye muscles, some the upper arms, some the back and calf muscles, while some affect all the muscles. A few are present at birth; some begin in adolescence or adulthood. In one type, the muscles seem enlarged but weakness is pronounced—the child has to pull himself up on a chair to achieve the standing posture. He walks with a broad base and leans backward with the small of his back curved in (lordosis). The pseudohypertrophy is due to fatty infiltration of the muscles. Some children with one form of the disease waste away and eventually succumb to heart failure or intercurrent infection.

Electrical reaction of muscles, reflex changes, muscle *biopsy,* evaluation of *gait* and strength may all be necessary to diagnose muscle weakness or *muscular dystrophies.*

No treatment except supportive care is available. (See *Atrophy;* Spinal muscular atrophy, Section 15.)

Myositis is a muscle infection or inflammation. *Viruses* (Coxsackie), bacteria (*streptococcus, staphylococcus* with *abscess* formation), fungi (*actinomycosis*), and parasites (trichina) may all invade the muscle and create pain, spasm, fever, and swelling.

Myositis ossificans is a rare familial disease of unknown cause in which inflammatory masses form in muscles, subside, and are replaced with calcium and bone. The whole body eventually becomes rigid and hard. No treatment is available.

Traumatic myositis is a deep muscle bruise with *hemorrhage.* If severe enough, muscle tissue can be damaged and replaced with fibrosis (scar) with some loss of size and strength. Occasionally the blood ossifies and a dense calcium deposit appears. (For example, Rider's bone in the inner thigh muscles.)

Nails and toes on stomach-sleeping babies may curve down or up depending on how much the babies move about in bed. Sleeping with shoes on will allow the nails to become straight again. If the feet turn out, the big toes may develop an *ingrown toenail* and secondary paronychia. Hot packs and/or protective shoes will relieve the condition.

Many children are born with horny, thick little toenails that resemble a dog's claw. It is a familial trait. No treatment is necessary. They need to be cut with animal claw cutters.

Orthopedics is the special branch of medicine dealing with birth defects, injuries and diseases of bones, joints and muscles. The orthopedist evaluates the dynamics of weight bearing and posture. He is basically a surgeon, but prescribes treatment carried out by the physiotherapist or brace maker.

Osgood-Schlatter's disease is an irritation of the upper growing end of the tibia (shin bone) about an inch below the bottom end of the knee cap. Local pain and swelling in this area in a twelve- to fourteen-year-old boy is diagnostic. It is aggravated by running, kicking, and kneeling. Symptoms last about a year and knobbiness in the area is usually permanent, but not disfiguring. An orthopedist may put the leg in a cast for six weeks if the patient cannot or will not limit his activity. Calcium, zinc, and vitamin D will speed healing.

Ossification centers refer to the appearance of *calcium* (visible by X ray) in the newly forming bones. Skull and collarbones are the first to show calcium. When the upper humerus (upper arm) growth center fuses with the humerus in a maturing female, it suggests that her menses will begin in a year or so and that growth is almost finished. (See *Bones, Epiphyses.*)

Osteochondroma is a painless knob of bone and overlying cartilage usually found at the end of a long bone at the point of tendon attachment. Surgery is necessary only when the size interferes with function or pain is persistent from compression of nearby structures.

Osteogenesis imperfecta, or brittle bones, is a congenital defect of connective tissue. The *calcium* is laid down properly, but the matrix is defective. (Bricks without straw to bind them would crumble more easily.) The bones are fragile and sometimes are broken at birth or by slight torsion (when diapers are changed or when the child throws a ball). Muscles are flaccid; dislocations are common. The sclerae (white part of eyeballs) are bluish. Deafness is common in adults. The bones heal well but with grotesque distortions, especially in the legs.

Osteoma is a benign, slowly growing bone tumor of face or skull. It is hard, nontender, and the overlying tissues freely move over it. Removal is indicated if pressure on nearby organs causes symptoms (eye, brain, nose).

Osteomyelitis is a serious bacterial infection of the bone usually due to the staphylococcus. The germ gets into the system from a nasal, throat, or skin infection and is carried to a capillary in the bone, where it lodges and multiplies. It often involves the nearby joint. High fever, prostration, and pain suggest the diagnosis. A blood culture may catch a germ which can be identified and tested to see which antibiotic would be most effective. An X ray of the area is not helpful (except to rule out scurvy and bone cancer) as it takes at least ten days for the infection to distort the bony architecture sufficiently to be visible.

If treatment is delayed, however, the infection will destroy the bone, produce sinus tracts with pus, and preclude complete healing, as bits of dead bone are trapped inside. The doctor usually initiates massive antistaphylococcus treatment as soon as he suspects osteomyelitis, then continues or changes the medicine, depending on later culture and X ray reports. A reduction in fever and pain on about the third day would encourage him to believe that he is using the appropriate antibiotic. It is wise to continue medication in large doses for a month or six weeks, because a recurrence is difficult to treat due to the emergence of resistant bacteria.

Surgical drainage is infrequent nowadays. If, however, the infection has tunneled through the cortex of the bone, surgical drainage is indicated.

Osteopetrosis—see *Albers-Schönberg disease*

Osteosclerosis—see *Albers-Schönberg disease*

Paralysis of a muscle or limb is usually due to interruption of nerve function. It may be central, caused by infection or bleeding in or near the motor area of the brain, inflammation of nerves originating in the spinal cord (*poliomyelitis*), injury to these nerves anywhere between the spinal cord and the muscle (lacerations, tick bites [Section 1], needle injection), or malfunction of the neuromuscular junction (*myasthenia*). (See *Cerebral palsy,* Section 15; *Brachial palsy, Facial nerve palsy,* Section 5; *Guillain-Barré syndrome,* Section 15; *Lead poisoning,* Section 1; *Myasthenia, Neuritis, Poliomyelitis,* Section 15; *Rabies,* Section 2.)

Familial periodic paralysis is a rare inherited disease characterized by the spreading of weakness from limbs to trunk which may last several hours. It is more common in males; attacks are usually precipitated by stress or cold and occur at night following exercise. The blood *potassium* level is low, and ingestion of this salt may abort the attack. Some cases are related to excess aldosterone secretion by the adrenal glands. (See *Hypokalemia,* Section 10.)

Patella (knee cap) may slip sideways from its normal position. A small, high-riding patella, severe knock-knees, a low lateral femoral condyle, and tight lateral capsule, may all contribute to this problem requiring surgery. Minor forms of this malalignment will cause softening of the cartilage on the inner side of the patella. Surgical adjustment is necessary before pain and arthritic changes occur.

Perthes' disease—see *Hip, Coxa plana*

Pigeon toe is the common turned-in appearance of the feet most easily seen when the child is walking. The feet point toward each other, and the child steps off using the outside of his foot. He may be clumsy and trip frequently.

Most children are somewhat pigeon-toed at birth, since they have held their legs crossed against their abdomen in the confining uterus. If they prefer to sleep prone in the knee-chest position with the buttocks resting on their heels, this turned-in tendency will be aggravated. The tibia (shinbone) will grow spiraling inward (tibial torsion), and the inner borders of the feet will angle inward (metatarsus varus). Parents may not be aware of the problem until their child is toddling, at which time the awkward pigeon-toed gait and instability are obvious.

If mothers are aware of the tendency, early exercising and positioning may preclude its development; at each diaper change the feet are angled out; each time the baby is held and cuddled, his feet are turned out against the mother's body in the spread-eagle position; each time he is put to bed his feet are put in the frog position (toes turned out). Side- and back-sleeping babies usually have no problem outgrowing this; it only seems to be the ones who sleep prone with their toes turned in.

By the sixth to eighth month of life if the baby has not begun to sleep in the frog position, some bracing (Denis-Browne splint, shoes glued or riveted to a board with the toes pointing out, or shoes with heels buckled together) must be tried while growth is still rapid. (One clever fisherman tied eight-ounce weights to the last lace hole in his son's shoes. After the baby was deeply asleep he lowered the weights over the sides of the crib. The constant traction pulled the feet out to the frog position, but still allowed some freedom of motion.) Simply securing the feet together at bedtime may be all that is necessary. Shoes worn to bed with a strap to appose the heels is one method.

The condition must be overcorrected as there is a tendency to return to the inward position.

The older child is usually fitted with a sturdy shoe, plus a 3/16-inch outer sole wedge. When he steps off in walking, this wedge acts as a pivot, and the foot turns outward. Some doctors prescribe a spring cable which runs from a waist belt to a sturdy shoe and holds the foot turned outward. All these devices will be negated if the child reverts to the knee-chest buttocks-resting-on-the-turned-in-feet sleeping position.

Sometimes the turned-in feet are due to an anteversion of the femora (thigh bones) at the hip socket. This can be inferred if the knee caps are facing inward (instead of straight forward). To compensate, the tibiae must spiral outward so that the feet, at least, are aimed straight forward.

Poliomyelitis—see Sections 2 and 15

Posture, if abnormal, suggests disease in bone or muscle. Poor posture, especially if associated with marked sway-back (lumbar lordosis), can lead to arthritic changes in the spine. It is also cosmetically undesirable. Muscular fatigue occurs more readily if the spine and pelvis are held in abnormal positions. Pain follows fatigue.

Poor muscle tone is the chief cause of poor posture. The adolescent rapid growth period is more frequently associated with poor muscle tone, especially in the long, slender ectomorph. His chest sags, his spine rounds forward, and the small of his back flattens. Others develop a marked sway back and tip their pelvis forward. Exercises to strengthen back muscles (lying prone on stomach, raising head and shoulders) are helpful, especially if accompanied by sit-ups to strengthen abdominal muscles which prevent the pelvis from tipping forward so much.

Along with exercises the adolescent must be taught to develop consciously correct ways of standing and walking until he acquires automatic postural reflexes.

Pott's disease, *tuberculosis* spondylitis or tuberculosis of the spine, is rare now that tuberculosis is under better surveillance. The TB germ in the lung breaks off into the bloodstream and lodges in one of the vertebral bodies (backbone). It slowly destroys the bone, which collapses, causing the hunchback appearance (Quasimodo kyphosis). The X ray of the spine reveals the tuberculosis process and the chest X ray reveals the primary lesion, or cavity or miliary spread. The TB skin test is almost always positive.

Treatment is slow (taking years) and demands antituberculosis drugs as well as positioning on a frame which keeps the back in extension (arched backward). A body plaster cast and/or surgical bone fusion of the three or four adjacent vertebrae is the next step when the lesion shows some healing.

Rheumatic fever is characterized by migratory joint pains in the wrists, ankles, knees, or elbows, associated with tenderness, swelling, and redness. It is apparently the joint lining's reaction to a *streptococcal* infection (strep sore throat) in the previous three weeks. Treatment consists of *aspirin, penicillin* (if the strep is still present), bed rest, and possibly *cortisone* drugs. The heart is more liable to injury than the joints, but the joint pains are more likely to get the patient to the doctor. Preventing further strep infections is the most important step. (See *Rheumatic fever,* Section 2.) Big doses of vitamin C can facilitate healing.

Rheumatoid arthritis—see *Arthritis*

Rib syndrome is a painful area of the chest, appearing in active children usually between six and twelve years of age. The sore spot is about two inches to the right or the left of the sternum (breastbone). It is usually just a dull ache in the rib at that point, but it may be a sharp, stabbing pain that stops his activity. It is thought to be due to an irritation or inflammation where the bony rib joins the cartilage. It heals in time without treatment. A left-sided pain might indicate heart pathology, but this would be revealed by rapid *pulse, cyanosis,* or at least persistent inability to exercise. Tenderness of the rib on firm pressure would suggest the rib syndrome; the treatment is reassurance.

Scheuermann's disease (juvenile epiphysitis of the spine) develops at puberty with vague pains most commonly in the lower thoracic spine. Examination early is usually not revealing, but over the subsequent months a gradual rounding of the mid-back occurs. The spine eventually becomes rigid in this area. The growing end plates of the vertebral bodies (epiphyses) ossify imcompletely; the vertebral bodies become wedge-shaped, allowing the spine to flex forward.

Treatment is most effective if early. Rest with back in hyperextension, exercises to increase strength of the back muscles, and braces (Milwaukee) or casts to counteract the forward flexion may all have to be tried.

Scoliosis is the curving of the spine to one side. Its cause is unknown. It is felt that an uncomplicated lateral deviation is due to a muscle weakness like *poliomyelitis.* The true idiopathic scoliosis is a lateral and a rotational deviation. Adolescent girls not uncommonly develop this condition at the time of the growth spurt usually associated with the onset of puberty. It is not painful and may easily be overlooked until far advanced. An alert mother may notice, while fixing a skirt for her daughter, that one hip is held noticeably higher that the other; the doctor may find some asymmetry of the girl's back during a routine physical. It is easy to diagnose if one looks for it.

X rays show the extent of the curve. If the girl has not reached her adult height, an elaborate brace (Milwaukee) from chin to hips may partially correct the bend to an acceptable position. Casting may hold it. Some orthopedic surgeons favor use of special metal (Harrington) rods secured to the vertebrae to arrest the process.

Sever's disease (see *Epiphyses*) is an inflammation of the heel bone where the epiphysis attaches. It is usually seen in the rapidly growing, athletic male, so is assumed to be due to the pull of the Achilles' tendon on this nonfused plate of bone. The sufferer has a dull ache in the heel which disappears with rest. His motivation to play ball is usually greater than the discomfort. It lasts about a year until the epiphysis become a part of the heel bone. A doughnut of sponge rubber under the heel may soften the pain.

Shoes are used for comfort and protection. Children's shoes should be light and pliable, and have adequate toe room for growth and exercise. The only real reason for wearing shoes is to protect the feet from broken glass, snow and ice, nails, worms, and bacteria in the soil. Moccasins or tennis shoes are quite adequate. High-laced shoes stay on better; strong ankles are a function of time and exercise. (Witness the novice ice skater: his ankles flop around until his muscles are strong enough; it has nothing to do with how tightly the skates are laced.) (See *Flat foot.*)

A special reverse-last shoe is used for the inverted foot (metarsus varus, the inner border of the foot, curves in instead of being straight from heel to big toe). Using it in the first year during rapid growth will correct this condition easily.

Spondylitis, ankylosing, is considered to be an inheritable disease, since males are the usual victims. It begins in adolescence with low back pain followed by stiffness and inflexibility of the lumbar spine.

At first only occasional sacroiliac discomfort at rest is noted, especially in the morning before arising. With activity the pain disappears. Pain and stiffness spread to the remainder of the spine within a year. Some arthritis of the hips, shoulders, and knees may be an early sign. Some fever and anemia are often associated. X rays are helpful in diagnosing the condition after the disease is established.

Aspirin, cortisone, postural exercises, heat, and occasionally surgery are the available therapies. Without treatment these patients end up severely doubled forward; the entire back is rounded.

Spondylolisthesis is the slipping forward of lumbar vertebrae. It is a congenital *anomaly,* but low back pain and lumbar lordosis (sway back or curved-in lower back) usually are not manifest until adolescence.

A special brace may control the symptoms; spinal fusion may be necessary if the condition progresses. Postural strengthening and corrective exercises frequently correct the discomfort.

Still's disease—see *Juvenile arthritis*

Synovitis—see *Hip*

Tennis elbow is common in those whose occupation requires frequent rotational movement of the forearm (carpenters, screw-ball pitchers). It begins as a dull ache at the outside of the elbow which progresses to weakness of grasp. It is assumed that some muscle fibers have been torn loose and continued activity precludes healing. Treatment is rest (by splinting) and heat; local anesthetic and/or cortisone injections may help. Surgery is recommended if pain continues.

Tibial torsion is the common spiral twist of the shinbone (tibia) which is the result of crowding in the uterus, and continued pressure on the growing leg bones as a result of sleeping in the knee-chest position with the buttocks resting on the turned-in feet. It results in a *pigeon-toed gait* with awkward steps and much stumbling and falling. It is frequently associated with metatarsus varus. (See *Pigeon toe.*).

Toe (*overlapping little*) is a common familial trait. The extensor tendon to the toe is shortened so the toe rides high and overrides the adjacent toe. Taping and exercises are of no value. If painful, tendon surgery may allow it to regain its normal position.

Torticollis, or wry neck (see *Torticollis,* Section 5, for congenital form), may occur following an injury which causes a fracture of one of the cervical vertebrae. Careful transport to the hospital is necessary to avoid accidental spinal cord injury.

One not uncommon form follows rotating the head to look backward. The patient notes a sharp painful snap and his neck becomes locked in a turned, cocked position. This subluxation (or partial dislocation) is reduced with traction after X rays to rule out fracture. Anesthesia is suggested.

A frequent pediatric wry neck occurs after a cold draft exposure or a minor respiratory infection. No injury can be elicited. The child is comfortable when lying still, but complains of pain and cocks his head to the affected side when standing. To turn his head he moves his whole body. A massive continuous hot, wet pack—like a horse-collar—relieves the distress of this muscle inflammation; possibly a myositis due to a virus. It lasts three days.

Vertebrae are the bones of the backbone. They are arranged one atop the other like a column of blocks with bony extensions surrounding the spinal cord. (See *Klippel-Feil syndrome* and *Pott's disease.*)

Wasting—see *Atrophy*

SECTION 8
The Circulatory System

PART I
The Heart and Blood Vessels

A. Shortness of breath, rapid pulse, cold sweat, pallor (or cyanosis), weakness (also Sections 1 and 9)

Carditis
Congestive heart failure
Endocardial fibroelastosis
Endocarditis
Glycogen storage disease
Myocarditis
Pericarditis
Pulmonary hypertension
Rheumatic endocarditis
Ventricular fibrillation

B. Heart murmur (see Congenital heart defects, Section 5)

Innocent, functional, non-organic
Organic
- *Cyanotic (blue)*
  - *Congenital heart lesions* (Section 5)
    - *Finger clubbing*
- *Not cyanotic*
  - *Aortic insufficiency*
  - *Aortic stenosis*
  - *Mitral insufficiency*
  - *Mitral stenosis*
  - *Pulmonary valvular disease*
  - *Tricuspid valvular disease*

Tests
- *Arteriography*
- *Cardiac catheterization*
- *Electrocardiogram*
- *Heart sounds*

C. Pulse, heart rate

Irregular
- *Arrhythmia*
- *Atrial fibrillation*

Rapid
- *Fever* (Section 2)
- *Hyperthyroidism* (Section 10)
- *Intraabdominal bleeding*
- *Tachycardia*
  - *Paroxysmal*

Wolff-Parkinson-White syndrome

Slow

Athlete in good condition (Heart rate)

Carotid sinus reflex

Head injuries (Section 1)

Heart block

Hypothyroidism (Section 10)

Stokes-Adams syndrome

D. Blood pressure

Hypertension

Coarctation of aorta (see Section 5)

Glomerulonephritis (see Section 13)

Pheochromocytoma (see Section 10)

Pulmonary hypertension

Ventricular hypertrophy

Low blood pressure

Blood loss (see Section 1)

Postural hypotension

E. Blood vessels and clots

Aneurysm

Aorta

Embolism

Infarction

Phlebitis

Thrombosis

Vena cava

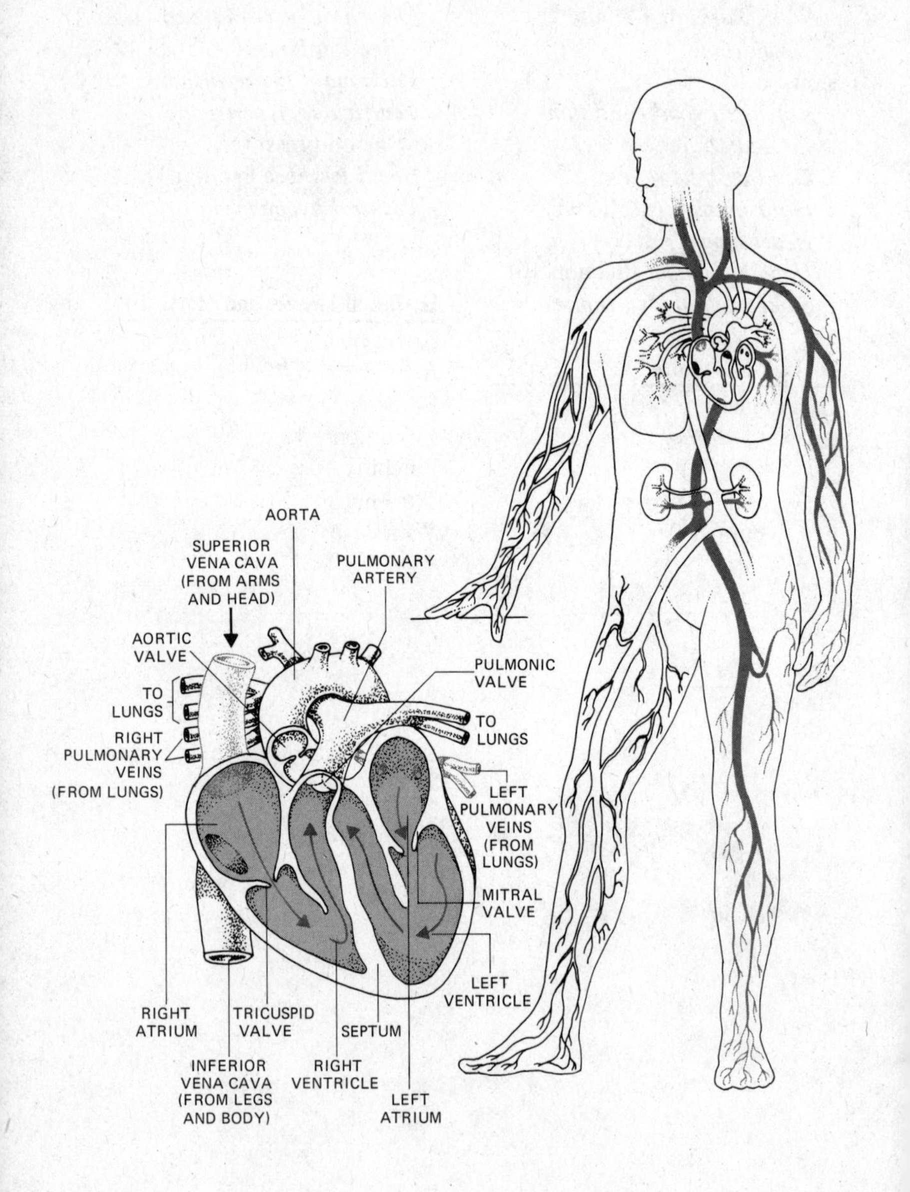
AORTA
SUPERIOR VENA CAVA (FROM ARMS AND HEAD)
PULMONARY ARTERY
AORTIC VALVE
PULMONIC VALVE
TO LUNGS
TO LUNGS
RIGHT PULMONARY VEINS (FROM LUNGS)
LEFT PULMONARY VEINS (FROM LUNGS)
MITRAL VALVE
LEFT VENTRICLE
RIGHT ATRIUM
TRICUSPID VALVE
SEPTUM
INFERIOR VENA CAVA (FROM LEGS AND BODY)
RIGHT VENTRICLE
LEFT ATRIUM

Aneurysm is the ballooning out of a blood vessel wall, due to a weakness of the wall—as an innertube pushes through a hole in the tire just before a blowout. The weakness may be present at birth, but the vessel may not blow until middle age. If occurring in the brain, a stroke results. Aneurysms are rarely found or diagnosed in children. (See *Cerebral aneurysm,* Section 15.)

Aorta is the large blood vessel that receives the oxygenated blood pumped from the left side of the heart. Branches from this supply head, arms, trunk, organs, legs.

Aortic insufficiency (or regurgitation) is the condition in which the aortic valve, scarred usually by rheumatic fever, is unable to close and prevent blood from leaking back into the left ventricle, while the heart is relaxed and filling. The left ventricle thus has to pump out its usual load plus the amount which has just leaked back. This results in enlargement of the heart, and may cause *congestive heart failure,* with shortness of breath, cough, and inability to exercise. Surgery, with replacement of the valve, may be required if heart failure cannot be controlled by *digitalis* and other medical treatment.

Aortic stenosis is a narrowing of the aorta, usually at its valve, but occasionally just below or, more rarely, just above the valve. This abnormality in young children is most often congenital. In older children, adolescents, and adults, the narrowing may be a result of rheumatic fever. Surgical correction is frequently possible after the exact site of stenosis has been defined by angiocardiography.

Arrhythmia is the term applied to irregular heartbeats. Most children have an arrhythmia related to respiration—more rapid on inspiration, slower on expiration. Erratic heartbeats and extremely rapid rates are best diagnosed with the aid of the *electrocardiogram.* (See *Heart rate, Heart block, Pulse.*)

Arteriography is the procedure of outlining abnormalities in arteries or the organs or areas supplied with blood by these arteries. A radio-opaque dye, or contrast agent, is injected directly into the *aorta,* or one of its branches, such as a coronary artery, to demonstrate size, position, course, narrowing or ballooning of the artery, and can outline tumors by defining the arteries that enter them. (See *Cardiac catheterization.*)

Atrial fibrillation is the inefficient, uncoordinated contraction of different areas of the wall of the atrium (upper heart chamber, formerly called auricle). Normally, the muscles of a heart chamber contract at the same time, squeezing like a fist, forcing the blood forward into the next chamber, or into an artery. When fibrillation occurs, it is usually a sign that the atrium is enlarged and its wall overstretched. This may result from congenital abnormalities, but is more often due to rheumatic fever. Atrial fibrillation is uncommon in children.

Blood pressure is the measurement (in millimeters of mercury) of the force required to pump blood from the left ventricle of the heart against the resistance of the arteries (systolic or upper value). The diastolic pressure is that pressure sustained by the arterial vessels between heartbeats. The standard for adult systolic pressure is 120 millimeters or so; for the ten-year-old, 100 millimeters. The diastolic pressure is usually 20 to 40 millimeters below the systolic (75 to 80 in an adult; 50 to 70 in a child). Elevation would suggest *kidney* disease, *aortic coarctation,* or, rarely, *adrenal gland* disease.

(*Pheochromocytoma* produces hypertension in episodic attacks, and it may be missed if the pressure is taken between attacks.)

Reduction of blood pressure would be seen in *shock. Postural hypotension* is diagnosed by a fall in blood pressure when the patient stands up.

Maintenance of the blood pressure assures that blood, and hence oxygen, is getting to the brain. A patient will faint when his cerebral circulation is inadequate; his new horizontal position will restore oxygen to the brain.

Cardiac catheterization is a procedure of diagnosing heart disease by the passage of a hollow tube or catheter into a vein or artery and then into the heart. Information is obtained by three methods during catheterizations:

1. X ray or fluoroscopic observation of the course and location of the catheter during its passage.
2. Pressures to determine an area of obstruction.
3. Oxygen saturation of the blood in a chamber or vessel to determine the source of that blood (e.g., blood from the left atrium to the right atrium in the case of an *atrial septal defect*).

Patients for cardiac catheterizations, even infants, do not have to be asleep since there is no pain connected with the manipulation of the catheter within the heart.

Carditis is an inflammation or infection of the heart. This may involve the heart lining (*endocarditis*), or the heart muscle (*myocarditis*), or the covering heart sac (*pericarditis*). The inflammation may be caused by a *virus,* but is most commonly due to a rheumatic fever. The pulse rate is rapid, even at rest and even after there is no fever. The X rays usually show an enlarged heart. The sounds of the heart are distant and weak sounding. *Murmurs* may appear if the heart valves are inflamed and swollen, thus failing to close properly. Recovery from carditis is slow, measured in months. No specific treatment is available. Rest, *digitalis* in some cases, and in rare instances one of the *cortisone* drugs are used to treat carditis.

Diphtheria toxin as well as some virus diseases can produce a similar set of symptoms and signs—enlarged, rapid heart. The heart may be weakened enough to fail, producing fluid in the lungs (*Congestive heart failure*) and—commonly in children—an enlarged liver.

Carotid sinus reflex causes slowing of pulse, anoxia, and fainting in susceptible people when the carotid sinus in the neck is pressed. A tight collar may initiate a *fainting* spell.

Congenital heart defects—see Section 5

Congestive heart failure occurs when the heart is unable to move forward all of the blood that returns through the veins. In childhood, this failure usually results from a congenitally malformed heart (see Section 5). *Rheumatic fever* and virus infections of the heart muscle (*myocarditis*), as well as extremely rapid pulse rates, may be other causes of congestive failure in children. It may be seen as a late development of rheumatic fever if the heart valves have been damaged by scarring.

The inability of the heart to propel blood forward results in a backup of blood in the tiny blood vessels of the lungs, causing fluid to accumulate, with shortness of breath, rapid breathing, and cough. It may also engorge the liver, causing it to swell. Infants in congestive heart failure usually breathe rapidly, cough, eat poorly, tire easily, perspire excessively, and gain weight slowly.

Congestive failure usually appears gradually but may develop suddenly in an infant with *congenital heart disease.* Immediate treatment is with *digitalis,* oxygen, a sitting position, low salt diet, *diuretics,* and occasionally *morphine.* If the condition is surgically correctable, surgery should be done in any patient who fails to respond well to these medical treatments. Many patients, however, respond satisfactorily and surgery can be postponed until they are bigger when the operation will be less risky. This decision should be made by the cardiologist and the cardiac surgeon as a team.

Electrocardiogram is the recording on graph paper of the electrical current flowing through the heart. It is an important diagnostic technique which, when used with auscultation of the chest, X rays, and *cardiac catheterization,* reveals the abnormality in virtually all cases of heart disease.

Embolism is a condition in which a blood clot becomes free and travels in the blood circulation, eventually lodging where a vessel branches or narrows. This condition is rare in childhood, but may occur following injury or in a heart congenitally malformed. If the clot lodges in the brain, a stroke would result; if in the blood vessel to a toe, gangrene might occur.

Pulmonary *embolism* usually rises from a clot in the leg veins that flows through the right side of the heart, and lodges in an artery in the lungs. Chest pain, fever, coughing up blood, and shortness of breath are the symptoms. This almost never occurs in children.

Endocardial fibroelastosis, or sclerosis, is the condition of thickening of the inner lining of the heart chambers and inflammation of the heart muscle. The cause is unknown, but possibly it is a result of a virus infection before birth. The infant may have difficulty breathing, with wheezing, blueness, and failure to gain. Congestive heart failure almost always develops. Formerly, endocardial fibroelastosis was thought always to be fatal. Recently, with careful medical management and digitalis treatment, many children survive and eventually have no further signs of this disease.

Endocarditis is an infection of the inner lining of the heart and/or heart valves. It may be caused by a strep or staph germ, usually on a heart lining previously damaged by *congenital malformation* or by *rheumatic fever.* The germs may enter the body through a skin infection, sore throat, or most often through a periapical tooth abscess.

The child with endocarditis may have fever, weakness, pallor and anemia and weight loss. A *murmur* is often heard. Diagnosis is made by growing the germ from a culture of the blood. The culture also tells the doctor which antibiotic would be most effective.

Children with heart lesions should usually have penicillin before and after dental work to avoid the possibility of developing endocarditis.

Finger clubbing is a late sign of any condition depriving the tissues of adequate oxygen supply. Clubbing results more often from cyanotic *congenital heart disease* ("blue-baby") and only rarely in children from chronic lung disease, such as *cystic fibrosis* (see Section 9). The ends of the fingers become bulging, widened, and the nails are rounded like the bowl of a spoon.

Glycogen storage disease. Deranged glycogen metabolism of the heart muscle may cause increased storage, leading to *cyanosis* and *heart failure.* Death is almost assured in the first year. (See *Glycogen,* Section 10; *Glycogen storage,* Section 12.)

Heart is the muscular pump which supplies oxygen-containing blood and nutrients to all tissues of the body. The right side of the heart receives the blood returning from the body and pumps it into the lungs where carbon dioxide is removed from the blood and oxygen is acquired. This blood then returns to the left side of the heart which pumps it out to the body.

Defects of formation of the heart (*congenital heart disease*) develop during the first five to eight weeks of the mother's pregnancy. Fortunately these are rare, occurring in about one baby in two hundred. The heart anomalies discussed in Section 5 are but lightly reviewed, to provide the reader with a superficial view of their complexities.

Heart block is the lack of normal conduction from atrium to ventricle. The rate is usually slowed to 50 beats per minute or slower and the atria do not beat in phase with the ventricular beat. The patient may have no symptoms or he may faint or develop congestive failure requiring a pacemaker implant to produce a more reliable and rapid beat.

Heart failure—see *Congestive heart failure*

Heart murmurs are the hums, squeaks, whooshes, and growls heard between the normal heart sounds. Most commonly murmurs are functional or innocent; no defects are demonstrable in the heart. It is assumed that they are due to swirling of blood about the cords and muscles in the chambers. A third of all children have these at various times; most disappear by adolescence. Reassurance is the only treatment.

Organic murmurs are produced by septal defects and valvular anomalies. Their intensity, duration, timing, and location will provide clues as to the underlying disease process, but X rays, *cardiac catheterization,* and ciné X ray may be necessary to find the true nature of the lesion.

Heart rate, or arterial pulse, is the number of heartbeats per minute. It is a measure of the contraction of the ventricles pumping blood out of the heart. The systolic pressure or thrust can be palpated in the neck or groin arteries, but is traditionally felt at the wrist (on the thumb side). It is rapid in the newborn (80 to 150 beats per minute, average 120) and gradually slows to 80 to 90 in childhood. An athletic adolescent in active training may have such an efficient heart that its slow beat can alarm the observer. (It may be as low as 40 to 50 beats per minute.)

Rapid rates (over 180 in the newborn or persistently over 120 in a child) suggest heart disease or conduction anomalies. An *electrocardiogram* is called for.

Heart sounds are assumed to be due to the closing of the various valves. The first heart sound is really the mitral and tricuspid valves closing simultaneously (*lub*); the second is the closing of the pulmonic and aortic valves (*dup*). The latter sound is often split or slightly asynchronous as the pulmonic valve closes just after the aortic (less than 0.1 second later). Doctors are supposed to listen to four or five areas over the precordium to evaluate each valve. Some smartalecky children will ask, "What's the matter, Doc? Can't you find my heart?"

Hypertension is elevated *blood pressure.* It is uncommon in children and its discovery must initiate a full scale investigation to determine its cause. Very often, it will be found that the pressure is normal if the patient is allowed to relax, or returns to be rechecked after taking a mild sedative. This patient does not have true hypertension in most cases, but was merely anxious or apprehensive at the time of the first examination.

Infarction is the plugging of blood vessels—usually arteries—by *emboli* or bits of clotted blood. The pulmonary embolus usually comes from the pelvis or leg veins and is rare in children. It would be more likely to follow surgery, malnutrition, or some other problem causing sluggish venous return. If the embolus causing the infarct is infected, a *pulmonary abscess* forms.

Symptoms are chest pain, weakness, and a cough, often producing bloody mucus.

An infarct in the *kidney* is usually associated with a clot (or *thrombosis*) in the vein from the kidney and most frequently accompanies a severe infection or dehydration usually in babies under a year of age. If blood and protein are present in urine and *shock* occurs with a flank mass, a kidney infarct and/or vein thrombosis is considered. Treatment is surgery.

Mitral insufficiency (or regurgitation) allows blood to flow back from the left ventricle into the left atrium. This increases pressure in the left atrium, the pulmonary veins which enter the left atrium from the lung, and may cause fluid to collect in the lung, which causes a cough, in this case a sign of *congestive heart failure.* Heart surgery, with repair or replacement of the mitral valve is the treatment.

Mitral stenosis is a narrowing of the mitral valve which separates the left atrium from the left ventricle. The left atrium must raise its pressure in order to force blood through this small diseased mitral valve. This pressure is transmitted back to the lungs as in *mitral insufficiency,* resulting in *congestive heart failure,* often with coughing of blood. Mitral stenosis may be congenital, but more often is a result of *rheumatic heart disease.* Surgery on the mitral valve, with enlargement of the opening, or replacement with an artificial valve is required.

Myocarditis is inflammation or infection of the heart muscle. It may be caused by *rheumatic fever, polyarteritis nodosa,* or by *viral, rickettsial,* or *bacterial* infection. The heart muscle may be damaged by poisons or toxins produced by bacteria (e.g., *diphtheria*) or by actual invasion of the muscle cell by a virus. The muscle and consequently the heart as a whole is weakened, dilates, and is unable to empty itself by pumping blood forward. The pulse becomes weak, blood pressure low (shock), the patient is short of breath and in *congestive heart failure. Digitalis* helps in most cases to strengthen the force of the heart beat. Bedrest, occasionally with oxygen, is also important in treatment of myocarditis.

Other endocrine or nutritional diseases produce damage to the heart muscle, but are not strictly an infection. *Hyperthyroidism* will make the pulse rapid because of the stimulating effect of the *thyroid* on the muscle. The same muscular wasting seen in *muscular dystrophy* affect the heart muscle. *Beriberi* and profound *anemia* will disturb the nutrition of the muscle and lead to *electrocardiogram* changes, rapid *pulse,* weakness, murmurs, and heart enlargement. Treatment to correct the underlying condition seems obvious.

Patent ductus—see *Ductus arteriosus,* Section 5

Pericarditis is an inflammation of the sac-like covering of the heart (pericardium). This may be caused by *rheumatic fever,* a virus infection such as influenza, or by bacteria. Fluid or at times pus, may accumulate between the pericardium and the surface of the heart. If fluid develops rapidly the pressure on the heart may prevent effective filling, thus impairing the heart's work as a pump.

Pain frequently is present with pericarditis. Often a rub (like sandpaper) can be heard with the stethoscope. Chest X ray and *electrocardiogram* may help in the diagnosis. Often pericarditis is best detected by withdrawing some of the fluid through a needle. The type of fluid dictates treatment. Pus indicates need for antibiotic therapy.

Trauma to the chest may cause inflammation or leakage of blood into this space. *Lupus, leukemia, anemia, hypothyroidism,* and *kidney* failure may be associated with fluid or blood in the pericardial space.

Phlebitis is a vein inflammation. The most common cause is continued presence of a needle or a catheter in a vein. It usually heals rapidly and seldom progresses when the object is removed. Hot packs may be necessary to localize the infection.

Postural hypotension is the reduction of blood pressure when the patient stands. Normally the pressure rises to counteract the effects of gravity on the blood. The brain will not be oxygenated adequately if the pressure falls; giddiness and fainting will follow.

The peripheral vessels normally constrict to increase the pressure, and the heart contraction is increased to force the blood up to the brain. In hypotension the blood "puddles" in the veins of the legs and abdomen so that insufficient blood reaches the heart to provide adequate outflow.

The wearing of tights, if they are sufficiently constricting, may prevent the pooling of blood in the dependent areas. (A gravity suit may be necessary.) *Ephedrine* sulfate may be helpful; a *cortisone* drug has been used to control symptoms.

Pulmonary hypertension is elevated pressure in the blood vessels of the lungs. This requires high pressure in the right ventricle. Heart failure may develop late in this situation. Occasionally children with pulmonary hypertension die suddenly, usually of an *arrhythmia,* ventricular fibrillation.

A few cases have been reported of right-sided heart enlargement subsequent to the intravenous self-injection of dissolved pills. Many of these pills have *talc* to act as a filler and hold the medicine together. This injected talc will plug up the lung capillaries, causing back pressure in the right side of the heart.

In the rare variety of unknown cause, the small arteries taking blood to the lungs develop thickened muscular walls. The blood can pass through these small tubules only with difficulty, thus creating a back pressure. The compromised right side of the heart enlarges, since it cannot pump all the blood out with each beat.

The patient has chest pain, weakness especially with exertion, and if failure occurs, the veins in the neck become distended, the *liver* may enlarge, and ankle *edema* appear.

X rays, the *electrocardiogram,* and *cardiac catheterization* confirm the diagnosis. Treatment with *digitalis* to encourage the heart to pump more forcibly is about all that can be offered for this progressively downhill problem.

Pulmonary valvular disease is the inflammation or defective function of the pulmonary valves (between the right ventricle and the pulmonary artery). It is rare in rheumatic *carditis.* It may be seen in *pulmonary hypertension,* because back pressure dilates the pulmonary artery, forcing the valves to separate. If the valve's edges cannot meet during diastole, blood will run back into the right ventricle, dilating it (pulmonary valvular insufficiency).

Usually the right ventricle tolerates pulmonary insufficiency (regurgitation) very well, since the pressures involved are not high in most patients.

Pulse is the beat or pressure wave noted in the peripheral arteries (the wrist is the one traditionally used) synchronous with systole or the emptying of blood from the ventricles (see *Heart rate*).

A rapid pulse persistently elevated over 150 to 200 beats per minute suggests *hyperthyroidism* (sleeping pulse stays elevated), *Wolff-Parkinson-White syndrome,* or an adrenalin producing *pheochromocytoma.*

A child (or adult, for that matter) may become alarmed by the occasional skipped beat that feels as if the heart flipped over inside. The heart fills with twice as much blood as usual during the pulseless interval. Then, when it beats, the force makes the heart bang against the ribs. This is common and innocuous.

Almost all normal children have sinus or respiratory arrhythmia. The heart speeds up when the child inhales and slows when he exhales. This is caused by the vacuum in the chest increasing the return of blood to the heart, requiring a faster beat to move this blood forward.

Rheumatic endocarditis (see *Rheumatic fever,* Section 2) is the most common type of heart inflammation and most often involves the mitral valve (between the left atrium and left ventricle). Inflammation leaves the valves thickened with irregular edges that fail to close properly. Blood may flow backward from the left ventricle into the left atrium with each heartbeat (see *Mitral insufficiency*). This insufficiency or regurgitation may cause back pressure in the lungs and right side of the heart, with possible heart failure. Later the valve may become scarred and fail to open completely. This is *mitral stenosis.*

Many children escape permanent heart damage with the first attack of rheumatic fever. It is very important to protect them from *streptococcal* infection so that further attacks of rheumatic fever will be prevented. This is done by regular doses of penicillin (daily by mouth or monthly by injection) which will almost always prevent the *streptococcal* infection that precedes rheumatic fever.

Not every murmur means *rheumatic fever,* and not every rheumatic-fever victim is crippled. Doctors may do much harm by restricting the activity of a child because he has a murmur. If the scarring is severe enough to compromise the blood flow, the child will become weak and short of breath while active, and he will limit his own activity automatically.

Endocarditis is the active inflammation; rest is required until the pulse has slowed and the *sedimentation rate* of the blood is normal. Once this has been achieved the heart may return almost to normal, and full activity may be allowed.

Stokes-Adams syndrome occurs in *heart block;* the slow heartbeat does not supply sufficient blood and oxygen to the brain, and the patient faints.

Tachycardia is rapid *heartbeat.* It is expected in fright or anger (as a result of *epinephrine*), *fever* and *hyperthyroidism* (increased metabolism), *anemia* (response to increased need for oxygen), and, of course, exercise.

Paroxysmal tachycardia is the occurrence of sudden attacks of rapid *heart rate* due to some stimulus in the atrium or ventricles or the nerve conducting tissue (nodal). Rates of over 200 and up to 300 per minute have been recorded, and if prolonged may lead to *congestive heart failure,* as the chambers do not have time to fill and empty properly. It may last seconds or days. The patient may notice only a fluttering sensation in his chest, or he may become dusky and develop heart failure. Pallor, irritability, and cold sweat may be the only signs noted in a baby, and they may suggest colic.

Pressure over the eyeballs, breath-holding, drinking ice water, or pressure over the large neck arteries may abort the attack. *Digitalis* controls the attacks and should be continued for a year or so, as it makes the heart less responsive to the stimulation. (See *Wolff-Parkinson-White syndrome.*)

Thrombosis is a blood clot occurring in an artery or vein, thus blocking off the local circulation. It is rare in children unless the blood is especially thickened from *dehydration, polycythemia,* or *cyanotic* heart disease. The clot causes an infarction. If the artery is infarcted or thrombosed, the tissue supplied by that circulation cannot be nourished. If the clot is arterial, gangrene may set in. If venous, reduction of function may be temporary, or at least not as serious. (See *Lateral Sinus thrombosis,* Section 14.)

Tricuspid valvular disease is usually the result of rheumatic heart disease. Insufficiency of the valves would create enlarged neck-vein pressure and enlarged *liver.* Stenosis from rheumatic disease would enlarge the liver, produce *edema* and *ascites.*

Vena cava is really two large veins: the inferior one brings venous blood to the right atrium from the body below the heart; the superior vena cava carries blood to the right atrium from the head and arms.

Ventricular fibrillation is the uncoordinated contraction of the various muscle fibers of the ventricles. (See *Atrial fibrillation.*) It may occur with sudden heart strain associated with some congenital anomalies (see *Aortic stenosis,* Section 5).

Ventricular hypertrophy is the thickening of the walls of one or both ventricles, usually due to excess pressure work; that is, the need to raise the pressure in the ventricle in order to eject the blood. Left ventricular hypertrophy may be seen in *hypertension, coarctation of the aorta,* and *aortic stenosis.* Right ventricular hypertrophy occurs in *pulmonic stenosis* and *pulmonary hypertension.* The ventricles may be dilated and thin-walled in atrial septal defects, however. This ventricular dilatation should not be confused with ventricular hypertrophy.

Ventricular septal defects—see *Congenital heart defects,* Section 5

Wolff-Parkinson-White (W-P-W) syndrome is a defect in the conduction of electrical impulses through the heart. *Paroxysmal tachycardia* occurs in a high percentage of patients with this problem. W-P-W can usually be recognized in the *electrocardiogram,* but in some instances, the electrocardiogram is normal between episodes of fast *pulse.*

PART II

Blood, Blood Cells, Immunity, Anemia, and Bleeding Disorders

A. Blood

Blood cells
Blood type
Exchange transfusion
Hemoglobin
Platelets
Red blood cells (Erythrocytes)
Reticulocyte
Sedimentation rate
Spleen
White blood cells

B. Too many infections; no immunity

Antibodies
Autoimmunity
Congenital dysplasia of thymus
Globulins
Congenital agammaglobulinemia
Dysgammaglobulinemia
Gamma globulin
Immunoglobulins A, G, M
Spleen
Thymus
White blood cell defects
Agranulocytosis
Neutropenia

C. Pale, weak, tired

Anemia
Blood loss (see *Duodenal ulcer,* Section 10; *Bleeding,* Section 1)
Hemolytic (Coombs test)
Autoimmunity
Drug induced
Erythroblastosis (Section 5)
Fava beans
Mediterranean (see *Thalassemia)*
Sickle cell
Spherocytosis
Thalassemia
Megaloblastic
Pernicious
Red blood cell
Hypersplenism
Banti's syndrome
Hypothyroidism (Section 10)
Tuberculosis (Section 9)
Rheumatic fever (Section 2)
Nephritis (Section 13)
Leukemia
Neoplasms (Section 10)

D. Plethoric, cyanotic

Congenital heart defects with cyanosis (Section 5)

Erythrocytosis (polycythemia)
Heart murmurs with cyanosis (Section 8, Part I)
Methemoglobinemia

E. Pale, yellow, waxy

Hemolytic anemias
Hyperbilirubinemia
Jaundice
Hepatitis (Section 12)
Hypothyroidism (Section 10)
Infectious mononucleosis (Section 12)
Leukemia
Neoplasms (Section 10)

F. Blood spots, excessive bleeding, easy bruisability (see Bleeding, (Hematoma)

Clotting disorders (coagulation)
Hemophilia
Vitamin K deficiency
Hemorrhagic disease of newborn (Section 5)
Leukemia
Liver disease (Section 12)
Von Willebrand's disease
Purpura
Low platelet count
Diffuse intravascular clotting
Drugs
Infections (Section 2)
Leukemia
Thrombocytopenia
Platelets adequate
Henoch-Schönlein vasculitis
Meningococcemia (Section 2)
Scurvy (Section 11)
Tests (coagulation)

Agranulocytosis is the absence of the polymorphonuclear cells due to drugs (*chloramphenicol, sulfa,* etc.), one type of *leukemia,* or overwhelming infection. If the body is in this condition, fever, prostration, ulcers of the throat and skin may be rapidly fatal. Treatment would depend on the cause.

Patients develop ulcers in the *mouth* and *rectum.* When the white count drops below 3,000 per cubic millimeter, all suspected drugs are discontinued, and the patient is supported with appropriate antibiotics until the count returns to normal.

AHG deficiency—see *Hemophilia*

Anemia is weak or thin blood and is almost always due to an iron-poor diet. At birth the baby has just so much iron in his body. As he grows (tripling his birth weight in the first year), this quantity of iron is spread through a larger volume. If he started at birth with a *hemoglobin* level of 16 grams in his veins, and if he does nothing but drink milk (containing no iron) for his entire first year, this level will be reduced to 8 grams or less, which indicates severe anemia. Modern formula milks have iron added to them, and some solids with iron should be begun by the third month. If solids, including fruit, vegetables, and meat, are given after age six to eight months, and an effort made to discourage milk drinking, the baby will almost never develop milk anemia. Breast-fed babies rarely get anemia.

The two-year-old child usually loses his appetite. Many mothers feel that adequate nutrition is provided if the child drinks his milk because "milk is a perfect food." The child then gets more anemic, and for some reason is even less eager than before to eat the foods that would correct his thin blood. If he doesn't eat, the mother should *stop* the milk, bread, and cheese—anything that is white is usually devoid of iron—in an effort to force him to eat the iron-bearing foods (meat, eggs, fruit, and vegetables). A few drops of an iron tonic daily will always increase the appetite of a child who suffers from an iron-deficiency anemia.

The rapidly growing preadolescent frequently needs an iron supplement, even though his diet may be rich in iron-bearing foods; he is simply growing faster than his diet can keep up with him. Once mature, a boy need not take extra iron regularly, as there is a chance of overloading his system. A girl may find extra iron will prevent anemia during her menstruating years.

Some feel that vitamin C enhances the absorption of iron from the intestine.

Anemia results from the reduction in numbers or size of red cells or lowered concentration of the hemoglobin molecules in the cell. It is a secondary condition or a sign of some more specific disease. Loss of blood after injury, surgery (such as *tonsillectomy*), or bleeding from *Meckel's diverticulum* or *duodenal ulcer* or *glomerulonephritis* are obvious reasons for anemia.

The vast majority of children who become anemic suffer from the iron-deficiency type; therefore, most anemias in children are treated with an iron tonic. If an unequivocal response is not manifest in the hemoglobin level in thirty days, a thorough search must be made for infection, hereditary factors, metabolic diseases, and hidden blood loss. Most patients, however, at least feel better in ten days.

Other much less commonly found kinds of anemias are:

Drug suppression of blood formation in bone marrow

The low thyroid state (see *Hypothyroidism,* Section 10)

Chronic disease (*rheumatic fever, nephritis, tuberculosis, neoplasm, lead poisoning*)

Pernicious anemia

Sickle-cell anemia

Spherocytosis

Thalassemia

Erythroblastosis

Hemolytic anemia

Pure red-cell anemia (red cells alone are not manufactured in sufficient quantities)

Antibodies are the proteins of the body largely responsible for the development of resistance to infection. *Immunoglobulins,* or *gamma globulin,* are large particles which "remember" to fight bacterial and viral diseases. When a baby gets a DPT shot (see *Diphtheria,* Section 2; *Allergy,* Section 3), his body manufactures *antibodies* to the *antigens* thus injected. If the real, live bacteria try to invade him at a later date, the immune "memory" is mobilized, and increased amounts of antibody are produced to neutralize the bacteria.

Three clearly recognized immunoglobulins differentiated by size have been identified.

Autoimmunity refers to a group of poorly understood conditions in which the body forms *antibodies* against certain normal body cells or tissues. This "allergy to self" is considered to be the mechanism in certain *hemolytic anemias* and *rheumatoid arthritis,* since cortisonelike drugs will have an effect on them. *Cortisone* is a hormone able to interfere with the antigen-antibody reaction.

Thyroiditis, myasthenia gravis, and *scleroderma* are considered to be autoimmune diseases. They have the common characteristic of forming an autoantibody (protein) or sensitized lymphocytes capable of reacting with specific tissues of the host. Some feel that these diseases are an expression of excessive immunity response; however, the diseases are more likely to appear in people who have a deficient immune-globulin system. These people may be more likely to develop mutant lymphocytes that are unable to recognize "self" and set about to destroy the host tissue. Genetic defects of immunity formation triggered by virus invasion alter the host reaction, and an autoimmune disease may appear. (See *Allergy*, Section 3.)

Banti's syndrome—see *Hypersplenism*

Bleeding (for treatment, see Section 1) is the escape of blood from its usual passage inside the vessels. It usually follows a cut or tear in the skin (laceration) or in a mucous membrane. (See *Nosebleed.*) Pressure, if applied directly on the bleeding area, will usually collapse the vessels so that blood cannot leak out. Bleeding into an internal organ is not so easily controlled. (See also *Head injuries,* Section 1; *Infectious mononucleosis,* Section 2; *Kidney injury:* see *Hematuria,* Section 13.)

Blood is the red liquid which flows in the blood vessels. It contains red cells to carry oxygen, *amino acids,* minerals, and sugar. Waste products are taken to the *lungs, liver,* and *kidneys* for excretion. It contains *white cells* to fight infection, *protein* to aid in immunity, and *platelets* and protein coagulation precursors.

Blood cells are of different types:

The red cell or *erythrocyte* imparts the red color to the blood and carries oxygen from the lungs to all the cells of the body. Red cells may be deficient in number (as following hemorrhage), or in amount of iron (iron-deficiency *anemia*), or may deviate from their normal doughnut shape (*sickle-cell anemia* or *spherocytosis*).

The white cells (*leukocytes*) are classified in several types, depending on nucleus shape and staining properties made visible when a dye is added to a blood smear. They are formed in the bone marrow and are a part of the immune mechanism.

1. Polymorphonuclear (nucleus has many shapes or segments) leukocytes (white cells) usually increase in number in response to a bacterial infection. If patient has signs of appendicitis, doctor asks, "What's the white count?" Technician: "18,000." Doctor: "We'd better operate." If the patient has a fever but the doctor can find no source of infection and white blood count is normal or low (7,000), "It's that virus that's going around."

2. Lymphocytes are white cells whose nuclei appear round and have different staining characteristics. *Infectious mononucleosis* (glandular fever) may reveal itself by the atypical appearance of the lymphocytes in the victim's blood. Leukemia in children is usually of the lymphocytic cells, and counts may rise to 100,000 cells in a cubic millimeter (normal—3,000 to 5,000).

Lymphocytes, one kind of white cells, are unable to ingest bacteria, but appear responsible for some immunoglobulins. Large numbers of lymphocytes are found in *whooping cough.*

3. Monocytes are large cells able to phagocytize (engulf and destroy) bacteria and debris. They normally constitute only a small percentage of the total white cells but will increase in *tuberculosis,* protozoan (*malaria*), and fungus diseases.

4. *Eosinophiles* are white cells which have granules in the cytoplasm that have an affinity for the dye eosin. These cells are characteristically increased in allergic conditions or parasitic infestations. Large numbers may be found in the nasal secretions of hay-fever sufferers.

5. Basophils account for only one or two percent of the white cells. They may be increased in *tuberculosis.*

6. *Platelets* are smaller than white cells, have no nucleus and aid in the clotting mechanism.

Blood transfusion may be needed after acute severe loss of blood from injury or a bleeding intestinal disease, from *hemophilia,* or in a chronic *anemia* associated with severe weakness. Some risk is involved: transfusion reaction (shock, *hives,* kidney damage), *hepatitis* or malaria transmission, heart failure. (See *Exchange transfusion.*)

Blood type refers to the designation of A, B, AB, or O types of blood found in humans. If a person of type O receives type A or B blood, he may have a reaction (shock, hemolysis, kidney damage) as O blood contains antibodies against A and B red cells. Although type O blood (the "universal donor") can usually be transfused into a person with A, B, or AB blood without a reaction, safety demands A recipients get A blood, B get B, etc. The Rh factor is found in 85 percent of whites, and Rh negative recipients should *not* get Rh positive blood.

Many people wear identifying tags with their blood group noted in case of the need for immediate transfusion. One laboratory, however, will not believe another laboratory's results, so the information is not *too* important. Typing and crossmatching can be done in just a few minutes.

Coagulation is the solidification or clotting of blood that serves to prevent its loss when a blood vessel is opened. The various coagulation factors must always be present in the blood so that clotting can occur if necessary; it must not occur spontaneously and thus block the blood flow of nourishment to vital organs. (See *Thrombosis.*) When a blood vessel is cut, the walls of the vessel constrict, slowing the flow. The *platelets* and/or tissue enzymes activate the various factors in the blood (about twelve of them) which finally allow fibrinogen to be converted to the fibrin clot. Various tests have been devised to pinpoint missing components in the chain of reactions leading to coagulation.

Hemorrhagic or bleeding disorders are divided into coagulative disorders and purpuras.

Coagulation investigation usually includes the following:

1. *Tourniquet test.* Blood-pressure cuff is pumped up to just below systolic pressure for five minutes. If a number of small skin hemorrhages appear, it suggests vascular incompetence or decreased number of platelets.
2. *Platelet count* is done with the microscope. If platelets are inadequate, one of the *purpuras* is suggested.
3. *Bleeding time* is measured by the length of time it takes a standard finger stab to stop bleeding. Normal is less than six to eight minutes. (The time may be doubled two hours after aspirin ingestion.)
4. *Whole-blood clotting time* is the time required for a clot to form in a glass tube. (Normal is less than ten to twelve minutes at body temperature; up to sixteen minutes at room temperature.)
5. *Thrombin time.* Cow thrombin is added to plasma; the time required to clot is measured.
6. *Prothrombin time.* Calcium and thromboplastin are added to plasma; the time required to clot is measured.

7. *Prothrombin consumption time* is a test used to evaluate one of the steps of the blood-coagulation mechanism. Serum is the fluid remaining after the cells and clot have been removed. Prothrombin is usually absent from serum, because it has been used up in the clotting process. If this test reveals a significant amount remaining, it suggests a coagulation defect.

8. *Partial thromboplastin time* is used to detect coagulation disorders. Bleeding and clotting times are usually determined prior to surgery, but may not reveal one of the rarer coagulation defects. Aspirin must be avoided for at least a week before these tests or any surgery. (See *Sodium salicylate* and *Codeine,* Section 4.)

Coagulation disorders

Acquired

a. related to vitamin K

b. associated with uremia, liver disease, *leukemia*

c. abnormal presence of anticoagulants (for example, heparin)

Hereditary

a. deficiencies of coagulation factors

b. Von Willebrand's disease

Factor deficiencies cause blood-clotting defects or bleeding problems. These are genetically controlled and include hemophilia (three types: factors VIII, IX, and XI). Some factors (II, VII, and X) require that *vitamin K* be available to initiate *liver* synthesis; hence vitamin K is administered routinely to the newborn, because the vitamin K from the mother may not be in sufficient amounts to protect the baby from significant hemorrhage (navel, bowel, kidney) in the first three days of life. After this time, he manufactures his own by intestinal bacterial action. (See *Hemorrhagic disease of newborn,* Section 5.)

Congenital agammaglobulinemia (Bruton's) is seen in boys and appears after eight months of age. Severe bacterial infections follow one after another with exasperating frequency; they require heroic antibiotic treatment. *Pneumonia, otitis media, sinusitis, pharyngitis, septicemia,* or *meningitis* may overwhelm the victim; resistance to bacterial infections is nonexistent as IgM, IgG, and IgA are all greatly reduced in the blood. Treatment is large and frequent injections of gamma globulin. Acquired and secondary forms may be seen. It is very rare.

Congenital dysplasia of the thymus, or Di George's syndrome, produces *tetany* and poorly functioning lymphocytes. Viral and fungal infections are poorly tolerated.

Coombs test detects antibody in the red cells. It is especially important in hemolytic diseases such as Rh incompatibility (*erythroblastosis*) when red cells are destroyed by an immunity reaction.

Dysgammaglobulinemia is the name given to immunity deficiency diseases in which only one or two of the *immunoglobulins* are deficient. Repeated infections are common. Intramuscular injections of *gamma globulin* are helpful only if IgG is low, as there is little IgM or IgA in commercial gamma globulin.

Many doctors give injections of gamma globulin because the child "has been sick too much." Reports of severe reactions are not infrequent. If the blood test does not specifically reveal a deficiency, gamma-globulin injections should be withheld while a search for some predisposing condition, usually an allergy, is made.

Erythrocyte is the red blood cell. It is really not a true cell, because the nucleus is absent by the time it comes from the bone marrow where it is formed. Its chief function is to carry oxygen from the alveoli of the lungs to all the cells of the body. When saturated with oxygen, the cell is red and imparts its color to the blood. Unoxygenated (venous) blood returning to the lungs has a blue tinge.

Most of the red cell is composed of *hemoglobin.* One type, fetal hemoglobin, is the predominant form before birth and is gradually replaced by adult hemoglobin in the first year of life. In *Cooley's anemia,* some defect prevents this changeover, and fetal hemoglobin persists. (See *Thalassemia.*)

Erythrocytosis, or **polycythemia,** is an excess of red cells and *hemoglobin,* usually stimulated by a low oxygen level in the blood. The bone marrow responds by manufacturing excess *erythrocytes* in an effort to increase the blood's oxygen-carrying capacity. This thick, rich blood would be found in victims of cyanotic heart disease, in those living at high altitudes (where there is less atmospheric oxygen), and for the first few days of life of some babies born with high counts (low oxygen content *in utero*).

Patients with severe *cystic fibrosis* or chronic *asthma* or *bronchitis* are unable to saturate the blood with oxygen, and erythrocytosis occurs.

Exchange transfusion is a blood replacement usually done on a baby with *erythroblastosis.* A fine plastic catheter is inserted into the vein in the umbilical-cord stump. This is connected to a syringe and a bottle of compatible blood. Being careful to monitor the baby's pulse and respiration, the operator, usually a pediatrician, removes 5 to

20 cubic centimeters (one to four teaspoons) of blood from the baby, discards it, and replaces it with the same amount of donor blood. The threefold purpose is to remove the antibodies (anti-Rh) which are destroying the baby's Rh positive blood, to remove the already formed *bilirubin* which can damage brain cells, and to correct the anemia. If the baby's venous pressure is normal, more blood is pushed in than is pulled out to counteract the anemia that is usually present.

The exchange transfusion may be used in older infants who have ingested certain poisons, such as aspirin or iron. (Obviously, other vessels than umbilical ones must be used.)

Fava beans hemolysis may occur in those who are deficient in a red-cell enzyme. This enzyme lack is responsible for the hemolysis of the red cells when they are exposed to oxidants like fava beans, some sulfa, fever-reducing, and antimalarial drugs.

Gamma globulin is a protein responsible for some of the body's immunity memory. (See *Immunity.*)

Globulins—see *Immunity*

Hematoma is a swelling due to a collection of blood that has leaked from nearby broken blood vessels. Symptoms are due to pressure on neighboring organs.

Hemoglobin is a complex *protein* molecule in the red cells which imparts red color to the blood and is responsible for oxygen transport. Numerous varieties are now recognized and classified according to structural differences. Hemoglobin F is the form in the red cells of the fetus and newborn. By the end of the first year of life the red cells produced contain mostly hemoglobin A, which type is normally produced for the remainder of life. Deficient production of hemoglobin A will lead to anemia. (See *Thalassemia.*) *Sickle-cell anemia* victims carry a form of hemoglobin in many of their cells which, under stress, elongates and distorts the red cells into sickle shapes. The body recognizes the abnormal shape and destroys these cells, causing *hemolysis* and *anemia.*

Hemolytic anemias are those due to increased red-cell destruction (hemolysis). Some defect of the red cell acts as a stimulus to the body to destroy it. In response to the anemia thus produced, the bone marrow produces more red cells. If the increased production-destruction rate is balanced, no big troubles occur except *jaundice,* gallstones, and enlarged *spleen* (the graveyard of red cells). Most growing children are unable to keep up, and anemia will follow. (See *Spherocytosis, Thalassemia, Sickle cell anemia.*)

Other types of hemolysis causing anemia are due to Rh immunization, malaria, drug sensitivity. One type occurs violently in association with an infection. The body apparently suspects the red cells are a foreign substance and destroys them. *Jaundice, anemia,* fever, enlarged *spleen,* and prostration require heroic treatment. Cortisone will reverse the hemolysis. Blood transfusions will counteract the anemia.

Hemolytic anemia is sometimes caused by defects inside the cell—the hemoglobin is made improperly, so the spleen destroys these cells. Sometimes an enzymatic defect is responsible; if this energy store is absent or depleted, the red cell dies prematurely. If certain drugs (sulfa) are taken by a person with a deficiency in this enzyme system, his cells may hemolyze.

Other hemolytic anemias are caused by an autoimmune mechanism—the cells are normal, but the body has developed an antibody against them (causing the Coombs test to be positive). *Lupus erythematosus* may cause hemolysis; some drugs and diseases may do this (mycoplasma *pneumonia*).

Hemophilia is the general name for a group of bleeding disorders now found to be due to lack of a specific substance in the blood. Classical hemophilia blood has little or no Factor VIII. Another type, Christmas disease, is deficient in Factor IX. Factor XI, when low, will produce a similar picture—nosebleeds, easy bruising. It is important to know which variety is present, because treatment is different, and genetic counseling would vary since the diseases are carried on different *chromosomes.*

Classic hemophilia is due to the deficient amount and/or function of the antihemophiliac *globulin* or Factor VIII. The gene responsible for this is carried on the X chromosome (sex-linked); thus females carry the trait, and half of each woman's sons on the average, will have the disease. The first clue may be bleeding from the *circumcision.* By the time the boy is a toddler, he will begin to develop large bruises and hematomata from minor injuries. Bleeding into the joints is painful and leads to arthritic stiffness. (See *Arthritis,* Section 7.) Plasma, or concentrates containing AHG, injected intravenously is the only treatment. Rapid intravenous injection of several units of cryo precipitate builds up the blood level of AHG to ninety percent of normal. Slow injection seems to permit the AHG to be used up almost as fast as it is being infused. (Like trying to fill the tank with gas with the engine running.)

It is difficult for a family to avoid overprotection. Some activity must be allowed, but rough play and contact sports are taboo.

Other factor deficiencies are felt to be genetic in origin and require plasma for treatment. But Factor VIII and IX deficiencies account for about ninety percent of all inherited coagulation disorders. Queen Victoria bore an affected son and two carrier daughters. Among their children and grandchildren, nine hemophiliac boys were produced.

The other coagulation disorders are carried by recessive genes. If a couple have one affected child, it means they are both carriers, and they have a one-in-four chance of producing another so affected. It is possible to identify female carriers of the gene for hemophilia in about fifty percent of cases.

Henoch-Schönlein vasculitis is a disease assumed to be of allergic onset manifested by a skin rash which becomes hemorrhagic (blood spots, *ecchymoses, petechiae*), abdominal pain with bloody stools, *arthritis,* and *kidney* failure. The disease may be mild or severe, acute or chronic, and may resemble *rheumatic fever, nephritis, mesenteric adenitis,* or other diseases. Treatment is symptomatic, but *cortisone* may be lifesaving.

Hyperbilirubinemia is excess *bilirubin* in the blood. (See *Bilirubin,* Section 5.) *Jaundice* is the sign of excessive destruction of red cells beyond the ability of the liver to handle and excrete it in the bile. If, however, there is no excess destruction of red cells (hemolysis), jaundice would be due to obstruction of bile flow, and bilirubin would "regurgitate" out of the liver cells into the circulation. In the jaundice of *hepatitis,* the bilirubin remains in the blood, because of the damaged cells' inability to move the bilirubin on to the bile, and also because the swelling of the liver obstructs the flow of bile.

Hypersplenism is not a disease but only a term used to include a variety of observations. Low white or red cell counts accompanied by an enlarged *spleen* indicate that the spleen has overreacted somehow, trapping and destroying some blood cells. Correction of the problem by a splenectomy is necessary. A number of poorly understood diseases also qualify for the term "hypersplenism," so efforts must be made to find the real cause.

Banti's syndrome is the name given to a group of findings which include an enlarged spleen, low white and red blood cell count, and enlargement of veins entering the liver. The victim is weak, pale, has an enlarged abdomen, and usually grows poorly. A variety of liver conditions can produce this obstruction of blood flow from spleen to liver. Treatment is to remove the cause and/or shunt the circulation around the liver.

Immunity is the sum total of the body's defenses against foreign substances—germs, *viruses,* dust, allergens, fungi, and even to parts of an individual's own body (*auto-immunity*). Sneezing could be part of the body's reaction to rid itself of undesirable inhalants. The withdrawal of the foot on painful penetration by a rusty nail is the body's way to avoid further introduction of noxious germs. A *globulin* (IgA) secreted by the nasal mucosa may be able to neutralize respiratory infection invasions. The *tonsils* and *adenoids* are composed of lymph tissue, and their strategic location at the gateway to the respiratory and digestive systems suggests that they have some responsibility for trapping viruses and germs. The fact that tonsils and adenoids normally increase in size during the first five years, when respiratory infections are so common (one every six to eight weeks), must mean that they are part of this immune mechanism. *Lymph nodes* swell from absorption of local poisons to save the body from another invader.

If a germ is terribly persistent and gets into the tissues—under the skin or mucous membrane—white blood cells (phagocytes) attack, engulf, and destroy the invader. If it slips by this defense, multiplies, and moves into the bloodstream, other immune processes are called up. The infection stimulates the lymphocytes to become plasma cells (which have a different appearance when stained); they manufacture specific *globulin* proteins against the particular invading organism. If the organism reinvades, the globulins and the "memory" stored in the cells will be brought into battle more rapidly. The continuous remanufacture of these immune substances accounts for the body's inability to become reinfected by most of the childhood diseases such as *measles, chickenpox,* and *mumps.*

The thymus, a large blob of lymph tissue in the upper front of the chest, is responsible for the origin of the lymphocytes found in the blood, *spleen,* and lymph nodes. *Immunoglobulins* begin to develop in the fetus at about the same time these cells appear. (See *Allergy,* Section 3.)

Immunoglobulin A (IgA) is the antibody protein found in serum and secretions (nasal, intestinal) and would thus be in the first line of defense. It is usually increased after viral respiratory infections.

The child who is "sick too much" is usually being exposed to too many children with infections at a time when he is unable to organize his own immune defenses. He may be subject to allergies (milk or inhalants) which allow frequent secondary infections. He may, however, be genetically susceptible because of a deficiency of any of the various cellular, organic, or globulin fractions.

Immunoglobulin G (IgG) is passively transferred from the mother via the placenta and is largely responsible for the newborn's immunity to *poliomyelitis, mumps,* and *measles.* This *protein* rapidly disappears, but the baby soon manufactures his own due to the stimulation by ingested and inhaled bacteria and viruses. (A baby reared in a sterile atmosphere would not manufacture this substance and would run a dangerous risk when suddenly exposed to the real, germy world.) This fraction of the Ig constitutes the chief storage of immune memory and gradually increases in amount during childhood. Injections of adult gamma globulin into a child will provide passive or short-term immunity against *rubeola* (hard measles), *hepatitis, mumps,* and *chickenpox.* Most adults have had these diseases, and this "memory" can be temporarily provided for the exposed child.

Temporary hypogammaglobulinemia is only a transient increase in susceptibility, because there is a lag in the baby's synthesis of his own immunoglobulins. A blood test reveals a low level, and therapy with periodic injections of adult *gamma globulin* dramatically reduces the severity and frequency of bacterial infections.

Immunoglobulin M (IgM) is found in a newborn if an intrauterine infection has occurred. Babies are susceptible to gram-negative infections (*E. coli,* Pseudomonas, Klebsiella) presumably because this Ig is so low in their blood. The level rises rapidly to normal adult levels by one year of age.

If IgM is elevated in the cord blood, *rubella, syphilis, cytomegalic-inclusion disease, bacteremia,* and *toxoplasmosis* should be looked for. These diseases may produce no clinical signs at birth, but may account for slow or retarded mental development before the first birthday. Early treatment based on the early detection of these devastating diseases may reduce the incidence of mental retardation.

Iron deficiency anemia—see *Anemia*

Jaundice is due to retained bilirubin (*hyperbilirubinemia*) and results in a yellow discoloration, first noted in the whites of the eyes. Its appearance suggests liver disease or increased red cell destruction. (See *Bilirubin* and *Erythroblastosis fetalis,* Section 5; *Hemolytic anemias; Hepatitis,* Section 12.)

Leukemia is a disease in which the *white blood cells* proliferate without control. The bone marrow is so busy manufacturing these cells that red cells and *platelets* decrease in number, and *anemia* and hemorrhages occur. The onset is usually acute, may seem to be a slight cold or flu with fever and lassitude. Within a week the child—usually of age three to five years—is quite obviously going downhill with pallor, yellow waxy skin, swollen glands, enlarged abdomen (the *liver* and *spleen* are infiltrated with white cells), loss of appetite, various aches and pains, and nosebleeds.

The white blood count is usually abnormally high but may be within normal limits or low. The immature cells (lymphoblasts, precursors of lymphocytes) seen are suggestive; the confirmation of the disease is the discovery of increased numbers of blast or early forms in the bone marrow. Anemia is the rule.

Most childhood leukemia is of the lymphocyte series and is fairly susceptible to a variety of chemical agents. Cortisone is often given first, and the patient may appear so normal (physically and hemotologically) in a very few days that one wonders if the diagnosis was correct. These remissions are short-lived, however, so another drug is given to confuse the white cells. Each succeeding remission is shorter, and each new drug may take longer to produce the desired effect. Combinations are tried or four-week cycles of different agents may be used, in an effort to forestall the inevitable recurrence. "Cures" of five- to six-year remissions are now on record, however. Usual drugs besides cortisone are chemicals with known ability to destroy cells or inhibit mitosis of rapidly dividing cells (vincristine, amethopterin, mercaptopurine). Without these agents, the average life expectancy is six months.

Most people are aware that leukemia is a fatal disease. These new agents raise hopes that early and adequate treatment may result in a lasting remission. Once the diagnosis is confirmed, the doctor and parents must discuss future plans. No child should be made to suffer unduly with prolonged hospitalization and/or painful procedures. Doctors and parents must honestly express their hopes and fears. The child must be answered honestly if he asks key questions.

Consultation must be provided for if questions arise, and parents must be dissuaded from traveling afar with false hopes of magic cures. Every large city has adequate facilities for handling the problem. Parents must be made aware that nothing they have done or not done is responsible. The cause is unknown, but research strongly suggests a virus link. Some increased incidence in children with Down's syndrome and in identical twins would imply some genetic possibilities.

I remember a beautiful mother who had decided to keep her out-of-wedlock son, since she had precious little else to sustain her. She assumed that her son's leukemia was her punishment.

Fortunately it is a rare disease. Many mothers will ask us to rule out the disease by taking a blood count. We are happy to do this, but if a parent seems obsessed with the disease, it may suggest some unconscious hostility which would best be explored psychiatrically.

Mediterranean anemia—see *Thalassemia*

Megaloblastic anemias are red-cell deficiencies caused by lack of folic acid and/or vitamin B_{12}. The red cells are larger than usual (iron deficiencies produce small red cells). Folic acid is minimal in goat's milk, and powdered milk may have little, so diets of these without supplementary cereal, fruit, or vitamins may bring about this anemia in the first year.

Malabsorption diseases, *celiac disease,* and some drugs interfere with folic-acid absorption and cause this anemia.

Vitamin B_{12} combines with a chemical in the stomach before it is absorbed from the small bowel. *Pernicious anemia* is the megaloblastic anemia that results from lack of this stomach factor even in the presence of adequate oral B_{12} intake. (See *Pernicious anemia.*)

Methemoglobinemia is the result of the *iron* in the *hemoglobin* molecule being in the ferric form (instead of ferrous). The *erythrocytes* are unable to transport oxygen, and the victim's skin becomes dusky and cyanotic. It may be an inherited trait, but may also be the result of exposure to aniline dyes (shoe polish or clothing dyes) or ingestion of well water containing nitrites, oxidizing agents capable of converting the ferrous (normal) ion to ferric state. Nitrites in plant foods may also produce this. *Phenacetin* (in A.P.C.), acetanilid, sulfa drugs, and aminophenol are occasionally responsible for methemoglobinemia. Vitamin C and methylene blue will reduce the ferric form of the ion back to ferrous.

An inherited form of methemoglobinemia may not respond to these agents, but fortunately results in few symptoms except the dusky hue.

Neutropenia is a deficiency of the polymorphonuclear leukocytes (the usual *white blood cell*). This rare hereditary defect has serious consequences, for the patient becomes susceptible to bacterial infections. If it is congenital, no therapy is available, and the baby is soon overwhelmed by some sepsis.

White cells are often decreased during *roseola, rubeola, typhoid fever,* and *brucellosis.* If a baby has a high fever and neutropenia is present, it usually means *roseola.* But a low white count occasionally means that a bacterial infection is overwhelming the patient. *Leukemia* may show a low count, as will *benzene poisoning* and some drug reactions (*Dilantin®, sulfonamides,* some *tranquilizers,* and *chloramphenicol*) which have suppressed the formation of phagocytes in the bone marrow.

Neutrophils—see *Blood cells,* polymorphonuclear leukocytes

Pernicious anemia is unusual in children but is suspected if a pale child fails to pink up after adequate doses of iron or oral vitamin B_{12}. This rare condition is due to a genetic lack of an intrinsic factor normally secreted by the stomach. B_{12} will not be absorbed if the intrinsic factor is absent.

It begins at about the toddler age, when the normal blood-forming stores from the mother have been used up. Pallor, irritability, unsteady gait, and sore tongue suggest a blood count. The red cells are larger than normal.

A rapid response to the injection of the vitamin B_{12} will clinch the diagnosis. B_{12} must be injected monthly for life; the absence of the intrinsic factor precludes the body's utilization of the ingested vitamin.

Platelets are small bits of cell cytoplasm that have broken away from a large cell in the bone marrow (megakaryocyte). They are essential to plug breaks in blood-vessel walls as well as to clot blood.

If platelets are reduced in number, petechiae or small blood spots appear. These look like spots of red ink dotting the skin; minute amounts of blood have leaked through microscopic holes in the capillary walls that the platelets were supposed to plug up.

Polycythemia—see *Erythrocytosis*

Purpura is a blood spot. A small, red dot like red ink is called a petechia; a larger area is called an ecchymosis. The leakage of blood from a blood vessel suggests a weakness in the blood-vessel wall or a low *platelet* count. If the number of platelets is adequate, the condition is called nonthrombocytopenic purpura. The blood spots may be due to an allergic response. (see *Henoch-Schönlein vasculitis,* also *Meningococcemia* and *Septicemia,* Section 2), vigorous crying or vomiting, or occasionally scurvy, drugs, and chronic diseases.

A low platelet count (see *Thrombocytopenic purpura*) may be due to some immune mechanism following a mild infection (*infectious mononucleosis*) or due to some drug (quinidine) idiosyncrasy, or be caused by an inherited condition (*Wiskott-Aldrich syndrome*) or *leukemia.* Platelets may be trapped or lost in the large capillary bed of a *hemangioma,* and effective clotting would then be denied to the remainder of the body. This is called diffuse intravascular clotting. (The bleeding tendency is a manifestation of the clotting.) These screening tests will allow the doctor to decide to what general category of hemorrhagic disorder the patient may be assigned: (a) partial thromboplastin time, (b) *platelet* count, and (c) bleeding time.

If the first PTT is prolonged, a *coagulation* disorder must be searched for.

If the platelet count is reduced and the bleeding time is prolonged, but PTT is normal, the patient is in the *thrombocytopenic purpura* group. If the platelet count and the PTT are normal, but the bleeding time is prolonged, the disorder falls in the nonthrombocytopenic purpuras. (This qualitative abnormality of the platelets is most commonly due to aspirin ingestion.)

Bruises or small (quarter to half inch) ecchymoses on the shins of children from toddler age to about twelve are so common from the daily bumps of climbing and playing that, if they are *not* present, it suggests the child is not normally active.

Ecchymoses appearing in unusual places—upper arms, face, thighs, lower back—would require an investigation of the child for a blood disease (bleeding tendency, *scurvy, leukemia,* etc.) or of the home for excessive punishment. (See *Battered child,* Section 1; *Cruelty to children,* Section 16.)

Red blood cell—see *Erythrocyte*

Reticulocyte is a young *erythrocyte* (red blood cell). Its appearance in the blood smear suggests that the bone marrow is active in manufacturing red cells (as in hemolytic anemia). A rise in the percentage of reticulocytes compared with the total red cell count is a clue that the therapy for the *anemic* (iron deficient) patient is successful.

Rh sensitization—see *Erythroblastosis fetalis,* Section 5

Sedimentation rate is a blood test of great value in ascertaining the seriousness and origin of a variety of diseases. Fresh blood is placed in a narrow glass tube; the rate of fall of the red cells in the serum is noted. A very slight drop of the red cells is normal (less than 5 millimeters in 15 minutes and 15 millimeters in 45 minutes). A rapid sedimentation rate (greater than 15 millimeters in 15 minutes and 40 millimeters in 45 minutes) suggests *abscesses, anemia, peritonitis, rheumatic fever, tuberculosis* or *glomerulonephritis,* and bacterial infection in general. It has been of great benefit in ruling out serious, chronic, debilitating diseases. For example, if a child has growing pains or vague aches in his muscles, bones, or joints, a sed-rate test, if normal, would tend to rule out *rheumatic fever* or *rheumatoid arthritis.*

Virus infections and *Rickettsial diseases* rarely affect the sed-rate.

Sickle-cell anemia is due to a genetic defect in the manufacture of *hemoglobin.* About 10 percent of American Negroes have some sickle hemoglobin. Under conditions of reduced oxygenation of the blood (high altitudes, shock) this abnormal hemoglobin reshapes into an elongated molecule which plugs up small capillaries.

A child might inherit the disease if both his parents have the trait (a one-out-of-four chance). All his blood cells contain this abnormal hemoglobin-S. Because the sickle-shaped red cells have difficulty squeezing through the capillaries, obstruction to blood flow occurs (*thrombosis*) and infarcts of *kidney, spleen, lung, bones,* and *brain* (stroke) may occur.

Hemolysis of the abnormal red cells leads to *anemia, jaundice, liver* damage, gallstones, and *kidney* damage. The spleen becomes fibrosed. Secondary infection is common, and most patients succumb to these multiple problems before reaching maturity.

Blood tests reveal the sickle-shaped cells and the hemoglobin-S. Treatment is supportive. Iron is not indicated.

All gradations of severity are seen from mild, iron-resistant anemia to severe anemia, frequent abdominal pain (thromboses of abdominal blood vessels), cerebral vascular accidents (strokes), nonhealing skin sores, and frequent severe infections.

Every Negro child with *anemia* unresponsive to *iron* should have a blood test for the sickling phenomenon and a determination of the presence of hemoglobin-S.

Spherocytosis is an inherited hemolytic *anemia* characterized by spherically shaped red cells. Some defect of the red cell membrane allows them to assume this shape; the spleen traps and destroys these abnormal cells. *Anemia* and *jaundice* follow. The *spleen* becomes enlarged, and most patients develop gallstones by early adolescence.

After the spleen is removed at age four years or so, the anemia disappears, although the red cells remain abnormal.

Spleen is a blood-forming and blood-destroying organ lying in the upper left side of the abdominal cavity, well protected by the lower ribs. It is a maze of capillaries and venules through which the blood is filtered, allowing the spleen to pick off old or abnormal red cells (see *Spherocytosis* and *Sickle-cell anemia*). In times of exaggerated blood-cell need, the spleen produces as if it were bone marrow. It plays a role in immunity; if the spleen is removed in an infant, he is more susceptible to overwhelming bacterial infections.

The spleen becomes enlarged in a number of conditions and when palpated below the rib margin, the following diseases must be considered: *hemolytic anemias,* infections (*infectious mononucleosis, malaria*), vein obstruction (*cirrhosis, congestive heart failure*), *lipidoses, leukemia, Hodgkin's disease.* (See *Banti's syndrome* and *Hypersplenism.*)

Rupture of the spleen occasionally follows a severe blow to the upper left abdomen or lower rib edge. Very minor trauma will rupture an enlarged spleen. Removal is standard if evidence of internal bleeding is present.

Absence of the spleen poses a threat to a child who is invaded by bacteria, since the cells of the spleen are important in clearing the bloodstream of potentially lethal bacteria. When splenectomy for any reason is contemplated, this susceptibility to severe infection must be considered.

Thalassemia, or Mediterranean or Cooley's anemia, is an inherited form of anemia that may be mild or severe. Hemolysis of the *red cells* may be prominent. The thalassemia trait manifests itself by mild, persistent *anemia,* unresponsive to *iron,* and red cells smaller than usual. It is caused by inheriting the *gene* from one parent (heterozygous) and is compatible with a fairly comfortable life. *Hemoglobin* synthesis of adult type (A) is defective in the trait and absent in the major form.

Thalassemia major is the severe form. The patient is homozygous for the genes (inherited from both parents). Frequent transfusions are necessary because of the few circulating red cells. The marrow of skull bones produces distortion of the head and face; the spleen and liver are huge. *Congestive heart failure* and stunted growth combine to produce an early death—usually by adolescence. Hemosiderosis (excessive iron storage) is common because of all the transfusions.

The only treatment available is the transfusion. Large, frequent transfusions will result in hemosiderosis, but the chronic anemia of too little blood keeps the patient weak, listless, and uncomfortable. Enough blood should be given to make the patient barely comfortable and able to be minimally active. Splenectomy in infancy may lead to susceptibility to severe infections. The removal of the *spleen* will not alter the disease; the chief reason for splenectomy is the large size of that organ.

Thrombocytopenia is the capillary leakage of blood caused by an insufficient number of *platelets.*

Idiopathic thrombocytopenic *purpura* is the result of some immune reaction to the platelets. The number of the "parent" cells in the marrow (megakaryocytes) is adequate, but they do not produce a sufficient number of platelets. It is often triggered by an infection.

Easy bruisability and small hemorrhages in the skin (petechiae) and mucous membranes are seen early. Hemorrhage into the brain is possible but rare.

Most children recover completely in a few weeks, so if the condition is mild, no treatment is necessary except to avoid trauma until the platelet count rises. Severe cases respond nicely to cortisone drugs.

Idiopathic thrombocytopenia is a form of *hypersplenism,* although the spleen is not enlarged. Some factor in the blood conditions the platelets for destruction by the spleen. This allows the disease to qualify as an *autoimmune* condition. Women with thrombocytopenia often deliver babies with transient thrombocytopenia; this suggests an antibody might have traversed the placenta and affected the infant's platelets. Even though a normal platelet count can be maintained with steroids (cortisone), splenectomy is the preferred treatment if the disease drags on beyond six months.

Thymus is a gland whose function is not clearly understood, but it is essential in the formation of some lymphocytes and of a hormone, both of which play key roles in the body's immune defenses. If the thymus is congenitally absent (Di George's syndrome), the baby is soon overwhelmed by a variety of viral and/or fungal infections. His lymphocytes are inadequate to meet the challenge of invading organisms; eventually some infection that would be no more than a "flu bug" in a normal child will take his life.

For a time in the 1930s it was thought that the thymus was responsible for the not infrequent, sudden-infant-death syndrome. The thymus when observed by X ray is often enlarged at age two to six months when the frequency of SID is highest. Because these babies were thought to have suffocated and the thymus is directly in front of the trachea, the natural conclusion seemed to be that the thymus compressed the trachea. Every "good" pediatrician fluoroscoped or X rayed babies routinely in those days, and if the thymic shadow was enlarged, the baby was subjected to X-ray therapy. In spite of this the incidence of SID remained the same. It has now been observed that the incidence of cancer of the thyroid may have been increased in those so irradiated. (My father conscientiously fluoroscoped infants in his search for large thymus glands; all it netted him was a crippling cancer of his hands.)

Von Willebrand's disease resembles *hemophilia.* It is inherited and manifests itself by nosebleeds and excessive hemorrhage after trauma or surgery. Bleeding time is prolonged and Factor VIII is deficient in amount or function. Treatment is similar to that of classic hemophilia.

White blood cells—see *Blood cells, Leukocytes*

SECTION 9

The Respiratory System

A. Cough, no fever, shortness of breath

Asthma
Atelectasis
Bronchiogenic cysts
Cysts in lungs
Emphysema
Foreign body (see Bronchi, Larynx, Trachea)
Löffler's syndrome
Nasal polyps
Parapertussis
Pigeon breeder's lung
Pneumothorax
Pulmonary edema (see also Section 8)
Pulmonary embolism (Section 8)
Respiratory distress syndrome (Section 5)
Silofiller's disease (Section 1)
Thyroglossal duct cyst
Tracheo-esophageal fistula (Section 5)
Vascular ring
Whooping cough (Pertussis)

B. Cough, fever, shortness of breath

Blastomycosis
Bronchiolitis
Bronchitis
Coccidioidomycosis
Cryptococcus
Empyema
Histoplasmosis
Influenza
Nocardiosis
Parrot fever (Psittacosis)
Pneumocystis carinii pneumonia
Polyarteritis (Section 2)
Pulmonary abscess
Q Fever (Section 2)
Tracheitis
Tracheobronchitis
Tuberculosis
Virus pneumonia (Mycoplasma pneumonia)

C. Croup, bark, hoarseness (see also Larynx)

Allergy (Asthma) (see Hay fever, Section 14; Milk, Section 11)
Croup
Epiglottitis
Influenza
Papilloma of larynx
Sinusitis (see Nose, Section 14)
Tracheitis
Tracheobronchitis

D. Cough with clear phlegm

Allergy
Asthma
Bronchiolitis
Croup
Influenza
Mycoplasma pneumonia
Parapertussis
Pulmonary edema
Vascular ring
Whooping cough (Pertussis)

E. Cough with purulent material

Bronchitis
Cystic fibrosis
Pneumonia
Pulmonary abscess
Sinusitis (see Nose, Section 14)

F. Chest pain

Devil's grip (Pleurodynia)
Empyema
Herpes zoster (Section 6)
Löffler's syndrome
Pericarditis (Section 8)
Pleurisy
Pneumonia
Pulmonary embolism (Section 8)
Rib, fractured (Section 1)
Rib syndrome (Section 7)

G. Special problems

Asphyxia
Cyanosis (also Sections 5, 6, 8)
Lung tumors
Nasal polyps
Sweat electrolytes
Tracheotomy
Zonking chart

H. Anatomical parts

Bronchi
Chest
Circumference
Funnel
Pigeon
Larynx
Lungs
Pleura
Sternum
Trachea

Asphyxia is the condition of decreased oxygenation of body tissues as caused by drowning, inhaling an object into the windpipe, strangulation, a *head injury* causing cessation of respiration, or oversedation. The patient is dusky or blue or ashen and pale. *Brain damage* will result if the condition is not relieved. (See *Cyanosis, Anoxia,* Section 5.)

Asthma occurs when the bronchial tubes fill with mucus and go into spasm, usually following some allergy or infection. Asthma produces a characteristic wheeze (more on expiration, less on inspiration) which can easily be detected by having the victim breathe into the observer's ear. The victim has considerably more trouble exhaling than inhaling. This is a reasonably serious condition, and the doctor's advice should be sought. In most children, asthma is usually triggered by some infection or when an infection is superimposed on an inhalation allergy. Antibiotics are usually indicated.

Asthma is a reversible, controllable condition. A large percentage of children can be helped if parents will do some careful detective work and elimination tests. If asthma occurs fairly constantly in the first year of life, milk is a likely offending agent. Soybean milk may be curative.

If asthma always follows a cold and a fever of 100° or so, and a purulent discharge is present, a bacterial allergy is likely. (See *Bronchitis.*) This victim may respond to antibiotics as well as to a series of dead bacteria injections (either a stock solution or one made up from the patient's own mucous secretions). (See *Allergy, Desensitization,* Section 3.)

If wheezing occurs only in early spring, tree and grass pollen may be the culprit; if in spring and summer, grass pollens; in summer and fall, weeds. (Many Midwesterners and Easterners come to Oregon from August to October to escape ragweed.) (Only plants which launch their pollen in quantities into the air, such as ragweed, give hay-fever sufferers any real trouble. Goldenrod, despite its wicked reputation, is pollinated by insects and will not usually provoke allergy unless brought into the sensitive's immediate presence.) If the wheezing lasts all winter, house dust and mold spores may be the cause. Most of the sufferers then usually have watery eyes and some nasal itch symptoms. If the inhalants cannot be avoided, a program of desensitization will control the symptoms in 70 percent to 80 percent of cases.

If symptoms occur when near cats, dogs, furniture, wool rugs and blankets, feather pillows, etc., these must be eliminated. Some children will wheeze after eating dairy products, peanuts, chocolate, corn, wheat, eggs, pork, or fish. Some are mildly sensitive to all the above, but have no symptoms unless some emotional trauma occurs—school difficulties, loss of a parent, or tension at home, for example.

Some allergic people develop a reaction to aspirin. A single tablet may induce a severe attack of asthma, but because an hour has elapsed, the causal relationship may not be obvious. (See *Cough,* Section 4.)

Status asthmaticus is the condition of refractory asthma unresponsive to the usual *epinephrine* injection. Infection is such a common complication of childhood allergy that *antibiotics* are usually administered to the asthmatic child who does not respond to the usual bronchodilators. *Cortisone* drugs may stop the attack, but are considered to be a last resort and only for short-term treatment.

Because of the risk of pulmonary failure with *cyanosis,* exhaustion, and death, the patient in status needs hospitalization and the attention of pulmonary experts. *Acidosis* develops because of the inability to exhale carbon dioxide. Machine-assisted breathing with mask, tent, or tracheal tube may be lifesaving.

ALLERGY CHECKLIST

Most Common Inhalants Causing Nasal or Lung Trouble

House dust—usually a mixture of molds, spores, fur, cottonseed

Animal hair or dander from cats and dogs, birds, horses, pigs (in upholstery)

Pollens from trees in spring, grass in spring and summer, ragweed in summer and fall

Chemical irritants such as sprays, deodorants, cleansers

Cottonseed in furniture and mattresses

All surroundings should be as free as possible from dusts of all kinds. Most people cannot control the dust conditions under which they work or spend their daytime hours, but everyone can, to a large extent, eliminate dust from the bedroom. The following simple instructions describe the preparation and maintenance of a dust-free sleeping room for those with perennial nasal congestion and/or nocturnal cough and/or asthma:

CLEAN THE ROOM THOROUGHLY

1. Remove all furniture, rugs, curtains, and draperies from the room. Empty all closets.

2. Clean the walls, ceiling, and floors. Scrub the woodwork and floors in the bedroom and closets. Wax the floors.

KEEP THE ROOM FREE FROM DUST

1. Any flues that open into the room should be sealed. If you have hot-air heating, seal the opening with oilcloth and adhesive tape and use an electric heater. If this is not practical, then place a common screen over the hot-air outlet behind the grating, and change the screen frequently.

2. The furniture that has been removed from the room should be thoroughly cleaned before it is returned. The room should contain a minimum amount of furniture and furnishings. A wood or metal chair may be used (not upholstered). Use plain rag rugs and plain light curtains (both of which must be washed at least once a week).

3. The room must be cleaned daily, and given a thorough and complete cleaning once a week. Clean the floor, furniture, tops of doors, window frames, sills, etc., with a damp cloth or oil mop. Air the room thoroughly. Then close the doors and windows until the child is ready to occupy the room.

4. Keep the doors and windows of this room closed as much as possible, especially when the room is not occupied. Use this room for sleeping only. Dress and undress in another room.

BEDDING IS IMPORTANT

1. Scrub the bed. Scrub the bedspring.

2. Box spring, mattress, and pillows must be encased in dustproof coverings. These are impervious to dust, and keep the child from coming in contact with the harmful allergens that are present in all bedding material.

3. Be sure to clean the bed and encase the pillows, box spring, and mattress outside of the bedroom before they are returned to the room.

4. Do not use any kind of mattress pad. Sheets and blankets should be laundered weekly.

5. If there are two beds in the room, both of them must be treated as described above.

GENERAL SUGGESTIONS

1. Care must be taken to keep down the dust throughout the entire house. Go over all floors and furniture with a vacuum cleaner at frequent intervals—once daily if possible. Following this, the house should be aired thoroughly. Cleaning must be done while the child is away from the house. Use a damp or oiled cloth to avoid raising the dust.

2. Pets, birds, and animals must be kept out of the house. Cats and dogs should be particularly discouraged. A difficult decision must be faced by a family who finds their child has become allergic to the dog or cat. Some people put up with allergic symptoms rather than "lose" the animal. Keeping the animal in the garage and maintaining a strictly "sterile" room, plus adding an electronic air filtering machine (tax deductible), might be a suitable compromise.

3. Avoid cosmetics, perfumes, insect sprays, or powders, and odoriferous substances such as camphor, tar, etc.

4. The child should not go into any room while it is being cleaned. He should be careful not to handle objects that are covered with dust, such as books, boxes, or clothing that have been stored on shelves or in cupboards over a long period of time. He should be kept away from attics and closets.

5. Keep out of the room all toys that will accumulate dust. Use only unstuffed, washable toys.

6. Keep bedroom door closed. Attach a flap at the bottom.

Most parents compromise with the above suggestions. If a few things are done and the symptoms disappear, that would seem sufficient. If trouble returns, the remainder might be done. If improvement is not obvious in a few weeks, a consultation with an allergist would be the next step. Skin tests may pinpoint the offending inhalant. (If molds give a big skin reaction, some relief may occur by drying out a basement or putting plastic over bare earth under the house.)

Atelactasis is the collapse of *lung* tissue due to infection (*bronchitis, asthma, pneumonia*), trauma (chest injury where the entry of air inside the chest wall collapses the lung), aspiration of a foreign object (peanut inhaled into and occluding a bronchial tube, thus preventing air exchange to lung below), or incomplete expansion of lungs at birth (prematurity with incompletely developed air sacs). (See Section 5.)

The patient is usually short of breath and *cyanotic*. The treatment is directed to the relief of the cause.

Blastomycosis is a fungus disease that presents as small abscesses in lungs, skin and/or bone. It is endemic to the Mississippi valley areas. Apparently the victim inhales the spores and after a lung infection begins, it may spread to skin and bones. X ray of lungs may have the appearance of tuberculosis.

Bronchi are the breathing tubes which carry air to the microscopic alveolar sacs where the oxygen and carbon-dioxide exchange is completed with the blood in adjacent capillaries. The *trachea* is the largest bronchus and branches into smaller bronchi, then to bronchioles.

A *foreign body* in the bronchial tube of a toddler is usually the result of his need to mouth objects in an effort to learn about his environment. Coins, marbles, nuts, pins, nails, screws, buttons, can be inhaled into the bronchial tubes. The object will wedge itself and defy efforts of coughing and gravity to dislodge it.

This is the usual story the doctor hears: "He had a penny in his mouth, and I was trying to get him to spit it out when he cried, inhaled, coughed, and turned blue. He's comfortable now, but he has a wheeze." The location of the object will determine the symptoms and signs. Hoarseness would indicate the larynx is the obstructive point. No air moving in or out of the right side of the chest would indicate the right main stem bronchus is obstructed. X rays determine the position accurately if the object is radiopaque. Bronchoscopy is the usual method of discovery and removal.

Prevention is obviously the best cure. Dolls and toys should not have detachable buttons. Candy should not contain nuts; no candy would be even better. Safety pins should always be kept closed and out of reach. Stop the habit of carrying objects—including cigarettes—in your mouth; imitative children don't know the dangers.

Bronchiolitis is a *viral* illness, usually occurring in the child under eighteen months, and frequently requires oxygen and cold mist in the hospital, as *cyanosis* commonly accompanies it. The victim breathes rapidly, and wheezing is heard on both inhaling and exhaling. (With *asthma,* wheezing is worse on expiration.) Most doctors will treat bronchiolitis with *antibiotics* because of the severity of the symptoms, but, of course, the virus does not respond.

Bronchitis is an infection of the bronchial tubes, usually of bacterial origin. The victim has a hard cough and may raise purulent material. It tends to be triggered by a cold and requires some antibiotic for its cure. An abnormal number of bronchial infections—especially if each one is accompanied by an audible expiratory wheeze—suggests an allergy in the background. Most often it is an inhalation *allergy,* but it can be related to milk drinking and/or an allergy to the person's own bacteria. Appropriate measures are necessary to cut down the frequency of these attacks, because a bad bronchitis attack decreases the amount of oxygen that is getting to the brain, with resultant brain injury. (A rare, inciting condition is *Hiatus hernia,* Section 12.)

Asthmatic bronchitis is common in children whose bronchial tubes frequently overreact to infection by increased mucous secretion and spasm. The characteristic expiratory wheeze, fever of 100° to 101° F. following a cold or influenza is the giveaway.

The mucus formed by the cold is a good medium for bacterial growth. The pus created as a result of this invasion inflames the tubing into the lungs, increasing the cough and fever. Children frequently develop a wheeze because of the spasm of the bronchial tubes and an asthma sound (wheezing on exhalation) results. This noisy, short-of-breath sound is easily audible to the parents and can frequently be diagnosed over the phone by the doctor if the child's open mouth is held close to the mouthpiece. The wheeze is usually accompanied by rales (the sound of dropping sand on metal) which is the noise produced by exhaled air bubbling through the pus-laden tubes. Treatment with *antibiotics* (and perhaps *epinephrine*) is required. The child who has this affliction more than two or three times a year would be a candidate for an *allergy* workup.

Bronchogenic cysts arise from the *trachea* or *bronchial tubes* and may produce coughing, wheezing, or choking attacks.

Chest is that part of the body covered by ribs between the neck and the abdomen.

Chest circumference roughly parallels the head circumference for the first two years of life, after which time the chest grows more rapidly and is about one to two inches greater than the head at age five. The difference may be important in evaluating *nutrition, dwarfism,* or *hydrocephalus.*

Funnel chest (pectus excavatum) is the indentation of the lower end of the sternum (breastbone) usually congenital and due to a shortening of the diaphragm muscle attached to the back side of the sternum. On deep inspiration this area is further retracted, and may lead to

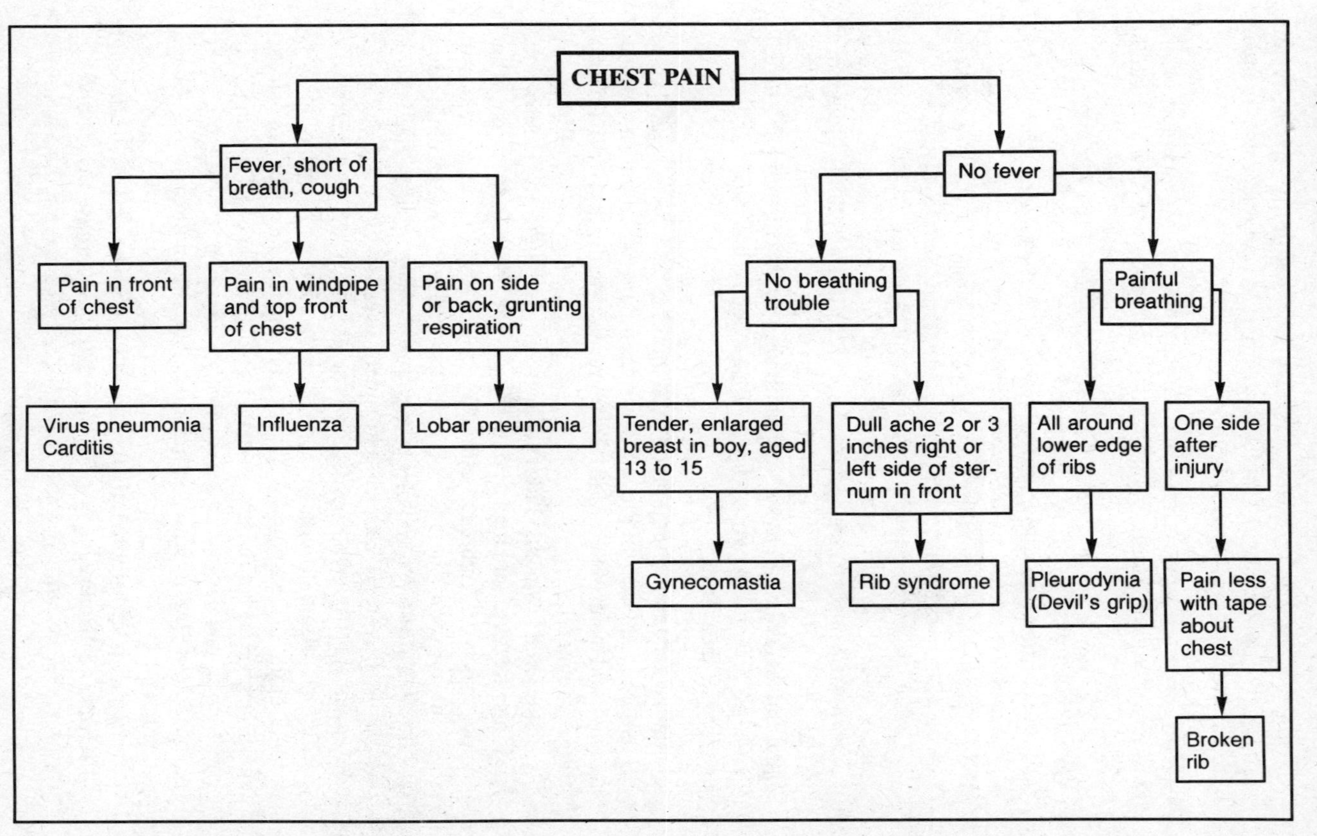
CHEST PAIN
Fever, short of breath, cough
Pain in front of chest
Virus pneumonia
Carditis
Pain in windpipe and top front of chest
Influenza
Pain on side or back, grunting respiration
Lobar pneumonia
No fever
No breathing trouble
Tender, enlarged breast in boy, aged 13 to 15
Gynecomastia
Dull ache 2 or 3 inches right or left side of ster-num in front
Rib syndrome
Painful breathing
All around lower edge of ribs
Pleurodynia (Devil's grip)
One side after injury
Pain less with tape about chest
Broken rib

shortness of breath or at least an unsightly deformity. Maturity improves the appearance of mild forms, but surgery is recommended for the more severe depressions.

Pigeon breast is, in contrast to funnel chest, a prominence of the lower end of the sternum and relative narrowing of the side of the rib cage.

Coccidioidomycosis, or San Joaquin Valley fever, is a fungus infection usually confined to the lungs of residents of the dry, dusty areas of the southwestern United States. Chills, fever, and cough may suggest the flu. An X ray would reveal shadows suggestive of *tuberculosis,* but the skin tests would help to differentiate the two diseases.

Most patients recover with rest, but a rare case may have the fungus widely spread over the body to meninges, bones, and skin. A new drug, *amphotericin,* may control the infection if diagnosed in time. Several recent cases have occurred in fossil hunters and others handling or digging in soil contaminated with this fungus (usually in California and Arizona desert areas, but it has recently been diagnosed in East Texas).

Croup is a common childhood affliction. It usually appears rather dramatically in the middle of a winter night, when the air outside is clear and cold. The air in the house is usually dry, and this may trigger the attack.

The child awakens suddenly between midnight and one o'clock, clawing the air, choking, and barking. The mother first may think the dog has been frightened until she realizes that the racket is coming from the nursery. She may be quite frantic because her child seems scared to death, but after twenty minutes of being upright and inhaling steam, he should be relaxed and quiet. Because most drugstores are closed at this time of night, the best cough syrup is a mixture of equal parts of gin, lemon juice, and honey. For the twenty- to forty-pound child, a teaspoonful is usually adequate to cut and loosen the phlegm and to reduce anxiety for all concerned. Gargling is ineffective as the larynx is below the gargle area. If available, syrup of ipecac (one teaspoonful) is helpful for laryngeal spasm. (See *Cough,* Section 4.)

Croup is considered to be basically a *virus* affliction, although *allergies* and bacteria may play their parts. It almost invariably lasts for three nights and, if under the influence of steam, the victim can

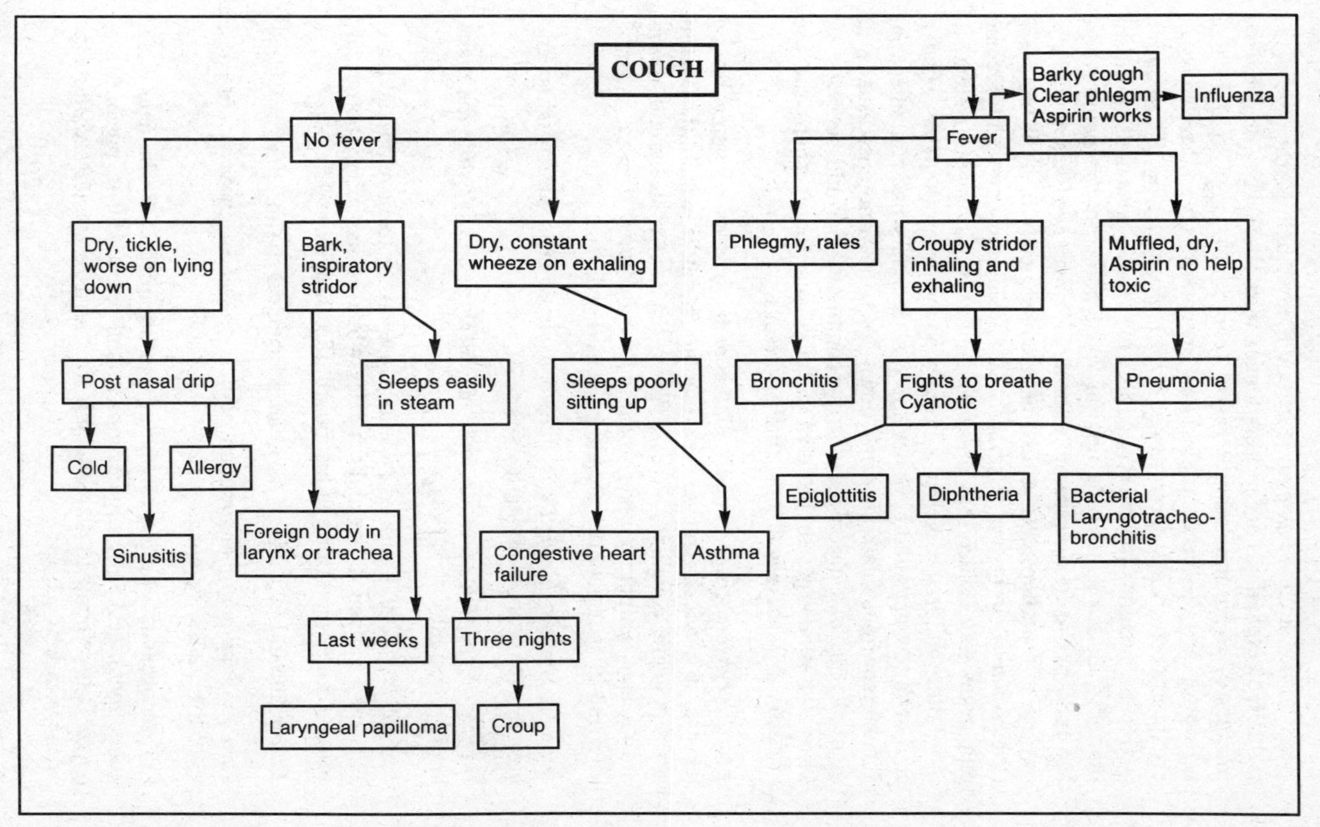
COUGH
No fever
Fever
Barky cough
Clear phlegm
Aspirin works
Influenza
Dry, tickle,
worse on lying
down
Bark,
inspiratory
stridor
Dry, constant
wheeze on exhaling
Phlegmy, rales
Croupy stridor
inhaling and
exhaling
Muffled, dry,
Aspirin no help
toxic
Post nasal drip
Sleeps easily
in steam
Sleeps poorly
sitting up
Bronchitis
Fights to breathe
Cyanotic
Pneumonia
Cold
Allergy
Epiglottitis
Diphtheria
Bacterial
Laryngotracheo-
bronchitis
Sinusitis
Foreign body in
larynx or trachea
Congestive heart
failure
Asthma
Last weeks
Three nights
Laryngeal papilloma
Croup

sleep for an hour or two in between the strangling, then he is all right. However, if his croup lasts longer than three days, or if twenty minutes of steam inhalation does not relax him enough to allow him to sleep, then he needs professional attention. One severe type of croup, almost always accompanied by a *temperature* of 103° or more, is due to bacterial infection. In this case, thick, tenacious, purulent matter occludes and swells up the vocal cords to the point where the child has to fight desperately for air. He may need hospitalization, oxygen, and perhaps even a tube inserted surgically into the windpipe (*tracheotomy*). If his air is severely restricted, the child will become blue or *cyanotic,* which may do some damage to his nervous system.

Some children develop a croupy sound after they have had a cold for a few days and have developed a secondary bacterial infection. Thick, tenacious material drips down into the windpipe, usually at night. If this is a chronic, recurring condition, it would suggest that the child is allergic to his own bacteria and that perhaps the use of bacterial vaccine will abort further attacks.

Acute laryngotracheobronchitis is due to a virus, is accompanied by fever and *headache* for seventy-two hours, after which the victim has a phlegmy cough for a week. (See *Influenza.*) If steam and *aspirin* do not give temporary relief, then acute *epiglottitis,* a severe bacterial infection of the epiglottis, should be considered.

Acute spasmodic laryngitis is due to a virus, lasts three nights, and has no fever accompanying it.

Diphtheria may cause croup, but this develops slowly while the membrane grows into the larynx.

Foreign bodies, if aspirated, would cause croup to develop suddenly. This may happen if the child inhales while he has a toy, bottle cap, coin, or some such thing in his mouth. (See *Larynx.*)

Tetany due to low calcium may cause laryngeal spasm.

Tumors, papillomas, or *cysts* on or near the vocal cords would cause a croupy cough, requiring surgery.

Cryptococcus is a fungus capable of causing infection in humans (skin, lungs, meninges). The organism is in soil, especially in pigeon droppings. It is difficult to diagnose and treat as it resembles *toxoplasmosis* or *tuberculosis.*

Cyanosis, or blue discoloration, means that not enough oxygen is getting into the system. It implies that there is some obstruction that prevents oxygen from reaching the bloodstream. There may be an obstruction in a small baby's nose, and he will be unable or unwilling to breathe through his mouth. He may have an infection in, or a congenital anomaly of, his throat or windpipe that prevents the easy inflow of air into his lungs. He may have a collapsed lung, *pneumonia,* or some problem that reduces the area of functioning lung tissue, or a heart anomaly where the unoxygenated blood is mixed with fresh, or where not enough blood is going through the lungs to become properly oxygenated. The nervous system suffers the most from lack of oxygen, and if prolonged or severe, this can result in *brain damage.* The obvious answer is to relieve the condition that is producing the lack of oxygenated blood and/or to give the patient increased amounts of oxygen. If the condition appears suddenly, it is a real emergency. The most important thing to do, besides calling the doctor, is to get someplace—such as a hospital emergency room or a doctor's office—where there is oxygen equipment. The local fire station and/or police usually have this, and this is often the easiest and fastest place to call or get to and find relief. (See *Congenital heart defects,* Section 5.)

Cystic fibrosis is an inherited disease characterized chiefly by chronic lung infection and intestinal *malabsorption.* Afflicted children have repeated attacks of *bronchitis,* often due to resistant bacteria, frequent, large, greasy, foul-smelling stools, wasted, malnourished bodies—especially buttocks, and shortened life expectancy.

Approximately one in twenty people carry the *gene* for cystic fibrosis; if carriers mate, one of four of their children will have the disease, half will carry the gene, and one quarter will be unaffected. About one child in two thousand in our country has the disease.

It is a disorder of the exocrine or mucus-producing glands; therefore, a few of these babies are born with an intestinal obstruction due to a plug of hard, dry stool which formed in the absence of the digestive enzymes. After the newborn period, *diarrhea* of large, smelly, greasy stools results from the lack of protein-, starch-, and fat-digesting *enzymes;* undigested food ferments and the irritated bowel pushed it on out as if it were a laxative. Of course, the child's body gets little nourishment, so the victim is wasted despite a ravenous appetite. Daily ingestion of pancreatic enzymes serves to control this problem fairly well, but *cirrhosis* of liver *intussusception,* and *rectal prolapse* are common.

The pulmonary complications are thought to be due to the lack of production of normal mucus in the bronchial tubes. *Bronchitis, bronchiolitis,* pulmonary *abscesses, atelectasis,* and *emphysema* may be seen singly or in various combinations. This pulmonary inflammation leads to hypertension of the pulmonary blood vessels and pressure on the right side of the heart. Thus heart failure may be a secondary complication to the already ravaged system.

When antibiotics became available, the pulmonary infections of cystic fibrosis were rapidly brought under control, but resistant strains (*Staphylococcus, Pseudomonas,* etc.) soon appeared. Now, most doctors use antibiotics intermittently or only if fever and an acute infection is present. Postural drainage and finely atomized inhalation (mist tent) are helpful to promote the flow of secretions out of the lungs.

These patients have excessive salt concentration in their sweat, and hot weather may cause them to develop shock from salt depletion. Extra salt is necessary in warm weather. In addition to the history and physical findings, the diagnosis is usually confirmed by assaying the sweat for *sodium* and chloride. The fingernail clippings also contain increased amounts of sodium. (See *Sweat electrolytes.*).

Because antibiotics, enzymes, postural drainage, and mist tents have prolonged the life expectancy of these children into adolescence and beyond, a variety of psychological problems has appeared. Some of these are due to the parents' natural desire to protect their child from the knowledge of an unhappy outcome. Honesty may hurt, but if a family is living a lie, the confused, frustrated child becomes angry and resentful. The doctor must be truthful, especially to the normally suspicious adolescent. A recent study of cystic-fibrosis patients who had been diagnosed early and treated vigorously showed a survival rate of 77 percent at age twenty years.

Absence of obvious signs of *anxiety* and *depression* does not mean that these feelings do not exist. A wise parent or doctor must at least ask occasionally, "How do you really feel about your disease?" "What do you think will happen to you?" Sometimes nothing can really *be* done, but we all need to feel that someone at least *cares.*

There is no cure for the condition, only control. The financial and emotional drain on the family can be enormous, but the Cystic Fibrosis Foundation can help with therapy and guidance. Research is uncovering new aids. Relatives of victims should seek genetic counseling if parenthood is contemplated.

Cysts in lungs may form from air trapped in the lung alveoli during *pneumonia, bronchitis,* or following an injury. The pressure of the air distends the lining of the elastic walls into a cyst which would be incapable of resuming its original size after the obstructive mechanism had been removed. Most cysts produce no symptoms and are an incidental finding on a chance X ray. If large enough to cause respiratory embarrassment, cysts should be removed. Most, however, will disappear spontaneously after a few weeks or months; the surrounding tissues will absorb the air and fluid they contain.

Emphysema is the dilation (occasionally to the point of rupture) of the alveoli, the microscopic sacs at the end of the bronchial tubes where gas exchange with blood is effected.

It occurs during an *asthma* attack or *bronchitis* because the air is trapped distal to the obstruction, distending the alveolar sacs. It may arise from a partial obstruction due to aspiration of a foreign object such as a peanut. The object acts as a ball valve, allowing air to be inhaled but preventing its exhalation. This accumulated air will cause emphysema in the area served by the obstructed bronchial tube.

If it is congenital, it is due to a narrowed bronchial tube segment or a fold of membrane acting as a valve.

The victim usually is short of breath and makes an audible wheeze on exhalation. If much *lung* tissue is involved, he will turn blue. (See *Cyanosis.*)

Empyema may develop during *pleurisy* when more fluid accumulates and becomes infected from an underlying bacterial pneumonia. The *staphylococcus* is the more common bacterium to cause extensive pus formation. Shortness of breath, high fever, and cyanosis become more severe as the empyema grows. The chest must be surgically tapped to remove the pus: one end of a drainage tube is placed in the empyema space and the other is connected with an underwater trap bottle to prevent air entering the chest. This drainage is required, as the antibiotics used for the underlying pneumonia are unable to penetrate the pus pocket and resolve the empyema (see *Pneumothorax*).

Epiglottitis is an inflammation of the epiglottis and is a severe form of bacterial croup. The child may become dusky (slightly cyanotic), he makes a loud noise on *both* inspiration and expiration, he usually has a high fever (and elevated white blood count), his chest heaves in and out, he is anxious and restless fighting for air, and his pulse is elevated above 160/minute and respirations are over 50 to 60/minute. The child will respond to oxygen, mist tent, and antibiotics in the hospital, but the disease may progress so rapidly that a *tracheotomy* (airway made surgically through the lower windpipe at the base of the neck) may have to be done while awaiting improvement.

(Acute spasmodic laryngitis responds to home measures; he sleeps—albeit noisily—for an hour or two between spasms of barking.)

Flu—see *Influenza*

Foreign bodies—see *Larynx, Bronchi*

Histoplasmosis is a fungus disease widely found in animals and man. The fungus Histoplasma is found in soil, especially near chicken and pigeon roosts. The fungus is either swallowed or inhaled, and its effect on the body is similar to that of *tuberculosis.* It may sneak into the lungs and cause a tissue reaction that walls itself off and does not make the host ill. An X ray might show some spots resembling tuberculosis. The disease, however, may sweep through the body and involve the bone marrow, *spleen,* and distant *lymph nodes,* and resemble *leukemia.* The severe form is usually fatal, as medicines against fungus diseases are toxic to humans.

Influenza is a virus respiratory infection (the "virus that's going around") that usually occurs in epidemics from December to March. It is especially harmful to very young or weak or very old victims, and the incidence of secondary bronchopneumonia is greatly increased as a sequel.

It begins suddenly with fever, malaise, chills, muscle aches, and soreness in *larynx* and windpipe area. Fever lasts seventy-two hours and is followed by a week of "choke, cough, and strangle." Phlegm produced is clear or milky; if it turns green or yellow, a secondary bacterial infection has been superimposed, and *antibiotics* might be worthwhile. (See *Bronchitis.*)

Treatment is *aspirin,* steam, *antihistaminics,* decongestants, cough remedies (equal parts of gin, lemon juice, and honey), extra fluids, hot baths. These cure nothing, but make the patient comfortable while living through the distress. Use of antibiotics during the virus phase does no good and may only serve to allow a resistant germ to develop and possibly *monilia.*

Several virus types have been found responsible for the epidemics that sweep through every winter. Vaccines of these influenza viruses have been developed and are about 50 percent to 60 percent reliable. The major problem is to try to predict which variant will be in vogue for the next go-around, then try to manufacture enough vaccine to distribute and inject before the epidemic hits. Results are occasionally gratifying in large military installations because absenteeism is reduced, but the doctor in private practice usually hears only the complaints. ("I got your——shot, but still got the flu," or "I was sicker from the shot than if I'd had the disease.") Newer, purified vaccines and better predictions should eliminate some of these difficulties.

Laryngitis—see *Croup*

Larynx, or voicebox, is the area in the windpipe containing the vocal cords (Adam's apple).

Foreign bodies may be trapped on or between the cords because of the narrow, slitlike opening. The usual story: a two-year-old with a peanut, diced carrot, plastic toy, marble, or coin in his mouth suddenly laughs or inhales. He is overcome with coughing, gasping, barking, or voice loss. He turns red and frantically clutches his throat and/or mouth. (Croup or barking in the middle of the night would suggest a virus, as a foreign body lodged in the larynx would not allow the child to fall asleep.) He may cough the object up, or it may remain stuck and have to be removed after direct observation with the laryngoscope, or it may move down into a bronchial tube and cause wheezing and/or bronchial-tube obstruction. (See *Emphysema.*)

It is amazing how a child may cough and choke on a bit of bone or shell, seem to rid himself of the object, but retain it in the laryngeal area with a minimum of symptoms. X rays may miss it if it is not opaque. Direct viewing is the only way to solve the mystery of a vocal change that cannot be explained by a virus.

Warts or nodules on the larynx are calluslike growths on the vocal cords. They may be due to shouting or singing too much, too loudly. Vocal rest will allow them to disappear from disuse, but the treatment is usually impossible to enforce. Surgery may be necessary if aphonia or severe hoarseness is a problem.

Löffler's syndrome is an unusual, transitory lung infiltration of *eosinophils* assumed to be an allergic reaction to intestinal *parasites* (*as-*

caris) or to the direct invasion of the lungs by the larvae of dog or cat roundworms (see *Toxocara canis*).

Cough, wheeze, and chest pain are the usual symptoms. The chest X-ray shows scattered densities (as in miliary *tuberculosis*) and the eosinophils are especially numerous in the blood count. Many eosinophils mean allergy and/or worms.

Lungs are the tubes and air-filled, microscopic sacs that allow for the absorption of oxygen from the air and the removal of carbon dioxide (and some volatile gases, contained in garlic, onions, spirits) from the body. Obviously bacteria, *viruses,* smoke, and chemicals can be inhaled along with air, so the lungs are frequently irritated and infected.

The *trachea* has cilia (little hairlike projections) which serve to propel bacteria and small foreign substances up to where they may be coughed out. Mucous glands in the lining serve to moisten the inhaled air and trap the unwanted particles. An *immunoglobulin* (IgA) is secreted along the lining and helps neutralize some viruses.

Muscles surrounding the bronchial tubes will contract when irritated by *allergens* (grass pollens, animal danders) or irritants (smog). The narrowing of the bronchial tubes will cause wheezing, especially on exhaling (*asthma*). Bacterial and viral infections may produce this same picture, but infection is more likely to cause wheezing on inspiration and expiration. Bacterial infections (*bronchitis, pneumonia, bronchiectasis*) produce a green or yellow purulent material. Viral or allergic conditions may cause no discharge, or it may be gray, white, or watery. A wheeze on inhaling is more likely to be produced by laryngeal pathology (or a foreign body).

The worse the cough, the higher up (closer to the throat) is the problem. Lobar pneumonia (way down in the lung) usually produces little or no cough; only a slight, muffled, feeble "eeaugh" may be elicited. The deeper the sound of the cough, the higher up is the problem; the croupy, brassy bark is a low note from the larynx.

Doctors thump on the chest with their fingers just as a shopper thunks a melon, testing for ripeness. The lungs, if full of air, will have a resonant, low-pitched note, in contrast to the liver (a muscle or solid organ) which has a dead, but high-pitched percussion sound. The stethoscope allows the doctor to listen to different areas of the lungs for breath sounds and rales, the noises made by the bursting of bubbles of air and pus or air and fluid inside the alveoli or bronchial tubes. When it is pressed against the child's back, the untrained ear of a parent may hear only loud rhonchi (phlegm rattling in the trachea) and the small, important rales may be missed. Without the stethoscope, the naked ear may hear the rales when the child breathes forcefully into it; they sound like sand falling on metal. If these are heard and the child has a fever, a cough with purulent sputum, the diagnosis is surely a bacterial lung infection worth treating with more than just aspirin.

Lung tumors usually occur as a cancer spreads from other parts of the body. Persistent cough, blood in sputum, wheezing, finally necessitate a chest X ray. A shadow suggests bronchoscopy or chest surgery.

Mycoplasma pneumonia is the organism causing atypical (or *virus*) pneumonia. It acts like most viral respiratory infections with *headache,* fever, sore windpipe, dry cough, and occasionally bloody sputum. "It's that flu that's going around," but the patient doesn't seem to get better after the usual seventy-two-hour wait. An X ray of the chest reveals a shadow fanning out from the heart. If the patient's condition warrants, a trial of a mycin drug might be helpful. If he gets better in twenty-four hours, the doctor might be credited, but the disease was probably about to abate anyway.

Nasal polyps are usually the result of chronic nasal allergy. They are pale, obstructive bags of cells and fluid. They are removed surgically. An *allergy* control program must be initiated. (See *Nose,* Section 14.)

Nocardiosis is a fungus disease primarily involving the lungs. The symptoms and signs mimic *tuberculosis,* so identification of the organism is all-important, as a *sulfa* drug—worthless for tuberculosis—is helpful early in nocardiosis.

Papilloma of *larynx* is a dangly clublike bit of tissue, considered benign, but may cause obstructive symptoms. If on the vocal cords and causing only hoarseness, it may be left as they frequently disappear at puberty. Some consider them due to a virus. If removed, it frequently regrows.

Parapertussis is a disease resembling *whooping cough* but is less severe and lasts only three weeks; whooping cough lasts six. It probably explains the occasional two-week night cough with a whoop in a child who has had his DPT shots. It responds poorly or not at all to antibiotics. There is no fever, the chest sounds are clear (no moisture heard) and any phlegm raised is clear or milky.

Pertussis, or whooping cough, is a bacterial respiratory infection that typically lasts six weeks. Two weeks of dry, irritating, usually nocturnal cough without fever are followed by two weeks of whooping. The child coughs, coughs, coughs in spasms until all his breath is exhaled; he then inhales suddenly and deeply with a characteristic whoop. He may become *cyanotic.* He may cough so hard that he breaks capillaries in the skin of his face (petechiae) or in the sclerae (*subconjunctival hemorrhages*). *Vomiting* may be a problem severe enough to cause *dehydration,* weight loss, or *malnutrition.* Secondary *otitis media* or *bronchitis* are common complications. Because of the complications, infants are more likely to succumb to this disease, but all ages are susceptible. The cough in the last two weeks of the disease reverts to the dry, irritating cough of the initial stage.

Examination of the chest usually is negative unless a secondary infection is present. The doctor should consider pertussis when confronted with a patient with such a severe cough with so few physical findings. An elevated *white blood cell count* (20,000 cubic millimeters or more), predominantly *lymphocytic,* is found. A culture revealing the causative organism clinches the diagnosis, especially if the patient had never received his baby DPT shots.

A hyperimmune serum (*gamma globulin* from humans with high immunity to pertussis) is effective in decreasing the course of the disease from six to two or three weeks. Antibiotic treatment with ampicillin has some effect on the course of the illness, but its use is questionable unless bronchitis or otitis is present.

DPT injections should be begun in the first two months of the baby's life to ward off this still common disease. It is still possible to acquire the disease after DPT shots, but it is milder and of shorter duration in the immunized child.

Pigeon breeder's lung is a type of sensitivity to pigeon feathers and droppings which produces a mild chronic cough, some dyspnea, weight loss, and an X-ray picture compatible with miliary tuberculosis. The symptoms and X rays are similar to other occupational pulmonary hypersensitivities (for example, sugar-cane worker's disease, thatched roof worker's disease, maple bark stripper's disease, paprika splitter's disease, and others). *Tuberculosis* must be ruled out by the skin test; pigeons must be removed.

(A fungus in the air conditioning system of an office was responsible for an "epidemic" of nodular pneumonitis. Cleaning the system cured the coughs and lesions.)

Pleura is the thin tissue over the surface of the lungs and on the inner side of the chest wall. This closed space between these two layers is under negative pressure, so when the chest expands and the diaphragm muscle moves down, air rushes into the lungs.

Pleurisy is an inflammation of the *pleura,* usually due to a lung disease that has extended to the surface of the lung. Pneumonia due to pneumococcus or other bacteria can cause this. It may occur with *tuberculosis; rheumatic fever* or *lupus* may also be associated with pleurisy.

The first signs are usually fever and pain in breathing or coughing. The victim prefers to lie on the affected side to reduce the chest movement when he breathes. The doctor's stethoscope may reveal a friction rub as the roughened pleural surfaces ride over one another.

If fluid fills up this space between the lung and the chest wall, the breath sounds are more difficult to hear through the intervening fluid, and the acute pleuritic pain on breathing may be replaced with a dull ache. (See *Empyema.*)

Pleurodynia, or Devil's grip, is a virus inflammation of the diaphragm, the large flat muscle (between the lungs and the liver) which draws air into the lungs. The disease causes pain about the circumference of the lower chest as if the victim were being squeezed each time he inhales. Fever and *headache* usually accompany the chest pain which may suggest *pneumonia* with *pleurisy* or *hepatitis.* As with other *virus* infections, *aspirin* and rest are the only treatment. Moist heat applications or chest taping may provide some relief.

Pneumocystis carinii pneumonia is an unusual lung infection seen in premature infants, debilitated children, or those with low immunoglobulins. *P. carinii* is a protozoan (like malaria or amoeba) so will not respond to *antibiotics.* The X ray shows granularity of the lung fields. Treatment is unsatisfactory. Most patients recover, but the condition may drag on for several weeks.

Pneumonia is a lung infection usually due to bacteria, but *viruses,* fungi, and aspirated matter (kerosene, food, dust) may be responsible. Most respiratory infections in infants and children are due to viruses, but once the lung tissue is involved with inflammation of any sort, bacteria may invade and cause a secondary, more severe infection. Smog, weather change, *allergies,* dry winter air, or low levels of *immunoglobulins* can predispose the lungs to the invasion of disease-producing agents. The inciting agents appear to be the cause because of the time relationship; but they are only enabling mechanisms to ease the growth of germs or viruses. (A patient once got a Staphylococcus pneumonia after he ate chocolate. He was allergic to chocolate; it gave him a pimple on his lip. *Staphylococcus* grew in the pimple; it somehow was inhaled into his lungs where it continued its growth.)

A patient ill with pneumonia, although loaded with bacteria, is less of a health menace than a carrier of a pneumococcus commonly found in the family of a pneumonia case.

The usual story starts with a minor cold, watery nose, and dry cough. On the second to fifth day, usually associated with a green or yellow nasal discharge, a shaking chill, and 104° to 106° temperature occurs. *Convulsions, cyanosis,* and prostration may be present. A dry muffled cough (the infection is below the cough reflex) is common in pneumonia and bronchopneumonia; in *asthma* the cough is frequent and noisy. *Aspirin* usually has little effect on the fever, so the doctor cannot call it "that virus that is going around."

Physical examination early may not reveal much to the doctor as the infection is too far from his stethoscope to be obvious to his ears. Grunting respirations, shortness of breath, lack of response to aspirin, and a high *white blood count* would just about give away the diagnosis of pneumonia even without an X ray. Doctors love this disease because it almost always responds to *penicillin;* it's what we save penicillin for. We can almost guarantee that in about ten hours after a substantial intramuscular injection of penicillin, the child will begin to respond. Fever will fall, breathing becomes easier, cough loosens or lessens, and the child can play or eat or at least act better. (I told a boy with pneumonia that he would start to feel better eight hours after the shot I gave him at 7 P.M. He set his alarm for 3 A.M. and called me because he said he was still sick. I responded with, "From *now on,* you'll feel better." Now I say ten hours.)

If the response is adequate, the treatment can usually be continued orally for a week or so. It may be worthwhile to get an X ray on the seventh to tenth day of treatment to ascertain the stage of resolution. Frequently a resolving shadow or a bit of pleural fluid remains, although the child seems quite normal.

Most lobar (involving one whole lobe) or bronchopneumonia cases (*bronchitis*) also respond rapidly to penicillin because the organism is almost always the pneumococcus, which has not figured out how to become resistant. Streptococcal pneumonia is rare but, of course, always responds nicely to penicillin. Some forms of the dreaded staphylococcus will respond to penicillin, but if the response is not clear-cut in ten to eighteen hours after adequate penicillin, the resistant forms should be considered, and a change of therapy is then mandatory. Infants are more likely to develop this variety; frequently there is some associated skin infection that has seeded the germ for transfer to the lungs. Staph pneumonia patients frequently develop *empyema,* and chest drainage is often necessary.

Pneumonia due to Hemophilus, Klebsiella, or *Pseudomonas* is rare and, of course, does not respond to penicillin. Lack of suitable response indicates the necessity of a culture of pharyngeal secretions for identification purposes.

Pneumonias due to viruses include *bronchiolitis* and primary atypical pneumonia (due to Eaton agent or *Mycoplasma pneumoniae*). It is probably this disease that people call "walking pneumonia," although one can have any pneumonia and still drag around.

Kerosene pneumonia, or lung inflammation following aspiration or ingestion of any *hydrocarbon,* can only be treated with oxygen and prophylactic antibiotics. It is uncertain whether the petroleum distillate has been absorbed from the stomach and circulated to the lungs or whether it has been inhaled at the time of ingestion or emesis.

A reasonable compromise: if a large amount (greater than a tablespoonful of a hydrocarbon) has been swallowed, flush out the stomach with the patient's head down; if less than this, just give a tablespoon of olive oil to retard the absorption of the material.

Lipoid pneumonia usually appears following the administration of some oily medication (oily nose drops, castor oil, mineral oil, cod liver oil) to an unwilling child. The lungs may suffer from the effects of this with cough, wheezing, and secondary infection.

Pneumothorax is air in the pleural space between the lung surface and the chest wall. The lungs are contractile and will shrink (collapsed lung) thus preventing optimum air exchange. It may result from a penetrating wound which allows air into this space. A blob or air sac in the lung may rupture, allowing inhaled air to fill the space. *Pneumonia* (especially *staphylococcus*) will break down lung tissue and allow pus and air to move into the pleural space (*empyema*).

Symptoms are sudden chest pain and shortness of breath. *Cyanosis* will occur if much lung tissue is collapsed or compressed. Usually the chest must be tapped with a needle and the air aspirated so the lung can re-expand. If *pneumonia* and *empyema* are present, a drainage tube is left in the pleural space to drain the pus.

Psittacosis, or ornithosis, is a viral lung infection assumed to be passed from birds to humans. Parrots, parakeets, or turkeys may carry the organism without appearing ill. It may be mild with fever and a dry cough—acting like *influenza.* Severe forms may produce severe dyspnea and *cyanosis.*

Tetracycline drugs are not lethal to the causative organisms, but will slow down their multiplication.

Pulmonary abscess is an *abscess* in the lung tissue (not *empyema*). It is usually due to the *staphylococcus,* contains pus (bacteria and white blood cells), gives rise to a high fever and prostration. If large enough it will embarrass respiration and cause *cyanosis.*

Multiple abscesses will occur with *cystic fibrosis,* wasting diseases, or in victims of low *immunoglobulins.* Solitary pus pockets may arise in a congenital *lung cyst* or follow lobar *pneumonia. Tuberculosis* might be the agent causing an abscess, but the symptoms are less dramatic. Inhalation of foreign or infected material (following *tonsillectomy*) might be the inciting event. The bacteria thus lodged in the lung tissue will grow and spread until the abscess is formed. If the abscess breaks, the pus may be coughed up (it usually has a dead smell), or flow into other areas and start new abscesses.

Vigorous antibiotic treatment may be effective in healing the abscess. If a foreign substance is present, it must be retrieved before healing can take place. Bronchoscopy and suction may aid in the healing, as medicine alone will not heal an abscess once it has formed; it only keeps it from spreading while nature and drainage allow the cavity to shrink or scar. If all else fails, surgical removal of the infected lobe or segment of the lobe will be curative.

Pulmonary edema is fluid in the lungs, most often due to *congestive heart failure.* (See Section 8.) Serous fluid leaks out of the capillaries of the lungs into the air sacs and bronchial tubes, thus interfering with the exchange of oxygen and carbon dioxide. The patient is short of breath, usually complains of chest pain, may cough up bloody, frothy fluid, and if severely affected, becomes *cyanotic.*

Hypertension, rapid administration of intravenous fluids, *nephritis, pneumonia,* inhalation of poisonous gases, and aspiration of volatile *hydrocarbons* may all present this ominous sign of serious involvement. Something must be done about the underlying disease, if possible, as pulmonary edema signals a fatal complication. A patient with rheumatic *myocarditis* with murmurs and a failing heart is in very serious trouble.

Oxygen therapy helps to allay the symptoms while more definitive treatment is effected against the underlying cause. Withdrawal of blood is still occasionally used if the edema is due to a failing heart.

Pulmonary embolism—see *Embolism,* Section 8

Pulmonary infarction—see *Infarction,* Section 8

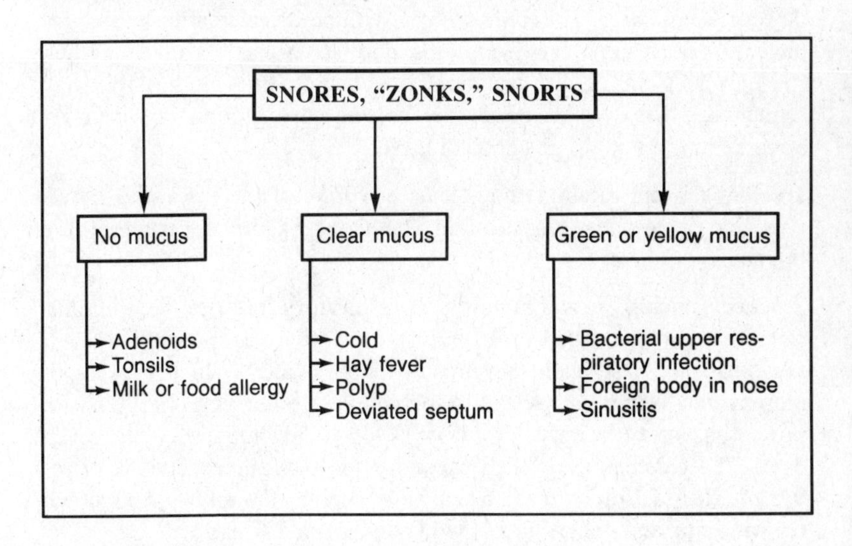

Sternum, or breastbone, is the bone in the front center of the chest. It may be divided due to a congenital lack of fusion.

Sweat electrolytes are measured in making a diagnosis of *cystic fibrosis.* The concentration of *sodium* and chloride are increased in this disease. A previously weighed piece of gauze is placed on the child's back under an occlusive dressing. After a period of perspiring the gauze is weighed wet and dry. A high salt content in sweat associated with chronic *bronchitis,* insufficient pancreatic *enzymes,* and a family story would implicate cystic fibrosis.

Thyroglossal duct cyst may be found anywhere from the lower midline area of the neck (mid-*thyroid*) to the base of the tongue deep in the throat where it may cause choking, noisy breathing, or difficulty in swallowing. Infection may occur. If symptomatic, removal is justified. (See *Neck,* Section 14.)

Torulosis—see *Cryptococcus*

Trachea is the tube that carries air from the larynx down into the chest; it divides into two bronchi which subdivide further into bronchial tubes, etc.

Foreign objects in the trachea produce a sudden, uncontrollable coughing and stridor sound. If the object is not too large or obstructive, it may be forgotten; symptoms of cough and stridor may reappear days or weeks later. The foreign object will be revealed after antibiotics have failed to cure the symptoms and an X ray is taken. When the object (a nickel, for instance) is shown to the mother she may remember: "Oh, yes, I recall now he *did* have a coughing spell for a while, but I thought he coughed it out."

Tracheitis is an inflammation—usually *viral*—of the *trachea.* Hoarseness and a burning sensation in the front of the upper chest are the clues.

Tracheobronchitis is a common *viral* respiratory infection seen in children and is often called *influenza.* A dry, often croupy cough, fever, and headache last about seventy-two hours, after which the cough loosens and brings up phlegm which, unless other complications are present, is clear, watery, or milky. This lasts another five to seven days. The patient feels well because his fever and headache are gone, but his sleep is interrupted; when he is supine, the mucus runs down his windpipe and chokes him. (See *Influenza* and *Croup.*)

Tracheotomy is an opening made into the windpipe at the lower end of the neck to relieve a respiratory obstruction due to swollen vocal cords, *diphtheritic* membrane in the *larynx,* a foreign object in the larynx, *epiglottitis,* or *laryngotracheobronchitis.* A curved tube is inserted to maintain the opening so that air may then get to the lungs. The laryngeal condition is thus alleviated once it is cleared, the tube is removed and the usual breathing passageway is then reused.

Tracheotomy may be needed for patients in shock or coma to permit the trachea and bronchial tubes to be aspirated adequately. The tracheotomy is often lifesaving.

Tuberculosis is a bacterial infection due to the tubercle bacillus. Fortunately, the vast time and expense devoted to case finding has practically wiped it out.

It is usually acquired by inhaling the bacteria exhaled from the tuberculous cavity in the lung of a diseased victim. The victim may be able to trap and wall off the bacteria so that adjacent tissue is not destroyed. At the height of this reaction, an X ray of the lungs may reveal a small shadow at the periphery of the lungs plus an enlarged lymph node close to the main bronchus (called a primary complex). About six weeks after this initial contact, the body forms a sensitivity to bacillus and the skin test (see *Tuberculin test,* Section 6) becomes positive.

If not walled off and calcified the original contaminated area may grow, erode through, and spill bacteria into a bronchial tube, thus allowing new patches of lung to become involved. Or bacteria may be carried to other organs of the body. This latter condition is called *miliary tuberculosis* and is usually fatal unless treatment is instituted rapidly.

See *Meningitis,* Section 2; *Peritonitis,* Section 12; *Renal tuberculosis,* Section 13; *Pott's disease,* Section 7; *Lymph nodes,* Section 6; *Neck,* Section 14. For diseases whose X rays of lungs resemble tuberculosis, see *Sporotrichosis,* Section 6; *Coccidioidomycosis, Cryptococcosis, Blastomycosis,* Section 6; *Nocardiosis, Pigeon breeder's lung, Löffler's syndrome, Histoplasmosis,* this section; *Toxoplasmosis,* Section 2.

Childhood tuberculosis is usually diagnosed by the positive skin test (see Section 6) performed in the doctor's office, at the public health clinic, or as a screening test in school. Positive reactors are X-rayed to determine the extent of the disease and all contacts are similarly investigated.

Treatment is instituted for:

1. All children under five years of age with positive skin tests.
2. All children and adolescents who have demonstrated a recent tuberculin skin test change from negative to positive.

3. All who have been in recent contact with an open case (contagious or usually cavity-containing adult) regardless of the skin test response.

Vascular ring is the congenital anomaly in which major blood vessels (aorta, subclavian, innominate arteries) surround the esophagus and *trachea* high in the chest. If they fit snugly about these tubes, they may constrict them sufficiently to cause difficulty in swallowing and/or breathing. A barky cough or frequent lung infection may draw attention to this area. X rays with barium in the esophagus reveal an indentation in the posterior aspect of the esophagus.

Surgery relieves the symptoms.

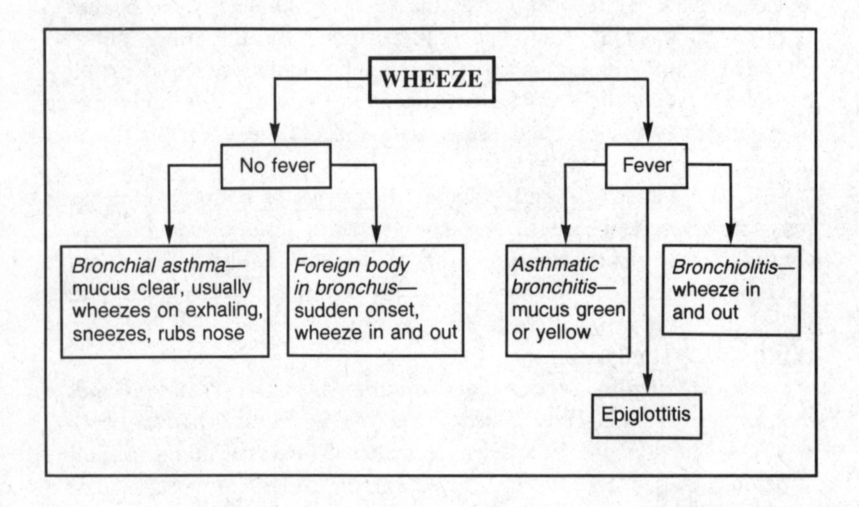

SECTION 10

The Endocrine System, Growth, and Metabolism *

A. Growth

Ectomorph
Endomorph
Growth
Mesomorph
Obesity (Section 11)

Growth disorders

a) *Dwarfism*
- *Achondroplasia*
- *Anemia* (Section 8)
- *Asthma* (Section 9)
- *Chondrodystrophies*
- *Congenital heart defects* (Section 5)
- *Cranio-pharyngioma* (Section 15)
- *Cretinism*
- *Cystic fibrosis* (Section 9)
- *Diabetes insipidus*
- *Diabetes mellitus*
- *Down's syndrome*
- *Enzyme deficiencies (Enzymes)*
- *Failure to thrive*
- *Food allergy* (Section 12)
- *Gargoylism*
- *Glycogen storage disease*
- *Hunter's syndrome*
- *Hypogonadism*
- *Hypopituitarism*
- *Hypothyroidism*
- *Kidney disorders* (Section 13)
- *Malabsorption* (Section 12)
- *Morquio's disease*
- *Parasites* (Section 12)
- *Pituitary dwarf (Dwarfism)*
- *Rickets* (Section 11)
- *Turner's syndrome (Hypogonadism)*
- *Ulcerative colitis* (Section 12)

b) *Excessive growth*
- *Acromegaly*
- *Adrenogenital syndrome (Adrenal glands)*
- *Gigantism*

B. Endocrine glands

1. *Pituitary*
   ACTH (Adrenocorticotrophic hormone)

*Read **Growth** first.

FSH (Follicle stimulating hormone)
Gonadotrophic hormone
HGH (Human growth hormone)
Acromegaly
Gigantism
Hypopituitarism
TSH (Thyrotrophic hormone)
Vasopressin (Diabetes insipidus)

2. *Adrenal*
   a. *Cortex*
      Aldosterone
         Hyperfunction (Aldosteronism)
      Androgens
         Hyperfunction (Adrenogenital syndrome)
      Glucocorticoids (Corticosteroids, hydrocortisone)
      Hyperfunction (Cushing's syndrome)
      Hypofunction (Addison's disease; Meningococcemia under Septicemia, Section 2)
   b. *Medulla*
      Adrenalin (Epinephrine, Section 4)
      Pheochromocytoma
3. *Thyroid*
   Calcitonin
   Goiter
   Hyperthyroidism
      Thyrotoxicosis
      Thyroxine
   Hypothyroidism
      Cretinism
   Thyroid function tests
   Thyroiditis
4. *Parathyroid*
   Hyperparathyroidism
   Hypoparathyroidism
5. *Pancreas*
   Diabetes mellitus
      Glucose tolerance test
      Insulin
   Hypoglycemia
      Leucine-induced
6. *Female hormones and organs*
   Breast enlargement
   Estrogens
   Menstruation
      No periods (Amenorrhea)
      Painful (Dysmenorrhea)
      Onset (Menarche)
   Ovary
   Puberty
      Delayed (Hypogonadism)
         Turner's syndrome
      Early onset (Precocious puberty)
         McCune-Albright syndrome
7. *Male hormones and organs*
      Enlarged breast (Gynecomastia)
   Puberty
      Delayed (Hypogonadism)
         Klinefelter's syndrome
         Laurence-Biedl syndrome
         Turner's syndrome
      Early onset (Precocious puberty)

C. Enzymes

Alcaptonuria (Section 13)
Amino-aciduria (Section 13)
Cystinosis
Disaccharide deficiency (Section 12)
Enzymes
Fanconi syndrome (Section 13)
Galactosemia
Glycogen storage disease
Hartnup disease
Inborn errors of metabolism
Lipidoses
Lipodystrophy
Marfan's syndrome
Phenylalanine, PKU
Porphyria (Section 13)
Renal tubular acidosis (Section 13)

D. Chemicals in blood metabolic

Acidosis (see also Section 5)
Alkalosis
Basal metabolism
Calcium
Carbon dioxide
Cholesterol
Dehydration
Electrolytes
Fructose
Glucose tolerance test
Hypercalcemia
Hypercholesterolemia
Hyperinsulinism
Hyperkalemia
Hyperlipidemia
Hypernatremia
Hypokalemia
Hyponatremia
Ketosis
Lipids
Phosphatase
Water

E. Heredity

Chromosomes
DNA (deoxyribonucleic acid)
Gene
Phenotype
RNA (Ribonucleic acid)
Sex chromatin
Trisomy

F. Cancer, Neoplasms, Growths

Adenoma
Biopsy
Carcinoma
Cystic hygroma
Fibroma
Granuloma
Eosinophilic granuloma
Hand-Schuller-Christian disease
Letterer-Siwe disease
Hodgkin's disease
Lipoma
Lymphangioma
Lymphosarcoma
Neoplasms
Nephroblastoma
Neuroblastoma
Pheochromocytoma
Polyp
Sarcoma
Teratoma
Reticuloendotheliosis

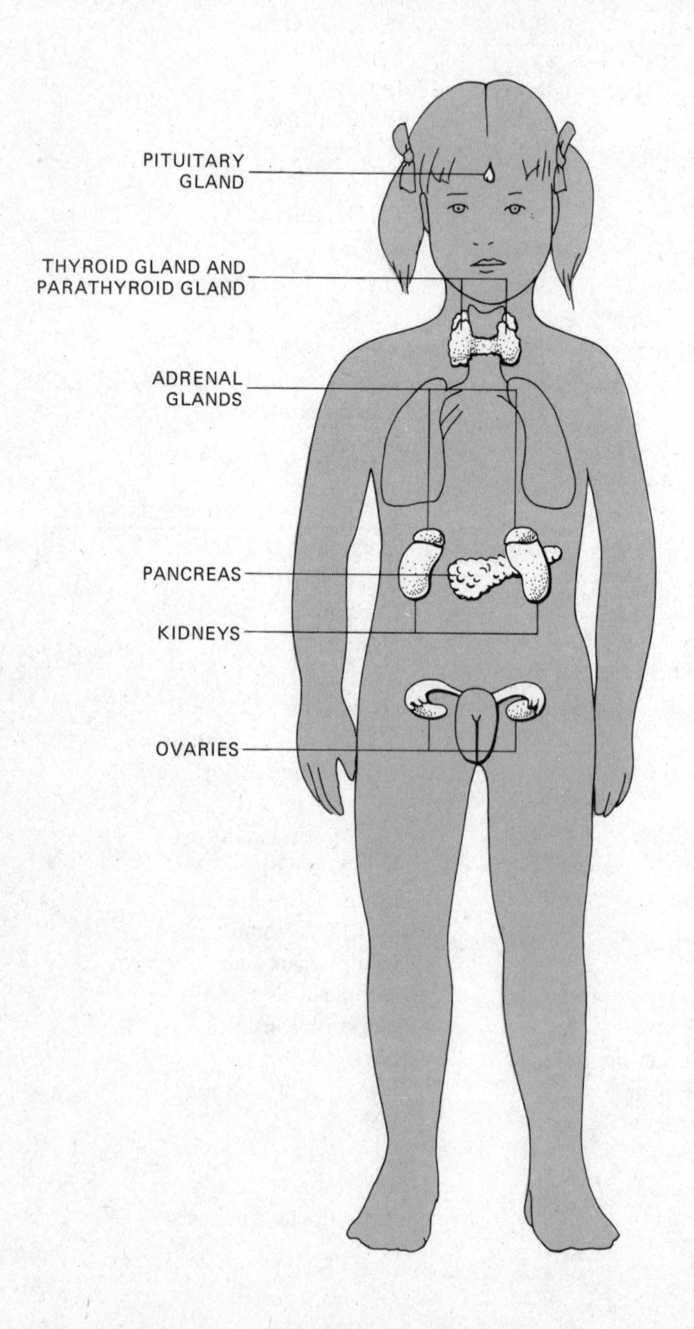
PITUITARY GLAND
THYROID GLAND AND PARATHYROID GLAND
ADRENAL GLANDS
PANCREAS
KIDNEYS
OVARIES

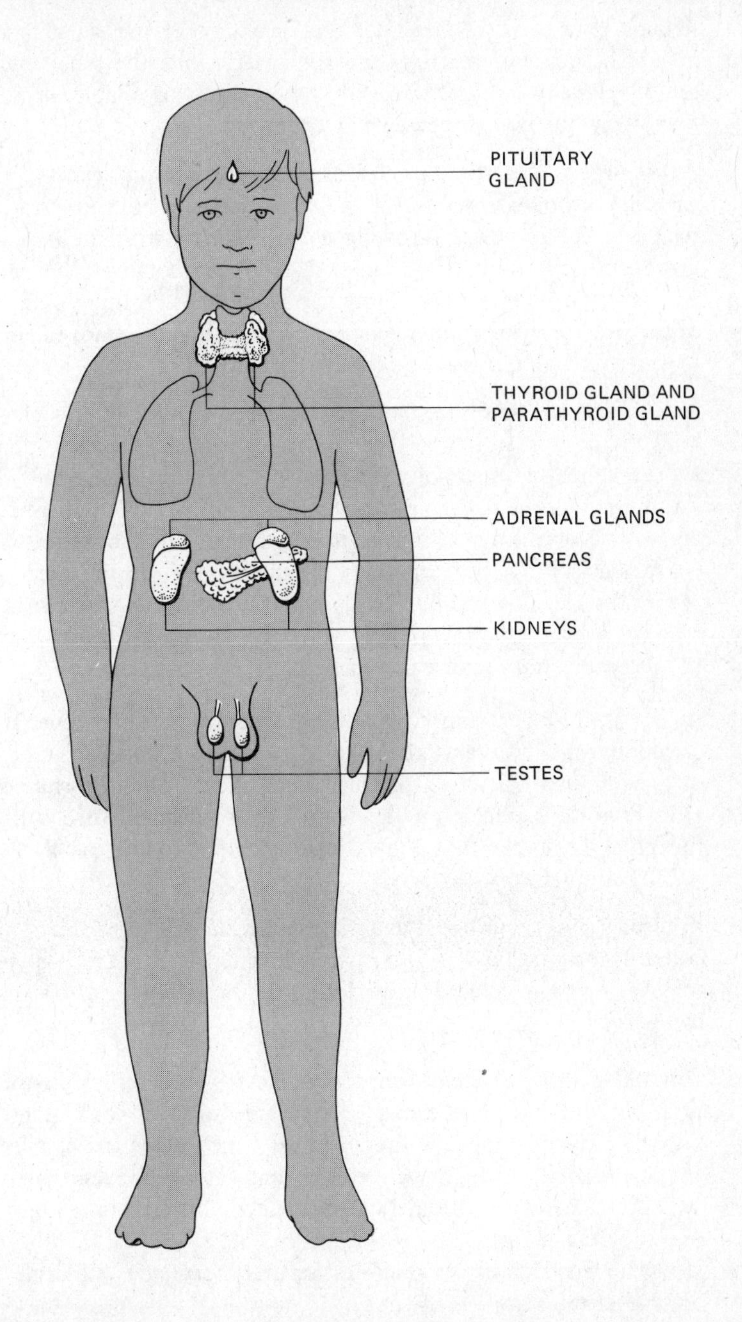
PITUITARY
GLAND
THYROID GLAND AND
PARATHYROID GLAND
ADRENAL GLANDS
PANCREAS
KIDNEYS
TESTES

Achondroplasia is a congenital malformation of the skeletal system, in which the arms and legs are shortened while the trunk and head are of relatively normal size. No known cure is available; it is usually hereditary but sporadic cases may occur.

Achromegaly describes a condition resulting from excess *pituitary growth* hormone secretion. If the hormone is produced prior to the fusion of the *epiphyses* (growing ends of bones) with the bone shafts, *gigantism* will result. If full growth has been obtained, the hormone will produce a large jaw and big hands and feet. A functioning tumor of the *pituitary* gland must be sought and, if found, removed surgically or destroyed by ultrasound waves or radiation.

Acidosis is an abnormal state of increased acidity of the blood and body fluids due to loss of base or alkali (due to *diarrhea,* abnormal *kidney* function, metabolic *acidosis*) or retention of carbon dioxide (as in *lung* disease or respiratory acidosis). The acidotic patient requires correction of the condition as it may prove fatal, but the cause of the acidosis must be eliminated simultaneously or the acidosis will recur. Intravenous alkaline fluids may be lifesaving. Aspirin is acidic and its overingestion will lead to acidosis, because of its effect on the body, but not because it is an acid.

ACTH is the abbreviation of adrenocorticotrophic hormone. It is secreted by the pituitary gland to stimulate the cortex (outer layer) of the *adrenal gland* to produce and secrete other hormones that have important effects on the body's metabolism. Hydrocortisone is the chief hormone that the adrenal glands produce as a result of ACTH stimulation.

Addison's disease (adrenal insufficiency) results from a lack of adrenal cortical hormone and is rarely seen in children. In the past it most often arose from a destructive lesion in the *adrenal glands* from *tuberculosis.*

Adrenal glands are small, important, hormone-secreting bits of tissue atop the kidneys. The center section (medulla) of each gland is responsible for epinephrine, the chemical which helps the startled body prepare for fight or flight. A rare secreting tumor (pheochromocytoma) will produce hypertension, flushing, pallor, excessive sweating, thirst, and rapid heartbeat.

The adrenal cortex secretes several hormones essential to life and/or metabolism:

1. Glucocorticoids (*corticosteroids*), the chief of which are hydrocortisone and cortisone. These are essential to sugar and fat metabolism.

2. Aldosterone is essential in sodium conservation.

3. Androgens promote growth and influence development of male sex characteristics. Only a small portion of androgen arises from the adrenal glands in the normal male; most is from the testes.

The adrenal cortex may not produce enough hormone, and in the newborn this may show as vomiting, diarrhea, and dehydration because the body is losing salt and water. *Hemorrhage* or infection destroying the cortex may cause shock, *cyanosis,* and *death.* (See *Addison's disease.*) The need is obvious for therapy to replace the proper hormone.

Hyperfunction, or excess secretion of various hormones, of the cortex leads to a variety of syndromes:

1. Adrenogenital syndrome (congenital adrenal hyperplasia) is manifest by precocious sexual development; children will develop pubic hair, a girl will develop an enlarged clitoris. The newborn female may be mistaken for a male. The androgens are overproduced, and hydrocortisone is deficient. Some victims also lose excessive salt in the urine and become dehydrated.

2. Aldosteronism is caused by a tumor secreting aldosterone or hyperfunction of the adrenal cortex. The patient is weak (*hypopotassemia*). He urinates a great deal. The body is especially low in potassium, but sodium is retained. Elevated blood pressure is associated.

3. Cushing's syndrome is the result of overproduction of hydrocortisone. Hypertension and a moon face appear, along with fat deposits in the upper trunk. A secreting tumor of the adrenal cortex or pituitary must be sought and removed if present. This syndrome occurs in patients treated with cortisone for inflammatory (see *Autoimmune disease*) or allergic diseases (for example, chronic asthma). (Also see *Corticosteroids.*)

Adrenal hemorrhage may occur at birth occasionally following breech delivery. Shock and collapse may occur. Death is rare. (See *Addison's disease.*) It may accompany *meningococcemia* (see *Septicemia,* Section 2) when bacteria lodge in the capillaries of the gland forcing their rupture (Waterhouse-Friderichsen syndrome).

Adrenalin—see *Epinephrine,* Section 4, and *Adrenal glands*

Alkalosis is the opposite of *acidosis* and may result from excess *vomiting* of stomach acid or *hyperventilation* (exhaling of carbon dioxide, thus lowering carbonic acid in the blood). Restorative acidifying fluids may be needed while the cause of the vomiting is corrected. Hyperventilation may be emotionally caused.

Amenorrhea is the absence of the menstrual flow. A fully mature girl with developed breasts and pubic hair should have at least one period within a year or so of such development. Failure to have menses by age sixteen should be investigated. (Ovarian, *adrenal, pituitary,* and *thyroid* function must be evaluated.) A possible cause is the imperforate *hymen*—easily diagnosed and corrected.

If a female has at least one period at *menarche* and then fails to menstruate, it implies she has all the necessary structures and hormones, but she has failed to ovulate. For the first two years after the menarche, most girls are irregular; frequent periods will alternate with months of amenorrhea. By far the most common—and suspected—cause of amenorrhea after the menarche is pregnancy; but nutritional and emotional factors may lead to menstrual irregularity if not amenorrhea.

Basal metabolism is the measurement of the calories utilized by the body at rest at normal temperature. It is a reflection of the work done by the body cells in order to function, maintain life, *temperature, heartbeat,* etc. In addition to this basal or basic rate, more *calories* are needed for fever, exercise, digestion, and growth. Babies need about three times the basal calories that adults do. Because *hyperthyroidism* increases the basal metabolism rate of calorie utilization, the oxygen-consumption test has long been used as a test of *thyroid* function: the greater the oxygen consumption, the greater the thyroid activity.

Breast enlargement in the female is normally expected just before *menarche.* Early development of breasts would raise the suspicion of a feminizing tumor of the *ovary* (rare).

Breast enlargement in the male—see *Gynecomastia*

Calcitonin is a hormone secreted in the thyroid gland, which helps maintain normal calcium blood levels. Its role is not fully understood.

Calcium is a mineral found chiefly in bones and teeth and is a necessary blood element to aid clotting and neuromuscular function. If the level of calcium in the blood is decreased (if it is deposited in bone, if it is not absorbed sufficiently from the intestines, if *alkalosis* is present, or if too much is excreted via the kidneys), *tetany* may occur. (See Section 15.)

Vitamin D, the sunshine vitamin, is essential to the absorption of calcium from the intestinal tract and its deposition in the bones. Apparently a diet low in calcium may still be adequate to calcify the bones if some vitamin D is provided. (See *Calcium, Rickets,* Section 11.)

Cancer—see *Neoplasms*

Carbon dioxide is a gas formed as the end product of carbohydrate metabolism. It is higher in amounts in the veins which carry it from the cells of the body to the lungs, where it is exhaled. It is in equilibrium with carbonic acid ($CO_2 + H_2O = H^+ + HCO_3$), a weak acid. If a lung disease prevents the release of CO_2, it accumulates in the blood, the concentration of the hydrogen ion builds up, and acidosis sets in. An hysterical patient may hyperventilate (breathe excessively), exhaling large amounts of carbon dioxide; alkalosis appears, conversely.

The determination of carbon dioxide and other chemicals in the blood is essential in disease states involving fluid and respiratory imbalances (*asthma, respiratory-distress syndrome, diabetes, renal failure,* severe *diarrhea,* and *vomiting*).

Cholesterol is a blood *lipid* (*fat*) which is elevated in certain hereditary, metabolic, or acquired liver, *kidney,* or *thyroid diseases* (*Glycogen storage disease, diabetes mellitus, nephrosis, hypothyroidism,* and biliary atresia).

Chondrodystrophies are a variety of growth deformities, usually genetically determined. These usually result in misshapen bones and/or dwarfism. (See also *Achondroplasia.*) Some surgical treatment may help the appearance.

Chromosomes are small threadlike strands in the nuclei of cells. They contain genes, composed of *DNA,* which determine the inherited characteristics of the organism. The human sperm and ovum each have twenty-three chromosomes which pair when the egg is fertilized; thus half of the baby's chromosomes are derived from the father, half from the mother. The father's chromosomes determine the sex of the offspring, for half of the sperm have an X chromosome and the other half a Y. All female eggs have X. X + Y yields a male infant; X + X produces a female. (See *Gene.*)

The Y chromosome does little else but help determine maleness. The X chromosome has a variety of genes (hemophilia, color-blindness, etc.) which would not affect a female carrier but only the male, as the paired Y chromosome has no ameliorating normal gene.

In the last decade a technique has been developed to stain and identify chromosomes. This allows abnormal chromosomes to be identified. If a couple produces a baby with an abnormality, genetic counseling, including this chromosome examination, may be helpful in determining if the anomaly is truly genetic or a temporary accident of chromosomal arrangement. It is possible to examine fetal cells for chromosomal defects by *amniocentesis.*

If a part or all of a chromosome is missing, the infant usually does not survive. If a germ cell does not divide properly, some extra chromosomes may be included in a sperm or egg cell. If fertilization occurs, the superfluous chromosome will be in every cell—one result is *Down's syndrome,* or mongolism. This inclusion of extra chromosome segments is called *trisomy.*

If a chromosome breaks and parts are attached to other chromosomes, the term "translocation" is used. Down's syndrome may develop from this anomaly. If the translocation is found in either parent, the risk of abnormal children is increased.

Chromosomal breakage is associated with *viral diseases, X radiation, leukemia,* and *drug* ingestion.

DNA is the abbreviation for deoxyribonucleic acid, the genetic material that forms the chromosomes found in the nuclei of all cells. It is a long chain of purines and pyrimidines linked in a specific orderly way with phosphate molecules and is the repository of genetic information. Another molecule, *RNA,* transfers this information to the cytoplasm of the cell where amino acids are assembled and do the work of that particular cell. A misplaced amino acid will derange the function of that cell (the abnormal hemoglobin of *sickle-cell anemia* is an example).

Gene is a division of the chromosome. Hundreds—or thousands—of genes lie along the length of each chromosome; each has a specific location on its particular chromosome.

DNA is the main material of the gene. DNA is a polymer (chain) of nucleotides (phosphate esters of purines and pyrimidines combined with a sugar, deoxyribose). Each chain is arranged in a double helical structure; these provide the specific function of the gene.

Other nucleotide polymers (RNA or ribonucleic acid) are able to transcribe this genetic information from the DNA of the nucleus to the cytoplasm of the cell. Protein chains are assembled with this information (for example, thyroid hormone, hemoglobin, muscle protein, immune globulins). If the genetic DNA is faulty, the specific protein for which that gene is responsible will be faulty.

Since genes are paired on the chromosomes, function of the cells may be altered if the paired genes are similar (homozygous) or dissimilar (heterozygous). Some genes are dominant. If a person has a gene for brown eyes on one chromosome and its corresponding gene on the paired chromosome is for blue eyes, his eyes will be brown (heterozygous). If he mates with a brown-eyed partner who is also heterozygous for brown-blue, they have a 25 percent chance of having a blue-eyed child. A recessive gene on one chromosome does not manifest its trait if the corresponding gene on the paired chromosome is dominant (*cystic fibrosis, albinism, galactosemia,* PKU disease, *cystinosis,* etc.).

Pathological conditions will be passed on in a similar manner. If the trait (*sicklemia, spherocytosis, achondroplasia, Huntington's chorea,* etc.) is dominant, and the partner does not have it, roughly 50 percent of the children will be affected, but none of the normal children will have the gene and hence cannot pass it on.

Some genes carried on the X chromosome only manifest themselves as a disease if a male (Y chromosome paired with X) is produced. The female (one X chromosome carries the abnormal gene, the other X chromosome is normal and would suppress the activity of the abnormal gene) would be a carrier but not show the disease. Half of her sons would manifest the disease she carries (*hemophilia, color blindness*).

Some genetically produced traits will only become manifest if the environment is stressful (some *diabetes,* some hemolytic diseases only if the victim is ill, some enzyme deficiencies if challenged by diet).

The above is only a sketchy outline of a complex phenomenon. Geneticists are now knowledgeable enough to be able to provide prospective parents with valuable information, so they may elect to terminate a pregnancy or to rear only adopted children.

Phenotype is the term applied to the observed features of a person in contrast to the genotype or the genetic makeup. For example, an individual may carry a gene for blue eyes and a gene for brown eyes, but his eyes will be brown because brown is dominant. Genotype: brown, blue; phenotype: brown.

Ribonucleic acid (RNA) is a nucleotide polymer which transcribes chromosomal information from DNA in the nucleus to the cell cytoplasm where protein synthesis is accomplished.

Corticosteroids are hormones secreted by the cortex of the *adrenal glands.* They are essential to life, have salt- and carbohydrate-regulating functions and anti-inflammatory properties. They are frequently used to suppress hyperimmune reactions. Thus they are commonly used (and abused) for *poison oak, asthma, drug reactions, arthritis,* bursitis, *hay fever, urticaria, nephrosis,* and *rheumatic fever.* As ointments and creams their use is common in *eczema, psoriasis,* and *contact rashes.* Overdoses may lead to stunted growth, temporary *diabetes,* or stomach *ulcers.* Corticosteroids are necessary at times of stress. If surgery is required for a patient who has recently discontinued the use of these hormones, it may be necessary to begin their use again, as the suppressed adrenal cortex may not function.

Cretinism is the result of the congenital lack of the *thyroid* hormone. It is usually not diagnosed at birth because the mother's thyroid tissue is adequate for both herself and the fetus. But as the weeks progress, the baby slowly runs down, like a watch. He becomes sluggish, cold, constipated, and cries little. With time his skin becomes thick, yellow, and coarse, his tongue seems too big for his mouth, his abdomen becomes protuberant, and he may develop an *umbilical hernia.* His growth is stunted and X rays reveal that his growth centers have failed to ossify properly for his age (see *Ossification centers, Bones,* Section 7). Blood tests for thyroid function confirm the diagnosis.

Thyroid or thyroxine is given as soon as the diagnosis is made. Improvement in appearance, activity, and growth is noted within a few weeks, but the outlook for adequate mentality is not as predictable. The growth of the normal brain is closely dependent on an adequate metabolism. Apparently deficiencies of thyroid hormone before or after birth—even for short periods of time—have a permanent effect on intellectual functions.

Cushing's syndrome—see *Adrenal glands*

Cystinosis is an inherited enzyme deficiency in which cystine, an amino acid, is stored in excessive amounts in the body, especially the *liver, spleen,* and *lymph nodes.* The condition is related to the *Fanconi syndrome.* These children are dwarfed, excrete sugar and amino acids in their urine, develop *rickets,* and die in the first few years of life, usually of kidney disease.

Dehydration is the excessive loss of body fluid, usually caused by *vomiting, diarrhea,* diabetic *acidosis,* or *pyloric stenosis.* The dehydrated victim is lethargic, has sunken eyes, dry skin and mouth, and the skin loses its usually elastic snap. Weight loss may be one to five pounds overnight. If allowed to continue, therapy may be fruitless as cells are irreversibly damaged. It may be seen to a lesser extent in a feverish child who refuses fluid or vomits because of an illness. Minerals are invariably lost with the fluid; chlorides and acid are lost in a proportionately larger amount than sodium in pyloric stenosis. Alkalosis is more likely, as a result, and extra chlorides are sometimes given in the water and salt solution intravenously to rehydrate the victim. Diarrhea usually produces dehydration and acidosis, because relatively more base ions (sodium) are lost in this condition.

Dehydration and mineral loss can become so complicated that a case requiring hospitalization is best treated by estimating the levels of sodium, chloride, the acidity, and bicarbonate levels in the blood. More accurate replacement is then possible.

Mild to moderate forms of dehydration can usually be treated rapidly if the *kidneys* and *lungs* are functioning properly, as they can compensate for some deviation if fluid intake (oral or intravenous) is adequate. The small infant (under five months) needs special attention because of his relative inability to concentrate urine.

Intestinal flu (*gastroenteritis,* see Section 12) is the most common condition that leads to fluid loss. The child vomits for twenty-four hours, and, if no fluid is retained, the dehydration resulting from the vomiting, fever, and diarrhea will produce *acidosis* and *ketosis*—which causes more vomiting. A vicious cycle may be perpetuated unless the vomiting is stopped (antiemetic rectal suppositories [see *Thorazine*®, Section 4] and intravenous fluids are used).

Home treatment consists of fluid—cola drinks, gelatin water, carbonated beverages—in small amounts (one ounce) at frequent intervals. If these are not retained after twelve hours, a suppository to tranquilize the vomiting center of the brain may stop the emesis. If the child is able to move about and can urinate at least twice in the twenty-four-hour period, he will probably "make it" at home. If this is not effective, medical attention and/or intravenous therapy of water, sugar, and minerals in the hospital would seem appropriate.

Development—see *Growth*

Diabetes insipidus is the passage of large amounts of dilute urine, and is due to the lack of a hormone (*vasopressin*) secreted by the posterior portion of the pituitary gland and the hypothalamus. This hormone promotes conservation of water via tubules in the kidneys. Without it much of the water in the blood flowing through the kidneys is lost, and the patient becomes dehydrated unless he consumes large amounts of water—often several quarts daily.

The diagnosis is made by a history of insatiable thirst, inability to concentrate urine when fluids are restricted, excretion of quarts of urine, growth failure, *anemia,* and inability to attend to normal activity because of the compelling thirst. A brain tumor in the *hypothalamus* or *pituitary* may cause this hormone deficiency, but it may be hereditary or the result of *head injury, tuberculosis, leukemia,* etc.

There may be a defect in the kidneys which makes the tubules unresponsive to the hormone; occasionally psychological factors may be the cause of high fluid ingestion.

A tumor obviously must be removed if present; the hormone must be supplied by injection or sprayed in the nose. The membranes will allow its absorption here as it is not effective orally.

Diabetes mellitus is an inherited disease in which *glucose* is poorly metabolized and/or stored. When the amount of glucose in the blood rises to a critical level, it appears in the urine. This produces excessive loss of water, leading to dehydration. Without sufficient glucose to convert to energy, the body burns *fat* and *protein,* which leads to *acidosis* and weight loss.

Diabetes was once thought to be due purely to a lack of *insulin* production by the *pancreas,* but research seems to indicate a number of factors are involved: low insulin production, lack of tissue response to normal amounts of insulin, antibody production against insulin, formation of defective insulin, and so forth.

The overt disease may be precipitated by infection, stress, rapid growth, or old age. Juvenile diabetes usually has a rapid, dramatic onset with thirst, weakness, and coma, while older people may slip into it without fanfare, often displaying only mild symptoms. Children's insulin requirements are remarkably changeable for the first year or two of their disease; the daily dose is usually given as a regular or short-acting insulin. Quick sources of sugar must be nearby for the occasional low-blood-sugar reactions. Insulin injections may be necessary three times a day with each meal. Long-acting insulin may be substituted when the insulin requirements become more stable. Infections and rapid growth at puberty require careful adjustment of insulin to avoid reactions.

Excessively rigid control of the diet and nit-picking calorie counting are to be avoided, but an overly permissive attitude can be dangerous since degenerative changes in the eyes and kidneys will occur more surely if reasonable control has been too erratic.

The rebellious adolescent diabetic has the most trouble with control, because his disease makes him different from his peers, and he seems to want to deny its reality. He may purposely go out of control in a passive-aggressive, manipulative effort to gain attention.

Guidance and encouraging personal responsibility are essential. The family and the doctor must foster the notion that the child is normal but has a controllable defect.

Sir William Osler said, "Get a chronic disease and take care of yourself, and you'll live a long and healthy life." I think I agree with that 70 percent of the time.

Down's syndrome, or mongolism, is a syndrome complex manifested by *mental retardation,* short stature, hypotonic musculature, epicanthic eyelid folds, protruding furrowed tongue, a simian crease in the palms, susceptibility to *respiratory infection,* and *leukemia.* Most cases are felt to be due to a chromosomal breakage and fertilization of an egg with twenty-four chromosomes instead of twenty-three. Each body cell thus contains forty-seven chromosomes, which apparently distorts maturation enough to produce the above anomalies.

Chromosome analysis of the child and parents may be helpful in evaluating the risk of recurrence. About one child in seven hundred has Down's syndrome, and the incidence increases along with the mother's age.

The diagnosis is occasionally difficult at birth, and some confusion with cretinism may exist.

The most difficult decision for parents to make is whether they should keep the child. Some would be able to accept the child without question; some would be completely revolted by the very idea. Little counseling need be done in these two situations. A large group of parents are unable to decide what to do for a variety of reasons. Once the child has become a part of the family, it is difficult to give him up; some parents who anticipate the child's ultimate placement in an institution would just as soon not become involved and would elect to board him out from day one without seeing him at all. Some parents might feel guilty if they did not care for a child they produced and would care for and cherish it until their old age forced them to seek outside help for the child's continuing dependent needs. Still others might find the child was a fulfillment of their own needs. The number of situations is as long as there are families who must adjust and adapt to this tragic surprise. Parents do what they must do, and their own doctor must only point out alternative solutions and then support them in whatever path they have chosen. Guilt must be avoided.

These children are friendly and docile, but suffer an inordinate number of respiratory infections frequently requiring antibiotics. Intellectual achievement is varied, but a stimulating home appears to be the best place to attain the maximum.

Dwarfism is short stature or less than optimum growth for any reason. Congenital anomalies associated with metabolic defects or enzyme deficiencies are rare and largely untreatable. One cause met in practice is that due to *malabsorption* or intestinal *allergy;* growth resumes normal rates when diagnosis and appropriate diet are established. If calories and protein are not being supplied in adequate amounts to the body cells, growth will fail. A diabetic child out of control would not be nourished well enough to grow. A *cretin* or child with inadequate *thyroid* hormone would not grow well because body cells need this hormone. Chronic infection, *diarrhea, kidney* disease, *parasite* infestation, *anemia* might slow growth somewhat. A *congenital heart lesion* with *cyanosis* would retard growth because of lack of oxygen in the tissues. Emotional deprivation might cause growth retardation and apparently not from just low calorie intake.

The *pituitary* dwarf is very rare; growth hormone from the pituitary gland is not formed, because a tumor (*craniopharyngioma*) or inflammation has destroyed the cells producing the hormone. In most cases the cause is unknown; the assumption is that some failure of stimulation from the hypothalamus occurs. A familial history may be noted. If a tumor is the cause, it must be removed. If no obvious reason is found, growth hormone will correct the failure, but the hormone is in unfortunately short supply.

Constitutional growth delay may be diagnosed by a family history of retarded growth and delayed onset of puberty in relatives. Bone age (see *Ossification centers,* Section 7) is usually delayed, and ultimate height is within normal limits.

Familial short stature accounts for the vast majority of syndromes. The child's height will be below the average for his age in a proportion dependent on the average of the heights of his closest relatives. Bone age is normal.

Hypopituitary dwarfs may be lacking in other pituitary hormones. A midbrain tumor should be searched for. Bone age is retarded.

The Short Child—Clinical Evaluation and Treatment

A standard workup for a short child who has no obvious disease to explain his problem includes complete blood count, urinalysis, creatinine blood level, thyroid function tests, pituitary hormone assay and X rays of wrists for assessment of bone development (see *Ossification centers,* Section 7). A buccal (cheek) smear for nuclear sex determination in a short female is helpful in ruling out Turner's syndrome. Differential diagnosis:

1. Bone disease—*chondrodystrophies, osteogenesis imperfectum,* dyschondroplasias, rickets, *hypophosphatasia* (see *Phosphatase*).
2. Generalized disease—*deprivation* (lack of love, mental stimulation, and food), chronic infection, *glycogen storage disease, Down's syndrome, gargoylism, reticuloendotheliosis, lipidoses, cystic fibrosis,* other inborn errors of metabolism.
3. Organic disorders—heart disease, renal disease (*renal tubular acidosis,* peylonephritis, *Fanconi's disease*), ulcerative colitis, regional enteritis, asthma, bronchiectasis, *anemia, malabsorption, hepatic insufficiency* (*cirrhosis*), endocrine (*pituitary, thyroid, parathyroid, adrenal, gonadal, diabetes*).
4. Genetic—African pygmies, *primordial dwarf* (perfectly miniature), delayed adolescence (constitutional), *Turner's syndrome.*
5. Others—*progeria,* intrauterine deprivation, bird-headed dwarfism, iatrogenic (steroid therapy).

Dysmenorrhea is painful menses severe enough to prevent a girl from engaging in normal daily activities. If ten to fifteen grains of aspirin are not sufficient to control the symptoms, an investigation to exclude pelvic abnormalities must be done. Monthly pains without flow might be due to an imperforate hymen, an obvious bluish bulge at the vaginal opening. A uterus tipped forward or backward may possibly cause excessive pain, but the usual case reveals no cyst or narrowed uterine opening or infection. Some feel that the increased vascular congestion in the pelvic area is the culprit; therefore exercise or calisthenics seem a logical treatment. Being up and about is the usual compromise of most girls who find they notice the backache, leg pains, and cramps less if they keep busy. A wise mother might be sympathetic with her crampy, irritable daughter but not indulge her unduly. The girl might just feel rewarded for this distress and perpetuate the difficulty. *Aspirin* and *codeine* mixtures are safe to use for cramps bad enough to make the victim bedridden. Although codeine is a narcotic and should be treated with respect, the chance of addiction appears almost nil, since it does not produce the systemic euphoria common to the morphinelike narcotics. 500–1,000 milligrams of calcium lactate daily will calm the irritable uterus if calcium absorption has been inadequate.

Ectomorph is the term popularized by William Sheldon* for the body build that is predominantly thin with poorly developed muscles, long fingers, and light weight proportional to body length. This type is felt to have a characteristic personality and disease tendencies. (*Schizoids,* for instance, are more likely to be ectomorphic.)

Electrolytes are the dissolved minerals in the blood, body fluids, and cells that allow the body to carry on its work. A complex control mechanism must maintain these in a narrow margin of concentration; otherwise sickness will result. The diet and intestinal absorption is largely responsible for the intake of various salts, while the *kidneys* and *liver* are in charge of the excretion of excess amounts or waste products of metabolism.

Sodium is the principal ion in the blood and body fluids. Potassium concentration is higher in the cells. Chloride is the other important chemical, then follow calcium, magnesium, sulfate, phosphate, and bicarbonate.

Blood studies to determine the concentration of these electrolytes in the blood are important in the diagnosis and treatment of diseases of *intestines, kidneys, adrenal glands,* and *lungs.*

The most common childhood disease which alters the electrolyte concentration is *intestinal flu.* Vomiting leads to excessive loss of chloride, water, and hydrogen ion, producing alkalosis. *Diarrhea* tends

* *Varieties of Temperament* (New York: Harper Brothers, 1942).

to cause acidosis, as the fluids lost contain sodium. A common error of home treatment is the use of boiled skimmed milk which is relatively high in sodium. Since *water* is the chief constituent lost, replacement fluids should be weak in electrolyte solutions. An example would be six teaspoons of sugar, a half teaspoon of salt to a quart of water, to be given in small (one to three ounces) amounts every fifteen to twenty minutes. Lethargy, weakness, and lack of urine suggest the use of intravenous fluids and monitoring of the electrolyte levels in the blood.

Endomorph is the term used to describe the body build with a prominent abdominal area, fat deposits about trunk, upper arms, and thighs, plus short, tapering fingers. Children with this body type are usually identifiable by one year of age: height is twenty-nine inches; weight is thirty pounds. The implication is that this baby will be a fat child, and a fat adult, with all the related disease susceptibilities that obesity is heir to. A long-term plan of discouraging food intake is about the only weapon the mother has in dealing with this proclivity. (See *Obesity,* Section 11.)

Enzymes are *protein* molecules which are responsible for structure or function of the body cells. The ultimate responsibility for the formation of the enzymes resides in the genes in the nucleus of the cells. If a gene is defective or its component chemicals are misplaced or absent, the enzymes will be deficient or nonfunctional, and disease or structural anomalies will occur. The list of entities due to absent or malfunctioning enzymes grows yearly.

The formation of the *hemoglobin* molecule was the first to be studied. If the child inherits an abnormal gene for hemoglobin formation, each hemoglobin molecule will be abnormal, but he may not manifest symptoms. If he inherits the abnormal gene from *both* parents, the hemoglobin protein he manufactures may be so abnormal that he becomes severely anemic. (See *Sickle-cell anemia,* Section 8.) There are as many potential disorders of metabolism as there are chemical components in the protein enzyme chain, but not all will disturb function sufficiently to cause disease. A partial list of more common anomalies due to inherited enzyme defects:

Defective immunoproteins, *hemophilia,* PKU (phenylketonuria) disease, *albinism, cystinosis, Marfan's syndrome, Hurler's disease, diabetes, galactosemia, glycogen storage disease, gout, lipidosis, porphyria, cystic fibrosis, celiac disease, periodic paralysis.*

Estrogens are hormones produced by the mature *ovary* and *adrenal glands.* They are responsible for the secondary sex characteristics of the female (maturation of uterus, *vagina,* breasts, body hair, and wide hips). They also stimulate growth of the uterine mucosa in the first half of the menstrual cycle. (Progesterone, the other ovarian hormone, is more active in the second half of the cycle after ovulation.) There is little estrogen activity until the female is about eleven years old, or about a year or so before the *menarche.*

Failure to thrive is a multifaceted syndrome in which a baby appears underweight and apathetic. Although a physical cause may be evident (heart, lung, kidney, intestinal malfunction) the classical case is presumed to be due to physical and emotional neglect. These babies lie quietly, show no emotion, do not respond to cuddling, eye everyone constantly—even suspiciously—reject food and are slow in arriving at developmental milestones.

If organic components preventing normal growth can be ruled out, these babies must be placed in a warm, loving, stimulating environment. Consistent display of mothering finally convinces the baby he is wanted and accepted at last; he finally begins to trust people, and his indifference turns to love—if he has not been deprived too long. *Schizophrenia* can be the end result of this syndrome. (See *Deprivation, Autism,* Section 16.)

Fructose is a simple sugar found in fruits and honey and is combined with dextrose to make sucrose (table sugar). Deficiencies of enzymes responsible for fructose metabolism will allow this sugar to build up. One form is especially harmful, as it leads to *hypoglycemia* (low glucose in blood) with associated lethargy, *convulsions,* and *growth failure.*

Galactosemia is the condition of elevated amounts of galactose in the blood. Galactose is formed by the enzyme action of lactase in the intestines upon lactose, the milk sugar. (Glucose is the mate of galactose in the lactose molecule.) Another enzyme in the tissues converts it into metabolically useful glucose. If the enzyme is lacking, the elevated galactose levels in the blood will lead to listlessness, *failure to thrive,* feeding problems, and weight loss. Enlarged *liver, jaundice,* and *cataracts* soon appear. Death is inevitable in the untreated case; mental retardation might occur if treatment is late.

No milk or milk products can be consumed, or the galactose

will reaccumulate. This treatment is simple and dramatic, if thought of in time and if the patient will stick to the necessary diet.

Gargoylism is a combination of defects, including *dwarfism, mental retardation,* cloudy *corneae,* enlarged *spleen* and *liver,* and various bony changes; short thick hands, club-shaped ribs, thickened arm and leg bones. The *tongue* protrudes, the brows are prominent, the head is enlarged. The condition is genetic, and no treatment is available.

Gaucher's disease—see *Lipidoses*

Gigantism is the condition of excessive height due to increased amounts of growth hormone produced by a *pituitary* adenoma. This is very rare but operable, as the tumor may be removed. A cerebral form due to some defect in the nervous system is more common but is untreatable. The latter patients are usually awkward and *mentally retarded;* growth hormone is normal. The rapid growth is obvious at or near birth.

In the pituitary giants the rapid growth appears when the adenoma begins to secrete the hormone. Great linear growth will occur if the epiphyses (growing ends of bones) have not fused together. If they have, the hormone will enlarge the jaw, head, hands—a condition called acromegaly.

Glucose tolerance test is a method of assaying the body's ability to absorb, transport, utilize, store, and excrete a standard amount of glucose given orally. After oral ingestion blood glucose levels are determined at half-hour, hour, two-, three-, four-, five-, and six-hour intervals. The test is valuable in detecting equivocal cases of *diabetes,* renal glycosuria, and *hypoglycemia.*

Glycogen is a complex sugar composed of glucose molecules linked together. It is stored in the *liver* and muscle cells where it is readily available as fuel. A large number of enzymes are involved in the synthesis of glycogen from glucose molecules and in the breakdown again to glucose. Congenital absence of any of these enzymes will lead to inability to form glycogen, excess storage of glycogen, deficient release of glucose or formation of deformed glycogen.

Glucose and glycogen utilization yields energy and lactic acid, carbon dioxide (exhaled via lungs) and water. If carbohydrate is not stored as glycogen or burned up for energy, it is converted to *fat.*

Glycogen storage disease (von Gierke's) is a genetically determined condition in which glycogen is stored in abnormal amounts in the *liver* and kidney cells. This glycogen cannot be degraded into its *glucose* parts due to an enzyme lack. These patients have enlarged livers (swollen with glycogen; see *Glycogen storage,* Sections 8 and 12) and low blood sugar (*hypoglycemia*). (The glucose is all stored in the glycogen molecules in the liver cells.) The body's principle source of energy, then, must be *fat.* When fat is utilized, fatty acids, *ketosis* and *acidosis* result.

The disease usually sneaks up on the victim, and the enlarged liver, *dwarfism, hypoglycemia* (with drowsiness and convulsions) become manifest in the second or third year.

In other forms of deranged glycogen metabolism the heart muscle may be the focal point of increased storage leading to *cyanosis* and *congestive heart failure.* Death is almost assured in the first year.

In another type of the disease glycogen storage is normal in the *muscles* but it cannot be broken down to glucose. The patient may do well unless he overexerts; severe *cramps* and *weakness* force him to slow down (Section 7).

Goiter is an enlarged *thyroid* gland found low in the front of the neck just above the breast bone. It may be associated with normal thyroid function or *hyper-* or *hypothyroidism.*

Endemic and/or congenital goiter is due to a deficiency of iodine in water and foods; this has occurred in the Pacific Northwest and Great Lakes areas in the United States, in Switzerland, and in some other regions. This condition is now rarely seen because of the use of iodized salt in the diet. In response to low levels of thyroid hormone, the pituitary gland compensates by increasing the production of thyroid stimulating hormone. This makes the gland enlarge. A pregnant woman taking iodides or antithyroid drugs for hyperthyroidism may deliver a baby with a huge thyroid gland, large enough to compress his trachea and cause asphyxia. A woman with a goiter due to iodine deficiency may produce a child with cretinism.

Sporadic goiter usually appears in maturing females and is not related to iodine deficiency. It may be due to an inflammation (*thyroiditis*) or excess iodide therapy (for *asthma*) or some unknown defect. The gland enlarges to produce thyroid hormone to maintain the body in normal balance. If the goiter is unsightly, it may be advisable to give thyroid hormone in order to reduce its size.

Gonadotrophic hormones—see *Pituitary*

Growth is the increase in weight and length from birth to the end of adolescence. It will vary depending on heredity, intrauterine conditions, environment, disease, hormones, emotional factors, and diet. Under optimum conditions it is predictable once a pattern has been established in the first year. Adult weight is too variable to be estimated, although a fat baby at a year of age is destined to be an obese adult.

Growth is most rapid *in utero,* but is still accelerated in the first few months of life. If the rate of length increase continued at the pace of the first few weeks, the child would be twenty feet tall at ten years of age! Growth is predetermined by genetic factors, but intrauterine nutrition and postnatal diet and environmental influences may alter the rate significantly. *Protein, iron, calcium,* and *phosphorus* seem to be the key nutrients for optimum growth.

An average baby will weigh about seven pounds at birth. Water loss accounts for the weight loss in the first few days, but he should be back to birth weight within seven to ten days. Twenty inches is the standard length at birth, but measurement is difficult since the nursery nurse may not be able to stretch the baby's legs out fully. Between three and five months the baby will double his birth weight, and his length at six months should be close to twenty-five or twenty-six inches. He adds only three or four inches to his length the remainder of the first year and perhaps another six or seven pounds.

Just as the mother becomes accustomed to the rapid growth and huge appetite, her child stops eating and growing. He has grown three to four inches in his second year, but after age four or five he grows only two to three inches a year until his prepuberty growth spurt.

Weight gain is much more variable than linear growth, and frequently is related to hereditary predisposition to *obesity.* Efforts to alter the weight increase are usually fruitless; it seems axiomatic that the harder the mother tries to keep her fat child slim, the more obese he becomes. There was a time when doctors suggested an ideal weight to go with a certain height. The rule now is that if a person looks thin, he is thin; if he looks fat, he is fat. (See *Obesity,* Section 11.)

The doctor who tries to evaluate growth must be able to observe a continuum of weights and lengths so deviations may be discovered rapidly and appropriate steps taken to evaluate the change. Each child has his own pattern of growth which becomes obvious as time goes by. A two-inch growth per year may be abnormal in one child but optimum in another. Most parents try to have a yearly checkup for their child so that growth deviations can be detected early.

Some prediction can be made. Doubling the length of a girl at eighteen months gives close to ultimate height as an adult; for a boy the two-year-old height should be doubled.

Various organ systems grow at different rates, apparently controlled by the thalamus and the *pituitary.* The brain grows most rapidly *in utero* by increasing the number of cells. After the first few months of life, however, it increases by increasing the size of the cells. The thymus gland (located in the chest) is large in infancy, then atrophies after many of its cells migrate to other tissues, as part of the body's immune mechanism. Lymph tissue grows to its peak at four to six years, then subsides to normal adult size after age seven. Secondary sexual characteristics (breasts, body hair) and size of sexual organs become obvious at puberty; this is mediated by the pituitary and *adrenal glands.*

Gynecomastia is breast enlargement in the male generally due to transient *estrogen* secretion from the maturing testes. About one third of pubertal boys will develop enlarged, tender breast tissue that feels as if ten or twelve BB shots were implanted directly beneath the nipple. It is a source of acute embarrassment to the boy, for it may last several months and give him some doubts about his masculinity.

Reassurance is the only treatment. Rarely is it associated with testicular or *adrenal* tumors.

Hartnup disease is a rare genetic, metabolic defect involving *tryptophan,* an amino acid.

Heredity is the sum of the genetic influences that determines physical and mental potential. The environment is supposed to nurture this potential and allow its full fruition in adulthood. Many traits are obviously inherited—height, eye color, *flat feet,* and many others. Some tendencies are inherited but only become manifest through environmental pressures—*diabetes, epilepsy, obesity, enuresis,* intelligence, some talents and abilities, certain *psychoses.* Controversy is apparent among psychiatrists, sociologists, grandmothers, astrologers, and pediatricians regarding the etiology of personality and behavior disorders. Many of us who deal exclusively with children are convinced that the personality development is multifaceted. A poor genetic background plus neurological damage plus a deficient diet in an unstable home should lead to a poorly functioning adult. Frequently, however, it motivates an individual to try harder; frequently he succeeds. Apparently luck and skill are the ingredients (with a little geography thrown in) that make an adventure out of what might otherwise seem routine growing, mating, and dying. (See *Chromosomes, Gene.*)

Human growth hormone (HGH) has just recently been synthesized. It contains almost two hundred individual amino-acid units, each having a specific position in the long chain protein molecule. The twisting or coiling of the chain—like a snake—also is a factor in determining the activity of this hormone. HGH is not available for the estimated 200,000 dwarfs who might be benefited; a few are now being treated by extracts of human pituitary gland (from cadavers, usually donated by request in a donor's will). One gland supplies about enough hormone for one or two injections; daily injections are continued for months or years. Response is dramatic in the early months of treatment and then slows, perhaps due to anti-HGH antibodies. The best response is in the five- to ten-year age group. One dwarf grew twelve inches in four years of daily injections; the untreated dwarf grows no more than two to four inches in this space of time. (A normal child grows two to three inches a year.)

Actually the pituitary dwarf is the least common of the dwarf syndromes.

Hunter's syndrome resembles *gargoylism* but is determined by a defective sex *chromosome.* Physical deformities, *mental retardation,* and *deafness* are characteristic.

Hurler's syndrome—see *Gargoylism*

Hydrocortisone (see *Adrenal gland*) is one of the chief hormones produced by the adrenal cortex and is necessary for life. It is widely used by physicians for allergic disorders (*asthma, hay fever,* poison-oak *dermatitis*), autoimmune diseases (*arthritis, rheumatic fever, nephrosis*), and as an anti-inflammatory drug (ointment for *eczema,* injection of acutely inflamed joints).

Hypercalcemia is excess calcium in the blood, and has been assumed to be due to excess vitamin D intake or to an exaggerated response to normal intake. If excessive vitamin D intake is early and prolonged (too much given to a pregnant woman or high doses given to a newborn), the effects may be permanent. The child with idiopathic hypercalcemia of infancy will have an elfin face, *mental retardation,* short stature, and X rays show dense bones. *Aortic stenosis* (Section 5) may be associated. If the *vitamin D* excess does not occur until late infancy, fever and irritability may be the only consequences.

The obvious treatment is discontinuation of vitamin D (even excluding sunshine) and lowering dietary calcium (no dairy products).

Vitamin D intake is normally kept to 400 international units a day. Whole or homogenized milk in our country usually has this amount in a quart. If the baby is getting this much from his milk, plus a vitamin supplement, plus sunshine, he may be getting too much vitamin D. Usually hypercalcemia is not a problem unless consumption of the vitamin is over 2,000 to 3,000 units per day over a few weeks time.

Hypercholesterolemia is excess of cholesterol in the blood. It is usually a familial trait. If the child inherits the trait from one parent, his *cholesterol* is elevated, and he is susceptible to early coronary-vessel disease (age thirty to forty years). If he inherits this from both parents, his cholesterol level goes up to very high levels and yellow, fatty (*xanthoma*) deposits are found in skin and tissues.

Hyperinsulinism is an excess of *insulin* in the system and causes *hypoglycemia* (low blood sugar). It may be due to an insulin-secreting tumor of the *pancreas* (rare) or to hyperfunction of the normal insulin-producing cells of the pancreas (found in newborns of diabetic mothers). (See *Hypoglycemia.*)

Hyperkalemia, or hyperpotassemia, is excess potassium in the blood. This affects the heart (which may beat rapidly or slowly) and muscles. It may stimulate the excretion of aldosterone from the *adrenal* cortex. Excess potassium is often due to overreplacement of potassium in intravenous fluids when *kidney* function is poor. (See also *Hypokalemia.*)

Hyperlipidemia is excess fat in the blood and is characteristically increased in von Gierke's disease, diabetic *acidosis, nephrosis, hypothyroidism,* and *liver* tumors. Lipids are increased in the hyperlipoproteinemias; these are familial or inborn errors. The victim is usually predisposed to vascular disease and early coronary occlusion due to the deposits on the vessel walls.

Hypernatremia is the excess of the sodium ion in the blood. It is common in *dehydration* in small infants with vomiting and diarrhea who are offered boiled skimmed milk (rich in sodium); the young infant's kidneys are unable to concentrate urine, so more sodium is going into his system than is coming out. High sodium levels will cause *convulsions* and *brain damage.*

Hyperparathyroidism is overactivity of the parathyroid glands which are located just behind the thyroid gland. It may be due to a secreting tumor, but is usually due to overactivity in response to a low calcium condition resulting from *rickets, malabsorption,* or *renal* diseases.

Calcium levels in the blood increase, and *phosphorus* decreases. X rays reveal low density of bones because of resorption of calcium from them. The patient is weak, nauseated, constipated, and may pass calcium *kidney* stones. Surgery is usually performed in anticipation of finding an *adenoma.*

Hyperthyroidism is the result of an excess of *thyroid* hormone. It is rare in children, but becomes progressively more common with age. Girls are much more susceptible than boys.

As thyroid increases the metabolism, the patient gradually becomes *hyperactive,* emotionally unstable, and restless. Appetite is increased, tremors develop, skin is warm and moist, *pulse* rate is increased and remains rapid in sleep. The eyes become prominent. The thyroid gland (in the lower neck) is swollen. Growth rate is increased. A baby may have these symptoms if born of a mother with a toxic thyroid.

The primary treatment is medical; anti-thyroid drugs prevent the synthesis of thyroid hormone. If medication is ineffective, surgery is sometimes necessary.

Exophthalmic goiter, rare in children, is due to excessive *thyroid* hormone secretion. The eyes are prominent, as the upper lid is elevated. (See *Hyperthyroidism.*)

Graves' disease, or hyperthyroidism, is usually the term applied to the condition of oversecretion of thyroid hormone that causes the eyes to appear prominent (exophthalmos).

Hypoglycemia means low blood sugar. Glucose levels in the blood normally rise and fall depending on food intake, exercise, insulin, thyroid function, epinephrine (adrenalin), fever, and other factors. It is normally at its lowest ebb after nocturnal fasting and rises in response to meals three times a day. The level rises higher and more rapidly after a sugary or high-carbohydrate meal and rises more slowly but is more sustained after a protein meal.

Adult levels vary from 60 to 120 milligrams percent. Newborn babies have glucose levels (20 to 50 milligrams per 100 milliliters of blood) in a range that would put a normal adult in coma. (Perhaps this is why a baby's hunger appears to be such an emergency.) After the newborn period, levels of 50 to 100 milligrams percent are usual. The metabolism of the brain is completely dependent on oxygen and glucose; therefore, hypoglycemia first gives rise to symptoms referable to the nervous system; *convulsions,* somnolence, fatigue, pallor, *headache,* poor or slurred speech, tremor, *fainting, behavior problems.* A new baby might have cold, clammy skin, twitches, eye rolling, drowsiness, poor feeding or sucking. Hypoglycemia may lead to *brain damage* and *mental retardation,* so diagnosis and therapy should not be delayed when the above symptoms are noted.

A fasting blood-sugar test (blood drawn after eight hours without food) is usually enough to establish the diagnosis if the glucose level is low and the symptoms are present. A rapid fall of the glucose level is more likely to produce symptoms than a low level slowly attained.

Possible causes of hypoglycemia include a diabetic mother (baby produces extra insulin in response to his mother's hyperglycemia), poor absorption from intestines, large losses via *kidneys* (*glycosuria*—lead poisoning), *galactosemia, glycogen storage disease,* islet cell adenoma of the *pancreas,* leucine sensitivity, liver damage (*alcohol, carbon tetrachloride*), ketotic hypoglycemia (akin to cyclic vomiting), *pituitary dwarfism, Addison's disease,* low *epinephrine* release.

Immediate oral sugar is the emergency treatment of the hypoglycemia attack. Children with reactive hypoglycemia (rapid fall of blood glucose three to four hours after a carbohydrate meal) should be provided with three protein servings a day. Protein gives up its calories more slowly. Carbohydrate meals quickly stimulate insulin to utilize and store the glucose; blood-sugar values are more likely to be reduced to low, symptomatic levels.

A doctor called to see a child with "peculiar symptoms" may be tempted to overutilize the laboratory. We used to get X rays, *kidney* studies, *calcium,* sugar, and *urea* levels hoping something would show up. A baby with convulsions may not need extensive testing, but should at least have a fasting blood-sugar test. If the convulsions are due to hypoglycemia, he will surely be brain damaged if it is not corrected rapidly.

(A patient I knew with a blood-sugar level of 20 to 30 milligrams percent at age three months had to have seven eighths of his pancreas removed before his seizures stopped. The investigation, however, was not made early enough to prevent brain damage. His IQ ended up at about 50.)

Hypogonadism in the female may be caused by surgical removal of ovaries (necessitated by cancer) or X radiation. The girl fails to become a woman. Breasts, pubic hair, and menses do not appear. In primary hypogonadism, the ovaries fail to function.

Turner's syndrome becomes obvious when adolescent sexual development and the *menarche* do not occur at the usual time. The ovaries are only bits of nonfunctioning tissue. This condition is a sex chromosomal abnormality. Other associated anomalies are short stature, webbing of the neck with a low hairline, heart and ear abnormalities, and frequently mental retardation.

Female sex hormones are successful in producing the breasts and other female characteristics but, of course, these women are infertile, as there are no ova.

Secondary hypogonadism in the female caused by pituitary failure results in short stature and sexual immaturity.

Hypogonadism in the male (sexual infantilism) is the deficient function of *testes.* It may be primary (little androgen hormone and decreased sperm production) or secondary and due to deficent *pituitary gonadotrophic hormone.*

Delayed adolescence in the male is frequently a familial trait, but if no signs of sexual maturity appear by age sixteen, an investigation is appropriate. This lack of sexual maturity in the male is called *eunuchism.* Castration before maturity will cause this condition. Eunuchism may occur in either sex after prepubertal gonadectomy.

In secondary hypogonadism the pituitary has failed to produce the testicular, stimulating hormones, so the otherwise normal testes fail to achieve adult function, and no masculinizing androgens are formed. *Pituitary dwarfs,* for example, are short and sexually infantile. Growth hormone is absent also.

Laurence-Biedl syndrome shows symptoms of hypogonadism, obesity, extra fingers, mental retardation, and retina changes.

Undescended testes will impair the production of sperm, but not of the androgen hormone. *Mumps orchitis* may have a similar effect, so these are not examples of complete hypogonadism.

Hypogonadism is usually not noticed until adolescence when the signs of puberty fail to appear—no acne, no pubic or axillary hair, no voice change, no enlargement of *penis* and *testes.* Fat accumulation in breasts and hips and arms and legs is disproportionately large compared to the trunk. Muscles fail to fill out.

Examples of hypogonadism usually due to sex chromosome anomalies:

Klinefelter's syndrome: mental retardation, gynecomastia, delinquency, bone defects, malformed ears, wide mouth, and wide-set eyes. These boys usually have extra *X chromosomes,* and their mothers were often over age thirty-five at the time of the child's birth.

Testosterone is administered to achieve sexual maturity if necessary.

Male Turner's syndrome: short stature, webbing of the neck, heart murmur, mental retardation, ptosis of eyelids, malformed ears.

Hypokalemia (low potassium in the blood) may follow *vomiting* and *diarrhea* when extra fluids containing no potassium have been given. The heart and skeletal muscles may be affected. (See *Paralysis,* Section 7.) Laboratory tests during replacement therapy for fluid loss would detect a dangerously low (or high) level. *Aldosterone* (an adrenal hormone) is instrumental in potassium metabolism.

Hyponatremia, or low sodium in the blood, is usually the result of fluid loss from *diarrhea* and *vomiting* with inadequate replacement of salt.

Hypoparathyroidism is the deficient excretion of the *parathyroid* hormone. It may be congenital (if the mother was *hyperparathyroid*) or a genetic defect or a surgical one (removal of the *thyroid* plus inadvertent parathyroid removal), or the cause may be unknown.

This hormone is chiefly responsible for *calcium* metabolism and maintenance of an optimum level in the blood. A low calcium level in the blood ordinarily stimulates the parathyroid to produce more hormone, which mobilizes calcium from the bones. If the glands are unresponsive, the low calcium produces *tetany:* twitches, numbness, tingling, *seizures,* abdominal pain, *headache,* and vomiting.

Calcium by injection is the emergency treatment. Large doses of vitamin D help to raise the calcium level.

Hypopituitarism is the condition of deficient production of one or more of the pituitary hormones, including the growth hormone. If a child stops growing and all the diseases usually responsible have been ruled out, a lesion in the pituitary might be responsible (craniopharyngioma, *tuberculosis, Hand-Schuller-Christian disease,* adenoma). If no lesion is found, the dwarfism may be due to lack of growth-hormone production or production of an inferior hormone or lack of response of bone and muscle to the normal amount of hormone (as in pygmies).

The disease may not be obvious until a year or so goes by, after which the small child is quite obviously way below the lower end of the growth chart. Signs of *thyroid* and *adrenal* insufficiency may develop if the lesion destroys the part of the pituitary that manufactures the hormones that stimulate the thyroid and the adrenal glands.

A growth hormone assay can be made to diagnose hypopituitarism and, if the level is low, a search for an operable lesion is undertaken. X rays of skull and determination of visual fields are helpful.

Hypothyroidism appears if the thyroid hormone is less than adequate to maintain metabolism. If congenital, it is called *cretinism.* If it develops after a few years of normal functioning, it is usually due to an inflammation, albeit unnoticed (*thyroiditis*).

The child gradually grows sluggish, sleeps a lot without becoming refreshed, becomes constipated, and the skin is cold, dry, and waxy looking. (Obesity is rarely a result of hypothyroidism. If the child has warm, moist palms and grows two inches a year, he is just fat, not low in thyroid.) Growth stops or decreases to an inch or so in a year; the yearly checkup provides a way to keep an accurate growth record.

An attempt must be made to differentiate primary hypothyroidism from secondary (inadequate thyrotrophic hormone due to deficient pituitary function). In the secondary type other pituitary hormones are altered also.

A few reliable blood tests are enough to establish the diagnosis.

Treatment is replacement for life with a daily dose of *thyroxine* or thyroid extract (animal source). Dosage is adjusted to secure optimum growth and normal blood thyroxine levels.

Usually mental ability will not suffer if the onset occurs after infancy.

Inborn errors of metabolism constitute an ever-increasing list of genetically determined syndromes which manifest themselves by *enzyme* deficiencies. Specific enzymes that are essential to proper cellular function are lacking. The following is a list of common and not-so-common disorders, followed by the enzyme that is deficient and hence responsible for the problem:

PKU—phenylalanine hydroxylase deficiency
Hemophilia—deficient Factor VIII of clotting mechanism
Hypogammaglobulinemia—deficient production of *immunoglobulins*
Sickle-cell anemia—defective *hemoglobin* synthesis
Albinism—deficient tyrosinase
Diabetes mellitus—inadequte insulin

These are but a few of the now known to be hundreds of enzyme deficiencies to which our flesh is heir. Research will no doubt be able to supply these missing factors, but substitution therapy is difficult at present. Identification of carriers of these traits and limitation of the number of children born with such defects seems appropriate.

Insulin is a hormone secreted by the islet cells of the pancreas. Its chief role is in lowering blood glucose by aiding its storage as glycogen in the liver and muscle. Insulin is the drug used by injection to treat the diabetic. Because the onset of *diabetes* in children is usually characterized by rapidly changing insulin requirements, it is best to use the regular or short-acting insulin until some stability is obtained. The average patient then gets a long-acting insulin injection (twenty-four-hour duration), plus the quick-acting, regular insulin at or before breakfast. Insulin dosage is increased during infection and decreased during exercise. Monitoring the urine for sugar is usually satisfactory to determine if the insulin dose is sufficient. Insulin shock or coma must be relieved immediately because of the potential harm to the brain cells from hypoglycemia. The patient rapidly becomes hungry, then pale, sweaty, and weak. He may faint and have a convulsion.

A child must be taught to recognize the symptoms so that he may ingest a remedial candy bar.

Ketosis is the abnormal accumulation in the body of ketone, a chemical formed by the breakdown of fat stores. It is usually associated with *dehydration* from *diabetic acidosis* or vomiting and as a precipitating condition in *cyclic vomiting.*

Klinefelter's syndrome—see *Hypogonadism*

Laurence-Biedl syndrome—see *Hypogonadism*

Leucine-induced hypoglycemia occurs in some people when fed leucine, an *amino acid. Insulin* is overproduced and drives the blood sugar down to dangerously low levels.

Lipidoses are inborn errors of fat enzyme production. Excessive accumulation of various lipids is end result.

Gaucher's disease is an inherited condition in which a glycolipid is stored in cells in the *lungs, liver, spleen, brain,* and bone marrow. It may be mild or severe, acute or chronic, and associated with growth failure. If it develops rapidly in infancy with hypertonia, strabismus, stiff neck, vomiting, and respiratory difficulties, a fatal outcome is predictable by six years of age. Slowly developing forms may be compatible with long life, but susceptibility to fractures (due to invasion of the bone marrow by large numbers of these fat cells) and hypersplenism (low blood counts) are troublesome to the patient. Splenectomy may be necessary. There is no known treatment.

Niemann-Pick disease is inherited. A phospholipid is stored in the *brain* and/or *spleen* and *liver. Blindness, seizures, mental retardation* usually occur and end the patient's life before adolescence.

Tay-Sachs disease is characterized by the invasion of a glycolipid into the nerve cells. Early infancy appears completely normal, but deterioration sets in by six to ten months of age. The baby becomes unresponsive, eats poorly, and loses his sight. Death is inevitable by age three. It occurs almost exclusively in Jewish infants.

Lipids, or fats, are found naturally in all tissues, but are more concentrated in the *blood, brain,* subcutaneous tissues, bone marrow, and *liver.* Excessive intake, poor utilization, local accumulation may be factors in the *lipidoses,* conditions of pathological storage.

Lipodystrophy is the partial (face, arms, trunk) or complete loss of fat between skin and underlying bones and muscles (prisoner-of-war look). Girls are more likely to be the victims. Although it is an inherited trait, it may not develop until late childhood. It is usually associated with liver diseases and skin changes (excessive pigmentation and hair).

Marfan's syndrome, or arachnodactyly, is the extreme case of being long and thin (*ectomorph*)—*really* long and thin. The fingers, toes, hands, and feet are abnormally long. Eye defects are common; a dislocated lens is supposed to clinch the diagnosis. *Heart anomalies* and a weak-walled *aorta* are frequent. If these anomalies do not cause the patient's demise, he may grow to adulthood and transmit the condition to his offspring.

Lincoln was supposed to have had this problem, but his early life as a rail-splitter and wrestler seems to negate the diagnosis, as victims are asthenic and have poor muscular development.

Menarche is the onset of menstruation. It may vary widely, is hastened by good *nutrition,* genetic factors (if the mother was early, the daughter often is), and race. It is not unusual for the menarche to occur at age ten.

When the mother notices *breast development* and pubic hair in her daughter (age nine to twelve), she would be wise to open the discussion about menses by asking, "What do you know about menstruation?" She may be surprised to learn how much her daughter knows. Most schools have a health class for ten- to twelve-year-old girls in which menstruation is discussed. This emotionally charged subject may have been taught, but the girl may not have learned. It is the duty of the mother to discover if her daughter has learned the essential facts and has a reasonably nonneurotic attitude about her female role.

Menstruation is the periodic loss of the endometrium (cellular lining of the uterus). If the egg released that month is not fertilized, the lining sloughs off. It soon rebuilds again, undaunted.

The *pituitary,* under some influence from the hypothalamus, sends hormones to the *ovaries* which respond by producing *estrogens.* Estrogens stimulate growth of breasts, uterus, and female sexual characteristics. They also build up the endometrium. About halfway between the periods, the ovary discharges an egg, and progesterone hormone takes over and further prepares the uterus for possible nesting of the fertilized ovum.

For the first few years of the adolescent's menses, few or no eggs are discharged from the ovaries; this confuses the hormones and frequently results in no periods for several months. This may alarm the girl—and her mother.

If menstruation has not begun by age sixteen, an examination is worthwhile. Age thirteen is about average. (See *Amenorrhea.*) The length and frequency of periods are irregular and inconsistent for the first two years after the menarche.

A growth prediction can be made at the time of the menarche: the girl's height has been almost attained, and she will rarely grow more than another inch or two.

Mesomorph is the term used to describe the muscular husky, broad, stocky type of body build: blocking halfbacks, wrestlers, shotput throwers. The body emphasizes its mesodermal tissues—muscle and bone. Some psychologists feel there are personality types that are associated with somatic types; the mesomorph gradually finds that he can get things by being "tough" (he is harder than the endomorph, stronger than the ectomorph), so he adopts this as a life style. (See *Ectomorph.*)

Mongolism—see *Down's syndrome*

Morquio's disease is an inherited chondrodysplasia that deforms the spine and chest. The head seems to rest on the broad chest, for many of the vertebrae of the neck are fused or absent. Arms are long, joints are large, abdomen protrudes, back is bent.

No treatment is available other than some orthopedic help for severe deformities.

Neoplasms are abnormal growths which are a leading cause of death among children, especially in the first five years. Many of these malignancies develop from cells which first appear in the embryo but never have matured. Something (possibly a *virus*) triggers their uninhibited growth; the rapidity of onset usually produces symptoms quite rapidly (*leukemia* and *brain tumors*), but frequently abdominal tumors (*Wilms's tumor* and *neuroblastoma*) may reach a large size before parents become suspicious of trouble. For this reason mothers should develop a casual, at least monthly, habit of general abdominal palpation at bath or bedtime. This just might bring an involved child to surgery earlier and with a better chance of cure than if parents relied only on the yearly checkup. Abdominal tumors in children are often completely asymptomatic.

There is a proved increase of *thyroid* cancer in children who received X radiation to the thymus gland in infancy. A similar increase in incidence of leukemia has been seen in children born of mothers who had much pelvic or abdominal X radiation during the pregnancy.

The outlook for cancer is more hopeful than ever before. Research will no doubt have the answer in a few short years. In the meantime, the doctor caring for the dying child's physical needs has the burden of holding the egos of all participants together. He has his own problems when he realizes he has nothing more to offer and so feels guilty about return appointments. The doctor may be evasive when asked by the child about death, growing up, being cured, but he should be encouraging without promising too much. The child must be made to feel safe, secure, and free of pain. He needs to know that a trusted person will be available if he feels helpless and alone.

Parents, for a variety of reasons, may not want their child to know that he has a fatal illness, although most children ultimately become suspicious. The doctor should respect the parents' wishes in the matter, although a frank discussion of the fatal outcome is usually anxiety relieving. If the child suspects his illness and cannot get the doctor to say even the name of the disease, he may feel his condition is so bad that even the doctor is afraid to talk about it.

In general, the honest approach is the best, as it suggests to the child that doctor and parents are to be trusted.

Adenoma means glandlike internal tumor. Some are benign—do not spread; others are malignant. They can be found anywhere in the body. The symptoms arising from their presence are related to their position (if in a bronchial tube, coughing and wheezing) or function (an *insulin*-secreting tumor in the pancreas causes low blood sugar).

When discovered, surgical removal seems appropriate, as some innocuous-appearing adenomata may be—or later become—cancerous.

Biopsy is the removal of a piece of tissue, usually in surgery, for closer inspection under a microscope. This examination aids in the diagnosis of a diseased organ when palpation or inspection are inadequate. For example, a small piece of a breast lump is often removed so that the pathologist can determine if cancer is present in a frozen section of the tissue. He can then rapidly signal the waiting surgeon, and a decision can be made regarding radical breast removal.

Carcinoma is a fortunately rare tumor growth in children. It may be found in almost every organ, and if not removed by surgery or destroyed by X ray or chemotherapy, will eventually kill the victim. "Malignant neoplasm" and "cancer" are synonymous. If leukemia can be included in the definition, then cancer is the second leading cause of death in children in the United States (accidents are the major cause). *Brain tumors* are second to *leukemia* in frequency. Tumors of *salivary glands, thyroid, adrenals, liver,* and *kidneys* usually grow rapidly without many disabling symptoms; they may become huge before being noticed. Early discovery and rapid treatment have led to a number of cures; the outlook should be hopeful.

Although X-ray irradiation is frequently used in the treatment of cancer, its use has been implicated as a possible inciting agent in the onset of certain other cancers. (X-ray treatment for thymus enlargement may be causally related to later thyroid cancer, and so forth.) Some evidence indicates that X-ray treatment for adolescent acne may be related to skin cancer in adulthood.

Cystic hygroma is a lymphangioma, which means an enlarged or dilated lymph vessel. It is not cancerous but, because of its large size, may impair function of nearby compressed organs. The most common site is the neck or center of chest; breathing problems may develop because of tracheal compression. Surgery may be necessary, but recurrences are common.

Eosinophilic granuloma is a tumor containing *eosinophiles.* An attempt has been made to classify this and other granulomatous diseases under one heading: histiocytosis. These conditions share this one type of cell but differ in location and rapidity of spread. The eosinophilic granuloma is a histiocytosis confined to one or a few bone lesions. It may lie unrecognized in a bone and be inadvertently revealed when an X ray is taken for some unrelated condition. It may be a tender lump in a skull bone which, when X-rayed, shows a calcium-free area. Microscopic examination reveals eosinophilis; X-ray therapy usually eliminates these solitary lesions (Section 7).

Fibroma is a benign tumor which may occur anywhere in the body. Symptoms would vary depending on its relationship to vital structures. It consists of fibrous tissue, collagen, and sometimes cartilage or bone. Removal and microscopic examination determines how radical treatment must be. If it arises in the muscle, it might be only a painless lump. If in or on a nerve (near the "funny bone" on elbow), shooting pain might force removal. If the tumor is in the heart muscle, it might grow large enough to cause heart dysfunction. A common fibroma grows in the jawbone and slowly calcifies. Surgical removal is standard treatment.

Granuloma is a tumor; the many varieties are classified depending on location and the cells they contain.

Hand-Schuller-Christian disease is the name for the condition of those patients who have more extensive destructive bone disease. Letterer-Siwe disease applies to those patients with rapidly advancing lesions in liver, lymph nodes, spleen, bone marrow, lungs, and skin. Anemia, weight loss, bone pain usually continue until the fatal outcome. Cortisone, anticancer drugs, X-ray treatment, and surgery are only palliative.

Hodgkin's disease is a malignant disease of *lymph* tissue for which early treatment may be curative. It characteristically begins as swollen lymph nodes unrelated to infection. Neck, axillary (armpit), or inguinal (groin) nodes will swell and remain swollen despite antibiotic treatment. A biopsy of such a node would reveal a cancer. Swollen glands in a lung tissue would be found in an X ray. The patient becomes wasted and anemic. Various chemicals (nitrogen mustard and others) are palliative but with repeated use become ineffective. Newer chemicals have controlled the disease in many; huge doses of vitamin C taken intravenously have been curative.

Lipoma, or fatty tumor, is a benign, round, firm but not hard growth usually easily felt just under the skin anywhere in the body. Surgical removal is recommended, as these tumors frequently grow large enough to make delayed surgery more difficult. They are occasionally found deep in the abdomen or growing from the *parotid (salivary)* gland.

Every unidentified tumor should be considered malignant until removed and identified under the microscope.

Lymphangioma is a collection of *lymph* vessels which may be large enough and cystic enough to press on adjacent organs (cystic hygroma). Lymph vessels in the tongue may cause the tongue to become large enough to interfere with eating or talking. Surgery affords relief. A lymphangioma may occur in the spleen, abdomen, or chest.

Lymphosarcoma is a malignant growth of the *lymph node.* Immature lymph cells replace the normal lymphocytes; the tumor grows rapidly as these cells divide rapidly. One form (lymphoma of Africa, Burkitt) is thought to be due to a virus, responds temporarily to X radiation and antitumor medicine. It is felt to be a cousin to leukemia.

Nephroblastoma, or Wilms's tumor, usually appears in the first three years as an abdominal mass. It arises from the kidney and may fill up the entire side of the abdomen before surgery.

Surgery, chemicals (actinomycin D), and X radiation constitute the treatment. Rapid care has brought about some exciting statistics: more than 50 percent of patients are considered cured (no recurrence two years after initial surgery).

Neuroblastoma is a common malignant tumor in infancy and early childhood. It usually arises from the medulla of the *adrenal* gland, but may begin from any of the nerves of the sympathetic nervous system which lie alongside the vertebrae (in the chest and pelvis). A mass palpated in the abdomen might be the first clue. X rays would reveal the approximate size and location on or near a kidney. It metastasizes (spreads) to the *liver, lymph nodes,* bone, and if to the *eye* orbit, its pressure of growth pushes the eyeball forward (exophthalmos).

Surgery and postoperative chemicals and X radiation are standard. Only about one out of three survives.

Pheochromocytoma is a tumor usually developing from the adrenal (medulla area) glands. There may be a familial tendency to this and other tumors. The tumor secretes excess amounts of *epinephrine* which causes *hypertension*—often in sudden spurts. Throbbing *headache,* palpitation of heart, sweating, pallor, and *vomiting* may be noted intermittently or continuously.

If urine collected for twenty-four hours has an excess of these adrenal-gland chemicals, the diagnosis may be strongly suspected, and a surgical search must be made. The operation is risky, as these tumors may be small and multiple, blood pressure may rise suddenly and dangerously if the tumor is traumatized, or the blood pressure may fall suddenly and dangerously when the tumor is removed.

Polyp is a club of tissue (skin or mucous membrane) representing an overgrowth of tissue. They are considered benign, but may cause obstruction in the passageway where they grow. (See *Nose,* Section 14.)

Sarcoma is a malignancy arising from muscle, fat, or connective tissue. Surgery is the best treatment, as these tumors are very resistant to X radiation. Lumps or masses of unknown origin should be removed surgically. Upon removal, the tissue is usually examined microscopically, and if malignant changes (especially signs of rapid cell division) are present, the area is usually widely excised including surrounding normal tissue.

Teratoma is a tumor, usually cystic, with a variety of well-differentiated tissues scattered through it (teeth, hair, bone, cartilage). If an X ray of a tumor reveals teeth, teratoma is likely. Surgical removal is curative. They are usually found between the neck and pelvic area; it is as if the victim were carrying his own unformed twin.

Niemann-Pick disease—see *Lipidoses*

Ovary (see *Hypogonadism; Abdominal pain—lower right, Hernia,* Section 12) is the female organ that produces eggs. The anterior *pituitary* activates the *ovaries* to mature function with its follicle-stimulating hormone which causes ova maturation. The pituitary also releases the luteinizing hormone which regulates the corpus luteum (the progesterone secreting bit of ovarian tissue formed after ovulation). These two hormones suddenly increase in amounts just a year or so prior to the *menarche.* (See *Menstruation.*)

Lesions of the ovary frequently produce *estrogens.* The granulosa cell tumor will cause *breast development,* axillary and pubic hair, accelerated growth in the child, plus menses. Surgical removal of the tumor is obviously indicated.

Parathyroid glands are four small endocrine glands located on the posterior surface of the thyroid gland. They are chiefly responsible for the maintenance of an optimum level of *calcium* in the blood stream. If the calcium falls, the *parathyroid glands* secrete hormone. If the level rises, the parathyroid hormone secretion is slowed. Calcium is necessary for muscle contractility, blood coagulation, bone formation, and other less well-understood functions. If the calcium in the blood falls, the parathyroid attempts to maintain the normal level by dissolving calcium from bone.

Calcitonin, secreted by the thyroid gland, counteracts parathyroid hormone. When *hypercalcemia* occurs, calcitonin tends to reduce the excess by depositing calcium in the bones.

If a pregnant woman has *hyperparathyroidism,* the excess calcium in the circulation will inhibit the baby's parathyroid gland secretion. At birth his sluggish parathyroids will not respond to the falling calcium level, and newborn *tetany* will occur.

Since hypoparathyroidism allows blood calcium to fall, the condition may resemble epilepsy, as *convulsions,* twitches, coma, and rigidity may be the only manifestations of the disease. A blood-calcium level might be taken as part of a workup for *epilepsy,* especially if muscle cramps or numbness and tingling of hands and feet are noted.

Phenylalanine is an *amino acid* used by the body in protein synthesis. If the enzyme which converts excess phenylalanine to tyrosine is absent, this chemical accumulates in the body and results in a condition called phenylketonuria or PKU, one of the *mental-retardation* syndromes. Pigment metabolism (tyrosine) is also altered, so these patients are blue-eyed blondes. All newborns should be checked for this chemical at birth. If the test is positive, milk with only trace amounts of phenylalanine as a diet control should be instituted early (at about one month). If the blood level of phenylalanine can be maintained at low levels, the mental retardation may be avoided. After age three or four years, the body can usually tolerate larger amounts of phenylalanine. It is difficult to maintain the diet, as it is boringly unpalatable.

Some babies have a temporarily immature enzyme system and are able to handle normal amounts of phenylalanine in their diet after a few months of life.

Phosphatase is an *enzyme* responsible for the breakdown of compounds containing phosphoric acid It is formed in the liver and secreted in the bile, so its determination helps to diagnose *liver* disease. *Rickets* and some other diseases of bone or *calcium* metabolism will show elevation of this enzyme.

Pigment metabolism—see *Porphyria,* Section 13

Pituitary is the master gland that sends a variety of powerful hormones to stimulate most of the endocrine glands and acts directly on all body cells. The gland lies at the base of the brain just behind the orbits and the sphenoid sinus. The anterior portion produces the following as a result of hormone stimulation from the hypothalamus:

ACTH (adrenocorticotrophic hormone) stimulates the *adrenal* cortex to produce its various hormones. Since a reciprocal feedback relationship exists between the pituitary and the adrenal glands, cortisone treatment of a patient must be tapered off so the suppressed excretion of ACTH will have a chance to increase to normal levels.

HGH (human growth hormone) affects all body cells. Its absence will result in dwarfism; excess will cause *gigantism* or *acromegaly.*

FSH (follicle stimulating hormone) stimulates growth of ova in the female and spermatozoa in the male.

Luteinizing hormone controls the corpus luteum in the female (see *Menstruation*) and the interstitial cells in the *testes.* Follicle stimulating and luteinizing hormones are called gonadotrophic and appear at puberty.

TSH (thyrotrophic hormone) stimulates the thyroid gland to produce thyroid hormone. If excess thyroid hormone is produced, it signals the pituitary to produce less thyrotrophic hormone. The pituitary will excrete increased amounts of thyrotrophic hormone if the level of thyroid hormone drops.

The posterior section of the pituitary is chiefly responsible for the secretion of *vasopressin,* the absence of which causes *diabetes insipidus.*

Precocious puberty is the abnormally early onset of secondary sexual changes. Breasts, pubic and axillary hair, and *menarche* normally develop in that order about one year apart, with the first *menstrual period* occurring at about eleven to thirteen years of age. Therefore, if breasts enlarge (not just tenderness in the nipples) before age eight, it suggests that there is some glandular pathology worth investigating. If the girl comes from a family of early developers, it may be normal.

Similarly, if a boy develops coarse, curly pubic hair and an enlarged penis, disproportionate to his age and size, something is wrong. His puberty onset is usually at age twelve to thirteen, so if there are changes before the age of nine or ten, investigation seems reasonable.

Tumors of the *ovaries, testes,* and *adrenal glands* should be searched for, but *brain* pathology might be responsible. A familial or idiopathic type is most commonly responsible. Full sexual development may be attained by age five or six. (South America won the prize for *La madre mas joven del mundo* some years ago. The mother was six years old.) Because sexual maturity encourages epiphyseal closure, these children are usually short as adults, rarely growing to a height of five feet.

McCune-Albright syndrome includes early sexual development, skin pigmentation, and bony deformities (dysplasia).

Lesions of the hypothalamus may cause early development; stimulation of the *pituitary* is assumed to be the mechanism of onset. Tumors in this area or pressure from nearby lesions in the pineal body or scarring following encephalitis may cause precocity. *Behavior problems, mental retardation,* neurological signs or physiological aberrations (*diabetes insipidus, temperature* irregularities, *seizures*) are usually associated.

With the availability of birth-control pills (containing hormones) a medicational puberty has been observed. Treatment is abstinence from the pills.

Progesterone (see *Menstruation*) is a female hormone secreted by the ovary after ovulation.

Protein-bound iodine (PBI)—see *Thyroid function tests*

Puberty (see *Menstruation*) is considered to be the onset of adolescence. It is clearly heralded in the female by her first *menstrual* period, which usually occurs at age eleven or twelve but may happen as early as age eight or as late as sixteen or seventeen. Pubic hair, *breast development,* and increased pelvic girdle width all have occurred as prepubescent changes. The boy shows growth in length and muscles plus pubic hair; his puberty is associated with the formation of spermatozoa. Thirteen to fourteen is the usual age for puberty for the male, with ten to eighteen as the outside limits of normal.

Reticuloendotheliosis is another name for a group of diseases which produce granulomas in various organs. (See *Neoplasms.*)

Sex chromatin, Barr body, is a dark spot in the nuclei of females' cells; it represents an inactive X *chromosome.* A normal male cell has no Barr body. The presence of two Barr bodies indicates an anomalous XXX female who may be mentally deficient; the absence of sex chromatin in a female's cells occurs when one of the two X chromosomes is deleted (*Turner's syndrome* or XO).

Tay-Sachs disease—see *Lipidoses*

Thyroid is an important *endocrine* gland placed low in the front of the neck. It concentrates iodine from the bloodstream, manufactures the thyroid hormones, stores them as a protein (globulin) molecule, and releases this substance at the request of the thyroid-stimulating hormone (TSH) of the pituitary.

The thyroid hormones (chiefly *thyroxine*) are essential for growth of all cells. (See *Cretinism* and *Hypothyroidism.*) A mutual control keeps the balance between the TSH and the thyroid hormones at an optimum level; if the thyroid secretes excessive hormone, this high level inhibits the release of TSH which effectively slows the release of thyroid hormones from the thyroid.

New and accurate blood tests for thyroxine have largely replaced the BMR (basal metabolic rate) or breathing test for thyroid function. The serum thyroxine (T_4) is fairly standard. If the level is low, it suggests *hypothyroidism.* If the level is high, it may mean *hyperthyroidism.*

Radioactive iodine may be ingested as a test; the amount of iodine taken up by the thyroid can be measured by a Geiger counter. A low uptake of the iodine indicates decreased function or hypothyroidism. (See *Goiter* and *Hyperthyroidism.*)

Thyroid function tests:

PBI, or protein-bound iodine, and BEI, or butanol-extractable iodine, are now considered obsolete by some because of the false values produced by other medicines—*estrogens,* iodides in cough syrups and radiopaque dyes, Dilantin®, and salicylates. T_4, or serum thyroxine, assays the thyroid more accurately.

RAI, or radioactive iodine uptake, test is done by giving the patient a dose of I^{131}; the amount of the dose that is absorbed by the gland is measured by a Geiger counter.

The oral temperature taken before arising in the A.M. should be 97.8°–98.2°F. If below this, hypothyroidism may be suspected.

Thyroiditis is an inflammation of the *thyroid.* The cause is unclear, but a *virus* or autoimmune mechanism (the body manufactures immune substances against its own tissues) have been suspected. It occurs almost exclusively in school-aged girls. The thyroid slowly increases in size and becomes firm. The swollen gland may remain enlarged or decrease in size; the patient may become *hypothyroid* or *hyperthyroid* or remain normothyroid.

Blood tests (PBI and T_4) may help diagnose this, or a needle *biopsy* may show the inflammation. Thyroid gland extract is the therapy and may have to be taken for the patient's lifetime if the disease has made her hypothyroid.

Hashimoto's thyroiditis is one cause of goiter, more likely seen in prepubertal and young adolescent girls. It may be due to a virus infection.

Thyrotoxicosis—see *Hyperthyroidism*

Thyrotrophic hormone, or thyroid stimulating hormone, TSH, is secreted by the pituitary and regulates the thyroid gland activity.

Thyroxine (T_4) is the chief hormone secreted by the thyroid gland.

Toxic goiter—see *Hyperthyroidism*

Trisomy refers to the anomalous situation in which each cell carries three of a particular *chromosome* instead of the usual two. In the process of cell division to make the sperm or the ovum, a paired chromosome fails to separate and remains whole. If this paired chromosome is involved in fertilization, the resultant cell will have twenty-three pairs of chromosomes plus one unpaired chromosome.

A variety of defects has been identified, depending on which chromosome is trisomic. If it is number 21, *Down's syndrome* will be produced.

Trisomy 18 may result in low-set ears, heart murmurs, cleft lip and palate, kidney anomalies, and chest and limb deformities. Most babies so afflicted die in the first year. Trisomy 13 is associated with facial and brain defects. Death is expected in the first few months.

Turner's syndrome—see *Hypogonadism*

Vasopressin is an antidiuretic hormone. Its absence allows *diabetes insipidus* to become manifest.

Water is essential to the body. All chemical reactions require water, as the ions must be dissolved before they can be utilized. Waste products need to be washed out with water. Nutrients need to be dissolved before absorption, and water is required to regulate body temperature.

The water content of the infant is almost seventy-five percent of the total weight. (Sixty percent of an adult is water.) The infant needs to ingest daily about ten percent of his weight in water or he may dehydrate, because he is unable to concentrate his urine as efficiently as the adult. Since milk is about ninety percent water, two to three ounces of milk per pound of weight per day should be enough to satisfy his needs. Extra fluid is necessary if vomiting, fever, or diarrhea is present or if environmental temperature is elevated. (About half of water loss is by vaporization from the skin and lungs.) If urine is passed in fair amounts at least twice a day, it suggests that dehydration is not serious.

SECTION 11

Diet, Feeding, and Nutrition *

A. Nutrition

Amino acids
Calcium
Calories
Carbohydrates
Cereal foods
Chloride—see Salt
Cobalt
Copper
Cow's milk
  After infancy
Fat
Fluoride
Glucose
Iodide
Iron
Kwashiorkor
Linoleic acid
Magnesium
Malnutrition
Manganese
Nutrition
Phosphorus
Potassium
Protein
Salt
Sodium—see Salt
Sulfur
Vitamins
  A
    Night blindness
    Hypervitaminosis A
  B
    B_1 (thiamine)
      Beriberi
    Riboflavin
    Niacin
      Pellagra
  B_6 (pyridoxine)
  B_{12} (folic acid)
  C
    Scurvy
  D
    Hypervitaminosis D
    Rickets
      Refractory rickets
  E
  K
Water (see Section 10)
Zinc

B. Feeding

Anorexia
Appetite
Bottle feeding
  Cow's milk

*Read **Diet** and **Nutrition** first.

Goat's milk
Meat milk
Soybean milks
Breast feeding
Colic
Allergy
Anal ring
Anxiety
Cold feet
Hunger
Inadequate feeding
Nipple holes
Non-intestinal causes
Obstructions
Pacifier
Position
Diet
Eating
Formula
Obesity
Pica
Weaning

Amino acids are the nitrogen-bearing chemical compounds that form protein. Two dozen different amino acids have been identified; their number and arrangement in different combinations give protein its various characteristics. When ingested, meat, milk, fish, eggs, nuts, and beans are broken down in the intestines to amino aicds. These are absorbed and circulated to all cells of the body where they are synthesized into human protein. If a particular amino acid is not present in the cell at the right time, the corresponding protein cannot be manufactured—hence, a deficiency. Some genetic diseases arise from a lack of an *enzyme* responsible for changing one amino acid into another (*phenylketonuria*) or for manufacturing protein molecules from amino acids (*agammaglobulinemia*). Essential amino acids are those the body is unable to synthesize. They must be included in the diet almost daily or the body is unable to manufacture the more complicated proteins necessary for structure or function. They are histidine, isoleucine, leucine, lysine, methionine, phenylalanine, threonine, tryptophan, and valine.

Anorexia is loss of appetite and occurs as the first symptom of almost all diseases. The mother, who is serving the food, is therefore usually the first to know if her child is sick. If the child's general attitude and physical behavior do not change, it suggests that the anorexia is physiological and not due to disease or emotional factors. Many parents are not aware of the tremendous reduction in appetite that occurs between the ages of two and four, and continue to insist on maintaining the previously established calorie intake. Mealtime then becomes a battle, and the child learns to manipulate his parents' frustration so as to tyrannize the family.

Many children—and adults—have major food likes and dislikes, sometimes based on *allergies,* sometimes on a mysterious built-in mechanism the body uses to provide internal balance (fluid needs, acid-base balance, various mineral requirements, etc.). These should be respected.

A good rule for the anorexic child: if he eats some protein and fruit almost every day, his bodily needs are usually satisfied. Vegetables provide much the same minerals and vitamins found in fruits, so the two are reasonably interchangeable. White foods—starches, cereals, potatoes, bread—are carbohydrate foods and supply extra calorie needs, depending on growth, size, and activity level. They are bonus foods. B-complex vitamins, as in brewer's yeast, may act as an appetite stimulant.

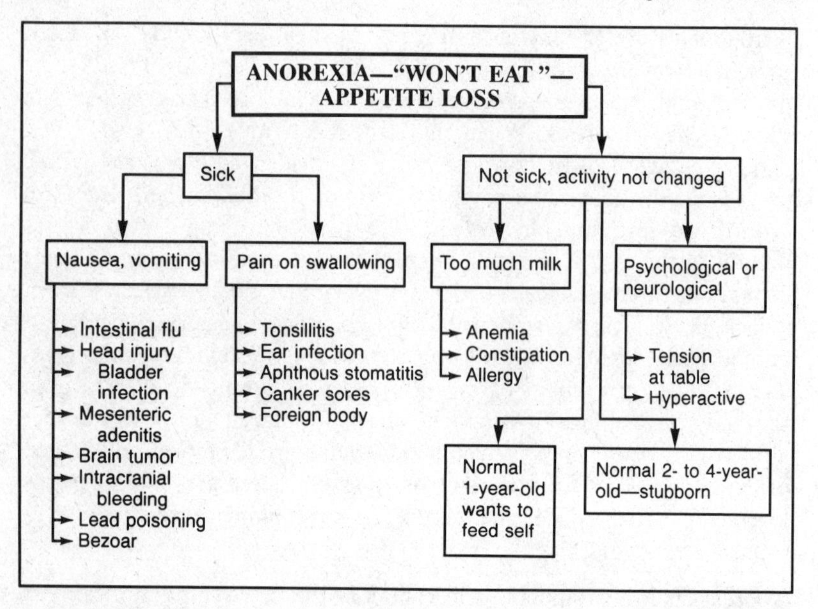

Appetite is related to parental attitudes, congenital factors, ability to absorb and digest food, state of the bowels, state of mind, age, and rate of growth. The wise parent can whet the child's appetite by offering nourishing meals pleasantly served in congenial, unhurried surroundings. Although a bad appetite does not imply ill health, a good appetite generally is, of course, a good sign. A *change* in appetite suggests a possible problem. If a child laughs and smiles more than half the time, and is up and moving around, he is probably getting enough to eat. Encouraging him to eat more will only make him fat or frustrated—and some children will go hungry if they know it bothers their parents. (See *Anorexia.*)

Beriberi is a group of symptoms and signs resulting from the deficiency of thiamine (*vitamin* B_1). *Thiamine* is needed in the formation of certain enzymes which regulate carbohydrate and nerve metabolism.

Thiamine is present in so many foods that the lack of it is rare in our country—except for the breast-fed baby whose mother is on a deficient diet. The symptoms are vague and generalized: weakness, appetite loss, irritability. The baby becomes apathetic, pale, and flabby. The heart rate is rapid, the liver may be enlarged, *cyanosis* or *convulsions* may occur.

In beriberi, other vitamins are usually deficient in addition to thiamine. The diagnosis may be difficult without a dietary history; the treatment is simply providing a vitamin supplement. People eating some meat and vegetables do not require vitamin B supplements, but stress may require them.

Bottle feeding is a poor substitute for breast feeding. Most authorities agree that a baby should be fed when he's hungry. This seems to make so much sense that it's hardly worth mentioning. A normal seven-pound new baby who is reasonably awake and alert needs from fourteen to twenty ounces of milk every twenty-four hours. If there are about twenty *calories* per ounce in the milk that he is consuming, he should get at least two ounces for each pound he weighs in his first two or three months. A baby on milk can empty his stomach in just an hour and a half, so if he can be fed every hour and a half or two hours, he will get his nutritional quota during his twelve waking hours and may possibly sleep all night long. If he can take two ounces eight times a day, he is going to get enough to take care of his needs.

If he's growing at a terrific rate or he's very active, then he may have to get more because his hunger will undoubtedly be greater. A baby destined to be a small adult can get all his calories during his twelve waking hours and not have to wake up in the night; he is unlikely to eat as much as a baby who will eventually be six feet tall. But if he's active and going to be a good-sized adult—it both parents are five feet ten or six feet tall—he won't be able to sleep through the night until he's three or four months old, because he's growing too fast to get all his calories during his twelve waking hours.

Milk provides fluid and enough *protein, calcium, carbohydrates*, and *calories* to take care of a baby's needs in those first months. In a warm environment add an ounce or two of water to each bottle as infant kidneys cannot conserve fluid. Most babies choke on plain water from the bottle.

Just about any good type of milk (homogenized milk or any of the standard prepared formulas to which water is added) will provide the necessary twenty calories per ounce. (See *Formula.*) Incidentally, if it is safe for adults to drink the water without boiling it, it is not necessary to boil it for the baby. But if a mother has any disease or skin infection, or if one is not sure about the water that comes from the well, it's probably better to boil it for ten minutes before using it for the formula. The bottles need not be boiled. If a bottle brush gets the milk curds out, then washing them along with the dishes is good enough.

Bottle feeding attempts to simulate breast feeding. The parent usually tries to hold and love the baby when bottle feeding, but a number of babies are upset if they are held. It does not mean that there is anything wrong with a baby if he prefers to have the bottle propped. These babies just do not want to be touched and handled when they are eating—it is too distracting. A nervous baby is more aware of his environment and easily overstimulated. Many parents have found that, if the bottle is propped, the baby is less likely to spit up the milk; he drinks the milk faster and seems to be more content. The stomach curves from left to right, so if he's fed while lying on his right side, the air bubbles will remain on the top and he's less likely to spit up his milk. (See *Colic.*).

Obviously, the most comfortable way to handle a baby is to cradle him and hold him. Singing and talking to the baby should not be too distracting, because he is busy eating. This is the usual picture of parenthood—the warmth, the cradling, the loving, the cooing, and the satisfactory warm milk going down to fill his stomach.

Breast feeding has become popular again now that bottle feeding has proved a disappointment. Rooming-in and home deliveries have aided its resurgence. Mothers who have nursed their babies successfully become evangelical in their efforts to encourage others to do likewise. The La Leche League, a mutually supportive organization, finds that mothers, given enough encouragement and facts, are able to nurse their babies.

Advantages. Human milk is cheap, safe, delivered at the proper temperature, free of bacteria, may possibly discourage some infection, and helps provide an important intimacy between mother and child. Babies are not allergic to it. Breast-fed babies are almost never constipated. The uterus contracts when the baby is nursing and returns to normal size more quickly. Breast feeding helps form a better dental arch.

Disadvantages. A baby may demand more than the mother can supply in the first ten days, and thus discouraged, both quit. A baby cannot get hold of an inverted or severely retracted nipple. Painful cracks and fissures may develop in the areola. Some women are embarrassed to feed their babies in public. A mother must be prepared to eat an adequate diet; she must also refrain from certain foods that might get in her milk and upset the baby (fish, cabbage, garlic, onions, chocolate, and beans).

A mother who does not succeed at nursing may feel guilty and inferior if her baby does not thrive or cries unduly. Her doctor might like to encourage nursing but cannot insist that she do so. Whatever decision she makes, her doctor—and her family—must encourage her and provide comfort, quiet, and freedom from anxiety. Preparatory information and exercises will permit an easy introduction to breast feeding on the natal day.

Complete emptying of the breasts is the only way to stimulate milk production. For a month before delivery a mother should strip her breasts three or four times daily, ending by squeezing with thumb and forefinger at the areolar margin while pushing back against her ribs. Some colostrum is usually obtained and allows the mother to become practiced in this ritual that may often be necessary in the first few days of nursing when the baby is unable to empty the breast.

A normal, alert, hungry baby needs only to have his cheek brush against the nipple to initiate a reflex that allows him to turn, open his mouth, and clamp his gums onto the nipple. If the breast lacteals are turgid with milk, he may not obtain a sufficient hold just beyond the areolar border. The mother should flatten this area by manually squeezing it to a size that can be accommodated. The baby does the rest, but after a few minutes of sucking, he may tire and drop off to sleep without emptying the canals holding the milk. It may thus be necessary for a few days to strip the breasts to encourage the formation of new milk. Within ten to fourteen days the baby and the mother work out a rhythm and a flow to achieve an adequate supply that permits satisfaction of hunger and *growth* needs.

Most find it best to allow only two to five minutes per nursing in the first few days to allow a toughening-up process. Demand feeding—not nibbling—is best for both participants; this is ideally arranged by rooming-in arrangements in the hospital. Try to ignore the discouraging words heard in many OB wards. Encouraging feeding every two to three hours during the day may allow the baby to sleep five to six hours at night—if he is cooperative. Milk usually does not appear until the fourth day, but removing the colostrum is an important prelude to the later flow of milk. Mothers usually find that they do better at home where they may cooperate with the baby's erratic schedule; the trick is to nurse him when he is vigorously hungry.

The baby's hunger may force the mother to offer a cow's milk supplement in these early days, but this usually weans him off the breast, as the bottle is less work for him. Some water as an extra might fill him without completely satisfying him so he will still want to return to his mother. He may develop a dehydration fever on the third day if fluids are insufficient.

Ordinary soap and water is an effective cleansing agent for the breast, and careful drying is necessary to avoid cracks and maceration. Some bland oil or lanolin may be used. Manual expression of milk is safer than using a pump which might further crack a nipple. A metal tea strainer worn inside the brassiere will provide an air cushion for sore nipples. Judicious sunshine exposure will promote healing and serve to toughen the areolar skin.

Sucking stimulation to the breasts sends a message to the thalamus in the mother's brain that signals the pituitary to send hormones to the breasts; milk will drip from the breast not being serviced. This same breast-brain reflex is utilized by women who have adopted newborns and successfully nursed them. It takes a little doing and determination, but can be accomplished.

With rest, fluids, a lusty baby, and some encouragement from doctor and family, most women can nurse a baby who cries and sucks. (See *Weaning.*)

Calcium is necessary for teeth and bones, for muscle contractility, and coagulation of blood. One gram a day is suggested as an optimum intake although its absorption may be more related to presence of *vitamin D* and the state of the bowel lining (see *Malabsorption,* Section 12) than to the amount swallowed. Dairy products are full of it, but many people who cannot eat cheese or drink milk have good teeth and bones if they get green leafy vegetables, seafood, and sunshine. From infancy to old age, we all need 1,000 milligrams of calcium daily. Dolomite and bone meal are good sources. (See *Tetany,* Sections 5 and 15; *Calcium,* Section 10.)

Calories are a measure of energy stored in food. Water has none; fat has the most. If a person consumes and absorbs into his system more calories than he utilizes, he gains weight.

The ideal diet provides sufficient calories for growth and exercise, adequate protein for muscle and brain, enough minerals for blood and bone, vitamins to prevent deficiencies, and fat for energy—and is also palatable. If normal, the human being has a fantastically accurate set of regulators that signal the brain to eat more or less, to consume more grains or fruits or meat to provide for certain needs. (See *Anorexia.*).

Cultural, family, and individual differences in response to food intake will determine overall body size. Most fat children eat a great deal, but so do some thin children. All the beautiful charts prepared by doctors and dieticians indicating what and how much food is to be consumed are usually disregarded by the harassed parent trying to cater to a variety of caloric needs and food prejudices in a family. A basic rule: provide enough calories for growth and energy using nourishing foods; for example, meat, vegetables, fruits, grains, milk. Sugary foods (cookies, jams, jelly, dessert) should not be permitted in the house. A frankfurter or beef patty plus a piece of fruit may be all the two- to three-year-old can choke down in a day, but will provide his protein, minerals, iron, and vitamins.

Urging a small child to eat large amounts may create a lifelong pattern of overeating and the related problems of obesity. Some families are mistakenly convinced that a big appetite is equated with health or that extra fat will protect the body from disease.

Carbohydrates are the chief sources of energy for the body. (*Fat* and *protein* provide energy also.) Sugars and starches in fruits, vegetables, milk, and grains have to be converted to simple sugars (dextrose for example) before they can be absorbed into the capillaries lining the intestines. These sugars are used throughout the body for cellular metabolism or are stored as *glycogen* in the *liver* and *muscle.*

Enzymes are necessary for all these steps. Saliva and pancreatic digestants reduce starches to sugars which can be split by enzymes in the cells lining the intestinal tract. If *lactase* (the enzyme responsible for splitting lactose, the milk sugar) is absent due to *diarrhea* or genetic defect, the undigested lactose ferments and irritates the intestine, resulting in *gas, cramps,* and *diarrhea.* It is best to avoid quick sugars (white, brown, corn syrup, maple syrup, molasses, and honey). (See *Malabsorption,* Section 12.)

Cereal foods are the usual first foods offered to the baby after his milk intake has been established. Rice cereal is the least upsetting and least allergenic. Pressure from friends and relatives, boredom or longing for a night's sleep are among the reasons parents begin cereal at three to four weeks of age. A doctor usually suggests using cereal as soon as parents indicate they want him to suggest it. It takes about twenty minutes to prepare the cereal and poke it down the often unwilling offspring's throat. The extra calories may allow the baby to last twenty minutes longer before hunger sets in. The chief advantage of cereal may lie in its iron content—which could be supplied more efficiently by concentrated drops. No harm will come to the baby if he is offered milk only, enriched with vitamins and iron, until eight months of age. Early solid-food intrduction will not establish better feeding habits later when solids become more important than milk.

Rice is the safest but is constipating. Barley and oats have some laxative action, but cereal with wheat is most likely to cause reactions: *gas, cramps, diarrhea,* or spitting. It is best not to start wheat until close to one year of age.

Adult-cooked cereal is satisfactory, but the powdered cereals for babies are most convenient. In the beginning it is made soupy enough to be easily sucked off the spoon. Some find it convenient to use a dull knife and wipe the cereal off the baby's upper gums, allowing the blob to fall on the tongue. If spitting is a problem, the powdered rice might be added directly to the formula until thick; obviously the nipple holes must be greatly enlarged to accommodate this resultant paste. Never buy or use boxed cereals; use only whole-grain cereals and breads.

Cobalt is part of the B_{12} molecule. It is widely distributed in many foods so a specific deficiency is unknown. The function of the spinal cord is dependent on cobalt.

Colic is any crying that cannot be related to hunger. The pediatric textbooks dismiss this distressing condition by stating that it is an overreactive intestinal tract in a baby who is being overstimulated by his environment.

The following possibilities should be considered when dealing with a fussy, crying, unhappy baby:

1. *Hunger.* If giving him an adequate supply of nourishing milk does not stop his screams, his condition is called colic. But if he is quiet for an hour and a half and then cries, his unhappiness is most likely caused by hunger. Babies can be fed every hour and a half during the day, and if they are comfortable and relaxed after each feeding, they do not have colic. However, if he gets an adequate supply of milk and bellows within twenty or thirty minutes, it is probably colic.

2. *Allergy.* If a baby is not suffering from hunger but is full of gas and seems bloated, a change of milk is worthwhile. If he is better within twenty-four to forty-eight hours after the change and remains so, it implies that he has a milk allergy. If the original milk is again tried and screaming returns, he should remain on the substitute milk. A number of babies will get better after a change to soybean milk or goat's milk, but after a week or two start to scream and cry with cramps. Of course, they have become allergic to the new milk, and another substitute will have to be tried.

3. *Position.* Some babies do not like to be held when they are fed and seem to be irritated by any effort to soothe them. It is perfectly acceptable and *not* psychologically damaging to let him lie flat on his back or tipped slightly to the right (stomach curves from left to right) with the bottle propped. Some mothers get quite skillful at thumping the baby's abdomen in the upper left portion—as if testing a melon. When the *thoonk* is just right, he should be picked up and burped.

4. *Nipple holes.* Obviously nothing can be done about the nipple holes used by breast-fed babies, but many people assume that the manufacturers of bottle nipples calibrate them so that they are exactly the right size. This is not so. In general, they're too small. To test rubber nipples: put cold formula in the bottle and turn the bottle upside down. Without shaking, the milk should drip out at the rate of about one drop a second. If it doesn't, the holes are too small and need enlarging. Using a knife, a crosscut is made over the hole so there are four flaps in the nipple top. When the baby sucks, these flaps will open and let the milk flow to him quite rapidly. The milk should flow into him at a rate that almost chokes him. A baby swallows *more* air if the nipple holes are too small, because he sucks air *around* the nipple. If the holes are large or if the crosscut method is used, he'll get less air and less bloat. Breast-fed babies get their milk at a rather rapid rate, so bottle milk should also come at a rapid rate. The baby should be able to take almost all his quota in five to ten minutes.

5. *Inadequate feeding.* A few mothers report their babies have colic after they gave them what they thought was an adequate amount of milk (four to eight ounces). Because the bottles held only eight ounces, they assumed it was enough. But when offered ten ounces, the babies were completely satisfied. This seems like an outrageous amount for a small baby, but it is clearly what some babies prefer.

Before the others stumbled on this, they were offering six ounces five times a day, but the babies wanted ten ounces three times a day. They were perfectly happy when they finally received this amount. (Of course, their total twenty-four-hour intake was the same in each case.)

6. *Obstructions.* About one out of four babies is born with a slight narrowing of the anal-rectal junction, just one half or one fourth of an inch inside the anal opening. It acts as a partial obstruction. When the baby's stomach is filled with milk, a reflex begins bowel action in the colon. If there is even a slight obstruction to the passage of stool and gas through the anal opening, the baby often doubles up and screams. He usually opens up this area after having passed a few stools, but sometimes the parent or the doctor has to pass a lubricated little finger inside his anus—no farther than an inch—to dilate the constricted area. If this is the cause of his distress, the baby will show immediate improvement. (Sometimes this maneuver is accompanied by the passage of a drop or two of blood.) Some babies have pockets of gas inside the anal opening; a glycerine suppository inserted into the rectum can help the baby express the stool and gas. However, this only relieves some of the gas in the last six inches or foot of the colon, not in the twenty feet of intestine between the *stomach* and *anus.*

7. *Nonintestinal causes.* Because the urinary department is located in the abdomen, a congenital urinary obstruction can sometimes cause colic. The doctor must be notified of any symptoms a child may have in this area—such as not being able to urinate for some hours at a time, or seeming to be in distress when he does urinate, or his urinary stream being thin and feeble (see *Urethritis,* Section 13). Any of these indicate some obstructive problem. The opening of the *urethra* at the head of the *penis* should be not just a pinhole but a slot usually measuring about one sixteenth of an inch. Sometimes a urine irritation or a urine burn can cause a stricture at the opening that results in back-pressure to the urinary stream, colic, and even damage to the kidneys. This opening must be inspected to make certain that it is adequate.

The colic due to an incarcerated *inguinal hernia* should be easily diagnosed by noticing a tender mass to one side of the base of the penis in the pubic area. (See *Hernia,* Section 12.)

8. An old wives' tale says the baby has colic because his feet are cold. I had always thought his feet were cold *because* he had

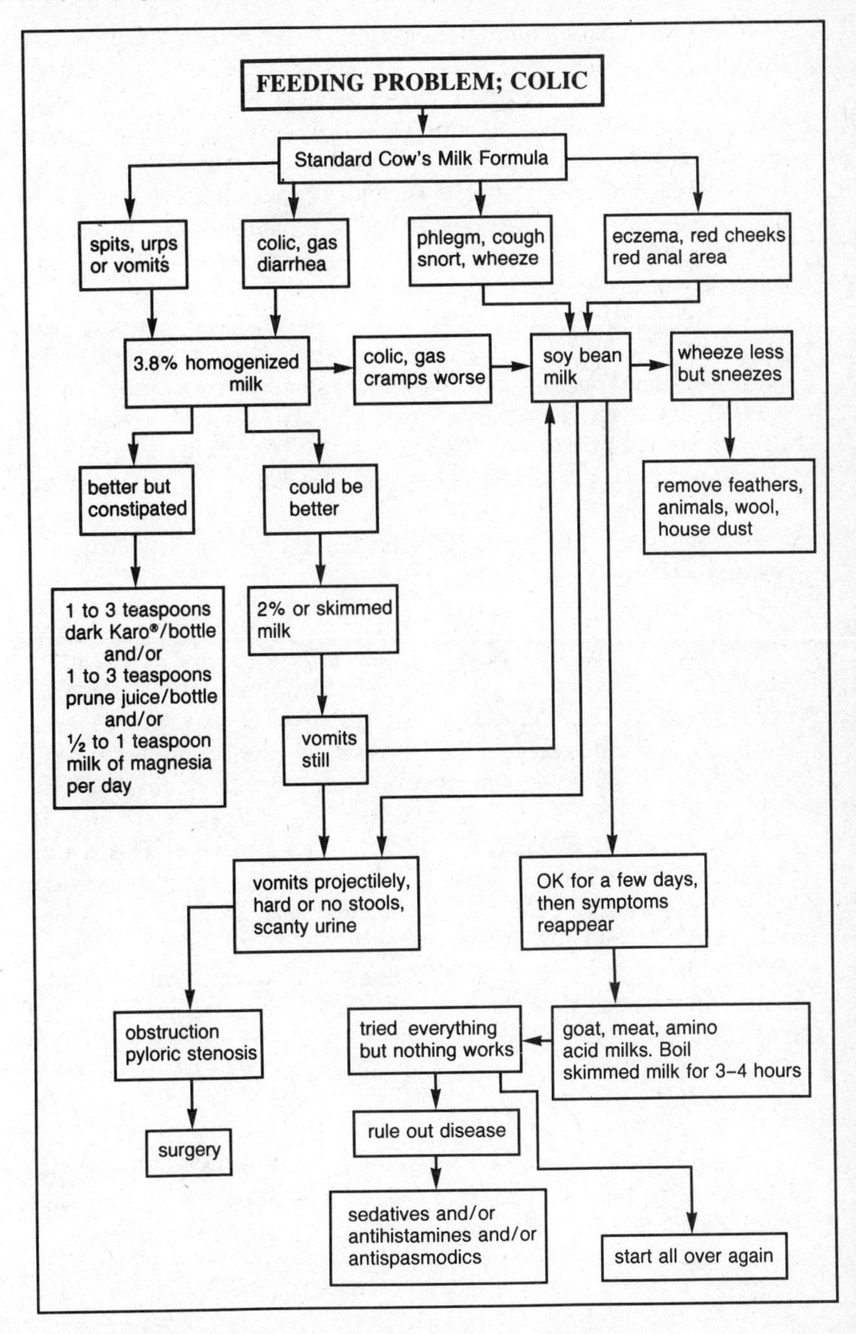
FEEDING PROBLEM; COLIC
Standard Cow's Milk Formula
spits, urps or vomits
colic, gas diarrhea
phlegm, cough snort, wheeze
eczema, red cheeks red anal area
3.8% homogenized milk
colic, gas cramps worse
soy bean milk
wheeze less but sneezes
better but constipated
could be better
remove feathers, animals, wool, house dust
1 to 3 teaspoons dark Karo®/bottle and/or 1 to 3 teaspoons prune juice/bottle and/or ½ to 1 teaspoon milk of magnesia per day
2% or skimmed milk
vomits still
vomits projectilely, hard or no stools, scanty urine
OK for a few days, then symptoms reappear
obstruction pyloric stenosis
tried everything but nothing works
goat, meat, amino acid milks. Boil skimmed milk for 3–4 hours
surgery
rule out disease
sedatives and/or antihistamines and/or antispasmodics
start all over again

colic. Keep his feet warm anyway; if it soothes him, then *that* is the answer.

9. Most babies need to suck on something for digestion, relaxation, and security. If sucking pleasure (oral drives) is not satisfied during the feedings, the infant should be urged to suck a pacifier (NUK® is best) before thumb or finger sucking becomes a fixed habit. The pacifier can be "lost" some day when the child is older (about age six). Usually less orthodontia work is necessary with the use of this substitute for the bony thumb.

10. A mother's anxiety may not cause the colic but may perpetuate it after the baby starts to cry. In her effort to soothe the baby, she may be overstimulating him. Some hyperresponsive babies have to cry themselves to sleep. If the baby has been eating well all day and begins to cry after his 6 to 10 P.M. feeding, it may be assumed he has an overloaded gut and needs to cry a little. Twenty minutes is about the standard time for allowing him to work it out for himself. If he is still at it after this interval, a little sedation is a sanity saver.

When all efforts have failed to reduce the baby's screaming attacks and he seems to need to be carried around a great deal of the time, parents should seek some medical relief. Most doctors will prescribe one of the *barbiturates* or a drug that has an effect on gastrointestinal spasms. These drugs seem to be quite safe if given in proper dosage, and can be given over some weeks or months with no ill effect. He should outgrow his colic by the time he is three to six months old, but if he is really touchy, he may need some type of sedative medicine, *tranquilizer,* or antispasm medicine for some months or years after infancy. Calcium, magnesium, zinc, manganese, or potassium may be deficient in these babies.

I assume such overreactive babies simply notice their intestines more than others. I see babies who are burping, passing gas, and bloated, and it doesn't bother them at all. Others can get one little bubble in their intestinal tract and go wild. Their nervous systems are more easily stimulated.

Copper is essential in many enzyme systems of the body, especially in those related to absorption of iron and synthesis of hemoglobin. It is needed for the nerves and pigmentation. *Wilson's disease* is a rare disorder of copper metabolism (see *Proteins*).

Cow's milk is meant for calves, but most human babies will thrive on it. It contains a percentage of water equivalent to that in human milk (88 percent), lactose for sugar as in human milk, twice as much protein (extra casein), and usually a standard amount of fat (3.5 to 4 percent), although types of fats vary in different milks. *Calcium* and *phosphorus* are adequate, but *iron* is insufficient in both milks and must be provided by six months of age or anemia will develop. Iron is unabsorbable from cow's milk. Both milks provide vitamins A and B, but C and D may be deficient and should be supplemented. Modern sanitation has reduced the number of bacteria in cow's milk, so there is little chance of milk-borne *streptococcus* sore throat, *diphtheria, dysentery,* and *tuberculosis.* Pasteurization of milk destroys these bacteria without significantly affecting the milk's taste or content. Heating makes for a smaller curd. Homogenization evenly spreads fat globules throughout the milk and allows a smaller curd to form when the milk mixes with stomach acid. Babies may be fed homogenized milk (3.8 percent) from birth, but usually an ounce of water is added per each four ounces of milk for the first three weeks. Babies rarely spit it up, but it is very constipating, and some magnesium oxide is usually added per bottle to keep the stools soft. If a baby spits homogenized milk, 2 percent or skimmed milk may be substituted, but these milks usually contain no *vitamin D,* which must be added.

Problems from fat, *lactose,* or *protein* incompatibility are common in 10 to 15 percent of babies. Some are truly *allergies,* but some experts prefer to use the term "intolerance." *Enzyme* deficiencies explain some feeding difficulties.

Simmering skimmed or homogenized milk denatures the protein and makes the milk more easily digestible. A can of evaporated milk with one small hole punched in the top (to preclude an explosion) may be placed in a pot of boiling water for an hour or two to produce a more agreeable milk. This denatured milk is mixed with water in the usual proportion. The length of time of exposure to boiling water is important; *cramps, colic, gas,* and *diarrhea* persisting after use of milk treated for one hour may disappear after use of milk boiled for three hours. Longer heat treatment than this is usually of no benefit.

Cow's milk after infancy has been highly overrated, chiefly by the dairy council which exists solely to promote dairy products. Nutritionists in medical schools extol the virtues of milk as the perfect food; doctors thus carry this message to their patients, so the myth is perpetuated. Most doctors have discovered, to their surprise, that a number of their patients are in excellent health in spite of low milk intake, or even *because* of an absence of ingestion of all dairy products! We all have found from experience that growing children who have consumed excess milk are more likely to become *anemic.* Anemic children may have double the *respiratory infections* that non-anemic children have. When a child becomes anemic, he dislikes the very foods that would correct his *anemia* and prefers to drink milk and eat white foods. Because these foods are lacking in *iron,* he becomes only more anemic and aggravates his original problem.

Milk is a common allergen. A rule most of us have learned: if a baby or child has any chronic respiratory, intestinal, skin, or urinary problem, milk and dairy products must be withheld from the diet, as they may be the cause of the problem. About one out of ten to fifteen babies is sensitive enough to milk to require a substitute; they may outgrow this later or have only minor upsets. Many babies have minor gas, snorting, and rash problems, but these are not upsetting enough to require a milk change.

Milk is constipating to most people. The frequent use of laxatives in our country is probably directly related to the high milk ingestion.

Mother Nature is trying to tell us something when teeth begin to appear at six to eight months. (The human is the only animal that drinks milk after infancy; the other mammals stop nursing when their teeth begin to bite the nipples.) Milk intake should be reduced. Children are normally poor eaters from two to four years of age; they will suffer from *anemia* and *constipation* if milk intake is not cut down. We all have lots of patients who have beautiful teeth and bones and are infrequently sick, yet had no milk from infancy because of their allergy.

There are patients who get *ear* or *kidney* or *bronchial* infections if they drink milk. Some *wet the bed* because of it. *Headaches,* pallor, and irritability can frequently be traced to milk (see *Tension-fatigue syndrome,* Section 15). Growing evidence suggests dairy products as one of the factors in the morbidity from vascular diseases. *Calcium* can be found in other foods, and animal *protein* provides a greater variety of *amino acids* than does milk. Dolomite is a good source of calcium; 1,000 milligrams a day.

Parents say: "I don't care if he doesn't eat as long as he drinks his milk." This should be changed to, "Stop the milk and maybe he will eat better."

Diet of children must provide adequate *calories, protein,* minerals, and *vitamins.* A rigid adherence to a prescribed, balanced diet usually leads to frustration, as most children consume either more or less than what is thought to be optimum. If offered eight ounces, he only takes seven; if one jar is opened, he wants a jar and a half.

The science of dietetics must be permissive, as *growth,* intestinal absorption, and activity levels are quite variable.

General rules:

1. Milk is the main diet in the first six to eight months, because of rapid growth and need for *calories, calcium,* and *protein.*

2. Iron-bearing foods become more important after five to six months, because anemia develops if milk continues to be the main diet staple.

3. Animal protein is a more efficient provider of all essential amino acids and B vitamins.

4. Self-feeding after twelve months of age allows the child to take some responsibility in balancing his own calorie requirements.

5. Meat and fruit or vegetables after infancy is a good rule; these two basics seem to provide the essential ingredients. Milk, grains, starches are used as "fillers" to supply the caloric or energy needs.

6. Supplementary vitamins should be given until one to two years of age. If the diet is adequate after this age, enough vitamins will be found in foods.

Amounts:

1. Birth to three months of age: two ounces of a standard milk per pound per twenty-four hours should be adequate, although most babies take more than this. Milk with iron preferable.

2. Rice or barley cereal added at seven to ten months of age should be given in the amount of two to ten tablespoons once or twice a day.

3. Fruit (applesauce, banana, pear) is added at eight to eleven months of age. Two to ten tablespoons a day can be mixed with cereal. Vegetables (carrot, squash, sweet potato) are added at nine to twelve months of age. It is best to limit the introduction of new foods to one a month.

4. Veal, lamb, and beef may be added at ten to twelve months and are best used singly, not in mixtures. Two to four teaspoonfuls can be given per day, and may be combined with fruit or a vegetable.

5. Solid foods are to be offered first after six months in an effort

to cut down on milk consumption. (Protein and iron are more important.)

6. At eleven months, four-ounce meals of cereal, fruit, vegetable, meat are offered three times a day. Teething biscuits and Zweibach are usually begun here; this is the first time wheat enters the diet. Fluoride may be given cautiously in small doses (0.25 milligram fluoride two to three times a week, along with dolomite) if not present in the drinking water.

7. At twelve to thirteen months, eight ounces of solids are offered three times a day with milk consumption determined by the baby—depending on *his* requirements. Some big, active babies still consume eight ounces of milk three or four times a day; small quiet ones may only need two to four ounces after their solids.

8. After one year of age, self-demand is the best rule to follow, and if appetite falls off, the starches, fats, white foods, and milk should be the first foods subtracted from the diet so that the child will get the basic meat and fruit. Egg, peaches, and green vegetables may be added at one year, cautiously, and one new food every few days. Finger foods are fun; but no raw carrots or nuts.

9. Age two to four years is traditionally a poor eating age. Most babies find one poor meal a day quite satisfactory. Offering small amounts that are sure to be consumed is better than a big helping that might completely discourage the child. Let *him* ask for more; it's a better ploy.

Eating (see *Diet*) should be associated with pleasant, warm, secure feelings. These may be sabotaged by the tense mother and her spitty baby or by the mother of the two- to four-year-old who feels that her child's appetite loss is a direct threat to her mothering ability. Parents may force-feed a reluctant child only to find the child goes hungry for attention or complies by become fat. (See *Dawdling,* Section 16.)

So many factors are involved with the eating process that a simple overall statement about "normality" is impossible. Some children eat huge amounts and stay thin; others eat "nothing" and get fat. If there is a rule to follow, it would be that if a child seems happy, plays normally, and grows two to three inches a year after age three, he is probably taking in at least enough *calories* to maintain his energy requirements. The first thing that a doctor does in evaluating an eating problem is to have the mother write down every bite the "non-eating" child takes during a typical twenty-four-hour period. The usual error is allowing him to fill up on milk, which cuts his appetite for more essential foods. Many mothers will add chocolate syrup to the milk in an effort to get it down! Six ounces of chocolate milk might have enough calories to destroy the three-year-old's appetite for the next twenty-four hours.

Some nervous children have an active gag reflex and refuse to eat more than the minimum metabolic requirements for fear of losing what little they have swallowed.

Most hyperactive children eat little because of distractions at the table. Some eat huge amounts but gain little because of their perpetual motion which burns up calories as fast as they are consumed.

Eating habits are big concerns for parents, especially mothers who feel that a child who eats well is well. A mother may not anticipate the tremendous drop in appetite after age two years and foster neurotic attitudes about diet. Great variations in appetite and food likes become obvious after age three. These idiosyncrasies should be respected within the context of good nutrition. (Encourage meat and fruit or vegetables; discourage milk and white foods.) An aversion may represent an *allergy,* a craving for sweets suggest *hyperactivity* or *hypoglycemia,* or sour-food likes may suggest the body's desire to stabilize a faulty acid-base balance. Many of these are genetically determined. It makes a cook's job difficult when various eating styles are scattered through the family. Some children are nauseated by breakfast and can barely choke down some juice; some need a hearty breakfast with *protein,* or they faint at 11 A.M. Compromise, compromise. Some cannot chew well until all the molars are in and need ground-up meats until age twelve years. Others have such an active gag reflex that a pea will bring up all of the meal.

Fat in the diet is a source of energy, essential to metabolism, and makes food taste better. A palatable diet usually derives about one third of its calories from fat; fat provides almost twice as many *calories* per ounce as carbohydrate or protein. The ingested fat is split by a pancreatic *enzyme,* lipase, into glycerines and fatty acids. Bile salts help dissolve these so that absorption takes place. *Linoleic-acid* deficiency will result in dry skin, but excess fat will lead to *obesity.* Saturated fatty acids (no double chemical bond, usually solid at room temperature) are thought to be causally related to streaks of fat in the blood-vessel linings of adults; these deposits are found in coronary heart-attack victims. Although evidence is not conclusive, research indicates that generally reducing fat intake and substituting unsaturated fatty acid preparations will cut down incidence of vascular accidents.

Fluoride may be important for teeth and bones. Every parent should determine from the local water bureau if *fluoride* is present. If not, a prescription from the doctor is obtained to supply this deficient, essential mineral. Less than one milligram every few days is probably safe until age eight years. Fluoride use extended through adolescence will continue to aid decay reduction by 10 percent. Best given with dolomite (calcium and magnesium).

Some evidence suggests that osteoporosis (deficient mineralization of bones) is less prevalent in the aged who have been drinking fluoridated water all their lives.

Folic acid is found in a wide variety of foods, but a deficiency will result in an anemia called *megaloblastic* in which red cells are larger than usual. (See *Anemia,* Section 8.) Folic acid is present in cow's milk and human milk; if goat's milk or powdered cow's milk is used, folic-acid supplement must be given, or the baby will become anemic after five or six months of life.

Formula is a combination of milk (usually cow's milk), water, and sugar made to resemble breast milk as closely as possible. Most babies are now fed prepared milks to which only water need be added. Because the newborn baby's *kidneys* do not concentrate fluids well, it is wise to make the milk a little dilute, especially in hot weather.

Examples:

1. Evaporated milk is a standard for babies. It has been heat-treated to vaporize the water, to provide a smaller curd, and to kill the bacteria. It has about 40 calories per ounce, so it is mixed with a little more than an equal amount of water (one 13-ounce can of evaporated milk, 18 ounces of water, and no sugar). If the baby's stools are hard and dry, some stool softener, such as magnesium oxide, would be safe.

If this is tolerated well, the amount of water is reduced gradually so that at one month of age the formula is half evaporated milk and half water. Tap water is safe to use without boiling. If the family can drink it, the baby can.

The chief disadvantage is the tendency of this milk to irritate the stomach (fatty acids?) and thus be regurgitated. It usually produces sloppy stools.

2. Homogenized milk with 3 percent to 4 percent fat is well tolerated by most babies, although a little water should be added for the first two to four weeks. Start with three ounces of homogenized milk plus one ounce of tap water, then four to one, then five to one. After three to four weeks, it is usually offered straight. If stools are hard, which they frequently are on a diet of homogenized milk, $^{1}/_{4}$ to $^{1}/_{2}$ teaspoon of magnesium oxide per day might help.

3. Skimmed or 2 percent milk may be used if spitting up is a problem. Some babies cannot tolerate much fat in the milk. Boiling or simmering for a few minutes to an hour may further improve the digestibility of the milk if spitting, gas, and/or sloppy stools occur. (Lost water must be readded, see *Hypernatremia,* Section 10.) Because of the low number of calories in skimmed milk, the baby may drink almost twice as much. It usually does not contain vitamin D, so this should be given as a supplement.

4. Most babies are now fed a modified type of milk in which the fat and protein are altered to facilitate digestion, reduce vomiting, and create a more normal bowel movement. These milks (Similac®, Enfamil®, SMA®, Modilac® etc.), are cheap, sterile, and more closely resemble breast milk—but are still basically from the cow. Most have vitamins and iron added in appropriate amounts.

A quick way to fix a feeding: at the first hunger cry, baby is picked up. Parent carries baby to kitchen. Parent talks reassuringly to baby, explaining that relief will be soon. Parent turns on hot water tap, puts baby bottle (previously washed, but boiling is not necessary) on counter. Parent opens refrigerator door, grabs can of concentrated formula, pours two ounces of milk into bottle, puts can back, closes refrigerator door. By this time the water is running hot, and two ounces of hot tap water are run into bottle. Parent shuts off water, screws on nipple, and puts nipple into baby's open mouth. Twenty-five seconds is the record. Sometimes the bottle can be held under the chin like a violin to free a hand to mop up the milk that has been spilled. (See *Bottle feeding.*)

Glucose is the simple sugar used in the metabolism of the body. It is the only compound the brain is able to use, hence a constant level of blood glucose is essential. Glucose is the end product of the breakdown of starches, milk sugar, table sugar, *glycogen,* and *amino acids.* Utilizing various enzymes and *hormones,* the glucose is metabolized in the cells and may go into the formation of amino acids, fatty acids, acetone, or pyruvic and lactic acid and thence to carbon dioxide and water.

Insulin is one of the agents responsible for maintaining a reasonably constant level of glucose in the blood and tissues. *Epinephrine* aids the release of glucose from glycogen, thus increasing the amount of circulating glucose. Gluco-corticoids from the adrenal cortex increase blood-sugar levels. (See *Diabetes* and *Hypoglycemia,* Section 10.)

Goat's milk is a satisfactory breast-milk substitute and is occasionally used if a *cow's-milk allergy* is suspected. Because of its similarity in allergenic properties to cow's milk, it is usually used after *soy* and *meat* formulas have been tried. It has no iron or folic acid and is usually devoid of vitamin D, so these must be given as a supplement.

Hypervitaminosis D is the disease caused by excessive vitamin D intake. (See *Hypercalcemia,* Section 10.) The usual dose considered adequate is 400 units per day. Cod-liver oil, sunshine, and most milks have *vitamin D.* More than 10,000 units a day can accumulate over a few weeks and produce symptoms. Some babies are sensitive to its effect and become toxic after receiving lower doses. Most babies get 400 units in their daily vitamin supplement plus the 400 units in the approximately one quart of milk per day they drink in the first six months of life. Keeping the daily intake under 1,000 units per day would be wise. Irritability, constipation, poor weight gain, poor muscle tone, pallor, excessive urination suggest vitamin D intoxication. If prolonged, *kidney* damage will occur.

Hypoproteinemia—see *Kwashiorkor*

Iodide is a salt essential to the function of the body, especially of the *thyroid* gland. A deficient intake will lead to simple *goiter* or endemic *cretinism.* People who live in areas where there is a natural deficiency can be maintained easily with the use of iodized salt in the *diet.* (See *Thyroid,* Section 10.) Kelp is a good source of iodine.

Iodides are incorporated in cough syrups as they help to liquify secretions (Calcidrine®). They are especially useful for asthma. Excessive use of iodides will produce iodism—skin rashes and disturbed thyroid function.

The protein-bound iodine test for thyroid function may be falsely elevated for several weeks after the use of iodide-containing cough syrups or X ray dyes.

Iron, a metal, is an essential part of the *hemoglobin* molecule and of muscle *protein.* Inadequate amounts in the diet are usually due to excessive milk intake and inadequate ingestion of meat, fruit, and vegetables. (See *Anemia,* Section 8.) Most of the iron ingested in the diet is passed out in the stool; however, if the body is anemic, it becomes more efficient in absorbing iron from the intestinal tract. Iron must be in the ferrous state to be absorbed; absorption is enhanced if it is accompanied to the intestines with *vitamin C.*

Some patients become *anemic* even when on a diet high in iron. Apparently some binding effect by minerals or protein in the intestines interferes with iron absorption—for example, phytic acid in grain. In some people milk ingestion produces a condition in the bowels that hinders iron absorption.

An iron tonic can safely be given to growing children who "eat poorly" or to mature, menstruating adolescent girls and women. It is best to monitor the *hemoglobin* level in the blood by a blood count every six to twelve months. Excessive iron will cause *hemosiderosis.*

Kwashiorkor, or protein malnutrition (hypoproteinemia), develops more easily in a growing child because of the need for *amino acids* for growth and maintenance. The total protein intake may be adequate, but if the essential ones (those the body is unable to manufacture) are lacking in the diet, proper protein cannot be put together for muscle, brain, and *metabolism.* The development of the condition is enhanced if chronic illness is also present, especially *diarrhea, nephrosis, burns,* or *hemorrhage.* This usually develops after the baby is weaned and his diet is suddenly devoid of good protein.

The child becomes edematous (water retentive), develops *dermatitis,* has sparse hair, fails to grow, becomes lethargic and quick-tempered. Muscles are weak and thin. The *liver* is enlarged by fat infiltration.

Treatment consists of slow introduction of foods of high protein value and elimination of infection.

During fetal life and throughout the first postnatal year, the brain grows largely by cell division. Protein deficiencies at those times would produce permanent brain defects. Protein deficiencies after that age might be less disastrous but would retard learning during the time of subnutrition.

Linoleic acid is an unsaturated (some double bonds between carbon atoms) acid which cannot be synthesized by the body and must be supplied in the diet. Its absence will lead to dry, thick skin. These unsaturated fatty acids are more prevalent in vegetable oils and are assumed safer for continued use than dairy fats. The latter are supposed to be at least partially responsible for atheromatous plaques in the blood vessels of adults in developed countries.

Magnesium is a mineral essential to body metabolism. Its excess or depletion depends on *vitamin D, parathyroid* function, *calcium* ingestion, *diarrhea, malabsorption,* severe *malnutrition.* Excessive intravenous fluid given over prolonged periods may wash out the magnesium, producing high calcium levels and renal *calculi. Tetany,* muscular twitchings, and *seizures* can occur.

Excessive magnesium in the system can cause coma and *electrocardiogram* changes. It might occur after a magnesium sulfate treatment for *hypertension* or when used as a purge.

Malnutrition may be caused by insufficient food or dietary imbalance due to poverty, ignorance, or emotional factors; *malabsorption* (see Section 12) may also result in wasting. *Iron* and *vitamin C* deficiencies are the chief defects in the American diet, but inadequate protein nutrition is a close third. (See *Kwashiorkor.*)

Manganese is found in grains and vegetables. It is important for *enzyme* activity.

Meat milks are usually used if a cow's milk allergy cannot be controlled with soy milk or if the infant acquires an allergy to the soy milk. When all else fails, some mothers will rotate the milks: boiled cow's milk in the morning, soy milk at noon, meat milk at supper, and whatever is handy at night. Apparently the baby is sensitive to *all* these milks but doesn't get enough of any one to upset him.

Nutrition (see *Diet*) to be adequate must provide enough of all essentials to allow for energy and growth. Babies and children require more water and protein proportionately than adults; short periods of *dehydration* and *protein* deficiency that can be handled easily by adults will produce permanent damage to the growing human. (See *Dehydration,* Section 10; *Kwashiorkor.*)

Water is obviously essential. Daily intake for a baby must amount to more than 10 percent of his body weight, depending on environmental heat and loss in the stools. A seven-pound baby needs about a pint of fluid daily. (An average adult could get by on four or five pints a day.) Almost half of the water loss occurs through evaporation from skin and lungs; the remainder is excreted in the urine. A baby urinating but twice on a hot day needs extra fluid to prevent dehydration and/or fever.

Protein requirements are greater for infants than children and adults. *Amino acids* are the basic chemicals (containing nitrogen) which constitute protein. Milk will supply the needs until animal protein (veal, beef, lamb) is added to the diet after six or seven months of life when the milk intake is reduced. It is much easier to supply a child's amino-acid requirements with animal protein than with the protein in grain, beans, peas, and nuts. About one teaspoonful of protein for every four or five pounds of body weight per day should keep the infant and child in positive nitrogen balance. One hot dog or a small hamburger patty should be enough each day for the growing child. (See *Fat, Protein, Carbohydrates.*)

Obesity is the accumulation of fat throughout the body. Until recently, doctors were trained to accept a certain weight as ideal for each height, but the rule now is: if someone looks fat, he *is* fat. The most acceptable cause of pure obesity is a genetic proclivity enhanced by psychological factors. Physiologic tendencies often initiate the problem, and family attitudes promote it. The fat baby is more likely to become the fat adult. The well-nourished baby who eats well is a joy to the mother, who needs to be needed and wants her baby to be dependent—and his oral demands are easily satisfied. His warm smile when his stomach is full rewards her. When he becomes a toddler, his growing independence and appetite loss suggests rejection to her, and she may respond with increased efforts to maintain him at the oral phase when he wants to go on to the anal or genital phase of development. He either goes hungry to upset her, or acquiesces and becomes fat.

The fat person, usually *endomorphic* (see Section 10), has a large intestinal capacity (up to forty feet of bowel); it takes a lot of food to fill all that up. The increased surface area enhances the absorption of every last calorie consumed. The satiety center in the thalamus may have a higher than normal threshold, so the eater gets a delayed message about potatoes and dessert. Fat people have short tapering fingers; this suggests a genetic difference in the way they handle calories. Research indicates that endomorphs have an increased number of fat storage cells under their skin, as if nature expects them to store more.

Why the concern then, if they are destined to be fat and it is such a fight to lose weight? Statistics indicate a higher morbidity in the obese due to increased incidence of *hypertension, diabetes, gall-bladder* pathology, and vascular disease. You should hear surgeons groan when they must tunnel through four inches of fat to a diseased gall bladder.

A mother can teach some preventive techniques of eating to her growing, cute, but plump child. Like a balloon which is easier to blow up the second time, the body finds it easier to gain than to lose. Prophylactic underfeeding and overexercising seem to be the only reasonable answer. No matter what the basis is for the extra lard, reduced caloric intake and increased *calorie* use will burn up the fat. But these people love to eat and hate to exercise.

Hypothyroidism, or glandular obesity, is rarely encountered although many respond to thyroid extract. Low thyroid in a growing child is fairly easily detected, since linear *growth* is slowed (to less than one to two inches per year), hands and feet are always cold and dry; sluggishness and drowsiness are usually present. Many of us have seen children become fat after tonsillectomy or a serious infection (*pneumonia, meningitis*). I wonder if the child has heard, "We'll get his tonsils out, and maybe he'll eat better." The child thinks, "I'd better eat, or they'll take them out again!" I wonder if the severe infection or the anesthesia knocked out the thalamic calorie-control center, or the stress exhausted some enzyme system.

Preventive measure: if both parents and all four grandparents are thin, nothing need be done except satisfy infantile oral demands. If family fat runs thick the baby's oral needs must be satisfied with large volumes of calorie-poor milk (two percent) and a pacifier. Candy must not be used as a bribe, as it seems to suggest eating as an answer to all frustration. Sugarless gum; low-calorie fruit drinks, fruits, vegetables, and meat should be established as a *family* habit. Exercise must be promoted. Fat adolescents and adults do well at summer camps or in group therapy where their food hang-ups can be bared. Bickering and needling seem only to push the lonely fat one into quiet, sullen, oral solitude.

A mother may find that—to avoid a mealtime confrontation—her obese child is stealing bread and candy bars, hiding them under the mattress or in the closet for midnight snacks. She may force him to cheat and lie. When he is sixteen and complains that his weight precludes social popularity, his mother says, "Well, I tried." His response: "You didn't try hard enough." The mother again is the handy scapegoat. Who else?

Phosphorus is a mineral important in bones, teeth, in the nuclei of cells, in the metabolism of chemicals and foods, and in the work of nerve cells. It is found in most foods, grains, and dairy products. Excess ingestion proportionate to *calcium* may lead to *tetany.*

Pica is the persistent ingestion of nonfoods. Dirt, sand, plaster, animal excreta, paint, glass, and grass have all been reported. This perverted craving is most often due to an *iron-deficiency anemia,* but *vitamin* and mineral lack may also account for it. The toddler has a need to investigate most things orally. When he notices his mother's frantic response to this natural desire, he is rewarded for his act, so he continues. He might not have found it interesting but for his mother's reaction. Somehow the mother has to pretend that she doesn't care, and at the same time she must provide a balanced *diet,* extra *iron,* and plenty of opportunity to satisfy oral drives. (Permit and encourage pacifier and thumb-sucking, let him mess in his food, let him place harmless toys in his mouth.) Sometimes the pica produces other diseases *(lead poisoning, worm infestation, acrodynia)* which by their nature heighten irritability and subsequently foster more pica.

Potassium is a mineral found in each cell. It is essential for nerve conduction, muscle contraction, and sugar metabolism. It acts in a reciprocal manner with *sodium.* If much sodium is ingested, potassium is excreted as a compensation, but if potassium falls to low levels, *aldosterone* secretion is reduced, and the potassium level will rise. Potassium levels are low in *aldosteronism, muscular dystrophy,* and *diarrhea.* (See *Hyperkalemia* and *Hypokalemia,* Section 10.)

Proteins are the building blocks of the body. Animal protein supplies human protein best. A vegetarian adult might be able to avoid protein *malnutrition,* but parents should not saddle their children with this practice, for malnutrition is common in the growing body. When the child is fully mature, he may elect to become a vegetarian with less risk of protein starvation, for his protein needs are then less, and if he tries, he may be able to consume all the essential amino acids required. A diet chronically low in protein usually results in lowered resistance to disease and growth retardation; if severe, *mental retardation* is usually associated.

It is possible that many vegetarians are suffering from *hypoproteinemia,* as it is difficult to ingest a diet complete in all essential amino acids without consuming an uncomfortable amount of nuts and beans. A few bits of meat every day are often sufficient to supply these amino acids that the body is unable to manufacture.

Plasma proteins may be low in *nephrosis* (they are lost into the urine), defective protein diet, and some hereditary problems.

In *Wilson's disease* (ceruloplasmin deficiency or hepatolenticular degeneration) the body is unable to manufacture a specific *globulin* which contains some copper atoms and/or copper metabolism is disturbed. Excess copper is deposited in the body. In the eyes a ring of copper is formed; the kidneys are damaged and allow glucose and amino acids to be excreted. Therapy attempts to reduce the body copper before it becomes toxic. (See Sections 12 and 15.)

Rare and bizarre diseases due to inherited deficiencies of *enzymes* responsible for synthesis of other proteins in the blood will cause liver, lung, and blood disorders. These diseases occur despite an adequate protein intake. The building blocks are present, but the enzyme that puts them together for the body's use is not functioning.

For adequate growth and nutrition a child requires about three times as much protein in proportion to weight as does the adult. The average adult needs about two or three ounces of protein per day. A fifty-pound six-year-old should get almost as much for optimum nutrition (about two ounces of hamburger, for example).

Rickets, or vitamin D deficiency or soft bones, has largely disappeared because of the universal knowledge of its cause and the addition of *vitamin D* to most milks. The disease is due to the deficient mineralization of bone; the connective tissue and cartilage are normal, but the *calcium* and *phosphorus* are not deposited therein.

Vitamin D is the sunshine vitamin; sunshine converts a vitamin precursor to vitamin D. Sunshine through window glass is of the wrong wave length to effect this change, hence rickets is more common in the northern climes. Vitamin D must be provided artificially in milk or vitamins or by a sunlamp. Breast milk contains little. (See *Vitamins.*)

Refractory rickets is a rare form of the disease that does not respond to the usual vitamin D doses. The symptoms are the same, but the vitamin in the usual dose will not increase mineralization of the bone because the phosphate in the blood is low (*hypophosphatemic* rickets). Defective calcium absorption, renal tubular inefficiency, and compensatory *parathyroid* imbalance may all play a part. It is often familial; the males in the family may all be severely *bow-legged.*

Extremely large doses of vitamin D are necessary to arrest the disease, but care must be taken to avoid the poisoning effects (fever, enlarged *liver,* bone pain, irritability, and *kidney* damage).

Other form may be due to low calcium as a genetic defect, *Fanconi syndrome,* or other diseases of the kidney tubules. (See *Cystinosis,* Section 10.)

Salt, or sodium chloride, makes food more palatable, but an excess is known to have some distant relationship to the development of *hypertension.* (The chief reason for salt restriction in the adult is to discourage fluid retention or edema.) Baby foods are high in salt content; it is wiser to use home-cooked foods, either strained or pureed in a blender. The salt content can be more easily restricted this way; in addition, it is cheaper. Additional seasoning should not be added to baby food in the jar.

The accidental ingestion of large amounts of salt can cause brain *hemorrhage* and *seizures.* Boiled skimmed milk is a concentrated salt solution; salt poisoning may occur if boiled skimmed milk is given to a baby already in some *dehydration* from *diarrhea.* (See *Hypernatremia,* Section 10.)

Soybean milks are a reasonable substitute for breast or cow's milk. They provide all the protein, calcium, and minerals necessary for growth and nutrition. If a baby vomits, has *diarrhea,* is screaming with gas, two days of soy milk will usually quiet these symptoms if they are due to an allergy. (It takes at least 48 to 72 hours to rid the intestines of the offending cow protein.) It is worth trying for the baby with chronic phlegm, snort or wheeze. Most respiratory allergies in infancy are due to milk sensitivity. The distressing sloppy stools may be controlled with pectin and kaolin.

Sulfur, an essential to body protein, is found in almost all tissues, incorporated as part of certain amino acids. The body can only utilize that sulfur that is consumed as organic or amino-acid-bound sulfur.

Vitamins are compounds that the body is unable to synthesize. They must be provided in the diet or, as in the case of vitamin D, sunshine is the needed ingredient to allow the body to manufacture this essential compound.

Vitamin A is a fat soluble vitamin found abundantly in egg yolk, liver, fish oils, milk fat, green and yellow vegetables, and yellow fruits. It is needed for retinal pigments (allowing vision in dim light), *bone* and *tooth* development, and integrity of skin and mucous membranes. Its absence causes night blindness, thickening of skin and membranes, and defective tooth and bone development. Its excess will lead to enlargement of *liver* and *spleen,* bone pain, appetite loss, and yellow, cracked skin.

Studies of large groups of people reveal that next to iron and vitamin C, vitamin A is a common dietary omission. Vitamin A intoxication is usually found in those who ingest large daily doses (more than 50,000 units) over several weeks' time to reduce the severity of their acne.

In infancy 1,000 units per day is usually sufficient. This should be gradually increased to 5,000 per day in the adult. After infancy a child on a diet containing a few of the above foods does not need vitamin A supplement. On the assumption that if a little is good, a lot is better, a mother might give big doses daily. After several weeks or months the child might show irritability, loss of appetite, peeling and itching of skin, tender bones, enlarged *liver,* and even *headache* and other symptoms to suggest a *brain tumor.*

Vitamin B is a mixture of about six distinct vitamins. All of these are contained in cereal, meat, fruit, vegetables, and milk, so a deficiency of one is usually associated with the deficiency of another.

Vitamin B_1 is thiamine, the anti*beriberi* vitamin. It is water soluble and is poorly stored in the body, so it must be supplied almost daily in the diet. But it is widely found in grains and meats. About one milligram per day seems to be adequate. (See *Beriberi.*)

Vitamin B_2 is riboflavin, one of the B-complex vitamins essential to some enzyme systems. Very little is necessary, but because it is not stored, it must be supplied frequently. Abundant amounts are found in meat, milk, eggs, and cereals. A deficiency will cause burning, itching, and redness of the eyes, and a smooth, magenta colored tongue.

Another B-complex vitamin is niacin, necessary for a number of enzyme activities. Pellagra is the disease which occurs as a result of its absence from the diet. Only 10 to 20 milligrams of this are necessary in the daily diet. It is found in meats, peanuts, whole-grain cereals, and green vegetables; it takes a really poor diet for pellagra to develop.

Niacin forms a part of some enzyme systems, and thus its absence causes generalized body symptoms: *anorexia,* weakness, dizziness, *diarrhea,* red skin on exposed areas (hands and face) which look like sunburn, red tongue, and sore lips. Other deficiency diseases are usually associated.

The treatment obviously is to provide niacin by means of a balanced diet and vitamin B supplement.

Vitamin B_6 is pyridoxine, normally found in milk, grain, meats, and vegetables; only a small amount is needed daily. The body uses it in its *enzyme* systems. Its absence from one of the canned milks a few years ago was responsible for *convulsions* in infants receiving this as their sole food; when cereal was added or B_6 given, the seizures promptly stopped.

Vitamin B_{12} and related compounds are essential to prevent the occurrence of *pernicious anemia.*

Folacin is another group of related chemicals, the absence of which causes *megaloblastic anemia.* (See *Folic acid.*)

Vitamin C is ascorbic acid. The absence of this enzyme will lead to scurvy, the chief manifestation of which is internal bleeding or seepage of blood and easy bruisability.

Vitamin C is not stored well in the body, so almost daily ingestion is necessary. Fresh fruits are good sources, and lightly cooked vegetables contain some.

It facilitates many enzyme systems in the body and enhances the absorption of iron. Its efficacy in stopping virus infections has been proved, but big doses are needed early. Most infants will respond to 500 milligrams of C every hour. Once the infection is controlled, the dose is tapered off. It is safe and occasionally cheaper than other methods. Most animals can synthesize their own; primates (and guinea pigs) need vitamin C supplied in the diet, or they will get scurvy. The action of ascorbic acid in the body is related to the integrity of collagen and connective tissue, which holds the body together.

A deficiency, therefore, will lead to hemorrhages (the capillaries are fragile), loosened teeth, and disorganized bone growth (*calcium* is deposited, but the bone-connective tissue is not adequate, and hemorrhages form between the bone and the periosteum).

A baby rarely has scurvy at birth unless the mother's diet has been wholly inadequate. If his diet during the first year is limited to milk (breast milk has little vitamin C in it), without fruit, juice, or vitamin supplements, he begins to show irritability, lethargy, and bone tenderness at about age six to ten months. His gums, especially near erupting teeth, will be swollen and hemorrhagic. Leg pains progress to refusal to move, and he assumes the frog position. Knobs of bloody, swollen bone tissue appear on the ribs. Blood in the stools or urine and skin hemorrhages are common.

X rays of the bones will reveal the characteristic changes. The low vitamin C blood level helps to confirm the history of poor intake. A mother who boils fruit juice to kill the bacteria will also destroy the heat-susceptible vitamin. (One obvious scurvy case was confusing because the mother insisted that she gave the baby orange juice. After the third interrogation session she mentioned the name of a popular brand of orange pop.)

If the body needs vitamin C, it will soak it up like a sponge. In the well-vitaminized body, a dose of vitamin C will be excreted in the urine in the subsequent few hours. In a case of scurvy, almost none will be found in the urine, as the tissues will have absorbed it. People on a reasonably balanced diet with fruits and/or vegetables may still need extra vitamin C for colds or stress.

I read about a nut who existed on eggs and wine for six months; he finally got scurvy. It does take some doing to develop the disease. Common sense dictates vitamin C supplement for the first year of life and then, when the growth rate is slower and the child is eating a variety of foods, it may be discontinued. Some unsure mothers will continue some vitamins and/or iron just once a week. There is good evidence that extra vitamin C (500 to 1,000 milligrams an hour) will discourage colds and flu, but it must be started early, and it doesn't work for everyone. It helps develop interferon, a natural antiviral substance. It increases the antibacterial effectiveness of the white blood cells. Some of us give 10 to 100 grams intravenously to help very sick people recover and to help addicts get off their narcotics.

The usual daily dose of 25 to 50 milligrams is more than adequate for the baby. For adults 50 to 75 milligrams is about right. Increased amounts may be required during fever and diarrhea. The nursing mother should double her dose. The scorbutic infant should receive 100 to 200 milligrams daily until healing is obvious. The bones will continue to heal with time and continued adequate vitamin C intake.

Vitamin D is transformed in the liver to calciferol. This metabolite moves to the intestine and bone, where its chief effect is to mobilize calcium into the circulation. *Calcitonin* (see Section 10), an enzyme secreted by cells in the *thyroid,* has the property of depositing calcium in the bone. The calciferol picks up the calcium from the intestines, and the calcitonin deposits it in the bones.

Usually a baby must be deprived of vitamin D for the whole of his first year before developing rickets. The skull bones are soft, and plunk in and out like a Ping-Pong ball on pressure. Knobs appear on the ribs at the junction of the bony rib and the cartilage rib (in the front of the chest—rachitic rosary). Wrists and ankles become thickened. As the disease progresses, an indentation around the chest appears due to the pull of the diaphragm on the soft ribs. The head becomes misshapen from pressure, and a prominent forehead develops; from the top, the head appears like a hot cross bun. The spine flexes forward to almost a hunch-backed appearance, the leg bones curve, and the toddler displays an exaggerated bowing to his legs. X rays of the bones show widening at the ends and decreased density. Other signs of *malnutrition,* such as *growth* failure and *anemia,* reflect the general poor diet.

Treatment is the giving of five to ten times the usual daily dose of vitamin D (usual dose—400 to 800 units). Rapid treatment may decrease the blood calcium level (the calcium is moving into the bones) so precipitously that *tetany* occurs.

Vitamin D is a storable, fat-soluble vitamin, so a three-month supply may be given once every three months with the same beneficial effects.

Grandmothers often discouraged early walking because they feared the development of bowed legs. If an infant wants to walk early and is receiving prophylactic vitamin D, he will show no more than the usual physiological bowing of the normal ten- to twenty-month-old. (See *Rickets.*)

Vitamin E is a group of related compounds called tocopherols. They are oil soluble. Their action is little understood but has something to do with muscle metabolism. A deficiency is rare and is usually associated with chronic diarrhea. *Anemia,* muscle weakness, and wasting are present in vitamin E-deficient people, but the exact relationship to the vitamin is unclear. The recommended amounts are easily obtained from the ingestion of nuts, peas, beans, and green, leafy vegetables. Vitamin E is an antioxidant, so it is used for premature infants to prevent the capillary proliferation in their eyes. (See *Retrolental fibroplasia,* Section 5.)

Vitamin K is a chemical necessary for the production of some coagulation factors. (See *Hemorrhagic disease of newborn,* Section 5.)

Weaning from the breast is usually accomplished after one year of age, when teeth tend to interfere with nursing comfort. The eruption of teeth is nature's way of telling the mother that solid foods are more important than milk. After six months of age, the baby is filled with solids, and then he decides how much milk he wants or needs. After six to nine months, one nursing is usually replaced with a four- to six-ounce bottle or cup of juice. After two to four weeks, another nursing is replaced by a bottle or cup. This gradual diminution of amount and frequency of milk intake is easier on both participants. Milk is less important after six to ten months, but adequate protein must be supplied in the solid foods. This method of substituting solids for milk after six months usually precludes the milk *anemia* so common in exclusively cow's-milk-fed babies.

Zinc is needed by the body as a trace element. It is essential in many enzymes. Its absence over long periods of time will lead to *anemia* and *dwarfism.* An excess irritates the intestine and may occur if galvanized iron pots are used for cooking. Enough of this metal is found in all foods to satisfy daily requirements. Zinc at about the 30-to-60 milligram level will help clear adolescent acne.

SECTION 12

The Abdomen and Digestive Tract *

A. Abdominal pain

Generalized
- *Abdominal epilepsy* (Section 16)
- *Colic* (Section 11)
- *Mesenteric lymphadenitis*
- *Parasites*
- *Peritonitis*
- *Pneumonia* (Section 9)
- *Regional enteritis*
- *Rheumatic fever* (Section 2)

Central
- *Appendicitis*
- *Gas*
- *Gastrointestinal allergy*
- *Intestinal flu (Gastroenteritis)*
- *Intestinal polyps*
- *Intussusception*
- *Irritable colon*
- *Mesenteric lymphadenitis*
- *Tension-fatigue syndrome* (Section 15)
- *Volvulus*

Lower right
- *Appendicitis*
- *Intussusception*
- *Kidney infection* (Section 13)
- *Mesenteric lymphadenitis*
- *Ovulation* (see Abdominal pain, lower left)
- *Torn muscles* (Myositis, Section 7)
- *Ureteral obstruction* (see Hydronephrosis, Section 13)

Upper right
- *Gall bladder disease*
  - *Cholecystitis*
  - *Cholelithiasis*
- *Liver disease*
  - *Abscess*
  - *Cysts*
  - *Hepatitis*

Upper mid
- *Bezoars*
- *Epigastric hernia*
- *Gastritis*
- *Hiatus hernia*
- *Pancreatitis*
- *Peptic ulcer* (see Duodenal, Gastric)
- *Ulcer*
  - *Duodenal*
  - *Gastric*

Upper left
- *Colitis*
- *Kidney* (Section 13)

*Read **Abdomen** first.

Spleen (Section 8)
Lower left
Colitis
Constipation
Diverticulitis
Gas
Irritable colon
Ovulation
Parasites
Polyposis
Worms (see Pinworms, Parasites)
Lower mid
Cystitis (Section 13)
Dysmenorrhea (Section 10)

B. Abdominal masses and distension

Ascites
Cirrhosis
Congestive heart failure (Section 8)
Galactosemia (Section 10)
Gas
Glycogen storage disease
Hepatitis (also Section 2)
Hydronephrosis (Section 13)
Hypersplenism (Section 8)
Hypervitaminosis A (Section 11)
Ileus, paralytic
Infectious mononucleosis (Section 2)
Leukemia (Section 8)
Lipidoses (Section 10)
Liver cysts
Echinococcus
Polycystic (also Renal, Section 13)
Tumors
Megacolon
Neoplasms (Section 10)
Letterer-Siwe
Nephroblastoma
Neuroblastoma
Teratoma

C. Vomiting

Achalasia
Adhesions
Appendicitis
Bezoars
Brain tumor (Section15)
Chalasia (cardioesophageal relaxation)
Cyclic vomiting
Dehydration (Section 10)
Gastroenteritis
Hematemesis
Hernia, incarcerated
Malrotation
Meningitis (Section 2)
Migraine (Section 15)
Motion sickness (Section 14)
Otitis media (Section 14)
Peritonitis
Pneumonia (Section 9)
Pyelitis (Section 13)
Pyloric stenosis
Pylorospasm
Regional enteritis
Rumination
Volvulus

D. Diarrhea

Amebiasis
Bacillary dysentery
Celiac disease
Cholera
Chronic nonspecific
Colitis

Cystic fibrosis (Section 9)
Disaccharide enzyme deficiency
Lactase deficiency
Sucrase deficiency
Enteropathy
Flu, intestinal (Gastroenteritis)
Food poisoning
Botulism
Clostridium perfringens
Salmonella
Staphylococcus
Gastroenteritis
Gastrointestinal allergy
Giardiasis
Irritable colon
Malabsorption
Parasites
Steatorrhea (see Malabsorption)
Typhoid fever (Section 2)

E. Blood in stool

Amebiasis
Anal fissure
Aspirin
Bacillary dysentery
Bleeding into intestinal tract
Colitis
Epistaxis (Section 1)
Gastric hemorrhage
Hemorrhagic disease of the newborn (Section 5)
Hemorrhoids
Intussusception
Iron poisoning (Section 1)
Meckel's diverticulum
Rectal polyp (see Intestinal polyps)
Regional enteritis
Ulcer
Duodenal
Gastric

F. Constipation

Diet (also Section 11)
Hypothyroidism (Section 10)
Megacolon
Psychological (see Bowel and bladder, Encopresis, Section 16)
Pyloric stenosis
Stool

G. Alimentary canal

Esophagus
Achalasia
Chalasia
Esophagitis, corrosive
Foreign bodies
Stomach
Barium meal
Bezoars
Gastric ulcer
Gastritis
Gastroenteritis
Heartburn
Pylorus
Stenosis
Duodenum
Bands (malrotation)
Ulcer
Small bowel
Gas
Gastrointestinal allergy
Intestinal flu (gastroenteritis)
Meckel's diverticulum
Regional enteritis
Volvulus
Worms (see Parasites)
Large bowel
Amebic dysentery (Amebiasis)
Barium enema
Colitis

Diverticulitis
Gas
Intussusception
Irritable colon
Megacolon
Rectum
Bowel control
Constipation
Enema
Laxatives
Polyposis
Prolapse
Anus
Fissure
Fistula
Hemorrhoids
Pruritis

H. Organs

Liver
Abscess
Cirrhosis
Cysts
Echinococcus (cyst)
Galactosemia (Section 10)
Glycogen storage disease
Hypervitaminosis A (Section 11)
Lipidoses (Section 10)
Polycystic disease
Gall bladder
Bile
Bile ducts
Cholecystitis
Cholelithiasis
Pancreas
Lipase
Pancreatitis
Mumps
Trauma
Neoplasms
Spleen (Section 8)
Infectious mononucleosis (Section 2)
Leukemia (Section 8)

I. Peritoneum

Ascites
Adhesions
Peritoneal dialysis
Peritonitis

J. Hernia

Diaphragmatic (Section 5)
Epigastric
Femoral
Hiatus
Inguinal
Umbilical

K. Tests

Barium enema
Barium meal
GOT (Glutamic oxaloacetic transaminase)
GPT (Glutamic pyruvic transaminase)
Intestinal biopsy
Liver function

L. Worms

Ascariasis
Enterobiasis (see Pinworms)
Fluke infections (Schistosomiasis)
Hookworm
Nematode infections
Oxyuriasis (see Pinworms)
Parasites
Pinworms
Strongyloidiasis
Tapeworm infestations
Diphyllobothriasis
Hymenolepiasis
Teniasis
Toxocara canis and cati
Trematodes
Trichuriasis (Whipworm infections)

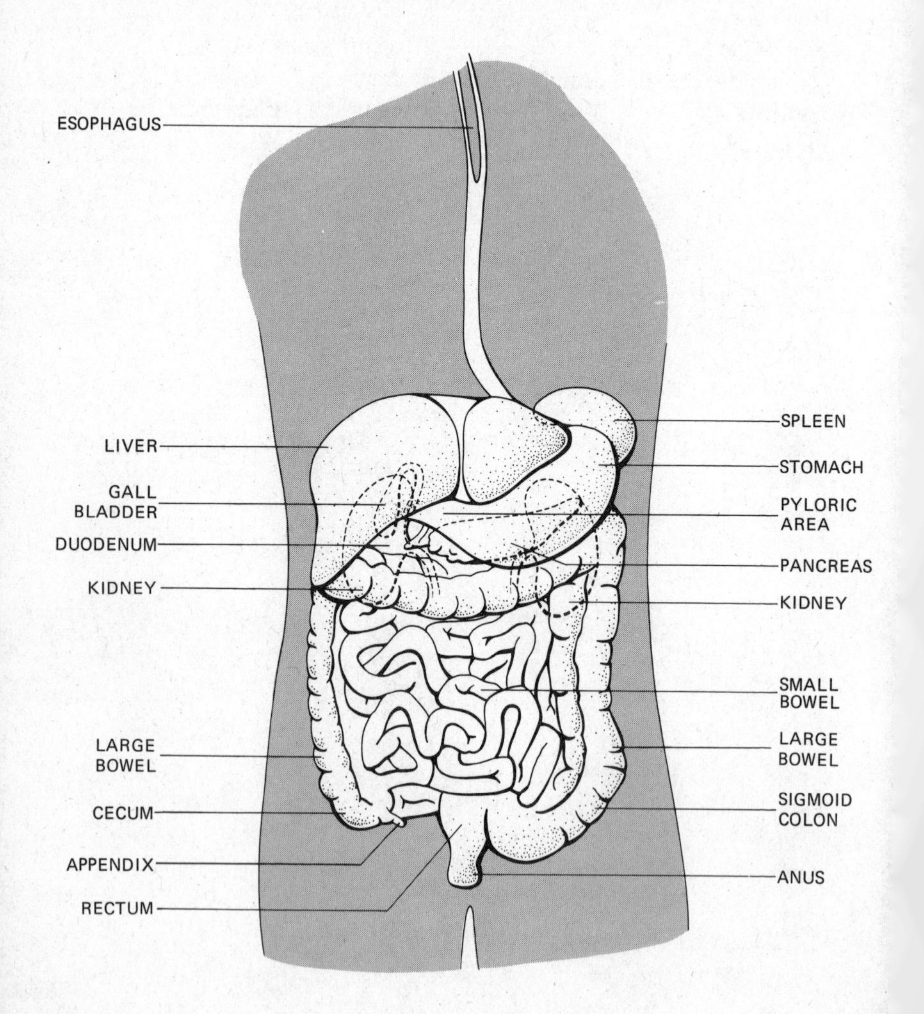
ESOPHAGUS
LIVER
GALL BLADDER
DUODENUM
KIDNEY
LARGE BOWEL
CECUM
APPENDIX
RECTUM
SPLEEN
STOMACH
PYLORIC AREA
PANCREAS
KIDNEY
SMALL BOWEL
LARGE BOWEL
SIGMOID COLON
ANUS

Abdomen. The region between the lower rib edges and the pelvic and pubic bones holds the *liver* (upper right), the *spleen* (upper left), *stomach* (upper central and left), *kidneys* with *adrenal glands* (upper left and right toward the back and spinal column), and the small and large *bowel* (all areas) with the *appendix* in the lower right area. The *bladder* is in the central lower area, the *rectum* just behind the bladder in this same area.

Every mother should practice palpating her child's abdomen (and her own) occasionally to become familiar with the feel of a normal abdomen. The doctor always palpates the abdomen as a part of the routine examination, but a swollen organ or tumor mass may develop silently and require immediate investigation long before the time of the yearly checkup. Bathtime provides a good opportunity for this home checkup. Under the pretense of tickling or playing "get you," the mother can practice a little preventive medicine without alarming her child or producing navel-gazing hypochondriasis.

Abdominal pain

Midabdominal pain centered at the navel, accompanied by nausea, *vomiting,* pallor, listlessness, and *diarrhea,* provides the classic indications of intestinal flu or viral *gastroenteritis.* The pain should come and go. The child usually feels almost normal between the spasms and seems happy and content at play; then a wave of pain, pallor, and nausea overwhelms him, forcing him to lie down, *vomit,* or try to expel a *stool*—usually loose.

Adults have this for one day, and it is called twenty-four-hour *flu.* A child has not developed his immunity sufficiently, so his diarrhea lasts seven days. One of the days—usually the first—is devoted to vomiting. If fever remains more than two days, if the child is toxic and listless between pains, if the diarrhea lasts more than seven days, and the stools have a particularly dead or fetid odor or blood is noted, it suggests *dysentery, intussusception,* and/or *dehydration.*

Pains caused by *colic* or food *allergy* are also likely to be located here. (See *Gastroenteritis, Diarrhea; Dehydration,* Section 10, and *Bacillary dysentery.*)

Midabdominal pain may indicate early appendicitis.

Lower right-side abdominal pain suggests *appendicitis.* This pain is usually constant and accompanied by muscle spasm and local tenderness. The victim feels that it is the worst *gas* pain he has ever had and that, if he had a good bowel movement, it would go away. If the pain remains exactly the same after a bowel movement, appendicitis is most likely the cause. The doctor's evaluation of the abdominal muscle spasm compared with other areas of the abdomen, plus a rectal temperature of 99.5° to 101° F., plus an elevated *white-blood count* of 12,000 to 16,000, plus tenderness on the right side by rectal palpation, is classic for appendicitis.

Upper right abdominal pain is associated with *liver* and (rarely in children) *gall-bladder* disease. A dull, constant ache or fullness in this area is chiefly found in *hepatitis*—a *virus* illness, usually accompanied by a yellow tint to the whites of the eyes (sclera) and, if severe enough, to the skin. The color is more easily seen in daylight than in artificial light.

Upper midabdominal pain is usually associated with the stomach itself. Burning, distress, or fullness in the area between the navel and the rib edge which is relieved by food and/or antacids is the cardinal symptom of an ulcer or at least hyperacidity. In a child the feeling of fullness or distress in this area indicates that the victim is frustrated, under pressure, overwhelmed with anger or hostility that he cannot release. A definite family connection has been observed for this syndrome, especially in boys; they are usually neat, compulsive, strive to attain perfection, and become depressed when their performance does not match their own expectations. Family attitudes may exaggerate the symptoms. Medicine and psychiatric aid may be necessary to allow these children to live with themselves.

Upper left abdominal fullness or distress, at or under the rib edge, suggests spleen enlargement (found in 50 percent of *infectious mononucleosis* victims) or *gas* in the large bowel or colitis. If pain is referred to the shoulder (shoulder-strap pain), the disease or injury is affecting the diaphragm. An enlarged or diseased left kidney can present pain in this area, but usually it is more toward the back.

Lower left abdominal area may be painful, tender, or bloated if *constipation* or *pinworms* are present. Gas in the colon resulting from the ingestion of irritating foods (milk, corn, onions, cabbage, garlic, beans) may produce severe cramping pains; usually these irritants first create pain in the umbilical area, and *then* in the lower left area. A bowel movement provides temporary relief because the painful distention is relieved.

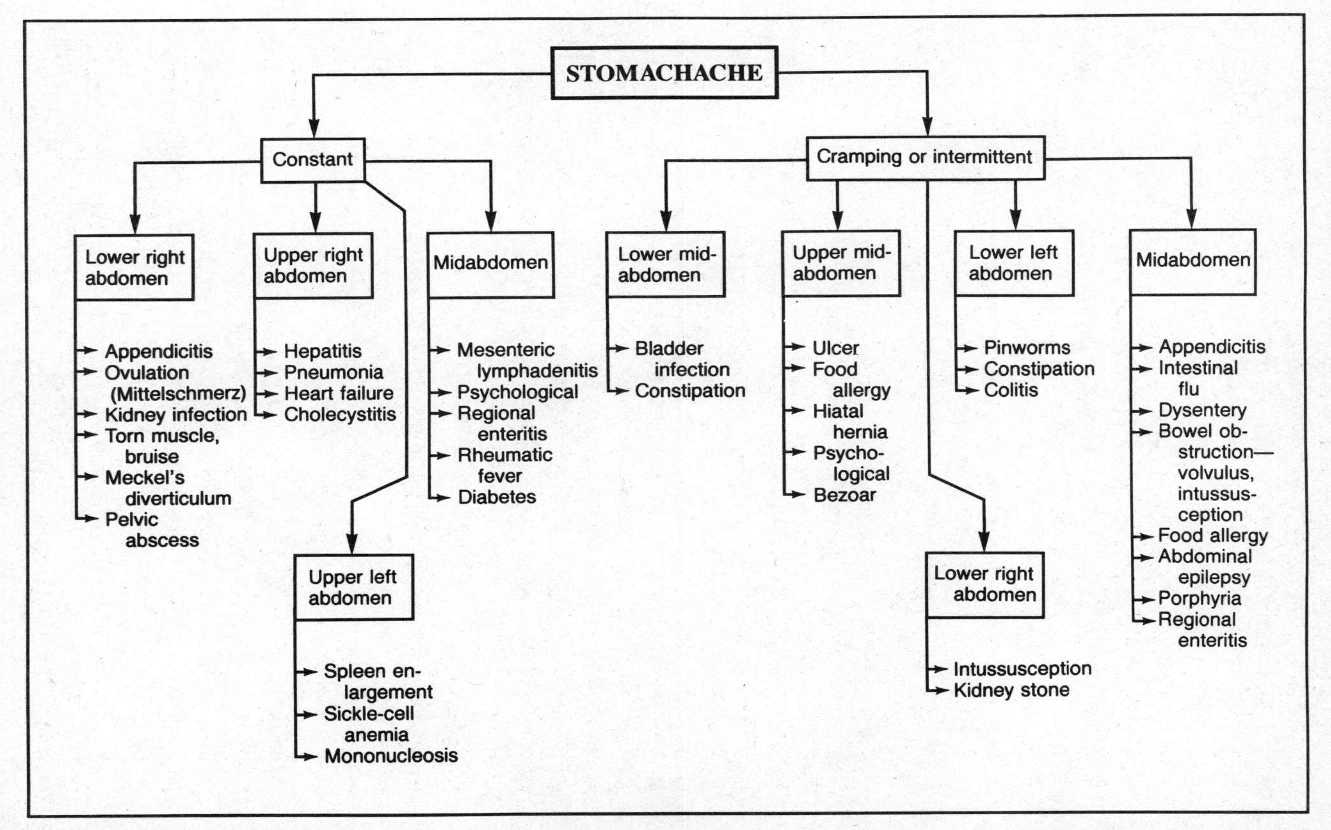
STOMACHACHE
Constant
Cramping or intermittent
Lower right abdomen
Appendicitis
Ovulation (Mittelschmerz)
Kidney infection
Torn muscle, bruise
Meckel's diverticulum
Pelvic abscess
Upper right abdomen
Hepatitis
Pneumonia
Heart failure
Cholecystitis
Upper left abdomen
Spleen enlargement
Sickle-cell anemia
Mononucleosis
Midabdomen
Mesenteric lymphadenitis
Psychological
Regional enteritis
Rheumatic fever
Diabetes
Lower mid-abdomen
Bladder infection
Constipation
Upper mid-abdomen
Ulcer
Food allergy
Hiatal hernia
Psycho-logical
Bezoar
Lower right abdomen
Intussusception
Kidney stone
Lower left abdomen
Pinworms
Constipation
Colitis
Midabdomen
Appendicitis
Intestinal flu
Dysentery
Bowel obstruction—volvulus, intussusception
Food allergy
Abdominal epilepsy
Porphyria
Regional enteritis

Midmenstrual cycle *lower abdominal* pain, left or right, is assumed to be due to egg extrusion from the ovary, called *Mittelschmerz,* because this foreign word is an euphemism for "laying an egg." (Really midway-between-periods-pain.)

Lower midabdominal pain usually means a *bladder* infection—almost exclusively found in the female. Burning and frequency of urination accompany the pain, and a urinalysis reveals pus cells. Appendicitis due to an abnormally located appendix must also be considered. Girls usually recognize uterine cramps during menses as no more than a minor discomfort accompanying menstruation.

Abdominal pain is sometimes assumed to be a pain or a cramp when actually it is a "misery" (or discomfort or nausea or distress), a rumbling, burning, or "something in there." Many patients have had a variety of diagnostic procedures and/or operations for symptoms no more definite than these. The real trouble is abdominal *epileptic equivalent, depression, schizophrenia, migraine,* or neurosis. The brain is playing tricks on these people. Once these patients have had surgery and, of course, with no relief, recurrence of the pain is especially hard to evaluate because *adhesions* may be causing the new pain.

Achalasia is a rarely occurring narrowing of the area at the lower end of the esophagus at the entrance to the stomach. It is present at birth or develops shortly thereafter. The baby vomits its formula unchanged, as it has had no opportunity to be soured or curdled by the acid in the stomach. Attempts to relieve the spasm and stenosis with mechanical stretching or relaxing medicines are usually not permanent, and surgery is almost always necessary.

Adhesion is the abnormal fusion or growing together of adjacent tissues due to scarring—following injury or infection. After surgery, adhesions and scar tissue inside the abdomen may cause kinking of the bowel and obstruction.

Amebiasis, or amebic dysentery, is due to the invasion of the colon by a one-celled parasite. Symptoms may be mild or severe, but mainly appear as *cramps,* bloody *diarrhea,* and weakness. Fever and liver pain suggest liver involvement. This disease is related to poor hygiene and is prevalent in the tropics but is rare in the United States.

Anal fissure is a crack or tear at the anal opening usually due to a hard, dry stool or irritation from a food sensitivity. Softening the stool by discontinuing white foods and lubricating the fissure with an antibiotic ointment to "grease the skids" usually heals such a fissure within one week.

Most cracks or tears are due to vigorous rubbing with dry toilet paper in an attempt to clean the anal opening and the adjacent skin. The skin is abraded, bacteria are introduced, and inflammation follows. The itch-scratch-itch cycle begins (see *Pruritus ani*). Just as water is necessary to clean muddy hands, so *moist* toilet paper (or a cotton ball) is safer and more efficient in cleansing the anal area. Blot, don't rub. Every home should have a bidet or half-bath for rinsing after defecation. Tucks® pads (cotton pads saturated with glycerin and witch hazel) are ideal for cleaning up after a bowel movement.

Anal or rectal fistula may be congenital or may arise from an untreated fissure. A bit of hard stool may impinge on the valves just inside the *anus* and burrow through the wall. An *abscess* forms, then grows, points (comes to a head), and may burst through the skin of the buttocks an inch or so from the anus. Much foul pus may be evacuated. An abscess about the anus is an emergency; the surgeon must drain this as some bacteria may burrow up into the abdomen (see *Peritonitis*).

Anus is the opening at the lower end of the intestinal tract through which the solid wastes of the body are evacuated, along with bacteria and undigested food. It is lined with many sensitive nerve endings. The opening is controlled by a fantastically efficient purse-string muscle which will allow gases (or flatus) to escape while retaining fluid or semisolids.

Appendicitis is an inflammation of the appendix, which in most people is found in the lower right area of the abdomen. If the inflammation is great enough, the appendix abscesses and ruptures, causing *peritonitis* (see Section 2). The trick is to diagnose appendicitis while the appendix is still intact, and get the surgeon to remove the dirty thing. It is now well-documented that appendicitis attacks can run in families; if parents had appendicitis when they were children, their children are more likely to develop it. I have seen it occur in twins within a few months of each other. Good rules to remember are (a) appendicitis feels like the worst gas pain one has ever had, but it does not go away, (b) if one has a good bowel movement and the pain does *not* go away, it is probably appendicitis. (See *Abdominal pain, lower right*.)

The use of laxatives, sedatives, enemas, pain killers, or hot or cold applications is extremely dangerous, since they may mask the findings and delay the surgical treatment. Surgical removal of an intact appendix is fairly simple and standard. A ruptured appendix leads to peritonitis, toxicity, and complications, or surgical drains and further surgery. Abdominal pain associated with *pneumonia, mesenteric lymphadenitis, volvulus, intussusception, gastroenteritis, kidney* infection, and ovulation of the female's right (occasionally left) ovary can all appear to be classical appendicitis. Even sore abdominal muscles may seem to be a surgical emergency. The very young and very old patients characteristically do not have the standard findings. All good surgeons remove one normal appendix for every four diseased ones; but this risk is worth taking, compared to the possibility of waiting and entering a pus-filled abdomen with the increased risk of mortality. A surgeon may elect to remove an appendix prophylactically if the patient going to a remote area has had some suspicious symptoms suggesting previous attacks, and there is a strong family tendency.

Ascariasis means infestation by the roundworm. The adult worms live in the intestine, and the female lays thousands of eggs a day. If unsanitary conditions prevail, children will pick up eggs from the ground where they play and will inadvertently swallow them. The eggs soon hatch, and the small worms migrate to the lungs and throat only to be swallowed again, winding up in the colon where they become adults. Abdominal pain, distention, liver inflamation, and lethargy suggest the presence of roundworms. Appendicitis may be caused by worms. In some endemic areas, parents treat their children (and themselves) once or twice a year just to keep the worm population subdued. (See also *Parasites, Pinworms, Liver.*)

Ascites is an abnormal collection of fluid in the abdominal cavity usually due to back pressure from a failing *heart,* a diseased *liver,* or from leakage of serum from capillaries due to nephrosis. A swollen abdomen and shortness of breath are the chief symptoms. Needle tapping the abdomen and draining the fluid will relieve the pressure temporarily.

Bacillary dysentery is a more dramatic, fulminating form of intestinal inflammation than intestinal flu (see *Gastroenteritis*). It is usually manifested by sudden onset of fever, prostration, *cramps, vomiting,* and foul-smelling *diarrhea* which may be bloody. Because it is due to a bacterium, the stools are more likely to have a dead, fetid, or putrid odor. The victim is more likely to go into shock or become dehydrated with this illness than with the viral intestinal flu. Typhoid fever would not be properly included here but only the diarrheas due to the *salmonella* or shigella groups of germs.

The disease is spread from human carriers to other humans usually because of crowded living conditions, flies, and poor sanitation. In the salmonella group, animals may be the chief source of infection.

If a patient seems quite ill with "intestinal flu," a stool culture might best be done to identify the germ responsible. Tests can be run to determine the most appropriate antibiotic or sulfa drug to be used for treatment.

Barium enema is the X-ray examination of the rectum and large bowel as the barium flows into the colon under fluoroscopic control. *Colitis, diverticula, intussusception, megacolon, malrotation,* and tumors are usually revealed by this method. A purge the day prior to the examination is standard; this removes much fecal material which might cloud the view.

Barium meal is the technique of using barium sulfate (radiopaque) in an X-ray examination. After its consumption by the patient, the radiologist observes the material as it moves through the *esophagus, stomach, duodenum,* and most of the small bowel. *Chalasia,* lesions of *esophagus, hiatal hernia, stomach* and *duodenal ulcers,* and tumors may be revealed.

Bezoars are balls of hair, fur, or fibers which may mat together in the stomach after ingestion. Most children swallow a few odds and ends of nonfood substances from the bed, clothing, or rugs, or will occasionally eat strands of their own hair. If they consume enough to form an obstructive ball which cannot be passed, surgery is required.

Symptoms of this rather rare problem are those of *cramps, anorexia, vomiting,* but a history of the peculiar eating habits would be the *sine qua non* for the diagnosis. Only strange children persist in this habit, so their minds must be straightened out as well as their stomachs.

Bile is secreted by the *liver* and flows into the *duodenum.* It serves to emulsify fats so they may be digested. It neutralizes acid from the stomach and has other digestive enzymes. The green pigment is the breakdown product of old red cells, and its presence or absence in the intestines is a reflection of the function of the liver. Babies usually have yellow stools because the pigment has been converted from green to yellow. Clay-colored or pale stools suggest the absence of bile, and usually are associated with jaundice and dark urine. Watery stools are often green because the pigment does not have a chance to be converted to the yellow color; food intolerance, *gastroenteritis,* or *dysentery* may produce green stools. Emesis containing bile indicates a more serious, surgical abdominal problem than does vomiting of only stomach contents.

Bile ducts are the canals which carry *bile* from the *liver* cells to the *gall bladder* and the *duodenum* (first segment of the small intestine). *Atresia,* absence, or *stenosis* of these ducts causes an obstruction to this free flow. This backup forces bile into the blood where the pigment causes jaundice or a yellow-green color of the skin. The stools are light in color because of the absence of bile; the urine is dark due to bile pigment. Surgical correction is possible in some of these cases, and it should be attempted for death is inevitable if bile cannot flow out of the liver.

The body conserves the bile salts it excretes into the intestine; they are almost completely reabsorbed during the passage to the *rectum.* They travel in the veins to the liver for reuse. Bile salts form units (micelles) with ingested *lipids* (fats), thus rendering them soluble.

Bleeding into the intestinal tract is difficult to pinpoint, as massive bleeding may come from a minute ulcer in the lining. (See *Gastric ulcer.*) The vomiting of fresh blood suggests swallowed blood from the nose or a mouth cut. If blood has been digested in the stomach, it looks like coffee grounds. A stomach ulcer might produce this, but it is rare.

Red blood on the surface of the stool suggests an *anal fissure.* If the blood is old, dark, and mixed with stool, bleeding from higher up is to be suspected. (*Gastric* or *duodenal ulcer, Meckel's diverticulum, intussusception, volvulus, colitis,* or *regional enteritis* might be considered.) Polyps and hemorrhoids are rare in infants, but would be a possible cause of bleeding as adulthood is approached. (One teaspoonful in the toilet bowl may look like a pint has been lost.)

Milk allergy can cause blood leakage from intestinal capillaries. Red, copious, frequent stools require immediate investigation, usually in a hospital; transfusion may be necessary. Upon surgical investigation,

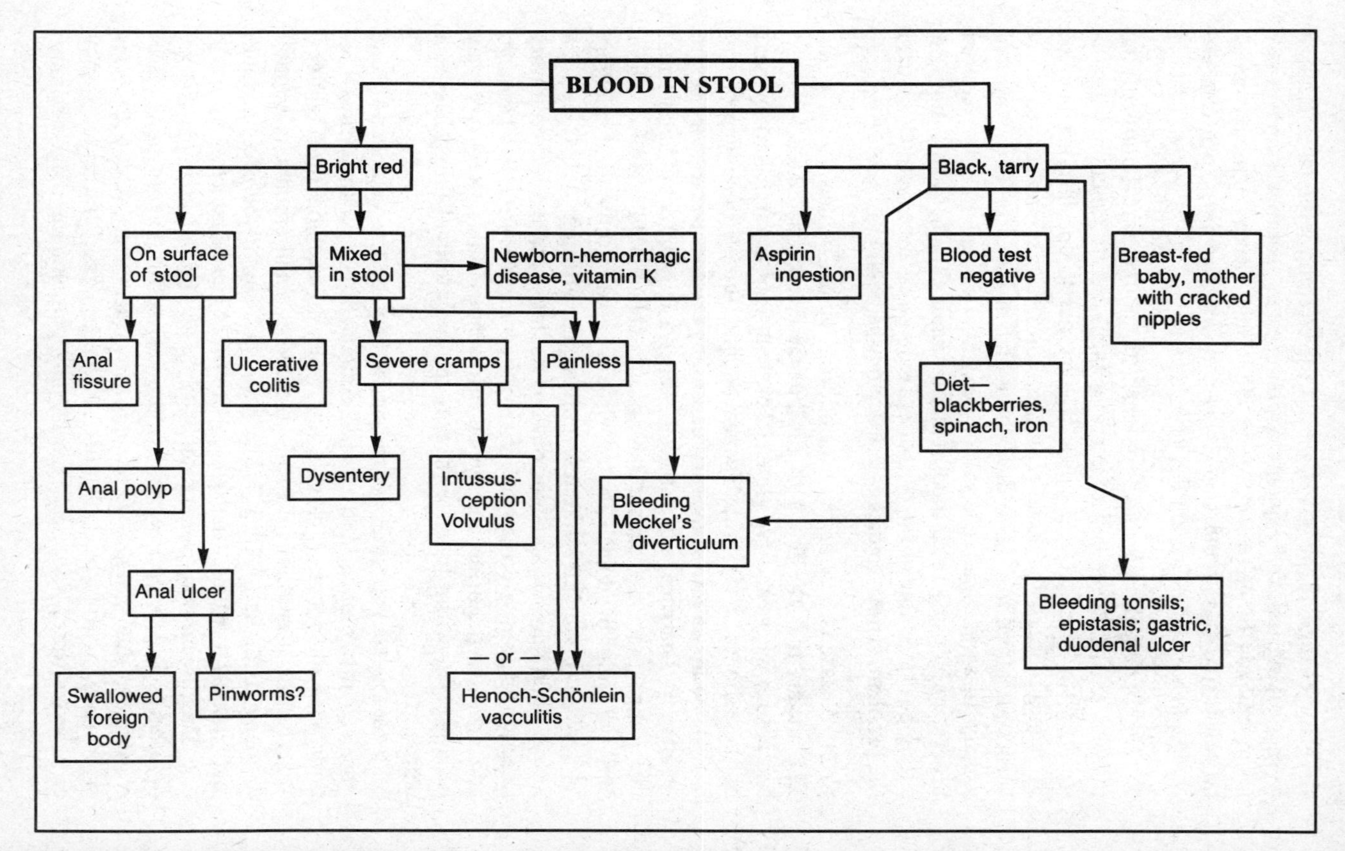
BLOOD IN STOOL
Bright red
Black, tarry
On surface of stool
Mixed in stool
Newborn-hemorrhagic disease, vitamin K
Aspirin ingestion
Blood test negative
Breast-fed baby, mother with cracked nipples
Anal fissure
Ulcerative colitis
Severe cramps
Painless
Diet— blackberries, spinach, iron
Anal polyp
Dysentery
Intussus-ception Volvulus
Bleeding Meckel's diverticulum
Anal ulcer
Bleeding tonsils; epistasis; gastric, duodenal ulcer
— or —
Swallowed foreign body
Pinworms?
Henoch-Schönlein vacculitis

the color change of the bowel wall at the bleeding level calls attention to the leaking lesion. Frequently careful search is unrewarding—there is no obvious blood vessel to tie off. Some bleeding diseases must be considered (low *prothrombin,* low *platelet, purpura*). (See *Henoch-Schönlein vasculitis,* Section 8.)

Cardioesophageal relaxation, or chalasia, is the rare failure of the muscles at the lower end of the esophagus (at its junction with the stomach) to constrict effectively. It gives rise to an alarming amount of regurgitation. The milk return is effortless and most frequently occurs after feedings when the baby is flat in the crib. This symptom usually disappears after eight or ten months, but can be reduced in severity by using thick foods and maintaining the baby in an upright sitting position most of the time after feedings. If these methods control the problem, X rays to diagnose it are not necessary.

Celiac disease is now better referred to as gluten-induced *enteropathy.* This means that the lining of the intestinal tract is unable to digest and absorb wheat and rye gluten, a protein—not a starch—component of these flours. It is probably genetic and thus a lifelong problem, but its manifestations may vary depending on age, being more severe in infancy. Diarrhea, malnutrition with wasted buttocks, but normal facial appearance are classic findings in a celiac child ingesting wheat and rye flour products. The stools are large, foamy, foul-smelling, and greasy, inasmuch as fat absorption is also affected.

A child may not show the obvious findings until a mild respiratory infection triggers a crisis, with severe *diarrhea, vomiting, dehydration,* and *acidosis,* requiring emergency intravenous fluids. Recovery may be slow even with gluten restriction, as the intestinal lining has been damaged.

Associated with the *malabsorption* may be the depletion of the *iron, calcium, protein,* and *vitamin* content of the blood. Growth retardation will occur if care is not taken to exclude these glutens. Wheat flour is especially difficult to avoid as small amounts are found in many foods as a "filler." The basic diet should be protein, milk, and bananas to which other gluten-free foods can be added.

The disease may be confused with *cystic fibrosis,* intestinal *allergy,* or other starch *malabsorption* syndromes. Most doctors lump cases of *diarrhea* into one of two categories: (a) infection due to virus or bacteria, or (b) allergy to milk, wheat, or eggs. "Intolerance" may be a better word. A variety of tests may pinpoint the diagnosis more accurately, among them a biopsy of intestinal lining using a tube passed orally.

Cholecystitis is inflammation of the *gall bladder.* It is rare in children, is usually associated with other bacterial infections, and acts like an intestinal obstruction (fever, pain, nausea, etc.). If the pain is localized, it occurs in the upper right side of the abdomen.

Cholelithiasis are *gall-bladder* stones and are rare in children. They would most likely be seen in children suffering from *sickle-cell anemia* or *spherocytosis* and would consist of *blood* pigments. They might be seen in the upper right side of the abdomen in an X ray taken for a lung or stomach condition. They would not be seen unless they contain calcium. Surgical removal is indicated because of high incidence of complications.

Cholera is a severe bacterial intestinal infection characterized by constant "rice-water stools" which rapidly cause *dehydration.* It is endemic in India and appears to spread east and west of that country during epidemics. Poor sanitation allows the disease to reappear frequently. Cholera-vaccine shots are recommended for travelers to these areas. *Tetracycline* and intravenous fluids are used for victims.

Chronic nonspecific diarrhea is the name given to the passage of three to ten big, sloppy stools a day without fever or other signs of illness. The child is happy, plays well, and even gains weight. No cause can be found. It usually begins as an ordinary attack of *gastroenteritis* with vomiting and diarrhea, but after the usual seven days it doesn't stop. Diet changes and constipating medicine (Kaopectate®) are of no value.

A temporary enzyme deficiency is blamed but is unproven. Sulfa drugs (triple sulfa suspension or Gantanol®) may give temporary relief, suggesting a bacterial infection although no pathological bacteria can be demonstrated in stool culture. A few intramuscular injections of B-complex vitamins will often revitalize the malfunctioning intestinal enzymes and normalize the stools in just a few days.

Cirrhosis is the loss of liver tissue by disease, injury, or drug and its replacement by scar tissue. The symptoms usually include *jaundice,* enlarged abdomen, weakness, *pruritus.* Some patients seem to have suffered only a mild form of *hepatitis* but they don't seem to recover.

Only 1 percent or 2 percent of hepatitis victims develop cirrhosis.

A specific liver test (SGPT) will reveal if hepatic damage is persistent. No specific therapy is indicated except rest, low fat, high carbohydrate diet, and avoidance of alcohol.

If an infant is born with stenosis of the bile ducts, the retained bile will scar the liver. If the obstruction can be relieved, the diseased liver will recover.

The liver may become cirrhotic as a result of or in association with *cystic fibrosis,* ulcerative *colitis, galactosemia, glycogen storage disease,* and the *lipidoses.*

Colitis, as the name implies, is an inflammation of the colon, the large intestine. Symptoms (mild or severe) include *cramps,* fever, *diarrhea* with or without blood, *dehydration,* and weight loss, depending on cause and natural host resistance.

Ulcerative colitis is a chronic inflammation of the large bowel characterized by exacerbations and remissions of bloody *diarrhea,* cramps, weakness, weight loss. The cause is largely unknown, but genetic, psychological, *allergic,* infectious factors are all considered as at least contributing to the continuation. Some disorder of immune mechanisms (body sensitive to itself, see *Autoimmunity,* Section 8) has been favored, because *cortisone* drugs and surgical removal of the colon have led to improvement.

At first the disease may act like any bowel upset, like *gastroenteritis* (intestinal flu), but as it progresses on to weight loss, *anemia, arthritis,* skin rashes, and severe *malnutrition*, it becomes obvious that a general bodily disease is present with bloody colitis as the chief manifestation. No pathogenic organism is grown from the stool cultures, and no source of infection is found in any corner of the body (tooth *abscess, sinusitis, tonsillitis*).

Examination with the sigmoidoscope reveals the inflamed colon that bleeds easily. A barium enema shows a narrow, shortened lumen. The patient is dependent, withdrawn, tense, and pathologically attached to the mother who becomes more tightly pulled into the child's emotional orbit. This psychological interdependence seems to enhance the continuation of the symptoms. It is not presently clear which is primary and which secondary.

Long-term care by pediatrician, surgeon, and psychiatrist is required for remission. Cure is never absolute; if control by *cortisone* drugs fails, surgery is usually advised well before the patient becomes a poor risk. Cancer of the bowel is a not uncommon complication.

Constipation is the passage of hard, usually dry, usually large stools. Constipation is determined by the consistency, not the *frequency.* The chief cause of constipation is the consumption of dairy products (milk, ice cream, and cheese) and foods low in roughage (usually white foods—breads, starches, potatoes, macaroni, rice, applesauce, bananas, etc.). These foods hold little moisture, so they become dry and packed by the time they get to the rectum.

(Inattention to the call of nature can lead to constipation, also.)

A child may withhold his movement because his last one was painful, thus setting up a cycle: the longer he holds it, the harder it gets, the more it hurts when he *does* go. He may refuse to defecate on command when he is being *toilet-trained* because of a stubborn, *passive-aggressive* attitude, and thus become constipated. His psychological refusal may allow a large fecal impaction to build up inside his *rectum,* causing *cramps* and irritability and occasionally a paradoxical leakage of soft stool around the mass, staining his underwear. (See *Encopresis,* Section 16.)

Dairy products and white foods must be eliminated from the diet; stool softeners, bulk laxatives, or milk of magnesia may be used. (These all take about three days to get down to where they will cause benefit.) Enemata and suppositories may be required to dislodge the first impacted portion. Occasionally the physician may have to insert his lubricated finger to break up and remove the big, dry chunks. These manipulations are painful and if repeatedly necessary can cause some psychological problems; it is better to soften the stools via the oral route.

Most breast-fed babies have loose, almost watery stools; frequently these babies pass them only once or twice a week. This is *not* constipation. Babies fed whole or homogenized milk are often constipated because the stomach acid produces a large curd when it contacts cow's milk. This curd becomes harder and drier until it may appear as a firm lump of clay at the rectum and crack the anal mucosa. One or two teaspoons of dark Karo® in each bottle may hold moisture. One half to one teaspoon of milk of magnesia in one bottle a day may keep the stool soft. Extra water usually only makes more urine. Addition of solid foods (not rice) may add roughage. Prune juice or grape juice may help. Cascara or castor oil are not recommended, because the bowel may become dependent on them. In general, as the baby approaches one year of age, milk should be reduced in amount. The two- to four-year-old eats very little, and hence has less bulk to pass. If he drinks a lot of milk, he may become severely constipated and may also develop anal fixations requiring psychological help later on.

The baby who develops *pyloric stenosis* usually has normal movements until vomiting has occurred for a few days, at which time the stools become hard and infrequent. Projectile vomiting in a month-old firstborn male in the springtime, who has developed scanty stools and urine, almost surely means pyloric stenosis.

Hypothyroid (cretin) babies are usually constipated.

Cyclic vomiting is the periodic, recurrent attack of violent emeses. At first it appears to be only a bout or two of *gastroenteritis* (intestinal flu), but when the attacks occur every few weeks and are not followed by diarrhea, some nervous-system disorder is possible. Children with this affliction are usually of a nervous, *hyperactive* disposition, and the attacks seem to be triggered by some emotion-charged event. As these children grow, the vomiting becomes less prominent, and headaches increase in intensity. A significant number of victims grow up to have *migraine* or at least sick headaches. There is a family history of this, usually on the mother's side. Efforts to tie this condition in with *epilepsy* have been fruitless.

It is felt that the victims of this condition are unable to mobilize sugar from *glycogen*. Under stress they burn up fat for energy and become acidotic, which induces vomiting. Ketones are found in the urine for a few hours prior to vomiting, so a suspicious mother might test the urine for them. If ketones are present, a strong sedative plus a sugary drink may abort an attack. Treatment after the attack begins consists of antiemetic suppositories (*Phenergan®, Thorazine®, Compazine®*). Treating the victims for hypoglycemia with frequent feedings and extra B-complex vitamins usually cuts down on the frequency and severity of the attacks.

Cystic fibrosis—see Section 9

Diarrhea is the passage of frequent, loose, or watery—usually bile-colored—stools. In our country it is most commonly due to a virus, and the disease is called intestinal flu (see *Gastroenteritis*). People who live in countries with poor sanitation facilities are more likely to have bacterial dysenteries due to *salmonella,* shigella, *typhoid, cholera,* or *amebic dysentery.* It is dangerous in infants, because of their susceptibility to dehydration and salt imbalance.

Diarrhea in the first few weeks of life is most likely due to a milk allergy (a breast-fed baby may be allergic to the cow's milk in the mother's diet), a fat intolerance, or a congenital absence of one of the sugar enzymes (see *Malabsorption*).

After this age, viral intestinal flu is the most common cause, although many children will have a few loose, explosive stools at the onset of a viral respiratory infection. Ten to twenty percent of children will develop diarrhea upon oral ingestion of antibiotics used for other infections. One wonders if the medicine is being flushed out without being absorbed and hence is not being utilized to treat the original disease.

Intestinal flu, *gastroenteritis,* the "virus that's going around," lasts seven days in children. If it lasts longer, it suggests a bacterial infection, a temporary absence of the sugar-digesting enzymes, or that the flu has "stirred up an allergy" to some food that was safe before.

The treatment is fluids containing diluted, suitable salts. Boiled skimmed milk must be diluted with at least the same quantity of water, or too much sodium will be consumed. Tea, gelatin water, bouillon, cola drinks are the safest of the fluids. White foods—bread, starches, banana, rice, applesauce—are the only foods to be offered during the week; anything else adds fuel to the fire.

Remedies containing kaolin and pectin may hold the stool together a little, but will not stop the inevitable seven-day course. Whatever is used on the sixth day will be credited with stopping the flu on the seventh. Anticramp medicine (*paregoric*) may make the victim comfortable. Most children have intestinal flu at least once a year; as they grow and develop immunity, the disease is less severe. Most adults call it the one-day flu because they can shuck it off faster than an infant.

Attention must be paid to hydration if diarrhea is accompanied by fever and *vomiting.* Antivomiting tranquilizing suppositories will depress the vomiting center of the brain and allow the baby to retain fluids. If the baby can hold up his head, smile occasionally, and urinate two or three times a day, he probably can get by, but responsibility for his care should be shared with a physician. Intravenous fluids should be considered if fever, *vomiting,* and lethargy are present as *dehydration* (Section 10) may lead to *acidosis* and irreversible changes in *brain, kidneys,* and *liver.*

Mild diarrhea—home treatment. Give nothing by mouth until *vomiting* is no longer occurring; then give a water-sugar-*electrolyte*

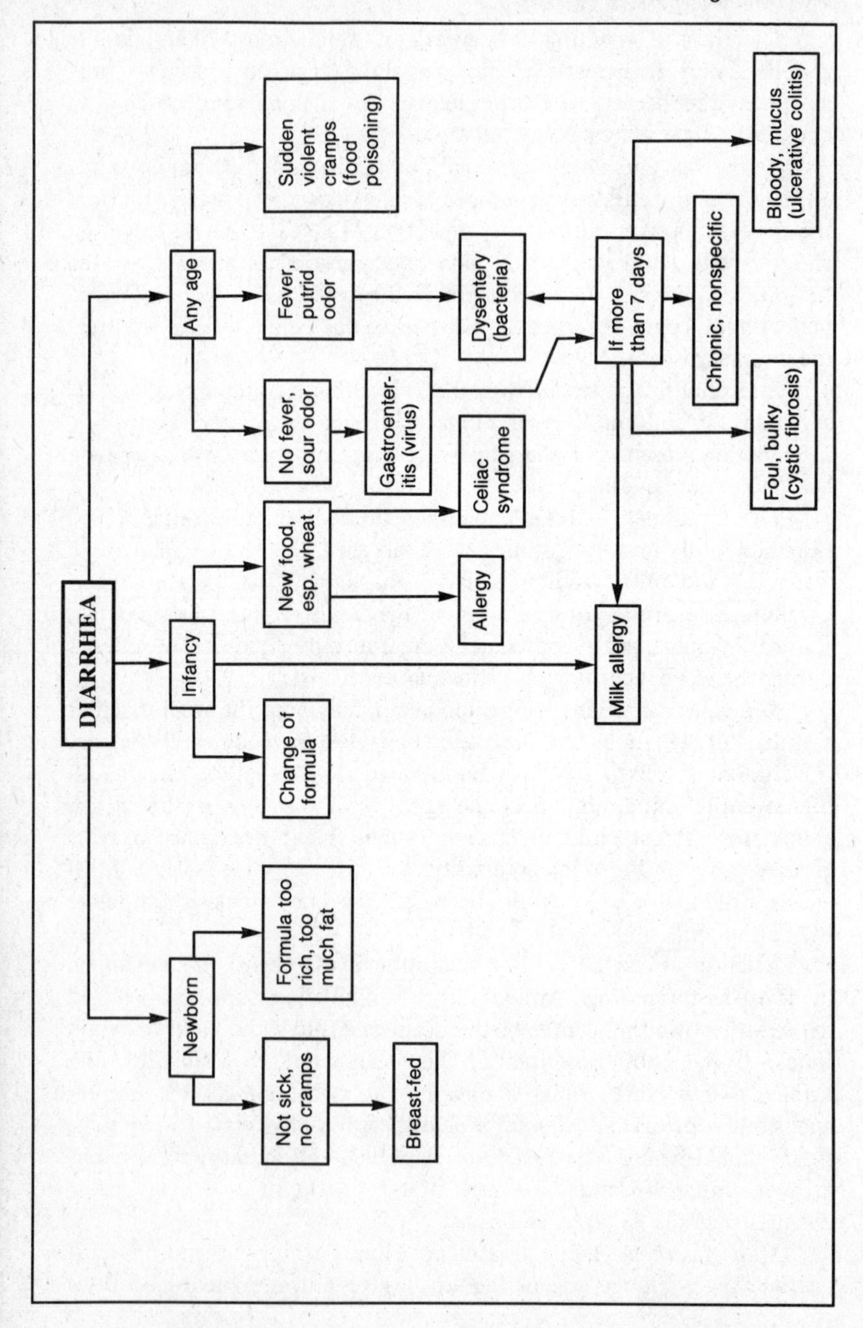
DIARRHEA
Newborn
Not sick, no cramps
Breast-fed
Formula too rich, too much fat
Infancy
Change of formula
New food, esp. wheat
Allergy
Celiac syndrome
Milk allergy
Any age
No fever, sour odor
Gastroenteritis (virus)
Fever, putrid odor
Dysentery (bacteria)
Sudden violent cramps (food poisoning)
If more than 7 days
Foul, bulky (cystic fibrosis)
Chronic, nonspecific
Bloody, mucus (ulcerative colitis)

solution (6 ounces of water, 1 teaspoon of sugar, and a pinch of salt). One ounce of this should be given every one half to one hour for six to twelve hours. Try to get a quart of this down in a twenty-four hour period. On the second day give four to eight ounces of this solution three times a day; then four to eight ounces of unboiled, half skimmed milk and half water three times a day. The third day change to skimmed milk (do not boil); on the fourth day give whole milk or formula. If symptoms are immediately exacerbated, a nonmilk (soy or meat) formula might be tried while awaiting the seven-day period to pass.

Breast-fed babies have loose, sloppy, almost watery stools which should, however, be yellow, infrequent, and have only a faint acid odor. Some babies have four of five of these a day; some have only two a week. If they do not fit into this pattern, the mother should alter *her* diet.

Various foods may cause loose stools, either because of an *allergy* or because of sugars they contain. Such stools would be obvious within six to twelve hours after ingestion of the offender; a diet calendar may be helpful to pinpoint it. Milk, usually constipating, is probably the most common cause of diarrhea, but wheat (see *Celiac disease*), eggs, nuts, fish, chocolate, green vegetables, pork, corn, and citrus could be irritants. (See *Gastrointestinal allergy.*)

Psychologically induced diarrhea must be considered in a tense, overly restricted child who is not allowed physical and/or verbal release of energy and frustration—or in a child who is simply nervous about some approaching event—school, etc. (also see *Malabsorption*).

Diarrhea (tourist's—la turista) is a mild intestinal disorder lasting a day or two that occurs in many people traveling abroad. It usually occurs in the first week of the visit and is ascribed variously to new foods, chemical, and biological irritants, and according to one Mexican physician, "imponderable psychogenic factors." Doctors in foreign countries are understandably disturbed by the American's insistence that poor sanitation is the cause of this inconvenience. Studies in Mexico, at least, reveal a low incidence of shigella or *salmonella.* It is noteworthy that the same temporary, nonpathological condition occurs in foreigners visiting the United States.

Disaccharide enzyme deficiencies are a rare cause of digestive malfunction. Because starch and sucrose (cane sugar) and lactose (milk sugar) are eaten almost daily by humans, inadequate amounts of the enzymes to break these foods into absorbable monosaccharides will quickly lead to *gas,* bloat, distention, and *diarrhea.*

The condition is genetically determined, and symptoms may be chronic, but a temporary loss of enzyme activity may follow a bout of intestinal flu.

Negroes and Orientals are more likely to be deficient in lactase, so they may become severely ill and assume their "friends" in the U.S.A. furnishing foreign aid have sent them "bad" skimmed-milk powder.

Diverticulitis is almost never seen in children. It is an inflammation of a diverticulum (outpouching from colon—like an appendix) and if present may require surgery.

Duodenal ulcer has been found more frequently in children of late, because doctors look for it more when confronted with a patient who has upper midabdominal pain. Too, X-ray diagnosis has become more accurate, so the lesion is found more easily. Some authorities feel that children are under more stress now than formerly, and the ulcer is the end result of the patient's inability to cope with stress-anger-frustration.

Actually an ulcer-oriented doctor discovered that ulcers *do* occur in children and told the rest of us, who now order more barium-meal stomach X rays—and hence, more ulcers are discovered. Usually behind a child's ulcer there is a family history.

An ulcer may occur in association with severe burns, injuries, and infections. Stomach (or gastric) ulcers are very rare, but duodenal ulcers (in the segment of small bowel connected to the stomach) increase in frequency with age.

Upper abdominal pain usually at night, before meals or at least on an empty stomach, is the usual symptom suggesting the condition, but the pain may be about the navel. *Blood*—usually black—in the stools would require an X-ray evaluation. Often an irritable duodenum is the only X-ray finding.

Frequent feedings—six to eight meals a day—with antacids and dairy products is the chief therapy. Some reorganization of the emotional climate in the home is required. Pain should subside within a few days. The condition is chronic, and recurrences are common.

EEG studies done on children with duodenal ulcers revealed the majority to have brain wave abnormalities. This neurophysiologic weakness might make the patient more susceptible to the ulcer.

Most observers of these ulcer-prone children find body tension, conscientiousness, overt compliance but intense underlying, unexpressed hostility, feelings of inadequacy, discomfiture when expressing hostile feelings, and need for approval by becoming servile and dependent. Many children try to excel for a demanding teacher. They frequently come from rigid homes where high value is placed on achievement.

Many children with ulcers are trying to fulfill unmet dependency needs from a mother who was cold, rejecting, or at best indifferent. (Genetic susceptibility coupled with this environment seems to be necessary to produce the ulcer.) The incidence is about four boys to one girl. Headaches are often related (50 percent in one group studied); they subside when the ulcer pain is gone. As Henry Maudsley said, "The sorrow that has no vent in tears may make other organs weep." (See *Gastric ulcer.*)

Dysentery—see *Bacillary dysentery*

Echinococcus cyst is the larval stage in man for the dog tapeworm. Somehow man ingests the eggs the dog passes. The larvae invade the system and colonize a cyst which over many years may grow to two- to three-inch size. Spillage or removal may cause spread of the organisms or fatal shock. The *liver, brain,* and *lungs* may have these cysts. (See *Skin test,* Section 6.)

Enema is removal of stool from the *rectum* by hydraulic pressure. Fluid (water, salt solution, or oil) is forced into the rectum, hopefully above the stool. This stretches the wall of the intestine, which responds by contracting, and thus the stool is pushed out.

In past centuries this was a common practice used to eliminate wastes from the body. Increased knowledge of diet has largely eliminated the need for such a procedure except in some disease states (*megacolon,* old age) or for preparation for X rays or surgery.

Constipation is better treated by the oral route (eliminating constipating foods, use of magnesia salts, bulk *laxatives, psyllium seed,* or—least used—*mineral oil*) as it is felt, especially in children, that undue attention to this area may lead to some psychic distortion. Reports of rectal perforation are not uncommon. Large amounts of plain water may lead to water intoxication *(cerebral edema),* for the large bowel very efficiently absorbs water. High, hot, and heavy enemata given to a victim of *appendicitis* have been known to burst the appendix even though it is five feet away.

However, a rectal insertion of six ounces of water plus two pinches of salt might rehydrate a vomiting infant.

A struggling child might be given an enema better by placing him face down (prone) on a chair by the bathtub so his legs are hanging down into the tub. The operator can see what is being done more easily and also be able to place his knee on the child's back to stabilize the moving target. Some type of lubricant facilitates the passage of the enema tip. (Fleet® enemata come ready to use; they are disposable.)

Enterobiasis—see *Pinworms*

Enteropathy—see *Celiac disease*

Esophagus is the tube connecting the throat and the stomach. It is the most narrow passageway encountered in the digestive process and the one most likely to cause problems for infants who swallow almost anything they can put in their mouths. If the mother is positive that the object was swallowed, if there are no symptoms, and if the child can swallow some food without immediate regurgitation, the object probably has reached the stomach; if the foreign object can arrive in the stomach, it will usually make the remaining journey without incident. Straining the stools may be rewarding if parents are that curious or if the object is valuable enough to warrant it; most parents do nothing unless symptoms of abdominal distress are noted. If the child suddenly refuses food or chokes or vomits at mealtime, an object in the esophagus should be considered.

X rays will demonstrate its position if it is radiopaque. A bit of barium-soaked cotton in some food would lodge on a nonopaque (plastic or leather) object and reveal the level of obstruction.

Esophagitis is an inflammation or infection of the esophagus. It may be common, but is usually associated with other diseases whose symptoms would draw attention away from the esophagus itself.

Corrosive esophagitis is an obviously sore, raw, bleeding esophagus following the ingestion of chemicals that eat away the lining. Lye, acids, especially drain cleaners and electric-dishwashing soap, will burn the gullet. Before the doctor is called, the mother must pour down the child's throat as much water as possible, even to the point of vomiting. A quart would be ideal. No effort is made to neutralize the chemical; just dilute it with water as fast as possible. (See *Alkalis,* in Poisons, Section 1.)

It heals of course, but scar tissue about the esophagus will frequently constrict and cause narrowing or obstruction to the passage of food. Intravenous feedings, *antibiotics, cortisone* may all be lifesaving at first, but dilation of the narrowed esophagus by passing catheters may be necessary to keep the lumen open. If no opening is present, the surgeon may be able to fashion a functioning gullet from a loop of intestine, thus connecting the throat with the stomach.

Fluke infections are due to invasion of flatworms. (See *Schistosomiasis.*)

Food allergy—see *Gastrointestinal allergy*

Food poisoning is the nonspecific term applied to a variety of food-borne toxins, bacteria, *viruses,* or *parasites.* The health department usually finds that some break in good, clean, food management is responsible or that one of the food handlers is a salmonella carrier.

Botulism is a severe, frequently fatal disease resulting from the ingestion of the poison produced by the *Clostridium botulinum* germ.

Seventy-five percent of the cases are due to home-canned food, obviously inadequately prepared. String beans are a likely offender, but beets, vichyssoise, spinach, peas, and chicken have all been responsible for botulism when improper canning methods have been employed.

The germ *C. botulinum* is found in the soil in all parts of the world; food grown in such soil can be contaminated. There is extremely little danger in foods that are commercially canned, since canning methods are so standardized and controlled, but home canning with unsterilized containers and without sufficient pressure can lead to lethal results. The spores of the botulinus are extremely hardy and can survive as much as six hours of boiling or fifteen pounds of pressure for six minutes. However, fifteen minutes of boiling in an open vessel will destroy the toxin even though the spore may still survive.

The disease may appear as an intestinal upset and then progress to muscle *paralysis,* double vision, trouble swallowing and talking, respiratory paralysis (possibly requiring an iron lung), and death.

This neurotropic (affinity for nerve tissue) toxin can be neutralized by a specific antibotulinum serum or antitoxin.

Clostridium perfringens is widespread in the feces of man and animals. A recent investigation of raw meat uncovered positive tests for this bacterium in over 50 percent of the samples. Adequate cooking is the common-sense control measure. Beef is the chief repository for this germ.

In a study done following an outbreak, rather characteristic findings resulted. One hundred people were served at a banquet. The four who did not eat the chicken salad had no symptoms. Of the ninety-six who did, seventy-five became ill twelve to fifteen hours later with *cramps* and *diarrhea,* but no fever. The duration of the symptoms was eight to twelve hours. Symptoms appear later than in *staphylococcus* food poisoning but sooner than in *Salmonella* infection and do not last as long. It causes fewer attacks, but affects a higher percentage of those exposed. It is not serious, but it should be recognized, because some of these infections come from nationally distributed canned foods, and the distribution must be stopped.

Salmonella infections (see *Bacillary dysentery*) are usually manifested by fever, *vomiting,* smelly *diarrhea,* and prostration. The responsible bacterium may come from another person or animal, or may grow and remain for long periods of time in meat, milk, and eggs. Recently, powdered eggs were found to be contaminated; pet turtles may have the disease (who can tell?) and spread it to the household. It is more easily spread in warm, summer weather. It is the most common cause of food poisoning. A recent outbreak affected nine thousand people before it was controlled.

The symptoms may be mild or severe, sudden or slow in onset, but fever, stomachache, and *vomiting* suggest the infection. Usually the *white blood count* is elevated, the stools are foul-smelling, and the patient is sicker than he is with *gastroenteritis.* Ampicillin is the drug of choice. Stool cultures indicate when a cure has been effected. Some people become carriers.

Staphylococcal food poisoning accounts for 25 percent of food poisoning cases, and is produced by a toxin elaborated by some strains of the staphylococcus. The bacteria grow in custards, ham, beef, fish, chicken, and salads improperly prepared and allowed to stand without refrigeration before consumption. The violent vomiting, *cramps,* and *diarrhea* appear within a few hours of ingestion. Severe prostration may require intravenous fluids. Symptoms abate in another few hours.

Foreign bodies in the stomach, such as buttons, marbles, small toys, beads, bits of bone, coins, are easily passed. The narrowest passageway is the esophagus (the tube from throat to stomach); if the object arrives in the stomach, the remainder of the journey is usually routine. If a child has swallowed an object and can then consume and swallow some cereal or bread, the esophagus is assumed to be open. Usually no X rays or worry are indicated. I observed a six-year-old girl who was able to swallow a quarter with some tears and substernal chest pain. Eating was normal for a day or so until she began to have some nausea and upper right abdominal pain. An X ray revealed the coin stuck at the pylorus (exit from the stomach). A day or two of atropine relaxed the muscles there, and the quarter passed on.

Pins, needles, sharp bones, and small open safety pins may drop straight into the stomach from the mouth, but be unable to make the turns in the small bowel. Stomach pain, tenderness, and fever suggest impingement and penetration through the wall. Surgery is indicated. The paucity of complications suggests that the bowel wall recoils from the sharp point as the object tumbles on down (like a worm retracting from a sharp stick). The object may have scratched the throat on the way down and allowed the patient to believe it is still stuck there.

Gall bladder is the storage sack for *bile.* It is tucked under the *liver* in the upper right side of the *abdomen.* It is rarely a problem in children. (See *Cholecystitis* and *Cholelithiasis.*) If bowel and liver problems have been ruled out, persistent problems in this area of the abdomen would suggest gall-bladder disease.

Gas may be produced by the action of gas-forming bacteria (*Clostridia*). As everyone knows, bean products produce a large amount of gas (carbon dioxide and hydrogen). Some *antibiotics* will destroy these gas-forming bacteria.

Flatulence from certain foods is common and evil-smelling (see Food Allergy Checklist); gasses may be absorbed from the colon and exhaled from the *lungs,* producing a foul breath. The bowel mucosa has the ability to blush as easily as the cheeks, and fullness, cramps, and flatulence may be enhanced. Most gas comes from swallowed air, but some is diffused into the lumen from the bloodstream and some by bacterial action. Eighty percent of swallowed air is nitrogen which is poorly absorbed into the bloodstream and must travel through the intestines to be eliminated as gas. Carbon dioxide, oxygen, and methane will be absorbed and exhaled in the lungs.

Air swallowers may be helped by exhaling before swallowing. Belching aids may prevent the gas from passing from the stomach to bowel. (One tablespoon of apple-cider vinegar in a small glass of water is a belch aid.)

Some people have gas because of too much acid; others because of too little acid. *Acidophilus bifidus,* a friendly bacterium, can help the intestines digest food instead of letting it sit and ferment.

Gastric hemorrhage may be due to an ulcer, *hemophilia, purpura,* lack of *vitamin K, scurvy, leukemia, neoplasm,* and the late effects of *cirrhosis* of the liver. The most common cause of a bloody emesis is swallowed blood from a nose bleed or following a tonsillo-adenoidectomy. If blood bounces right back, it will be red, but if allowed to digest, it appears the color of coffee grounds when vomited and loose tar when defecated.

Gastric ulcer, or stomach ulcer, is being diagnosed in children more frequently now, since doctors are aware that it occurs in the pediatric age group. New, skillful radiological techniques make it possible to find it more easily. Frequently its first manifestation is in an infant who has a bloody emesis or a tarry, black stool (melena) without pain. (The more frequent duodenal ulcer usually appears in the older child or adolescent and is heralded by upper midabdominal pain on an empty stomach.) A family history of ulcers or at least of "dyspepsia" is usually noted. Frequently ulcers are found in compulsive, competitive, need-to-win types of people. The child is often neat and ritualistic from birth, and these traits are reinforced by parental drives to squeeze success out of the child. Many doctors are convinced that there is a genetic ulcer type and that stomach symptoms are part of the personality makeup and not totally the result of some environmental mechanism.

A bland diet and antacids are routine. The condition may be controlled, but usually not cured. Uncontrolled bleeding caused by the ulcer eroding into a blood vessel or perforation of the ulcer completely through the wall of the stomach requires immediate surgical intervention. (See *Duodenal ulcer.*)

Gastritis is an inflammation of the *stomach,* usually caused by a *virus* and usually associated with *gastroenteritis.* It may follow a severe burn or infection or cortisone therapy. It may be seen with *chickenpox* or *scarlet fever;* the patient may vomit blood associated with his stomachache. *Aspirin* can erode the stomach lining if taken repeatedly, causing moderate blood loss. Iron-medicine overdose will usually cause bleeding as will caustic *alkalis.* (See Section 1.)

Gastroenteritis is a *virus* inflammation of the stomach and small and large bowel, which is the most common infection—next to the common cold—seen in the pediatric age group. It has a characteristic pattern. *Vomiting* and nausea occur periodically for twenty-four hours, with or without fever. Simultaneously or on the second day, *cramps* and *diarrhea* occur which last about a week. Most children have this disease about once a year. As they get older and develop immunity, the body is able to shake it off sooner. The adult usually has the condition only one day—hence the term "one-day flu." (See *Diarrhea.*)

It is difficult to differentiate it from a Salmonella infection (see *Food poisoning*), and occasionally *appendicitis* acts in a similar manner. With the flu the pain is usually cramping (off and on) and the abdomen is soft between spasms. In conditions requiring surgery, the pain is constant and abdominal palpation is painful.

Gastrointestinal allergy is a term loosely applied to the inflammation of the intestines following ingestion of specific foods (see Food Allergy Checklist). The convenience of the term to explain *gas, diarrhea, cramps,* bloody stools, may delay a more accurate determination of a more specific disease. Lactase deficiency, gluten-induced *enteropathy, cystic fibrosis,* may appear to be *allergies,* but are the result of enzyme deficiencies. It is interesting to see, however, what appears to be an intestinal wheat allergy in a baby disappear when he is two, only to reappear as a nasal allergy to grass pollens when he is three.

Conditions variously related to food allergies include *cheilitis* (from contact), *angioedema* of lips, palate, *stomatitis* (mouth inflammation), recurrent canker sores (*herpes* virus triggered by an allergy), *hay fever, asthma,* edema and spasm of throat, hoarseness, nausea, dyspepsia, *vomiting,* cramping, fullness, *gas, diarrhea, constipation,* mucus in stool, and *pruritus ani.*

Response to the food may be immediate—sometimes even before the food is swallowed. The whole protein is more likely to be involved in this reaction; fish, seafoods, berries, nuts, and egg white are the common allergens. Skin tests are fairly reliable in these cases.

A delayed response to ingested foods occurs after a few hours or up to a day or so. Wheat, corn, milk, eggs, beef, pork, white potato, oranges, chocolate, and legumes are more likely to cause delayed reactions as some breakdown product of the food protein is the usual offender. Children often absorb food proteins before complete digestion; this is supposed to account for the greater frequency of food allergies in the younger age group. Skin tests are not reliable if the body reaction stems from food breakdown products.

Ragweed-sensitive people are often sensitive to melons; grass pollen-allergic people seem to be more sensitive to cereal foods, although a different part of the plant is responsible.

Confusion in establishing the diagnosis is related to the following:

1. Cooked foods may be safe but raw ones dangerous. (Toast is okay, bread bad.)
2. Quantity is a factor. (Two strawberries are okay; six cause hives.)
3. Cumulative effect. (Daily bacon; gas on Sunday.)
4. Concomitant effect. (Milk okay; milk and wheat, gas.)

An elimination diet must be adhered to for three weeks; choices are made from the safe list. If symptoms are gone, then add one new food every four days. (See *Tension fatigue,* Section 15; *Allergy,* Section 3; *Colic,* Section 11.)

FOOD ALLERGY CHECKLIST

Foods Most Likely to Cause Trouble

Milk
Cottage cheese
Ice cream
Chocolate
Wheat
Corn
Fish
Eggs
Berries (especially strawberries)
Pork
Green vegetables
Citrus fruits and tomatoes
Vitamins
Spices
Garlic
Onions
Nuts

Safest Foods

Veal
Beef
Lamb
Rice
Barley
Applesauce
Bananas
Pears
Yellow vegetables

Giardiasis is the intestinal upset—weakness, cramps, diarrhea—assumed to be due to the protozoa, *Giardia lamblia.* It is transmitted from person to person by unwashed food and flies. It is not a clear-cut pathological agent, as many children have it in their stools, but have no symptoms.

It is, however, easily eliminated by use of Atabrine® or Flagyl®.

Glutamic oxaloacetic transaminase (GOT) is an enzyme found in *heart, liver,* and muscle. When cells are destroyed—as in *hepatitis*—large amounts are released into the blood. A test for this helps confirm disease in the heart, muscle, or liver but the enzyme is nonspecific. A patient with a low-grade fever and a dull ache in the liver area might have hepatitis. If these symptoms are accompanied by *jaundice,* the diagnosis is almost certain; if jaundice is not present, an elevated serum GOT helps to confirm it.

Glutamic pyruvic transaminase (GPT) is a similar enzyme, but is concentrated in liver cells and might be a more reliable test of liver-cell destruction or disease.

Gluten-induced enteropathy—see *Celiac disease*

Glycogen storage disease, von Gierke's disease, is a genetically determined condition in which glycogen is stored in abnormal amounts in the *liver* and *kidney* cells. This glycogen cannot be degraded into its glucose parts due to an *enzyme* lack. These patients have enlarged *livers* (swollen with glycogen) and low blood sugar or *hypoglycemia* (the glucose is all stored in the glycogen molecules in the liver cells). Their principal source of energy, then, is fat, and when fat is utilized, fatty acids, *ketosis,* and *acidosis* result.

The disease usually sneaks up on the victim, and the enlarged liver, *dwarfism, hypoglycemia* (with drowsiness and *convulsions*) become manifest in the second or third year. (See *Glycogen,* Sections 7, 8, and 10.)

Heartburn is the sensation of burning (occasionally described as heat, fullness, *gas,* distress) at the lower end of the sternum (breastbone). There is almost never anything wrong with the heart. It is assumed that stomach acid is being regurgitated up into the esophagus to create the sensation; in this situation the victim usually describes a mobile pain that moves up the chest into the throat. It may or may not be associated with stomach contents rolling up into the throat (on bending or lying down). It may be found in the pregnant woman whose stomach is distorted by the swollen uterus. If liquid antacids relieve it, acid is assumed to be the offender. Food *allergies* (milk, pork, chocolate, and others) may produce the sensation.

If the victim states his pain does not move, then a *neuritis* may be blamed or at least a nervous condition—the tight feeling before Monday school in the tense, worried child (see *Duodenal ulcer*).

Some people feel heartburn with little demonstrable stomach acid; some notice it only after a bout of unresolved anger or hostility. It sometimes runs in families.

Persistent distress suggests the advisability of a *barium meal* to rule out an ulcer or *hiatus hernia* (a portion of the stomach knuckles into the lower part of the chest).

Hematemesis is vomiting of blood. It usually follows swallowing of blood from a bloody nose. Nursing infants sucking from a cracked nipple will often get enough blood to cause vomiting. If these causes are ruled out, and no foreign object is responsible, then an ulcer in the stomach *(Gastric ulcer)* may be *bleeding,* or the child may have consumed corrosive poisons, *iron* tablets, or *aspirin,* or esophageal varices may have opened.

Hemorrhoids are distended veins protruding at the anal opening. They are so rare in children that, if suspected, some venous obstruction in the pelvis must be sought. Although many children are constipated, the hard stools and straining to defecate rarely result in hemorrhoids. *Fissures* are more common, and when they heal, a skin tag may form at the *anal* opening that may be mistaken for a hemorrhoid.

Hepatitis is a *virus* inflammation of the *liver.* Two types are recognized. Infectious hepatitis (IH) is passed from person to person mainly by the oral route and takes about a month to manifest itself after exposure. Serum hepatitis (SH) is passed by the injection of contaminated blood fluids or needles; the virus is carried by the bloodstream to the liver. It shows itself about two months (or more) after the virus is introduced to the host. Immunity to one form does not provide immunity to the other. *Gamma-globulin* administration will attenuate IH but not SH.

The liver shows destruction of cells and inflammation throughout. New cells regenerate, fortunately, in the majority of cases.

The patient usually feels as if he has stomach flu because the initial symptoms are nausea, *vomiting,* stomachache, fever, and occasionally *diarrhea.* The stomachache is usually high up under the right rib edge and is dull and constant. (A flu stomachache is usually at the navel and cramping.) After a few days of sickness, the patient begins to feel a little better, only to notice that his eyeballs are yellow. *Jaundice* and a tender *liver* in an other wise healthy child almost surely mean IH. (In the elderly, *gall-bladder* disease, pancreas cancer, and *cirrhosis* must be considered.) The urine becomes deeply yellow because of the bile that backs up into the circulation. The stools may be light in color.

Prophylactic gamma globulin is indicated for travelers in Africa, Asia, Central America, South America, the Philippines, and South Pacific Islands. (Australia and New Zealand apparently are not endemic.)

It is estimated that for every one patient with obvious IH (jaundice and tender liver), nine patients have a mild case that is assumed to be flu. These latter only have weakness, nausea, heavy abdominal feeling for a week or two, and recover. No harm has been done if they recover without an official diagnosis.

The patient should be allowed to be active after the fever and weakness have diminished. An army doctor once put a group of men back to duty when signs of acute inflammation had passed and noted no difference in the ultimate outcome of these men as compared to another similar group required to stay quietly in the hospital ward.

The contagious period with IH is probably the two weeks preceding the height of the illness (fever, tender liver, jaundice), and the patient may shed virus for two to four weeks after this. Food handlers, teachers, and children are usually allowed to return to their jobs or school three weeks after the onset of symptoms, although the virus can still be recovered from their stools. It is now felt that some patients carry the virus for months or years, and chronic hepatitis with gradual liver-cell destruction and scarring may occur. Big doses of vitamin C (10 to 20 grams a day) are now used by many to help the body fight off this virus. The patient is encouraged to move out of bed as much as is comfortable; complete bed rest only serves to weaken the patient further and retard convalescence. Patients are usually away from school or play for three weeks and may be "out of sorts" for a month afterward.

Gamma globulin is recommended only for the household contacts of IH patients. Severely ill patients might be helped with cortisone drugs.

SH patients are not contagious as no virus can be demonstrated in the stools. Prophylactic gamma globulin does not seem to be effective in protecting a patient inoculated with SH.

Hernia is the extrusion of body contents from the normal location into another area. Almost all are in the abdominal cavity. Pressure plus weakness in the muscle wall allow loops of bowel to push out.

Diaphragmatic hernia—see Section 5

Epigastric hernia is located in the midline between the navel and the sternum (breast bone). It is small and painful as it may pinch a nerve. It is demonstrated by straining. Surgery is the solution.

Femoral hernia is a protrusion of an intestinal loop into the upper front area of the thigh, just below the groin crease. A mass appears and disappears depending on intra-abdominal pressure. Surgery is indicated. It is a rare condition in children.

Hiatus hernia is the protrusion of a portion of the stomach up through the *diaphragm* into the chest. It was formerly thought to be rare in children, but more skillful X rays now are able to demonstrate this lesion. Heartburn and pain low in the front of the chest suggest the problem. Children frequently have nocturnal cough (stomach contents rolling up the esophagus and irritating the *trachea*). Frequent *bronchitis* and *asthma* may be associated with the regurgitation.

If medical management is unsuccessful, surgery is frequently curative.

Inguinal hernia is more common in boys than girls because the openings in the lower part of the abdomen which hold the sperm ducts provide a natural pathway for a loop of bowel to tunnel through. Some are as small as a half inch; some are huge enough to push into the scrotum. The mother might notice a squishy lump in the groin just to the left or right of the base of the penis. It would swell out on crying and recede after a nap.

Few symptoms are noted except fussiness; an intuitive mother might feel that her child is fretful—he is vaguely uncomfortable. These hernias must be surgically repaired, regardless of the paucity of symptoms, as trusses are worthless and an occasional hernia becomes stuck or *incarcerated,* requiring an emergency operation. In the latter case the lump would be hard and tender, and the infant would be screaming with pain and perhaps vomiting. Surgery is always indicated, whether for a ten-day-old baby or a hundred-year-old man.

If a female develops an inguinal hernia, it is often associated with an ovary, as this organ is close to the inguinal canal.

Umbilical hernia develops after birth if the opening previously occupied by the cord vessels does not close sufficiently. Fibrous and elastic tissue surrounding this opening should cinch the hole up tight like a purse string. If the opening is not closed, slight crying or straining will push a loop of bowel into this skin sac, often with an alarming gurgle. It is *not* due to improper cord ligation done in the delivery room. Parents, of course, are sure that this huge (as big as a fist, occasionally) balloon will burst, and intestines will fall out. This does not happen, although these ugly bags will enlarge until about one year of age, at which time the surrounding muscles will tend to close the navel hiatus. Some parents prefer to have this area taped so that they won't have to look at it. To tape it properly, the skin from each side must be pulled together over the defect so that it will act as a plug for the hole. The closing will always take place spontaneously, although it may take up to four years to do so. The chief job of the pediatrician and parents is to keep these babies away from the surgeon; he likes to operate and will be likely not to wait for it to disappear spontaneously. Some surgeons will compromise; if it is getting larger at age two years, operate. A small defect in a girl at two years of age may later become large and uncomfortable during pregnancy.

Hirshsprung's disease—see *Megacolon*

Hookworm infections are common in barefoot children in the warm Southern states. The larvae invade the skin, migrate to the *lungs,* pass up the *trachea,* down the esophagus, and attach themselves to the lining of the intestines. They suck the host's blood, copulate, and lay eggs. The victim's stool may contain thousands of eggs, and if sanitation is minimal, they will lie on the ground to await another barefoot child.

Anemia is the chief debility, but toxic symptoms, stomachaches, and general lethargy may be present. Usually two or three other *parasites* are present as well, so they all must be treated.

Ileus, or more properly paralytic ileus, is a paralyzed bowel. The patient shows signs of intestinal obstruction such as no bowel action, bloat, and vomiting. It is usually due to some infection nearby (*pneumonia* or *peritonitis*). Kidney failure with *uremia,* abdominal operations, or injuries and *electrolyte* imbalance will produce this problem.

Peristalsis (the intestinal-wall contractions that propel food from stomach to rectum) is not functioning. No tinkles or gurgles are heard when the abdomen is listened to.

Treatment is gastric suction to relieve distension and I-V fluids to prevent *dehydration,* and, of course, treating the cause.

Intestinal flu—see *Gastroenteritis*

Intestinal polyps may occur anywhere in the intestinal tract and might help an *intussusception* begin. Usually they are rectal; bleeding and painful defecation suggest their presence. Because of the "neck" with which the blob may be attached, the polyp may be extruded through the anal opening as if the rectum thought it was a stool.

Intussusception is an acute abdominal emergency in which part of the intestine telescopes into the segment just next to it. It occurs most commonly in the one- to two-year-old age group. The usual segment affected is the small bowel just near to the cecum, the first portion of the large bowel in the lower right side of the abdomen. It is like an inside-out sleeve. The bowel assumes that the contained intestine is food and tries to push it on through. This is accompanied by screaming *cramps,* alternating with *shock.* Blood (usually red) in the stools is often associated. The mass may be palpated in the lower abdomen. Vomiting of bile suggests an obstruction, and treatment cannot be delayed, as gangrene will develop.

Early in the course of the condition a *barium enema* may diagnose as well as treat the protruding mass. The column of barium in the large bowel may provide sufficient pressure to push the intestine back to its original position. Surgery may still be indicated to assure that all is well. If gangrene is present, the involved bowel must be removed.

Irritable colon describes bowel-movement irregularities (hard, small pellets or loose, big, sloppy stools) associated with abdominal cramps in an overachieving, driving, success-oriented child. The condition is aggravated by parental concern and a smothering desire to keep the child dependent.

It is defined by some as a benign, self-limited condition beginning in infancy and disappearing at age three years (perhaps coinciding with toilet training and the mother's boredom with stool gazing). The child grows, eats, and sleeps well, but his stools may be big, loose, and frequent for a day. These episodes alternate with constipation.

This condition is a collection of little-understood bowel problems that include food *allergies* (especially to milk and wheat), abdominal *seizures* (abnormal EEG), and psychosomatic predispositons—the parents have the same thing. Could there be a gene for stomachache?

Attacks may be triggered by respiratory infections, teething (always a safe bet), eating chilled foods, and emotional crises in a child whose parents have gastrointestinal "weaknesses."

The child may have had colic or a milk intolerance as a baby, the mother was forced to be concerned and eventually taught the child to report every twinge. His recital at breakfast is rewarded by a day in bed, so his hypochondria is reinforced.

It is often amazing how a pale, weak, whiny child can be transformed into a happy, outgoing, pink-cheeked athlete when milk or wheat or corn is eliminated from the diet. Not *every* obscure symptom is psychosomatic.

Cystic fibrosis, gastrointestinal allergy, salmonella infection, parasites, disaccharide deficiency, and *celiac disease* must be ruled out.

Lactase deficiency is the state of inadequate production of lactase, an enzyme that breaks down milk sugar (lactose), into glucose and galactose, the simple sugars. The larger molecule has a *diarrhea* effect; this, plus the bacterial fermentation of the sugar, produces watery, gas-filled stools which severely burn the skin at the *anal* opening.

Some babies are born with the condition and can never tolerate lactose. The more common deficiency follows a bout of *dysentery* or *gastroenteritis* which might erode the intestinal cellular lining wherein the *enzyme* is produced.

Removal of lactose-containing milk from the diet is the method of control.

Laxatives are agents that soften the stool (by holding moisture) and/or increase intestinal activity.

Many people feel they need a laxative because of the misunderstanding that if they do *not* have a daily bowel movement, poisons in the stool will be absorbed in the body and make them sick or drive them insane. Everyone has a different rhythm for elimination, varying from three bowel movements a day to one a week. If the stool is hard and big enough to cause pain and fissuring, changes in the diet should be tried before anything else. (See *Constipation.*)

Cascara, made from the bark of the cascara buckthorn, is a laxative not much used because of its tendency to induce cramps and dependency.

Castor oil is a laxative, the use of which was time-honored "to clean out the bowel poisons." Its use is now limited to special occasions such as bowel preparation for surgery or X ray examination (see *Barium enema*).

Most surgeons prefer to use a bulk, moisture-holding preparation (L-A® formula, see *Constipation,* Section 4), as it produces a more natural bowel movement and tends to prevent the anal opening from constricting after anal surgery.

The constipatee might become dependent on cascara or castor oil; a purge on Monday might produce the Sunday, Monday, Tuesday, and Wednesday movements on Tuesday. He might be so cleaned out that when Friday rolls around and nothing happens, the purge would be repeated. He thus would be kept a day or two ahead of his natural tendencies.

Milk of magnesia (magnesium hydroxide) is a mild and safe laxative. If diet changes are not effective in changing the stools from hard and dry to soft and moist, a teaspoonful of this liquid given daily should produce some results by at least three days; if not, an *enema* may have to be considered.

Magnesium citrate and sulfate hold moisture and are safer and less habit forming than cascara or castor oil.

Many doctors will use *thyroid* as a laxative, assuming that the sluggish bowel is a sign of *hypothyroidism.* If all other measures above fail, it might be considered, but it is cheating unless good clinical and laboratory evidence confirms the low thyroid state.

Mineral oil will lubricate the passageways but may be overdone. One of our professors in medical school told us "In America, the only contraindication to mineral oil seems to be a slippery pavement." It seems to be safe for the elderly who eat poorly and are able to pass only a "little dust." But it may inhibit the absorption of *vitamins A* and *D* (which are oil soluble) and sometimes will produce an opacity in the lungs if an occasional drop has been inadvertently aspirated. A thirty-pound child needs about two or three teaspoonfuls a day to do the job.

Lipase is an enzyme secreted in the pancreas and passed into the intestine. It digests fat after bile has emulsified it. Its absence is suggested if the stools are malodorous, large, and greasy, as in *cystic fibrosis.*

Liver is the large digestive organ that did some eighty-five different things when I went to medical school. Now, research has found it is responsible for at least five hundred separate important functions. It stores glucose as *glycogen* and reconverts it to glucose to maintain the blood sugar at a fairly constant level. It stores *protein.* It is responsible for *fat* metabolism. *Urea,* albumin, *clotting* factor precursors are formed in the liver. *Vitamins A* and *D* are stored in the liver; a single dose every three to six months is a satisfactory method of administering these two vitamins. The newborn baby's liver stores the *iron* it has received from the mother; this is gradually depleted by six months of age, so oral iron must be added to the diet by that time (cereal, fruit, vegetables, meat). The liver can also detoxify a number of medicines and poisons as well as make bile.

Liver *abscess* is a rare infection due usually to the *Staphylococcus,* but any organism may be responsible. Chills, high fever, pain over the liver would suggest the problem. Surgery is usually necessary to rule out *peritonitis* or *gall-bladder disease;* at that time the abscess is needled for drainage and identification of the organism. Amebic liver abscess is formed by the coalescence of small areas of liver destruction due to the invasion of the amebae. *Ascaris,* or round worms, may migrate into the liver and form a cyst or abscess (if the worms drag some bacteria along).

Liver cysts may be hereditary, due to *neoplasm, Echinococcus,* retention of bile or lymph, or a manifestation of generalized *polycystic* disease. If large enough to produce symptoms, their removal seems to be justified. (See *Polycystic disease.*).

Liver function tests help to determine what and where lies the pathology of the patient with *jaundice* and an enlarged *liver. Bilirubin* accounts for the yellow skin; the bilirubin test will reveal if the bilirubin is due to hemolysis or obstruction to flow of bile through the liver. Certain bile salts in the urine reveal if the liver trouble is infectious or obstructive. Increased amounts of an enzyme in the blood *(Glutamic pyruvic transaminase)* will help to diagnose an early case of *hepatitis.* BSP test is a sensitive way to find out if liver function is adequate.

Liver tumors must be considered when an abdominal mass is discovered. Usually they are the result of metastatic spread from cancer in other organs. (See *Neoplasms,* Section 10.)

Malabsorption is the general wasting of body tissues that occurs when food passes through the intestines without being digested and/or absorbed. Stools are usually bulky, greasy, foamy, loose, and malodorous. This is called steatorrhea (fat *diarrhea*), but impaired fat digestion is not the primary cause; the greasy stools just contain a great deal of unabsorbed fat.

Stomach acids and pepsin, bile, and pancreatic digestive *enzymes* (*lipase,* protease, and amylase) may all be working efficiently to digest and emulsify that *fat, protein,* and *carbohydrate* in the meal. The pathology lies in the lining of the small bowel which has lost its ability to move these products of digestion from the lumen of the intestine into the capillaries and lymph channels on the other side of these lining cells. Microscopic projections, villi (like fingers waving in the intestinal breeze), are flattened; intracellular enzyme systems fail to provide energy to pump the nutrients across the length of the cell. Bacteria digest the unabsorbed protein and sugar, causing gas and cramps. Fat soluble *vitamins A, D,* and *K* are poorly absorbed and skin changes, low *calcium tetany,* and *bleeding* problems occur. General body wasting is the rule.

Although some cases of *steatorrhea* are due to specific enzyme deficiencies, the above picture may eventually occur, for those enzyme systems and absorptive mechanisms are mutually interdependent. For instance, the large amounts of unabsorbed lactose molecules present in *lactase deficiency* act as a purge and flush out fat and protein.

Babies have poor tolerance to intestinal irritations and will develop steatorrhea if their diet is too rich in fat (especially dairy or animal fat). A not uncommon chronic diarrhea (with fat) will prolong an ordinary case of *gastroenteritis.* This *virus* infection usually lasts seven days, but it may impair the enzyme function of the lining cells and perpetuate the diarrhea condition long after the virus has been eliminated.

If diarrhea lasts more than the usual seven days, the usual regimen of white foods, applesauce, bananas, and milk for diarrhea may be the wrong diet. The child may have developed enzyme deficiencies which prevent gluten (wheat) absorption, lactose (milk sugar) digestion—or secondary bacterial invasion may be fouling up the enzyme function.

Milk and dairy products are first discontinued. If the stools become normal in two days, the answer is milk *allergy* or a temporary *lactase deficiency.* If that is unsuccessful and wheat *(celiac disease)* has been eliminated from the diet, a trial of an intestinal antibiotic (*neomycin* or *sulfa*) may control bacterial growth so that normal function may resume. (See *Chronic nonspecific diarrhea, Cystic fibrosis,* Section 9, *Celiac disease, Regional enteritis, Diarrhea, Malrotation.*)

A number of tests have been devised to determine more accurately the specific cause of *malabsorption: barium meal* with X rays, measurement of fat intake and excretion, B_{12} absorption tests, and biopsy of the intestinal-lining cells. The latter is done by passing a flexible tube through the mouth on down to the small bowel. The tube has a cutting device that can catch a bit of the lining for biochemical and microscopic analysis.

Malrotation of the bowel is a congenital defect in which the intestines do not assume their normal position in the abdomen. Usually the cecum is high in the abdomen instead of in the lower right side. Bands from it may compress the *duodenum* or a *volvulus* may form because of the anomalous position.

Meckel's diverticulum is a pocket or pit in the wall of the small bowel with three or four feet of its junction with the cecum, the beginning of the large bowel. This anomaly occurs in about 5 percent of the population, but becomes a surgical emergency if it bleeds (causing bloody or tarry stools), helps start an *intussusception,* or becomes inflamed and suggests *appendicitis.*

Megacolon, or large colon, is a congenital lesion that becomes fairly obvious within the first month of life. A defect in the innervation in a segment of bowel near the rectum prevents the smooth, integrated, peristaltic waves from pushing the stool into the rectum whence voluntary muscle action expels it. Stool and *gas* back up as in an obstruction, and the abdomen becomes distended. Unless the stools are quite loose, passage is effected only by repeated *enemata.* This story of difficult passage from birth on would lead to a *barium-enema* examination. The narrowed segment makes the diagnosis, and surgical correction is the next step. The entire area must be removed and the normal bowel above connected to the normal rectum below. Decompression must first be obtained, because the large, distended colon cannot be anastomosed to the smaller rectum easily (it would be like trying to connect an automobile tire to a bicycle tire).

Occasionally this condition is confused with a psychological stool-withholding problem or chronic constipation (which invariably begins after infancy), or a valve or stenosis at the *colon-rectum* junction.

Normal saline solutions or mineral-oil enemata are best used;

plain water may be absorbed from the abnormally distended colon to such an extent that water intoxication (cerebral edema) may result.

Mesenteric lymphadenitis is the inflammation and swelling of the *lymph nodes* in the abdomen. Lymph glands are found all over the body and respond to infection with tenderness and fever. The mesenteric glands (in the supporting tissue between the intestines and the back abdominal wall) become involved secondarily to a throat infection, possibly because of swallowed germs, or independently—in which latter case it may mimic *appendicitis* with fever, local pain, and tenderness in the lower right abdomen and an elevated *white blood-cell* count. Surgery is the only way to differentiate these conditions, and although finding a normal appendix produces some embarrassment for the surgeon, he must not wait if appendicitis is a consideration.

Adenitis of the mesenteric glands may smolder for weeks or months following a throat or bowel infection. The child is not too sick, and his temperature when taken rectally is no more than 99.5°, so the parents assume that he is a *neurotic,* a goof-off, or a hypochondriac. The doctor can find nothing in the examination to suggest disease (the affected glands are too deep to palpate), and the blood count may be normal. However, the lethargy, appetite loss, and circles under the eyes would put the diagnosis into the organic rather than the psychological column (especially if he comes in from play to lie down). The story is frequently common in the four- to six-year-olds who are especially prone to infections and swollen lymph tissue anyway. A few days' trial of an *antibiotic* will relieve the dull, achy fullness the child experiences, his color and appetite will improve, and the mother may feel some guilt that she had been assuming her sick child was faking the whole thing. (See also *Tension-fatigue syndrome,* Section 15.)

Nematode infections, or roundworm infections, include *pinworms, whipworms, hookworms, ascariasis, trichinosis* (Section 2), *filariasis,* dracunculosis, and *strongyloidiasis.* The dog and cat roundworm (*Toxocara canis* and *cati*) produce *brain, eye, liver,* and *lung* symptoms as they migrate through the human host rather than cause intestinal problems.

Oxyuriasis—see *Pinworms*

Pancreas is an organ with a dual function. It produces digestive *enzymes* (trypsin for protein digestion, amylase for starch digestion, and *lipase* for fat digestion), and *insulin* for the metabolism of glucose. A tube may be passed into the *duodenum,* where the pancreas dumps these enzymes, and some of the pancreatic juice can be retrieved for analysis. In *cystic fibrosis* these enzymes are absent; this accounts for the patient's large, foul, greasy stools.

Pancreas neoplasms are rare. *Hypoglycemia* may lead to the consideration of an islet cell (insulin secreting) tumor of the pancreas.

Pancreatitis is rare in children except when associated with *mumps.* The victim may or may not have *parotid* swelling, but tenderness in the upper abdomen (*intestinal flu* pain is usually around the navel), fever, and *vomiting* should suggest pancreatitis. Antivomiting suppositories and/or intravenous fluids may be necessary for the four or five days of prostration.

Ascaris (roundworm) invasion of the pancreatic duct or injury to the upper abdomen may cause pancreatitis.

The powerful *enzymes* secreted by the pancreas are not activated until they meet the *duodenal* juices. Trypsinogen becomes trypsin, which activates the other pancreatic enzymes. These enzymes rapidly digest *proteins* into their simple amino acids which are then absorbed. Obviously, if these enzymes become active inside the pancreas, they assume the tissue is food and begin to digest it. Trauma, *mumps,* alcoholism, *peptic ulcer,* and *gall stones* are associated with pancreatitis.

Paralytic ileus—see *Ileus*

Parasites are organisms that live in or on the body. Bacteria, *viruses, fungi,* and their relatives might all be considered parasites, but the term usually refers to worms. (See *Ascariasis, Giardiasis, Flukes, Trichuriasis, Toxocara, Schistosomiasis, Hookworm, Nematode infections, Pinworms, Strongyloidiasis, Tapeworms.*) Some of these worms are smart enough to live comfortably inside their host without creating a disability severe enough to motivate the host to seek relief. Biting insects and the itch mite (*scabies,* see Section 6) are parasites whose enthusiasm for the host is so irritating that their elimination is assured. (See also *Cercaria dermatitis, Creeping eruption, Filariasis,* Section 6; *Loeffler's syndrome,* Section 9; *Trichinosis,* Section Section 2.)

Peptic ulcer—see *Duodenal ulcer* and *Gastric ulcer*

Peritoneal dialysis is a method for removing wastes or poisons from the body. Sterile fluid is allowed to run into the peritoneal cavity through a catheter passed through the abdominal wall. By diffusion various undesirable materials migrate in this fluid and then flow out of the body via another catheter.

This method is used in renal failure, when the *kidneys* are unable to put out enough urine to clear the blood of uremic poisons. Some poison cases are salvaged by dialysis if the toxic material has passed beyond the victim's stomach into his circulation.

Peritoneum is the lining of the abdominal space. It consists of a thin, glistening sheet of cells that cover the *intestines, liver, spleen,* and the abdominal walls. It allows the loops of bowel to slide against one another during digestion. (See *Ascites.*)

The small bowel begins at the exit of the stomach and includes the *duodenum* (a few inches), jejunum, and *ileum* (twenty to forty feet). It is chiefly responsible for digesting and absorbing the products of digestion.

The large bowel begins in the lower right side of the abdomen with the cecum. It is about five feet long, absorbs water, and passes feces on to the rectum.

Peritonitis, purulent, is an infection of the peritoneal lining most commonly following a ruptured appendix or bowel. A germ floating through the bloodstream from some other infected area may settle here and begin to grow. It may occur as a complication of *nephrosis* or *ascites,* since the fluid in the abdominal space makes a good culture medium.

Severe abdominal pain, high fever, elevated white blood count, and prostration suggest emergency abdominal exploratory surgery. For the nephrotic or ascitic case, however, usually some fluid is removed from the peritoneal space by needle aspiration to establish diagnosis. Appropriate and large amounts of antibiotic are lifesaving. (See *Peritonitis,* Section 2.)

Pinworms are the most common cause of night wakefulness in children. One of my four-month-old patients acquired worms from his four-year-old sister who was "helpful" in feeding and changing him. (A child does not develop worms without someone to act as carrier.) The mother thought her baby had colic, but one day when she was changing his diaper, he happened to discharge a stool with a great number of quarter-inch white, crawly, squirming worms. Both children were treated with the appropriate medicine, and both were soon cheerful and happy.

In infant girls, these small worms may migrate forward into the vaginal opening. In rare cases they may move on into the *bladder* and *ureters* into the *kidney.* Or, again in the case of girls, into the *vagina,* through the uterus, out the fallopian tubes, and into the peritoneum. A large series of studies indicate that worms can obstruct the appendix, causing *appendicitis.* Pathologists are no longer surprised to find segments of worms in an infected appendix—and not just pinworms either. Many other kinds of worms afflict humans, but in children, the most common is the pinworm.

The pinworm's life cycle is: the pregnant female worms come out at night to lay their microscopic eggs around the anal opening. Each female may lay several thousand. This causes intense itching; the child usually scratches this area, picking up a number of eggs underneath his fingernails. He may be bathed daily and his fingernails may be short and clean, but he will still harbor some eggs under his nails. Then when he handles books, toys, or athletic equipment, he leaves some of these eggs behind. Another child may pick up these toys and, of course, transmit the eggs from his hand to his mouth. It does not take more than two eggs (one male, one female) to start a new cycle in a new child. When these eggs get to the colon, they hatch, male meets female, female gets pregnant, and lays her thousand eggs outside the anal opening. Again the itch, and again the cycle is repeated.

The cardinal symptom of worms is night wakefulness. If a child is wakeful at night and not sick with sore throat, ear infection, or *gas* attack, he may have worms. Other worm symptoms to check for are stomachache, teeth grinding, and an itchy, burning sensation around the anal opening. Most afflicted children are also irritable and tense because they have not been sleeping properly. They cry easily, are grouchy, fussy, and often mean, suggesting a behavior problem. Most remedies are now quite effective, and within seventy-two hours after the proper dose, the sufferer should have been relieved of enough of his internal population to show noticeable improvement. (See *Worms,* Section 4.)

Some doctors refuse to treat the patient with worms unless they see the evidence. They may ask the mother to bring in a sample of her child's stool or a piece of transparent tape that she has pushed against the anal opening, thus perhaps picking up minute eggs that the doctor can examine under the microscope. This seems unnecessary. If the child has worm symptoms and has not had adequate treatment for them for a few months, he should be treated on the assumption that he has them again. The treatment will not hurt him in any case. One dose is given by mouth and repeated in ten days. It only kills the adult worms, so the repeat dose is needed to kill those that have developed from the eggs present ten days previously. Side effects from the medicine are rare, and no enemas are necessary.

A number of old wives' tales should be dispelled:

1. Worms are found in all strata of society, though unsanitary habits certainly encourage them.
2. Sitting on cold cement does not cause worms.
3. Neither does eating candy.
4. A huge appetite is not a symptom of worms. When afflicted with any type of worm the victim usually has a poor appetite.
5. A child who picks his nose does not do so because he has worms. But the child who picks his nose or sucks his thumb is more likely to ingest some worm eggs because he always has his hand at his face.

Pediatricians receive calls about worms daily. Some authorities feel that upward of 60 percent of all children have them at one time or another. Pinworms are more common in some areas of the country (such as the South) than in others. Until recently, they were considered to be signs of poor care and an unclean home. Anybody with worms was automatically considered to be of a lower social order and obviously did not bathe regularly. Even today, the general public does not hear about worms, because when a horrified mother discovers that *her* child has them, she seldom broadcasts the news.

This attitude echoes the teaching that we received in medical school: only a "certain type of person" gets worms, and if you washed regularly and kept reasonably neat toilet habits, you would never be afflicted. However, the worms have proved us all wrong by being found in the cleanest homes as well as the dirtiest. I have developed a new theory (perhaps based mainly on the fact that my own children have had worms periodically): children have worms because they have friends. If a child does not socialize too well, he may not have any friends from whom to get worms. So I would say, if your child gets worms frequently, he may be just relating to his peers. (If he *never* gets worms, he either has antisocial tendencies or uninfected classmates.)

Some form of controlled medication in the classroom seems prudent. There is no reason why the children who are usually playing and exchanging toys, books, and worm eggs with each other could not all be treated together. If a whole school class or neighborhood, city, or county (ideally, the whole world) could be treated at one time, we might be able to get rid of these pesky creatures and stop their cycle. Pinworms are really a social disease among children. However, because of the widespread but mistaken belief that worms are the product of dirty and inadequate home care, most mothers treat their children in secrecy, without letting school or neighbors know what they are doing. Thus, by the time a mother has her child free of worms, those defunct worms' grandchildren are incubating in her neighbor's child, who in a couple of weeks will be ready to give his worm eggs back to their original donor.

Often a child with worms will wake up screaming with terrible nightmares. I think worms irritate a child, so that he is more likely to dream, and of course he does not dream about worms. He has to have some content for his dreams, so he will be dreaming about the last thing he remembers—usually the horror show he watched on television. TV gets blamed for a lot of symptoms that are really due to worms.

Polycystic disease of the *liver* is usually associated with renal cysts. It is an inherited problem. Few or no symptoms occur unless the cysts are large enough to obstruct *bile* flow, in which case the enlarged *liver* and *jaundice* will appear. The renal cysts are usually more of a problem than the hepatic ones. (See *Renal cysts,* Section 13.)

Polyposis, multiple, familial, is a rare inherited condition in which dozens of polyps grow on the lining of the colon and rectum. As it frequently leads to a malignant cancer, the entire polyp-bearing colon is removed surgically. Solitary polyps are usually removed during sigmoidoscopy (direct vision through a tube in lower colon).

Prolapse of the rectum occurs when part of the rectal lining extrudes through the *anal* opening upon straining; a tube of very red membrane may extend an inch or so out from the anus. With suitable lubrication it is easily inserted. It is fairly common in small babies but rarely observed, as few mothers watch every stool action and are content to wait until the diaper is full before changing. Eventually growth and scar tissue serve to prevent its recurrence, but surgery may be wise if it is out all the time. Constipation or polyps must be taken care of, obviously.

Protein-losing enteropathy means the loss of significant amounts of the proteins from the blood due to some leak into the intestines. It may be seen as an "allergy" (usually an abnormal response to milk), or in *nephrosis,* in gluten-induced *diarrhea,* or in intestinal disease *(diarrhea, colitis).*

Pruritis ani is an itchy *anus.* The most common cause is *pinworm* infestation, but a variety of foods (citrus, peaches, melon, tomatoes, corn, nuts, and milk) may all cause this. Some scented and/or colored toilet papers will cause a contact rash with an accompanying itch. (Wiping the anal area with posion-oak leaves after a bowel movement in the woods seems too obvious to mention.) Bubble bath usually causes a generalized body rash but may be accentuated about the anus. A hard, dry bowel movement may cause a fissure with an associated itch, which is self-perpetuating as the scratching will keep the crack open. Even softening the stools will not allow the fissure to heal promptly.

Causes: *anal fissures* and fistulae, *candidiasis,* fungus, *allergy* (food or contact), *worms.*

Treatment: *Burow's solution* compresses twice daily, antihistaminics by mouth, cortisone ointment applied three times a day, cleansing

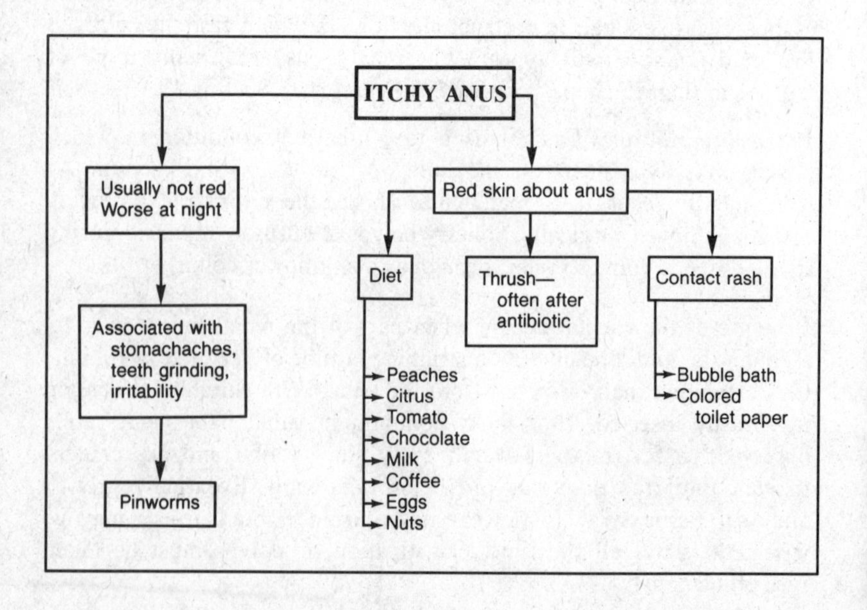

after bowel movements with moist absorbent cotton (see *Anal fissure*), low roughage diet, no peaches, citrus, or chocolate, and the use of a bulk laxative.

Pyloric stenosis is the obstruction of the pylorus (outlet of the stomach) due to the hypertrophy of the muscles in the wall of this portion of the intestinal tract. It has an affinity for the firstborn male child in the springtime. (Of course, I once had a second-born female patient develop this in the fall.) The symptoms develop in the first six weeks of life. (A prematurely born baby may not have symptoms until he is seven or eight weeks of age.)

Initially there is only an occasional spit-up, but after a few days projectile vomiting shoots the stomach's contents across the room. The initial symptoms suggest a milk *allergy,* but it is quite obviously a mechanical problem when even water is blasted back. Urine and stools become scanty, and *malnutrition,* lethargy, *dehydration,* and *alkalosis* become late findings in the undiagnosed, neglected case.

The swollen muscle feels like an olive deep in the abdomen above and to the right of the navel. After a few ounces of milk are swallowed, gastric waves can be seen through the upper left abdominal area moving from left toward the navel; they appear like a gold ball rolling under the skin and indicate the stomach contractions trying to force the milk through the narrow pyloric tunnel. In a doubtful case, some radiopaque dye can be added to the milk. The X ray would show no stomach emptying or a thin ("string sign") column in the pyloric area. *Emesis* is milk and stomach juices; *bile* returned indicates that the obstruction is further down the *duodenum.*

Surgery is the treatment. Under light anesthesia, after appropriate I-V fluid correction, the surgeon finds the knot of muscle and cuts the fibers that encircle the pylorus. He tries to cut enough to relieve the narrowing, but tries to avoid entering the lumen which might invite peritonitis.

Pylorospasm can be confused with pyloric stenosis, but because it is due to muscle spasm and not hypertrophy it is usually relieved by intestinal tranquilizers (barbiturates and *atropinelike* drugs) and a calmer environment.

Rectum is a holding area for solid wastes that allows us to be socially acceptable for long periods of time. It is a tough and distendable tube, but sensitive to touch and pressure. It is a miracle how a human can learn to pass *gas* around or through loose fecal material in the rectum without dislodging any of it. The sphincter (purse string) muscle at the anal opening is under both conscious and involuntary control. (Most people must consciously send a message to this muscle to hold tight when they feel a big cough, sneeze, or laugh coming on.) With all the traffic here, it is amazing that there are so few big problems.

Regional enteritis is a disease of the bowel wall; the cause is unknown. (Crohn's disease, or granulomatous enteritis, is another name for the same or a closely related condition.) Thickening and scarring of the small intestines cause stomachaches, low-grade fever, nausea, and constipation alternating with *diarrhea* and *anemia.* The pain is usually about the navel and is intermittent, like the cramping of *intestinal flu* but the symptoms go on for weeks and months.

Inflammation of a segment or segments of the bowel is most common in the *ileum* just proximal to the *cecum* and the first portion of the *colon.* The wall of the bowel becomes thickened and the lumen narrowed. A palpable mass develops in half of the patients. Symptoms can be mild and chronic with constipation alternating with *diarrhea,* vague abdominal pains, low-grade fever, *anorexia.* Occasionally the onset may be sudden and resemble *appendicitis* or *mesenteric lymphadenitis.* If chronic, *mesenteric lymphadenitis,* psychogenic stomachache, abdominal *seizures, tuberculosis, colitis,* and food *allergy* all have to be ruled out. Diet change is not helpful, antibiotics are of no value, *Dilantin*® does not stop the attacks, and a TB skin test is negative.

In the presence of the above symptoms, plus anemia and an elevated *sedimentation rate,* the diagnosis should be confirmed by the *barium-meal* X ray. Thickened, rigid bowel walls and narrowing of size of the lumen may be seen early in the disease; later fistulae and ulcers can be identified. Signs of intestinal obstruction may require surgery, at which time the diagnosis is made. *Abscesses* and *fistulae* may develop in chronic cases. *Cortisone* treatment may control the inflammation and the symptoms. Surgery to remove the involved areas may be curative. It is a difficult condition to diagnose and a challenge to treat; fortunately, it is not common.

Children with this condition are emotionally unstable, depressed, and fearful of new situations. Surgery may be necessary, but even though the surgeon may feel he has removed all the diseased segment, a recurrence in a new area can be expected months or years later. Diet change and vitamins are helpful; antibiotics are of no value.

Because of its chronic, inflammatory nature, it is classified with other diseases of similar obscure etiology (*rheumatic fever, glomerulonephritis, rheumatoid arthritis*).

Roundworm infections—see *Nematode infections*

Rumination is the self-induced emesis of all or part of the stomach contents. The initial event may be fortuitous, but if the child learns that he receives extra attention for this deed, he may perpetuate this form of *passive aggression* even to the point of *malnutrition* and, rarely, death. The child is displaying the ultimate in nonverbal rejection of his environment. This attention-getting device is the only way he has to signal that love and acceptance are inadequate. Consistent, warm, human mothering must be provided along with antiemetic medicines.

Schistosomiasis is a common fluke infestation found all over the world except in North America. Part of its life cycle is spent in certain snails. When a human goes in the water, swimming larvae enter through his skin and end up in the veins of the rectum or bladder. The pregnant worm lays so many eggs that the veins rupture and the eggs are passed in the excreta. The small larvae from the hatched eggs invade specific snail hosts.

It is quite obvious that the disease is perpetuated by poor sanitary habits; central collection and treatment of sewage and/or protection of the wading workers would eliminate the disease rapidly.

Skin lesions, enlarged *liver* and *spleen,* chronic *diarrhea, anemia,* debility, and *fever* may all be present. Treatment is difficult, but cure with antimony salts is possible if the disease has not advanced too far.

Intestinal flukes attach themselves to the lining of the intestinal tract, where they cause *anemia, diarrhea,* abdominal fluid (*ascites*), and associated weakness. These *parasites* are ingested with unwashed fruits and vegetables or with improperly cooked fish. They are found chiefly in India and the Orient.

Liver flukes are ingested the same way but migrate to the liver, setting up inflammation which leads to biliary obstruction and *cirrhosis.*

Lung flukes are found in Pacific areas and are swallowed when inadequately cooked, contaminated crab is ingested. The larvae migrate through the intestinal wall into the *lungs,* but may end up in the *brain* or *groin*. *Cough* and bloody sputum may suggest their presence. Flukes in the brain may cause convulsions.

Treatment sufficient to eradicate flukes is hazardous, as it may eliminate the host.

Steatorrhea (see *Celiac disease*) is excessive fat in the stools. The term is used interchangeably with "*celiac syndrome*" and "*malabsorption.*" A variety of conditions may produce the same picture of *malnutrition,* large, foul-smelling, greasy stools, and an enlarged, *gas*-distended abdomen including *cystic fibrosis, gluten-induced enteropathy,* intestinal *allergy, disaccharidase deficiency,* and *diarrhea* of nonspecific nature.

Stomach is the collecting area for food. People put a large variety of substances into their stomachs and call it food. The stomach is tough and distendible and can withstand much insult.

Stool is perhaps a better term for a fecal evacuation than "go-go," "number two," "big job," or "big potty." Doctors use "bowel movement" (BM) or "defecation." Families would be well-advised to use a specific medical term that will never be confused with some other activity. (If you say, "Let's go for a ride," and the child goes to the bathroom instead of the car, it would be wise to revise some terms.)

Strongyloidiasis is a thread-worm infection. The worm enters the body through the skin of the bare feet when they are in contact with warm, moist, infected soil. The larvae pass to the lungs, migrate up to the trachea, and are swallowed. The fertile females living in the bowel wall lay eggs into the intestinal tract. These hatch, are passed, and wait in fertile soil for another human contact.

The larvae are found in the feces, and appropriate treatment is usually curative. Reinfection is easy unless proper sanitation and footgear are provided. Cough accompanies the passage of the larvae through the lungs; *diarrhea,* bloat, and malnutrition are associated with the intestinal phase.

Sucrase deficiency is the absence of the *enzyme* in the intestines that is able to hydrolyze table sugar (sucrose) into simple sugars (glucose and fructose). It is an inherited trait if present from birth. It is temporary (or secondary) if it follows a bout of *diarrhea* which may have eroded away the lining cells where the enzyme is formed; when the cells regrow, the enzyme returns.

The condition leads to diarrhea, as the undigested sugar acts as a purge. *Malnutrition* follows if sugar is not withheld. (See *Malabsorption.*)

Tapeworm infestations, or flatworms or Cestoda, are found in all countries. The head of the worm has suckers and frequently barbs for attachment to the bowel wall. The body is a series of segments in which egg fertilization takes place. The eggs are passed in the stools, and if hygiene is not practiced, they are passed on to the next victim.

Symptoms may be vague and few, or severe, with *anemia, cramps,* weight loss, and *diarrhea.* Eosinophilia is common. Atabrine and purges usually dislodge the worms.

Diphyllobothriasis is infestation with the fish tapeworm, found in those who eat raw fish. Anemia and intestinal distress are suggestive.

Hymenolepiasis victims usually have been in contact with rat or mouse fleas. Insomnia, irritability, and weight loss may occur.

Teniasis develops in those who ingest raw meat from infected cattle or hogs. The mature worms may be several feet long and cause intestinal obstruction. Anemia, hunger, and increased appetite associated with weight loss and eosinophilia would suggest a stool examination for eggs.

Toxocara canis (dog roundworm) and **cati** (cat roundworm) live in these animal hosts. Children playing in and eating dirt ingest eggs laid by the adult worms. The eggs hatch in the child's intestines; the larvae begin a migration through the body. They are trapped and walled off by an inflammatory process; the body attempts to seal them off as it would any foreign object. No symptoms occur if only a few worms are to be dealt with, but a massive invasion may lead to *liver, lung, brain,* and eyeball disease. These worms have been observed migrating through the chambers of the eye. Convulsions may be the clue to their presence in the brain.

Household pets should be dewormed occasionally. Treatment of children who have these larvae migrating through them is limited to the removal of the individual invader when it arrives in an organ accessible to surgical intervention.

Trematodes—see *Schistosomiasis*

Trichobezoar—see *Bezoars*

Trichuriasis, or whipworm infection, is another roundworm or *nematode* widely distributed in warm climates. Somehow eggs from contaminated soil in areas where adequate toilet facilities are unavailable are transferred to the mouths of children. The swallowed eggs hatch, become worms, and attach to the wall of the lower bowel. The females become pregnant and lay thousands of eggs daily which pass out with the stools. The cycle is repeated unless sanitary facilities are provided.

If infestation is slight, symptoms are minimal. Large colonies of worms living in the intestines may cause *anemia,* bloat, lethargy, and growth retardation, however. The microscopic eggs may be seen in the stools.

Antiworm enemas with *hexylresorcinol* may eliminate the majority of the worms.

Ulcer—see *Duodenal ulcer* and *Gastric ulcer*

Ulcerative colitis—see *Colitis*

Umbilicus—see *Navel,* Section 5; *Hernia*

Visceral larvae migrans—see *Toxocara canis*

Volvulus is a type of internal intestinal hernia. A loop of bowel becomes trapped in an anomalous fold or defect of the mesentery, twists, and becomes incarcerated. Shock, severe cramps, and vomiting of bile require emergency surgery before gangrene develops.

Vomiting is the rejection of *stomach* and/or *intestinal* contents. Spitting up to one mother may seem violent heaving to another. It is difficult for a doctor to estimate the severity of a telephone report of "vomiting" without additional clues as to amount, frequency, duration, force, and content. The following may be helpful in evaluating relative severity.

The general condition of the vomiter is perhaps more important than what is coming up; if there is fever and lethargy in addition to the vomiting, the condition is more serious than it is in the child who vomits and then resumes normal play.

Spit up or *wet burp* is common in babies who overload their stomachs with milk or who may have swallowed air and bring up an ounce or two of milk when they burp. The milk may be slightly soured (a good sign that stomach acid is present). The stomach may curve like a fish hook, so feeding a baby while he is lying on his

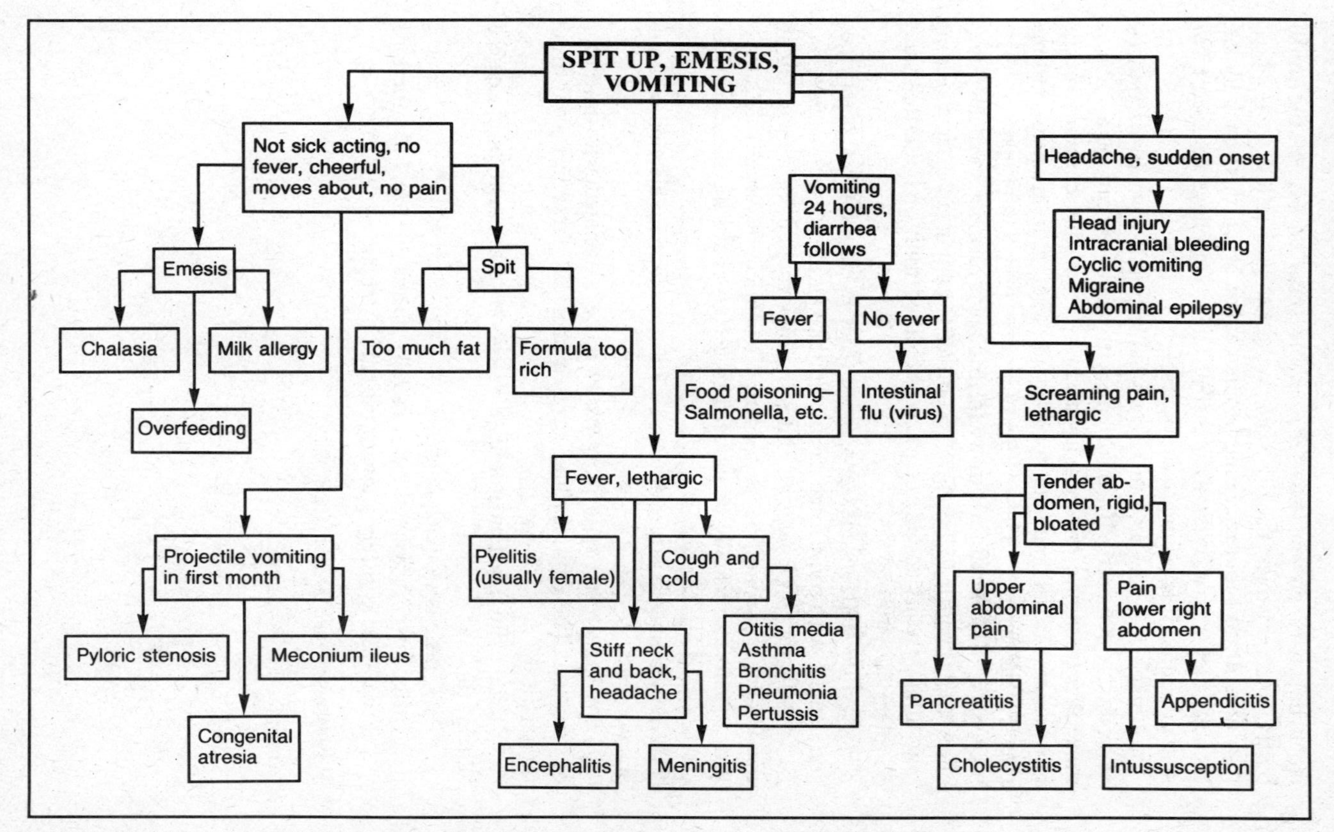
SPIT UP, EMESIS, VOMITING
Not sick acting, no fever, cheerful, moves about, no pain
Emesis
Chalasia
Milk allergy
Overfeeding
Spit
Too much fat
Formula too rich
Projectile vomiting in first month
Pyloric stenosis
Meconium ileus
Congenital atresia
Fever, lethargic
Pyelitis (usually female)
Cough and cold
Otitis media
Asthma
Bronchitis
Pneumonia
Pertussis
Stiff neck and back, headache
Encephalitis
Meningitis
Vomiting 24 hours, diarrhea follows
Fever
Food poisoning–Salmonella, etc.
No fever
Intestinal flu (virus)
Screaming pain, lethargic
Tender abdomen, rigid, bloated
Upper abdominal pain
Pancreatitis
Cholecystitis
Pain lower right abdomen
Appendicitis
Intussusception
Headache, sudden onset
Head injury
Intracranial bleeding
Cyclic vomiting
Migraine
Abdominal epilepsy

right side may prevent this (the bubble stays on top of the milk). Spitty, burpy babies usually have a "good gag reflex," an inborn trait difficult to suppress. Some people cannot brush their back molars because they gag and vomit so easily. They often have decayed *teeth,* as their stomach acids erode the enamel.

Emesis is a nice way to say a small amount (two to six ounces) of vomit is returned. If consistent with each feeding in a baby, a milk allergy should be considered. In spite of this constant return, most babies do well and gain normally. Smaller, more frequent feedings may be the answer. Thickening the milk with a tablespoon of rice may make it difficult to throw up. Stomach-relaxing medicines may allow the stomach to be more receptive. Propping up after a feeding may allow gravity to aid retention. Acidified milk or buttermilk may be tolerated better.

Vomitus suggests a larger amount (four to eight ounces) is returned and usually with some force. It may initiate an illness such as *intestinal flu, meningitis, pyelonephritis,* intestinal obstruction, or *concussion.* If the underlying condition is serious, the patient is usually lethargic. Flu patients can usually be induced to get up and walk about between emeses.

Heaves suggest larger amounts and more forceful ejection of stomach contents.

Projectile vomiting is more likely to be associated with intestinal obstruction. The emitted fluid is often shot out three feet away from the victim.

If the child is articulate, his description of the taste of the emesis is helpful:

Acid taste is stomach contents.

Bitter taste suggests bile and usually means intestinal obstruction.

Fecal taste is surely a low intestinal obstruction.

Whipworm—see *Trichuriasis*

Worms—see *Parasites*

SECTION 13

The Genitals and Urinary System

A. Kidneys

Glomerulonephritis
Hydronephrosis
Kidney failure
Nephritis
Nephroblastoma (Wilms's tumor, Section 10)
Nephrosis
  Lipoid
Oliguria
Pyelography
Pyelonephritis (pyelitis)
Renal cysts
Renal rickets
Renal tuberculosis

B. Ureters

Calculus
Cystoscopy
Hydronephrosis

C. Bladder

Calculus
Culture
Cystitis
  Hemorrhagic
Cystography
Cystoscopy

D. Urethra

Dysuria
Urethritis

E. Genitals

Hymen
Ovaries (Section 10)
  Oophoritis
Penis
  Circumcision (Section 5)
  Micropenis
  Paraphimosis
  Phimosis
Scrotum
  Swollen
    Hernia, inguinal (Section 12)
    Hydrocele (Section 5)
Testes
  Absent (Cryptorchidism)
    Hermaphroditism (Section 5)
  Painful
    Epididymitis
    Orchitis
    Torsion
  Small (Hypogonadism, Section 10)
Vagina
  Labial adhesions
  Vaginal discharge

F. **Bed-wetting** (Enuresis)

G. **Excessive urination** (Polyuria)

Diabetes (Section 10)

H. **Painful urination** (Dysuria)

Allergy (Section 3)
Cystitis
Injury to genitals (see Emergencies, Section 1)
Pyelonephritis

I. **Scanty urination** (Oliguria)

Dehydration (Section 10)
Glomerulonephritis
Hemolytic-uremic syndrome (Section 2)
Kidney Failure

J. **Urinalysis**

Acetone
- *Cyclic vomiting* (Section 12)
- *Dehydration* (Section 10)
- *Diabetes* (Section 10)
- *Gastroenteritis* (Section 12)
- *Vomiting* (Section 12)

Albuminuria
- *Fanconi syndrome*
- *Glomerulonephritis*
- *Lead Poisoning* (Section 1)
- *Nephrosis*
  - *Lipoid*
- *Orthostatic albuminuria*
- *Renal tubular acidosis*

Alkaline urine
- *Ammoniacal diaper*
- *Renal tubular acidosis*

Aminoaciduria (see also *Inborn errors,* Section 10)
- *Alcaptonuria*
- *Cystinosis* (Section 10)
- *Hartnup disease* (Section 10)
- *Phenylalanine* (Section 10)

Red urine
- *Beeturia*
- *Blood* (Hematuria)
- *Phenolphthalein* (Section 1)
- *Porphyria*
- *Lead poisoning* (Section 1)

Specific gravity
- *Dilute urine*
  - *Diabetes insipidus* (Section 10)
- *Concentrated urine*
  - *Dehydration* (Section 10)
  - *Diabetes mellitus* (Section 10)

Sugar in urine
- *Glycosuria*
  - *Diabetes mellitus* (Section 10)

Urea

K. **Blood in urine** (Hematuria)

Ammoniacal diaper
Calculus
Cystitis
- *Hemorrhagic*

Glomerulonephritis
Hemorrhagic disease of newborn (Section 5)
Henoch-Schönlein vasculitis (Section 8)
Hydronephrosis
Kidney injury
Neoplasms (Retroperitoneal; also Section 10)

Nephritis
Pyelonephritis
Renal tuberculosis
Scarlet fever (Section 2)
Scurvy (Section 11)
Urethritis
Wilms's tumor (Neoplasm, Section 10)

L. Pus in urine (Pyuria, urinary infection)

Cystitis
Glomerulonephritis
Hydronephrosis
Nephritis
Nephrosis
Pyelonephritis
Renal tuberculosis
Urethritis

M. Tests

Culture
Cystography
Cystoscopy
Retrograde pyelography
Pyelography (IVP)
Urologist

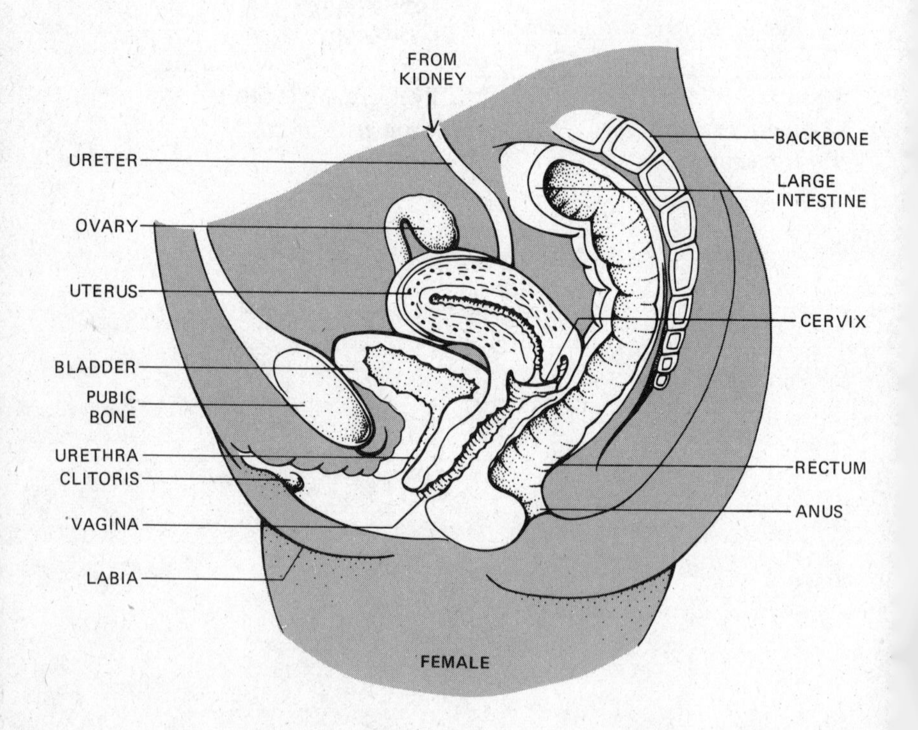
FROM
KIDNEY
URETER
OVARY
UTERUS
BLADDER
PUBIC
BONE
URETHRA
CLITORIS
VAGINA
LABIA
BACKBONE
LARGE
INTESTINE
CERVIX
RECTUM
ANUS
FEMALE

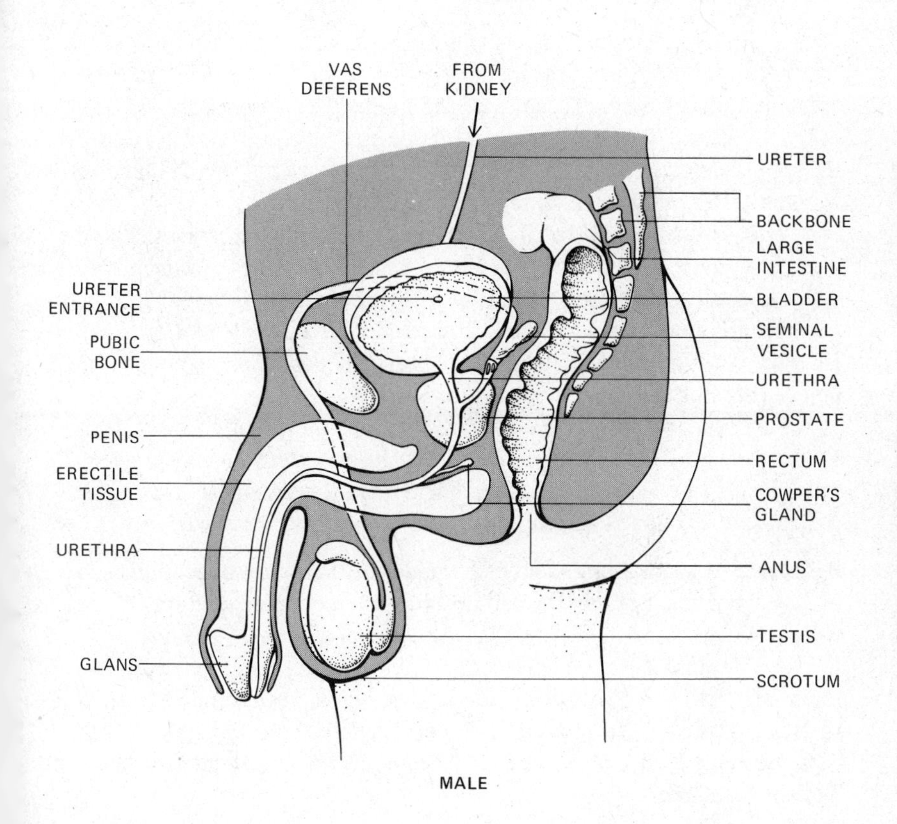
VAS DEFERENS
FROM KIDNEY
URETER
BACKBONE
LARGE INTESTINE
URETER ENTRANCE
BLADDER
PUBIC BONE
SEMINAL VESICLE
URETHRA
PROSTATE
PENIS
RECTUM
ERECTILE TISSUE
COWPER'S GLAND
URETHRA
ANUS
TESTIS
GLANS
SCROTUM

MALE

Acetone, a poisonous chemical, is commonly used as a fingernail polish remover. It is produced in small quantities by the metabolism of the body's fat. A diabetic in acidosis will have acetone in the urine. Acetone is found in the urine as a result of dehydration after prolonged vomiting. If discovered in the urine at the *onset* of *headache,* stomachache, and *vomiting,* it suggests the victim has *cyclic* or acetonuric vomiting—the childhood equivalent of a *migraine.*

Albuminuria, or proteinuria, is the presence of more than the usual amount of albumin in the urine. The presence of this protein indicates some abnormal disease (usually of the kidney; see *Pyelonephritis, Glomerulonephritis, Cystitis*), injury, or abnormal position of the kidney, or systemic infection such as *diphtheria* or *scarlet fever.* It may be found after exercise, or high fever.

The orthostatic form of albuminuria occurs after standing and does not appear after lying down. A morning urine specimen will be free of albumin, but a late afternoon specimen will reveal it. The patients are more likely to be tall, thin, and have a swayback (lordosis). Pressure on the renal veins in the upright position is thought to be the cause of this benign condition.

However, recent evidence from electron microscopy of renal biopsies indicates that these patients may have suffered some previous renal insult (for example, *glomerulonephritis*). This suggests that these patients should have followup urine and blood-pressure checks.

Alcaptonuria is an amino-acid-enzyme defect that allows accumulation of homogentisic acid in the blood and its excessive excretion in the urine. When exposed to air, this acid turns black. If the urine on the baby's diaper turns black, he should be checked for this rare metabolic error. Adults with this problem have accumulated enough of this pigment in their bodies to stain their sclerae (white of eyes), ears, nose, and checks; arthritis is common. No treatment is known. This disease is rare.

Amino-aciduria is the appearance of abnormally large amounts of *amino acids* (products of *protein* digestion) in the urine. It is a genetic defect in metabolism. Excess amino acids are presented to the *kidneys* to excrete, and/or defective kidney tubules are unable to absorb amino acids as they pass through. This is seen in *Galactosemia, Rickets,* and *Scurvy.* (See *Alcaptonuria; Cystinosis, Hartnup disease,* Section 10.)

These are rare defects of the various amino acid enzyme systems; there is a defect and a disease for each of the amino acids. Some inborn errors of metabolism may respond to vitamin therapy. B_6 has been used to control the debilitating effects of homocystinuria, one form of *anemia,* and cystathioninuria. B_{12} in huge doses aids in the control of a form of aminoaciduria. B_1 and B_2 have been linked with anemias.

Ammoniacal diaper results from the conversion of urea to ammonia by bacterial action in the diaper. The skin of many babies' buttocks is extremely sensitive to this chemical, and blisters and ulcers may form. A boy may develop a meatal ulcer just inside the urethral opening of his penis, which on healing may lead to a stenosis. Obstruction to urinary flow may result in bladder and kidney damage. (This is one argument against circumcision; the foreskin protects the meatal orifice.)

The most effective treatment of ammoniacal diaper consists of killing the diaper bacteria, by letting sunshine or ultraviolet light fall directly on the diapers or by the use of bacteriocidal rinses. Acidifying the urine (this may be accomplished by giving the child apple

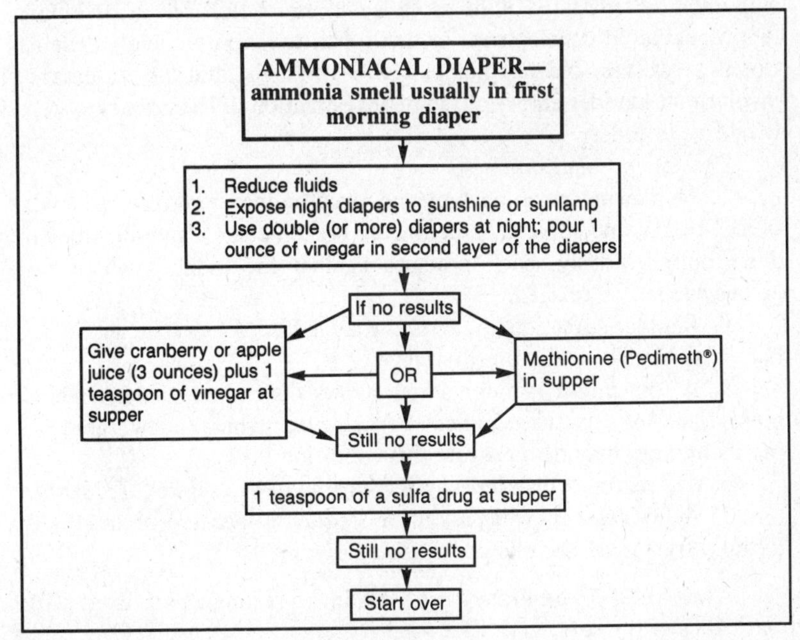

or cranberry juice, or by pouring an ounce of vinegar onto the second of double night diapers; an amino acid, *methionine,* or *vitamin C,* can be given in the supper to acidify the urine). Protecting the skin with heavy ointments and the reduction of fluid intake are of secondary importance. (See *Diaper dermatitis,* Section 6.)

Bed-wetting—see *Enuresis*

Beeturia is the appearance of red pigment in the urine after the ingestion of beets. If the red color is quite easily detected after a normal serving of beets (two to four ounces), it suggests that the patient is *anemic.* Iron in the blood should be checked.

Bladder is the hollow, distensible organ that collects urine from the *kidneys.* It allows humans to be socially acceptable for long periods of time. Many children have attained early control over their bladder, but this is rare under eighteen months of age. The development of voluntary control of the muscles descends from the neck, to the arms, to back (the child sits), to legs (he can stand), and then to bladder and *anal* sphincter muscles. Parents should expect some dry periods of two to three hours once walking has been mastered. The child will only be frustrated if he is expected to "hold" his urine before this time. Rapid development of this social function is mainly genetic. But if a two-year-old has not passed beyond his infantile, automatic, involuntary bladder emptying, some investigation of the urinary system would be in order.

Possible problems include:

1. Narrowing of a part of the *urethra* may produce, a small, weak stream, incomplete emptying of the bladder, straining to void and, more seriously, back pressure against the kidneys which can be permanently damaged.

2. Bladder infection or *cystitis* may go unnoticed in an infant, but cause bladder and kidney damage.

3. A congenitally small bladder cannot distend adequately to hold more than two or three ounces of urine at a time. New rapid X-ray techniques may demonstrate this condition.

4. A "nervous" bladder may force urine to be excreted frequently.

5. A few patients will pass urine frequently because of an allergy to milk, fruit juices, or chocolate. (See *Enuresis.*)

Anomalies of the kidneys and bladder are often associated with anomalies of the ears.

Blood in urine, Bloody urine —see *Hematuria*

Calculus is a stone formed due to precipitation of various chemicals in the urine. Stones may be composed of uric acid, cystine, oxalates, calcium, and other substances. Enzyme deficiencies, excess *vitamin D* intake, infection, alkaline diet, and other factors such as prolonged bed rest (with release of calcium from bone) may be inciting agents. *Hypercalcemia* and *hyperparathyroidism* may present large amounts of calcium to the *kidneys,* leading to the formation of calcium deposits.

The size of the particles may vary from "sand" to huge stones too large to pass. Symptoms of flank pain, blood in urine, *dysuria,* frequency, fever, suggest urinary problems. X rays reveal calcium but not uric acid stones. Analysis of the stone suggests the course of action to preclude further information: reduce vitamin D and calcium intake, alkalinize or acidify the urine, or if uric acid is precipitating, reduce meat ingestion.

Calculus in bladder is usually accompanied by blood, pain, and urgency of urination. The stone may suddenly occlude the exit from the bladder so the urinary stream will abruptly and painfully stop. *Cystoscopy* plus breaking up the calculus into small passable pieces relieves the condition. Calcium stones in urine may be due to low magnesium intake.

Cryptorchidism is the nondescent of one or both testes into the normal position in the scrotum. The *testes* normally are found in the scrotum at birth, but in many prematurely born males this does not occur until the baby is two or three months old. If one or both testes have not arrived by that time, the patient is a candidate for surgical correction. This is best done before the child is five years old, as the incidence of atrophy, injury, and malignant change is significant if the testis is allowed to remain high after this age.

Some doctors will give a hormone at age five; if the testes descend into the scrotum, it is assumed they will in adolescence, so surgery is not performed. Most surgeons feel that waiting is dangerous and that surgery is the only hope of salvaging the boy from the abovementioned problems.

Culture. A measured amount of noncontaminated urine is placed on a nutrient substance and put in the incubator. Usually in a day, colonies of bacteria may be seen growing. If the volume of urine is 0.01 milliliter and the number of colonies counted is 1,000, this is reliable evidence of a urinary infection (100,000 bacteria per milliliter). Counts of 10,000 to 20,000 are to be regarded with suspicion and repeating the culture is worthwhile.

Cystitis is a bladder inflammation and usually causes urinary burning, urgency, and frequency, but rarely fever or stomachache. It is most common in immature females and is rare in males, so it is assumed that infection is ascending; that is, the bacteria migrate up the *urethra* from the germ-laden *vaginal* and/or *anal* area into the *bladder.* The usual bacterium responsible is the *Escherichia coli,* the common intestinal germ. Urinalysis will reveal pus cells and usually albumin.

Most doctors have found that if a male develops this condition he must have some abnormality of urinary tubular structure (urethral stenosis, bladder diverticulum, ureteral stenosis, *kidney* or *bladder* stone, double kidney, etc.) that creates urinary stasis and, like stagnant water, encourages germ growth. Most doctors, however, allow a female to have at least two bladder infections before embarking on the investigation of her urinary department.

Usually the infection responds within forty-eight hours to sulfa drugs, but daily treatment must be continued for ten to fifteen days lest the infection recur because a few germs were left.

Sometimes a culture of the urine is taken by catching a few drops of urine in a sterile container about halfway through the female's act of urinating; called the midstream catch, it is simple and fairly reliable.

The most reliable method of obtaining a urine culture in a female is by inserting a small catheter up the urethra into the bladder. Urine obtained this way is not contaminated by vaginal or vulvar bacteria. The midstream catch in males is felt to be as reliable as catheterization. In the infant male a noncontaminated urine specimen suitable for culture can be obtained by placing a small, sterile plastic bag over the thoroughly cleansed penis. (Recently some investigators have aspirated urine by passing a needle through the lower abdominal wall into the bladder.)

The culture test is of most value in those cases that do not respond to sulfa. A culture of the bacteria would identify it more accurately. A sensitivity study could be made to find the most effective antibiotic.

The frequency of urination and burning symptoms must be accompanied by pus cells and bacteria to diagnose cystitis. If no pus is found, a nervous bladder may be operative, but an *allergy* (to citrus, chocolate, milk, etc.) must first be ruled out. (See *Hemorrhagic cystitis.*)

Cystography is the technique of X raying the *bladder* after filling it with an opaque dye. Size and contour are diagnostic factors. Cinecystography is an X-ray motion picture of the bladder excreting the opaque liquid. This investigation is important as it may reveal reflux of bladder urine up the ureters toward the *kidneys*—an abnormal situation which might be responsible for repeated kidney infections. The child does not need to be hospitalized.

Cystoscopy is the passage of an optical instrument into the bladder. The urethral and bladder mucosae can be visualized for color, strictures, and obstructions, tumors, signs of pressure, diverticula, anomalies, and the location of the ureteral openings. Catheters are usually passed up the *ureters* where radiopaque dye is injected. X-ray pictures (called retrograde pyelograms) reveal kidney anomalies and signs of obstruction in the ureters.

Dysuria is painful urination and usually suggests a *bladder* infection (*cystitis*), but may be caused by normal urine passing over an am-

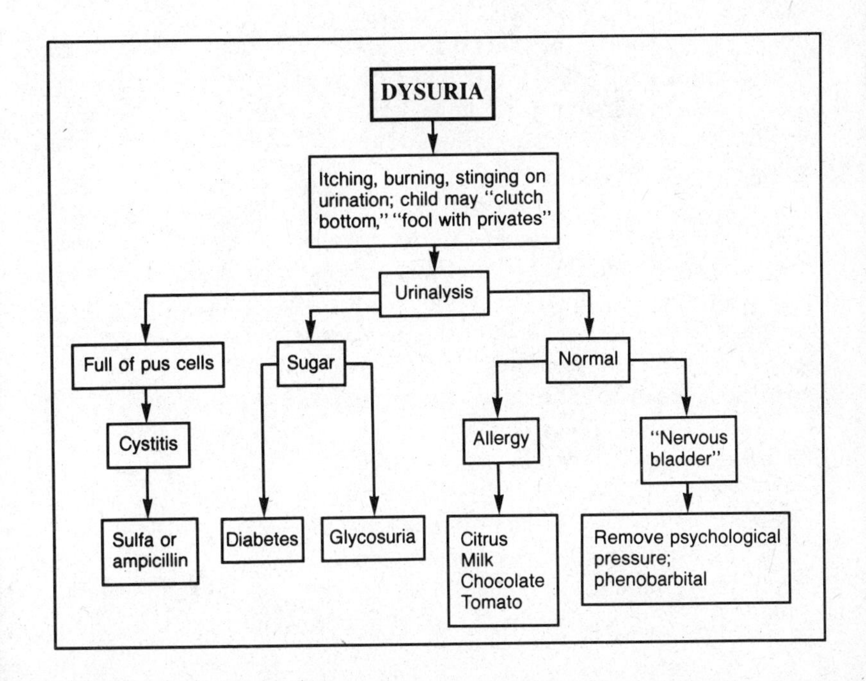

moniacal ulcer or other diaper-area rash. Frequency along with dysuria suggests bladder trouble. A urinalysis would confirm the diagnosis. If there is little pus in the urine and no obvious external lesion, an allergy (citrus, tomato, etc.) should be considered.

Enuresis, or bed-wetting, is the persistence of nocturnal wetting; in a girl, beyond age four years or a boy, beyond age five. The cause is unknown in the vast majority of cases, but a hereditary tendency is prominent in the family history. These children usually have a small bladder capacity and a penchant for deep sleep. Physical factors must be ruled out: (a) anomalies of the *urethra, bladder,* and *ureters,* and (b) *allergies* to milk, citrus juices, or chocolate. Poor school performance, unhealthy environmental attitudes, and other emotional disturbances may be causative, but many feel that these are secondary to the concern over the wetting. An uncontrolled *diabetic* or a patient with a urinary infection would obviously be likely to wet.

Genetic or inherited factors are felt to be the most common cause of bed-wetting (accounting for 80 percent). The remaining 20 percent wet because of fluid intake after four o'clock in the afternoon, allergies, structural abnormalities of the urinary system, and abnormal brain waves (see *Epileptic equivalents,* Section 15).

A normal mother becomes discouraged and frustrated when faced with mountains of smelly bedclothes to wash. She is supposed to know the child cannot help it, but he detects the look of disappointment in her face. He tries, but nothing short of sleeping on the toilet will keep the bed dry.

When a mother realizes that her child is a bed-wetter, the first thing she should do is have her doctor make a routine urinalysis to search for albumin, sugar, and pus cells. A normal urinalysis does not necessarily rule out structural anomalies. Some children have double kidneys. All sorts of oddities may occur in a child who appears healthy. If these are suspected, X rays and perhaps a specialist (urologist) are needed to determine the size and efficiency of the bladder and *kidneys.* (See *Cystoscopy, Cystography, Pyelography.*) If urine is not being excreted properly or completely, it is likely to become infected. Thus, if a bed-wetter has had a number of bladder or kidney infections, some structural deviation is usually present.

Some estimate of urinary health can be made by watching the child urinate. Without straining, the stream should be forceful, making bubbles in the toilet bowl. The stream size is important. A child who wets frequently during the day with poor control and constant dribbling should be investigated by a urologist. It can occasionally mean some nervous instability of the bladder or an allergic problem.

Because bed-wetting is reasonably rare in the female, and much more common in the male, a more extensive investigation is necessary when the patient is a girl. She might be more likely to have a structural abnormality. Obviously, any child should be investigated for other systemic conditions such as *tuberculosis, anemia, diabetes,* and *rheumatic fever* that may play a small role in bed-wetting. If the child is not feeling well generally, this could affect the urinary functions.

If the child still bed-wets after structural anomalies are ruled out and chronic infections cleared up, then consider an *allergy.* Perhaps one out of ten enuretics will wet the bed for this reason—it is as if their bladder were sneezing. A urinary allergy is usually related to something fluid in the child's diet, such as milk or orange juice, but it could conceivably come from chocolate, tomatoes, pineapples, or peaches. *What,* rather than *how much,* seems to irritate the bladder to push out urine at undesirable times. A child may be labeled a neurotic because he wets the bed, but his "neurosis" is cured when he forgets his evening milk. It is worth trying. Milk, ice cream, and cottage cheese are eliminated from the diet for one day. If he stays dry, milk is the culprit, and without it his bed-wetting is cured.

Many emotionally disturbed children wet the bed, but not all bed-wetters are neurotic or unhappy. After a child passes the age of six or seven, he usually becomes embarrassed about his condition, especially when he finds that he cannot spend the night with friends or go on camping trips. His mother is also getting discouraged. Her efforts to get him up at night, restrict his fluids, and undeprive him emotionally (if that is her working theory) have all come to naught. She often cannot conceal her disgust. Then, perhaps *because* he is wetting the bed, he may get neurotic or feel inferior or develop emotional problems that come as a *result* of the bed-wetting. So, when psychologists see a withdrawn child who is wetting the bed, it is frequently impossible for them to decide which condition came first, the bed-wetting or the emotional problems. "Passive aggression" is the psychiatrist's term, usually applied to a boy who resents his parents for some real or imagined insult. Unable to externalize or verbalize his aggression, he subconsciously bed-wets as a means of getting even. "Urethral aggression" is another, perhaps less savory term for this syndrome.

The child with a familial or inherited trait for enuresis, besides being a deep sleeper, usually has a small or "immature" bladder. His kidneys are fine, but his bladder is not able to store all the urine that has accumulated during the night. His bladder sends a message to the spinal cord saying it is full. But no message from the spinal cord comes to the social part of the brain that knows it is not acceptable to urinate in bed because Mother will get mad. It is as if the connections in the switchboard up in the brain were asleep, and no message could get through from down below. The spinal cord does not have any social awareness, so without the brain telling it what to do, it acts on its own authority. It sends back the message to the bladder: "Dump it!"

The bladder is properly formed, but the sphincter muscle designed to hold in the urine cannot seem to withstand the bladder wall's strong muscles. Magnesium helps the bladder muscles stretch.

The treatment for this frustrating condition is not universally satisfactory. All doctors have seen many bed-wetting patients. After ruling out anatomical abnormalities and allergies affecting the urinary tract, the first question is, "Is there a family history of this condition?" In many cases, the mother will admit that she had a couple of brothers and a father who wet the bed, but that she didn't. She usually doesn't know of any history of bed-wetting on her husband's side of the family. Few husbands, of course, want their wives to know that they were less than perfect males, and wet the bed as children.

Bed-wetters outgrow the problem, but later when saddled with children in the same fix, they usually react excessively because they don't like to see their own "forgotten" weakness showing up again. This seems to be a natural response, but only serves to aggravate the condition. Placing so much emotional emphasis on this one symptom almost always serves to make it worse. Many children seem to continue bed-wetting on purpose as if they knew it aggravated their parents.

Today, when so many remedies are available for so many other conditions, we doctors are embarrassed to say, "Sorry." We attempt treatment without raising false hopes of rapid cures. We play down the condition and provide reassurance. We try to get the mother to accept her child and stop nagging and punishing him for this unconscious act. There is no way to punish the unconscious ganglia of a child's nervous system.

Almost all children outgrow the condition when they fully mature.

Their muscle strength is greater, their bladder capacity has increased, and they may not be sleeping as deeply as they did in their childhood—they become more aware of the full-bladder impulses that suggest to the sleeping brain to do something about going to the bathroom.

Most parents try the obvious maneuver of awakening the child and taking him to the toilet. He often responds like an automatic toy, voiding on command, but his bladder doesn't "learn" anything. Something must be done to get the brain to help out.

Old-fashioned methods—strapping objects to the back, eating salty nuts or raisins at bedtime, or sleeping with head lower than feet—may work by preventing sound sleep and allowing the victim to be more aware of bladder distention, thus permitting a more socially acceptable response.

Devices that ring bells at the first bit of wetting usually serve to awaken the family, who must then arouse the child. The method does work, though, on the conditioned-reflex principle. A medicine (imipramine, Tofranil®) is reasonably effective in preventing deep sleep and also increasing the tone of the sphincter muscle (purse-string muscle at outlet of bladder). It appears to allow the enuretic child to establish new patterns of inhibitory control over the reflex emptying of the full bladder. When given in appropriate doses, imipramines will help control more than 50 percent of bed-wetters.

Imipramine is most effective two to four hours after administration. Parents must determine if the child is an early (8 to 12 P.M.) wetter, or late (midnight to 6 A.M.) wetter, or both. The drug should be given at supper for the early wetters, and at the parents' bedtime for the late ones—or both times for the double wetters. Sometimes, after several weeks of drug-induced dryness, it seems that a bladder habit is established that continues when the medicine is withdrawn. Imipramines seem to be safe, but should be given under a doctor's supervision.

Some studies indicate that enuretics as a group have a higher-than-normal incidence of abnormal EEGs. An impulsive, surly, aggressive bed-wetter might do better on an anticonvulsive drug than on imipramine. Five milligrams of *dextroamphetamine* at bedtime may work. Offering a protein food at bedtime and stopping all sugars may permit the social part of the brain to respond to the full bladder.

A logical training regimen can help supplement the above treatment, providing the child is at least seven years old and motivated. During the day he can be rewarded for holding his urine instead

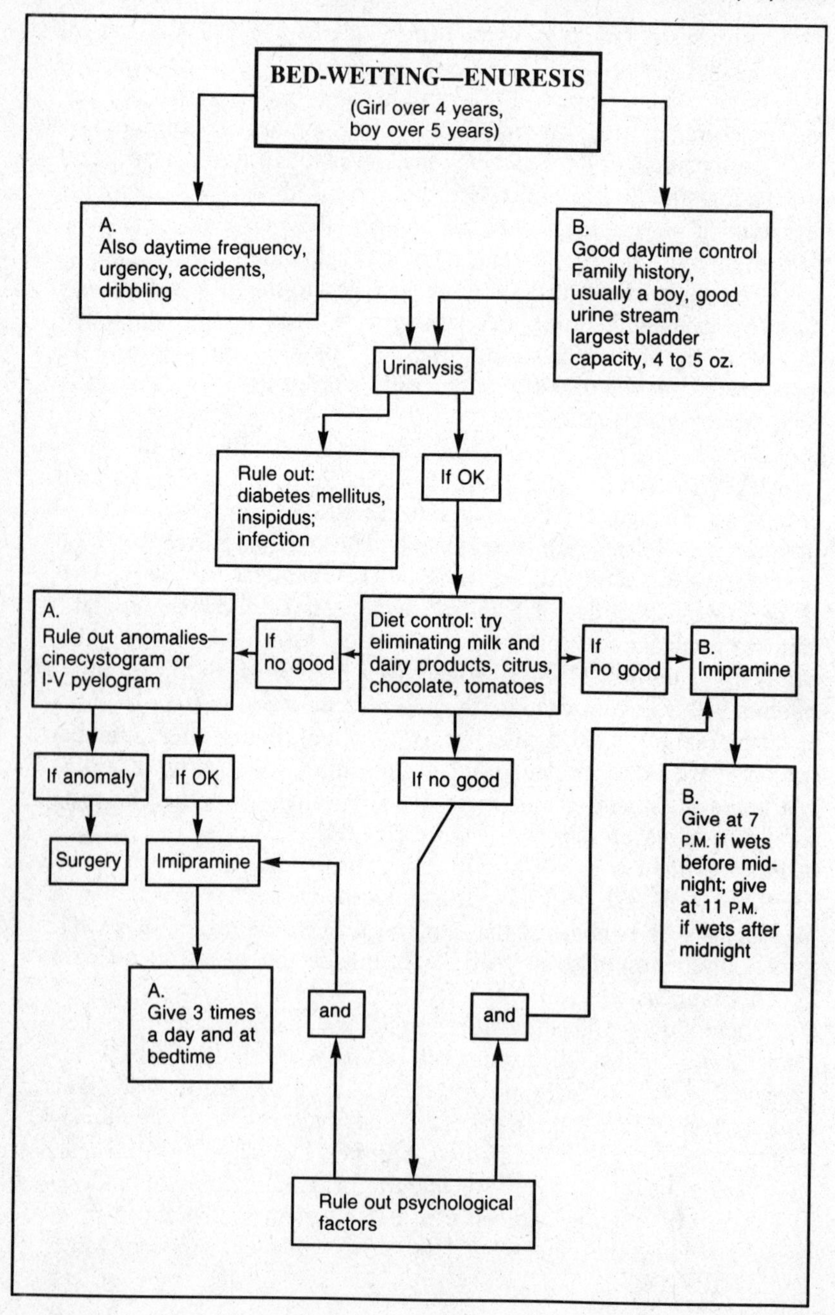
BED-WETTING—ENURESIS
(Girl over 4 years,
boy over 5 years)
A.
Also daytime frequency,
urgency, accidents,
dribbling
B.
Good daytime control
Family history,
usually a boy, good
urine stream
largest bladder
capacity, 4 to 5 oz.
Urinalysis
Rule out:
diabetes mellitus,
insipidus;
infection
If OK
Diet control: try
eliminating milk and
dairy products, citrus,
chocolate, tomatoes
If
no good
A.
Rule out anomalies—
cinecystogram or
I-V pyelogram
If
no good
B.
Imipramine
If anomaly
If OK
If no good
Surgery
Imipramine
B.
Give at 7
P.M. if wets
before mid-
night; give
at 11 P.M.
if wets after
midnight
A.
Give 3 times
a day and at
bedtime
and
and
Rule out psychological
factors

of passing it at the first urge. He should also learn to stop and start the stream a few times during urination. These exercises can stretch his bladder capacity and develop voluntary brain control over the sphincter purse-string muscle that holds urine in the bladder. To remain dry, a capacity of ten to twelve ounces would be required.

As with so many other children's problems, the family's attitude is all-important. A casual, relaxed approach to bed-wetting is much better than the frantic, we-are-going-to-do-something-right-this-minute, clenched-teeth attitude. If the child has wet himself every night since birth, he is most probably afflicted with the more common "immature bladder" that tends to run in families. If, however, he has been dry for some time and then develops this trait, one should look for physical problems, diseases, and, more importantly, school pressures or other emotional difficulties that may have cropped up.

Epididymitis is an inflammation of the sperm-collecting tubules. A tender swollen mass is noted on one side of the testicle. It is rare in children before puberty and may be associated with *orchitis.* Antibiotics are indicated if a bacterial infection is suspected.

Fanconi syndrome causes *dwarfing* and *rickets* and is due to loss of phosphate, *amino acids,* and sugar by the kidneys. It is assumed to be genetic, although some cases occur after heavy metal poisoning. Usually before one year of age, the infant fails to grow, becomes acidotic and feverish. Treatment with *vitamin D* and extra sodium and potassium compensates for the losses through the damaged kidney tubules. Victims die after a few years from *kidney failure.*

Genitals are the external sex organs. Parents would be well-advised to call these organs by their proper names and not "privates," "bottom," "down there," or "pee-pee place."

The male has a penis and a *scrotum* (or bag) containing two testicles. The head of the penis (or glans) has an opening for urine and sperm (urethral orifice) which should be at least one-sixteenth-inch slot—not a pinpoint hole.

The penis, highly sensitive to touch, readily becomes erect with slight stimulation or occasionally when the bladder is full. A male "discovers" his penis at about one year of age when he can see over his protuberant abdomen. It frequently itches because of diaper irritation or food allergy (to orange juice especially). He fools with it and finds the sensation pleasurable; so he continues. If his mother indicates disgust, his interest may be encouraged. Studied indifference should be the parents' attitude when confronted with genital play. (See *Phimosis* and *Paraphimosis.*)

Many obese boys accumulate a pad of fat over the pubic bone that allows the penis almost to disappear. It will become a normal-looking appendage after weight loss and/or adolescent maturation. (I wonder about a mother who says to me, "That's the strangest-looking penis I've ever seen.") (See *Micropenis.*)

The female genitalia consist of two labia (or lips) which converge at the pubic bone over the clitoris. The latter may be slightly enlarged at birth but is usually completely covered by the labia by childhood. Upon separation of the labia the *vaginal* opening is revealed to be about one-fourth inch in diameter, the bottom margin formed by the *hymen,* a crescent of tough but tender tissue. The *urethral* opening, about halfway between the clitoris and the vaginal opening, is a barely detectable pinhole. The most common adhesion seen is in infant females; the labiae may be joined together, producing an abnormal appearance to the vaginal opening. If the opening of the urethra is occluded, the adhesion may be separated by the application of an estrogen cream. Forceful tearing apart of the labia is painful, and the raw edges are more likely to readhere. Because this problem is almost never seen in the older girl, we assume it relieves itself.

Glomerulonephritis is an inflammation of the *kidneys* due to an antibody-antigen reaction that develops after a streptococcal infection of throat or skin. It is as if the body became allergic to its own kidney tissue. The capillaries in the kidneys become swollen and inflamed, allowing *blood* and *protein* to leak out in the urine. The patient becomes pale, irritable, feverish, and usually develops some *edema* or swelling (frequently of the eyelids only). There are few physical findings except elevated blood pressure. The urine is scanty, reddish brown, and contains excess protein (*albuminuria*). *Headache,* drowsiness, and *convulsions* are usually the results of *hypertension* and spasm of cerebral blood vessels. The heart may go into failure because of the increased blood volume and the elevated *blood pressure.* The swollen capillaries in the glomeruli of the kidneys (which filter the blood to make urine) may prevent urine formation (kidney failure). This is serious but may only be temporary; the patient may recover completely.

The disease may be so mild and transient that it goes unrecognized, or it may be so wildly explosive with edema, convulsions, blood in the urine, and fever that the patient may succumb. Hospitalization is required to monitor the urine volume and the blood pressure. *Penicillin* is indicated to eradicate any streptococcus infection.

Eighty to ninety percent of patients recover completely; the vast majority are well in the first two months. If the urine and sedimentation rate of the blood remain abnormal after six months, the disease is called subacute or chronic.

Chronic glomerulonephritis is common following *nephritis* in adults, but occurs in less than 5 percent of children so affected. It may be discovered in a routine urinalysis (albumin and red cells) or by finding *hypertension.* Some patients develop generalized *edema* with very swollen eyelids, abdomen (see *Ascites,* Section 12), and ankles (*nephrosis*). A rare type of glomerulonephritis is Alport's syndrome.

Cortisone therapy may alter the course of the chronic form, but these patients follow a gradual downhill course with hypertension, uremia, headache, listlessness, and heart failure.

Dialysis or cleaning of the blood with a kidney machine is of some temporary help, and kidney transplantation is occasionally performed in the hope of more lasting help, but the procedure is quite complicated and usually restricted to large research centers.

Glycosuria is the presence of *glucose,* a simple sugar, in the urine. This usually means *diabetes mellitus* and is one of the chief reasons for doing a routine urinalysis. The *kidneys* usually do not allow glucose to appear in the urine. If the amount of glucose in the blood exceeds a certain critical level, as in *diabetes,* the kidney tubules are unable to reabsorb this excess and glucose will "spill over" into the urine. In some cases the kidney threshold for glucose is low, and glucose will appear in the urine despite a normal amount in the blood—renal glycosuria. In the patient with renal glycosuria, a glucose-tolerance test is indicated to rule out the possibility of diabetes. This inability to reabsorb glucose is a genetic trait; no treatment is necessary. It may also occur in poisonings (*lead*) when kidney damage results.

Hematuria is blood in the urine; gross hematuria implies that the urine is frankly red, smoky, or brown. Microscopic hematuria implies that the urine is grossly clear, but that the red cells can be seen in small numbers under the microscope. The absence of frank blood delays treatment as the condition would go unnoticed. Red urine will follow ingestion of beets (especially if the patient is *anemic*), crayons, mercurochrome, and merthiolate, so the urine must be ex-

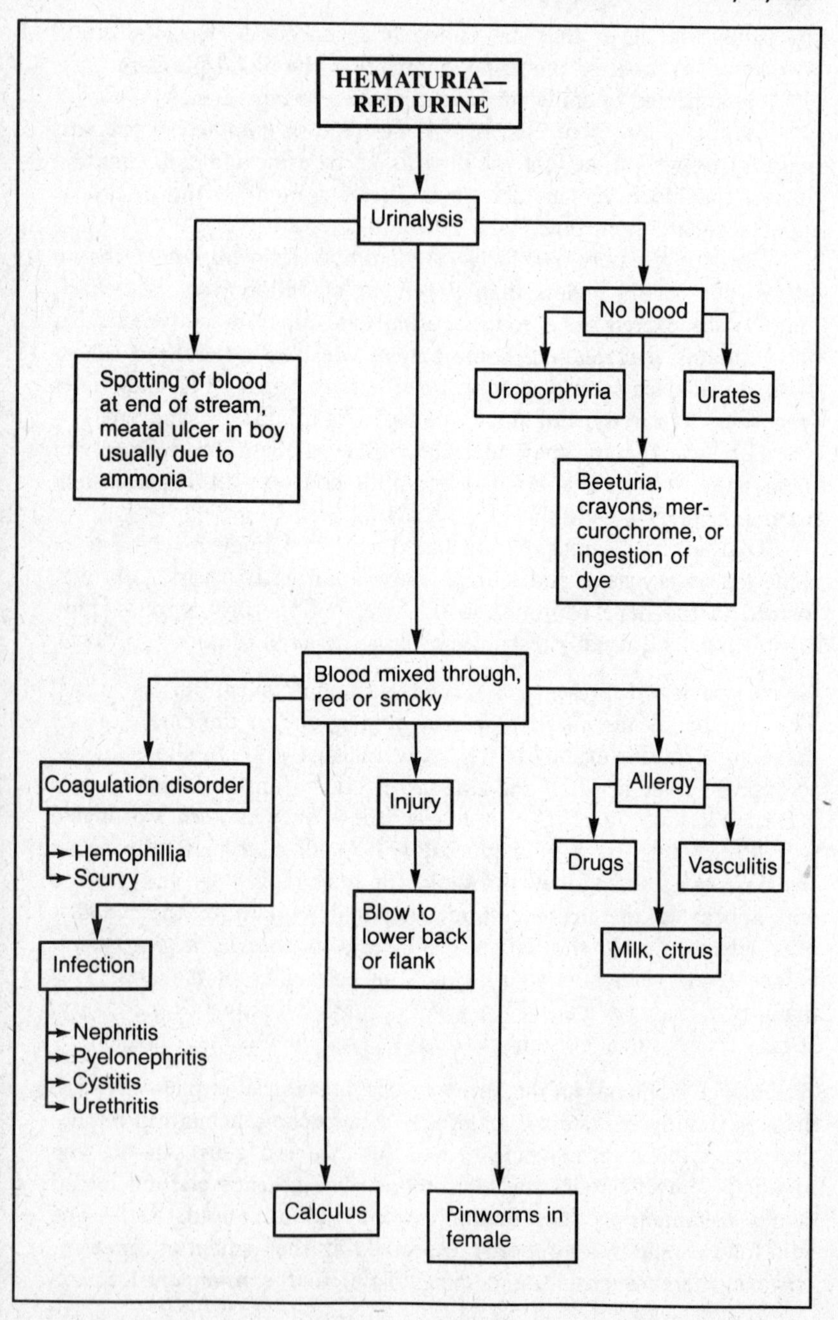
HEMATURIA—
RED URINE
Urinalysis
Spotting of blood at end of stream, meatal ulcer in boy usually due to ammonia
No blood
Uroporphyria
Urates
Beeturia, crayons, mer-curochrome, or ingestion of dye
Blood mixed through, red or smoky
Coagulation disorder
Hemophillia
Scurvy
Infection
Nephritis
Pyelonephritis
Cystitis
Urethritis
Injury
Blow to lower back or flank
Allergy
Drugs
Vasculitis
Milk, citrus
Calculus
Pinworms in female

amined under the microscope. Clots usually indicate trauma, stone (*calculus*), malignancy, or *tuberculosis.*

The most common cause of hematuria in a boy is an ammoniacal sore just inside the urethral opening. The ammonia erodes the lining, and the salty urine irritates and washes out a few drops of blood—usually passed at the beginning of urination. Small drops of blood may be noted on diaper or underwear.

Cystitis or bladder infection is the next most common cause; the infection erodes the bladder lining sufficiently to break open some capillaries.

Glomerulonephritis is usually associated with grossly bloody urine. *Pyelonephritis* (bacterial kidney infection) only infrequently is accompanied by hematuria.

Allergies to some foods may cause massive bleeding. Drugs (*sulfanilamide*), stones, cancer, *tuberculosis, congestive heart failure, hemophilia,* trauma, *hemangiomata, renal cysts, vitamin C* and *K* deficiencies, *leukemia, purpura, lupus, sickle-cell* trait, *renal-vein thrombosis, septicemia,* are rare conditions; a pertinent history or a physical examination suggests the diagnosis.

Recent vigorous exercise, acute infections elsewhere (strep throat), mild trauma, may cause blood in the urine. Repeated urinalyses will reveal normal findings, obviously. If blood is persistent, the condition must be investigated. If the source is undetermined, *cystoscopy* and X-ray examination of the kidneys are necessary.

Hemorrhagic cystitis is an infection of the bladder with the usual burning, frequency and urgency but associated with gross *hematuria.* The inflammation has eroded bladder capillaries.

Treatment is the same as for *cystitis.* A few are due to a virus. The condition may be confused with *glomerulonephritis or Henoch-Schönlein vasculitis.*

Hydronephrosis is an enlarged kidney caused by an obstruction in the urinary tract *(ureter, bladder, urethra*) which is the common cause of a large mass in the abdomen present at birth. When the condition is discovered, an effort is made to relieve the obstruction. Occasionally the kidney tissue has been destroyed by the back pressure, and the kidney is best removed. But frequently a damaged kidney will regain much of its normal function once the obstruction is relieved. The slowly moving urine is a good culture medium for bacterial infection. When this is suspected, an X ray of the kidneys reveals this hitherto silent but potentially lethal condition.

A mother might become suspicious if she noticed a weak or feeble urinary stream. Normal urination is a painless, effortless action. If a boy baby, lying on his back, must strain to urinate, and the stream is thin and does not arch over his knees and wet his feet, an obstruction in the urethra (the tube from the bladder to the outside) might be suspected.

A urinalysis is the minimum workup when uropathy is suspected. Red and white cells are found if infection is active; *albuminuria* may or may not be present in hydronephrosis. There may be no clue that a serious anomaly is present except for the infection. Tests would be helpful in determining the level of obstruction. (See *Cystoscopy, Pyelography, Cystography.*) In I-V *pyelography* a damaged kidney might not be able to concentrate the dye well enough for it to be seen in the X ray. The urologist next does a *cystoscopy.* He injects a dye to find the extent of damage with more X rays if the intravenous ones were not clear. This latter technique, retrograde pyelography, would reveal a common cause of hydronephrosis, a narrowing or kinking at the upper end of the ureter where it joins the pelvis of the kidney.

Most cases of hydronephrosis are benefited by surgical correction of the obstruction.

Hymen, or maidenhead, is a crescent-shaped bit of tender tissue at the posterior aspect of the vaginal opening. Its integrity is traditionally the hallmark of virginity, but some virgins have no hymen, and some women still have an intact hymen after intercourse. Use of intravaginal tampons by virginal girls is practical if comfortable. An imperforate hymen would obstruct menstrual flow and must be looked for in a nonmenstruating, mature adolescent female.

Kidney failure is usually the result of chronic *nephritis* with extensive damage to the glomeruli or tubules or of chronic urinary obstruction with pressure destruction of kidney substance. Acute renal failure as a result of prolonged inadequate blood flow due to shock, surgery, *septicemia,* injury or *dehydration* may irreversibly damage the kidneys, but function can be restored if treated in time. Intravenous fluids based on blood levels of various salts might sustain the victim until urine flows again.

Renal failure is first manifested by reduction in urine volume, lethargy, confusion, *edema, hypertension,* shock (depending on causative agent), and elevated nitrogen wastes in the blood (*urea* nitrogen not being flushed out).

Renal agenesis means absent kidneys. The condition is fatal; life usually ends within a month. Anomalies of the urinary or genital tract may be associated with odd facial features.

Unilateral absence is not uncommon. The single remaining kidney is usually larger than normal.

Kidneys are one of the chief organs of fluid and waste excretion. About one fifth of the blood pumped by each heartbeat passes to the kidneys. Arteries branch into small tubes, eventually knotting up in a capillary tuft (glomerulus) where water and small dissolved particles are filtered out into collecting tubules which carry this eventually (as urine) to the ureters and bladder. These tubules reabsorb most of the water (under the influence of a hormone; see *Diabetes insipidus,* Section 10) and much glucose and minerals. If the body becomes acidotic from *diarrhea,* for instance, the kidneys will compensate by increased retention of alkali and excretion of hydrogen (acid ions) combined with ammonium. The kidneys act to keep the blood in a narrow range of acid-base and fluid balance.

Infants up to six months of age are unable to concentrate urine as well as adults. This is the chief reason for using milk as the main article of diet during this period. The infant's poor ability to clear *sodium* in the first few months of life argues against the early introduction of solid foods with high sodium content. Because of this poor concentration ability, *diarrhea* during warm weather is especially dangerous. Extra fluid (watered milk) is important. Boiled skimmed milk is dangerous because of its high sodium content.

Floating or displaced kidney is usually asymptomatic and discovered on routine abdominal palpation. It may occasionally kink the ureter and produce urinary colic or repeated infection from static urine. X rays, after injection of X-ray-opaque dye, with the patient first upright and then supine would reveal the amount of movement. Floating kidney is more likely seen in the long, thin, droopy, nonmuscular *ectomorph.*

Horseshoe kidney is the name given to the condition of fusion of the lower poles of the kidneys. It may cause infection, obstruction, pain, blood in the urine, and stones.

Labial adhesions—see *Genitals,* female

Lithiasis—see *Calculus*

Micropenis is a small penis. If associated with absent *testes* or *hypospadias,* it may be a clitoris and some attempt should be made to determine the true sex of the patient.

Often a fat boy will be needlessly concerned because his pubic fat may actually hide his normal-sized penis. It is a source of great embarrassment to him, and constant reassurance must be provided until full adolescent maturation allows him to see it and believe.

Nephritis is an inflammation of the *kidneys.* This category includes *glomerulonephritis* (acute and chronic), nephritis associated with *Henoch-Schönlein vasculitis, lupus erythematosus, polyarteritis,* nephritis combined with deafness (Alport's syndrome, an hereditary disease), and *hemolytic-uremic* syndrome (see Section 2). Many diseases produce some transient kidney disturbance, but because the attention of the doctor is directed to some other part of the body, the urinalysis may be overlooked. *Pneumonia, strep* throat, and *dysentery* produce toxin severe enough to hurt the kidneys; the urine may show albumin and red cells. In most cases these changes are temporary, disappearing when symptoms of the primary disease subside. Nephritis may be associated with *diphtheria* and (rarely) with *mumps.*

Nephrosis is a complex symptom including generalized edema (fluid retention), much protein in urine, low level of albumin in the blood, and elevated cholesterol in the blood. The onset is most frequently at about two years of age.

If hypertension and blood in the urine are persistent, some doctors assume that the disease is due to *glomerulonephritis* (hyperimmune response to *streptococcal* infection).

In *lipoid nephrosis* the glomeruli are normal, but the *kidneys* are swollen and pale. Fat-like deposits are seen in the tubule cells. This disease usually does not cause blood in the urine or *hypertension.*

The *edema* may be slight in the beginning with swelling only in the eyelids. It may be overwhelming and almost double the patient's weight in a week or so. Remissions may occur spontaneously (occasionally after measles); recurrences frequently follow a mild respiratory infection. *Peritonitis* is a common complication, as the accumulated fluid in the peritoneum is a good culture medium. Skin infections (*cellulitis*) are common.

Recovery is possible in the majority of cases, but it may take months or years. The *cortisone* drugs have been helpful in speeding up the remissions and making the recurrences less severe. Response is more obvious in the lipoid type than in the glomerulonephritic variety. Some have found that the use of immunosuppressive drugs have induced remissions if cortisone resistance has developed. When a remission is obtained on cortisone, the drug is continued for months.

Oliguria is a reduction of urinary flow. It is temporary in *dehydration,* shock, *septicemia, acidosis, hemorrhage,* and heart failure, but might be the early stage of kidney failure, however, just prior to complete urinary shutdown. An ounce of urine a day obviously means oliguria and is associated with generalized *kidney* disease (glomerulonephritis), uremia, and *hypertension.*

Oophoritis is an ovarian inflammation and occurs in a few mature females as a complication of *mumps.* Lower abdominal pain is obvious, and if the right ovary is involved, may be confused with *appendicitis.*

Orchitis, *mumps,* is the testicular inflammation that occurs in about one out of four mature males who acquire *mumps.* It may occur simultaneously with or shortly after the *parotid* swelling. The involved side of the scrotum becomes red, hot, and tender. *Codeine* or narcotics might be advised if *aspirin* is of no benefit. Ice bags or at least a sling support (with the patient lying on his back) may help; it lasts about three or four days. Surgery may be needed to relieve the pressure. Fertility may be impaired, but not usually eliminated even if the inflammation is bilateral, as it is in about 20 percent of cases.

There seems to be no positive correlation between physical activity and the development of mumps orchitis. Statistics indicate that patients who have been flat on their backs in bed with mumps will develop this as frequently as patients who have been up.

Orthostatic albuminuria—see *Albuminuria*

Ovaries—see Section 10

Paraphimosis is the condition in which the retracted foreskin cannot be replaced back over the glans (head) of the *penis.* The mother may have pulled the foreskin back to cleanse the penis only to find that it acts as a tourniquet; the glans, turgid with blood, becomes larger and the constricting foreskin becomes tighter.

Plenty of lubricant plus firm, constant, cold, generalized pressure on the swollen glans usually will allow the foreskin to be replaced. If successful, it is no longer a paraphimosis. If unsuccessful, a surgical slit and possible circumcision are in order.

Penis—see *Genitals*

Phimosis is the extreme narrowing of the foreskin over the head of the penis so that retraction is impossible. A slit or a circumcision may be necessary to allow some mobility of the foreskin. A long, redundant foreskin may be an indication for *circumcision* (see Section 5).

Polyuria is the frequent passing of large amounts of urine. It is characteristic of *diabetes mellitus* and *insipidus,* and a variety of *kidney* diseases.

Porphyria is the general name for a group of inherited metabolic disorders in which pyrrole is involved. One type predominantly affects the liver and one predominantly the red cells. Porphyrins accumulate or are excreted in the urine or stool; tests can determine the type and amount. These chemical relatives of hemoglobin are formed and stored in skin tissues. Because they are photosensitive the patient develops swelling, redness, and blisters when exposed to the sun.

In a patient genetically disposed to porphyria, certain drugs will allow an enzyme to build up which leads to more porphyrins and symptoms. (*Sulfa* drugs, *barbiturates,* and some sex hormones may trigger the attack.) Intestinal symptoms, *hypertension,* muscle and back pain, confused and abnormal behavior, fever, and urinary complaints are the more common findings in an attack. Colicky pain may be severe and suggest a surgical condition, but examination reveals few objective findings. "Peculiar" personality changes may border on the psychotic. Sometimes *phenobarbital* is given to quiet the restless behavior, but the patient only gets worse. Red urine gives awav the disease. Blood, urine, and stools have abnormal amounts of porphyrins, and the diagnosis is confirmed.

The condition does not usually become manifest until adolescence. Diet control, avoidance of alcohol and certain drugs will help prevent the attacks. The skin must not be exposed to the sun. Patients must be properly identified so that surgery will not be performed during the abdominal-pain attacks.

Pyelography is the X-ray examination of the *kidneys* and *ureters* following an intravenous injection of a dye opaque to X rays. The dye is concentrated by the kidneys, and successive pictures reveal the integrity of the tubing through which the urine flows.

Pyelonephritis is a kidney infection due to a germ, usually associated with some obstruction, albeit minor, to the flow of urine. Like germs in stagnant water, the bacteria are not flushed out completely or rapidly enough to prevent them from multiplying in the *bladder* or the pelvis of the *kidney*. As it is more frequently seen in females, it is assumed that bacteria in the vaginal area migrate up the relatively short *urethra* (the tube from the bladder to the outside) into the bladder. The pressure inside the bladder at the time of urination may be great enough to force some infected urine back up to the kidneys through the inadequate valves at the junction of the *ureters* and the bladder. The bacteria multiply in the urine and invade the kidney substance.

The infection is usually ushered in with a violent chill, *headache*, stomach or back ache, followed by fever and usually an *emesis* or two. If *aspirin* (if retained) plus a hot bath are ineffective in reducing the high fever, this should alert the physician to seek a bacterial infection (*otitis media, tonsillitis, pneumonia,* or pyelitis). A chill and a fever in a female means a bladder or kidney infection until ruled out by an examination of the patient and a urinalysis. The urine usually has elevated amounts of albumin and is loaded with pus (*white blood cells*). A *culture* usually reveals the *E. coli* bacterium, thus suggesting that the infection came from fecal contamination.

Treatment with a *sulfa* drug or *ampicillin* almost always reduces the fever within twenty-four hours, but to be sure that the germs have been eradicated, it is best to continue treatment for ten to twenty days. A *culture* to determine the number of bacteria present per cubic millimeter is a reliable way to verify a bacteriological cure.

It is sometimes difficult to snatch a urine specimen on demand from a sick and uncooperative patient. (See *Cystitis.*) We can manually wring out a wet diaper and find a few pus cells (mixed with soap granules and cotton fibers); a plastic bag can be affixed to the perineal area and a teaspoon of urine may find its way into this. If the story of chills, fever, and dysuria are present in a female and no urine is forthcoming, an elevated white blood count (20,000 to 30,000 per cubic millimeter) is presumptive evidence of a pyelitis. Treatment can begin with this as the working diagnosis, and the urine could be brought to the microscope the next day. It would still be full of pus cells, but the antibiotic may prevent any bacterial growth in the culture.

There is some prophylactic benefit in providing enough fluid for a child to allow at least a minimum of three or four urinations a day. This helps to wash out any bacteria that might sneak into the bladder. Teaching a girl (especially a girl) to wipe her anus after bowel movements from front to back may discourage germ migration. Tight underpants may be a factor in setting up an irritation. Drinking apple and cranberry juice has been helpful in promoting an acid urine which discourages bacterial growth. A few patients will *not* get bladder and kidney infections if they do not drink milk, orange, or tomato juice. Some occult *allergic* mechanism makes the outlet tube opening (urethra) swell up, precluding the complete emptying of the bladder, and the full-blown infection follows. Daily vitamin C will help acidify the urine.

Because the infection is so common in females, it is standard to allow them two bona-fide infections before a full-scale investigation is made. (See *Hydronephrosis.*) Then it is best to consult a *urologist.* Surgical correction of any obstruction is necessary to avoid recurrent infection, kidney damage, and the late effects of *hypertension* and *kidney failure.* Some reports suggest evidence of chronic pyelonephritis in 2 to 3 percent of all kidneys at autopsy (higher in females). Routine urinalyses are worthwhile, and frequent follow-up examinations are a must in all those patients who have had this infection.

Renal cysts are large, single, or simple cysts (fluid-filled spaces) of the kidneys and are relatively common at all ages. They may be large enough to be palpable and may cause pressure atrophy of the renal substance; but, their most important significance is that the doctor cannot tell them apart from the mass produced by a kidney tumor without doing special tests (renal *angiography, retrograde pyelography*). Frequently surgical exploration is necessary to be sure that the mass is only a cyst and not a malignant tumor.

Multiple (or *polycystic*) *kidney disease* is a genetically transmitted condition in which the kidney tissue is partially replaced by thousands of small cysts which may grow larger and larger with growth of the child. The kidneys may resemble sponges, and cystic disease of the lungs or liver may be associated. In one form of the disease, *kidney failure, hypertension, oliguria,* and uremia develop early in life (within the first ten years) and the prognosis is very poor. In the most common form, however, the child grows into adulthood without serious problems and it is not until the age of thirty to fifty years that the symptoms of renal failure become manifest. Both forms carry a very poor prognosis and the only treatment thus far is chronic hemodialysis (artificial purification of the blood) or kidney transplantation—both of which are very complicated, expensive and available only in a few research centers. Obviously a diseased cystic kidney should not be removed without evidence of adequate function in the opposite kidney.

Renal rickets is bone demineralization (decreased calcium is visible in bone X rays) due to *kidney* disease (pyelonephritis, *glomerulonephritis, polycystic disease, hydronephrosis*). The kidney tubules are damaged by the underlying disease and are unable to maintain a normal acid-base buffer system in the blood; excess phosphate and acidity of the blood encourages dissolution of calcium from the bone into the blood; *calcium* in the diet is not absorbed properly.

The severity of the kidney pathology is enough to cause anemia and growth failure. Urinalysis, blood tests, and bone X rays will reveal the problem. Signs of *rickets* (Section 11) would be present if the disease had progressed.

If nothing can be done to correct the kidney lesion, large doses of *vitamin D* will increase calcium absorption and bone mineralization. (Tens of thousands of units a day may be necessary to correct this problem, in contrast to the usual 400 units per day for the normal child.)

Renal tuberculosis is a rare infection usually spread from a diseased lung to the *kidney* via the blood stream. Chills, fever, frequency, *hematuria* would suggest a kidney infection; pus in the urine would confirm it. Then if the patient does not respond after a few days of standard treatment with *sulfa* or *ampicillin,* and the usual germs do not grow in the culture, *tuberculosis* would be suspected. (Special and prolonged culture methods are necessary to grow the TB germ.)

If *streptomycin* and *isoniazid* do not quiet the infection, removal of the kidney must be considered. (Normal function of the other kidney must be assured, of course.)

Renal tubular acidosis is a disorder in which the *kidney* tubules are unable to excrete acid urine. The victim is in constant *acidosis,* passes *calcium* kidney stones, is weak, and grows poorly.

Treatment is to replace the minerals being lost in the urine. *Sodium* and *potassium* are the ones that will counteract the acidosis.

Retroperitoneal neoplasms are cancers that are derived from the kidneys or adjacent structures near the spine. They give few symptoms except some abdominal distention. They are rare, and if discovered early, the permanent cure rate is quite high. Their detection is one of the chief reasons for the annual physical (and the parents' more frequent abdominal palpation as a tickling game at bath or bedtime). *Wilms's tumor, neuroblastoma, teratoma, lymphosarcoma* are all serious, but cures are possible (see *Neoplasms,* Section 10).

Scrotum—see *Testes*

Specific gravity test of urine compares urine density with that of water (1.000). Very concentrated urine has a specific gravity greater than 1.025. The test is of some value in determining the ability of the *kidneys* to concentrate urine. Small babies are unable to concentrate it, but after six months this ability should be on a par with that of adults. Renal diseases (chronic *glomerulonephritis*) will impair the concentrating ability of the kidneys. (The specific gravity should be greater than 1.015 after twelve hours of limited fluid intake.)

Testes or testicles are the paired male organs for the production

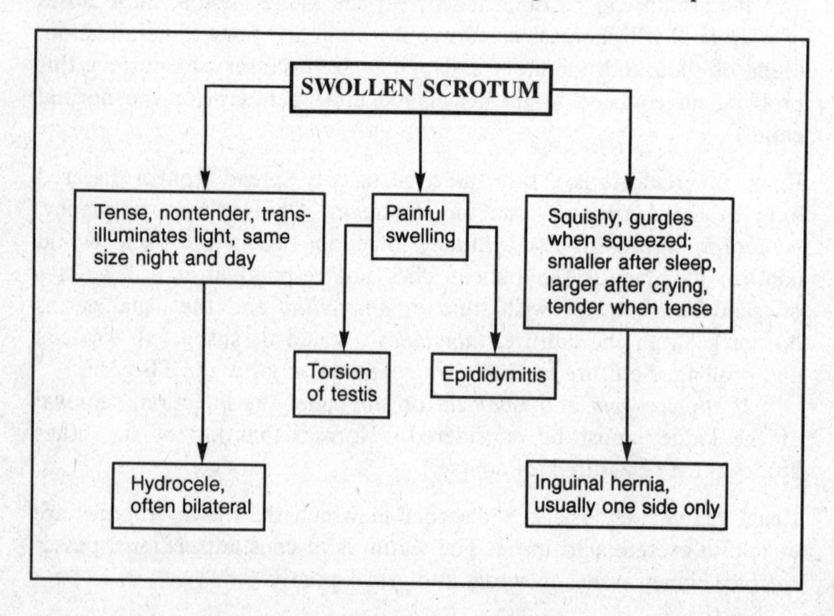

of sperm found in the scrotum. (See *Hypogonadism,* Section 10.) FSH from the pituitary stimulates the maturation of spermatozoa. The luteinizing hormone stimulates the interstitial cells of the testes to mature; these produce testosterone which is the hormone responsible for masculinizing the boy.

Torsion of the testis is a twisting of the testicle on the spermatic cord. This occludes the blood supply and if not relieved in a few hours, the testicle dies and must be removed. Vague discomfiture is followed by intense pain and tenderness, fever, and *vomiting.* Surgery is the only way to save the testis. After the cord has been untwisted, the blood supply should return; if not, the testis may have to be removed. If the surgery is successful, the testis is usually sutured to the lining to prevent its twisting again. The surgeon will usually surgically fix the opposite testis at the same time to prevent torsion of the opposite side in the future.

Urea is a nitrogen-bearing compound found abundantly in the urine. It is the chief chemical remaining after nitrogen compounds are metabolized. If increased amounts are found in the blood (uremia), it suggests *kidney* damage, dysfunction, or dehydration. As an I-V solution, it helps to reduce *edema* of the brain and body tissues, but must be given only if the kidneys are functioning properly.

Ureters are the tubes that carry urine from the *kidneys* to the *bladder*; anomalies are common. They may be doubled—one carrying urine from the top half of a kidney, and the other from the bottom half. The ureter may be dilated because of an obstruction in the urethra or where the ureters join the bladder. These narrowed points do not allow free passage of urine, and infection invades this stagnant fluid. Fever accompanied by flank or lower abdominal pain suggests the need for urinalysis, which usually reveals pus. If the valve at the ureter-bladder junction is malfunctioning, infection may be introduced into the ureters at the time of urinating. The pressure on the bladder to empty will force some urine back up the ureters (reflux); infection usually follows. Surgery is necessary if infections are repetitious. X rays are usually done to pinpoint the anomalous area.

Obstruction of urinary flow from ureter to bladder may be silent, may herald itself with intermittent flank pain, or as a mass that comes and goes. (With pressure urine would pass out of dilated ureter into bladder.) Abdominal pain or vomiting attacks that cannot be called "flu" suggest the need of X-ray studies of the kidneys.

The ureters may receive large volumes of urine from the distended bladder if the urethra is narrowed. After corrective surgery on the urethra, the reflux up the ureters usually ceases because the bladder resumes a smaller, more normal size, and the bladder wall acts as a valve to prevent this backflow. If X rays reveal that this reflux still occurs, then surgery must be accomplished to reimplant the ureters into the bladder.

Repeated infection may cause pathological changes in the various tubes which will give the X-ray appearance of some obstruction. So the problem works both ways; obstruction to flow allows infection to become superimposed; infection leads to distorted tubing, which allows urinary stasis and reinfection.

Urethra is the tube that carries urine from the *bladder* to the outside; in the male it is obviously longer, since it traverses the length of the *penis.* The circumcised male has no protection from diaper and ammonia irritation and may develop an ulcer just at or inside the opening of the penis (glans). On healing, this meatal ulcer may cause a narrowing (or stricture) that slows urinary flow. It may cause back pressure into the bladder, infection, and *kidney* damage.

It is important that a mother occasionally observe her boy's urinary stream (he usually cannot micturate for the doctor on command). A fine, misty, high-pressure spray that must be forced out by tensing abdominal muscles suggests this stricture, and operative intervention is required to preclude bladder and kidney damage. Occasionally the parent can eavesdrop at the bathroom door for healthy sounds of a good stream striking the toilet-bowl water; it should be forceful enough to produce bubbles. The opening (meatus) should be a one-sixteenth to one-eighth inch slit; a pinhole is not adequate. (See *Urinalysis.*)

If this stricture is discovered early in infancy at the time the ammoniacal ulcer is bleeding and about to heal and contract, the use of an antibiotic eye ointment may heal the ulcer as it maintains the normal opening. I say *eye* ointment because the tube (one-eighth ounce size) has a pinpointed dispensing end that can easily be inserted a few millimeters into the urethra; the inserted ointment and the stretching action of the conical end of the tube preclude the ultimate narrowing that occurs if the ulcer is untreated.

The girl has her problems, but not from ammonia. The short urethra in the female empties into the moist, dark, germ-laden area between the lips (labia) of the vaginal opening. Her anatomy thus makes her susceptible to ascending bladder and kidney infections. The germ that usually migrates "upstream" is the *E. coli,* so it is assumed to come from the *anal* area. Not all females are susceptible, so other factors such as tight underwear, wiping the anus from back to front (instead of from front to back), insufficient fluids, faulty voiding habits, and alkaline urine (germs grow better in alkaline urine than in acid urine) all play a role.

Urethritis is the inflammation of the urethra and is associated with *cystitis, allergy,* and irritating bath soap (bubble bath especially). Some urologists believe that there is a condition called chronic posterior urethritis. This low-grade infection causes local swelling in the lining of the urethra just adjacent to the *bladder.* A reflex spasm of the urethral sphincter may also prevent a complete emptying of the urine. Infection follows. If no other structural anomaly can be found to explain frequent urinary infections, the treatment is to stretch this area with catheters back to its normal size. *Allergies* (to milk or orange juice, for example) can occasionally be demonstrated as the triggering mechanism.

Urinalysis includes the determination of *protein* (more than a trace suggests infection, *nephritis, nephrosis*), *glucose* (diabetes), *pH* (acidity or alkalinity), and *specific gravity* (too dilute—*diabetes insipidus,* too concentrated—*dehydration*). A microscopic examination is made for *red cells* (infection, nephritis, injury, etc. [see *Hematuria*]), *white cells* (infection), crystals (uric acid, cysteine), and casts (agglutinated material from damaged tubules).

Normal urine is perfectly sterile provided that it has been collected in a sterile fashion. If only a few colonies of bacteria per millimeter of urine are present, then it is generally assumed that these are contaminants from adjacent skin surfaces; the patient does not have an actual urinary infection. (See *Culture.*)

Urinary infection, chronic or recurrent, suggests some obstructive process.

Other tests of kidney function include blood tests for urea nitrogen, pH, and bicarbonate levels. Kidney biopsy is usually reserved for kidney disease with obscure or equivocal findings.

One urologist suggested the use of a tape recording that could be brought to the office for analysis. Urine sounds may be as individual as a fingerprint: (a) the normal, full, strong fall, (b) the hesitant, wavering stream with dribbing at the end, (c) the on-and-off stream requiring use of abdominal muscles with audible grunts. The latter two indicate the need of further X-ray or urological workup, especially if associated with enuresis, frequency, accidents, or constantly damp underwear.

Every parent should observe the child frequently in infancy and occasionally afterward for signs of *dysuria* (straining), frequency, and inadequate stream. The infant boy should be able to wet his feet easily while lying on his back; the girl should flood the diaper without straining. When a child is old enough to use the toilet, the flow should be easily audible as it hits the water and should make bubbles. One may have to eavesdrop, as the older child may refuse to urinate for an audience.

The urine is usually pale yellow. Very dark yellow is usually caused by vitamin preparations or food (carrots). Red urine must be checked for blood, but may be the result of eating crayons, paints, merthiolate, or beets. Reddish deposits on the diaper are usually urates. Green or blue urine usually follows ingestion of methylene blue—the usual college dormitory joke.

Urinary system is that part of the body involved with excretion of wastes, conservation of water, maintenance of normal electrolytic (salt) balance in the bloodstream, and partially with stabilization of the blood pressure.

Urologist is a surgical and medical specialist whose field is the diseases of the kidneys, bladder, prostate, and various connecting tubes. He is an expert in evaluating kidney function and waste metabolism. He may work in a team with an internist or pediatrician and general surgeon in evaluating abdominal pathology. He treats with drugs or surgery. He understands and is frequently consulted about adult sexual problems.

Vagina is the distensible tube lying between the female external genitalia and the uterus inside the pelvis. It is located between the bladder in front and the rectum behind. It receives the *penis* during intercourse and distends widely to receive the baby during birth (at which time it is called the birth canal).

An imperforate hymen may bulge because of the secretions that have built up behind it. An incision is required. An absent vagina is rare and may be fashioned after maturity. The uterus, however, may be absent or rudimentary and non-functioning.

Vaginal discharge is common in the prepubescent female and should be white, gray, or mucoid. It is the response to female hormones and requires no treatment except for hygiene and extra changes of underwear. Some girls require a menstrual pad to contain the large flow.

A green or yellow discharge is the sign of vaginitis, common in young girls because the hormone-deficient vaginal lining is susceptible to bacterial invasion. Irritating alkaline soaps (especially bubble bath) may inflame the lining so that infection sets in. If the girl will sit twice a day in a shallow tub of water to which is added about two ounces of vinegar, it may acidify the area enough to discourage bacterial growth. Failing this, *estrogen* creams or estrogen vaginal inserts (*urethral* suppositories are narrow and slide into the immature vagina easily) will usually clear it up. (See *Nitrofurans,* under *Antibacterials,* Section 4.) Antibiotics may be necessary. A suspicious doctor looking for *gonorrhea* may do a culture.

If a the discharge is foul-smelling and/or bloody, a foreign object must be searched for (toys, a bit of carrot, or a pencil). The discovery of such an object suggests that the area is pruritic (itchy), and the possibility of *allergies* (chocolate milk, citrus juices) should be considered.

Special small instruments with lights may be necessary for examination. The doctor usually palpates the area via the rectum because the hymen is especially sensitive.

Monilia infection usually responds to *nystatin.*

Wilms's tumor—see *Nephroblastoma,* under *Neoplasms,* Section 10

SECTION 14

The Ears, Eyes, Mouth, Neck, and Nose

PART I

Ears

A. Hearing loss (deafness)

Cochlear (sensorineural)
Conductive
Adenoids (see Part V)
Foreign bodies
Serous otitis
Wax
Tests
Audiometry

B. Earache

Furuncle in ear canal
Herpangina (Section 2)
Mastoiditis
Mumps (Section 2)
Myringitis
Otitis media
Roseola (Section 2)
Swimmer's ear (otitis externa)
Teething

C. Vertigo

Allergy
Anemia (Section 8)
Ataxia (Section 15; also Gait, Section 7)
Drugs (Tranquilizers, Section 4)
Hypoglycemia (Section 10)
Motion sickness
Nystagmus—see Eyes
Otitis media
Postural hypotension (Section 8)

D. Deformed, prominent ears

Cauliflower ear (External ear)

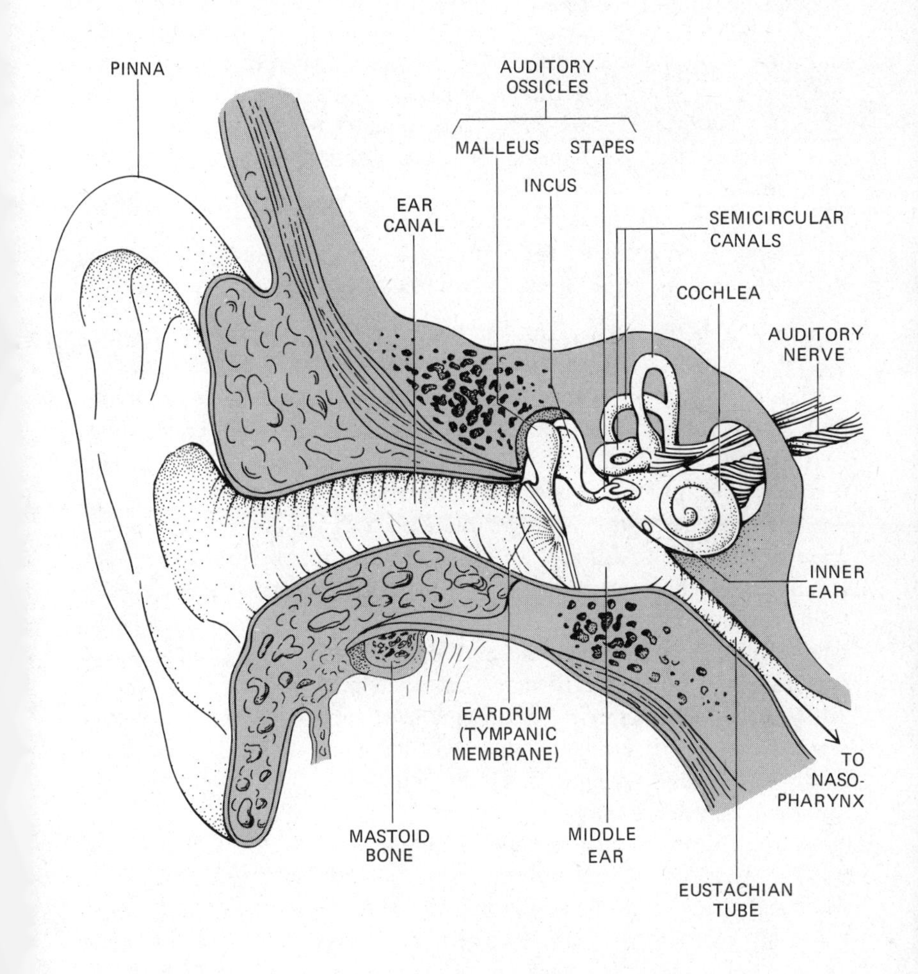
PINNA
AUDITORY OSSICLES
MALLEUS
STAPES
INCUS
EAR CANAL
SEMICIRCULAR CANALS
COCHLEA
AUDITORY NERVE
INNER EAR
EARDRUM (TYMPANIC MEMBRANE)
TO NASO-PHARYNX
MASTOID BONE
MIDDLE EAR
EUSTACHIAN TUBE

Audiometry is a form of hearing test. This test, when the patient is cooperative, will determine the decibel level and number of cycles per second at which sound is perceived. Many children have never had normal hearing, so are not aware that they have a deficit; their speech pattern may be affected. Many children, too, have lost gradually and imperceptibly some hearing in the higher range due to infection, and only this test will determine the extent of the loss.

It is best done in a soundproof room. The child is fitted with ear phones and asked to respond with a gesture when he first hears a sound. Each ear is tested through the whole range of tones (cycles per second) usually perceived by the human ear; the decibel level (loudness) at which the child responds to the sound is recorded. Persistent loss of over 20 decibels requires investigation.

Deafness is better called hearing loss; the term "deafness" suggests a total loss, which is rare. Congenital hearing loss, usually hereditary or due to intrauterine infection (*rubella*), must be tested for in the first few months of life because electronically amplified sound may be provided to allow some auditory stimulation early in life when it is so important for language development.

Hearing perception may be reduced because of wax impaction, retraction of the eardrum, scarring of the drum, fusion of the ossicles (small bones that carry sound impulse from eardrum to inner ear), fluid behind the eardrum (serous otitis, may be associated with respiratory or milk allergies, and enlarged tonsils and adenoids), perforated or bulging eardrum, and calcium deposits on the drum. All these cause conductive hearing losses: interference of the sound waves from the outside to the inner ear (nerve and cochlea). Conductive losses on the audiogram reveal that perception of high, middle, and low tones is reduced.

A cochlear (neurosensory) loss of hearing is due to defects of nerve conduction from the inner ear to the auditory area of the brain. Maternal influenza at the gestational age when the cochlea was forming can cause congenital neurosensory loss. Genetic factors cause some hearing loss. Infections such as mumps or encephalitis at any age may lead to auditory damage. The recent rubella epidemic caused severe hearing loss in the children born of mothers who contracted the disease in the early months of pregnancy.

These problems may reduce the decibel level of all sounds perceived or may selectively reduce the sounds of only certain frequencies. High tone loss suggests a mixed etiology.

When the eardrum of a child with a sensorineural loss is examined, the doctor can find nothing wrong. The eardrum of a child with a conductive loss is usually thick, dull, retracted, amber colored, and/or distorted or fixed in some way to suggest a problem. It may appear normal and still have fluid behind it.

Children rarely realize or express the fact that they are deaf. Peculiarities of speech or behavior may be the only clue. Inattention is so common in children that its presence alone is not enough to diagnose a deficit. Since many children become skillful lip readers, parents may need to resort to tricking the child with whispers or watches as testing devices. By age three or four, most can be tested with the audiogram machine. Because *adenoid* enlargement is maximal at five and six years of age, hearing difficulties due to this obstructive tissue are greatest at that time. The child may not complain and only seem bored, inattentive, or stupid.

Most school systems have—or should have—arrangements with a capable audiologist to test *all* children in kindergarten and/or first grade. Repeat testing for borderline cases follows. Retesting in third or fifth grades would catch most problem children before irreparable damage had occurred to their psyches or their ears.

Deafness may be associated with other bodily ills: *Goiter* and *Hunter's syndrome,* Section 10; *Albers-Schönberg disease,* Section 7; and *Treacher-Collins syndrome,* Section 5.

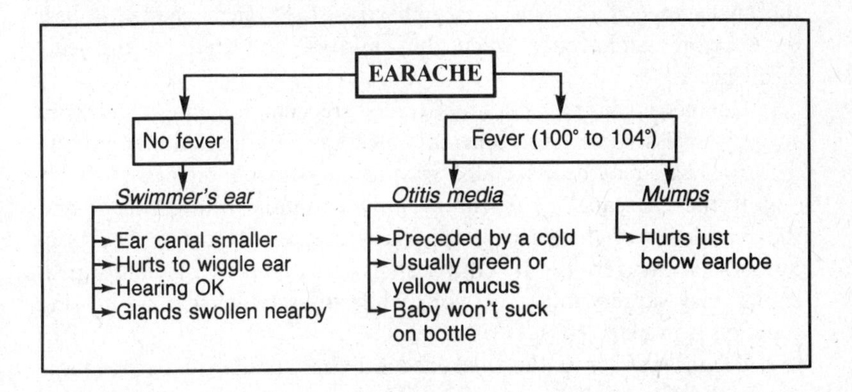

External ear is the skin and cartilaginous appendage found on the side of the head, constructed in such a way as to help direct sound waves into the ear canal to promote hearing and at the same time offer some protection to the eardrum from wind and flying objects such as bees and gnats.

Children, especially boys, have a rule that goes, "If you have a hole in your body, put something in it." Almost daily we doctors are pulling bits of paper, foil, pencil, erasers, crayon, or beads out of some two-to-six-year-old's ear canal. Most children who do this have forgotten when and are reluctant to tell why they put the object in there. It suggests, however, that something brought their attention to the hole: the canal itched because of an *allergy* or fungus infection or a middle-ear infection (*otitis media*), or fluid accumulation (serous otitis media) gave a sensation of fullness or deafness or pressure that required some form of probing investigation. Small objects may be teased or washed out; large impacted objects may require anesthesia in a small child, since the wall of the canal is tender. Bugs, beetles, flies, bees may be subdued with oil, alcohol, or whiskey and then removed. Vegetable matter (seeds, stems) should not be washed with water; the material swells up and may become impacted.

The composition of the ear cartilage is the end result of the embryonal fusion of a number of tissues; one small deviation at an early stage of development will result in a grossly abnormal appearance. Ears are rarely perfect mirror images of each other. (Next time you are in a crowd, look at the person in front of you and compare the left ear with the right; they are usually dissimilar in some minor way.) Plastic surgery is an acceptable retread method of changing the appearance if the bearer is embarrassed. Surgical change is best done before adolescence when the child is motivated by the jeers of his peers.

Cutaneous dimples or sinus tracts are common and require no surgery unless subject to recurrent infection. Low set and/or grossly deformed ears may be associated with urinary-tract anomalies.

If the ear canal is absent or only a dimple, the eardrum and the remainder of the hearing apparatus are usually malformed also. Surgery is dangerous. If both canals are congenitally unformed, exploratory surgery might be worthwhile to ascertain if some hearing function is present.

Cauliflower ear is the thickened ear that results from inadequate care following ear trauma—usually occurring during boxing or wrestling. If the blood clot (*hematoma*) between the skin and underlying cartilage is not removed immediately by needle aspiration or incision, a thickened scar may form.

Hearing disorders—see *Communication disorders,* Section 15; *Deafness*

Lateral sinus thrombosis is an infected blood clot in one of the veins just inside the skull near the ear hole. It is usually caused by an inadequately treated *mastoiditis* that has invaded this nearby vein. Chills, fever, headache, somnolence, and facial-muscle weakness might imitate a brain abscess.

Big antibiotic doses combined with surgery to remove the clot may be effective if done in the early stages of this very serious condition.

Mastoiditis is an infection of the mastoid cells which lie adjacent to the middle ear. The infection usually spreads from an untreated *otitis media.* It is obviously less common than before antibiotics were available, but it still happens. Frequently a mother will give medicine for a day or two and then quit when the earache is gone; some germs are left smoldering on, maybe spreading to the mastoid or perhaps developing resistance to antibiotics.

Chronic mastoiditis is a chronic bacterial infection in the mastoid spaces (like a sinus infection). Low-grade fever, headache, and chronic purulent drainage from the ear canal (through the ruptured drum) are suggestive. X rays might show a cloudiness of these mastoid cells. It is usually the result of inadequate treatment of an otitis media and/or acute mastoiditis. Antibiotics and possibly surgery are indicated. (See *Lateral sinus thrombosis.*)

Ménière's syndrome—see *Vertigo*

Motion sickness is a common problem of all age groups. It is an uncontrollable attack of nausea, vomiting, pallor, cold sweat, and weakness that persists in some people for the duration of a car, boat, train, or plane ride. It is due to the reflex action of the hypersensitive vestibular (balancing) apparatus in the inner ear.

It may be controlled by the calming action of *antihistaminics* on this mechanism or by the use of *anti-vomiting tranquilizers.* It is best to administer the drug about one half hour before departure. (See *Vertigo; Anti-motion sickness remedies,* Section 4.)

Myringitis is an inflammation of the eardrum and is painful. It may be associated with the irritation of wax in the canal or with *otitis externa.* The red eardrums often seen with *roseola* are myringitis, but because there is no bacterial invasion, no antibiotics are indicated.

Bullous myringitis is a virus infection of the eardrum, is painful until the blebs are opened, and is important only because secondary bacterial infection is a common sequel.

Otitis externa, Swimmer's ear, is any inflammation or infection in the ear canal (from the ear hole down to the eardrum). *Virus, allergy,* fungus, bacteria, yeasts may be primary, secondary, or mixed causes. *Swimmer's ear* occurs because the retained water macerates the canal skin and wax. This debris provides a good medium in which germs grow; it is dark, wet, and warm. An unpleasant odor is usually due to the growth of *pseudomonas* and *E. coli* germs. The ear-canal orifice is smaller than usual, the pain is aggravated by movement of the ear, and the local lymph nodes are swollen (in contrast to *otitis media*).

Swimmer's ear may result from bathing as well as swimming. Shampooing the hair may allow the water to run into the ear canals if the whole head is placed in the water. Shampooing in the shower is less conducive to retained ear-canal water.

A black material in the canal suggests a fungus growth more likely seen in the tropics.

Cleansing of the infected debris is more important than the medicinal drops usually instilled. (One doesn't paint a board without scraping off the old paint, grease, and dirt.) Then local broad-spectrum antibiotic (see Section 4) drops will arrest the condition. *Cortisone* may be included to dampen inflammation. Pain pills with *codeine* are usually necessary for three days. Prophylactic swabbing with alcohol on a fine wick of cotton after showers and swimming might prevent a recurrence. Protective oil might replace the washed-out cerumen.

A furuncle or pimple in a hair follicle is very painful (but usually no fever is associated); the victim complains of pain when chewing or when the ear is manipulated. These usually pop and drain by themselves. Aluminum subacetate with 2 percent acetic acid ear wicks (Domeboro Otic® with 2 percent acetic acid), aspirin, and codeine will ease the condition.

It is not uncommon for a baby to have itchy, smelly ears. If he likes to have his ears scratched and they smell like dirty socks or Roquefort cheese, he surely has at least infected debris. Cleansing (see *Wax* removal) followed by appropriate drops should clear this up.

Otitis media, or middle-ear infection is probably the most common bacterial infection seen in children. It is an inflammation just behind and on the eardrum. It is extremely painful and very common in children getting over colds, although less common after the age of seven. If not treated adequately, the infection can lead to hearing loss and/or perforation, scarring, mastoid inflammation, *lateral sinus thrombosis, Bell's palsy* (Section 15), or *meningitis* (Section 2). In patients who have been successfully treated, a secretion may be left behind the eardrum (*serous otitis*). Repeated middle-ear infections are usually due to enlarged *adenoids,* but are sometimes a complication of nasal allergies.

The story starts with an ordinary cold which follows the usual drippy nose, sneeze, and irritability routine. On the third to fifth day, the child becomes more irritable and/or begins to scream as if struck. He may indicate his ear; a baby may refuse to suck on his bottle as the negative pressure in his nasopharynx pulls on the inflamed drum. Fever of 101° to 103° usually suggests pus under pressure behind the eardrum; he may be more sick and miserable than in pain. Fever of 100° is often associated with more screaming pain and less toxicity. Usually there is a purulent (green or yellow) discharge from the nose. An occasional child will be only uncomfortable, then have sticky yellow pus pouring from his ear the next morning. This means that the eardrum burst as a result of the pressure of the pus which built up behind it. It is amazing, however, how quickly the eardrum heals over when the infection is controlled.

Treatment is indicated in almost all cases. The absence or disappearance of pain does *not* mean treatment is not necessary. A nose and throat specialist might prefer to see the patient at the onset of symptoms. Sometimes a doctor will treat an obvious infection over the telephone by calling a prescription in to the drugstore (especially if it is after office hours). If the infection is severe enough to cause vomiting, an antibiotic injection is the most efficient method to initiate treatment; lancing the eardrum (myringotomy) might be done also. An abscessed otitis media responds faster if the drum is lanced and the pus evacuated.

It takes at least eight hours for the medicine to be absorbed, find, and kill the germs sufficiently to reduce the inflammation and relieve the pain. If the child is still uncomfortable after twelve hours, he is on the wrong antibiotic and/or the drum needs lancing. Treatment, if successful, must be continued for at least four to six days (sometimes longer). The child should be seen on the fifth or sixth day to determine the extent of healing and whether medicine should be continued or changed.

Decongestants (see Section 4)—phlegm-driers and membrane-shrinkers—and/or *antihistaminics* are usually given simultaneously to allow the eustachian tubes (tunnels between pharynx and inner ear which equalize air pressure on the inner side of the eardrum) to remain open. Myringotomy is done less often nowadays since antibiotics seem effective in destroying the infection. (See *Serous otitis.*)

Keeping the feet warm or wearing ear coverings will not prevent ear infections; the germs crawl up the eustachian tubes on the *inside*—not the outside. Blowing the nose may blow bacteria through these tunnels to the middle-ear space. It is supposed to be better to let the nose drip or to snuff up the material and spit it out (ugh!).

Prophylactic *sulfa* or *penicillin* has not proved beneficial in warding off ear infections, although we sometimes use this protective method. Resistant bacteria emerge or *allergies* to the medicine may occur. A trial of a few shots of a bacterial vaccine may be helpful in teaching the body how to fight off infection. (See Nose, *sinusitis.*) Too-frequent infections may alert the doctor to check the patient's *immune globulin level* (see Section 8).

The *Hemophilus bacterium* is the usual offender in the first two years, so sulfa drugs or ampicillin (see Section 4) are best used. After three years of age the streptococcus seems to dominate, so penicillin or erythromycin are the drugs of choice. Tetracycline drugs are almost never used in this age group (see Section 4).

Serous otitis or fluid behind the eardrum frequently follows *otitis media.* The fluid is sterile because the antibiotics have killed the bacteria, but the fluid cannot escape (due to congestion caused by allergy or adenoids) via the eustachian tubes. This fluid may become thick, retract the eardrum, and cause hearing impairment. (See *Deafness.*)

Careful follow-up of the appearance of the tympanic membrane (eardrum) is essential in preventing hearing loss. Retained fluid may have to be drained (myringotomy) and/or a hollow plastic tube left in place for a few weeks to allow the equalization of air pressure to be maintained.

Tonsil and *adenoid* tissue normally enlarges until age five or six. Repeated ear infections are the chief indication for their removal. Frequent ear infections in the first two years may be controlled by discontinuing milk ingestion. Some children react with swollen nasopharyngeal tissue when milk is consumed; they may outgrow this when older.

Some parents find that they can reduce the chance of a secondary *otitis media* if they begin giving an antihistamine combined with a decongestant at the very onset of a cold and, of course, continue it for the full seven days of the cold.

Tympanic membrane is the eardrum.

Vertigo, or giddiness or dizziness, is rare in a child. It is suggested if the child lists and falls to one side as if drunk. Weakness and giddiness are not really vertigo and are more likely to be due to temporary cerebral hypoxia (decreased blood flow). *Anemia,* intestinal cramps or *flu,* low blood sugar (*hypoglycemia*), *hyperventilation,* sudden standing after lying down, or a shot in the doctor's office without crying may all produce a light-headed feeling. (See *Syncope,* Section 15.)

Equilibrium is controlled by the cerebellum, which receives messages from the eyes, the vestibular apparatus (canals near the inner ear that reveal if the head is upright or tipped), and from the muscles and joints. The cerebellum sends messages to the brain which then makes appropriate adjustments. Interruption of any of this input will distort the message; the brain may "see" double if eye muscles are unbalanced; it may assume that stationary objects are moving around if the vestibular apparatus or cerebellum is diseased.

The vertigo most likely to be seen in children is due to inflammation or *edema* of the inner ear (labyrinthitis) and adjacent balance-control structures. *Otitis media* is noted, and the vertigo disappears after antibiotic treatment. Allergic disturbances may produce vertigo and improve with allergic control and/or antihistaminics. (See *Motion sickness.*)

Ménière's syndrome describes recurrent attacks of sudden vertigo usually associated with ringing in the ears and/or impaired hearing. Sudden edema or fluid accumulation (ingestion of salty foods) in these balance canals may explain the problem; it is as if a hive had suddenly appeared in the inner-ear area. Antihistaminics help some, and nicotinic acid may help others. Diuretics and low-sodium diet are beneficial.

A *virus* infection may be responsible for vertigo. Brain concussion, *brain tumor, hypertension* or *hypotension,* drugs, *alcohol,* and other causes are less likely.

Wax in the ears is a clue to the mother that her child has not bathed properly. Friends and relatives are quick to judge a child's home care by how much wax is obvious at the ear hole. The mother's reaction is to tease it out with a cotton-tipped applicator (Q-tip®). She may get most of it out, but she usually pushes some farther down into the canal, where it becomes impacted. Adequate examination of the eardrum is impossible, and quick, painless removal of the wax by the doctor is difficult and frustrating. Although wax rarely causes deafness, it must be removed. If the doctor cannot remove it deftly the first time or two with a looped, curettelike scoop, he must wash out the ears. This "ear enema" is frightening to the patient and time-consuming for the doctor; tears, water, and sweat fall together on the floor.

Rules: Don't put anything in the ear smaller than your elbow. Don't use above-mentioned cotton swabs. Chronic, dry wax makers may obtain relief by dropping glycerine or mineral oil in the ear once a week; the wax may not stick to the hairs so tenaciously. Ask the druggest for an ear-wax softening solution (see Section 4). Most of these people just accept the fact they must have the doctor wash out their ears periodically.

But, if the doctor says it's okay, you can syringe the wax out of your child's ears yourself. Some doctors instill a few drops of hydrogen peroxide in the canal prior to washing; it speeds up removal. (I know an orchestra leader who comes in for ear cleansing when he has trouble hearing his oboist.)

PART II

Eyes

A. Inflamed

Conjunctivitis (see Conjunctiva)
  Allergic
    Chemosis
  Ophthalmia neonatorum and
    Eyes (Section 5)
  Plugged tear duct
    (*Nasolacrimal obstruction*)
  Purulent
Foreign body in eye
Subconjunctival hemorrhage

B. Defective vision

Amblyopia
Blindness
  Color
  Night (see also Vitamin A,
    Section 11)
Cataracts
Choked disc (Papilledema)
Chorioretinitis
Glaucoma (Newborn, Eyes,
  Section 5)
Optic atrophy
Optic neuritis
Refractive error
  Astigmatism
  Farsightedness (Hyperopia)
  Nearsightedness (Myopia)
Retinal detachment
Retrolental fibroplasia (Newborn,
  Eyes, Section 5)
Scotoma
Visual Field
Visual testing (see Cross-eyes)

C. Squint, strabismus, cross-eye, wall-eye

Alternating strabismus (see
  Cross-eyes)
Amblyopia ex anopsia
Blowout fracture (Eye injury,
  Section 1)
  Injury (Eye injury, Section 1)
Double vision (Diplopia)
  Botulism (see Food poisoning,
    Section 12)
Sixth-nerve paralysis

D. Nystagmus

E. Eyelids

Black eye (Palpebral hematoma)
Droopy lids (Ptosis)
Red, scaly edges (Blepharitis)
Red, swollen
  Itch (*allergic*)
  Scarred together
    (*Symblepharon*)
  Sty
  Tender (*orbital cellulitis*)

F. Cornea

Foreign body
Glaucoma (Newborn, Section 5)
Keratitis

G. Iris

Coloboma (Newborn, Section 5)
Uveitis

H. Lens

Cataract

I. Pupil

Unequal
  Horner's syndrome
  Skull fracture (Section 1)
White

J. Retina

Chorioretinitis
Optic neuritis
Papilledema
Retinal detachment
Retinoblastoma
Visual field

K. Sclera

Blue (see Osteogenesis imperfecta, Section 7)
Red (Subconjunctival hemorrhage)
Swollen (Chemosis)

L. Photophobia

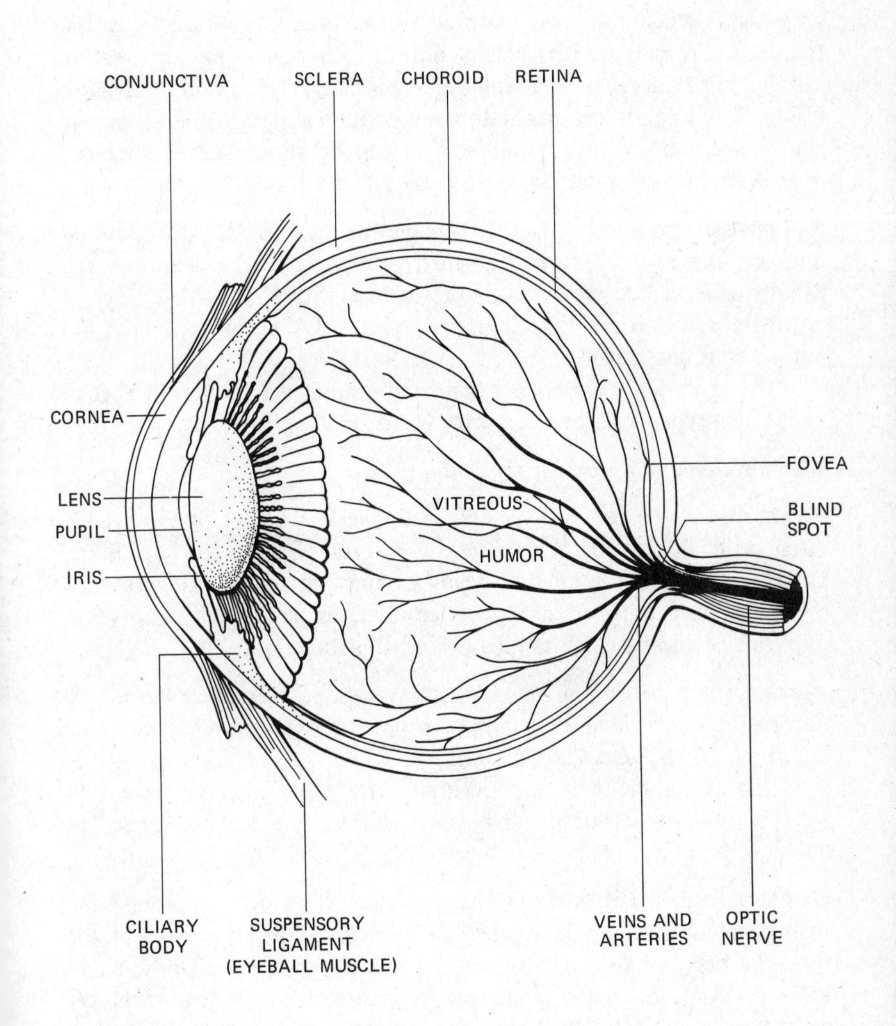
CONJUNCTIVA
SCLERA
CHOROID
RETINA
CORNEA
LENS
PUPIL
IRIS
VITREOUS
HUMOR
FOVEA
BLIND
SPOT
CILIARY
BODY
SUSPENSORY
LIGAMENT
(EYEBALL MUSCLE)
VEINS AND
ARTERIES
OPTIC
NERVE

Amblyopia is another name for blindness and usually refers to *amblyopia ex anopsia,* or suppression or disuse blindness. Central sharp vision fails to develop because of squint or *strabismus* (wall-eyes or cross-eyes) when the visual cortex of the brain, "confused" by the reception of two images, blocks out or suppresses one. Correcting muscle imbalance plus patching the good eye may help to restore vision if the condition is not too severe and is detected and treated before age four or five. But such treatment almost never succeeds if delayed until after age six.

Astigmatism produces a distorted image for the sufferer; all the radial lines on the eye chart are not clearly focused in the retina as the usually spherical cornea has an abnormal curvature.

Minor forms are very common; parts of the viewed object are out of focus or distorted.

Eye strain, headaches, and dislike of reading are the result. Special cylindrical type lenses are necessary for clear vision.

Black eye—see *Palpebral hematoma*

Blepharitis is the red, scaly, slightly thickened margin of the eyelids often associated with *seborrheic dermatitis* (see Section 6). Some crusting and matting of the eyelashes may occur. It is aggravated by dairy-product ingestion and pollen allergies. It may clear up when dandruff is eliminated. Vitamins B_2 and B_6 should help.

Blindness may be due to genetic factors, trauma, *glaucoma, retrolental fibroplasia, ophthalmia neonatorum,* suppression *amblyopia.* (See *Color blindness, Night blindness, Scotoma.*)

Photoflash pictures do not injure the eyes. Reading in a dull light or with light producing a glare will not damage the eyes, but will lead to fatigue of the eye muscles.

Cataracts are opacities in the lens of the eye, most commonly due to prenatal influences. If a pregnant woman contracts *rubella* at the time the baby's lenses are forming in her uterus, he will most likely have cataracts at birth. If no known cause is found, cataracts are considered genetically produced. Some metabolic disease (*galactosemia* and *hypocalcemia*) may be the cause. Trauma to the eyeball or some drugs may play a role.

Chemosis is the swelling of the thin membrane covering the eyeball (*conjunctiva*). The *cornea* with iris and pupil appears sunken in the gelatinous pillow surrounding it. The cause is almost always a pollen allergy, and intense itching and sneezing accompany the swelling. Removal of the victim from the irritant (animal, grass pollen, feather pillow) will help, and an antiallergic eye drop (see Section 4) would be soothing.

Choked disk—see *Papilledema*

Chorioretinitis is an inflammation or infection of the choroid and *retina* due to a variety of diseases. The retina is seen as patchy areas of atrophy with rearrangement of usual pigment pattern. Corresponding decrease in vision is dependent on the severity of the disease and how much damage has been done to the central vision area of the retina (*syphilis, cytomegalic-inclusion disease, toxoplasmosis,* and *tuberculosis* may cause this).

Color-blindness is almost unheard of in females, but occurs in about 5 percent of males as a genetically determined trait. The boy cannot differentiate between swatches of green and red colors or cannot see the pink dots mixed with the bronzy-green dots on a special test card. For pilots or drivers, night navigation may be difficult, because the green lines on the map may be indistinguishable from the red ones in the dim red light. Most color-blind people soon remember whether the green or red is above or below on the traffic lights.

Conjunctiva is a thin membrane that covers the sclera and lines the eyelids. Tears wash debris and dust from this thin layer.

Conjunctivitis or surface infection of conjunctivae creates inflammation and a yellow or green purulent exudate which may glue the lids together. An antibiotic ointment is appropriate. (See *Nasolacrimal duct.*) Allergic conjunctivitis produces a water discharge and an intense itching sensation. Occasionally the conjunctivae are ballooned out by edema (*chemosis*).

The conjunctivae may become inflamed due to sunlight, dust, foreign objects, or the common cold. A bright red spot of blood might appear on the sclera (subconjunctival *hemorrhage*) after an injury or the straining of coughing or vomiting. This blood disintegrates and is absorbed, changing from red to blue to green and yellow, taking about two weeks to disappear.

Conjunctivitis or *ophthalmia neonatorum* is rarely seen because of the use of prophylactic eye drops in newborns. It is contracted from the mother who has a gonorrheal infection.

Cornea is the transparent tissue in front of the pupil and iris through which light must pass as part of the visual process.

The luster of the cornea should be noted in the newborn. The tension of the cornea and eyeball can be felt through the eyelids (see *Glaucoma,* Section 5). Glaucoma is to be suspected if tension is increased, if eye seems enlarged, or cornea is "steamy."

An older child usually gets very uncomfortable if he has an ulceration or a foreign object on his cornea. These are often difficult to see and doctors use a special stain (fluoroscein); it would be wise to consult an ophthalmologist if corneal problems are even suspected.

Cross-eyes, or squint or esotropia, is a form of strabismus in which the eyes turn in. Two images are thus transferred from the retinae to the brain. As this is confusing, the brain suppresses one of the images, and suppression blindness (*amblyopia ex anopsia*) occurs. Once well established by age four or five, it is considered irreversible. Discovery and correction of this defect is considered mandatory by two years of age to preclude onset of deficient vision in the unused eye.

All children should have their visual acuity checked before the age of four or five.

Some infants with a prominent lid fold on the nasal side of the eye may appear to have crossed eyes because the skin covers the medial side of the eyeball. As the child grows, this illusion gradually disappears.

Infants frequently cry in the doctor's office, and visual testing is difficult. Parents should do some home testing. When a light is held in front of the infant's face, the light reflex from the corneas should be symmetrically placed in both pupils. If the light reflex is noted in the center of the pupil of the right eye and on the outer side of the left pupil, then the left eye is turning in (esotropic). The light reflex is seen as a tiny bright diamond and is a very sensitive test. The "cover test" can be used for the older child: he looks at an object with the right eye while the left is covered; the cover is moved to the right eye, and if the left eye does not move to fix on the object, the eye muscles are probably balanced properly.

In alternating *strabismus,* one eye will fix on an object for a while, then it will turn in while the other eye fixes. This is a sight saver, inasmuch as both eyes are being used. If only one is constantly used to fix on objects while the other eye deviates, the above-mentioned *amblyopia* will develop. If the eyes cannot focus on the same object (one eye nearsighted, the other eye farsighted) crossed eyes may develop.

Patching the good eye to strengthen the weak one, exercises, and lenses may be sufficient, but in about fifty percent of cases, surgery (sometimes multiple) is necessary.

Diplopia, or double vision, may have been present since birth, but due to the confusion of two objects, the child learns to suppress the vision from one eye (*amblyopia*). If diplopia develops after a blow to or near the eye, it suggests a fracture in the bony orbit with snagging of tissue or muscle in the fracture line. Surgery is obviously necessary. (Diplopia is an early symptom in *botulism.* See Section 12.)

Foreign bodies in the eye are potentially dangerous because of the possibility of corneal scarring. Not all serious wounds are painful. If the object is not obviously or easily removed, bringing immediate relief, a doctor should be consulted—preferably an *ophthalmologist.*

Acids, sprays, chemicals that get into the eye should be flushed out immediately with lukewarm tap water; don't bother to sterilize it. The dilution of the poison is essential. The longer the flushing can be continued, the better; twenty minutes would be ideal. The problem is the overwhelming eyelid spasm that occurs with eye injuries. Two people may be necessary; one to pry open the lid and the other to run in the water. Then call the doctor.

Hordeolum (see *Sty*) is a common eyelid *staphylococcus* infection.

Horner's syndrome is evidenced by a small pupil, partially shut eyelids, and absence of sweating on the same side of the face as the affected eye. It is due to a defect of the sympathetic nerves of the neck.

Hyperopia, or farsightedness, is due to a cornea that is flatter than normal. The light rays are not bent enough so the image is focused somewhere behind the *retina* and is blurred. The muscles controlling accommodation are working constantly to make the lens focus on the retina, and the result is fatigue, headache, and disinterest in reading. Most teachers hope the poor student has correctable vision trouble, and glasses will turn him on. It happens just often enough to make vision testing worthwhile for any suspected problem, especially if the above complaints are noted.

Hypertelorism is a greater-than-normal distance between the eyes. It is often associated with other congenital defects and frequently with *mental retardation.* It may also be seen in perfectly normal people. Obviously there is no remedy, since the eyes are imbedded in the skull.

Keratitis is an infection of the cornea, the clear tissue in front of the pupil. Lesions here are usually painful, cause redness, lid spasm, and much tearing.

Syphilis will cause a keratitis. Fungus and bacterial infection and ulcers are usually secondary invaders after injury.

Viral keratitis may be aggravated by cortisone eye drops which may soothe the inflammation but allow the virus to invade further.

Lens—see *Cataracts.* Dislocation of the lens is associated with arachnodactyly (spider fingers), seen in *Marfan's syndrome,* Section 10.

Myopia, or nearsightedness, is the inability to see objects clearly in the distance because the strongly curved cornea bends the light rays too much and the optical focus is in front of the retina. Concave type lenses in glasses are obviously necessary. There is a strong hereditary tendency.

Nasolacrimal duct (tear duct) obstruction is a failure of complete formation of the passageway from the inner corner of the lids into the nasal cavity. This common condition prevents the tears from flowing into the nose; as in stagnant water germs begin to grow. The baby has a purulent discharge at the lid edge and tears often run down the cheek. An antibiotic ointment or drop is used to control the infection; massaging the inner aspect of the lower lid against the nose may relieve the obstruction if it is but a mucous plug. If the obstruction continues after the first six or seven months, the ophthalmologist can usually open up the duct by passing a probe down the passageway into the nose.

Nearsightedness—see *Myopia*

Night blindness is the traditional clue that *vitamin A* is deficient. The victim has trouble adapting to darkness; this is evaluated subjectively, so if suspicion is present, a blood test for vitamin A level should be made.

Nystagmus is the rhythmic, alternating, lateral movement of the eyes. *Cerebellar disease* (*tumor,* inflammation) must be searched for.

Ophthalmologist is a medical doctor (M.D.) who has had extra training and experience in the diseases of the eye. He is the first person to consult regarding eye conditions; if he feels it necessary, he might refer his patient to an orthoptic technician for eye exercises. The *optician* fills his prescription for the patient's glasses.

The ophthalmologist's training includes study of diseases of the whole body so he can correlate eye conditions with other symptoms of a general nature (*hypertension, brain tumor, diabetes, cancer, allergies* may be detected first by the ophthalmologist).

Optic atrophy is the loss of vision due to death of the optic nerve which carries the visual message from the retina to the brain. The disk, the point of entry of the optic nerve into the back of the eyeball, is chalky white. *Neuritis, edema,* degenerative diseases involving the optic nerve can be responsible. *Glaucoma,* if not corrected, results in optic atrophy.

Optician is a technician who has been trained to fill the prescriptions of an *ophthalmologist.* He may give you advice and probably knows who is the best ophthalmologist in the area.

Optic neuritis is the inflammation of the optic nerve. It causes rapid visual loss and may be due to infections in the eye or in the orbit. The optic nerve is an extension of the brain, so *encephalitis* might initiate neuritis. Encephalitis or infection of the eye or tissues in the orbit involve this nerve and lead to blindness. (See *Tay-Sachs disease,* Sections 10 and 15.)

Optometrist is the person specially trained to measure visual function. He is not an M.D. The *ophthalmologist* is the first source person. He decides who else might be helpful.

Orbital cellulitis is the generalized infection of the eye socket area surrounding the eyeball. It usually follows a nasal or sinus infection, the bacteria having invaded the orbit. Fever of 103° to 105°, crushing headache, swollen, shiny, red eyelids suggest the diagnosis. Rapid, huge antibiotic doses may prevent abscess formation or bone infection.

Palpebral hematoma is a black eye. If a blow on forehead or on eyebrows is severe enough to break the vessels under the skin, the free blood will migrate down to the loosely attached eyelids, which become blue and distended. Ice and compression (or raw beefsteak from the refrigerator) at the time of injury may reduce some of the lid swelling that appears the next day. Once the swelling and blood are present, moist heat compresses or hot packs will increase the blood flow through the lids and allow the old dead blood to be absorbed more quickly. As the blood disintegrates, it becomes green, then yellow. Usually three weeks is required for the tissues to return to normal.

Papilledema, or choked disk, is the visual evidence of increased intracranial pressure. Ophthalmoscopic evidence of elevation of the nerve head (where the optic nerve enters the eyeball) makes a search for bleeding or tumor in the brain mandatory.

Photophobia, or fear of or avoidance of light, is noted in most eye inflammations or infections. Patients with *conjunctivitis, keratitis, blepharitis,* and hay fever dislike strong light. Victims of *acrodynia* (see Section 1) have a pronounced photophobia.

Ptosis of eyelids is droopy eyes. The muscles to the upper lids are deficient or defective so that the lids cannot be opened sufficiently to allow unobstructed vision. The child must tip his head back to look up. It is often a family trait and improves with age and height, since upward gaze is less necessary in the adult world. If the condition is bilateral, *myasthenia* might be considered. If unilateral, a *tumor, birth injury,* or *aneurysm* should be considered.

If the problem is severe and unimproved with time, surgical shortening of the muscle may be required.

Pupil is the round hole in the middle of the iris through which we see. One pupil may be larger than the other, but vision remains normal. If the eyelid opening on the side of the small pupil is narrow and that side of the face produces no sweat, there is a defect in the cervical chain of sympathetic nerve fibers; it is called *Horner's syndrome.*

If the pupil is white or otherwise different from the usual black space, a variety of serious disorders may be present: *retinoblastoma, cataract,* or *retrolental fibroplasia* (Section 5). Persistence of the embryonal blood vessels might be visible as strands of tissue behind the pupil.

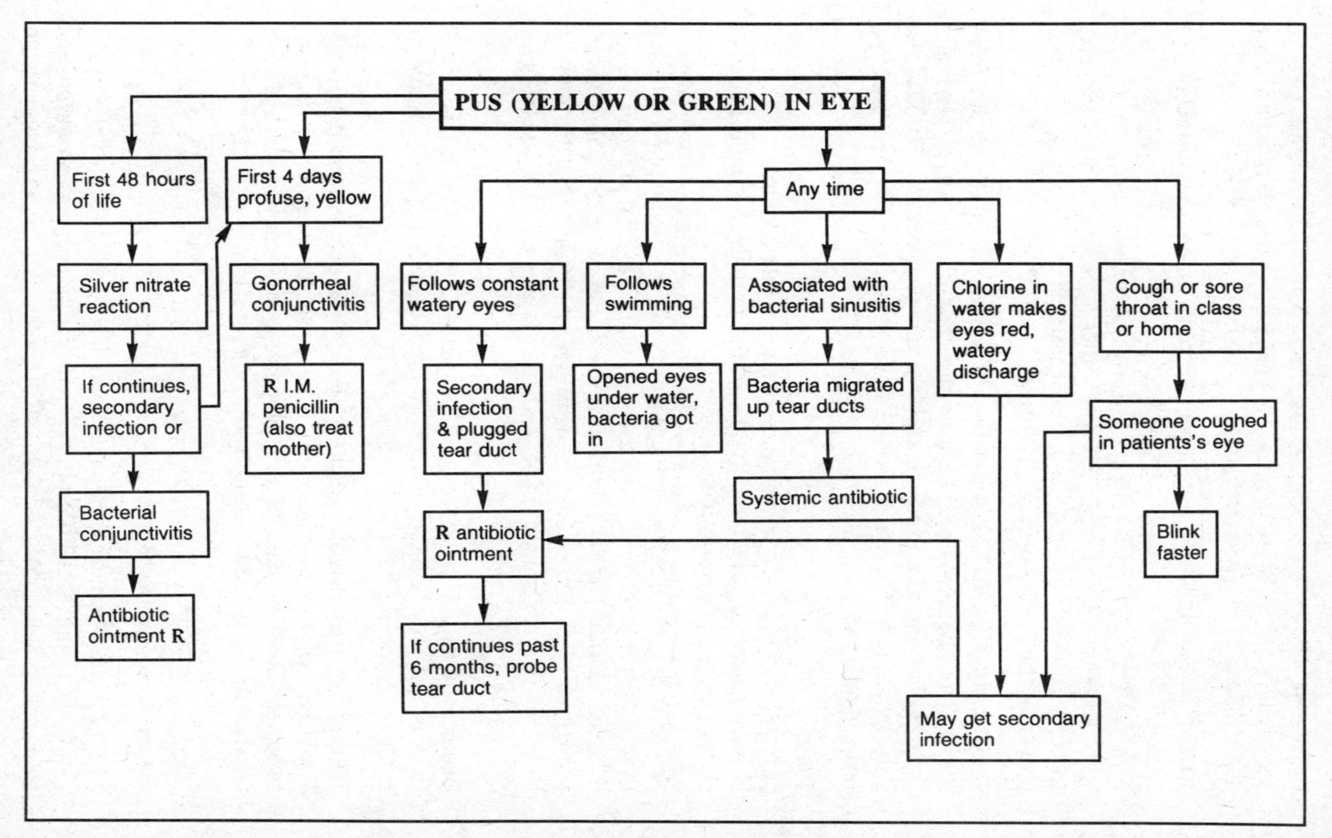
PUS (YELLOW OR GREEN) IN EYE
First 48 hours of life
Silver nitrate reaction
If continues, secondary infection or
Bacterial conjunctivitis
Antibiotic ointment R
First 4 days profuse, yellow
Gonorrheal conjunctivitis
R I.M. penicillin (also treat mother)
Any time
Follows constant watery eyes
Secondary infection & plugged tear duct
R antibiotic ointment
If continues past 6 months, probe tear duct
Follows swimming
Opened eyes under water, bacteria got in
Associated with bacterial sinusitis
Bacteria migrated up tear ducts
Systemic antibiotic
Chlorine in water makes eyes red, watery discharge
Cough or sore throat in class or home
Someone coughed in patients's eye
Blink faster
May get secondary infection

Refractive error refers to the inability of the lens and cornea to bend the light rays so a clear image focuses on the *retina.* (See *Astigmatism, Hyperopia, Myopia.*)

Retina is the photosensitive layer of cells lining the inside of the back of the eyeball. One type of light-sensitive cells called the rods pick up peripheral weak light. (To view a feeble star, look to one side of it—not directly at it.) The other type, the cones, are able to pick up color; they are more concentrated in the fovea, the area on which the incoming image is focused. (See *Chorioretinitis.*)

Retinal detachment is a separation of a portion of the retina from the wall of the eyeball. Trauma is the chief cause, but *diabetes* and *hypertension* may predispose a child to this problem. A loss of vision corresponding to this area is the chief symptom. Surgery and bed rest are required.

Retinoblastoma is a rare tumor of the eye. The first clue to the parent may be a white substance behind a dilated pupil. If the eye is not enucleated, the tumor will spread through the optic nerve to the brain. There is a family tendency.

Sclera is the white part of the eyeball. A bluish discoloration is noted in *osteogenesis imperfecta.* Red discoloration from dilated blood vessels is noted in *allergies* or *conjunctivitis.* An injury or coughing severe enough to break a blood vessel will reveal itself easily by the contrast between the red blood spot and the white of the sclera. (See *Subconjunctival hemorrhage.*)

Scotoma is patchy blindness or blind spot. One section of the visual field is not seen by the patient. *Retinal* disease or toxic poisoning must be searched for.

Sixth-nerve paralysis is present if the eye cannot be turned laterally (sideways) beyond the midline. It may be transient (*neuritis*), due to an infection of part of the temporal bone near the path of this cranial nerve, or due to a tumor in the brain stem.

Squint—see *Cross-eyes*

Strabismus—see *Cross-eyes*

Sty, or hordeolum, is a *staphylococcal* infection in one of the eyelid glands. It begins as a little pimple that rapidly progresses to a pustule and then a small boil. It takes about five days to get big enough to burst by itself, with the release of pus and blood. Hot packs may speed the progress. Antibiotic ointments are worthless to control the sty, but may prevent the spread of bacteria to adjacent tissues.

Sties are more likely to develop on granulating eyelids (*seborrhea*), in the eyelids of those children who rub their itchy, allergic eyes, or in the eyelids of families harboring a *staphyloccocal* carrier.

Recurrent sties must be managed by a diet eliminating chocolate and reducing milk to a minimum, careful bathing, prophylactic antistaphylococcal ointment applied daily in all noses in the household, and perhaps, the use of a staphylococcal vaccine. Once the frequency of recurrence decreases, a booster shot of the vaccine need be given only when the sty just begins to form; this seems to remind the body to mobilize its staph defense. The sty may melt away.

Symblepharon is the attachment of an area of lid to the eyeball due to the formation of scar tissue following eye injury (acid or lye burns). Surgery is obviously necessary.

Subconjunctival hemorrhage shows as a bright red spot of blood against the white of the sclera. A baby may nick his eye with his fingernail when he is waving his arms about signaling to be fed. It may appear after a bout of coughing and is not uncommon with *whooping cough.* It does no damage to vision, but inspection of the *cornea* would be advisable if the bleeding is a result of trauma.

The red turns to blue, then green, then yellow as the blood pigment is metabolized and absorbed in about two weeks' time.

Sympathetic ophthalmia is a rare condition in which the normal eye becomes inflamed some weeks after the other eye has been injured. It is assumed to be some hypersensitivity reaction to the breakdown products absorbed by the body from the injured eye.

Uveitis is an inflammation of the iris and the middle (choroid) coat of the eyeball. Pain, sensitivity to light (photophobia), and excessive tearing suggest this rare disorder. Vision is reduced, a cloudy fluid may be seen in the chamber just behind the cornea, and the pupil is usually small. It may be the result of trauma, or be associated with *rheumatic* disease, *tuberculosis,* or *syphilis.*

Visual field is the eye's peripheral vision. Disturbances in visual fields are due to lesions in the eye, optic nerve, or brain.

Visual testing—see *Cross-eyes*

PART III
Mouth

A. Lips

Blue
- *Asthma* (Section 9)
- *Congenital heart defects with cyanosis* (Sections 5 and 8)
- *Fever* (Section 2)
- *Methemoglobinemia* (Section 8)
- *Pneumonia* (Section 2)

Canker sores

Cracked
- *Chapped* (*Cheilitis*)
- *Cheilosis*

Harelip (cleft) (see Cleft palate, Section 5)

Red (see Carbon-monoxide poisoning, Section 1)

Swollen
- *Allergy* (see Angioedema, Section 3)
- *Frenulum tear*

B. Teeth

Amelogenesis imperfecta

Caries
- *Calculus*
- *Plaque control*

Colored teeth
- *Blue-green—erythroblastosis*
- *Brown—excessive fluoride ingestion*
- *Gray—blood pigment in recently injured tooth*
- *Yellow to green—tetracycline ingestion, amelogenesis imperfecta*

Dentition schedule
- *Crowding*
- *Delayed*
- *Eruption hematoma*
- *Natal teeth* (Section 5)

Injury to teeth
- *Avulsion*
- *Displacement*
- *Enamel hypoplasia*
- *Intrusion*
- *Mouth guards*
- *Replantation*
- *Splinting*

Malocclusion
- *Orthodontist*

Periapical abscess

Teeth grinding

Toothache

C. Gums

Canker sores

Gingivitis

Gingivostomatitis (Section 2)

Thrush (Moniliasis)

D. Palate, cleft

See Newborn, Section 5

E. Salivary glands

Calculus

Drooling

Parotid

Swollen
- *Bacterial infection*
- *Mumps* (see also Section 2)

F. Tongue

Big (Macroglossia)
Coated
Fissured
Geography
Hairy
Injuries (Section 1)
Smooth
Thrust
Tie

G. Tonsillectomy

H. Uvula

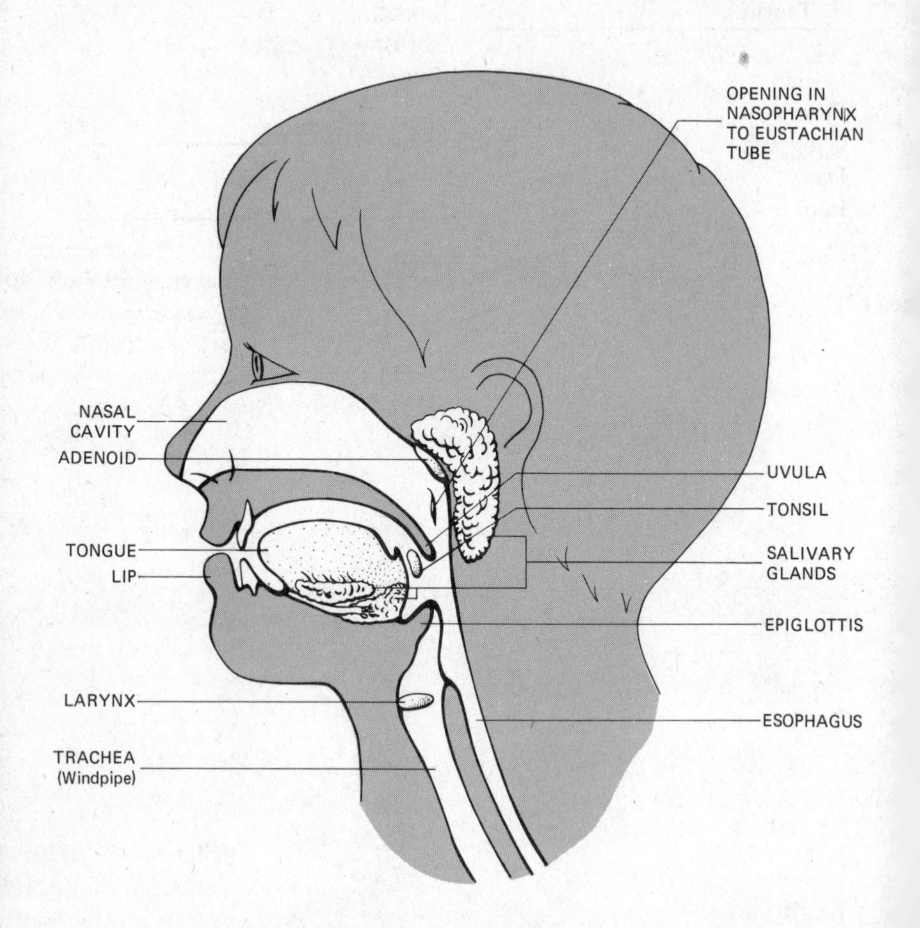
OPENING IN NASOPHARYNX TO EUSTACHIAN TUBE
NASAL CAVITY
ADENOID
UVULA
TONSIL
TONGUE
LIP
SALIVARY GLANDS
EPIGLOTTIS
LARYNX
ESOPHAGUS
TRACHEA (Windpipe)

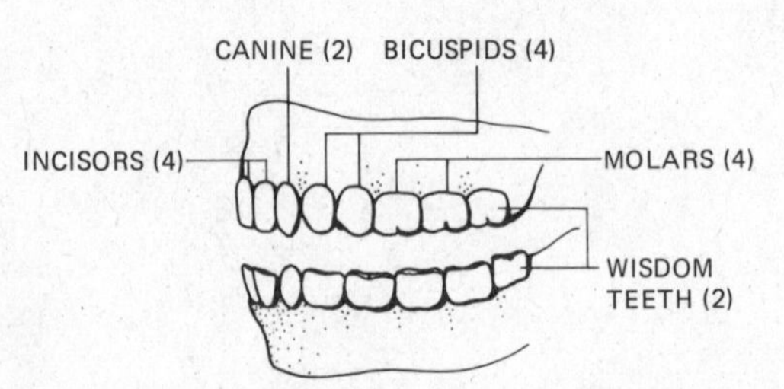
PERMANENT TEETH
CANINE (2)
BICUSPIDS (4)
INCISORS (4)
MOLARS (4)
WISDOM TEETH (2)

Amelogenesis imperfecta (thin enamel), dentinogenesis imperfecta (poorly calcified dentine), and ectodermal dysplasia are inherited conditions that make the primary and permanent teeth subject to easy destruction. The crown must be artificially protected at an early age.

Calculus is a calcium-like deposit in teeth, usually lower, which can irritate the gums. Gingivitis is a common sequel to this, so removal is important.

Candidiasis—see *Moniliasis*

Canker sores or aphthous ulcers, usually occur singly on the lips or gums as ulcers. They are painful and last about a week. They are assumed to be a *virus* infection but triggered by stress, sunshine, menses, or ingestion of chocolate, walnuts, or citrus. There is some cross-immunity against them from cowpox; hence, repeated *smallpox* vaccination may provide the sufferer with enough protection to fight off canker sores.

Local treatment of these pesky sores includes *cortisone ointment,* sodium bicarbonate, *antihistaminics,* and tincture of benzoin; most of these are ineffective, however.

Caries (*dental*) is the decay of the enamel and dentine of the teeth. Acid formed by bacteria in a matrix called plaque, feeding on retained food particles, especially sugar, will dissolve holes in the enamel and eventually into the pulp. Dentists now speak of plaque control—not just brushing the teeth. The plaque clings to the teeth usually near the gum line. It is composed of bacteria, sugars, calcium, and other material in a self-perpetuating colony resistant to ordinary tooth brushing, like a coral growth. Acids produced lead to caries growth. The teeth must be brushed to rid them of food particles, but dental floss is the real weapon against plaque and calculus. It usually requires instruction from the dental hygienist to start the program and motivate the patient in its continuation. Poor tooth brushing, sticky candies, and absence of fluoride in the water supply all tend to increase the incidence of this painful problem. A child who must go to sleep with a bottle in his mouth will have more caries because of the retention of milk sugar on tooth surfaces. A child who is subject to vomiting attacks will suffer an inordinate amount of decay, because the stomach acid will promote dissolution of surface enamel. The quality, acidity, and amount of saliva has an effect.

Baby or primary teeth will be shed but, if carious, they should be filled, as infected pulp may lead to periapical abscess with gumboil and associated complications.

Chapped lips, or **cheilitis,** is the cracking and scaling of the lips, usually due to food (chocolate, citrus, and tomato) or contact sensitivity, but aggravated by alternate moistening by tongue and drying by air or sunshine. It is frequently complicated by a secondary bacterial infection requiring an antibiotic ointment. An occasional baby becomes sensitive to the rubber nipple or pacifier.

Cheilosis is the fissuring and cracking at the mouth corners due to *vitamin B* deficiency. This is usually complicated by a yeast infection (*moniliasis*) which must be treated along with improving the diet in cereals and meats.

Dentition schedule is the approximate age of tooth calcification and eruption. The timing is largely determined genetically, but the sequence is fairly standard. The lower two central incisors appear first at about six months of age, although some babies have these near birth, and a rare one will not have them until twelve months. The upper central incisors follow closely. The laterals will appear by ten to eleven months, but some are delayed to fourteen months. The first molars come next (called two-year molars, as they should have arrived by age two). The cuspids, or eye and stomach teeth, fill in the space between the incisors and the molars by eighteen months or so. The second molars usually come all at once by age two years (called three-year molars).

If the first permanent lower incisors have not erupted by age seven, some deficiency disease (especially low thyroid) should be sought.

An old wives' tale blames *roseola* on cutting teeth. Roseola is a disease that appears between six months and two years of age, so teething is blamed. It is possible that the act of breaking the gums may provide a portal of entry for the *virus,* and thus teething appears causally related to the disease.

Infants may be irritable when the teeth are pushing through, and aspirin seems appropriate; chewing on a pacifier or rubber ring may be soothing (that pain that feels good.) Sometimes a blue *eruption hematoma,* or cyst of blood appears between the crown of a molar and the unbroken gum. It is never necessary to cut the gums; the growth force of the tooth is always stronger than the gum tissue through which it is emerging, and the tooth will erupt.

Hypothyroidism, rickets, and *hypopituitarism* may delay eruption of the teeth well beyond the average outlined above.

Crowding of primary dentition is obvious by age four. Most of these children will eventually need orthodontic care.

Permanent lower central incisors erupting behind (to the tongue side of) primary incisors may worry parents. Extraction of the baby teeth to allow for movement of permanent ones is rarely necessary. If the action of the tongue upon the permanent tooth does not move it forward enough to loosen the primary incisor, the latter might be extracted. Occasionally the deciduous teeth are ankylosed to the jaw bone.

Permanent upper central incisors and cuspids (eye teeth) may erupt labially (to the lip side) of the upper baby incisors. Sometimes extraction could allow for easier migration of the permanent tooth to its normal position.

Frenulum is a bridge of tissue extending from the center of the upper gum to the upper lip. It is sometimes very thick and appears to separate the upper central incisors. Cutting this membrane will not preclude separated teeth.

Many two-year-old children fall on their faces and tear this membrane, because the lip is pulled sharply to the side. Vigorous bleeding will follow as this tissue contains a big vein. Direct pressure from the outside against the lip will occlude this vessel flat on the gum and stop the leak.

Gingivitis is inflamed gums. If erosions, ulcers, pus, bleeding, and putrid odor are associated, it is called ulcerative necrotizing gingivitis or trenchmouth, rarely seen under age ten years. Malnourished children with scurvy and no mouth care are prone to this. Secondary bacterial infection would require antibiotics; dental prophylaxis and debridement of dead tissue is the treatment. It may be confused with *herpetic* or *gingivostomatitis* or oral *moniliasis.* (See *Acrodynia,* Section 1; *Canker sores, Gingivostomatitis,* Section 2.)

Harelip—see *Cleft palate,* Section 5

Injury to primary teeth occurs in about 25 percent of children, usually just before two years of age. *Displaced* baby teeth following injury rarely cause defects of the underlying permanent teeth, but X rays are suggested. If repositioning and *splinting* by the dentist is necessary, this should be done as soon as possible. The gray-blue discoloration of injured teeth is due to bleeding; follow up study of these teeth is important. A dead tooth should be treated or extracted.

Intrusions (teeth pushed into the gums) are seldom a threat to the permanent teeth. The displaced teeth, if pulp is not exposed, are allowed to re-erupt, but abscess formation could require extraction.

Some drifting of teeth is expected after tooth loss, but space saving appliances are usually not necessary for the upper front deciduous teeth as normal growth forces of the face allow adequate room for permanent teeth in this area.

A blow to the chin always suggests the possibility of a broken jaw; X rays may be indicated.

Avulsion of a whole baby tooth plus root is unusual. *Replantation* is not worth the effort. Injuries to the permanent central upper incisors is quite common in active eight- to twelve-year-old boys, especially if hyperactive and accident prone. Early orthodontic referral is a must for those with buck teeth.

The necessity for *mouth guards* for boys in contact sports seems too obvious to mention.

Complete *avulsion* (with root) of a permanent incisor is a dental emergency. A study indicated that if the tooth is washed, reimplanted, and splinted within thirty minutes, replantation will be successful in most cases. If the out-of-socket time was more than two hours, success was near zero percent.

Lips (see *Cleft palate,* Section 5) are often the clue to conditions elsewhere. Blue lips suggest heart or lung disease. Pale lips mean anemia or shock. Swollen lips are the sign of a food allergy (*angioedema*). Cracks at the corners are usually caused by an allergy which frequently becomes secondarily infected (see *Impetigo,* Section 6) but may be a sign of deficiency disease—see *Vitamins,* Section 11; *Chapped lips.*

Malocclusion (*dental*) is the inability of the teeth to contact evenly when the jaws are apposed in biting. The spatial relationship of the jaw may be the chief defect. The upper incisors may be placed forward of the lowers (overbite), or if the lower jaw is prominent, the upper incisors may fit behind the lowers (underbite). These discrepancies are more readily seen in X rays, and if corresponding molars are not making satisfactory contact top with bottom, some correction is wise. If a few crowns of a few teeth are the only ones making contact, dental disease will result from overuse or underuse, and some teeth will surely be lost.

Cosmetic deformity is not the only reason why crooked teeth should be straightened.

The first contact the patient has with the *orthodontist* is usually at age eight to ten years when much teeth shedding is occurring. Severe malocclusion problems (see *Treacher-Collins syndrome,* Section 5) would require his services in infancy. Banding a boy with an overbite at age eight is prophylaxis against tooth trauma.

Genetic factors are the chief cause of malocclusion, but they are aggravated by thumb-sucking. Thumb-sucking is not harmful until the permanent teeth erupt. Corrective measures should be performed before maturity. Clarinet lessons, if prescribed by the orthodontist for the child with prominent lower jaw, are tax deductible.

Periodic visits to the dentist are important not only to reinforce good dental care, but also to evaluate the proper time for intervention in jaw malalignment. (Sedation before dental appointments may sometimes be necessary for the apprehensive child.) The orthodontist may wish some teeth to be extracted to allow the others to "drift" or spacers may be used to prevent drifting. Most orthodontists are somewhat compulsive in their desire for perfect results; they know teeth will become unaligned if not watched and that a less than perfect cosmetic result is a bad advertisement. Orthodontists frequently straighten adult teeth that became crowded after the wisdom teeth distorted the alignment. No one is too old or too young for treatment. Motivation of the child is an important consideration in determining the starting date.

Moniliasis (or *Candidiasis*) is a yeast infection (called *thrush*) common in the mouth and diaper area of babies less than a month old. It is rare after that unless the child has had heavy antibiotic doses—it may regrow because of the temporary lack of competition from bacteria.

Pregnant women frequently have a mild, unrecognized case of vaginal moniliasis, and the baby will acquire it during the birth passage. He may also get it in the nursery, as the yeast is almost impossible to eradicate. He may get it from his mother anytime if her vaginal yeast infection continues.

In the mouth the colonies appear as white milk curds (but they won't rub off) over gums, tongue, and inside the cheeks. The baby may be fussy, but he's not really bothered much. In the diaper area the infection shows as a rather intense redness over the whole genital area with a well-demarcated border. On close inspection, small blisters can be seen at the margin.

Treatment is slow but simple now with *nystatin* (internal or external) and/or amphotericin B as a cream (see Section 4) for the diaper area. (See *Mouth, Moniliasis,* Section 5.)

Parotid glands are salivary glands which lie just below and in front of the ear lobe.

Rarely will bacteria invade the parotid glands. High fever accompanies an exquisite tenderness, and pus may be massaged out of the gland into the mouth. (The opening of the duct for the parotid glands is on the top of a papule inside the cheeks at the level of the six-year molars.) The white count is elevated. Heroic antibiotic treatment should rapidly be curative; otherwise the infection may become an abscess requiring surgical drainage.

A calculus (rare) may obstruct the salivary flow, causing swelling. An X ray would reveal a calcium stone. A tumor (very rare lymphosarcoma) causes a firm swelling.

Mumps is properly called *epidemic parotitis* and is easy to diagnose if it is "going around." If it recurs, it is called *recurrent parotitis* and is assumed to be due to another virus to which the patient is not immune.

Periapical abscess or gumboil is usually the result of infection due to deep caries or a blow. A tooth becomes carious down to the pulp. The infection tunnels through the gum after invading the root. Extraction is indicated if it involves a baby tooth. Pulp treatment may save a permanent tooth.

Salivary glands are six in number. The *parotid* pair are just below and in front of the ear lobes (the usual ones to swell with *mumps*), the submaxillary are just below the level of the six-year molars, and the sublingual pair are under the chin (when swollen, they produce a double-chin). Salivary-gland problems are rare in children except for mumps, which is slowly disappearing because of the use of the mumps vaccine.

There is a correlation between excessive dental *caries* and reduced saliva flow. Increased flow of saliva is usually due to teething or mouth infections, and is present in some forms of mental deficiency.

Drooling usually increases at about three months of age. The baby really does not care about his appearance, so lets his saliva run down his chin. Eventually, after a few months, he learns to swallow it, and no effort on the parents' part will speed up his social control. Most parents feel that a tooth is on its way, but they usually have to wait four months for that exciting day.

Drooling occurring with a fever in a two-year-old is almost pathognomonic of a common *virus* infection called *herpangina* (see Section 2).

Big *tonsils* will encourage drooling. A child who drools excessively after two years of age might have a neurological defect or *mental retardation.*

Teeth are formed from a layer of cells from the mouth epithelium that joins mesodermal cells in the jaws. As some development has begun early in pregnancy (the fifth month), the mother's diet, diseases, and medicine will be reflected in the baby's deciduous (milk) teeth. *Tetracyclines* taken by the mother for some infection will stain the baby's baby teeth that were being calcified at the time of the drug ingestion. They appear dirty, yellow or green depending on the dose and the length of time the medicine was administered. The same is true for the child's permanent teeth; if possible, he should *not* receive tetracycline in the first six years or so of his life, or the enamel of his permanent teeth will assume this stain. Some dentists report that bleaching is successful. Too much fluoride will cause mottling of his teeth. This may be a few white patches on the enamel or poorly formed brown enamel if the fluoride was heavy (5 parts per million). If severe jaundice was present at birth, bilirubin will be incorporated in the baby teeth.

Fluoride is usually taken by a pregnant woman to toughen her baby's first teeth. The child should have fluoride until at least age eight or nine years, when his permanent teeth are nearly formed. The ingested fluoride benefits only unerupted teeth. By age eight, the permanent teeth are well formed, so the tablets are less beneficial after this time, although they will cut cavities 20 percent if continued through adolescence. (Some evidence indicates fluoride reduces the tendency to osteoporosis in middle age.)

In addition, most dentists paint the teeth with topical fluoride at age three years and periodically thereafter. (Most dentists are now doing it every six months.)

A rule: toothbrush at two years; dentist at three.

Enamel hypoplasia is usually manifest as pits or areas denuded of enamel or permanent teeth. It is assumed to be caused by infection or metabolic disturbance, or trauma to primary teeth, during infancy when the enamel of these teeth was being deposited.

Enamel mottling is noted in the enamel of those who spent their infancy in areas with high fluoride levels in the water supply. It will show as white or brown patches.

A good diet *sans* sugar is more important than fluoride supplements.

Teeth grinding, or *bruxism,* suggests tension. If nocturnal and persistent, the child should be treated for worms. The physical presence of the worms does not have to be verified because teeth grinding is so common in a wormy child.

Thrush—see *Moniliasis*

Tongue is chiefly muscle with taste buds on the surface. Its color and surface moisture give some clues as to bodily diseases, but not as much as doctors thought years ago.

Atrophic glossitis is seen in *niacin deficiency.* The whole surface is denuded of papillae, is smooth and fiery red.

Bites—see Section 1.

Coated tongue covered with white debris suggests some illness. If the tongue is dry and furry, dehydration is present. Early *scarlet fever* displays a coated tongue; when the white material sloughs off, the strawberry red tongue is obvious.

A fissured tongue (like an erratically plowed field) is frequently seen in *Down's syndrome* or following scarlet fever, or may appear as an isolated condition.

Geography tongue is a benign allergic condition in which the usual papillae on the surface have been lost temporarily; the papillae at the edge of these areas give the tongue the appearance of a map. South America one day may be Africa the next.

Glossitis is an inflammation of the tongue. The surface looks like a red strawberry, and the condition is most likely to occur after *scarlet fever.* A more purplish red (magenta), smooth tongue is seen in *vitamin B* (riboflavin) deficiency.

Hairy tongue is due to the elongation of the papillae. Some drugs cause this. It may be associated with a bleeding disease that allows a little blood to ooze into the mouth over a long period of time. The blood pigment stains the papillae brown or black.

Macroglossia is a large tongue. It may be normal in a large, muscular (mesomorphic type) infant, but if it interferes with sucking or breathing, a lingual cyst or lymphangioma must be looked for. Some tongue cysts, if large and on the posterior area, cause breathing and feeding difficulties. Some are as large as golf balls; they are full of a mucoid material. Surgery is indicated.

A *cretin* (*hypothyroid* baby) has a large tongue, but there are some other clues to indicate this diagnosis.

A smooth, salmon-pink tongue is seen in chronic diarrhea and/or pernicious anemia.

Tongue thrust is the forward pressure of the tongue against the teeth during swallowing or speech sufficient to push the teeth forward or to interfere with articulation of "s" sounds (lisping). Speech pathologists claim that they can correct this if the child is referred to them by age six or seven. The dentist may place a "reminder" wire gadget just inside the incisors to break the habit of thrusting. Usually seen in people who were bottle fed.

Tonsillectomy (see *Adenoids*) is the surgical removal of the tonsils. The risk of the operation must be weighed against the risk of leaving them in. Despite technical advances, a few deaths from this operation are reported each year. Reaction to the anesthesia, bleeding, and aspiration of blood or tonsillar tissue into the lungs still occur.

The size of the tonsils is not the compelling reason for their removal, for it is normal for them to grow larger—along with the adenoids—up until five or six years of age, after which time they shrink, and, of course, as the body gets bigger around them, they look smaller.

The usual reason for tonsil removal seems to be that the adenoids need removal because of repeated otitis media. (Actually both tonsillar and adenoidal tissue contribute to ear infection.) If tonsils are chronically infected, and every cold or sore throat ends with swollen anterior neck nodes (just under the corner of the jaw bone) requiring antibiotics, removal seems justified. Adenoidectomy might properly be done at the same time (operation called T & A) even though the ears are not involved. A child rarely may have such big, pendulous tonsils that they flop down into his throat, occluding his airway when he lies on his back. Tonsil and adenoid removal often suggests the child had (or has) a milk allergy.

It is difficult for the doctor and the parents to arrive at some reasonable compromise about the operation. They must know that the operation will not stop colds (look to allergies instead), that the child will still get sore throats, and that age seven seems to have some curative magic to it.

The average child has about six to eight respiratory infections a year until age six. When he is seven years old, he should act like an adult—one sore throat, one attack of influenza, one cold, and one bout of intestinal flu a year. If he exceeds this arbitrary optimum (mine), then he should have his tonsils and adenoids out or have an allergy workup. The history of repeated infection is more important than the appearance of the tonsils. (But at one charity hospital some years ago, the waiting list for tonsillectomies was so long that it took a year to get the operation done. After the year had gone by, only 30 percent of the children still needed the operation.)

After tonsils are removed, some decrease in sore throats should be anticipated, and the chronically swollen anterior cervical nodes should decrease in size. *Allergies, colds, flu,* and *laryngitis* will not be affected, but repeated ear infections should be reduced after the T & A.

It is common to see children who had really chronically infected tonsils and adenoids become cheerful, energetic, and ravenous eaters after the removal of these offending tissues. The improved appetite must indicate that the child feels better. (I wonder if he eats more because he kept hearing his mother say he *would* once he had the operation. He may figure that, if he *doesn't,* he might have to go through the operation again.)

Toothache usually develops in a neglected carious tooth or as a result of a deep filling. Rubbing aspirin into a painful cavity is occasionally practiced by the pain-maddened layman. This can cause a severe burn. The aspirin is put to better use after ingestion; the dentist is the one to treat the holes in your teeth. (See *Codeine,* Section 4.)

Uvula is the fingerlike appendage hanging down from the middle of the soft palate. If excessively long, it may tickle the throat and produce an irritating cough. Some advise clipping a piece off, if this seems to be the only agent responsible for the irritation. Occasionally the uvula appears to be stuck to one tonsil; this is temporary and means nothing.

PART IV
Neck

Lumps and swellings

Branchial cleft cyst
Cystic hygroma (Section 10)
Hodgkin's disease (Section 10)
Lymph nodes
  Adenovirus
  Pharyngitis (Section 2)
  Scarlet fever (Section 2)
  Tonsillitis (Section 2)
  Tuberculosis
Mumps (see Salivary glands in Mouth, also Section 2)
Thyroglossal duct cyst
Wry neck (see Torticollis, Section 5; Muscles, Section 7)

Adenovirus is the name for a group of *viruses* responsible for some colds and a few of the respiratory influenzalike diseases—"that virus that's going around." (See *Virus,* Section 2.) Adenoviruses are more likely to cause inflamed eyes, sore throats, and swollen neck glands. Many of these are erroneously treated with antibiotics, as virus sore throats are often mistaken for strep throats.

Branchial cleft cyst is the remnant of an embryonic gill slit; its opening may be noted on the skin just in front of the sternocleidomastoid muscle (the muscle that extends from the mastoid bone to the clavicle). The cyst may be huge and have no opening. It may be small and the opening exude occasional drops of mucus. If infection occurs, surgical excision would be indicated.

Lymph nodes are small round glands packed with *lymphocytes.* They are located all over the body, becoming noticeable if local inflammation drains to them. The most common ones to enlarge are the *tonsil* glands found high in the neck just below the corner of the jawbone. They are normally at least one centimeter large (the size of a small lima bean), nontender, and movable between the skin and underlying muscle tissue. Within two days of an untreated tonsil infection, these glands swell—sometimes to walnut size—and become tender. Occasionally a bacterial infection in the glands produces pus; an abscess forms and surgical drainage must be performed. In the days before antibiotics, many tonsillitis infections ended with suppuration of these neck glands.

Tuberculosis of the cervical lymph nodes has largely disappeared because there is little bovine (cow-originated) tuberculosis; apparently the bacilli in the cow's milk infected the tonsils, and the infection moved on to the glands.

Thyroglossal duct cyst is a fluid-filled cavity located anywhere from the base of the tongue (near the pharynx) to the lower center of the neck near the *thyroid* gland. It is a remnant of an embryonal tube. If it causes symptoms such as difficult swallowing, neck mass (always in the direct center), or infection, surgery should be performed. Recurrences are likely if all the tissue is not removed.

PART V
Nose

A. Runny

Allergic rhinitis (Hay fever)
Common cold
  Complications
  Decongestants
  Nose drops
Sinusitis

B. Bloody

See Epistaxis, Section 1

C. Foreign body in nose

See Section 1

D. Nasal polyps

E. Nasal septum deviation

See Nose injury, Sections 1 and 5

F. Sense of smell

Adenoids are blobs of lymph tissue found just behind and above the soft palate, attached to the back wall of the pharynx. They are similar to the *tonsils* in structure and function. Although they cannot be seen ordinarily, they are assumed to be swollen and/or infected whenever the tonsils are. Normally enlarged from age four to six years, they create hyponasal speech and may occlude the opening of the eustachian tubes, which allow for the equalization of air pressure in the inner ear. The location of enlarged adenoids explains why children snore, breathe through their mouths, and have repeated ear infections and/or hearing impairment.

Adenoids should not be removed just because they're there. There is a risk to any operation. Adenoidectomy *may* be considered when repeated ear infections, hearing loss due to such infections, or persistent fluid behind the eardrum cannot be controlled in any other way. Nasal allergy due to house dust, bacterial allergy, and food allergy must be controlled or eliminated first. All doctors have seen the pathetic child with nasal symptoms who had his adenoids removed, only to become saddled with *asthma* or *bronchitis*—as if his adenoids were protecting his lungs.

Stop milk ingestion for a couple of months; if snoring and hyponasal symptoms persist, then consider adenoidectomy.

The adenoids are rarely removed from a child who has a short palate; he may develop hypernasal speech because the palate is not long enough to reach the pharyngeal wall without the adenoids to bridge the gap. This is especially true of the child with a repaired *cleft palate.* The surgeon may be forced to remove all or part of adenoid mass if hearing loss is due to the adenoids, however. Rule of thumb: the farther away the trouble is from the tonsils and adenoids, the less likely will their removal do any good.

Bloody nose—see *Epistaxis,* Section 1

Common cold, or rhinitis or nasopharyngitis, is the most common *virus* infection of children, because cold symptoms are caused by a wide variety of viruses. It is *always* going around.

There must be fifty to a hundred different viruses that produce similar symptoms. Rhinovirus is a general name for one group. (See *Cold,* Section 4.)

A child may become immune to one virus, but in three weeks be afflicted by a new—to him—virus. Within one to three days after exposure, the victim develops headache, fever, malaise, sneezing, and dry soreness in nose and throat. Within a day or two, the temperature returns to normal and is replaced with a clear, watery nasal discharge with or without a slight, dry tickling cough. These symptoms last five to seven days. If symptoms last longer or fever rises after the third day, a complication has occurred and may need treatment.

From the age of two to five years a child has an average of six to eight colds a year. Occasionally *anemia* and/or *allergies* will increase susceptibility. Some frequent cold sufferers find that dairy products trigger an onset. Exposure to cold, damp air, dry winter air, and emotions have all been implicated as causative factors, but proof is lacking; some conditions may allow the virus to multiply, but the virus has to be present to cause the cold.

The "snotty-nosed kid" is such a common phenomenon from two to six years of age we would like to consider the condition normal, except that most mothers view it as embarrassing evidence of inadequate care. The mother has heard that her child is not fed properly, is not getting sufficient vitamins or rest, is allowed to eat candy, his socks are wet and dirty, or he is bathed too much or too little. The pediatrician is asked to solve the problem, but all he can do is provide sympathy and treat the secondary infections. The child simply has to have about fifty to a hundred bad colds from birth to age seven, before he acquires enough immunity to settle down to the usual adult frequency of one bad cold a year. Only by strict isolation from others in a room of 70° F. and 50 percent humidity can colds be prevented.

Of proved benefit: correct anemia, eliminate allergens (inhaled or ingested; see *Allergy Checklist,* Section 9), control temperature and humidity.

Of some value: large doses of *vitamin C, antihistaminics* at the onset of a cold, wearing socks to bed.

Of no benefit: *adenoid* and *tonsil* removal, prophylactic antibiotics, chicken soup, purges, enemata, bed rest, vinegar and honey.

Aspirin in the dosage of one grain for each ten pounds of weight is effective only to relieve the headache, sore throat, and fever associated with the cold.

Steam or at least a moisture-laden atmosphere keeps the secretions liquid so they will drain more easily. The commercial cold steam vaporizer is safer than the kettle on a hot plate. However, hanging wet sheets and towels about the room is cheaper than a vaporizer.

If the humidity is high enough to be effective, the windows should fog up.

Most children are more comfortable in the prone position when their noses are full of phlegm; otherwise it rolls down their throats and produces a tickly cough. An older child might do better on his back with the head somewhat elevated by a blanket roll under the mattress. If pillows are used to elevate the head, foam rubber might be better if a feather *allergy* is an irritating factor.

Extra fluids might be urged during the febrile phase, but a regular diet can be resumed during the drip stage. *Vitamin C* is usually tried early in the disease in doses of about 500 milligrams for a child and 1,000 milligrams for an adult every hour for the first day or two, then is tapered off.

Fever is more prominent in the under-six-year-old, but should not last more than seventy-two hours. The drip and snort last about seven days. If the secretions become purulent (green or yellow), a bacterial secondary infection has become superimposed, and antibiotic therapy may be worthwhile.

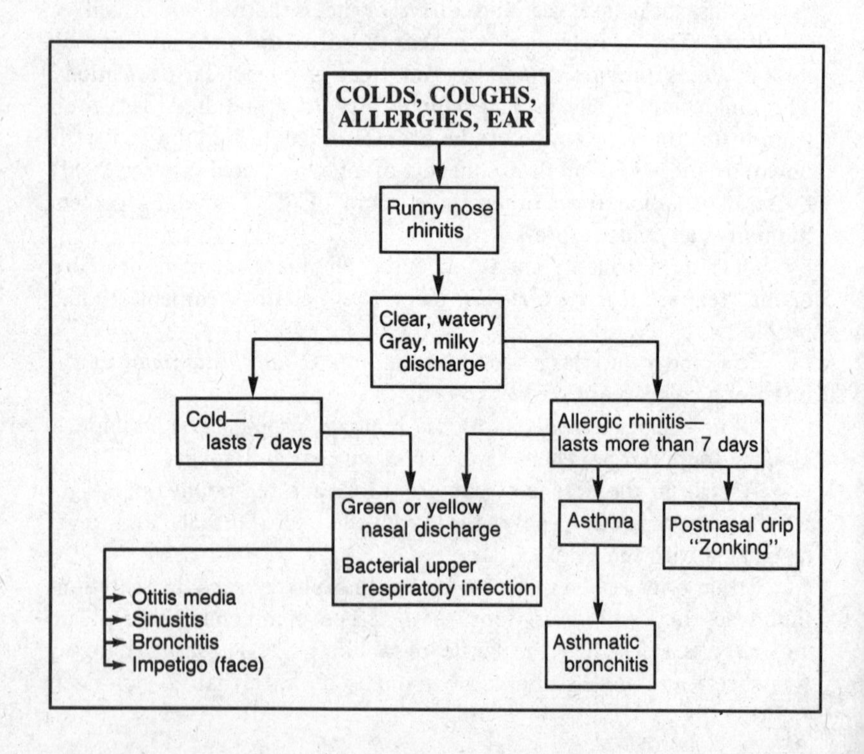

Complications of the cold include *otitis media, bronchitis, sinusitis,* and a bacterial *upper respiratory infection* (URI). the most common story that a pediatrician hears is, "My child has had a cold for four days. He seemed to be getting better until this morning at two A.M. He woke up screaming about his ear and his temperature was 101°." This usually means a bacterial secondary infection called *otitis media.* The germs migrate through the eustachian tube to the air space just behind the eardrum. There the bacteria multiply until the pus pushes on the tender eardrum, causing considerable pain. Antibiotics by mouth kill the bacteria, and the eardrum returns to normal.

The next most common complication of a cold is *bronchitis* (see Section 9).

Decongestants reduce the swelling and mucus drainage of the respiratory tract. Nose drops and sprays have drying and vasoconstricting actions which provide temporary relief from viral and allergic rhinitis. They are optimally used four or five times a day for two days, then discontinued for two days.

Oral decongestants are usually combined with *antihistaminics* and provide longer relief but occasional drowsiness (a possible blessing for a wakeful child). These rarely work in the presence of a purulent (thick green or yellow) discharge, but are suggested with or following antibiotic use for *otitis media* and *sinusitis* to promote adequate drainage. (See *Cold,* Section 4.)

Foreign body in nose—see Section 1

Hay fever is allergic rhinitis. It is a profuse, watery discharge from the nose (and eyes) accompanied by sneezing and an uncontrollable drive to rub, pick, or otherwise fool with the nose and eyes. The irritation may involve the throat and produce a burning sensation, postnasal drip, a dry cough, throat clearing, and a characteristic "zonking" sound—a reverse snoring as the patient attempts to suck the mucus from his palate. The nasal mucosa is a pale or bluish color in contrast to the redness accompanying a cold or bacterial infection. A smear of this mucus is full of *eosinophils,* the hallmark of allergy. Circles under the eyes suggest allergy. A crease near the end of the nose where it has been bent from rubbing may indicate hay fever.

The pollens (grass, animal danders, house dust, and molds) in the air irritate the membranes of the allergic sufferer, histamine is released, capillaries dilate, and serum leaks into the mucosa. The glands secrete mucus to protect the lining.

Avoidance of the offenders is the best treatment. (See Allergy Checklist, Section 9.) *Nose drops, antihistaminics,* and *decongestants* will provide temporary relief. *Cortisone* will stop the allergic response, but is never the initial treatment. *Desensitization* (Section 3) is the method of control if the allergens cannot be avoided.

Nasal polyps, rare in children, are usually the late result of an untreated nasal allergy. A pale blue blob of tissue may fill the nasal passageway, causing obstruction to the sinus cavity openings. A polyp arising near the tonsil may flop down into the pharynx or over the larynx and cause respiratory distress and cyanosis.

Nasal septum deviation is rarely congenital (a cyst must be ruled out). (See *Broken nose, Newborn,* Section 5.) It usually develops gradually by adolescence as a late sequel to a long-forgotten injury to the toddler's nose. It is difficult to break a child's nose, but the cartilage that constitutes most of his nose can be injured by trauma. An innocuous blood clot on or near the septum following childhood trauma may stimulate uneven growth later on; the end result is a deviated septum. A deviation may occur as a result of growth pressures on the thin septum by the skull bone above and the hard palate below; the thin plate of cartilage and bone will bulge into the nasal cavity. It can usually be seen by inspection: the septum protrudes into the passageway about an inch inside the opening. The other side has more space; occluding this opening will produce noisy, difficult air passage. The deviation may obstruct the openings of the sinuses leading to repeated infections. *Allergic rhinitis* becomes more troublesome due to the narrowness of the space. Septal deviation may resemble a *polyp.*

Surgery is the answer if symptoms are present, but it is usually delayed until full nasal growth comes—after midadolescence. (See *Nose injury,* Section 1.)

Nose serves to increase the humidity and warm the air breathed into the *lungs.* Debris, smog, dust, and bacteria are caught in the mucous layer in the nose, and cilia push this pollution back to the throat where it will be swallowed or spat out, depending on the preference of the afflicted postnasal drippee.

Nose drops are most effective if only used infrequently—three times a day for two days, then a rest period of a day or so. Patients rapidly develop a resistance to them, and they either don't work at all to shrink the nasal membranes, or if they do work, a rebound tissue swelling produces more congestion than was present in the original nasal condition. A purulent (green or yellow) discharge responds poorly to nose drops; a *virus rhinitis* or *allergic* drip responds well.

An older child might prefer a nasal spray injected into his nose; for maximum benefit his head should be placed in the upside-down position. A baby with a cold may be very uncomfortable when sucking and nose drops might allow him to breathe and suck at the same time. Place the baby on his back on top of your thighs with his head hanging over your knees. Two drops of a standard nose-drop solution are placed in each nostril. Clap your hand over his mouth; when he inhales, he will suck the drops through the passageway. Do this about fifteen minutes prior to feeding for maximum benefit.

Oral *antihistaminics* and decongestants serve to open up the passageways with less fighting and screaming. They may be helpful in maintaining the patency of the eustachian tubes and usually produce some sleepiness.

Nose injuries—see Sections 1 and 5

Sinusitis is a frequent complication of the cold but more common in the older age group when the sinuses are more fully developed. Fever, pain, and swelling of face over the involved sinus suggest this problem.

Sinusitis usually accompanies a purulent *rhinitis.* Only the maxillary (inside the cheek bones) and ethmoid sinuses (high in the nose between the eyes) are sufficiently developed at birth to become infected when the nose is involved. The frontal (forehead) and sphenoid (behind the eyes, in front of the pituitary) sinuses are not much involved until age six or so.

The symptoms are those of any collection of pus in an enclosed space: fever, *headache* (usually over the involved sinus—for example, a sore cheek indicates that the maxillary sinus is involved), purulent nasal discharge, and elevated *white blood count.*

Because of the location near the eyes, ethmoid sinusitis often produces swelling, pain, and redness of the eyelids. (See *Orbital cellulitis.*)

Antibiotics and shrinking of the swollen nasal membranes are standard.

Chronic *sinusitis* is due to obstructive lesions in the nose or adenoid hypertrophy. A deviated nasal septum may occlude a sinus opening and allow pus to build up. Nasal inhalation allergies or bacterial allergies are the most common reason for the chronic forms. A few patients develop sinusitis because of a milk allergy. The swollen tissues caused by the allergic reaction plug up the sinus cavities and allow bacteria to grow.

The headache of frontal and ethmoid sinusitis diminishes as the day progresses, since drainage is facilitated by the upright position. Maxillary and sphenoid sinusitis becomes worse as the day progresses, as the sinus opening is at a higher level than the floor of the sinus.

Many people are relieved of this chronic problem after receiving a series of bacteria (their own or a stock solution) injections. If every cold ends with a green or yellow discharge and other responsible allergies have been controlled, a few shots of this dead bacteria vaccine may cure the sticky mess by "teaching" the sufferer resistance to bacterial invasion. They are valuable for some zonkers and helpful for sufferers of asthmatic bronchitis.

If each cold leads to a secondary infection, some consideration should be given to *allergy* (milk, house dust, bacterial allergy) or obstructive tissue (tonsils and adenoids) or to lowered *immune globulins.*

Smell or olfactory sense is effected by special sense receptors in the nose which pass the information through the first cranial nerve to the brain. There the information is decoded into sensation with a large emotional charge, either pleasant or unpleasant. Taste and smell are interrelated; a person with no smell sensation is unable to distinguish between an apple, a raw potato, and an onion. (I knew a nurse who had lost all sense of smell after a skull fracture; she felt no nausea in the diarrhea ward but was a terrible cook.)

Some familiar odor is usually used to test the sense of smell and hence the first or olfactory cranial nerve.

Taste and smell are dependent upon adequate zinc ingestion.

SECTION 15

The Brain and Nervous System *

A. Convulsions, seizures

Due to cerebral dysrhythmia
- *Epileptic equivalents*
  - *Abdominal epilepsy*
- *Focus seizures*
  - *Jacksonian epilepsy*
- *Grand mal*
- *Petit mal*
- *Psychomotor epilepsy*
- *Salaam seizure* (*Myoclonic fit*)

Due to chemical changes
- *Hypernatremia* (Section 10)
- *Hypoglycemia* (Section 10)
- *Hypoparathyroidism* (Section 10)
- *Tetany* (also Section 5)
  - *Hyperventilation*

Due to fever and infection
- *Encephalitis*
- *Febrile convulsion*
- *Hemolytic uremic syndrome* (Section 2)
- *Meningitis* (Section 2)
- *Reye's syndrome*

Due to space-occupying lesions
- *Brain tumor or abscess*
- *Cerebral aneurysm*
- *Cerebral edema*
- *Intracranial bleeding*
- *Sturge-Weber syndrome*
- *Tuberous sclerosis*

Other
- *Breath holding (Section 16)*
- *Nodding spasms* (Section 16)
- *Seizure after head injury* (See Convulsions)

B. Alterations of consciousness

Amnesia
Cerebral edema
Cerebral embolism
Coma
Concussion (see Skull fracture, Section 1)
Delirium
Encephalitis
Encephalopathy
Epileptic equivalents (see Convulsions)
Hypoglycemia (Section 10)
Intracranial bleeding
Meningitis (Section 2)
Petit mal epilepsy
Reye's syndrome
Syncope (fainting) (see also Section 1)

*Read **Nervous System** first.

C. Brain damage

Cerebral degenerative disease
- *Dawson's (subacute sclerosing panencephalitis)*
- *Lipidoses* (Section 10)
- *Spinal muscular atrophy*
- *Tuberous sclerosis*

Cerebral palsy
- *Athetosis*
- *Paraplegia*
- *Spastic diplegia*
- *Spastic paralysis*

Mental retardation
- *Cerebral calcification*
  - *Sturge-Weber syndrome*
- *Down's syndrome* (Section 10)
- *Hydrocephalus*

D. Cerebral dysfunction, minimal

Accident prone
Awkward
Broad left thumb nail
Communication disorders
- *Clutter*
- *Dyslexia*
- *Echolalia*
- *Learning disorders*
- *Speech*
- *Stutter*

Distractible
Handedness (dominance)
Hyperactive
Impulse ridden
Short attention span

E. Headache

Headache with fever
- *Brain abscess*
- *Encephalitis*
  - *Infectious mononucleosis* (Section 1)
  - *Mumps* (Section 2)
- *Influenza* (Section 2)
- *Meningitis* (Section 2)
- *Polyarteritis* (Section 2)
- *Reye's syndrome*
- *Virus infections* (Section 2)

Headache without fever
- *Brain tumor*
- *Cerebral aneurysm*
- *Cerebral calcification*
- *Cerebral edema*
- *Cerebral fistula*
- *Concussion* (Skull fracture, Section 1)
- *Depression* (Section 16)
- *Encephalopathy*
  - *Hypertension* (Section 8)
  - *Lead poisoning* (Section 1)
- *Headache*
- *Hypervitaminosis A* (Section 11)
- *Intracranial bleeding*
- *Migraine*
- *Tension-fatigue syndrome*

F. Nervous system

Hypothalamus
Spinal cord

G. Paralysis, weakness

Botulism (Section 12)
Brachial palsy (Section 5)
Cerebral palsy
Cervical rib (Section 7)
Facial (Bell's palsy)
Fatigue

Floppy infant syndrome
Guillain-Barré syndrome
Hemiplegia
Muscular dystrophy (Section 7)
Myasthenia gravis
Multiple sclerosis
Neuritis
Paralysis (Section 7)
Postural hypotension (Section 8)
Spina bifida
Sturge-Weber syndrome
Tick bite (Section 1)

H. Gait disorders (see also Section 7)

Ataxia
Cerebellar
Friedreich's
Myotonic dystrophy
St. Vitus dance (chorea)
Wilson's disease (Section 11)

I. Head size and shape

Hydrocephalus
Microcephaly
Skull

J. Pain

Herpes zoster (Section 6)
Neuritis
Neurofibroma
Poliomyelitis
Ruptured intervertebral disk (Spinal cord)

K. Tests

Bender-Gestalt Visual Motor Test
Brain scan
Cerebral angiography
Cerebrospinal fluid
Lumbar puncture
Electroencephalogram
Hypsarrhythmia
Myelogram
Pneumoencephalogram
Transillumination (see Hydranencephaly)

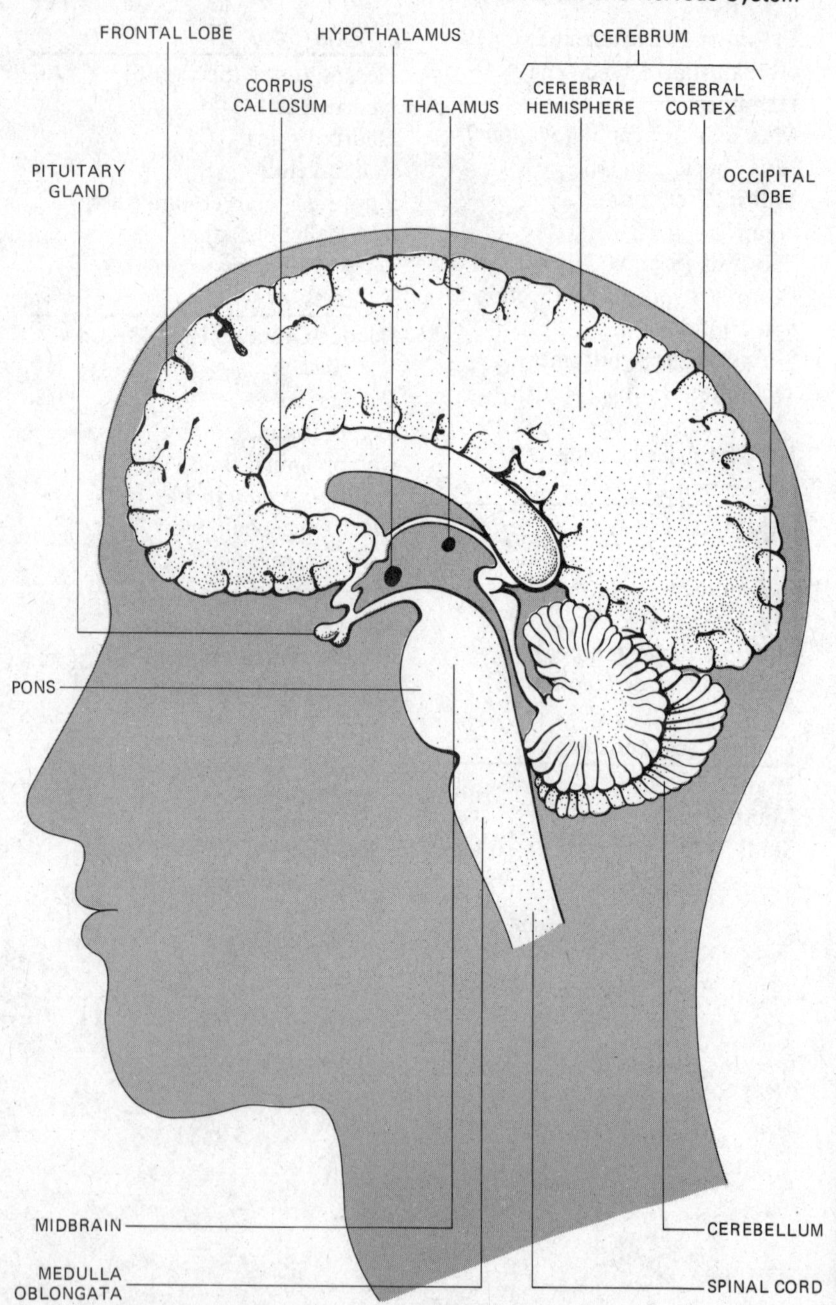
FRONTAL LOBE
HYPOTHALAMUS
CEREBRUM
CORPUS CALLOSUM
THALAMUS
CEREBRAL HEMISPHERE
CEREBRAL CORTEX
PITUITARY GLAND
OCCIPITAL LOBE
PONS
MIDBRAIN
CEREBELLUM
MEDULLA OBLONGATA
SPINAL CORD

Amaurotic familial idiocy, Tay-Sachs disease, begins at about six months of age and is characterized by reversal of development; *blindness,* wasting, and spasticity lead to death. This is the most common form; other forms develop later and involve loss of the myelin sheath about the nerves. The progressive wasting to death is inevitable. (See *Lipidoses,* Section 10.)

Amnesia is loss of memory, sometimes noted after a head injury, implying that a concussion has occurred. The victim is unable to recall the events leading up to the blow on the head (retrograde amnesia). As he recovers, memory returns, usually completely. (See *Skull fracture,* Section 1.)

Epileptics usually experience transient memory loss; the *petit mal* patient, for instance, does not realize that he has been staring into space.

Angiography (*cerebral*) is an X-ray technique. Radiopaque dye is injected into the vessels leading to the brain. The angiograms (X-ray pictures) produced aid the doctor in determining the location and size of *tumors, clots,* or *aneurysms* in the skull.

Astrocytoma is a slow-growing, cystic brain tumor. In the cerebellum it causes loss of muscle tone, *ataxia,* and *nystagmus.* Headache and vomiting occur later. Surgical cures are possible in some cases.

Ataxia is the unsteady gait that accompanies a variety of nervous-system infections, *tumors,* or drug reactions. Walking with feet separated, a weaving *gait,* nausea, lethargy, *nystagmus,* and tremors may be associated. *Encephalitis* may give rise to this sign, as can *measles* and *polio. Dilantin®, phenobarbital,* and *tranquilizer* overdoses may produce this "drunken" appearance. A cerebellar brain tumor may start with this but is soon associated with *headache* and nausea. Medical diagnosis is needed. (See *Limp,* Section 7.)

Athetosis is usually associated with cerebral palsy. It is most obvious in the hands and fingers: uncoordinated twisting, flexing, extending movements suggest one's attempt to don wet gloves. Writhing of trunk and leg muscles is usually associated. (See *Cerebral palsy.*)

Bell's palsy is a weakness or paralysis of the muscles on one side of the face, due to a malfunctioning of the facial nerve. The nerve passes near the middle ear and may have been hurt or injured by an ear infection or by forceps pressure at birth. (See Section 5.)

Bell's palsy is occasionally due to tooth disease nearby if not otitis media or mastoiditis; it may be associated with hypertension.

The Bender-Gestalt Visual Motor Test is used to sample perceptual-motor development and certain aspects of perceptual-motor impairment associated with central nervous system dysfunction. It is occasionally, but unreliably, used for general personality assessment.

The test consists of nine cards, each containing a relatively uncomplicated abstract design. The child's task is to copy each design as well as he can. The basic skills for handling the tasks reasonably well probably mature between seven and eight years. Significant deviations in performance after that age may be signs of central nervous system impairment, delayed generalized development, regression, etc. There are sound normative data against which to interpret a child's record.

Brain abscess is a localized bacterial infection of the brain. A spreading sinus, skull, or mastoid infection may be the source or an infected embolus from a lung or heart source may seed itself in the brain substance. Fever, drowsiness, and headache at first may be mild and respond to aspirin. As the infection spreads it may cause prostration, a convulsion or one-sided weakness (*hemiplegia*) if the abscess is near the motor area of the brain.

Antibiotics will eliminate a forming abscess, but surgery may be necessary if the pus pocket has developed. Seizures are a common sequel.

Brain damage may be slight (*cerebral dysfunction*) or severe (*cerebral degeneration*). Because nerves cannot regenerate like skin, any dead nerve is permanently lost; however, other parts of the vast brain complex may be able to assume the function of the damaged part. Slight insults to the brain are usually not detectable by *electroencephalogram* (EEG), neurological evaluation, or even inspection.

Because "damage" gives rise to visions of scars, clots, or holes to the nonmedical layman, other, softer euphemisms have been invented. "Minimal cerebral dysfunction" can be used to describe the child who seems to have everything, but doesn't use it efficiently. In these cases "something is wrong," but there is no specific observable defect (as one could note after a stroke or *polio* or *brachial palsy*).

The constant daydreamer might be included here if we stretch the definition to these absurd, vague extremes. (We are *all* probably brain-damaged to a certain extent.) The difficulty of definition is most acute for the purists who would like to draw a line between symptoms due to actual nerve dysfunction, damage, or loss, and symptoms due to psychological factors. Actually the areas of the brain may be so close and interdependent that it would never be possible to differentiate. Indeed, the victim of some malfunction of his nervous system is more likely to develop psychological symptoms because of his frustrations and feelings of inferiority.

The child, then, who has normal or above-average intelligence, has no detectable neurological fault, but does not learn or behave as other children, might be called brain-damaged but we really don't know if he is or not. Some of these children have had some history of injury or sickness that *could* have hurt them (difficult delivery, prematurity, cord about the neck, *whooping cough, pneumonia, asthmatic bronchitis, concussion, high fever* plus *convulsions, meningitis*). Occasionally a strong genetic factor is present. (See *Cerebral dysfunction.*)

Brain scan (isotope encephalography) utilizes the proclivity of tumors to take up radioactive substances. The material is injected intravenously and a Geiger counter indicates where the material has been concentrated.

Brain tumors in children have a grave outlook as many lie deep in the brain, making surgical removal difficult. Many are adjacent to vital centers of the brain stem. Early-morning nausea, *vomiting,* and *headache* are the most common early findings; unsteady gait and visual disturbances might follow. The head size may enlarge in the young child. Early investigation by a neurosurgeon is essential if suspicious symptoms are noted, for some of the tumors can be completely removed early; some permanent cures are recorded. X rays of skull, *electroencephalogram, cerebral angiogram,* radioactive brain scan, *lumbar puncture* (see *cerebrospinal fluid*) all may be required to help diagnose and localize the growth. (See *Astrocytoma, Medulloblastoma,* and *Ependymoma.*)

Carpopedal spasm—see *Tetany*

Cerebellar ataxia is a benign condition thought to be due to a *virus.* It may follow a cold. The child is unsteady and acts as if he had had alcohol or drugs. He may vomit, be lethargic, have *nystagmus* (see *Eyes,* Section 14), or refuse to get out of bed as if dizzy. The symptoms may suggest *polio* or a *brain tumor.* Recovery without treatment is usually complete in a few weeks.

Cerebral aneurysm is usually a congenital outpouching or ballooning of the wall of an artery at the base of the brain. If this dilated saccule compresses a nerve, pain in the face or weakness of eye muscles may result. If it ruptures, symptoms of a stroke appear suddenly: exquisite *headache, vomiting, coma,* or *convulsion.* Treatment, of course, is corrective surgery—elective as long as there is no danger of the aneurysm giving way.

Cerebral calcification is any *calcium* deposit inside the skull bones detected by X ray. It may occur as a late finding in *subdural hematoma* because the blood clot may stimulate the deposition of calcium. It may appear after *toxoplasmosis, cytomegalic-inclusion disease,* miliary *tuberculosis,* or calcium may be deposited in the body of a *craniopharyngioma* or other tumors such as angiomas.

The calcium is deposited as a late event of some disease usually involving stasis of blood flow. The appearance and location suggests the disease; a baby who is small at birth, fails to grow properly, and is retarded might have his condition diagnosed by a skull film. If a calcium deposit is seen inside the skull, the nature of the condition causing the retardation thus might be revealed. Appropriate treatment, if any, could be instituted.

Cerebral degenerative disease is a general term covering a variety of neurological states in which brain tissue atrophies, degenerates, or is functionally lost. The cause or causes are largely unknown, but genetic predisposition is common. In some there is *lipid* storage in the nerves, causing loss of nerve function. (See *Lipidoses,* Section 10; *Amaurotic familial idiocy.*)

Cerebral dysfunction in its strictest sense is the term applied to a child who is unable to learn or behave in a fashion considered normal for his age. A broad definition could be carried to the extreme of including the *mentally retarded,* the *blind,* the *deaf,* the *epileptic,* the *neurotic,* etc., *ad absurdum.*

Some doctors prefer to limit the diagnosis to the child who might respond to the amphetamine drugs, hence, it would be a therapeutic category. If a child with a learning problem does not respond to this drug, he would be excluded from that doctor's diagnostic category.

A psychologist might use the term for a child with normal or above-average abilities, but who shows marked variability in skills that cannot be accounted for by environmental events. A teacher might use the term for any child who is disruptive in her classroom because of distractibility and short attention span.

A mother would use the term for a child who was *hyperactive,* a race horse, accident-prone, or difficult to live with. Counseling to change negative parental attitudes, and to arrange a more concrete, routinized environment as compensation for the child's poor control may be necessary.

Accident proneness is a life style with some children. It is obvious in the hyperactive child who has some coordination problem; his inability to curb his motor drives coupled with his inability to adjust to the sensory messages from his environment allow him to bang into doors, fall down stairs, slam his fingers in the door, burn himself on the stove. He is not stupid. Some defect in the association pathways in his brain may be responsible. (He may be operating at the low end of the normal maturation spectrum, called a developmental lag.) Moreover, each severe head injury may knock out a few nerve cells whose absence might further increase his maladroitness.

Awkward is the adjective used to describe humans with a variety of neuromuscular disorders. The toddler just learning to walk may be described as awkward because he falls or bangs into things in his enthusiasm to find out about his environment and try out his legs.

Awkwardness as a single complaint used by a mother to describe her four-year-old may have more predictive significance than any objective findings the doctor can note on physical examination. If there is a family history of clumsiness, poor balance, and limited athletic skills, it may imply a constitutional lack of coordination. It may be a developmental lag and the child catches up in time, but his temporary maladroitness may have allowed a poor *self-image* to appear.

If coupled with immaturity, explosive temper outbursts, and lack of *impulse control,* such awkwardness might suggest minimal cerebral dysfunction. Hypoglycemia and food allergies will preclude optimal brain function.

The *EEG,* or brain-wave test, may provide supportive evidence but is unreliable in making a diagnosis of a nervous-system fault. As the years go by, the mother would be the best judge to intuit what hobby or athletic endeavors should or should not be stressed.

A poorly coordinated child senses his lack of skill and quickly despises any activity that would embarrass him, even though the parents may think he would profit by the training. To a certain extent a ballerina is born a ballerina.

Distractibility is usually associated with a short attention span and *hyperactivity.* The child who is excessively distractible is usually called immature because he jumps from one activity to another, a phenomenon seen almost universally in the one- to two-and-a-half-year-old. If the three- to five-year-old cannot focus his attention for more than a few minutes at a time on a story or project but is constantly moving from one area to another, he is distractible. The child is best diagnosed by a nursery-school or kindergarten teacher who has a few other children with whom to compare. The "problem child" is usually a boy. He is unable to disregard unimportant stimuli; if someone drops a pencil or sneezes on the other side of the room, he is the first one there to investigate. If his mother sends him to another room to get his shoes that he forgot the third trip ago, he calls out in fifteen minutes, "What am I doing in here?" He was sidetracked by a few attractions along the way.

It is a lovable but irritating trait; he must sit still in school, keep quiet, and learn something. If it interferes with his (or others') learning, he must be put into a special small group (one to one, teacher to pupil is best) or given medicine to extend his attention span and inhibit his stimuli response.

Hyperactive is the term used to describe motor activity not appropriate for a child's age or the situation. The term is often applied to a child with minimal cerebral dysfunction if it is associated with a short attention span and distractibility.

Major traits of the hyperactive child are:

- Hyperactive behavior
- Short attention span
- Distractibility

The doctor or psychologist may see:

- Strephosymbolia (confusing *p* and *q; b* and *d;* reversing *was* and *saw, dog* and *god*)
- Dyslexia (specific reading disability out of proportion to intelligence)
- Visuo-sensory conceptual disorder related to the above

Eye-hand coordination confusion
Scatter of IQ test results between verbal (usually high) and performance (usually low)

The mother and/or the doctor may have observed:

Hyperactivity in the womb
Some oxygen deprivation before, at, or after delivery
Premature, overdue, or postmature birth, smallness for age, or second of twins
Whooping cough, pneumonia, or bronchitis requiring oxygen in the hospital
Colic, fussy and demanding behavior, need to prop bottle
Refusal to be cuddled, squirminess, ease of stimulation, ticklish
Sleep resistance (either light or restless sleeper)
Tendency to be accident-prone, excessive climbing, falling, and swallowing poisons or adult medicines
Loves animals, especially dogs and horses
Constant asking of questions, and constant movement
Inability to sit still even to eat or watch television without rocking or fiddling with something, constant nibbling, loves sweets
Eager, enthusiastic, and stimulating qualities that make the child nice to know but awful to live with

The teacher notices:

Overactivity, frequent trips to bathroom or fountain, too much talking that is loud and out of turn, disruptive effect on class
Restlessness, fidgeting, foot-tapping, annoyance to other children, inability to keep his hands to himself, ticklish
Knowledge and interest in everyone else's work, but failure to finish own
Difficulty with arithmetic and spelling; failure in "self-control"
Popularity and usually a lack of aggression or meanness, but overresponsiveness with laughing or crying
Immaturity, daydreaming, *underachieving*

Drugs most commonly used:

Dextroamphetamine sulfate (Dexedrine; Smith, Kline and French)
Amphetamine sulfate (Benzedrine; Smith, Kline and French)
Methylphenidate hydrochloride (Ritalin; Ciba)
Methamphetamine hydrochloride (Desoxyn; Abbott)
Pemoline (Cylert; Abbott)

The diagnosis is made comparatively. A mother living with a hyperactive child may not realize it until she has another more placid, normal child. Or she may only realize that he is hyperactive after the teacher complains that he will not sit still or be quiet or finish his work. He may display hyperactivity only when forced to sit still and conform in the classroom; the teacher can compare him with others.

Parts of the nervous system have a stimulating effect on motor activity, while other parts have an inhibitory or slowing effect. This latter filtering effect seems to be deficient in the child with cerebral dysfunction, for he finds it necessary to respond immediately to stimuli; this inability to disregard unimportant sensations is his chief weakness. Because of it, he has a short attention span, is distractible, impulse ridden, talkative, ticklish, hyperactive, easily frustrated, unpredictable, and may be unable to fall asleep and have poor motor coordination. These children are occasionally labeled as retarded.

As an infant, he might have been wakeful, colicky, easily stimulated, and overreacted to pain and sickness. But his major problem arose when he was enrolled in the first grade, and he had to study and concentrate in spite of the many stimuli his brain was receiving from thirty not-so-quiet six-year-olds. He has no cerebral mechanism to prevent these sensations from being acted upon.

His work is unfinished. The teacher says, "I know he knows it, but he won't put it on paper so I can grade him." (See *Underachievement,* Section 16.)

In addition to the rather obvious disruptive behavior, these children are sometimes afflicted with dyslexia. There is frequently an inability to copy geometric shapes, particularly if they demand several refined discriminations simultaneously; for example, equal sides, different angles, and diamond shapes (see *Bender-Gestalt test*).

Other neurological signs such as clumsiness, poor balance, loud talk, slobbering, delay in tying or buttoning skills may be present. These children are usually exquisitely ticklish. They usually have mirror motion: when asked to turn one hand back and forth, the other hand mirrors the action. Visual and hearing deficits must be tested for and ruled out.

Medication with amphetamine drugs may control the whole picture. Counseling to alleviate psychological blocks and poor parental attitudes may be necessary. Diagnostic tests for reading disability and education on a close one-to-one basis would be ideal.

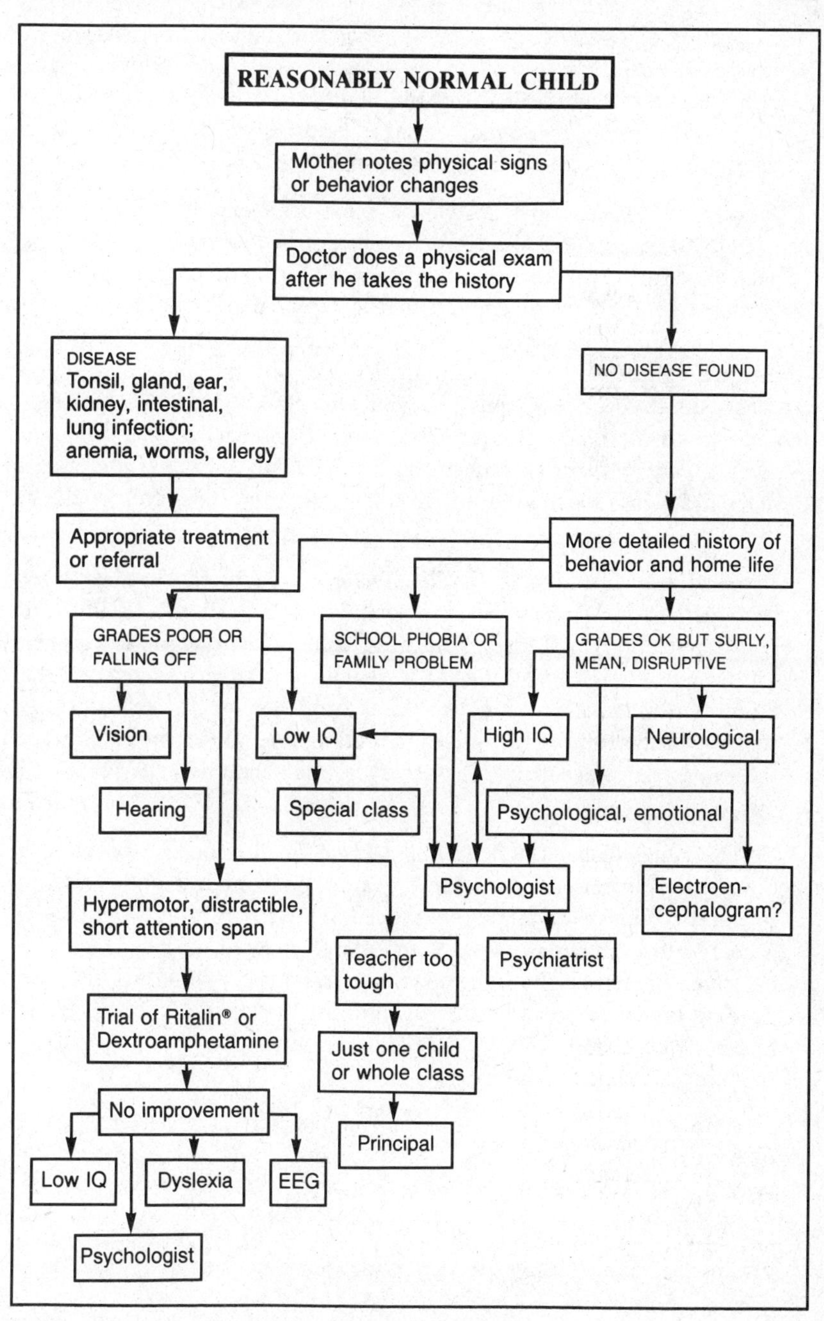
REASONABLY NORMAL CHILD
Mother notes physical signs or behavior changes
Doctor does a physical exam after he takes the history
DISEASE
Tonsil, gland, ear, kidney, intestinal, lung infection; anemia, worms, allergy
NO DISEASE FOUND
Appropriate treatment or referral
More detailed history of behavior and home life
GRADES POOR OR FALLING OFF
SCHOOL PHOBIA OR FAMILY PROBLEM
GRADES OK BUT SURLY, MEAN, DISRUPTIVE
Vision
Low IQ
High IQ
Neurological
Hearing
Special class
Psychological, emotional
Psychologist
Electroen-cephalogram?
Hypermotor, distractible, short attention span
Teacher too tough
Psychiatrist
Trial of Ritalin® or Dextroamphetamine
Just one child or whole class
No improvement
Principal
Low IQ
Dyslexia
EEG
Psychologist

Self-confidence, a good self-image, and immediate rewards for attainable goals are important in working with these children, who easily become depressed or hostile about their inability to succeed. Diet manipulation, avoidance of sugar, and ingestion of vitamins and calcium will often ameliorate all the symptoms.

Impulse ridden describes a level of immaturity expected in a normal one- to three-year-old child. Such behavior is less frequent after this age, as self-control becomes somewhat built-in, due in part to the development of control centers in the brain augmented by learning from discipline. An impulsive child is either *brain damaged* and neurologically unable to conform, or he has not had limits set by a consistent environment. (His behavior also could be a normal variant, a developmental lag.) He appears spoiled. Associated symptoms of *hyperactivity* and short attention span will usually serve to differentiate the child with minimal brain dysfunction from the psychologically impaired.

Cerebral edema means a swollen, waterlogged brain. It may result from concussion, infection, or a lack of oxygen. If the brain tissue is swollen enough, it may compress areas of the brain responsible for heartbeat and breathing. Intravenous injections of concentrated fluids may remove some of the water from the swollen tissue. Cortisonelike drugs may help. Fluid retention due to hormone effect is the cause of premenstrual headaches or headache due to birth-control pills.

Cerebral embolism is a condition caused by the lodging of a bit of blood clot, infectious material or fat globule in a blood vessel of the brain. This plug might have been released from a thrombus on a heart valve (rheumatic fever), an area of infected lung (pneumonia), or from the fat in the bone marrow (fracture). Symptoms vary depending on the size of the material and the area of the brain involved. Sudden *hemiplegia* follows the obstruction of the artery supplying the motor area in the cortex.

Cerebral fistula, the rare, abnormal connection of an arterial vessel to a vein, causes headaches, hydrocephalus, convulsions, and, if the vessels leak blood, subarachnoid hemorrhage.

Cerebral palsy includes a variety of injuries to the nervous system, leading to *muscular dysfunction* with or without mental deficiency, visual and auditory defects, seizure problems, and emotional disorders. Most of these are directly due to prenatal or birth injuries, *anoxia,* infections, or *hyperbilirubinemia.*

Spastic paralysis is a form of cerebral palsy in which the upper motor neurons are damaged from birth trauma or *anoxia.* These nerve fibers send uninhibited impulses to the spinal nerve fibers that activate the muscles. The lower neurons overact, putting the muscles into a state of increased tone or spasm. The legs pull together (scissors), the toes point down, the head may be pulled back (opisthotonus), and when the baby is put face down, he is unable to relax and turn his head to one side.

Physiotherapy is of some, but limited, benefit to these children. Water therapy with passive and active exercises helps to prevent contractures and muscle wasting.

Diplegia is a word usually following the word "spastic" to indicate a child with cerebral palsy who has movement malfunction of upper *and* lower limbs. The arms are flexed and held close to the chest, while the legs are stiff at knees and hips. Victims walk with a scissors gait, toes pointing down and in. The cause is damage, usually at birth, to the motor cortex of the brain.

Paraplegia is paralysis of the legs. If the legs are spastic or rigid and unmoving, a lesion is usually present in the brain (*cerebral palsy*). If the legs are flaccid (no muscle tone) and unmoving, the lesion is usually in the nerves that originate in the spinal cord (for example, *poliomyelitis*). *Spasticity, Athetosis, Ataxia,* and *Hypotonia* (see *Floppy infant syndrome;* also *Hypotonia,* Section 7.) May be seen singly or in various combinations. Neurological, orthopedic, and physical therapy may all be helpful.

About a million people in the United States are afflicted with *cerebral palsy.* Twenty-five percent are severe enough to be bedridden and usually succumb to some infection before age five. Half are seen by neurologists and orthopedic surgeons who perform tendon operations or prescribe physiotherapy. The remainder suffer minor hurts to the nervous system and are maladroit, have crossed eyes, or wear out their shoes in odd ways.

Cerebral vascular lesions—see *Cerebral aneurysm, fistula*

Cerebrospinal fluid is the watery solution surrounding the brain and spinal cord. The removal of a small amount of this fluid (*lumbar puncture*) is safe (does not cause paralysis) and is necessary for an accurate evaluation of a number of nervous-system diseases, especially *meningitis.* (See *Lumbar puncture.*) Sometimes fluid is removed and air injected. (See *Pneumoencephalogram.*)

Chorea is St. Vitus dance, a coarse, involuntary jerking of the large-muscle groups. The victim may appear awkward and clumsy and drop and spill things. Irritability and deterioration in school performance is typical.

Huntington's chorea is a genetic disease with increasing severity of uncontrolled movements. Brain atrophy and resultant dementia ultimately destroy the patient.

Sydenham's chorea is one, and sometimes the only one, of the manifestations of a *rheumatic fever* attack. The purposeless movements may be mild or may be severe enough to necessitate special restrictive confinement; drugs are necessary to sedate the wild thrashing movements. Recovery is usually complete, but may take weeks. The condition is thought to be some rheumatic brain involvement. About one third of chorea victims will eventually develop heart lesions compatible with *rheumatic heart disease.*

Coma is the condition of complete lack of response to stimulation. In addition to aspirin or tranquilizers or cough-syrup poisoning, one must search for diabetic *acidosis, hyponatremia* or *hypernatremia, hypoglycemia, lead poisoning, septicemia, Reye's disease, meningitis,* and *encephalitis.*

Communication disorders is the general term used to encompass defects of hearing, vision, perception, cognition, speech, or learning. Since meaningful *speech* is dependent upon adequate hearing, early assessment of gross hearing in infancy should be a part of the early examination of the child (by six months). If two or three words are not spoken appropriately by eighteen months or so, an exhaustive evaluation of the auditory apparatus must be made. Development of communication relies heavily on ability to hear.

Lack of early speech beyond the babbling in the first few months usually means a sensorineural defect (inner-ear, cochlear, or auditory-nerve malfunction). The cause of this type is usually genetic, maternal viral infection (for example, *rubella*), *bilirubin* excess, use of toxic drugs (for example, *streptomycin*), or *anoxic* insult at birth. (See *Hearing loss,* Section 14.)

The perception or recognition of sounds or words may be deficient, due to some defect or damage of the auditory area of the brain. Other nervous-system problems such as mental retardation, *hyperactivity, autism,* or *cerebral palsy* are usually present. Treatment is difficult and must be individualized; drugs such as amphetamines may increase the attention span and allow the audiologist some access to the patient's mind. Children who were premature, who suffered *anoxia, meningitis, encephalitis,* or *head trauma* are more likely to fall into this group.

It is vitally important that the babbling and syllabic repetitions the infant makes be reinforced by imitations from the adults—usually the mother—in the environment. A reflex speech pattern is established early, and communication is enhanced. If a baby says "da-da," and no one responds with a smile and a "da-da," he may stop saying it and remain silent for lack of a reward.

Half of his speech should be understandable at two years of age; this increases to complete understandability by age five.

It is axiomatic that speech delay or disorder is almost *never* due to mouth anomalies (except *cleft* lip and *palate*). *Tongue-tie* does not cause speech delay or stammering. *Hearing loss* (Section 14), neurological impairment, and (infrequently) environmental understimulation are the chief reasons for poor language achievement. (See *Speech*, *Learning disorders*, *Cerebral dysfunction*, *Stuttering*, *Dyslexia*.)

Convulsions, or epilepsy, are periodic attacks of unconsciousness, or at least alteration of the conscious state, and are usually associated with some involuntary muscle activity. They are but observable signs of a problem in the brain. Their cause requires investigation.

It is estimated that some 2 percent of children are thus affected. Information constantly repeated in medical literature would have us optimistically believe that 80 percent of spells are controllable, and in 70 percent of these, cures are possible. Recent new evidence indicates that these happy statistics must be reduced by half. It has been found that about one half of epileptics are involved with two different types of convulsions. If the *seizures* are mild, they may be controlled easily. If severe, control may be impossible, or at best temporary or difficult. Aggressive treatment should be instituted early.

Some strange forms of epilepsy are difficult to diagnose, but the following requirements must be fulfilled if the condition is to be labeled *epilepsy:* (a) seizures are recurrent, (b) they are usually the same, (c) the patient is relatively normal between attacks. There is no epileptic personality, although some believe psychomotor seizures may be associated with aggressiveness. The brain-wave test, or *EEG* (electroencephalogram), may be a useful tool in aiding diagnosis, but is not infallible, as some seizures have their origin deep in the brain too remote for the test to reveal. (Conversely, 15 percent of normal children have abnormal EEGs.)

Seizures due to birth *anoxia, meningitis,* metabolic disorders, *hypoglycemia,* PKU disease, congenital *syphilis, rubella, toxoplasmosis,* etc., are more likely to be associated with mental retardation or the *hyperactive* syndrome. The IQ range of the epileptic child has the same distribution as the normal population.

A seizure in a baby may be misdiagnosed as colic, for his immature nervous system responds with a massive, total body response. *Tetany* of newborn, *hypoglycemia, kernicterus* (*hyperbilirubin*), intracranial bleeding or severe *anoxia* at birth cause seizures in the newborn period. (See Section 5.) Except for tetany these are more productive of brain damage and mental retardation; hence, immediate corrective therapy is mandatory.

Salaam seizure, or myoclonic fit, is a jackknife seizure with flexion of the trunk, head and arms, usually appearing before one year of age. *Mental retardation* is the rule.

Grand mal is the more common type and is usually implied by the term "epilepsy." Usually an aura (noise, lights, pain) or some strange symptom (stomachache or headache, irritability, hyperactivity, appetite loss) gives warning of the explosion to come. The victim suddenly stiffens, cries out, falls, and his eyes roll up. Initial pallor is replaced by flushing, then *cyanosis* as he holds his breath. After this thirty seconds of stiffness, the body is overcome by a series of powerful, jerking, rhythmical movements that may go on for some minutes. Urine is usually forced out of the bladder by the straining. Sleep is the usual rule after this exhausting exercise. Some *headache* and mental confusion are present after awakening.

Petit mal is a rare form of spell in which the child momentarily loses consciousness and seems to stare vacantly into space, then resumes the preseizure activity. He does not fall, has no memory of the lapse, and is frequently accused of inattention or daydreaming. He may have many attacks a day. The *EEG* shows a typical pattern. Although control is sometimes difficult, some may outgrow the problem by adolescence, but *grand mal* may supervene. Hyperventilation (overbreathing) may bring on a *petit mal* attack.

Seizures after head injury are not common, but some authorities recommend the use of *phenobarbital* for six months to preclude their appearance.

Psychomotor attacks may vary from a minor emotional outburst without adequate environmental stimulus to a complicated body action, which, although coordinated, is purposeless (for example, plucking at clothes, chewing, swallowing, or rubbing hands). Some loss of posture is usually associated with the attack, and there may be hyperactivity before the spell and drowsiness afterward. Sudden unexplained outbursts of violence, aggression, or running away may be classified as psychomotor. The *EEG* may show nothing unless taken during an attack when the temporal-lobe area appears to be the focus. Sleepwalking, night terrors, temper outbursts, bizarre speech may be due to this. Spells of great fear or depression or the shakes or feeling odd may suggest this.

Epileptic equivalent is the name given to any one of a variety of otherwise inexplicable symptoms that may be the result of abortive seizures. *Headaches* suggesting *migraine,* stomachaches (*abdominal epilepsy*), followed by pallor and somnolence (some severe enough to require surgical evaluation), automatic purposeless acts, sudden, explosive, impulsive attacks on things or people may all appear to be psychogenic in origin, but might well be set off by an irritable electrical focus somewhere in the brain. *Fainting* attacks without a reasonable environmental stimulus or unaccompanied by hypoglycemia or anemia should be investigated for EEG abnormalities or *Stokes-Adams syncope.* Some forms of migraine are assumed to be related to epilepsy, but not all neurologists agree to this. *Breath-holding* (see Section 16), so common in the toddler, may lead to convulsive movements. Medication is not indicated. Some frantic mothers insist on something for the child so that household rules can be enforced without the constant worry of triggering a frightening spell.

The majority of *grand mal* seizures are idiopathic (cause unknown), but psychic strain, fatigue, loss of sleep, biochemical or infectious agents may precipitate a spell. There are documented cases of *grand mal* seizures being triggered by certain music or patterns of light. (A local neurologist told me of a girl who had a seizure whenever she heard sad cowboy music. Dilantin® was not effective in controlling the condition, so when she went to a dance she had to wear a buzzer device in her ear and turn up the sound when she heard the orchestra begin to play "I'm Heading for the Last Roundup.")

We have learned much about the brain from the investigations of *epilepsy.* A lesion in or near the motor area of the brain will produce the *grand mal* seizure. Stimulation in certain areas of the temporal lobe will produce attacks of dread or fear or fits of violence. These temporal lobes store emotional memory. Some epileptics have seizures of depression or dread without any motor component. Sometimes the miserable sensation precedes a falling spell. Recent EEG research now indicates that much episodic abnormal behavior is the result of some overflow or "take over" from these energized nuclei in the hypothalamus and/or temporal lobe area of the cortex.

The medical workup for an epileptic patient depends on his age and history, but the physical and neurological examination, X ray of skull, urinalysis, blood tests (*sugar* [see *Hypoglycemia,* Section 10], *calcium, urea*), EEG, and possible spinal tap would be included.

The care of the patient during the seizure involves protecting him from harm. Turning him to the side position, to prevent secretions from running down his windpipe, and loosening his clothing are all that is necessary. Most patients have bitten their tongues at the *onset* of the spell, so jamming a stick in the mouth is unnecessary and may only do more harm (break teeth). If the seizure does not stop after a few minutes the patient would benefit by being given some oxygen and perhaps an injection of an anticonvulsant (Valium® is standard.)

Status epilepticus is the repetition of *grand mal* seizures without an intervening recovery period. It usually occurs if a patient has recently and abruptly discontinued his medication.

It is difficult for parents to treat their epileptic child as they would a child not subject to seizures. Overprotection is the usual error made, and often the child is not allowed to engage in games and sports (see *Athletics,* Section 7). He may become excessively dependent or overtly hostile—especially in adolescence when he wants to be normal. He may refuse to take the medicine, which further intensifies parental anxieties. Public fears of the epileptic are a holdover from witchcraft days, and much needs to be done in schools and shops to educate the public about "the falling sickness." Most neurologists feel that the surly attitude of some epileptics is due to the attitude of society toward them rather than any inherent neurological nastiness. The Epilepsy League is working mightily uphill to dispel some medieval old wives' tales, but they have a long way to go.

Treatment involves the use of drugs which are increased in dosage until control is effective. If side effects are excessive before benefit is achieved, another drug is added or substituted. Phenobarbital is the drug of choice for most seizures, but *Dilantin®, Mebaral®, Zarontin®, Mysoline®,* valproic acid, may be considered (see *Anticonvulsants,* Section 4). Rashes, behavior abnormalities, low white blood counts, swollen gums may be disturbing side effects. Medication is usually continued indefinitely. Some doctors continue full doses until the period of rapid growth has been passed (pubescence seems to aggravate seizure tendencies), and then try to withdraw the medicine. Recurrence of seizures is too common; it is better to plan on lifetime drug maintenance.

Craniopharyngioma accounts for about ten percent of all intracranial tumors in children. It develops from embryonic cell remnants in the pituitary gland area. Cells multiply and cysts form. Increased intracranial pressure causes headaches. The victim may become obese because of the stimulating effect on the nearby appetite center of the hypothalamus. Intereference with growth hormone production causes short stature. Diabetes insipidus develops in one fourth of the patients. Many patients have delayed sexual development because of the decreased gonadotrophic hormone secretion. Visual defects are common because the optic nerves pass near this area.

A few of the above symptoms and signs plus a skull X ray showing bone destruction in the pituitary area are usually enough to make the diagnosis. Surgery is the only treatment, but the proximity to vital structures gives rise to gloomy mortality rates. Survivors usually need to be maintained on hormone therapy.

Delirium is a combination of excitement, confusion, disorientation, and restlessness, with elements of suspiciousness and suicidal or aggressive tendencies added in various degrees.

It is most frequently seen in the infant or child who has been given a *barbiturate* for colic, teething, or restlessness. A paradoxical excitement seems to overwhelm him, and he acts like a drunk in pain, crying and staggering.

The toddler who suddenly acts up may have gotten diet pills, *thyroid, tranquilizers,* or *barbiturates* from somebody's purse or the medicine chest. He may have taken a few sips from the liquor cabinet.

Sudden fever or head injury will produce the same picture. Lead *encephalitis* (paint ingestion) or vitamin deficiencies would have other signs to help determine the cause.

The cure is to remove that cause. If the child has not taken a toxic overdose but is suffering from an untoward reaction that will subside in a few hours, the wet-sheet pack may tranquilize him. With arms at his sides, he is wrapped from shoulders to toes in a snug wet sheet, then in a blanket so only his head can move. With little resulting stimulation from body to excitable brain, he frequently drops off to sleep from boredom.

Dyslexia is a specific reading disability; there is no known cause. By the narrowest definition, primary dyslexia applies only to children who have at least average intelligence, no measurable psychological, physical, or neurological fault, and have not been deprived at home or at school. About ten percent of the population have this to some extent. It is assumed to be due to a central brain problem rather than to any pathology of the eye itself. Most children with severe eye problems become readers despite their visual handicap; there is more to reading than seeing. It is a complex pathway involving *hearing,* and ability to perceive (recognizing the difference between a *b* and a *d*), and remembering the associated sounds.

Nothing is wrong with dyslexic children, except that they cannot read or they are reading one to two years behind the remainder of the class. They are unable to relate the printed word with its appropriate sound. (Japanese claim dyslexia is unknown to them as there is a specific sound for each character.) They reverse letters in their minds, read "was" for "saw," substitute whole syllables, and cannot spell. They are frequently disruptive, distractible, and have a short attention span, which may be secondary to reading difficulty. They are usually males, and their fathers have had similar problems; this is the genetic type. They may have mixed eye-hand dominance (right-handed, left-eyed), or some visual acuity or eye-muscle imbalance problems; these, however, are not the *determinants* of dyslexia.

There are two major types of dyslexia: the first is a phonetic deficiency—the child cannot sound out the words and makes a response to the whole word by a substitution ("chair" might be called "table"; "bus" might be "car"), the second is an inability to respond to the whole word—the child must sound out every letter, even familiar ones ("listen" is spelled "lisn"). Some children have a mixture of these problems; they are difficult to treat and frequently become adult nonreaders.

Early childhood clues that dyslexia may develop: delayed speech, marked *stuttering, cluttering,* poor self-expression. After the first grade the dyslexic child shows poor memory for printed (in contrast to spoken) words, word and letter reversals (especially *p, q, d, b*) are common, spelling is bizarre, handwriting is atrocious (sport skills may be excellent), handedness uncertainty (not related to *thumb nail* breadth) may be present, and there is difficulty with time and up-down concepts.

The problem is obvious by the second half of the first grade; a thorough investigation must be made by this time and appropriate remedial measures taken.

Some compromise in the learning process is essential while awaiting the remedial efforts to produce benefits. Oral testing and reading assigned material to the child will still allow him to learn the subject matter so he doesn't fall too far behind.

If a child is *hyperactive* and dyslexic, a trial of Ritalin® or an amphetamine is indicated. If his attention span is controlled but his dyslexia is unimproved, he needs the special skills of a professional remedial reading teacher. Secondary dyslexia may have an emotional cause (rare) or be due to a low IQ. The rare *schizophrenic* child may have dyslexia. Obviously visual and auditory function must be evaluated. Food allergies and hypoglemia can cause dyslexia.

Most schools have remedial reading programs successful with the first or second grader who has a developmental lag in reading skills. The severely dyslexic victim is unreachable via the usual visual pathways, so auditory and kinesthetic (touch) methods must be used. The phonetic (sounding-out) works better than look-and-say methods. The teacher's expertise and enthusiasm are all important.

Education is rooted in reading ability, so the child who cannot read becomes frustrated by his embarrassment, hates school, develops antisocial and/or psychological symptoms. Every effort must be made to bolster his ego and give him success as quickly as possible before he develops damaging feelings of self devaluation, drops out and becomes delinquent. Fire setting and vandalism directed at schools are often the end result of school failure.

Educators get a variety of different remedies thrust at them by advocates of many theories of causation. All seem to claim success. The enthusiasm of the therapist may be more important to success because the child is getting individual attention; motivation is kindled to overcome his handicap.

Electroencephalogram, or EEG or brain-wave test, is the record of amplified electrical waves that arise from the surface of the brain. It is helpful but not specific, in diagnosing convulsive disorders, blood clots on the *brain, tumors,* and other lesions. Its value has not been clearly demonstrated in behavior problems which have a large psychogenic flavor, but a high percentage of children—and adults—have abnormal EEGs associated with an impulsive, explosive, destructive personality. Fifteen percent of normal children have abnormal EEGs; some severely retarded patients have normal EEGs.

Predominate brain waves vary according to age, being slow in infancy and faster in adulthood.

Patients with *grand mal* epilepsy may have normal waves in the intervals between seizures, but usually some spikes or slow waves are found. *Petit mal* epilepsy is quite characteristic, with a spike and dome pattern occurring three times a second.

Fluid, blood, or *abscess* over an area would prevent the registering of waves and would thus localize the lesion.

Encephalitis, or sleeping sickness, is a virus inflammation of the brain. It is usually associated with a respiratory infection but it may be carried by flies and mosquitoes. The severe headache that accompanies most virus diseases can be assumed to be due to edema; the brain swells, and the resultant pressure creates the headache.

Encephalitis may also accompany *infectious mononucleosis, measles,* vaccinia, *chickenpox,* and *influenza.* It may be due to the canker-sore virus (*herpes simplex*) and be severe, prolonged, and crippling.

Mosquitoes and ticks can carry a virus from animals to the human; this form is called equine encephalitis. *Rabies*—almost invariably fatal—is a viral encephalitis.

Mumps encephalitis, which occurs in about 10 to 20 percent of patients with mumps, is associated with fever, headache, *vomiting,* stiff neck, and back. If there is no parotid gland swelling, *polio* may be suspected, but mumps encephalitis rarely produces muscle weakness.

Treatment depends on the severity of the symptoms. If coma is present, hospital nursing care is necessary. *Cortisone* drugs may decrease some of the swelling due to the inflammation. Reducing the fever helps.

It is not unusual for the patient to suffer emotional or behavioral changes from encephalitis. Hyperactivity, impulsivity, and temper outbursts would most likely be seen.

Encephalopathy is the general term that simply means something is wrong with the brain. Drowsiness, coma, confusion, *headache, vomiting,* instability, etc., are associated with a variety of diseases (see *Polyarteritis,* Section 2) or poisonings. If the *liver* is diseased and cannot excrete the waste products (ammonia), the patient will have hepatic encephalopathy. In *nephritis* with elevated blood pressure, the vascular spasm in the brain reduces the amount of oxygen to the brain, and hypertensive encephalopathy (with above symptoms) will follow. When the blood pressure falls, the symptoms clear. *Lead poisoning* will cause similar symptoms, because the metal produces brain swelling. Some older boxers have this (see *Athletics,* Section 7). Frequently, however, the cause cannot be found.

Ependymoma is a type of tumor that invades the brain, giving rise to *vomiting, headache,* and unsteadiness. Because of its proximity to vital functions, it is difficult to remove. X-ray treatment is helpful.

Epilepsy—see *Convulsions*

Fatigue is a common complaint of mothers. Either *they* are fatigued from child rearing and childbearing, or their adolescent children are so pooped they cannot make their beds, do the dishes, or be of any help around the house. The growing child is expected to be fatigued just from growing, but when this is combined with the pressures of schoolwork, competition with peers, *anemia,* and excessive television watching, fatigue can turn into tears, rebellion, and *anger.*

If a child wants to go to bed, sleeps adequately (twelve hours for the four- to seven-year-old, eleven hours for the seven- to nine-year-old, ten hours for the ten- to twelve-year-old, and nine hours up to maturity), and awakens tired, the following should be investigated: chronic infection (kidney, tonsils, lungs, *mesenteric adenitis*), *worms,* low *thyroid, rheumatic fever, diabetes, hypoglycemia, anemia, allergy,* and overstimulation or overwork.

Some children, because of genetic makeup, are self-stimulating

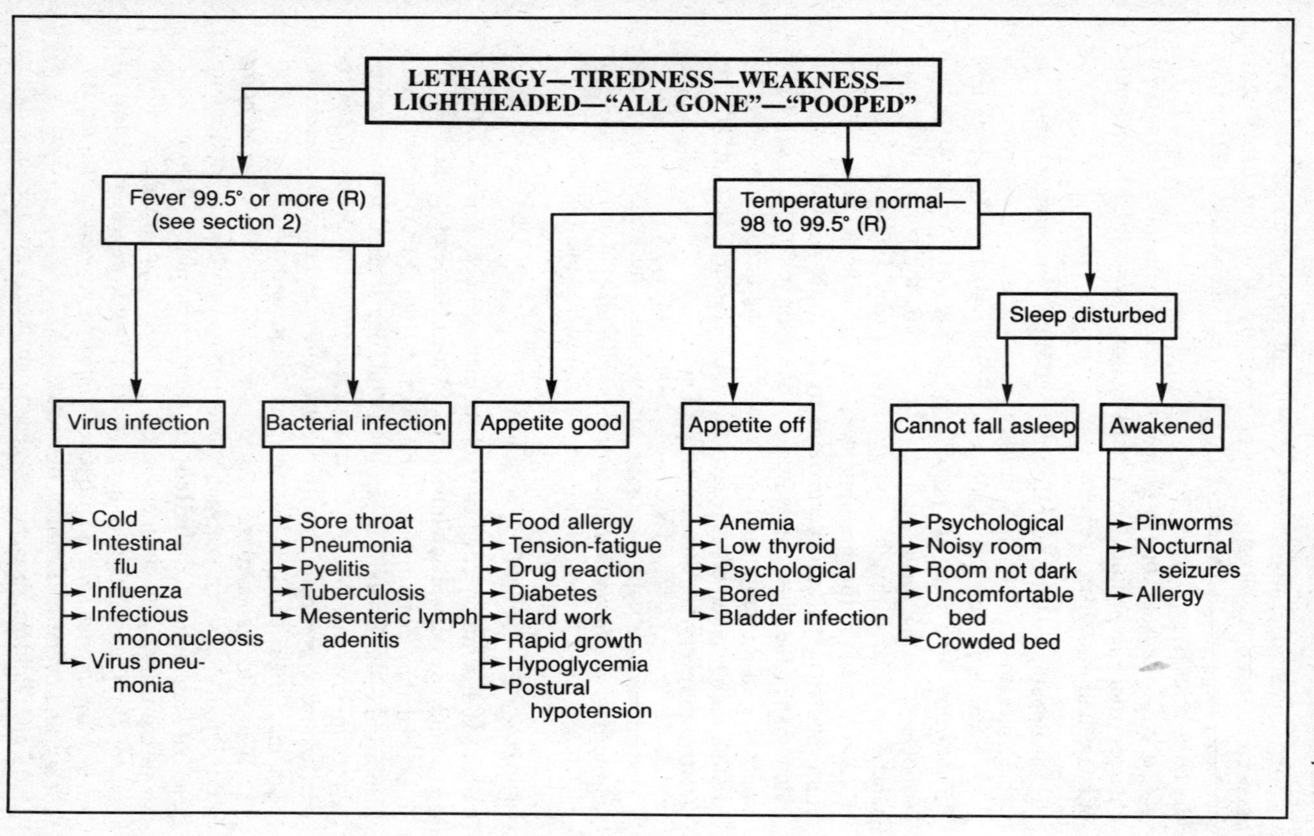
LETHARGY—TIREDNESS—WEAKNESS—
LIGHTHEADED—"ALL GONE"—"POOPED"
Fever 99.5° or more (R)
(see section 2)
Temperature normal—
98 to 99.5° (R)
Sleep disturbed
Virus infection
Bacterial infection
Appetite good
Appetite off
Cannot fall asleep
Awakened
Cold
Intestinal
flu
Influenza
Infectious
mononucleosis
Virus pneu-
monia
Sore throat
Pneumonia
Pyelitis
Tuberculosis
Mesenteric lymph
adenitis
Food allergy
Tension-fatigue
Drug reaction
Diabetes
Hard work
Rapid growth
Hypoglycemia
Postural
hypotension
Anemia
Low thyroid
Psychological
Bored
Bladder infection
Psychological
Noisy room
Room not dark
Uncomfortable
bed
Crowded bed
Pinworms
Nocturnal
seizures
Allergy

and are unable to turn themselves off at a reasonable time at night. As the frustrated parents find they cannot legislate sleep, they must compromise and allow the child to remain in his bed playing quietly or reading. They can sneak in later and turn off the light. (See *Sleep,* Section 16.)

Abnormal fatigue or inability to keep up with the peer group may be due to emotional problems (depression, especially) or some occult neurological condition. Giving B-complex vitamins and a protein snack at bedtime revitalizes many children.

A sometimes forgotten condition called *postural hypotension* would be discovered if the blood pressure is lower on standing than when lying down.

Most adolescents have energy to do what they want to do—but not what is required of them by their parents.

Febrile seizures, better called benign spells precipitated by fever, are observed in 10 percent of children during onset of fever, are most common in the one-to-four-year age group, have a family incidence, and are occasionally associated with *grand mal* epilepsy later. Most authorities believe daily phenobarbital treatment is worthwhile until the child is five years old, as an occasional patient may suffer *status epilepticus* (see *Convulsions*) with the next fever. Phenobarbital given only at fever times is usually too late to halt the spell.

Floppy infant syndrome is the term given to babies with generalized muscular hypotonia who cannot otherwise fit into any clear-cut diagnostic category. Once cerebral palsy and mental retardation (including Down's syndrome) have been ruled out, some rare and difficult-to-diagnose conditions must be considered before an idiopathic label is attached. *Cerebral degenerative disease, brain tumor,* congenital *muscular dystrophy,* and *myasthenia gravis* are rare, but if these can be ruled out, floppy infant syndrome is the term for the remainder. Electromyography and muscle biopsy may reveal a specific disorder. Many floppy infants gradually respond, and although they have gross lags in motor and adaptive development, they may do well as adults, albeit somewhat awkward. (See *Hypotonia,* Section 7.)

Focal seizures are uncontrolled spasms or movements of facial, arm, or leg muscles. The activity may spread to involve adjacent muscles. If consciousness is lost, it is called *Jacksonian epilepsy.* The presence of muscle twitches or shakes in the face, arm, or leg may spread to the whole body, producing a generalized seizure like grand mal.

Friedreich's ataxia is a progressively debilitating disease manifested by gradual appearance of clumsiness, unsteady *gait,* poor speech, loss of reflexes, *deafness, blindness,* dementia. The feet develop an abnormally high arch. *Heart anomalies* are common. Hereditary factors are present. There is no treatment.

Guillain-Barré syndrome, or infectious polyneuritis, is a disease of the nervous system often associated with some other illness (*mononucleosis, diphtheria, influenza,* etc.) in which the patient loses sensation and muscle use from feet to legs to abdomen to chest. Movement of muscles may be painful, although the skin over them has lost touch sense. If the muscles of respiration are involved, the patient may need to be placed in a respirator. The spinal fluid is usually devoid of cells, in contrast to *polio.* No causal virus has been isolated. Recovery may take months but is usually complete. (See *Paralysis,* Section 7.)

Handedness preference is genetically determined. The majority of people are right-handed, but recent investigations indicate an increasing number (up to 30 percent) of children preferring the left hand; this is probably due to their parents' general awareness that attempts to change dominant left-handedness cause frustration, stuttering, and learning problems. The breadth of the thumbnails is a clue: the right thumbnail is broader in a child who is genetically right-handed. If he prefers to use his left hand, it may suggest that he has suffered some neurological impairment to the left side of his brain, whence emanates the control of the right side of the body.

Cerebral dominance refers to this preferred handedness. Left cerebral dominance means the person is right-eyed, -handed, and -footed. Some people prefer to use the right hand for some things and the left for others; this is mixed dominance. Equal ability is ambidexterity. Attempts to change dominance once established are frustrating to the child and about as difficult as changing blue eyes to brown.

Headache in children is more likely to be a symptom of organic disease than of tension, worry, or neurosis. Most commonly it is associated with fevers of *viral* origin. Usually the child is unable to describe the type (throbbing, steady, dull, sharp) or severity of the pain until he is over eight years old. The mother can only infer a headache in a young child by his undue lethargy, furrowed brow, scalp rubbing, or ear pulling.

Distended blood vessels or distorted meninges are the chief reasons for the pain. A headache aggravated by activity and relieved by rest is an example of a *vascular headache;* hangover headaches are due to swollen blood vessels. A *brain tumor* or blood clot would stretch the meninges and cause pain. A *migraine* headache in a child is usually associated with vomiting to the point that the head pain is almost forgotten; the pain may be all over the head and not just on one side as is typical in the adult. The child may not be aware of any visual prodromal signals that his attack is coming, but the mother may note hyper- or hypoactivity during the day prior to the headache. The periodicity and the family history are confirmatory signals. Relief with caffeine would also suggest the possibility of migraine.

A similar headache associated with abnormal brain waves is called an *epileptic equivalent.* It comes on suddenly and is associated with pallor. The giveaway would be the child's falling asleep afterward, as if the nervous system were exhausted. *Phenobarbital* or *Dilantin®* would give relief in this case.

Food allergies frequently are the cause of headaches. The most common allergenic foods include chocolate, corn, pork, milk, nuts, fish, and eggs. A good plan would be for the mother to make a diet calendar, listing all the foods consumed in the previous three to twelve hours before the headache. After three or four headaches, it should be obvious that some one food was always included—if indeed it is an allergic headache. ("He has a chocolate bar every day after school, and by supper he is pale, has sunken eyes, and a crushing headache.") (See *Tension-fatigue syndrome.*)

Eyestrain can cause headaches, usually frontal, but a child with a refractive error usually dislikes reading. He avoids reading to avoid the headache. *Sinus trouble* to be severe enough to cause a headache will usually give other clues: purulent nasal discharge, fever, tenderness to bone pressure at the sinus site. *Tension headache* is supposed to be due to the neck muscles pulling on the scalp at the back of the head. Headache may also be due to neuritis or neuralgia of the sensory nerves of the scalp. The pain is sudden and radiates along the pathway of the nerve; the skin supplied by this nerve is usually extra sensitive. A common neuralgia pain is due to irritation of one of the cervical (neck) nerves supplying the back side of the head. Tension of the back neck muscles aggravates the neuralgia and a vicious cycle begins.

A careful history-taking is the most important diagnostic aid

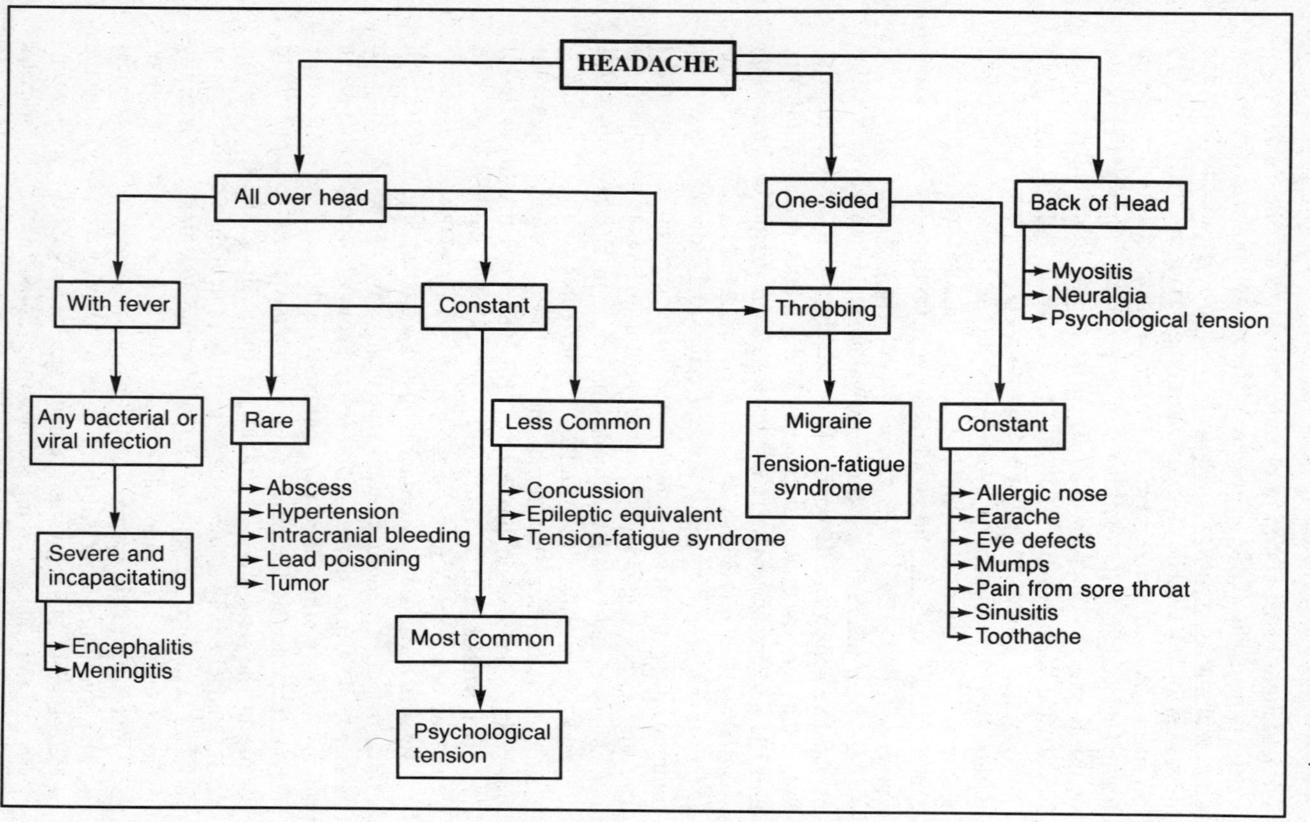
HEADACHE
All over head
One-sided
Back of Head
Myositis
Neuralgia
Psychological tension
With fever
Constant
Throbbing
Any bacterial or viral infection
Rare
Less Common
Migraine
Tension-fatigue syndrome
Constant
Abscess
Hypertension
Intracranial bleeding
Lead poisoning
Tumor
Concussion
Epileptic equivalent
Tension-fatigue syndrome
Allergic nose
Earache
Eye defects
Mumps
Pain from sore throat
Sinusitis
Toothache
Severe and incapacitating
Encephalitis
Meningitis
Most common
Psychological tension

in headache evaluation, but eye examination (*choked disk* and *refractive errors*), skull X ray, *EEG,* blood-sugar examination, *blood pressure* and *urinalysis* (*hypertension* due to *kidney disease*), spinal-fluid examination may be necessary. (See *Migraine.*)

Hemiplegia is weakness or *paralysis* of one side of the body. In the elderly the stroke is usually due to vascular disease in the brain. In a child it may be due to an infection, an embolus, a thrombosis, or unknown factors. It is of sudden onset with an overwhelming convulsion, coma, fever, and paralysis on one side of the body. Recovery is slow and often not complete. *Convulsions* and *retardation* may be sequels.

Hydranencephaly is a rare congenital absence of the cerebral hemispheres. This space is filled with a clear fluid so the general shape of the skull at birth is normal. Although sucking and breathing are normal, it becomes quite obvious in a few weeks that the baby is blind and retarded. The head will transilluminate light. No treatment is possible. The condition may be associated with cytomegalic inclusion disease.

Hydrocephalus, or water on the brain, is the excess accumulation of spinal fluid in the ventricles (inside the brain) and/or over the brain's surface (subarachnoid space). Spinal fluid is formed inside the brain from the choroid plexus (mass of capillaries in the ventricles), flows through the ventricles (spaces inside the brain substance), then out near the brain stem to bathe the spinal cord and the outer surface of the brain where the fluid is reabsorbed. Too much production of fluid or an obstruction of the flow to points of absorption causes excess accumulation. *Tumors, cysts,* or scar tissue after infection might be responsible for closure of various openings through which the fluid must pass.

The condition may be present at birth, but usually is not noted until two or three weeks pass and the soft spot seems too large or too tense. Appetite falls, the upper eyelids retract and the sclerae (whites) become visible above the irises, scalp veins become prominent, and the baby develops a high-pitched cry.

Diagnostic studies may be necessary to establish the obstructive point (*pneumoencephalogram,* sonar scanning).

The ideal neurosurgical procedure is to provide a shunt from the pool of excess fluid back to the circulation. The most common method is the insertion of a polyethylene catheter that carries the fluid from a ventricle in the brain to the right atrium of the heart. Infection and clotting are common complications. Surgery for this once universally fatal condition now has a more sanguine success rate, but many revisions may be necessary. Parents must discuss the pros and cons of the operation with their neurosurgeon.

Hypothalamus is a small area at the base of the brain (just above and connected to the pituitary gland). It has nerve control over the pituitary as well as humoral influences. Some of the cells secrete chemicals that migrate to the pituitary (*vasopressin,* see *Diabetes insipidus,* Section 10). The hypothalamus acts as a thermostat in body-temperature regulation, blood pressure, sleep, eating, and drinking. Some behavior and emotional responses of the body have their origin here; other behavior traits are modified by hypothalamic influences.

Lesions of the hypothalamus have been responsible for the following: *precocious puberty, hypogonadism,* fits of rage or laughing or crying, somnolence, *obesity,* emaciation, *convulsions,* and, of course, *diabetes insipidus.*

Hypsarrhythmia is an EEG pattern associated with salaam seizure, a type of myoclonic seizure seen in infants. (See *Convulsions.*)

Intracranial bleeding (see *Cerebral aneurysm*) is bleeding inside the skull. Bleeding after trauma includes *epidural hematoma, subdural hematoma,* intracerebral hemorrhage, and subarachnoid hemorrhage—a classification based on location. Spontaneous (no injury involved) hemorrhage is usually subarachnoid or intracerebral, usually the result of a ruptured aneurysm and more likely to be deep in the brain. Postinjury bleeding is more likely to be in the surface of the brain. *Angiography* would help to localize the lesion.

Epidural hematoma is a blood clot between the skull bone and the outer meningeal covering (like a thin sheet of plastic) of the brain. It is usually the result of a fractured skull which tears open a blood vessel. This brisk bleeding will rapidly compress the brain and cause drowsiness, *headache, vomiting,* weakness or numbness of face, arm, or leg on the side opposite the clot. The pupil on the same side may become enlarged and fixed (nonresponsive to light). (See *Skull fracture, Head injuries,* Section 1.) If symptoms are progressive, surgery is necessary to evacuate the clot and stop the bleeding, or the patient will succumb.

Subdural hematoma is a blood clot between the surface of the brain and the meningeal covering. It usually arises from a blow to the head or a fall. The newborn may develop this after a long, difficult delivery with much head molding. The bleeding is venous, so the blood may accumulate slowly and few symptoms are noted. A *battered child* may develop this condition. An infant may only be irritable, have a low fever, vomit, grow poorly, and develop an enlarged head with a tense soft spot (fontanel).

The original blood clot forms into a pocket (like a sandwich bag) with thick yellow fluid in the middle. This fluid increases in amount because of new hemorrhages and absorption of spinal fluid into it like a sponge; it perpetuates itself. The ultimate large size will compress the brain. Treatment is aspiration of the fluid by daily needle taps through the soft spot until no fluid re-forms. Surgery may be necessary to remove the membranes. If atrophy of the brain has occurred from the compression, the operation will not restore normal brain function.

Learning disorders is a general term suggesting some neurological problem which precludes adequate progress. It includes *mental retardation,* sensory impairment, short attention span, poor memory, deficient conceptualization, and *distractibility.* In its strict sense it would exclude emotional problems and physiological defects such as *anemia,* inadequate diet, and insufficient *sleep.*

No specific test can detect children who are destined to do poorly in school, but the kindergarten teacher would be suspicious, and the first-grade teacher would know. The brain-wave test is of no value in diagnosing this problem. Neurologically there are usually no obvious reflex or performance tests that really give it away. The psychologist can test; he will usually find normal abilities but a discrepancy between the "verbal" and the "performance" scores. If behavior modification techniques and/or medication do not route the child into normal class advancement, he becomes more disruptive because he is angry and frustrated. Inability to read at grade level must be investigated next. (See *Dyslexia.*) Remedial reading is the next step, and if success is early, he may yet keep up with his class. Maintaining a satisfactory self-image is all-important.

Early identification is the cornerstone of treatment; the farther behind the child is academically, the more difficult are the remedial techniques.

Lumbar puncture, or spinal tap, is a safe method of confirming a number of neurological diseases. With the patient lying on his side in the flexed, fetal position, some local anesthetic is injected into the skin and tissue of the midline in the lower back. A needle is inserted between the vertebrae until the spinal canal is entered. The fluid is normally as clear as water and contains a few cells. Pressure can be estimated; elevated pressure might indicate tumor or blood clot. Elevation of cell count indicates *encephalitis* or *meningitis.* Yellow fluid suggests an old injury (blood has hemolyzed); red fluid means a fresh hemorrhage.

Medulloblastoma is the most common of brain tumors in children, is the most rapid growing, spreads quickly to other parts of the brain or spinal cord, and because of all this is the most difficult to eradicate surgically. X-ray therapy is only temporarily palliative, and most children succumb less than a year after the diagnosis is made.

Mental retardation is intellectual impairment sufficient to slow learning ability. All degrees are seen from mild (common) to severe (rare). It usually becomes manifest by the delay in arriving at developmental landmarks. If undetected in the preschool years, it will then come to light when formal schooling is attempted. The child cannot cope with reading and simple arithmetic, and social and emotional problems are added to his burden. Memory, reasoning, abstract thought are usually equally reduced. Affected children frequently have other associated neurological problems such as *seizures,* clumsiness, *speech, hearing,* and *visual* disorders.

About 3 to 4 percent of the population (6 million) are involved to a point that school, social, and employment possibilities are affected, and sheltered (at home) or institutional care is necessary. Limited, menial job opportunities are the only outlook for most.

Severely retarded children (with an *IQ* below 35) need constant care, as they soil themselves and must be fed. The trainable (IQ of 35 to 50) need constant supervision, but may be able to accomplish some household chores. The educable (IQ from 50 to 75) could do simple farm, construction, or domestic work. Placement in jobs in the community is becoming an attainable goal.

Many children with sensory (auditory and visual) problems may appear retarded unless the defect is discovered. Many *dyslexic* children or those with minimal *brain dysfunction* or *petit-mal epilepsy, anemia,* or *malnutrition* might not function properly. Not uncommonly the teacher treats a child as if he is retarded, and he "becomes" retarded.

An unresolved controversy has one side believing that the chief predisposing factor is genetic and that no amount of environmental manipulation or stimulation will lead to achievement beyond a low normal. The opposition is equally cogent in showing that poverty, poor diet, and an unstimulating environment are the determining factors.

The first viewpoint is a discouraging blow to minority groups, and if accepted, might sabotage all the supplemental programs now being provided. Most conservatives believe that the truth lies somewhere in the middle: a mixture of genetic and environmental factors. The hopeful note is that innovative educational techniques, if applied during the first year, can improve intellectual function. (See *Kwashiorkor, Malnutrition,* Section 11; *Down's syndrome,* Section 10.)

Some examples of known problems associated with mental retardation are as follows:

Genetically determined: *phenylketonuria, galactosemia, lipidoses.*

Maternal infections: *rubella, syphillis, toxoplasmosis, cytomegalic inclusion disease.*

Chemical and metabolic: X ray to pregnant mother, low *thyroid* (*cretinism*), *hyperbilirubinemia* (*erythroblastosis*), *toxemia,* maternal drug ingestion.

Birth related: *prematurity, anoxia,* cerebral trauma, *hypoglycemia.*

After birth: trauma, infection, severe *anemia* or *protein deficiency, lead poisoning, deprivation.*

By far the majority of patients with mental retardation have no suspicious history of infection or trauma to bring the attention of mother or doctor to the problem until some observation at about ten or eleven months of age makes the diagnosis possible. ("He doesn't sit up well." "He doesn't care when I leave the room." "He doesn't do anything.")

If correctible conditions have been corrected (*anemia, cretinism,* environmental *deprivation,* low protein *diet, hearing* and *speech* defects, *phenylketonuria, subdural hematoma*), some management plan must be organized for long-term therapy. Somehow the parents must be supported and encouraged. Guilt is the common parental reaction to the realization that their child is retarded. ("I didn't take my vitamins when I was pregnant.") Parents should seek the counsel of a sympathetic doctor. Most find that joining the National Association for Retarded Children is the best thing they ever did. They are relieved to share the problem, are kept aware of research in the field, and are able to anticipate problems by communication with other parents.

Intelligence testing is fairly accurate by age five years, and some estimate of the child's functional capacity should be made so a program can be outlined. Achievement is enhanced is some successes are planned each day. Learning abilities can be improved if stimulation is optimum. If no positive efforts are made, the child may become even more retarded.

Microcephaly, or small brain, is always associated with some *mental retardation.* As the brain does not grow at the usual rate, the skull bones will not grow. The ears and nose appear abnormally large in proportion to the rest of the head. It may be an inherited trait, but may arise from maternal infection, X radiation, *anoxia,* or congenital brain defect.

Migraine is a severe headache caused by the dilation of blood vessels to the scalp and outer membranes (dura) of the brain. A short period of visual sensations (spots, flashing lights) may precede the actual headache. Strange feelings of numbness or tingling may occur on the face or arm on one side. These subjective symptoms are assumed to be due to the constriction of the above-mentioned vessels which supply blood to the sensory areas of the brain. After this spasm, relaxation of these vessels results in a pounding, incapacitating headache associated with flushing of the skin on the same side. Exertion aggravates the pain, and the victim prefers to lie quietly in the dark, hoping blessed sleep may come. The pain may last for hours or days.

In few other diseases of the nervous system do the influences of psychology, genetics, and organic pathology so intertwine as in migraine. Most authorities note the familial incidence (70 percent have a positive family history of sick headaches), higher incidence in females with rigid personalities and high personal standards of performance, attacks frequently triggered by a frustrating situation in which anger and hostility would be an appropriate outlet, but an unbending conscience will not permit this release (even verbally), a high percentage of brain-wave abnormalities, and a high rate of *allergic* manifestations in the history. Although a migraine "personality" is described, anyone can have such a headache even if all the above predisposing factors are absent. Food allergies and hypoglycemia can trigger migraine attacks.

Caffeine, ergotamine (*Cafergot®*), *antihistamines, tranquilizers,* and *antiemetics* constitute the medical treatment. An effective new drug, methysergide, is efficient in preventing the attacks, but a strange abdominal fibrosis is associated with prolonged use. Children may respond better to phenobarbital and/or *Dilantin®*.

Children with cyclic or periodic vomiting frequently grow up to have migraine headaches. The vomiting becomes less and the headaches worse with age. A defect in the release of glucose from glycogen stored in the liver accounts for acetone in the urine, and the vomiting apparently results from *acidosis.* If a child has headaches of such severity as to incapacitate him during exciting play, migraine should be considered. If headaches are frequent, a diet elimination should be tried first to rule out the possibility of an allergy; common offenders: chocolate, milk, corn, nuts, wheat, eggs, citrus, fish. An *EEG* would be worthwhile, and a trial of phenobarbital or *Dilantin®* appropriate. If none of these seem helpful (and tumors and clots are not present), a trial of *aspirin* and caffeine and/or ergotamine would be helpful. Improvement would at least suggest that the headaches are due to dilated cerebral blood vessels.

If headaches are associated with fainting, sensory or motor loss, stiff neck or confusion, some intracranial lesion must be searched for.

One authority feels that about 2 percent of children have migraine, but it is not often considered, as it is assumed to be an adult condition.

1. Abdominal pain and listlessness are the usual initiating symptoms. (The adult's prelude is irritability and hunger; confusion and slow responsiveness are more likely to be seen in children.)
2. Children's attacks are more frequent but shorter in duration than adults.
3. Fever, *vomiting,* and abdominal pain suggest intestinal flu in children; however, the absence of *diarrhea* tends to suggest migraine.
4. Headaches may be all over. (Adults usually have one-sided headaches.)
5. Boys are more frequently involved. (Women suffer more than men.)

Car sickness is often a precursor to migraine; many childhood breath-holders develop migraine.

Migraine is unlikely without a family history.

Relaxation after a time of stress may be a precipitating factor and would explain the headache occurring after school in a high achiever. Migraine is common in the premenstrual adolescent.

About 10 percent of epileptics have migraine, and about 5 percent of migrainous people have *epilepsy.* The percentages are higher than in the normal population. EEG abnormalities are more common in the patients with migraine than in the total population. It is difficult to differentiate "convulsive equivalents" (abdominal epilepsy) from migraine in children. *Dilantin*® may control both conditions. If it does not help, then caffeine and ergotamine are indicated.

The majority of patients with childhood migraine usually outgrow the symptoms when adults; the same driving, compulsive personality usually remains, however.

Multiple sclerosis is almost never seen or recognized before adolescence. It may be the result of a "slow acting" virus pinching and scarring widely separated parts of the nervous system. It beings as a sudden loss of motor function or control of a leg, or sudden blindness in one eye. Remissions may last for months or years, but eventually most patients lose much muscular control and become bedridden. A no-fat diet and large doses of vitamins C and B complex, intravenously and orally, show promise in cases recognized early.

Myasthenia is excessive weakness of muscles which are restored to normal strength by rest. *Myositis, hyperthyroidism,* neuronitis, and *malnutrition* may show this response, but in the absence of these conditions, the primary disease is due to some block between the motor end plate of the nerve and the muscle fiber. Acetylcholine is elaborated at the end plate and, if normal in type and amount, triggers the muscle fiber to contract. An *enzyme,* cholinesterase, destroys this chemical. Anticholinesterase drugs (neostigmine) will allow the acetylcholine to fulfill its function and is a specific in the diagnosis and treatment of primary myasthenia gravis.

Myasthenia congenita is a familial disease (the mother is not affected). Response to neostigmine is rapid here also.

Myasthenia gravis is rarely seen before early adolescence. It is most common in females. First symptoms typically occur in an older adolescent girl. Droopy eyelids, double vision, expressionless face, tired jaws after eating, nasal speech are worse at the end of the day and absent after a night's sleep. Neostigmine produces a rapid response; its use is necessary for life. In some cases a thymoma is present which must be searched for and removed; improvement then follows. (See *Paralysis,* Section 7.) About one out of seven babies born to women with MG will temporarily have the condition in the newborn period. Neostigmine is used until recovery.

Myelogram is the X-ray picture taken after a radiopaque dye has been injected into the spinal canal. It reveals herniated disks, obstructions from tumors, and other spinal-fluid-flow dynamic abnormalities.

Myoclonic epilepsy or salaam seizure—see *Convulsions*

Myotonic dystrophy is a familial disease characterized by an inability to relax muscular tension voluntarily. The victim cannot release his grip with ease. Chewing is difficult because his bite is sustained. Initiating a step often throws his body into a rigid contraction and his balance is lost; while waiting for a traffic light to change, the patient may have to "mark time." This increase in muscle tone is aggravated by cold weather. Many patients are mildly retarded. No effective treatment is known.

Nervous system is the network that allows for communication between one part of the body and another. Sensory nerves bring messages to the brain which organizes an answer and then allows the motor area to execute the order.

The brain and spinal cord are the central nervous system; the peripheral nervous system includes the nerves bringing messages to the central nervous system (sensory), the motor nerves which carry impulses out to the glands and muscles, and the autonomic nervous system. This latter is not considered under direct voluntary control; it allows the body to prepare for *fight* (rapid heart, extra adrenalin), *flight* (blood diverted from intestines to muscles of legs), *food* (increased intestinal activity, saliva, and digestive enzymes), *feces* (moving wastes to lower rectum).

Just as specific areas in the brain receive and organize messages from the environment, centers in the deeper areas in the brain (hypothalamus) store potentials of whole acts of behavior rage, hunger, sleep, sexual appetite, feelings of well-being, and other integrated emotional responses. These areas, when stimulated by electrodes, will force subjects to engage in activities. (A cat chasing a mouse when stimulated electrically in the sleep area will stop running, curl up, and nap.) Certain types of psychomotor epilepsy could be explained by a similar mechanism; an irritable focus in or near one of these hypothalamic or thalamic areas might "take over" the victim, surprising himself and his family.

Parts of the hypothalamus when stimulated provide pleasure, so it is rewarding to repeat the acts that reproduce these pleasurable feelings. (Eating when hungry leads to pleasurable satiety, so an animal learns to eat to avoid the displeasure of hunger.) If the neurons in the satiety center of the hypothalamus are stimulated, the animal stops eating; if the neurons are destroyed, the animal develops a voracious appetite and becomes grossly obese. (I have a patient who was afflicted at age two with *epiglottitis* with *cyanosis* requiring a *tracheotomy.* Since then he has become enormously overweight and maddeningly stubborn.)

Many responses of the human organism short-circuit the cerebral hemispheres or the socially-oriented part of the brain. A finger is burned and the hand is pulled away reflexly; the "thinking" part of the brain is not called into use. An angry crowd reacting after a ball game is operating on the collective hypothalamus of all the participants. A soldier in the heat of battle is functioning via his lower animal brain.

As a child grows, he learns by imitation and a reward system that he can get what his hypothalamus wants and still not lose his friends, parents, and peers.

The temporal lobes receive auditory sensation. They also store memory of past events which can be recalled by hypnosis or direct electrical stimulation of the brain. The emotion associated with the event is also recalled at that time.

Closely associated, then, to the areas that receive pure auditory sensation are the areas which endow meaning to what is heard. These association areas give us music, not sound. Sensation is innate, but perception is learned. These perceptions must occur at a certain time in the development of the nervous system or they will never be incorporated as a permanent stored memory in the association areas. Opportunities for spontaneous learning must come in the first few years of a child's life. Heat, cold, color, texture, the touch and sight of a round ball are stored simultaneously in the appropriate association areas. The smell, touch, sight, and sound of the baby's mother are all perceived as "good" in the cerebral association areas. The infant has learned that his mother is to be trusted and obeyed. (See *Family,* Section 16.)

Visual perception area lies just forward of the visual area for sensation. Dark and light colors are noted in the occipital visual sensation area; nerve connections in the visual perception areas receive these impulses and tell us we are looking at a house. If it is our home, emotions are brought to the conscious level. It now has meaning; secondary areas are being stimulated. These are all interconnected to the auditory areas (from the temporal lobe) and the touch areas from the sensory cortex in front. Conceptualization of speech occurs in the left cerebral hemisphere as a part of the intertwining of auditory and visual association areas. (The right cerebral hemisphere area is involved with spatial relations.) The victim of *dyslexia* is unable to use his association areas to give meaning to the word he is "seeing." Much of man's behavior has been learned, in contrast to the animals whose behavior is innate or inborn. Through experience, man learns to modify his behavior. Much of his early motor behavior is innate but not necessarily present at birth (ability to walk, talk, think). When the cerebral hemispheres mature (nerve fibers develop a myelin sheath) these potentials become observable abilities; the latent becomes manifest. Each child develops these capacities for learning at a predetermined, genetically controlled rate (one child may walk well at 10 months, another not until 18 months; both are normal). Rote memory of a three-year-old child is but a showoff gimmick utilized by a proud mother, but usable, meaningful learning of the material must await the development of the nearby associative pathways. Learning cannot be too early or too late; the neuronal pathways must be stimulated as they develop or their ability to function is forever lost. Constantly used pathways of neuron connections increase in size with use (somewhat like muscle and bone). Intuitive parents know how to stimulate their child appropriately so he may learn about the world in an atmosphere of mutual trust. Pushing a child beyond his capacity produces anger, frustration, and/or depression.

A hurt to the nervous system (*anoxia, convulsions, fever,* trauma, *deprivation, low protein diet*) may not reveal itself at the time it occurs, but becomes manifest only when the involved area is supposed to mature and become serviceable. Subtle inadequacies in behavior or learning will frustrate child, parent, and teacher. Reeducation, psychiatric help, behavior modification, and drugs may all be necessary.

Neuritis is an inflammation of a nerve. If several nerves are inflamed, it is called polyneuritis and is more likely to be due to a chemical (thallium or lead) or a dietary deficiency (pellagra) or an infection (diphtheria or scarlet fever). Weakness of the muscles supplied by the nerve and sensory loss of the involved skin are the common manifestations.

Traumatic neuropathy follows an injury (obstetrical palsies; see *Brachial nerve palsy,* Section 5), injection, or pressure. The general use of injections in the treatment of children has caused a number of permanent paralyses in an arm or leg. The large sciatic nerve that passes deep in the buttock to the leg may be injured by the needle or by the injected material. The safest muscles for intramuscular injections are the outer thigh and the deltoid (shoulder) muscles.

Surgical removal of scar tissue is of doubtful benefit for injection neuropathy, but is essential for crushing or lacerating wounds so the nerve ends may be apposed neatly. The nerve fiber will grow out through the nerve sheath and complete function may be restored in a few months.

Neurofibroma is a nerve tumor which, if compressed in a small space, will cause pain. Removal is in order. (See *Neurofibromatosis,* Section 6.)

Nodding spasms—see *Habits,* Spasmus nutans, Section 16

Paralysis—see Section 7

Petit mal epilepsy—see *Convulsions*

Pneumoencephalograms are the X-ray pictures taken after spinal fluid is withdrawn by a *lumbar puncture* and replaced with air. This contrast of fluid and tissue with the air usually outlines quite clearly the ventricles inside the *brain.* It reveals any shift of the brain caused by bleeding or the presence of a mass, and it outlines brain atrophy if present. The air is absorbed by the capillaries and excreted by the lungs over a period of a few days.

This test is helpful in diagnosing *hydrocephalus* and tumors but is of little diagnostic or prognostic benefit for victims of mental *retardation* or *cerebral palsy.*

Poliomyelitis is a *virus* infection with an affinity for the spinal motor nerve cells. The disease is infrequently seen now because of the widespread use of *polio vaccine* (injectable, killed Salk, or orally given, live, attenuated Sabin). Three types of polio virus may all produce *paralysis,* and immunity to one type does not provide cross-immunity to another, so all types of vaccines must be given. (See *Allergies and Immunizations,* Section 3).

We still hear of sporadic cases of polio—largely in the unvaccinated child—so the virus is still about. The oral vaccine allows the intestinal lining cells to develop an immunity, so if the natural virus is swallowed, the immune cells will neutralize its effect before it can invade the circulation and pass to the brain and spinal cord.

In the unimmune patient the virus may cause only a minor cold, headache, and a few muscle aches, or it may cause extensive destruction of the nerves controlling muscle use all the way from the palate to the lower limbs. A patient may recover from type I polio and then be reinfected with type II or III, as there is no cross protection.

If the virus invades the nerves, fever, *headache,* stiff neck and back will follow. Muscle pain may be generalized, and weakness soon follows.

(Anterior tibial muscle weakness is common; this causes a foot drop.) Most of the residual function returns in four weeks, but more will return over the following two years.

The dreaded bulbar polio results from involvement of the nerves to the palate, tongue, larynx, and diaphragm; swallowing will cause choking and food to return out the nose. The respirator (iron lung) may be needed to assist weak breathing effort.

Polio may be confused with *Guillain-Barré syndrome, meningitis, mumps,* or other *encephalitis* diseases, *lockjaw, scurvy, rheumatic fever, osteomyelitis, botulism,* or *hip* diseases.

Until Sister Kenny showed us the value of physiotherapy and hot packs, polio patients were put in plaster casts to prevent contractions. She demonstrated the value of heat (hot, wet wool blankets were wrapped about the patient's muscles to relieve spasm).

Psychomotor epilepsy—see *Convulsions*

Reye's syndrome is a *virus* infection (usually fatal) manifested by fat infiltration in the *liver* and *brain* (cerebral *edema*).

The young child appears to have a minor cold, but soon develops vomiting, headache, and lethargy. Fever may be only slight. In a day or two, coma develops and death occurs, apparently from the swollen brain tissue.

The course of the illness is rapid. What appears to be the flu one day is a terminal illness the next, and remedial measures (*cortisone* and hypertonic intravenous solutions to decrease the edema of the brain) are usually too late to be effective.

St. Vitus dance—see *Chorea*

Seizures—see *Convulsions*

Skull is the bony case protecting the brain. Lacunar (holes in the) skull is often associated with a meningocele and *hydrocephalus.*

Acrocephaly means pointed head. This congenital trait is assumed to be related to the early closure of the suture lines of the skull. If the sagittal (front to back) line closes early, the head becomes long and narrow.

Oxycephaly results when the coronal suture line of the skull (the one running from temple to temple over the top of the head) fuses prematurely. The head grows wide, the eyes push out (exophthalmos) and visual, heart, and skeletal defects are associated.

Because the space limitation compromises brain growth, some brain damage with possible mental retardation can be anticipated. Neurosurgery is worth considering to allow maximum brain growth as well as for cosmetic purposes.

Scaphocephaly is a long, narrow head due to the early closure of the sagittal skull suture line that runs from the forehead to the back of the head. By itself this anomaly usually does not prevent adequate brain growth, so surgery is rarely performed.

Speech (see *Stuttering, Communication disorders*) development depends on the development of the higher brain centers. Deviations from normal usually suggest some injury to the nervous system. Speech diagnosis and therapy have made vast strides in the last few years; speech anomalies should be investigated early.

A child should have a few intelligible words by two years of age. A child should be able to speak at least one or two sentences by age three, be able to pronounce initial consonants by age two or three. A child should not drop endings or stutter consistently after age five. A child should not speak too loudly, too softly, too nasally, or with a peculiar rhythm. (See *Tongue thrust,* Section 14.)

Spina bifida is a defect of the vertebral column usually in the lower lumbar area. The bony arch that protects the spinal cord is absent or deformed. It is usually discovered fortuitously when an X ray is taken for some other reason. Occasionally a dimple or a tuft of hair on the skin overlies the defect. Symptoms of clumsy gait, difficulty in gaining urinary and fecal control, loss of sensation over buttocks and back of thighs suggest that the lesion is associated with nerve pressure due to a fibrous band or a fatty tumor.

Spinal cord is that portion of the central nervous system contained within the vertebral column. Sensory nerves carry messages to the brain for touch, pain, heat, cold, and position sensation. Motor nerves from the brain stimulate the nerves activating the skeletal muscles and controlling the autonomic functions of the heart, lungs, intestines, vessels, and bladder.

Injuries to the spinal cord are usually due to falls or diving injuries; fractures of the vertebrae are usually associated. *Paralysis* of all function below the level of injury is common, and little return of function can be expected. *Cysts, tumors,* or infection of the nearby bones (vertebral body) will cause compression of the cord. *Ruptured intervertebral disk* (Section 7) is rare in childhood.

Transportation of a patient with a neck or back injury is tricky. As little motion as possible is important. Positioning the victim on his stomach with his back arched is the safest method.

Spinal muscular atrophy is an inherited, progressive, muscle-wasting disease occurring in infancy and is due to the degeneration of the motor nerve cells. After the disease has progressed, the child lies in a flaccid heap, unable to suck or move. Death usually is early, due to a respiratory infection. Some patients survive adolescence despite the severe debility.

Spinocerebellar ataxia—see *Friedreich's ataxia*

Sturge-Weber syndrome is a condition in which a facial port-wine stain is associated with an underlying complex of dilated capillaries of the skull and meningeal membranes overlying the brain. Calcifications are usually seen about these cerebral vessels in the X ray, the opposite side of the body may be weak because the motor area of the brain is involved, and *mental deficiency* is not uncommon. *Seizures* may occur.

Surgery to remove the irritating capillaries and calcium deposits may be beneficial.

Stuttering is nonfluency in speech, and is considered abnormal after age five. It is so common for the two- to four-year-old to try to imitate the fluent parent that he becomes trapped, and if he shifted into neutral with the motor running, his thought comes out like this: "I . . . I . . . I . . . I . . . go . . . go . . . go . . . to . . . Grandma's." If the "helpful" listeners try to slow him down or have him repeat the sentence correctly, he becomes involved in the *mechanism* of the idea, and his nonfluency is enforced. (Ask a musician or an athlete to analyze his technique. He just "does it." To pick it apart makes him slow and clumsy.)

When their child stutters, parents must discipline themselves to avoid comment. They must look on it as a normal developmental stage in the child's progress, like standing and falling precede walking. Most children sail through this if they are *not* told it is wrong. A very few with *psychological* and/or *neurological* problems will remain fixed at this immature level. Help is needed if improvement is not shown by the fifth birthday.

Cluttering is a speech imbalance frequently seen in a hyperactive, impulsive, outgoing child. He talks rapidly but repetitions, hesitations and incomplete sentences are frequent. Dyslexia is commonly associated. Amphetamines, Mellaril® or Benadryl® may help normalize him.

Echolalia is the seemingly mechanical repetition of words or syllables. The small child just learning to talk will say "ba" in imitation of hearing someone else say it. The child may originate the conversation by making a random babbling sound which the eager mother praises. Thus, if the child says, "Da," the mother may interpret it as the forerunner of "Daddy," and repeat it to the child, who in turn repeats in a circular kind of communication. The three-year-old may respond by repeating the last word or two of a sentence. This is a normal part of the process of learning to talk; if echolalia persists beyond early childhood, however, it is most often associated with *mental retardation* or *psychosis.*

Subacute sclerosing panencephalitis (Dawson's) is a virus disease of the brain which destroys brain cells. It is thought to be an atypical response to the measles (*rubeola*) virus as the patients have an elevated rubeola titer in their blood.

Cases appear a few months or years after a typical case of measles. Mood changes, intellectual deterioration, and *myoclonic* jerks may appear insidiously. Completely bedridden immobility (*coma*) soon follows; death is inevitable. This deterioration may take two months or ten years. No treatment is available.

Syncope is a fainting spell. It is common in the doctor's office after a shot has been given to a child who does not cry. The slowed heart rate and puddling of the blood in the dilated abdominal vessels prevent blood and oxygen from reaching the brain in sufficient amounts to keep the brain cells operative. Lying down, crying, straining (tightening the abdominal muscles), bending over are all effective in restoring cerebral circulation.

Some people are susceptible and faint on suggestion or while watching operations or standing motionless after a full meal. If anemia is ruled out as a predisposing condition, and no triggering event can be found easily, an *EEG* is valuable. If the waves are abnormal, an anticonvulsive drug (*phenobarbital* or *Dilantin*®) might be tried. Low blood sugar (*hypoglycemia*), *postural hypotension,* and hyperventilation must be ruled out.

(I used to feel faint while singing lustily in Sunday school, wearing a tight collar, after three sausages for breakfast.)

Tay-Sachs disease—see *Lipidoses* (cerebral degenerative disease), Section 10; *Amaurotic familial idiocy*

Tension-fatigue syndrome is a food allergy induced combination of dull, generalized headache, violaceous half-circles under eyes, ill-defined, periumbilical stomachaches and stuffy nose, usually associated with zonking (described in *Sinusitis,* Section 14). Some personal or family history of *atopy* (see Section 6) can usually be elicited.

The most common offending foods are milk (and dairy products), chocolate, and eggs. Wheat, corn, pork, and nuts may produce the same group of symptoms and signs. No skin test is reliable in determining the offender so a diet elimination program must be adhered to rigidly: no dairy products (most imitation milks have some milk protein in them) are to be ingested for a minimum of three to four weeks. If no improvement is noted, the other possible offenders are similarly dropped from the diet.

This long term approach must be followed because at least five allergy-induced, long-lasting chemicals may have been elaborated by the body's allergic response and it takes a few weeks for them to be metabolized and eliminated.

Tetany is the increased irritability of muscles usually from a lower-than-normal amount of *calcium* and/or *magnesium* in the blood, or higher-than-normal amount of *sodium* and/or *potassium. Alkalosis* may be a contributing factor. (See *Tetany,* Section 5.)

No matter what the cause, the signs are the same; neuromuscular irritability with facial twitching, flexion of wrists with stiff fingers flexed at the knuckle joints, toes flexed with the arch exaggerated. Crowing due to laryngeal spasm and convulsion may be late signs.

Carpopedal spasm is one of the signs of tetany. The thumb is pulled into the palm, and the stiff fingers flex at the knuckles. The wrist and toes flex also, and the foot flexes at the instep. It may be associated with *convulsions* and is usually due to the lowering of the calcium ion in the blood. When these characteristic signs of tetany are seen, blood tests for calcium and alkalosis are necessary. After a month or so of no vitamin D, low calcium tetany may develop. Renal disease may cause *hypocalcemia* (see Section 10). *Malabsorption* (see Section 12) problems will prevent optimum intestinal absorption of calcium. Liver disease may be a cause.

Tetany of alkalosis may result from *hyperventilation* (overbreathing) in which excess carbon dioxide is exhaled; this loss of acid produces alkalosis. Muscle irritability is increased because calcium is less available in alkaline solutions.

Tuberous sclerosis is an inherited trait that combines a variety of skin lesions (red, cystic lesions over the nose and cheeks) with calcified nodules over the surface of the brain. *Seizures* and mental retardation are common.

Von Recklinghausen's disease—see *Neurofibromatosis,* Section 6

Werdnig-Hoffmann disease—see *Spinal muscular atrophy*

SECTION 16

Psychological Health *

I. Behavior

Aggressive reactions
- *Anger*
- *Defiance*
- *Delinquency*
- *Fire setting*
- *Lying*

Drug abuse
- *Glue sniffing*
- *LSD*
- *Marijuana*

Habits
- *Breath-holding*
- *Head-banging*
- *Nail-biting*
- *Spasmus nutans*
- *Thumb-sucking*
- *Tics*
- *Trichotillomania*

Passive-aggressive reactions
- *Dawdling*
- *Encopresis*
- *Rumination* (Section 12)
- *School dropout*
- See also Coercion

Sex disorders
- *Exhibitionism*
- *Fetishism*
- *Homosexuality*
- *Masturbation*
- *Sexual molestation* (Section 1)

Sleep problems
- *Nightmares*
- *Sleep*

II. Family

Adolescence
Anal Phase
Attachment
Bowel and bladder control
Conformity
Developmental map
Discipline (see Superego)
Excitement
Failure
Guidelines for normality
Guilt (see Superego)
Identification
Permissiveness
Self-esteem
Superego or conscience
Temper tantrum
Whining

III. Special family problems

Adoption
Animals
Art

*Read **Behavior** first.

Bilingual home
Broken home
Chores and allowance
Coercion
Cruelty to children
Cultural influences
Dating
Daydreaming
Death in family
Deprivation
Excitement
Jealousy
Privacy
Sex education
Underachievement

IV. Neuroses

Anorexia nervosa
Anxiety
Compulsiveness
Depression
Fears
Obsessiveness
Perfectionism
School phobia

Seclusiveness
Shyness
Suicide attempt

V. Psychoses

Autism
Delusions
Paranoid disorder
Schizoid
Schizophrenia

VI. Tests

Bender-Gestalt test (see Section 15)
Denver Developmental Screening Test
Draw-a-man test
Intelligence quotient
Rorschach test
Thematic Apperception Test
Wechsler-Bellevue Intelligence Scale
Wide Range Achievement Test

Adolescence. Its onset and speed of passage is largely determined by genetic factors. It may follow a pattern inherited from grandparents as well as a combination of parental genetic influences. Childhood sickness—especially *allergies, diabetes, rheumatic fever, tuberculosis,* and *diet* deficiencies or excesses—will play a significant role in adolescent growth, development, and psychological resources. The ability of the adolescent to weather his emotional storms is correlated with the self-image he received from his parents in infancy.

The physician who has cared for a child since birth should be the best one to give health care and psychological support through this touchy period. In no other age group is medical care more closely coupled with mutual respect and honesty than during adolescence. The teen-ager is overly concerned with "self," and the doctor, like it or not, must show a genuine interest in that *person,* not in just "the acne" or "that case of mono." If possible, the postpubescent teen-ager should make the appointment and see the doctor alone as part of the blueprint for getting out of the nest. Some liaison, however, must be carried on with the parents (*with* the youth's knowledge) so the doctor has some idea of their various areas of concern. The doctor may be willing but the twelve- to eighteen-year-old may not. Courtesy and mutual respect suggest that the parent at least *ask* the teen-ager about *his* preference.

Adolescents must try to differentiate desire for independence from desire for dependence upon their parents. They must make an effort to consider themselves masculine or feminine, respectable and lovable. They must develop friendships to aid in mutual solving of social problems. They must try to discover who they are and what they want to become.

Parents who are most helpful: adults who are reasonably satisfied with their own lives; they do not depend on their children for this satisfaction. They also have their own standards of behavior and set limits of reasonable behavior for their children. They allow the adolescent more responsibility in decision-making with age. They trust and have confidence in their children; they try not to speak of failure except to their pillows.

Adoption is the provision of home life and parental love for a child whose natural parents are unable or unwilling to give this. The adoptive parents are rewarded by the love they receive from the growing child. The majority of children are adopted by nonrelatives; a large number of grandparents, aunts, and uncles, however, adopt homeless relatives. Some concerned mothers are adopting instead of conceiving to control the population explosion.

Although many doctors and lawyers can place children in compatible homes, it is still considered best for prospective parents to work through an agency specifically designed to handle adoptions. This may be time-consuming, but it gives the natural mother a chance to examine her own feelings about releasing the child as well as giving the adoptive parents an opportunity to investigate (with the assistance of a social worker) their own motivations for parenthood.

These efforts can help reduce "changes of heart" on both sides after the adoption has been executed.

Honest evaluation must be sought, for there are several households for whom adoption is not advisable:

1. The couple who feel that a child will cement their crumbling marriage can find only that the adoption has cracked their shaky union even more decisively and may perhaps have unnecessarily disturbed the innocent child.
2. The couple who quickly adopt a child to replace one of their own lost by illness or accident will discover the replacement is not the same; disappointment may follow.
3. The couple who, out of pity, adopt a child with a severe handicap may find they are not emotionally or financially able to cope with all the problems.
4. The couple who may adopt a child of a different race out of altruism or to prove their ability to love on a broad scale may find they are not strong or secure enough to endure neighborhood prejudice and end up frustrated and discouraged.

A pediatrician should have the opportunity of examining and evaluating an adoptee so that both agency and the adopters know of any potential risks. The baby given up for adoption may have had less than optimum prenatal and delivery care.

Some adoptive parents tend to overreact in their child-rearing methods, because slight deviations from normal behavior suggest to them that they are being improper mothers or they think they have not given the child what his natural mother would have given.

Most authorities recommend that the adopted child be informed of his status somewhere between the ages of four and six. Each family needs to work out the details of the timing and the method of explaining, but presenting the facts early is imperative. The adolescent who discovers for himself the news (to him, identity-shaking) may feel he has been cheated, or see this "secret" as just another hypocritical parental action, and become suspicious and hostile.

Aggressive reactions include anger, defiance, disobedience, delinquency, fire setting, and lying. With the help of his mother, the growing child learns what he can and cannot have. It is a sign of maturity to be able to reorganize and accept impulses but be able to tolerate delay of gratification. The child is maturing emotionally (becoming civilized) if he reaches this point between the ages of four and six. If it is impossible for him to control his anger by channeling or expressing it—not suppressing it—by that time, then something has gone wrong either psychologically or neurologically. He is fixed at an immature level of development. Physically he is six, but emotionally he still acts like a two-year-old. The kindergarten teacher is best able to detect this infantile behavior because she has the rest of the class with which to compare him. In some, hypoglycemia will prevent the conscience from operating.

Anal phase is the psychological development period when the child's bowel actions become important to him or his family—roughly at one to three years of age.

Anger is the response to pain and frustration, an appropriate emotion if some constructive good comes of it. Many children, because of their subservient role at home and in school, and lack of opportunity to learn how to express their feelings acceptably, will lash out inappropriately when they are pressured or see no way out of a frightening situation. Some children accept the world and its rules (gravity always works, night follows day), but some—and I'm sure it is due to some inborn trait or nervous-system fault—fight every step of the way. They seem to be mad at the world because they cannot control it. They are impulse ridden; they need immediate gratification of desires.

Animals as pets are important to most children. They can fill a void for a lonely child, and can be an aid in teaching responsibility to the indifferent child.

Known *allergic* children should not be saddled with one more furry object to sneeze and wheeze at. Snakes, frogs, salamanders, fish, or turtles would be more appropriate. An impulsive toddler can be dangerously mauled by a touchy cat or dog, and a defenseless puppy or kitten can be seriously harmed; it's best to wait until a child is old enough to realize the animal's needs and not set up a situation in which he can be hurt or experience the regret of having injured another living being.

Art that children produce should be limited only by the quantity of paper or mud or whatever medium is used. Attempts to place adult standards on children's production only stifle their work and inhibit creativity. Rhoda Kellogg, the expert on children's art, tells us that the expression and development of art follows a universal pattern with only minor individual cultural differences. This progression of ability is akin to the maturation of other bodily skills—the child sits before standing, he stands before walking. In an analogous way he scribbles (lines, dots, circles, spirals) before he makes designs. A form recognizable by an adult is not important to the child. He is trying to draw the essence of the dog—its *dogginess,* or the sun's warmth and brightness, not a yellow circle.

The joy a child (or an adult) has in creativity increases his learning and interest and curiosity. No restrictions should be placed on the content or form of art work; it is a projection of inner thoughts and feelings and must not be governed by adult rules.

Attachment to an accepting adult is the only way a human has to learn mutual trust. If a child is shut off consistently from attachment within the first two years of life because of severe neglect, abuse, or shifting about from one family to another, he is going to be hard-pressed to fulfill his role as an adequate social human. The human organism appears to force itself onto its environment with age-related mechanisms calculated to satisfy its needs. The hungry baby cries and is fed.

As his nerve fibers in the higher cerebral centers become capable of storing information, he incorporates the fact that a warm, loving, accepting adult is a dependable, necessary part of his existence. If he laughs, smiles, and eats, then this adult responds with love and satisfactory care. He is rewarded for being pleasant and is loved for being loving. This early attachment is necessary to develop a *conscience* as well as a good self-image.

Growth and environment testing lead to a series of compromises; the child finds that if he goes too far, he may lose the love and support he needs. As he marches on through his growth, his parents retreat a step at a time. He is supposed to be learning how far he can assert his individuality and gregariousness without hurting others.

Fortunately for the majority of our children, most parents are able to provide a warm, intimate, continuous relationship with their child in which both find satisfaction and enjoyment. In this climate *anxiety* and *guilt* develop in such a way that coping methods are not overtaxed.

A household with people is a small society and must have a few rules. Even a minimum of rules is enough to create some frustrations in a growing child. The anxiety thus provoked is uncomfortable (sometimes painful) and forces him to use some anxiety-reducing mechanism (thumb-sucking, bed rocking, head banging, crying, overeating). If this physical activity is satisfactory and *anxiety* is relieved, he has learned by this reward to reproduce the action with each subsequent appearance of *anxiety.*

One value of parents is to internalize automatic impulse control, so that the mature individual can operate comfortably as a socially responsible adult.

According to Freud, the child's psychological development passes from the oral phase to the *anal* (toddler to about age three) *phase* and into the Oedipal relationship with the parent of the opposite sex. Most parents are unable to understand these periods, but refer to them as infancy, *toilet-training* time, and sexual-curiosity age.

Each normal infant progresses through predictable *developmental* levels depending on health, genetic determinants, and environmental reactions to his presence. His nervous system develops from head to tail; he sits before he stands, stands before he walks, and walks before he develops sphincter control of his bladder and rectum. Speech progresses from simple to complex: "M—m—m" to "Mama" to "Mother," etc. Graphics progress from scribbling to forming words and representational art. Each phase must be successfully completed before the next can be added.

If his interaction with his environment is not satisfactory, he may be unable to pass on to the next level, and though he may grow intellectually and physically, his emotional response remains fixed at that unresolved level. (A baby frustrated at breast, bottle, nipple, or thumb may revert to this infantile oral level of behavior whenever adult problems seem overwhelming.)

Behavior is the observable, overt manifestation of a person's thoughts and feelings. Children usually reflect their moods in a fairly obvious way.

A behavior disorder is an action that bothers a child's parents, friends, or others who are significantly affected by his conduct. *Thumb-sucking* to one mother may indicate contentment and relaxation; to another mother it suggests that the child is immature and/or insecure. One mother may feel that the child will outgrow it in time; the other family may feel that if something drastic is not done, it will become fixed, showing the world that the child came from a "bad" home. A *hyperactive* child may be completely out of place in a quiet, controlled household—a frustrating disruption that needs strong control measures. The same driven child may be unnoticed in a highly verbal, physically active household.

In some babies, evidence of *hyperactivity,* restlessness, and more than average responsiveness to stimuli can be noted from birth. These attributes may remain all their lives. Others will be quiet, passive, and slow to rouse—spectators. Some respond more to physical pain and less to emotional shock; others do just the opposite.

Some children are basically fearful, tense, and anxious; these traits would be exaggerated in a tense, insecure home. Other children are rigid, unbending in their relationships with others or even themselves, and drive on in the quest of perfection. If their goals are not achieved, *headaches* and stomachaches may develop.

Theories regarding the cause of deviant behavior are frequently too simplistic; genetic, nutritional, infectious, anoxic, social, traumatic, environmental factors all play a role.

The fussy, colicky baby may be unable to disregard a bit of *gas* going "sideways" in his intestines because of a faulty inhibitory mechanism in the lower area of his brain. Everyone who eats has gas; one baby feels this more and responds to it more vigorously. He is usually more active—or hyperactive. This infancy problem seems to be predictive of his whole life style—he overreacts to minimal stimuli. His responsive parents may react in the only way they know: holding, cuddling, rocking. He is rewarded for crying. Judicious use of a sedative won't remove the gas, but will prevent his all-out response to it.

After a few sleepless nights, the tired or sick parents may become a little curt. This could lead to resentment and possibly subtle rejection. They may notice his ease of stimulation when cuddled. Instead of giggling and mutual satisfaction, a parent may be "rewarded" with a tense, vomiting child. The parent learns to respond more "softly."

A wobbly, clinging, *floppy,* "loosely strung" baby may be panic-stricken when handled or moved about. A poorly functioning cerebellar inner-ear neural connection may panic the baby as if on a broken merry-go-round. The parent of this child will avoid sudden movements or roughhouse. He may grow up to be "delicate"—touchy, insecure—not because his parent *wanted* him to be so, but because he insisted that he be handled so. If the father is an athletically oriented *mesomorph,* his disappointment in this boy may be a subtle but effective aloofness, or he may push him into impossible physical pursuits in which he is bound to lose.

His constitutional vulnerability when exposed to this unaccepting environment can turn his anger and frustration into internalizing symptoms (stomachaches, *headaches, encopresis, enuresis, fears,* and phobias).

Neurotic symptoms in childhood (anxiety and phobias) correlate well with *anxiety* and *depression* in adulthood. The fact that these children rarely become sociopathic adults may be some consolation.

Some children with congenitally poor muscular development (*ectomorph*) are usually late maturers, so adolescence is fraught with feelings of rejection and inadequacy and failure. They need to be dependent and supported. They belittle others and find much fault with the aggressive, athletic, *mesomorphic* "jocks."

The indulged, overprotected child reared in a permissive home (catered to every whim—smother love but no limits or control applied) will usually become egocentric (spoiled brat), disobedient, impudent, and demanding. His mother becomes the slave to every tyrannical whim. If he has not developed a *conscience* or *superego* or any control over his basic drives by age six or seven, he will not be able to do so later on.

Social-learning theorists believe that if the socially acceptable behavior of a child is rewarded and the unacceptable aggression is ignored, the child will grow to control egocentric drives from his lower animal brain. This is generally true, but firm limits must be applied to the child's physical aggression within the context of love. The trusted parent control is internalized into a *conscience* and the child becomes uncomfortable if he hurts someone. His cerebral hemispheres allow him, if he has time, to evaluate the total situation and compromise the pressures from the environment with the animal demands arising from his body via his hypothalamus.

In the rejecting home, in addition to the insults of an inadequate diet, little love, and a paucity of intellectual stimulation, a rigid, authoritarian (and usually physically aggressive) parent will almost certainly drive a child to one of the externalizing syndromes (defiant, vengeful, hostile, rude, or, at least, negative).

Oral deprivation in the first few months may determine oral habit patterns later on: *obesity* in the *endomorphic* child, *rumination* in the child who internalizes, high abdominal pain in the obsessive child—he can never satisfy his mother—*anorexia nervosa* in the *ectomorphic* type.

Harsh, punitive methods of enforced bowel control usually serve only to anger the child, and negativism and aggression may color all his responses to his mother and, as a continuum, to the school and the world.

The excessively aggressive adult will, in general, promote hyperaggression in a child. This sequence is most consistent if the child is a big, muscular, *mesomorph* anyway, but will almost surely develop if he is an *impulse ridden, hyperactive* child. Parents who stimulate their children erotically or who deprive them emotionally can count on rearing an aggressive adult. Battered children frequently grow up to batter their own children; very little guilt may be associated with this. However, some children reared in an aggressive, hostile environment may learn to inhibit completely their normal aggressive drives.

An alcoholic, delinquent (sociopathic), hostile father is much more likely to have a son who follows in his footsteps. A genetic influence is suggested, for this is likely to happen whether the father is at home or absent.

Family traits of sociopathy, *epilepsy,* alcoholism, *schizophrenia,* and *migraine* may allow a child (who might be a carrier) to be more vulnerable to birth trauma, infection, and a debilitating environment. An absent mother might be more traumatic to a four-month-old than to a two-year-old, although the latter may make more noise about it.

Emotionally handicapped children have a very high rate of learning difficulties (*dyslexia,* underachieving) which suggests concomitant neurological hurts as another causal factor.

It is worthwhile to note that in studies of children between the ages of six and twelve who are functioning adequately at home and school, 50 percent have fears, worries, and *temper tantrums,* 30 percent have *nightmares* and *nail-biting,* and 15 percent are *enuretic,* suck their thumbs, and have a variety of *tics* and twitches. Follow-up studies indicate a reasonably high percent functioning as non-neurotic adults.

(Go to your next grade-school reunion and note how "normal" the ones who came seem to be.) Shy, nervous, irritable, sensitive children with fears, tics, and speech defects frequently do very well as adults. Withdrawn types may do well especially if they marry a dependable spouse.

Physically ill parents usually have a low energy reserve and are more likely to be withdrawn or to become irritable with their children. A mother with a contagious-disease problem (*tuberculosis,* for example) cannot involve herself in the normal, intimate mother-child relationship. A disrupted family—mother or father frequently in the hospital—has more than the usual number of arguments about help and responsibility and broken plans. Some of the children from such homes develop a false maturity. They have not been allowed to complete successfully various childhood phases. They may need more dependency. They may develop bodily concern because of identification with the ill parent. They may just get mad, frustrated, and hostile.

Depressed mothers are especially disturbing to their children, who are often fearful, passive, infantile, and sickly.

A significant correlation exists between father loss and children who grow to delinquency, *depression,* drug addiction, and *schizophrenia.*

The loss of the mother when the child is under five years of age is correlated with *depression* in both sons and daughters.

The oldest child in a family is a little more likely to be seen in a guidance clinic; the most common complaint is temper outbusts. The only child is more likely to be timid, nervous, and *enuretic,* but rebelliousness may be the chief complaint. Sibling jealousy takes its toll, and the touchy one in the family is more likely to be the target. If the parents take sides, then the put-down sibling will become antisocial at school.

Home treatment of the variety of behavioral, neurological, and psychological problems touched upon is almost impossible because parental attitudes must be treated. Helping a sick child and sending him back into the pit is asking for more of the same. The understanding that parents may get from a sympathetic pediatrician or general practitioner should be a preventive to many of the above problems.

List of behavior disorders and areas of investigation:

Hyperkinetic reaction
- Attention span short
- Can't concentrate

Foolhardy
Hyperactive
Impulsive
Learning or memory poor
School failure
(See *Minimal cerebral dysfunction,* Section 15)

Epileptic equivalents
Clumsy, awkward, maladroit
Convulsions, tremors, jerks, whirling
Episodes of rage, low frustration threshold
Headaches, blackouts, dizziness, fainting
Jekyll and Hyde personality
Runs away
Sleep abnormalities
Speech disability
Unpredictable, variable
Will not compromise
(EEG might help. See *Disobedience, Hypoglycemia*; see also *Convulsions,* Section 15.)

Overanxious reaction
Anxious
Compulsive
Depressed
Fearful
Quiet
Shy
(Ambitious parents try to hold child to high, exacting standards. Child blames self for failure. See *Anxiety, Coercion, Compulsion, Depression, Guilt, Perfectionism.*)

Withdrawal reaction
Cold
Poor social relations
Sameness, perseveration
Unaffectionate
(Contact with others frustrating. Parents often detached. Discipline inconsistent: overpermissiveness, then punitive. See *Autism, Deprivation, Discipline.*)

Unsocialized aggressive reaction
Aggressive
Cruel

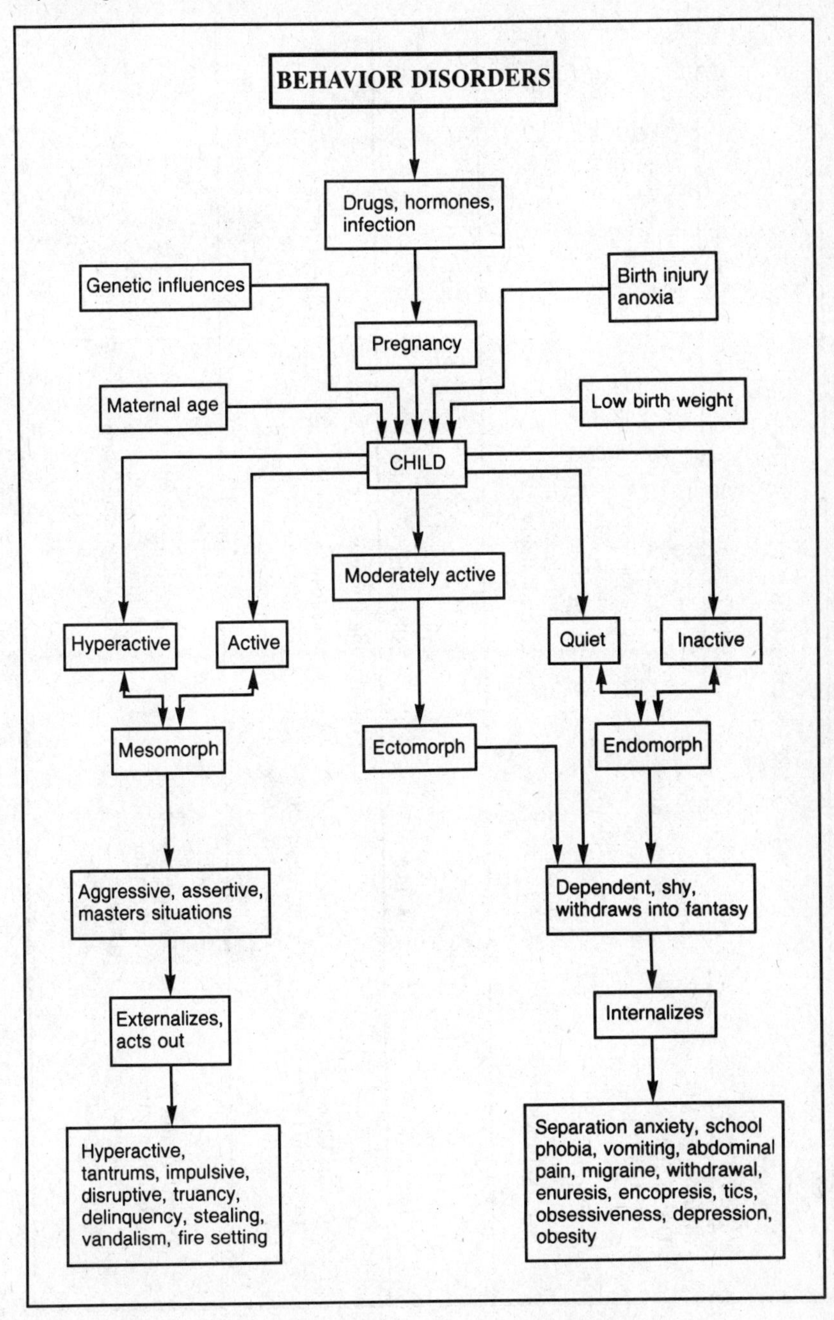
BEHAVIOR DISORDERS
Drugs, hormones, infection
Genetic influences
Birth injury anoxia
Pregnancy
Maternal age
Low birth weight
CHILD
Moderately active
Hyperactive
Active
Quiet
Inactive
Mesomorph
Ectomorph
Endomorph
Aggressive, assertive, masters situations
Dependent, shy, withdraws into fantasy
Externalizes, acts out
Internalizes
Hyperactive, tantrums, impulsive, disruptive, truancy, delinquency, stealing, vandalism, fire setting
Separation anxiety, school phobia, vomiting, abdominal pain, migraine, withdrawal, enuresis, encopresis, tics, obsessiveness, depression, obesity

CATEGORIES OF SICK CHILDREN

Hyperactive	*Surly, mean*	*Fearful, timid*	*Compulsive, neat*
Short attention span	Fights, no friends	Clinging, anxious	Tries too hard
Distractible	Has to win, rages	Tearful	Must be top of class
Talkative	Breaks toys	Cannot face new situations	Tense, tics, twitches
Underachiever	Projects blame	Clumsy, loner	Ulcer prone, stays up late
Immature	Acts out	Depressed, withdrawn	Migraine headaches
Restless	Aggressive	No friends	Nervous stomach
Accident-prone	Lights fires	Tired, sickly	
	Temper outbursts		
Causes			
Oxygen lack	High fever	Pregnancy late in life	Genetic
Prematurity	Convulsions	Intrauterine factors	
Contributing Factors			
No limits	No love	No love	Demands for achievement
Permissive environment	Punitive parents	Devaluation	Rigid home
	Constant devaluation		
	Genetic		
Treatment			
Amphetamine	Phenobarbital	Imipramine	Lower goals
Methylphenidate	Impramine	Dilantin	Less pressure
Social engineering	Dilantin	Behavior modification	Tranquilizers
Sugar-free, additive-free diet	Psychotherapy		Psychotherapy

Defiant
Delinquent
Lying
Stealing
Tantrums
Vengeful
(Child knows he was never wanted. No trust in any adult. See *Anger, Defiance, Delinquency, Disobedience, Fire setting.*)

Runaway reaction
Encopresis
Furtive
Noncompliant
Timid
(The child protests his parental rejection. See *Passive aggression.*)

Bilingual home means that two languages are spoken with equal frequency under the same roof. Some authorities fear this is an impediment to *speech* development in the growing child; others insist that it is an aid.

It would be difficult for the young child to learn either language adequately if the two were jumbled together with frequent and rapid shifts from one to the other. If there is a reasonable effort to avoid confusion for the child, there should be no adverse effects.

The ease the child of a bilingual home has in foreign-language study in school would suggest that more homes should make an effort to introduce a second language while the child is small.

Bowel and bladder control is eagerly sought by mothers as a sign of maturity and obedience in their children. It is axiomatic, however, that when full energy is applied to achieve the goal of toilet conformity, success is delayed. The rule then: the older the child, the shorter the training period. Age two years sees the majority of girls happily defecating in the pot. Most boys are willing by age three.

Voluntary sphincter-muscle control depends on genetic factors; cerebral ability to relax awaits full locomotion, since the nerves to the bladder and rectal muscles develop *after* the nerves to the leg muscles. This is usually after fifteen to eighteen months of age and just at the time when the child is likely to be willful and negative in his attitude. He suspects that the parent wants something, and the game of spiteful withholding leads to fixed *passive aggression* that may color all mother-child relationships.

Studied indifference is the best method of handling toilet training. Make the pot available; if parents use the toilet, so will the child.

(As the child grows old enough, use the Tom Sawyer whitewash-the-fence technique. At about age two, when the child says, "I go pee-pee in the toilet," parent responds, "You can't; it's mine." This may be enough motivation to increase the desire to grow up. After a little bickering, parent acquiesces, saying, "Okay, but if you wreck my toilet, it's back to the diapers for you." This device may work long enough to establish the habit pattern.)

Many mothers have set the goal of going back to work when their children are three years old and in nursery school, but at age two years and eleven months the indifferent frustrator is still disinterested in toilet cooperation. Nursery schools usually insist on toilet training as one of the entrance requirements, so a few sneaky mothers will try the following: they put the child in obviously used training pants and tell the teacher that he is trained but has a "few" accidents. (Six a day is a few?) At toilet time when everybody goes, the previously reluctant one will get the message and use the toilet because his peer group does.

There must be a *gene* for toilet-training time that is as immutable as eye color. Don't try to change this built-in timing device; you will only frustrate yourself and the owner of the clock.

In the *anal* phase, harsh or *coercive toilet training* may lead to *constipation* and/or *encopresis.* However, complete neglect in this area of training may allow *encopresis* to remain as a behavior problem after most children are bowel trained.

Some children become completely submissive; their adult personalities are characterized by parsimony, preciseness, and *compulsiveness.* These traits are determined more by the parents' total life style than the attitude toward his bowel functions; it may help to shape his life style about withholding or producing. In later life he may enjoy the game of setting up tasks for himself and then completing them.

Broken home is reputed to be the cause of the majority of childhood *anxieties, neuroses,* school phobias, *enuresis,* and behavior problems. It is also supposed to be the chief inciting event in the production of *homosexuality, psychosis,* alcoholism, and suicide in adults. According to some experts, if an individual has *any* problem and he came from a broken home, the two facts must be causally related.

Actually, the broken home is an observable indication of a family problem. Once the physical act of legal dissolution of the marriage has been accomplished, the children may be more relaxed and cheerful, because the tense ordeal is over. In the usual case, the children remain with the mother who now feels the release of tension and can reorganize her life and her home for the business of child rearing. The predivorce fights suggest to the child that his home is breaking up, and the insecure child reacts like anyone in a frustrating, adrenalin-producing bind—he has nightmares, he whines, he loses his appetite, his schoolwork deteriorates, and school phobia may appear. The child's doctor, aware only of the symptoms, may be sidetracked into an investigation of physical causes (*anemia, worms,* academic pressure), or may prescribe a *tranquilizer* when he should be devoting some attention to holding the child's disintegrating ego together. If the child is old enough and the doctor is willing, he may be able to help by sympathetic understanding and allowing the child to air his miseries and fears.

The child's problem is his inability to take sides in the battle. He may love both parents equally and cannot fathom their hostility, especially if each parent tries to enlist his support in the conflict. Up until age six or eight, a child will be reassured by knowing he is with one parent consistently and will not be shifted about, although he visits the other parent. Some of a child's anxiety may be coming from his belief that the other parent can whisk him away.

Although it is easy and natural for each parent to deride the ex-spouse in an effort to win the child to his side, the results are devastating to the child. When asked why Daddy is gone, the mother, though she may have to bite her lip to say it, must respond with something like, "He's a wonderful man, or I would not have married him, but we could not get along," or "Love your father; he had problems that made him hard to live with." If it is not realistic to praise an obvious cad, then simply avoid saying anything negative about the ex-spouse.

The timing of the parental separation (or death, divorce, or illness) is all important to the health of the child's psyche. The earlier the loss, the more damaging to the growing personality. The loss of the mother in the first year is cited as the biggest blow; the child's great love object disappeared—he may forever withhold his love for fear of a second hurt, especially if his caretakers are many and/or erratic.

The loss of the mother at age three, four, or five years, when the child has been experimenting with damaging phrases or even thoughts such as "I hate you!" "Drop dead!" "Go away!" may lead to guilt feelings. He somehow feels that his verbalizations or ideas were responsible, and his grief may be severe and chronic.

Once a child is a mature adolescent or young adult and capable of abstract thought, a more accurate account of the problem can be discussed. A good method is to ask the child what *he* thinks happened. An open, running dialogue is therapeutic for mother and child and father and child.

Some rules:

1. A cracked marriage will be more completely fractured by the burden of additional children.

2. Fighting and open hostility within sight or hearing of children produce fear and anxiety. If a fight does occur at the dining room table, the child must get the idea that both participants have survived and that each parent's relationship with the child is still sane and sure.

3. Separated parents must not degrade each other to their children, no matter how much hatred they bear. The child should not have to choose sides between parents.

Chores are the household duties assigned to children to teach responsibility as well as to make housekeeping a more efficient enterprise. The jobs should be considered as part of living together in mutual respect: "You live here. I do this for you, you do this for me." The tasks should be simple enough for the child to understand and accomplish. They should be equally divided among the children. There should be some leeway about time to accomplish them; the child should have some choice of when he wants to do routine tasks.

Each family must decide what philosophy is appropriate for them and at what age an allowance should begin and how much should be given. A firm commitment has to be made—and understood—by all family members as to when "pay day" is and what chores are required in return. Just because parents can afford to give a lot of spending money to the child who asks for it is no reason to hand it out. The child learns nothing except that his parents are a soft touch.

One clever motivational trick is to offer the child matching funds. For every dollar he earns toward a coveted bike, the parents add a dollar to his earnings. Some families post a list of extra jobs that need to be done with a scale of payment in accordance with the difficulty and time required for each one. The children in the family can then decide which job they want to do—if any. It is, however, not a good idea to withhold a promised allowance until a child is "nice." It only serves as a barrier, promotes belittling, and sets up a cycle of frustration-anger-hostility. The child finally gives up even thinking about being "nice" because his score card is so hopelessly in the negative.

In spite of rewards and praise some chores do not get done. A firm, nonnegotiable period of restriction or confinement seems appropriate.

Verbal appreciation of a task well done or commendation for the excellence of a job routinely expected is more important in molding a child's self-respect than money doled out. This positive reinforcement is best done at the dinner table so all may hear.

Coercion is the forced directing of a child to perform beyond his ability (for example, toilet training under one year of age). But sometimes a child will imagine that high goals of perfection exist even when the parents are content with modest performance. It is best to treat the child's distortion as real and meaningful to him. One approach might be, "This may be too hard for you, but you might want to try it." Or, "I don't know if you can do this, but . . ." Exaggerated praise ("That's fantastic!" instead of simply, "It's OK.") may be necessary to reach the inner ear and ego of a child who is down on himself because of what he assumes are high standards.

An overly ambitious parent who urges the child to achieve or lose love or suffer punishment might produce a lazy child who senses that doing nothing is safer than performing imperfectly. For the child this may be more satisfactory because the nagging may net him at least a distorted version of attention—second best to recognition, a more desirable choice but apparently unattainable. This same attitude can be seen in sports (child a little clumsy, but father wants a superior athlete) and even in normal household routines: expecting a fifteen-month-old to eat well with a spoon, punishing a child of eighteen months for untrained bowel function, blaming a sound-sleeping seven-year-old for wetting the bed, etc. This is one of the best ways to alienate a child. The child can do nothing to please his parents, so he stops trying. He has been called a lazy slob for so long that he becomes one.

Conformity is the self-discipline of one's actions to gain acceptance—

usually by a peer group. If the methods used by parents are too severe or too early, oversubmission or frustration and *anger* are the result. Nonconformity is often the result of rigid rules forced on a child with an inadequately developed self-image.

A parent must not sabotage the child by setting up impossible goals beyond the child's neuromuscular developmental level. (Learning waits on maturation.)

As he progresses from age six to twelve, his parents will encourage academic, athletic, or artistic interests wherein he can win or at least achieve recognition. Then they smile and praise. Pushing a clumsy child into an activity requiring agility on the supposition he will overcome his deficit will only make him more keenly aware of his inferiority. Then, if unable to hate his parents for getting him in that embarrassing spot, he will hate himself, become depressed, and/or develop bodily symptoms (*stomachaches* and *headaches, bed-wetting, encopresis, delinquency*).

Cruelty to children is, unfortunately, a common phenomenon. Most states have laws to protect those who report child abuse or battering, but the incidence seems to be rising. Most children involved are under three years old. The death rate is high—about 15 percent in first attacks and approaching 50 percent when the child is returned to the same home with no attempt made to treat or supervise the parents.

The parents are usually immature, impulsive, and frequently of low intelligence. They may be depressed, neurotic, and consider themselves failures. Child abuse is usually the result of anger or frustration and not necessarily the reaction to any specific act of the child. Hypoglycemia in the child and resultant loss of neocortical control may be precipitating factors. (See *Battered child,* Section 1.)

Some clues that a mother may hurt her baby are:

1. In the first few weeks of the baby's life she calls or comes to the doctor with imaginary complaints. She suspects something awful is about to happen.

2. She believes "discipline" should be begun in the first weeks of life. She is trying to communicate the fact that she is about to lose her control.

A team approach to this delicate health problem includes a psychiatrist, a pediatrician, and a social worker or nurse to make frequent supportive home visits.

Cultural influences, rate of learning to read, and intelligence are interrelated. Reading and poverty are negatively related. If parents read to themselves and make a point of reading to their children, motivation to imitate will be strong. An intelligent child will often figure out the symbols and technique long before school can get to him. I heard of a nonreading family who were so shaken by their bright four-year-old girl poring over books that they punished her, believing that she was mocking them.

On the other hand, pushy parents can thwart a child's interest by insisting on the child's use of books or classics beyond his comprehension or interest. The material must be available, but free choice is essential; the child has to progress through the comics, animal stories, and Mark Twain before Shakespeare, Dostoevski, or Kafka can be appreciated.

Dating is the American (mostly middle- and upper-class) phenomenon of adolescent boy asking adolescent girl to attend movie, dance, or game with him. The surging hormones and social pressures push these young people together, but not without many anxiety-producing moments. Both sets of parents have mixed feelings about the confrontation, because it represents their offspring's first stepping out of the nest and, of course, awakens in them long-dormant memories of their own first encounters with the opposite sex. They want their children to be socially comfortable and acceptable, but they don't want them to be hurt emotionally or burned sexually.

Insecure parents desiring popularity for their offspring will often force boy-girl parties well before optimum maturation. Early sexual stimulation of puerile couples in the absence of adequate adult impulse-controls leads to disasters.

Dating should be as spontaneous as possible and structured in the context of school function backed up by the support of the peer group. Perhaps several boys of freshman or sophomore class in high school would have a group date with a like number of girls to attend a school game and have ice cream afterward. Some unobtrusive parental supervision whould be provided to arrange for transportation. This safe crowd-date could advance to double dating in a year or two with single couple-dating at age seventeen or eighteen.

The boy should be instructed to call for his girl at her door (not honking the car horn and waiting in the street for her to come out), meet her parents (shake hands and look them in the eye), and clearly indicate when she will be returned home safely. Parents should set some sort of rule that is rigid-permissive: "The dance is over at midnight; you must be home at one A.M."

"Everyone else can stay out until two" means that maybe *one* other girl *says* she can get home by one-thirty. Adolescents need a framework within which they may operate. Most are not mature enough even at sixeen or seventeen to be able to handle their compelling chemistries; they need a fair limit set. Too much free time permits one thing to lead to another. Overtly they object to the limit, because it implies their parents do not trust them. But secretly they realize that concern is being shown.

This may sound a little old-fashioned. Earlier sexual maturity, new social pressures, and growing boredom in school have changed the adolescent dating scene. Somehow these youths must know their parents care for their safety and yet trust them to follow our *fair* rules. (See *Sex education.*)

Daydreaming sometimes borders on a sickness and might be due, if excessive, to *anemia, petit mal, neurosis,* or *depression.* Ideally each child—and adult—should have some daydreaming time set aside to plan, think, organize, contemplate his relationship with God and nature, or just look at his navel.

Mothers—or teachers who really know the child—are in the best position to judge whether the inactivity is a normal amount, whether it is a sickness, or whether it is boredom. An older child or adolescent may stop seeing his friends or schoolwork, previously good, may fall off. *Schizophrenia* or drug ingestion may be the cause. In the old days, daydreaming boys were assumed to be the victims of "self-abuse" (*masturbation*) but research has indicated that this is such a normal activity (95 percent of all boys practice it) that no positive correlation can be made. Excessive guilt rather than exhaustion would be an avenue of investigation by the personal physician.

Death of a sibling, parent, grandparent, or loved one should be faced with open, honest evidence of grief. A child should be allowed to witness appropriate adult emotion; he needs to work out his mourning of the loss just as his parents do. He must share in sadness just as he does in joy and anger. There is no better way to learn about love and emotion than in the security of a sharing family.

A last private view of the body of a close person may not be so traumatic to the child as an adult might imagine. If done, appropriate consideration of the child's age should be made (under six seems a little young). In any event, he will fare best if he can face the situation with a compassionate adult. The parents must accept the fact of the death before the child is able to do so.

Defiance in its broadest sense includes *dawdling,* reluctance, *passive aggression,* stubbornness, tuning out the parents' verbal orders, responding to suggestions with ugly facial grimaces, kicking, screaming, breaking toys or furniture, running away, etc. Anything that is not sweet, cheerful compliance could be called defiance.

Adolescent defiance is normal but usually takes the parents by surprise. Some toe-to-toe combat is a parental job requirement. It can be tolerated if the parents have a sense of humor, don't pick, and allow the child to verbalize in a non-punitive atmosphere. If his grades are acceptable and your adult friends think he is okay, he will survive. If it appears that he is underperforming out of a spirit of testiness, sometimes asking him what kind of grades he wants to work for might take some of the charge out of his brigade.

Physical defiance yields to verbal negativism with "no" to everything. The three-year-old can be tricked or cajoled into cooperation if given alternate paths to the same objective. A rule: don't fight on the child's level; he usually wins. *Do* motivate on his level. ("Take me to your bedroom" is better than "Be a nice boy.")

A child over five or six whose only response is physically violent defiance is immature because of a neurological hurt or emotional defect.

Unexpected defiance suggests the child has an overwhelming anxiety because of a feeling of helplessness; he cannot cope with a situation. The parents may have insisted the child perform some act that his immature neuromuscular apparatus cannot accomplish. Frustration leads to anger, and the child becomes stubborn or overtly hostile to all requests.

Delinquency is a term usually restricted to the adolescent and younger child who breaks the law (speeding, vandalism, stealing, arson, and, of course, assault and murder) or who repeatedly runs away. The causes are multifaceted, but some of the following are usually present: unwanted child; working parents who show little supervision or interest; mean, punitive parents; delinquent friends; hereditary factors; neurological defects. Hypoglycemia is a common contributing factor.

It is now felt that the severely deprived or emotionally starved infant is more likely to become delinquent. His poor self-image and uninhibited acts of hostility brand him as antisocial. Once so categorized, he tends to act in a way to suit his category.

A temperamentally aggressive or pushy, muscular child may so disrupt the mother bent on civilizing him that she may overreact in her discipline and become reactively punitive. He, in turn, adopts this as a way of life.

Deprivation of a child's environment is usually the result of the parents' unwillingness or inability to accept the baby as their responsibility. Sickness, poverty, or dietary defects may affect the nutrition of the fetus. Early in the fetal development, the brain cells are increasing in number by cell division, and a low protein diet and lack of iron may irreversibly impair the baby's growing brain. Severe early protein deprivation may result in a less-than-full component of brain cells. Drugs, smoking, and inadequate prenatal care by a girl who is not convinced she wants the baby add to the damage.

This physically deprived baby may now be insulted by an environment of hostility, low stimulation level, brutal reprisals for disrupting the status quo, or constant shifting from one home to another. If he is not battered, he will at least be unloved. He will soon suspect he is unwanted and avoid human contact—as he has learned it is dangerous: "If you show love, you may become hurt." Self-stimulation, poor growth, rumination, and *autism* can be traced to maternal deprivation. The process is felt to be reversible if interrupted in time and if persistent love, warmth, and acceptance are offered. However, the traits and reactions stemming from severe early deprivation are among the more persistent and asocial of known psychological problems. (See *Prematurity,* Section 5; *Failure to thrive,* Section 10.)

If cared for by an insensitive or unaware mother, the *brain-damaged, retarded, blind,* or *deaf* baby may set up his own self-destroying deprivation. The mother may be trying to offer love but become discouraged by a lack of response and abandon her efforts. The mother-child interaction is a two-way reflex, and each step in the development of mutual trust and respect builds on the successful completion of the prior one. Compensatory intervention is essential early for successful maturation of potential.

Along with the appropriate visual and auditory stimulation, the baby requires oral gratification. Cutaneous or tactile skin stimulation is felt to be important to a growing nervous system.

Experiments with families who display poor verbal interaction with their children indicate that increasing this one modality of communication significantly increased the child's IQ level.

Early evidence that a child has suffered deprivation—common in institutionalized babies and in some homes—would include (a) little or no smiling, (b) a suspicous watchfulness, (c) few babbling or gurgling attempts, (d) lack of enjoyment when cuddling is attempted, and (e) no anticipatory attitude when approached.

As the deprived child approaches one year, he treats furniture, strangers, and parents with equal indifference. Desire to explore the environment is lacking, as is the neuromuscular ability to perform.

Most of the mothers of these children have received inadequate nurturing from their own homes and so, in effect, are unable to pass on the love they never got. (See *Cruelty to children, Autism.*)

Follow-up studies of these emotionally deprived children indicate that they never quite catch up to the norm in physical, intellectual, or emotional functioning, and they have a host of behavior problems from aggressiveness to hyperactivity. Obviously the treatment must be early intervention, but birth control for a woman who is likely to deprive the child is the best approach to this personal and social waste.

Disobedience, or defiance of authority, is one of the most common complaints that parents bring to the pediatrician. The doctor may be insecure in his ability to determine the cause—as it may be the result of a sick or anemic child reacting to normal pressures of day-to-day living: a neurologically inadequate child who doesn't comprehend or remember the lessons of house discipline; a normally gregarious, impulsive child who is desperately seeking limits to his antisocial behavior; a child who is being overly punished for infractions of capricious rules; or a combination of these. A parent who is afraid to insist on obedience of home rules because the child might not like him is only encouraging disobedience. Although learning is enhanced by rewarding positive social acts, some effort must be made to control impulsive, aggressive acts, or they will continue in adulthood.

Frequently in an otherwise well-ordered, obedient, almost overly controlled family, one child will be openly defiant, mean, destructive, and have a terrible, explosive temper. After one of his scenes, he will become calm, subdued, overly affectionate—asking forgiveness for his behavior, as if he needs recognition that he couldn't help

DEVELOPMENTAL MAP

Age	*Tests and Immunizations*	*Diet*
1 MONTH	D.P.T.(1) Oral Polio	Milk, 2 ounces per pound per 24 hours Vitamins, fluoride, and iron
2 MONTHS	D.P.T.(2)	Rice or Barley
3 MONTHS	Oral Polio D.P.T.(3)	Applesauce
3–5 MONTHS		Bananas Carrots
6–7 MONTHS		Squash Give solid foods first
8–9 MONTHS		Sweet potato Veal, beef, or lamb Teething biscuit
ONE YEAR to 15 MONTHS (FEMALE)—28–30 inches at 1 year (MALE)—29–31 inches at 1 year	Hemoglobin test Measles vaccine Urine test	"Finger food" Discourage milk Cup Messes in food Egg, citrus, green vegetables, peaches

Motor Development	*What Environment Should Provide*	*Warnings, Suggestions, Comments*
Cries, sucks, swallows, blinks at lights Head sags, clenches hands	Touch, skin contact, motion, rocking Sounds to hear—especially human voices Objects to see—especially mother Full stomach, social contact Love, warmth, cuddling, security	Try to breast-feed Take a nap when he does Don't push solids—they're not important yet Baby should gain one to three pounds over birthweight
Stares at objects, follows objects with eyes		
Listens to sounds, raises head when prone "Social smile," smiles and laughs at people	Sucking pleasure (pacifier or thumb) Mobiles, TV, pictures, things to see Voices, songs, records, simple stories Smiles and laughter when he smiles Human voices to talk when he talks People to watch Toys to excite him	Carry him about house and to store and park Do simple vision and hearing tests Good age to travel Good age to photograph him Don't leave him where he may fall
Rolls over Looks at and reaches for toy Follows object 180° Laughs and squeals		
Sits, leaning on hands Transfers cube from hand to hand Turns when spoken to or when someone speaks		
Sits well Stands, hanging on Thumb-finger grasp Imitates speech Shy with strangers Resists toy removal Plays peek-a-boo Cries upon separation	Pillow to prop him up to see and grasp Toys to grab Sling or chair so his feet touch the floor Handy objects to fondle and bite Human contact	Toys too big to swallow (remove buttons) No lead in paint He develops a temper Get used to separation cry
Feeds self; creeps Shows temper Pull up to sitting Cries on separation Waves "bye-bye"; imitates gestures Stands with support Crawls well; says "mama," "bye-bye" Walks alone; investigates	Needs loving parent or baby sitter Reward and praise for accomplishment	Don't force spoon Don't wean suddenly Keep from undue contact with strangers

DEVELOPMENTAL MAP (continued)

Age	*Tests and Immunizations*	*Diet*
18 MONTHS to 2 YEARS (Double body length to estimate adult height; do this at 18 months for girls and 2 years for boys)	TB test D.P.T. Booster	Spoon Milk and white foods are *least* important Appetite decreases Meats, fruits, and fluoride *most* important One meal a day
3 YEARS	TB test Dentist	Definite food likes and dislikes
4 to 5 YEARS	Hearing test Rubella Vaccine	Appetite better Serve small amounts; let him ask you for seconds
5 YEARS (Grows 2–3 inches a year)	Visual Acuity Test Oral Polio D.P.T. Booster Mumps Vaccine TB test	3 reasonably good meals a day Meats most important; then fruits; then vegetables; then grain and cereal Milk and white foods least important

Motor Development	*What Environment Should Provide*	*Warnings, Suggestions, Comments*
Climbs stairs one at a time; kicks ball Says "no," pulls toy Three to five words Scribbles; uses cup without spilling Names objects in picture Bladder and bowel control Runs Sentences of three words Builds tower of several blocks Knows name Turns pages, uses scissors, can draw line ——— Draws circle, cross Rides tricycle, asks "what"	Consistent "no" or punishment for doing dangerous things Safe place to play, use muscles, and run—and have temper tantrums Chance to scribble and smear without adult supervision Answers to questions; ask him to name objects Nighttime rituals; tooth brushing, relaxing bath, story, cuddly animal, favorite blanket, prayers Love and limits Honest answers about sex and parts of body Reassurance or night light to counter sleep resistance, fear of the dark	Read to him Start using toothbrush He needs to mess in and smash food, imitate housework Remove poisons, paints, detergents, medicines (have Syrup of Ipecac ready) Ignore temper tantrums Turn pot handles around on stove Bad time to stop pacifier or thumb sucking—he's too stubborn Girl may be toilet-trainable If he won't eat and suffers constipation, stop milk and white foods Whining begins; try to ignore it
Can draw a man Plays with peers; can count three objects Balances on one foot for ten seconds Can jump on one foot; catch ball Prefers to play with other children Can tell a story	Nursery school or constructive social play Increased periods of separation from parents Praise for verbal accomplishment and "art" work	Stammering common; pretend you don't notice Rely on your sense of humor when he calls you names Introduce child to cooking, housework, machinery maintenance
Imitates adult activity Asks "why" Interest in sex differences Throws ball Knows three or four colors Dresses and undresses self Copies some letters Can tell a longer story	Chance to dress up and play-act Assumption that he is doing his best in school Pictures and books about history as well as "the facts of life" Sense of belonging in family Discussion of his opinions on menus, vacations, etc. Being read to Contact with culture: museums, films, etc. Reinforcement for acceptable behavior	School-phobia common; do all you can to keep him there Plan "show and tell" for whole family Encourage child in sports Assign daily chores: make the bed, feed the pet, do the dishes Allowance (?); help him respect property rights of others Ignore "dirty" talk—he's just testing Punish for lying, cheating, stealing

it. It almost seems that something made him do it—the devil, maybe. Some attacks are suggestive of seizures. Indeed, a brain-wave test (*EEG*) in some of these children (or adults) reveals an abnormality which can occasionally be controlled with *Mellaril®, phenobarbital* or *Dilantin®*. The calming of these wild episodes may allow the mother to continue her disciplinary measures with more consistency. Alternating good and bad behavior is also suggestive of a nutritional problem.

Once a disobedient child has established his life pattern of stubborn "no," the parents unwittingly perpetuate the self-destroying pattern because they feel the must fight back, thus somehow reinforcing the disobedience.

Divorce—see *Broken home*

Drug abuse. At the present time the average age of first experimenting with drugs is between age twelve and fifteen. Marijuana is more easily available, but LSD is used by many, although less frequently. Some studies indicate that about one youngster out of four has tried LSD at least once by age eighteen.

Most youthful users do not tell their parents of their drug experiences, but any reasonably intuitive parent should be alert enough to recognize if his child is a chronic user.

It is to be hoped that a young person is just experimenting, searching for a new experience. He is trying to match his peer group and might also be motivated by rebellious feelings toward his parents; he knows that they would disapprove. These motives predominate, and such an experimenter primarily requires acceptance and understanding. Recriminations, overly severe punishment, or name-calling serve to push the child into more drug use. "They think I'm a bum: I might as well act like one." (The self-fulfilling prophecy.)

When first aware that their child is on drugs, parents will run the gamut of disbelief, astonishment, disappointment, guilt, frustration, anger. Their initial reaction is to punish and ground him. This direct attack is as useful as telling the *thumb-sucking* two-year-old to stop his habit. Physicians know how hard it is to treat alcoholism and obesity. The rules are the same. The underlying cause of the user's need to seek this escape must be sought. Somehow he must be allowed to be understood; he must have some success in the "square" world. Academic goals must be changed. Some hobby, sport, or job must be found that holds his interest.

Many *hyperactive* children who have not had a successful learning experience in school become drop-out acid heads. They are tired of being told, "You could do better if you would sit still and try." The schizoid or frankly *schizophrenic* is attracted to drugs as he feels his ego structure eroding. Drugs provide some support. A severely disturbed adolescent is the *depressed* one who takes risks, as if he hopes to kill himself—and often does—with an overdose.

Schools could do a great deal to alter curricula so that each child feels successful. Parents could do much by accepting the adolescent when he is having a great deal of trouble accepting himself.

The ominous group that continues using drugs frequently and on a long-term basis is usually made up of those who have a low opinion of themselves, and the drug world is their only *real* existence. They do poorly at school, they cannot seem to live up to the standards imposed at home, they are too young for a job that is interesting, they feel alienated. They express hostility toward the establishment by copping out—as they are sure they would not be successful in it. They fight it as if they are afraid to join it. These young people are salvageable if quick action is taken; if not, heroin may be the next step they take.

Glue sniffing is the act of inhaling the volatile diluent in tubes of glue. Similar effects can be obtained from smelling gasoline, paint thinner, perfume, and other volatile substances. Usually dizziness, numbness, tingling, illusions, and other pleasant or unpleasant sensations follow. Unconsciousness and *convulsions* may occur. Most authorities feel it causes *brain damage.*

LSD, or lysergic acid diethylamide, is an easily synthesized and commonly used psychedelic agent called "mind-expanding" by its advocates and "an escape mechanism" by its detractors. First synthesized by a Swiss chemist thirty years ago, it was hailed as an investigative tool because it induced delusional symptoms similar to those of *psychosis,* lasting for four to eight hours. Indeed, it gave credence to the growing realization that *schizophrenia* might be a biochemical aberration. About one thousandth part of a gram (a gram is about one fourth of a teaspoonful) is enough to send the ingester into a wild dream world. A telephone pole is so beautiful that it makes him cry, interpersonal relationships become exquisite communications between souls, the whole world is truly one with God, heaven, and nature, growing things whisper truth, and the mind transcends all

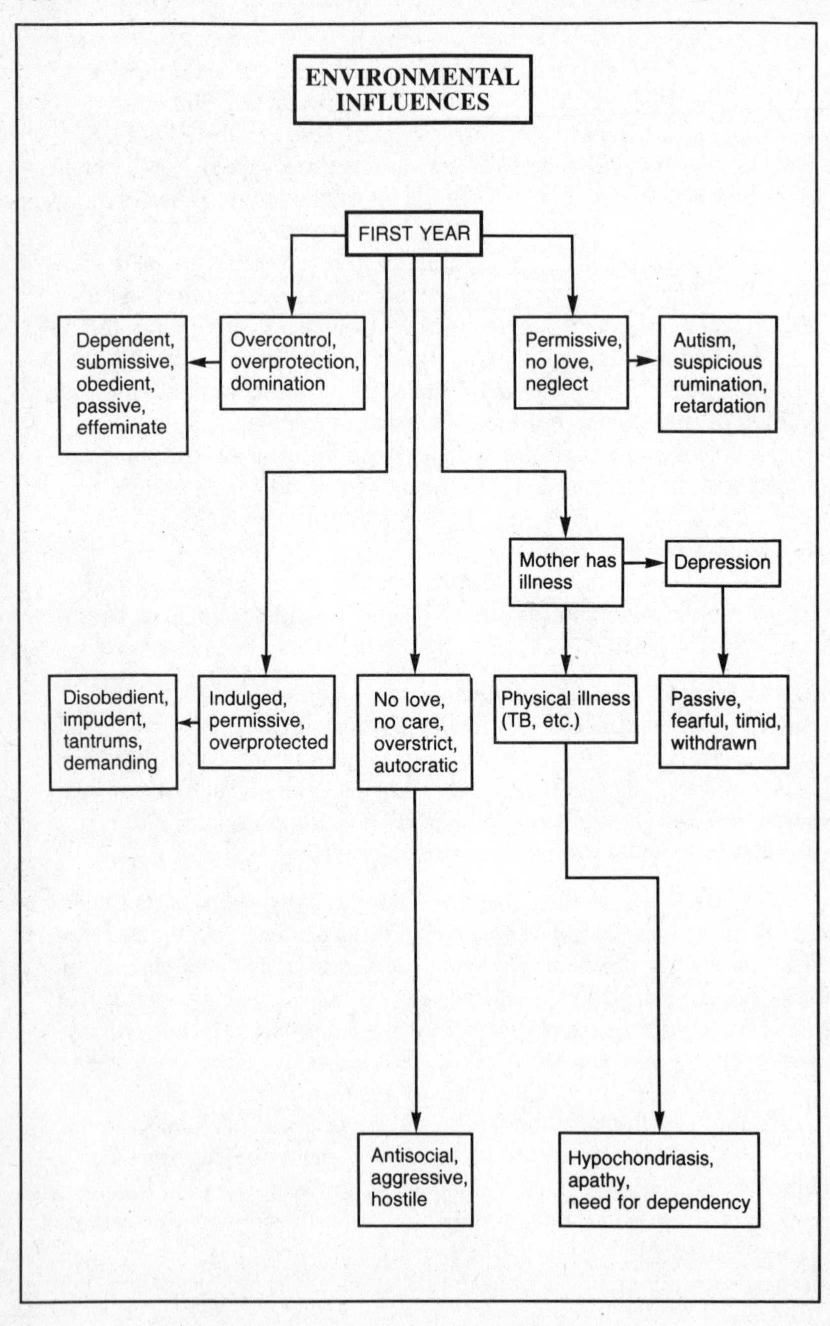
ENVIRONMENTAL INFLUENCES
FIRST YEAR
Dependent, submissive, obedient, passive, effeminate
Overcontrol, overprotection, domination
Permissive, no love, neglect
Autism, suspicious rumination, retardation
Mother has illness
Depression
Disobedient, impudent, tantrums, demanding
Indulged, permissive, overprotected
No love, no care, overstrict, autocratic
Physical illness (TB, etc.)
Passive, fearful, timid, withdrawn
Antisocial, aggressive, hostile
Hypochondriasis, apathy, need for dependency

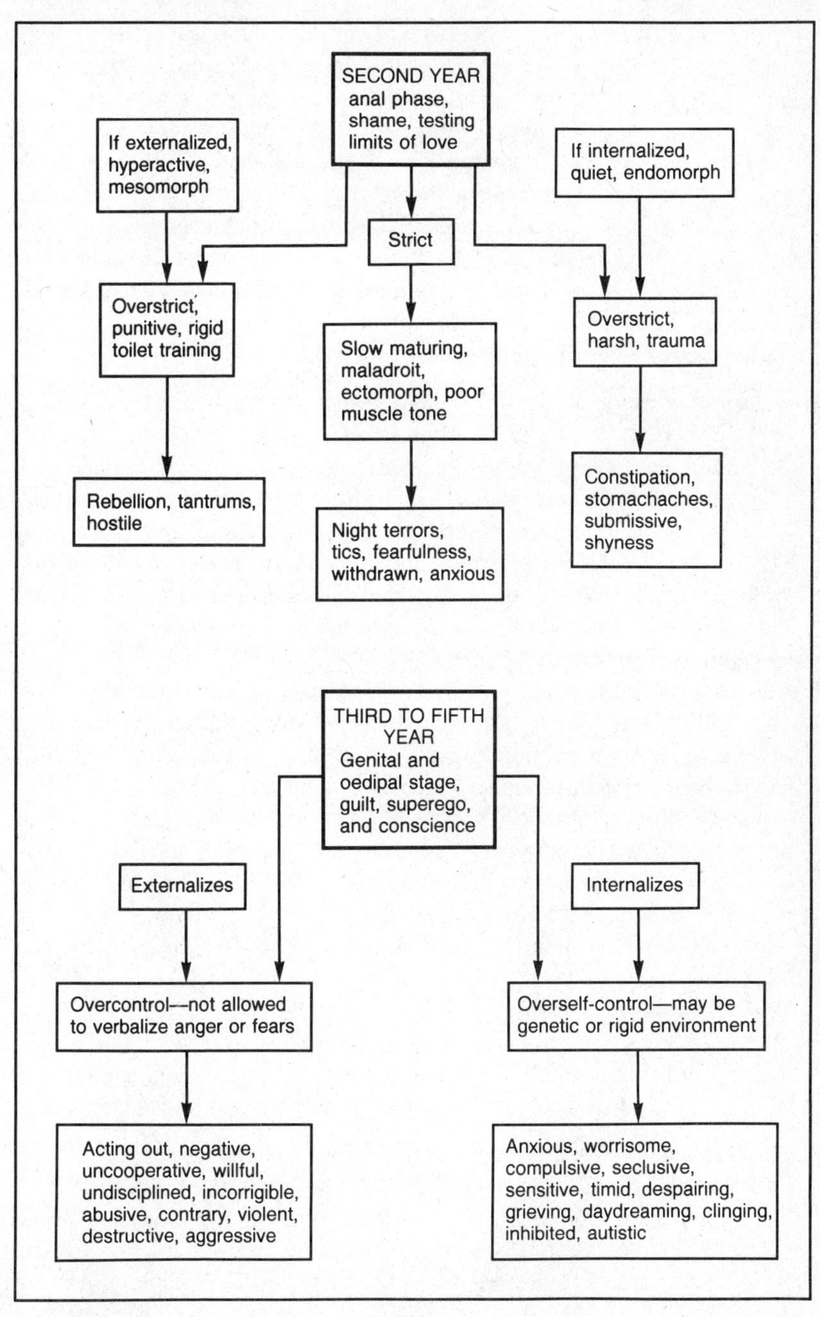
SECOND YEAR
anal phase,
shame, testing
limits of love
If externalized,
hyperactive,
mesomorph
If internalized,
quiet, endomorph
Strict
Overstrict,
punitive, rigid
toilet training
Slow maturing,
maladroit,
ectomorph, poor
muscle tone
Overstrict,
harsh, trauma
Rebellion, tantrums,
hostile
Night terrors,
tics, fearfulness,
withdrawn, anxious
Constipation,
stomachaches,
submissive,
shyness
THIRD TO FIFTH
YEAR
Genital and
oedipal stage,
guilt, superego,
and conscience
Externalizes
Internalizes
Overcontrol—not allowed
to verbalize anger or fears
Overself-control—may be
genetic or rigid environment
Acting out, negative,
uncooperative, willful,
undisciplined, incorrigible,
abusive, contrary, violent,
destructive, aggressive
Anxious, worrisome,
compulsive, seclusive,
sensitive, timid, despairing,
grieving, daydreaming, clinging,
inhibited, autistic

time. This ecstasy is so overwhelming that some can talk of little else between "trips"; it becomes a little boring to the nontravelers.

Not infrequent bad experiences motivate some to give it up. Some feel "ugly" or that their brains are "melting." Panicky feelings of loss of self are acute emergencies; some can be "talked down" by sympathetic friends or by an understanding physician who might use an injection of a *tranquilizer* to speed up return to normality.

An overdose of LSD can cause a bad trip to become a fatal one, or psychotic behavior might cause the user to leap from a window or walk into traffic. A few experience flashbacks or delusions long after the drug has disappeared from the body.

Marijuana is obtained from the flowering tops of *Cannabis sativa.* (Hashish is the more potent resin.) Smoking pot or joints is a recent common activity in the United States (and elsewhere). Along with the euphoria, inflamed eyes and sore throat are common concomitants. Users tell of increased awareness of surroundings and perceptive thoughts, all subjective. Group smoking may increase communication while solitary smoking usually promotes lethargy or quiet navel contemplation. A letdown feeling usually follows after four hours which suggests to the user that another joint would be therapeutic.

Chronic use is associated with school and social failure; the a-motivational syndrome is a vicious cycle. More failure leads to more smoking; more smoking inhibits the desire to get going with life. Sleep disturbances, flashbacks, memory failures, lowered threshold for sensory stimuli, tremors, weakness, and reduction of sexual potency may be seen in chronic users. Illusions and delusions suggest an early psychotic illness. Schizophrenia may become overt; no one can determine if schizoid traits nudged the patient into smoking or if the smoking was the inciting agent allowing latent psychosis to become manifest.

Parents should suspect marijuana smoking if they notice their red-eyed child emerge from the locked bathroom, where the unmistakable odor of burning leaves can be detected. Drug-takers are looking for comfort; most of them do not feel well; many are low in calcium.

Excitement makes life interesting. The anticipation of a party, a trip, a visit may be more exhilarating than the event itself. Exciting play prior to bedtime or to the point of overstimulation is not appropriate for preschool children who have not developed their abilities of impulse control. Frantic action and strident voices require adult intervention;

under this guidance the child eventually learns to call a halt before exciting play becomes out-of-control panic.

A little fear is usually associated with any excitement. An aware adult will sense when the child is losing control by the expression on his face. Children with minimal brain damage are easily overstimulated; even mild tickling becomes a sensory nightmare over which some of these children have no control.

Failure is the inability to compete successfully with one's peers or to satisfy one's own high standards. Elementary and high-school students are competing constantly on academic, social, and athletic levels; the struggle for success is a daily event. The student who is doing poorly knows it; there is no conspiracy to keep him from finding out. He usually becomes disruptive in some manner. He may know he can't do the assigned work satisfactorily, so he simply does not do it at all; he feels that no grade is better than a bad one.

Failure breeds failure. Before a degrading self-image becomes irreversible, the child's sense of worth must be retrieved with encouragement, a new environment, social engineering, or if he is neurologically handicapped, medication and/or placement in a small, ungraded class so that some success will brighten his day. Once labeled a failure, the tendency is to accept the label and act accordingly.

An overly conscientious child may be so tense because of a fear of failure that he develops stomachaches and/or tics. These symptoms suggest he is under some pressure or at least too much pressure for his particular physiology. Some children are built this way from birth, and very little environmental pressure is needed to imprint social conformity into them. (See *Duodenal ulcer*, Section 12.)

If each boy would grow up to be a farmer like his father, and each girl a farmer's wife, mothering would be easy, as the child would imitate the appropriate parent. With so many choices open, and so many mothers working outside the home, the child has difficulty learning his social and sexual role. Social responsibility comes late to the modern youth but sexual maturity begins earlier now.

Family. The family is a society's way of perpetuating itself. A society will not allow self-extermination. It sanctions large families in times of low birth rate and encourages limitations in family size if population density is uncomfortable. Parents are the agents of transmittal of the social customs and legends to the young; the conscience of a society is passed on to the young by parental reinforcement. Most societies discourage any action that serves to disrupt the family. Divorce is inconvenient, adultery is a crime, unwed mothers are disgraced, incest and rape are punishable acts. Overtly and covertly society encourages the solidarity, security, and continuity of the child's environment as if it knew that this was the optimum situation to rear a properly functioning member of society. Society "suspects" that the mother can do a better job of loving, feeding, and acculturing her child if she is old enough (laws against child brides), secure enough (marriage is encouraged *before* pregnancy), and adequately housed. Her unworried mind can be more fully devoted to mothering if her environment is supportive.

Whether we like it or not, whether it is "good" or "bad," the family is no longer the father-dominant, mother-dependent, or patriarchal institution so traditional before World War II. A more democratic, equal sharing partnership is the family mode now. Couples tend to live away from their parents. This may provide a certain independence of action, but deprives the parent of some expertise to fall back on in times of stress, and deprives the child of some chance to relate to the different influences of close relatives. The pediatrician is often the "grandmother." The parent now relies on the flood of child-rearing information from television, radio, magazines, and books rather than on some know-it-all, live-in aunt.

The principal task of the parents is to foster socially acceptable, mature behavior in their child without destroying his capacity for individual goal attainment. Development proceeds with nourishment—calories, protein, minerals, and vitamins—for the body, and stimulation and interaction from the environment, including love and encouragement by appropriate human adults.

Fire setting is dangerous. The curious three- to six-year-old must be protected from his impulsive acts. Tempting matches left about are an invitation to disaster. The child should be encouraged to light candles, fireplace fires, plum puddings, etc., with proper adult supervision. The six- to ten-year-old might be experimenting when he burns paper in the wastebasket or rags in the garage, but the recidivist or the adolescent is sick and needs help. His fire is a "smoke" signal to the world that he needs some attention to his disturbed psyche. Research has indicated that the school failure, the *retarded* who have a low success rate, the *hyperactive* are more likely to be fire setters, as if this activity were the only thing at which they had any success.

The punitive home with an indifferent or absent or overly aggressive father has a high incidence of this delinquent activity. The fire, like petty thievery, is the child's expression of a sense of losing out in his wish to be close to his family.

Find some socially acceptable activity at which the child feels a sense of accomplishment; find a way to restore closeness to someone he fears he is losing or has lost; and antisocial acts will be minimized.

Habits are routine, often stereotyped, practices that parents urge upon a child. It is hoped that good hygiene will become ingrained into the child's life style; he becomes uncomfortable if it is lacking. Bed routine, bathing, teeth-brushing, eating proper foods, social niceties, pleasant speech, concern for others are some of the activities that parents are supposed to brand into the child's nervous system. Many compromises are necessary between the mother's ideal of a "nice" child and what the child is willing to conform to. These good habits are usually incorporated into a child's (or the future adult's) daily life more by parental example than by admonishment. "Bad" habits frequently begin from a physiological need or nervous energy overflow. Once manifest they can become fixed because of the attention paid to them by a conscientious parent in an effort to eliminate them. Night wakefulness, for example, may actually be due to a disease (*epilepsy, pinworms, gas,* etc.). The mother goes to the bedside and comforts or feeds the child, thus rewarding him for the disturbance. Sedatives, worm medicine, and diet change may treat the original cause for awakening, but the child has been taught to expect some extra attention and will perpetuate the disturbance.

Continuation of undesirable habits suggests that the parents are pushing the child (or the child believes they are), usually a boy, into activities in which the child sees a limited chance of success. His anxiety and frustration seek some discharge in motor activity: nail-biting, *thumb-sucking, tics,* restlessness, inability to sleep, bed rocking.

The treatment is to stop the urgent prodding for perfection, drop the tight schedule, allow him to stare into space occasionally, accept and approve his own accomplishments, albeit below the parents' standards. Many children who have these rhythmical habits are actually low in calcium; 1,000 milligrams (dolomite or bone meal) daily for a week may calm his body enough that he does not need to do "his thing."

Breath-holding attacks occur at the time of fright, frustration, injury, temper tantrum, or a spanking. The infant—usually eight to eighteen months of age—cries two or three times, exhales, holds his breath, turns blue, arches his back, and passes out. He may have some convulsive movements or stiffening of arms and legs. He relaxes in a moment, becomes pale, then resumes normal activity.

It is important to differentiate this from *epilepsy.* In epilepsy there is no emotionally precipitating factor; usually the child does not cry; the *cyanosis accompanies* or *follows* the seizure. The *EEG* is normal in the breath-holder; medication is pointless unless the mother "must do something." Attacks may occur daily, weekly, or monthly.

The parents must understand that the breath-holding attacks are innocuous and will cease in a year or so, and if they pay any attention to them, they are telling the child that he should continue their use. Mothers of breath-holding children are reluctant to scold them or leave them for fear of precipitating an attack. Studied indifference to these attacks seems to be the best method of treating them; otherwise, the spoiled child will soon dominate the household.

This indifference should be a complete turning away from the child and/or leaving the room. If this is hard to do, the mother must discuss the problem with a knowledgeable counselor or physician and get support.

Head-banging, nodding, or *twisting* may be evidence of *neurosis, psychosis,* tension, *epilepsy, headache,* or occur in a normal child who has a need to perform this tic for release of energy. If the child seems happy and is eating well, it is well to consider it a developmental phase which should pass. An EEG might be useful; if abnormal, *phenobarbital* or *Dilantin®* might be tried.

Nail-biting is a common childhood habit that upsets most parents, because it suggests to them that their child is neurotic and they are somehow responsible. The more concerned they are, the more the child seems to continue the habit. Some evidence suggests a familial trait; a parent who struggled with his own nail-biting as a child would be overly concerned when his own flesh-and-blood does the same thing—almost as a taunt.

Spasmus nutans, or nodding spasm, is found in infants and consists of one or all of the following: head nodding, tipping of the head to one side or the other, and jerky eye movements usually in one eye. No cause is known, but some feel it is related to poor lighting, which prevents the baby from making adequate eye fixations. It clears spontaneously.

Thumb-sucking is an irritating childhood trait that seems to be a normal part of human growth. The parents who scold or punish their child about this only serve to reinforce its continuation. The child's peer group almost invariably will minimize the habit because of nonacceptance. Substitution of some other oral gratification (chewing gum?) may discourage it. A pacifier habit begun in the first few weeks (*Nuk*® is best) is less disfiguring to tooth alignment as well as easier to remove in childhood. Facial changes and *malocclusion* result from persistence of this habit after the age of five years. The child who must suck his thumb more than twelve hours a day after this age needs a discouraging appliance from the dentist and some counseling from the pediatrician or friendly psychologist. (The habit does not have to mean the child is insecure; it only means the child likes to suck his thumb.)

Tics are habit spasms of muscle groups that appear to be involuntary, although if the child "really tries," he can reduce the repetitive frequency. Blinking, turning the head, shrugging the shoulders, and wrinkling the forehead are all common. The affected child is frequently tense and perfectionistic; one has the feeling that he is trying to control his need to shout, jump, or run, and this bottled-up tension is released in the tic. It is assumed to be a neurotic expression, but some violent tics may be associated with *chorea* or *epileptic equivalents.* An EEG might be helpful in classifying the disorder. *Phenobarbital* or a *tranquilizer* (haloperidol is useful) may reduce the frequency so the parents will not have to berate the already tense child with constant repetitions of "Stop it!"

Most tics, however, are considered developmental disorders as they usually appear in boys just starting school. Eighty percent recover completely in eight years.

I watched a tic in one child progress from head turning to shoulder shrugging to body twisting to leg turning before it stopped; it took four years to go from top to bottom.

Trichotillomania is the name for the odd habit of pulling out scalp hair and swallowing it. It leads to the formation of the hairball. The child who does this is in need of psychiatric attention.

Identification is the process of patterning one's life or thinking after that of another. In the usual family the boy will attempt to imitate his father, the girl will try to be like her mother. This comes about naturally and easily if the adults are reasonably mature and comfortable as male and female. This development is reflected in the games children play. The four- to six-year-old boy plays Daddy to the little girl's Mommy.

If the father is terribly hostile or punitive, the child may identify through fear instead of love or respect. Such a boy would internalize this attitude and grow up to be hostile and punitive himself.

A girl at age three to five may be a tease and a flirt with her father, but she senses that this is a dangerous game to play as she may lose her mother's love. She turns to playmates to fulfill the love-and-be-loved drives until adolescence suggests heterosexual contacts.

If a child is unwanted or rejected, he may have no motivation to *want* to identify with a parent, and immaturity results. A mother may demonstrate to her daughter that womanhood is a rotten role; the girl might take the hint and become a tomboy. It is unfortunate that Women's Liberation is sometimes equated with the rejection of femininity; the impressionable little girl is unable to separate the two concepts.

A boy may have problems figuring out the male role when he sees his father only at the end of a harassing day. Many men come home with exaggerated stories of their hard day at the office which serve to suggest to a son that some other way of life might be more worthwhile.

The absent, distant, or aloof parent poses a problem; if the father is not around, how does a boy learn how to be a man? A grandfather, uncle, or teacher may be helpful. If the father's absence is due to a *divorce* associated with much acrimony, a mother might sabotage her boy's growth to maleness by constantly pointing out that his father is no good.

Jealousy is a normal phenomenon in any family, but doesn't have to lead to chronic, seething hostility. The more excessive the pampering and attention given to the firstborn, the more chronic will be the jealousy. If children are spaced about a year or so apart, the older child may be unaware of the new usurper. But the two- to four-year-old, if not properly prepared for the new baby (or even if he is), may show ill-concealed rage and frustration at being replaced.

He must absolutely be prevented from hurting the baby, but should be urged to verbalize his hostility as much as possible. Before the new baby's birth, some attempt should be made to explain the coming event and the child's expected role.

On the day the new baby comes home, it might be best to bring the baby in like the groceries, while the mother makes a big fuss over her older child. Then after calm is restored, she might ask, "Oh, by the way, do you want to see your new brother?" The conversation should be interspersed with "Our baby" and "We will feed him" to show how the responsibility is to be shared.

When friends come to see the baby, it would be wise to have the older child show him and answer questions. A thoughtful visitor, if bringing a gift for the baby, will also bring one for the older child.

Sometimes things go smoothly until the older child realizes that the new one is there to stay, or until he becomes a toddler and starts to appropriate the older one's best toys. A mother must not play favorites in her role as umpire. She will find out how consistent and fair she was when the children are adolescents and still remember the time and place of every one of her ill-judged decisions.

Some jealousy, intramural fighting, and jockeying for positions of favor in the house are good practice sessions for the grown-up world.

Lying is so common in preschool children that it is usually regarded as just an attention-getting device, a method of mastering a situation or of increasing self-esteem. Lying after age six may result from parental insistence on high standards that the child finds unrealistic. If the child's lies go undetected and unchallenged, the habit is encouraged. Too, children lie because they frequently note that their parents twist the truth a little and get away with it. A child may lie to build his own ego if no loving parent gives him any self-respect or shows trust.

Most parents who catch their child in a bold-faced lie insist that he confess. Reluctance may stem from fear of punishment. Some reward must be granted for the confession, but the child must still be punished appropriately for the original deed.

Neurosis may appear as *Anorexia nervosa, Anxiety, Depression, Fears, Guilt, Obsessiveness, Perfectionism, School phobia, Seclusiveness, Shyness, Suicide attempt.*

Anorexia nervosa is a fairly rare but potentially serious emotional disturbance usually found in adolescent girls. It starts as a psychological rejection or fear of growing up and then becomes a nutritional problem. Severe restriction of food intake, coupled with alarming weight loss, triggers the parents to be punitive at mealtime—which only seems to make the victim more determined to waste away. Logic is of no help. Psychiatric aid is needed. Early, conflictful mother-child relationships and/or schizoid traits seem to be ever present.

Anxiety is the conscious awareness of the symptoms of fear—rapid *heartbeat,* tightness in abdomen, flushing of skin, sweaty palms, tremor, crying, nausea, and such—without certain knowledge of the cause. Some psychic mechanism will not allow the victim to face his fear because he believes he is unable to deal with it. Falling blood sugar will release adrenalin and produce these same symptoms.

An anxiety attack may be precipitated by some minor experience; however, a long smoldering anxiety must have been just under the surface. Parental over-solicitude is frequently present in the home background of anxious children. Conflict in the home is a cause of anxiety.

Anxiety for no apparent cause may arise because guilt prevents normal resentful feelings from arising. In a home where outward tranquility and control are prized, a child may suppress anger but get the parents' attention and interest through bodily symptoms and/or anxiety attacks; this attention accomplishes a certain distorted discharge of resentment. Logic and punishment are useless in treating anxiety. Psychological testing, family interview techniques, or play therapy may give the therapist some insights as to what the child is *really* afraid of.

Depression in children is the result of the loss of some love object. (The loved object can be the child himself if he feels he is worthless and does not care for himself.) The depth or quality of the reaction may seem inappropriate by adult standards but should be respected by the adult family members. Some children are by temperament more easily upset, sensitive, or depressed than others in the family. Children who have been taught to control hostile feelings completely will more easily turn these feelings toward themselves, and their guilt will devastate them into depressive reactions more easily.

Sometimes a child will make depressive statements such as, "No one likes me," "I'm stupid," and he automatically gets a reassuring statement from the parents. The child receives this as "They need for me to be happy." But he might find it more useful to learn that ups and downs are part of the life game. If, at first, he is just listened to and allowed to think of his own way out, it may be less reinforcing of the depressing comments. An expert might have to be consulted to determine if the comments are an attention-getting device.

Adolescents are prone to flights into depression, as well as elation. It is assumed that they feel inadequate or unable to cope with what seems to be insurmountable problems (sex control, masturbation, grades, inability to communicate with peer groups, etc.). A poor self-image adds conviction to despondent feelings. Sickness, anemia, and poor school performance enhance the sadness. If appetite loss, constipation, and other bodily functions are altered, and reassurance by family, physician and/or minister are ineffective, psychiatric help is urgent.

Fears are so common that, if a child does not develop a few of them as he grows, he might well be considered abnormal. They are usually completely irrational but do not respond to calm reassurance or stern appeals to reason. The evils lurking in the dark or under the bed may be minimized (but not eliminated) by a night light or flashlight in bed for the four- to ten-year-old. Forcing the child to face his imagination in the dark is cruel, but establishing the habit of sleeping with the parents is not wise either.

The anxiety a child feels over new situations—visits, new toys, new foods, a new bed—may suggest some insecurity. But it very well could be that his nervous system is not mature enough to handle the situation and that a parent has overestimated his ability to cope with it. The child is torn between his desire to do what his parent wants him to and his worry that he may fail in the new project and thus lose approval. The anxiety produced may turn into anger, pouting, a temper tantrum, a tic, or a neatly timed stomachache which would resolve the frustration.

The child cannot explain his own fear, depression, guilt, worry, fantasy. He senses that some danger is sneaking into his consciousness and reacts according to his basic personality makeup. An oral type might overeat or bite his nails. An active child might be more restless or sleepwalk or rock the bed. An overcontrolled, constricted child might become deeply depressed or develop a peptic ulcer. If the child is unable to express anger over a lost contact with his parents, encopresis may appear.

Many four- to seven-year-olds suddenly realize how tenuous is our hold on life, and at that age they cannot develop a philosophical detachment from the inevitable end. They are, however, more concerned about whether their parents will be available to care for them than they are about their own passing on. Witnessing a car accident or the death of a relative may incite development of this fear. Reassurance seems of no avail. Insisting on silence usually allows the psychic pressures to build up until some other—or worse—symptom appears to funnel off the energy. Allowing the child to express his fears and worries is the most desirable therapy available. Grief must be allowed to be dissipated verbally and physically, as repression will produce depressive symptoms. (See *Death, Broken home.*)

Some children are congenitally prone to worrying. Some form of brain dysfunction may account for overwhelming fear of doctor, dentist, separation, animals, etc. Certainly not every skittish child has been made this way by his skittish mother. Some notice pain more than would be expected, perhaps due to a lack of built-in inhibitory control of pain stimuli. Some of these children need a *tranquilizer.* Children need to share their fears with an understanding adult. It is not wise to "pump" a child to find out what his fears are. If the signs of fearful attitudes are obvious, an open "hot line" to the parent is most reassuring.

Ridiculing a child makes him feel more alone than before. Sympathy and a genuine desire to help will convey the impression that he can eventually master the fear. Play therapy in which the child acts out the upsetting experience over and over may finally convince him that he is in charge.

Obsessiveness is usually associated with *compulsiveness* and implies a rigid, unbending personality structure and fear or inability to verbalize hostile or aggressive feelings. Many children at age five or six will develop obsessive thoughts, possibly to compensate for sexual feelings their strict homes find abhorrent. They may refuse to ride in the car because of fear of accident; they know that the thought is irrational but cannot ignore it. A compulsive act is a repetitious, persistent mechanism to dissipate the energy engendered by anxiety. An overly neat, controlled child who carefully hangs up his clothes and keeps his room neat without being told is trying hard to control his anger and frustration in the face of overdemanding parents or what he thinks are overdemanding parents.

There must be some genetic predisposition to overcontrol as one child in a large family of slobs might demonstrate this obsessive compulsiveness for no apparent reason. He would be rewarded with praise by the mother who points him out as an example; he also might develop tics, twitches, or ulcers as a further "reward" for his overconformity.

As a child becomes more verbal, he should be allowed to express his anger, frustration, and hatred without fear of loss of love from his parents. As he matures, he can deal with his conscious awareness of these feelings and take suitable action to relieve the emotion. If, as a child, he learned or was taught to suppress all hostility, obsessive thoughts or compulsive acts arise which usually end up irritating others and thus give a distorted reduction of anger. However, they are poor substitutes, not only for the person himself, but for those in his environment. They can't really label the child's actions as hostile, but they are victimized just the same.

Perfectionism as an adolescent trait is usually the result of parental dissatisfaction with the child's performance during his younger years. The parents did not accept the child's behavior (or he thinks they did not) no matter how hard he tried. Because the parents were always disappointed in him, he incorporates this as his own life style. Personal dissatisfaction may paralyze his involvement in school, sports, and interpersonal relationships. He figures he cannot do anything well enough to suit his high standards, so he may do nothing. His parents belittle and nitpick; this only frustrates him or forces him to quit altogether.

He must be told to stop belittling himself and the parents must "get off his back." He is punishing himself enough already; overcoercion leads to passive aggression.

School phobia is a form of anxiety. In primary school children it is ordinarily a separation anxiety that the child has transferred to the school; it looms as the obvious villain in the plot to wreck his daily routine. He senses that his home is about to break up (parental hostility, impending divorce, etc.), and it might happen *today,* while he is away at school.

School phobia in a primary school child may actually represent the presence of healthy assertive or independent feelings in a child who is somewhat dependent. They may frighten him.

School phobia is one of the few psychological syndromes that occurs more frequently in girls. The cure rate is high.

School phobia in high school is very serious as it is usually associated with a severe neurosis or psychosis.

As in most psychological problems one theory of causation is too simplistic. A child may hate school—not fear it—because he is unsuccessful due to some neurological impairment or *dyslexia;* he would prefer to avoid another day of "You could do better if you tried." Another child may be *depressed,* uncomfortable, or preoccupied because of a stressful home and need to absent himself from an environment that is unsupportive.

Seclusiveness to the point of isolation from contact with the peer group is usually the result of a fear of failure. The child's real or imagined feelings of inferiority prevent him from entering in activities where he knows he will be ridiculed. Avoidance will naturally preclude the frustrating situation. *Daydreaming* is safer. It may be a *passive-aggressive* act in response to a *coercive* home or the natural retreat of an easily stimulated child to an overly-organized life.

The home and school life of a child who avoids peer group contact must be reevaluated. Pressure to conform must relax; a demanding schedule must be dropped. Just getting out of bed, eating, and going to school is usually enough organization for most children.

Shyness or social isolation is related to *seclusiveness* but is different in the quality of feeling. The shy child (old term: introvert) seems to be more of a spectator. He acts as if he *wants* to join in the fun but doesn't know how; the seclusive child actively avoids participation. His social needs may get him close to the action but his fear of embarrassment or failure may be so strong that he cannot participate. Forced involvement will only make him seclusive, a real isolate.

Our culture prizes the outgoing, brash, vigorous *mesomorph.* The thoughtful quiet child with thin muscles and bones is sure he will make some clumsy mistake so he refuses to join in the games. When he finds he is always the last one chosen, he becomes convinced he is unwanted and self-respect plummets. If he has no other successes going for him in school or hobbies, his withdrawal and *depression* may become pathological.

Self-confidence must be improved. Nitpicking is to be avoided; many children who have been constantly told they are "bums" come to believe it and act like bums. Ashamed, guilty, depressed, they seek self-glorification in seclusive day-dreaming.

Seclusiveness in the adolescent is so serious that it should be investigated, as the ultimate goal of the withdrawn child may be *suicide.* Overwhelming guilt, poor self-image, and chronic illness (*epilepsy, diabetes, minimal brain dysfunction*) feed on each other; if the home environment is unaccepting, full of turmoil and physically and verbally abusive, the adolescent seems almost paralyzed to speak or act as everything going wrong seems to be his fault.

One of the chief values of playmates and school contacts is to allow the growing child to learn how to get his way in the world and still have friends. We are social animals; we need to satisfy our physical urges (eating, sleeping, sexual outlets, territorial rights) without hurting others. If parental force is great enough to suppress the usual physical and verbal expression of normal hostility, withdrawal may be the only pathway to adjustment.

Early social contacts are important in learning how to cope. Parents who isolate or protect their children from the world are only making the ultimate debut into the adult world more traumatic for their child.

Suicide attempts in adolescents are not uncommon. Boys are more successful but many more girls make the attempt. *Psychoses*—schizophrenia and depression—are less likely to lead to this than a situational frustration coupled with a feeling of abject inferiority. The youth with poor impulse control, doing poorly at school, who has been told he could do better if he would try, develops a rotten self-image. He seeks sympathy and attention; he swallows a handful of his parents' tranquilizers, sleeping pills, antihistaminics, and aspirin; not before, however, he has dropped a few clues. He has usually told a teacher or a friend or left a note for his parents. He has become seclusive, sleepless, and has lost his appetite. Because these children have often displayed a long history of immature behavior, their parents, in an effort to "protect" them from themselves, frequently apply rigid control which the adolescent feels is intolerable. The attempt is a retaliation: "I'll show you." The attempt and the subsequent concern may be therapeutic or, at least, serve to initiate psychological care. Prevention when the obvious signals are hoisted makes more sense. Some effort should be made to bolster their self-esteem and reorganize their school and home environment to allow a little hope in.

Passive-aggressive reaction is the psychiatric term for stubborn, bull-headed, usually silent refusal to cooperate. The child seems to know what behavior his mother is most anxious for him to display, and then seems to delight in not performing it—won't be *toilet trained,* won't say "How do you do?" or shake hands or get dressed. *Dawdling* and *encopresis* are part of this reaction. Pouting is common.

The child usually resorts to this rebellion because he feels there are too many pressures on him to produce or perform at some arbitrary standard. He must be allowed some free time and/or be encouraged to verbalize his controlled hostility. He must be allowed to feel successful at something.

Dawdling is a *passive-aggressive* act that drives parents wild, because the harder they scream and cajole, the more skillful becomes the dawdler in his obstructionism. It becomes a way of life to many children who find it secures great attention with little effort. It may begin when the one-year-old loses his interest in food for eating, but wants to use it to experiment with the effects of gravity. The mother who insists on "finish your plate" teaches her child that dawdling will be rewarded with attention. If she can be reassured he will not starve, she will recognize that the meal is over and separate child and food. She must pretend it is unimportant. Toilet training is the next dawdling phenomenon that must be treated with masterful unconcern.

When breakfast is on the table and the school bus is coming down the road, dawdling in dressing wrecks the morning for the whole family. The child's feeling of self-responsibility would be enhanced by waking him early enough, having breakfast ready, and the path cleared. No coercion is expressed. If he is tardy, *he* has to face the teacher with some fumbling excuse. He was late; he must alter his behavior. The success of this method depends on the child's love for teacher and school. He may dawdle because school is an enemy, or he is academically unsuccessful. (See *Anxiety.*)

Encopresis is the repeated soiling of underwear by the passage of small amounts of stool which the child claims he knows nothing about. It is a form of aggression which drives most mothers frantic because there is no way to fight it. It is almost exclusively seen in boys, especially *hyperactive, disruptive* underachievers who are being hounded to sit still and do better. This enforced conformity suggests a passive rebellion—soiling. The treatment is directed at the mind, not the stool, but some effort must be made to determine if the victim is neurologically sound and not constipated from milk intake. A baby is expected to soil his diapers, but if a boy is over three years and not trained, the diagnosis is considered. A boy who has been trained, then develops encopresis after age four to six needs remedial steps immediately, as this habit pattern is extremely difficult to dislodge. The parents' punitive measures somehow encourage its continuation.

It may have its origin at toilet-training time when parents were persistently insistent, and the child's immaturity prevented conformity. Frustration → anxiety → anger → stool withholding. This progression may have been enhanced by the normal appetite loss, big milk intake at two or three years which usually leads to *constipation.* Retention over a few days is impossible, and some stool leaks out. The insulted mother reacts in anger, which sets the pattern.

Diet change (stop white foods and milk), stool softeners, allowing a ten-minute BM time after breakfast with reward for accomplishment—but no remarks or punishment for failure—will usually allow the child to relax and respond more appropriately to nature's call. Obviously some attention must be directed to improving the atmosphere at school and/or home. Verbal *aggression* is encouraged as a substitute for his rectal hostility. Pressure to make him achieve must cease. Psychiatric help to alter behavior and mood may be necessary.

School dropout is a growing indictment of the school's and society's failure to provide for the adequate education of our children. The dropout rate is high among children whose parents:

1. Quit school at an early age
2. Show little interest in academic achievement
3. Submit to the impulsive whims of their children
4. Push and nitpick their children into defiance
5. Continually show disappointment, lack of interest, or no warm acceptance.

Children with low academic achievement relative to their classmates because of *minimal brain damage, low IQ,* or sickness, frequently quit because of low self-esteem and frustration from taunts of classmates.

Some children drop out because of boredom; they may be stronger psychologically than their submissive classmates.

Permissiveness is that environmental life style that allows free and immediate gratification of every desire. A permissive home will allow a child to mature without internalized controls; he becomes a petulant, spoiled brat.

It must be remembered that not all impulsive, restless, driven children have been reared in laissez-faire homes. Some of these children are the result of a defective nervous system. (See *Minimal cerebral dysfunction,* Section 15.) These children do not have the nervous system equipment that is capable of storing this control.

Privacy should be the right of everyone, child or adult. A child cannot respect a hypocritical parent who preaches the right of privacy but who insists in eavesdropping, opening mail, probing the child's every thought and action. The child who has no privacy or is belittled suspects he is not considered trustworthy by his parents and may react with a variety of responses: depression, hostility, passive aggression. His damaged self-respect could encourage him to become revengeful; he may grow to become a cheater or engage in a business that bilks the innocent, just as he suffered at the hands of those he wanted to trust.

Psychosis is a serious psychological disorder; usually a large segment of the patient's total behavior is influenced by and under the control of the maladaptive process. In contrast, a *neurosis* usually affects only one part of the personality. The psychotic is not as good as the neurotic at hiding the kinds of behavior the public doesn't like.

Psychosis includes *Autism, Delusions, Paranoid disorder, Schizoid personality, Schizophrenia.*

Autism is a form of early childhood *schizophrenia.* Some evidence of its presence in the first few months of life is signaled by the reluctance of the infant to engage in social interaction—smiling, responding—when fed or held or entertained. That this peculiar behavior appears so early suggests that the condition is genetically or congenitally controlled, for it is difficult to blame the parents entirely for this severe psychic encapsulation. This child relates to humans as if they were inanimate pieces of furniture. He is classified as *mentally retarded* or *deaf* because of his immature and indifferent social behavior. But when testing is sometimes successful, abilities may be found to be higher than suspected, albeit deficient. Various strange withdrawal signs are found along with his desire to maintain a pathological, monotonous sameness in his surroundings.

Treatment is generally unrewarding but possible. At least a quarter of all autistic children will need to be institutionalized because of their unpredictable outbursts or severe intellectual retardation. Diet change and extra vitamin B_6 and zinc can be helpful.

Delusions are false beliefs. These are usually associated with schizophrenia, but may also be associated with fever or delirium. The patient is convinced he has a disease, or people are talking about him, or he is wealthy or powerful; the *paranoid* believes that others are out to get him. These thoughts may be transient in a magically thinking three- to six-year-old, but if persistent in an adolescent—not on drugs—this would suggest a *schizophrenic* disorder.

Paranoid disorder is rarely seen in children, although most children frequently display hostility, envy, and suspicion. The magical thinking three- to five-year-old tends to blame people, objects, and gravity for his own immaturity or lack of skill. A maladroit, *brain-damaged,* neurologically impaired child may be so frustrated by his inadequacies that he tends to blame others or the world for some of his problems. It is really quite depressing and ego destroying to continue to blame oneself for everything that goes wrong. Persistent projections of hate toward teachers and classmates may be transient, but may be the early signs of paranoid schizophrenia.

Delusions of persecution that make the adult paranoid are rare in children. They are almost impossible to eliminate, as they are a defense which protects the personality from complete disintegration.

Schizophrenia is considered a psychosis, as are severe *depression* and manic-depressive states. These are rare in childhood (as is *autism*), but bizarre reactions to people and things may be indicative of early trends toward psychological disturbance.

The psychotic child is too loud and boisterous, or too quiet and withdrawn. His speech is garbled or nonexistent. He lives in his own dream world, laughing or crying as if responding to an inner voice. Brain damage or encephalitis is suspected because of the severity of his withdrawal from the world.

Schizoid personality, or character disorder, is a term applied to those people who are loners. They make only peripheral social contacts and are obviously uncomfortable when faced with warm human contacts. They may drift in and out of schizophrenia, depending on environmental stresses.

Schizophrenia is an affective psychosis. The emotions of the patient are completely inappropriate to the situation. The schizophrenic seems to have withdrawn from the real world into his own fantasy life, or has set up his own system of delusions and hallucinations out of keeping with the facts. The absence of facial response to social contact is called a flattened affect. The victim seems to be looking through the interviewer. All thought processes seem to begin and end with the self.

This mental illness claims more people than any other disease except perhaps cancer and heart conditions. Until the advent of *tranquilizers,* more hospital beds were occupied by schizophrenics than by any other category of patient. Usually the onset is in adolescence; in a high percentage of patients the disease becomes chronic and requires continuous custodial care or long-term heavy drug therapy.

A young person may come to the doctor with bizarre somatic symptoms that have no physical explanation: "Water is moving around in my head," "A rolling pain in my back," "My hands are shrinking." His thoughts of self occupy him completely. A car stops a block away; he believes that he had something to do with it (ideas of personal reference). Things seem unreal as if "I am standing to one side watching myself do things" (depersonalization).

Withdrawal, sleeplessness, suspiciousness, shyness, inappropriate facial response to the subject discussed, and depression all may be present singly or in various combinations. The personality change makes the parents suspect drug abuse. Ritualistic repetition of bizarre mannerisms suggest that the patient is governed by some odd inner voice. The onset may be acute with violence, acting out, or mania, and the police may have to intervene. This psychiatric emergency requires physical restraint and drug sedation. Some schizophrenics seem to feel the world is such a threat that they must retreat back to the uterus. They regress completely back to the dependent infantile level, requiring tube feeding.

Frequently the patient's early environment has been devoid of warm, accepting humans. His early attempts at love were frustrated by a cold, indifferent, or absent parent. Recent compelling evidence casts new light on the genetic-biochemical theory of etiology. Hypoglycemia, excess copper, food allergies, low niacinamide may all contribute to their dysperceptions.

Because youths take drugs and because youths become schizophrenic, it is difficult to decide which leads to which. A drug experience in an incipient schizophrenic may encourage him to slip into his *psychosis.*

Self-esteem is the opinion one has of one's self. Self-devaluation is common in our country and in the civilizations that use guilt as a motivating force to control selfish drives. Everyone should be provided with a little of this sense of right and wrong, but if it is overdone, severe depression and suicide may supervene.

Parental attitudes that lead to this frustrating, self-destroying devaluation:

1. Constant harsh discipline for everything the child does (spilling milk, stumbling, soiling himself). Punishment for behavior the child cannot control because of slow or poor neuromuscular control is one of the most destructive things parents can do. The *impulsive, hyperactive* child is especially vulnerable because he seems accident-prone and almost congenitally unable to learn by past experience. He becomes especially depressed at about twelve to fifteen years of age when he realizes he cannot control himself without a pill; he hates himself at a time when even *normal* children are struggling with a self concept.
2. Perfectionistic parents never seem quite satisfied with the child's performance; the child grows to belittle himself no matter how adequate his achievements seem.
3. Overconcern about health may suggest to the child that he is not strong enough to perform.
4. Rejection and distrust by parents will be incorporated in the child; he will treat himself the same way.
5. Extremely moralistic, religious family attitudes may become a way of life for the child who is overwhelmed with guilt for every odd thought he may have. Hopefully, he may rebel somewhat against this rigidity, but shame and *guilt* for less than perfect performance may make him depressed or lead him to develop an *ulcer.*

Frequently a therapist will suggest as part of therapy that a parent spend more time alone with a child—really listening, not lecturing or moralizing. One effective way to do this is to plan an outing to a museum or a surprise meal in a restaurant. No strings attached. No suggestions must be made that the child must be good or behave. The implication the child receives is that he is being treated because he is an important person to the parent.

Some guidelines for the development of a reasonably normal human with a good self-image:

1. Do not expect too much or too little from a child. Each develops at a different rate. Letting the child decide about weaning and bowel training seems permissive, but is less frustrating and precludes some childhood anger and aggression.
2. Do not punish thoughts and feelings, but antisocial behavior or aggressive acts are to be limited.
3. Conditioning by a system of rewards for good behavior and ignoring some bad behavior is more suitable in "shaping" a child's behavior than only punishment for bad behavior. Consistency is an obvious ingredient.
4. Do nothing to devaluate a child's self-image. Wanting a child before he arrives and loving him once he gets here is the basis of human relations.
5. Do not usurp the child's right of personal responsibility. The child's homework may suffer if he watches too much TV; he must answer to the teacher for his deficiency. Parents should provide some general rules of eating and bedtime, but the child should have the option of what he will do with his uncommitted hours.

Sex

Exhibitionism, or the display of the genitalia, is almost exclusively confined to males. It's cute in a four-year-old who is a show-off, but represents an immature attention-getting device in the adolescent or adult. Psychotherapy seems obvious.

Fetishism is sexual gratification from touch, sight, or smell of a garment in place of a person of the opposite sex. It is more common in males and is the result of poor parental relationship. The child cannot identify with the proper parent, so turns to fetishism as a "safe" release of sexual urges.

Homosexuality is sexual attraction between individuals of the same gender. Arguments are still raging as to its cause or even if it is all that bad; most psychiatrists and psychologists feel that it is the result of a faulty environment, but others are convinced that genetic forces are the determinants. Many pediatricians believe that a mixture of forces is involved.

The confusion in the layman's mind stems from the fact that homosexuality may arise if the child has a domineering, seductive mother, and/or a hostile, weak, or absent father. And, of course, a homosexual may come from a family with none of these; the safe answer, then, is heredity and/or environment.

Many pediatricians deal with the weak, sickly, "floppy," unathletic boy who does poorly in rough sports and is called "sissy" or "fairy" by his peers. This putdown creates anger, frustration, and withdrawal into areas of success—cooking, clothes, quiet hobbies. Continued success in these areas reinforces these activities despite parental encouragement of more masculine pursuits. The more parents insist that their son "go out and play with the boys," the more he avoids these activities. This kind of maladroit child might just upset a muscular, *mesomorphic* father who imagines his son duplicating his own athletic career. Such a father sincerely believes that he is doing his son a favor by pushing physical exploits. The son knows he cannot possibly live up to these expectations, so refuses to cooperate. The father may become punitive in his insistence; *his* hostility and frustration may be what the psychiatrist sees as the major influence in the boy's avoidance of traditionally masculine activities. In a neurologically damaged child (who is physically incapable of "making the team") his father's efforts to push him into activities in which he is incompetent to participate and in which he can only anticipate failure, serve to drive the boy toward things that he can do with some sense of achievement and success. There seems to be a genetic predisposition that is aggravated by neurological and environmental forces.

No matter what the cause of homosexuality, if the patient is motivated, it is treatable. Up to 50 percent of cases can be encouraged sufficiently to accept heterosexual life. It is generally agreed that reversal of the trend can be effected if it comes to the attention of a psychiatrist or psychologist at an early age. Effeminate behavior which is consistent and persistent at age four or five years will not be outgrown. Family attitudes must be changed. An overprotective mother must stop seducing her son. An overbearing or hostile father must be willing to accept him.

Nagging and criticism will not help. *The child must first be ac-*

cepted as he is. Masculine activities should be encouraged; it is almost always possible to find *some* sport or physical activity that a child will enjoy and become interested in—swimming, hiking, mountain climbing, skiing, tennis, rock collecting—there are many alternatives to the football team. And a boy should not be suspect just because he is interested in art, music, or drama. There are many examples of completely masculine writers, poets, composers, and playwrights who never made a touchdown. If the father is absent, has turned off his son, or is unavailable or unwilling to be of help, an uncle, brother, grandfather, or other male substitute is essential. If the boy's father (or his substitute) is someone he can admire, not fear, he will want to imitate him and grow up to accept his masculine role. A boy also needs to be with his own age group and not tied to his mother's apron strings. He must be exposed to dirt and age-appropriate dangers.

The *transsexual* boy seems convinced that he is a girl. He loves to dress as a girl, play feminine games, is always the mother when the group plays house, is fascinated with makeup, jewelry, and other strictly feminine things.

Parents and teachers should be alert to the early signs of transsexualism in little boys. The intensity of this desire to be a girl is the determining factor that should alert the parents to seek help. These boys would dress in female clothing daily if allowed to; when denied this desire they become frustrated and depressed. They consistently insist that they want to be women when they grow up. This persistent, all-pervasive drive is in contrast to the usual boy who tries on his mother's clothes as a dress-up pretend game. The evidence is usually obvious by age two or three years.

The *transvestite,* when young, has usually been dressed in female clothing by an older woman. He gets sensual pleasure from this, although his behavior is quite boyish at other times.

These two types are clearly recognizable by age six, and early treatment is essential. Their behavior must be differentiated, however, from the play-acting and mimicry that all normal children indulge in. Wearing his mother's shoes, hat, or jewelry is just indicative that a boy is "testing." If he is normal, he does not object to having these things removed and does not compulsively put them on again. Good-natured tolerance is the mood the mother should convey.

Kinsey's investigations of sexual activities revealed that one third of normal adult males had had some sort of sexual contact with another male before maturity. Apparently these contacts were not enough to "fix" homosexuality but, in many cases, did create guilt. Follow-up studies on boys who were enticed into a sexual affair with an adult male indicated that it had not led them to accept homosexuality as a way of life unless they were already so predisposed. The child participated out of obedience or curiosity and suffered no psychic damage.

Not until recent, large investigations have been made has anyone realized the amount and variety of sexual activities—most of them performed by otherwise well-adjusted heterosexual humans. Apparently our overt traditional adherence to a stereotyped acceptable norm has been too rigid and has done naught but foster anxiety, guilt, remorse, and depression in those who have felt that slight idiosyncrasies were equivalent to queerness.

Homosexuality is a medical, social, and psychological problem, not a criminal offense, and must be taken out of the courts and put into the doctors' offices. Doctors must be willing to accept the challenge and not force these people to rally round the banner of the "third sex." It is a disease of incomplete psychosexual development, a sign of a disturbed neuropsychic childhood.

Masturbation is genital manipulation. It is most common in adolescent males, frequent in adolescent females, not uncommon in married, sexually adjusted couples, but is still considered "sinful" by much of society. Kinsey allowed a little fresh air to waft over this problem when he discovered that somewhat over 90 percent of males practiced it with frequent regularity, and at least 40 percent of females had used this method.

The three- to six-year-old child will often rub genitalia against a pillow, mattress, or furniture; the concerned parent should be reassured that it is part of the child's exploratory attempts in his learning about body function. Overconcern about the activity will encourage its continuation, as the child thinks, "Hey, I'm really onto something." Frequently an itch will develop from *bed-wetting* or drinking citrus, tomato, or chocolate; the child scratches the genitalia and finds more than local relief. It feels good, so he continues even when he switches to apple juice. He feels guilt when he notices the angry frustration on his parents' faces. With a reasonable child a parent might be able to teach discretion, but threats of "I'll cut it off," "You'll go crazy," "The boogie man will get you" serve to make the adolescent guilt about masturbation more overwhelming.

Each adolescent must resolve his own physiological drives. Some prefer to allow seminal fluid to build up until released in a vivid, sexual but safe dream. Some furtively masturbate in bathroom or bed with accompaniment of sexual fantasies. Some need to relieve the agonizing pelvic congestion after a sexually stimulating but not climactic date.

The universality of the practice and the associated guilt is indicated by the common gambit of the upper high schooler saying to the fourteen-year-old neophyte, "Did you know that if you masturbate, hair will grow on your palm?" Of course, the naïve youth will examine his hand for the first signs of sprouting growth; the guffaws at the boy's embarrassment reveal the guilt that the older one is relieved to share.

Sex education is the process of providing information and passing on attitudes to children that allow them to function as reasonably non-neurotic adults: content with the sex assigned to them by their genes. Organ names and mechanics are learned from animals, playmates, parents, sex hygiene courses. Feelings, sex drives, acceptance of maleness or femaleness are largely determined by the tone of the child's early home environment.

The jurisdictional dispute over who teaches what is the basis for the concern of parents about sex education courses in the schools. Some parents feel that they should be the ones to instill a healthy attitude toward sex—in their own time and in the comfortable, natural setting of the home. Sex educators cite case after case involving otherwise intelligent young people who have fallen into sexual problems because of naiveté or simply a lack of accurate information. They feel that if the adolescent is given sexual facts in the objective classroom by a skilled teacher, he will be armed with enough common sense to make the "right decision" when hormones urge novel adventures.

Many well-meaning parents feel that if the subject is not discussed, the adolescent will not think about it and he or she can be maintained nearly virginal until safely placed in the marriage bed. The rising rate of venereal disease, unwed mothers, and pregnant brides, suggests that this attitude is not working. Religious teaching, threats of punishment or banishment have not served to stem the rate of sexual activity. Sex drives seem to overwhelm cerebral control in the most intelligent, moral young people. Desire is almost unavoidable if they are healthy and normal and together for more than twenty-five minutes. Mother Nature wants the race to go on.

Sleep problems. Someone said that sleep is our natural state, and that we arise only to eat and eliminate. Sleep is needed by everyone—for varying amounts of time. If deprived of sleep and dream time, humans become mean, irritable, and occasionally *psychotic.* Anxious people have trouble getting to sleep. *Schizophrenics* and the severely depressed have reduced REM (rapid eye movements) sleep, suggesting decreased time spent dreaming, thus adding to their distress.

The small infant, sans colic, will spend twenty hours a day in sleep; the exhaustion of his rapid growth seems to dictate this.

At one year of age, a child sleeps twelve hours a night and takes a one- to three-hour nap. This pattern is fairly constant until age four to six when he gives up his nap, although he still seems to need it. If his exhausted mother can compromise with a quiet time for an hour or so after lunch, she is doing well. If, however, he happens to sleep during nap time, he will be alert until 10 or 11 P.M.

REM sleep for normal infants is 50 percent of sleep time; by age two years REM is at the adult level of 20 to 25 percent of sleep time. A minimum REM time is a nightly requirement; if this is reduced, a debt accumulates which must be made up in subsequent nights, or symptoms mentioned above occur.

A typical young adult drifts down to deep sleep, and in about an hour and a half rises to light sleep and enters REM sleep. After ten to twenty minutes of this, he goes through the cycle again. There are about five cycles (ninety minutes each) per usual eight-hour sleep period. People who claim they did not sleep a wink may have been in a light sleep with much REM activity.

Enuresis, somnambulism, and night terrors have not been correlated with REM sleep but are associated with arousal from deep sleep. *Nightmares,* somnambulism and restlessness are common in children. Although emotional tension, family strife, school problems may be inciting agents, *pinworms* must be considered and searched for. Most pediatricians assume that a child (or adult) with any night problem has worms. A preliminary search for them may be rewarding. It is not necessary to see the worms, but it is nice to know what is being treated. A few days after the treatment has been initiated, the child should sleep restfully again. If there is no improvement, nocturnal *seizures* (an *EEG* is needed for the diagnosis) or psychic problems or an *allergy* should be considered.

A child with somnambulism usually wanders about the house with his eyes open. Most eventually return to bed and remember nothing the following day. If awakened during the act, he may be frightened but is usually just confused.

Sleep rarely comes by parental fiat, but rules are worthwhile as a security aid. An appropriate bedtime should be insisted upon. Consistency and firmness despite protests will help develop self-control and eventual respect for fair parents.

Positive influences: vigorous outdoor physical exercise, hot bath, hot supper, quiet, congenial atmosphere, single-bed occupancy, single occupancy in room, favorite toy, 500 to 1,000 milligrams calcium (dolomite), protein snack. No sugar!

Negative influences: noisy, unhappy home, multiple occupancy in room and bed, sedentary activities all day, *pinworms, allergies,* separation *anxiety,* stimulation, and roughhouse immediately before bed. About one in fifteen or twenty children is *hyperactive* to the point that minimal stimulation precludes relaxation; these children sing, toss about, and find excuses to get out of bed as if they know that relaxing with their eyes shut will bring sleep. They act as if they're afraid they'll miss something.

Won't go to sleep. This seems to be so typical of the two-year-old that it suggests normality. *If* the usual rituals have been completed *and* all inducements have been exhausted, a sedative about a half hour before bedtime might get the child started. The only trouble is that the usual sedatives that induce sleep in adults have a stimulating effect on most children. The barbiturates are usually worthless. They also have been found to reduce dream (REM) time. *Chloral hydrate, Thorazine®, Mellaril®,* and *Stelazine®* are more effective. The somnient effect of antihistamines may be taken advantage of here—*Phenergan®, Benadryl®,* Temaril®, *chlorpheniramine.* The use of these drugs is superior to allowing the child to fall asleep in the parents' bed—a terribly difficult habit to break.

Awakens one to six hours after falling asleep. This is not a habit. The habit is the child's expectation of reward once he has been awakened by his built-in arousal system or *worms, gas,* or other causes. The wise mother will go the child's bed, assure herself that he is not sick or has his foot caught, and return to bed *without* cuddling

SLEEP RESISTANCE AND NIGHT WAKEFULNESS

	Possible Causes	
Age	*Won't go to sleep*	*Awakens after going to sleep*
Birth to 6 months	Hunger Colic Overstimulation	Hunger; Colic; lost pacifier; too small bed; sickness; earache; cutting teeth; urine contacting open sores; urinary infection
6 months to 15 months	Overstimulation Fear of separation "Spoiled" (?) Nap too long Low calcium	Ear infection; fever; pinworms; diaper rash; gas from food; croup; allergy to pillow, blanket, or toy; low calcium
15 months to 3 years	Playing a "game" Anxiety, fear of separation Nap too long	Pinworms; diaper rash; sickness; teething; bed too small; refused to have bowel movement during day, relaxes and has it at night
3 to 5 years	Nap too long Overstimulated. Spoiled? No rules "Ghosts" or "snakes" in room Family arguments in next room	Pinworms; sickness; fall out of bed
5 years on	Doesn't need so much sleep Parents fighting House too noisy	Pinworms; sickness; full bladder; seizure

him, fooling with him, or feeding him. She does nothing that could possibly be interpreted as a reward for his wakefulness. He must learn to turn over and go back to sleep like the rest of us do. He may fuss and cry for one to six hours, but he must not be catered to. If the mother finally goes in after three hours, he assumes the next night that he must cry three hours before she will come.

The older child who cannot drop off to sleep until 9 to 11 P.M. should be allowed to read in bed with his own night light as he bothers no one and as long as he awakens refreshed in the morning.

Superego is the conscience, or set of values, that the child develops largely through his parents' insistence that he control his impulsiveness; otherwise he might lose their love. A "nice" adult has a built-in sense of social-moral values; if he deviates from this self-control, he feels guilty or depressed. His internalized "parent" punishes him.

Improper parenting, *brain damage,* or a combination of factors inherited and environmental may distort the development of the superego. An overpowering superego will hold an adult almost immobile or at least joyless. Little or no superego control is assumed to be the cause of the criminal or sociopath or antisocial personality, though low blood sugar from sugar ingestion or food allergy will also prevent the optimum functioning of the conscience.

Guilt is one of the motivating forces in Western civilization that pressures individuals to be law-abiding. If the parents have been successful, the child will grow into an adult who is able to control his impulses but not be too constricted.

Overwhelming guilt will lead to paralyzing depression—the result of saddling the child's personality with a poor self-image.

Discipline helps the child internalize impulse control so that as he grows, his sense of right and wrong is usually fixed. He cannot deviate from learned responses in his conscience without anxiety. But children come in all grades of sensitiveness, and a variety of methods is needed to control different children in the same family. One may need only a raised eyebrow to help him recognize a transgression; another may need a wooden spoon on his buttocks to help him control his impulsiveness.

Discipline is necessary to protect the toddler from self-destruction. Usual no-no's: "Don't run in the street; the car will run over you." "Don't climb up there; you'll fall and crack your head." "Don't eat that medicine [soap, polish, etc.]; you'll kill yourself." "Don't touch the stove; you'll get burned." Variations are endless. A child has to be exposed to a few dangers in the safety of a secure home so he may file the information away for future automatic avoidance—gravity works, fire burns, knives are sharp, and so forth.

As he becomes more socially aware at two years or so, he must learn that if he hurts others, he will get hurt or he will lose love of mother and/or new friend. If his nervous system is normal and his mother is balancing praise and love and limits, he will learn self-control of his normal aggressiveness.

When discipline sinks to constant nagging and haranguing, the parent should begin to wonder if the child is actually getting some reward out of all the aggravation he stirs up. Simple declarative sentences and brief isolation are worth more than continued reasoning—especially if the reasoning is not working.

A practical suggestion: if your two- to five-year-old has been a non-conforming pest all day, but none of his aggravations have been obnoxious enough to demand immediate countermoves, a period of isolation in his room (better still, a room without toys) might break the cycle of mounting anger. "Stay there five minutes until you feel better; I'll call you when it's time." Then if he deliberately defies, two smacks on his bare buttocks are supposed to let him know you are consistent and mean what you say. If punishment seems necessary, however, it suggests the child or the parent is sick.

Consistent limits must be set that are reasonable for the age. Force must not be used to make a child accomplish some act that he is not neurologically prepared to perform. (For example, don't hurry toilet training.) Shaming a child about behavior he could not control (bed-wetting) is self-defeating.

If they think it worked for them, parents usually adopt the attitudes they learned from their own parents and use similar child-rearing methods. Parents who must have autocratic, protective dominance over their children will usually rear obedient but shy or effeminate boys and inhibited girls. If a child in this type of household is impulsive, gabby, and *hyperactive,* he may come to grief because he is unable to internalize the self-control which seems to be the accepted norm in this household. He is labeled "bad" in this environment; he figures, since he is already classified, he might as well act that way. He is more likely to drop out of school ("If you would just sit still, you would do better work"), run away from home ("You are a pest; just get hold of yourself"), and/or take up drug use because he has no success at the "square" pursuits. The trick is somehow to indicate to the aggressive or destructive child that his behavior is inappropriate and he needs to apply some control. This has to be done without destroying his own self-respect. Praise must balance blame, although the balance is often precarious.

The small, helpless, cute, laughing, under-ten-month-old is such a joy to the home it is hard to believe that in another year and a half he will have turned into such an aggravation—not eating, not *trained, whining,* into everything. The parents still love him, of course, because of the earlier programming, but they don't have to like his behavior.

Temper tantrum is a form of communication by which the verbally inadequate fifteen- to eighteen-month-old expresses his anger and frustration. It must be a normal phase of development in social living because almost all children pass through this period. The child wants to put his finger on the hot stove, his mother says, "That's a no-no!" and the child falls on the floor kicking and screaming.

These episodes will decrease with time if the mother does not "reward" the child for them, either with cuddling and love, or spankings and punishment. Boys seem to be more prone to these tantrums, not only because they are innately physical in their responses, but because *speech* development is slower than it is in girls. As soon as the child learns to swear (he learned it at the neighbors') or imitate "No-no!" he is able to communicate on a higher level than the physical or acting-out level.

While the child is growing and is largely under the influence of his basic drives of hunger, aggression, "mine" and "gimme," the new brain is developing. As the nerve fibers of his neocortex become functional, the mother rewards him (and it) for increasing impulse control until these responses become automatic. It cannot be rushed, since learning waits on maturation. Self-control cannot be learned until the self-control nerves have matured.

The love-and-limits concept is difficult for some mothers to maintain if they are tired, neurotic, or unaided by a loving, sympathetic husband. A normal mother makes plenty of mistakes and is sometimes inconsistent or unfair, but if the child was wanted, her overall care will average out. She knows how to respond to his demands, to smile, to show her love appropriately, to set limits to aggression, and rewards his socially acceptable behavior with her approval.

Much of a child's feelings of frustration and pessimism can be traced to the parents' attitudes following infancy. They may have been loving and accepting so long as he was a baby, but by the time he was eighteen months old (with a nervous system just barely able to manage finger foods) have expected him to eat neatly. They may have punished him and called him a bad boy when he did not accomplish *toilet training* by age two years. They indicated that he was not living up to their (or what he thought was their) standards. (These parental demands are said to be more prevalent in the Nordic races.) The acceptance of failure becomes a part of his conscience and hounds him all of his days.

If his parents have accepted him with all his faults, a child develops a good self-image. If they cannot accept all his faults but at least do not look on them as a deliberate plot to unhinge their home, that probably is good enough. He controls his aggressive, elbowing ways because his loving parents disapprove. He matures.

Tests

Bender-Gestalt test (Section 15)

Denver Developmental Screening Test is designed for professional use only and is a practical method of evaluating the integrity of the growing child's neuromuscular apparatus. It gives guidelines for normal achievement of head holding, sitting, standing, running, and other motor functions, of babbling and speech functions (language), and of social or adaptive responses. It is somewhat predictive of general intellectual levels, neurological deficiencies, and some specific sensory problems. It mainly determines if a child is within normal developmental levels for his age.

Draw-a-Man test is one of a number of methods used to determine in a general way whether a child is retarded and if there are some organic defects in his nervous system. The beauty of the test is its simplicity. The child is given pencil or crayon and paper, and asked to draw a picture of a person. The four-year-old draws a circle for body-head, the extremities are represented by single lines, and a few dots indicate a face.

The six-year-old will divide the body into definite head and trunk sections; the neck usually does not appear until age seven. Eyes, nose, mouth, and ears are usually present by six, as are fingers and a few clothes. The nine-year-old's drawing is fairly sophisticated or photographic.

Deviations from these norms, if associated with *hyperactivity, impulsivity, distractibility,* or school failure would suggest psychological and neurological evaluation to pinpoint the problem more accurately.

The child's drawing can also be used as a projective test if he is asked to tell about the person he drew.

Intelligence quotient is the value determined by dividing the mental age by the chronological age and multiplying by one hundred. Roughly speaking, if a ten-year-old child scores at the eight-year-old level on an intelligence test, his IQ score is 8 over 10 times 100, or 80. After much testing and refining, intelligence tests are now perfected to the extent that the usual white North American child can be evaluated for his ability to get along in school. A psychologist once said that the intelligence test measures whatever the intelligence test is supposed to measure.

The development of the Stanford-Binet and Wechsler Intelligence tests was based on the concept that the average individual would achieve a score of 100, with the majority of the population in this country falling within the 90 to 110 range. If the child can see, hear, and is not too distractible, the tests are fairly accurate after age five years. Obviously, the test must make allowances for language and cultural differences.

Most intelligence tests can make a pretty good assessment of the child's general level of knowledge, reasoning, memory, and judgment abilities. They can detect a number of neurological defects and psychological problems.

School systems are relying on psychological testing for problem children as an aid in placing them in some academic holding area (special class for *mentally retarded* or *hyperactive,* brain-damaged, retention in first grade for a second year, or other adjustments to the academic program). The chief drawback is that once the child is labeled, he soon becomes what his label says he is. The intelligence quotient is a summary rating of how a person compares with large numbers of other people on intelligence test performance. The usefulness of an IQ score depends upon the test used, what it is being used for, who is using it, and occasionally, what the person had for breakfast on the day he was measured.

Ordinarily, a well-trained psychologist can provide the most professional interpretation of an IQ and an analysis of skills that make it up.

Rorschach test is a projective test that is widely used to measure a patient's cognitive (thinking) and affective (feeling) abilities. He is asked to describe what he sees in a series of ten inkblots, half of which have some color. His responses are graded and compared with more or less standard responses.

Thematic Apperception Test (TAT) allows the psychologist to measure and evaluate a patient's personal concerns and conflicts. He is shown a number of pictures and asked to make up a story about each. The patient usually projects his attitudes toward other people into the pictures.

Wechsler-Bellevue Intelligence Scale is usually considered a test of intelligence, but the individual's ego strength and his adaptive abilities can be noted also. There are ten parts to the test. The vocabulary subtest is the best prediction of overall IQ score. Using all the tests is the best way to evaluate all thinking (cognitive) functions or ego abilities. Ability to function in problem-solving situations is measured.

Underachievement is a discrepancy between what someone thinks the child's accomplishments should be and his actual attainments. One group of students is termed "socially oriented underachievers." They work for rewards of social interaction rather than for academic achievement. At some point the child anticipates he will be a failure and attempts to substitute social attention in place of the recognition for accomplishment he would really prefer to have.

The following signs will be recorded: These children work only when the teacher hovers over and heckles them. They display attention-getting behavior such as falling out of chairs, making noise, and annoying other students. They seek contact at an immature level through hitting, kissing, tapping, and pushing. They may be well liked and considered charming, or they may irritate other children and be called pests. Their written school work is usually incomplete and sloppy, even though their oral work may be satisfactory. They may know the material but do not hand in assignments; they begin work enthusiastically but do not finish. Dallying behaviors such as pencil-sharpening, daydreaming, and walking around the room are common. Teachers view them as challenges and show them a great deal of coercive and affectionate attention. They keep them after class or at recess, reason with them, help them with homework, cheer them on, and allow them free access to school counselors. This attention constitutes a reward for underachievement. They may be mistaken for children with the *hyperactive syndrome.*

A school counselor or psychologist aware of what is going on will be able to arrange 1) thorough elimination of attention for the underachieving behavior and 2) specific rewards from teacher and peers for productive work within the child's current skill level.

Whining is a trait peculiar to the two-year-old who is communicating his frustration to his parents. His language skills are rudimentary and he has not learned the value of an appropriate, incisive swear word. He has found that his mother ignores last year's temper tantrum. He also notes and is somehow rewarded by the exasperated look on her face when he whines, so he continues this until boredom or expressive language supervenes. Studied indifference should be the parents' role in coping with this temporary but entirely normal growth phase.

If excessive—whining more than 55 percent of the time—it might be worthwhile to treat for worms or search for an infection (ear or bladder) or change the diet.

Bibliography

ARENA, JAY M. *Poisoning.* Springfield, Ill.: Charles C. Thomas, 1970.

ARNOLD, ARNOLD. *Teaching Your Child to Learn.* Englewood Cliffs, N. J.: Prentice-Hall, Inc., 1971.

BELTZ, STEPHEN. *How to Make Johnny Want to Obey.* Englewood Cliffs, N.J.: Prentice-Hall, Inc., 1971.

BLOCK, WILLIAM A. *What Your Child Really Wants to Know About Sex—and Why.* Englewood Cliffs, N.J.: Prentice-Hall, Inc., 1972.

BRAIN, LORD, and JOHN N. WALTON. *Diseases of the Nervous System.* London: Oxford University Press, 1969.

CROSBY, R. M. N., and R. A. LISTON. *The Waysiders: A New Approach in Reading and the Dyslexic Child.* New York: Delacorte Press, 1968.

DREISBACK, ROBERT H. *Handbook of Poisoning: Diagnosis and Treatment.* Los Angeles: Lange Medical Publications, 1959.

GARDNER, LYTT I. *Endocrine and Genetic Diseases of Childhood.* Philadelphia: W. B. Saunders Company, 1969.

HARRIS, M. COLEMAN, and NORMAN SHURE. *All About Allergy.* Englewood Cliffs, N.J.: Prentice-Hall, Inc., 1969.

HENDERSON, NEIL C. *How to Understand and Treat Your Child's Symptoms.* Englewood Cliffs, N.J.: Prentice-Hall, Inc., 1971.

HYMES, JAMES, JR. *The Child Under Six.* Englewood Cliffs, N.J.: Prentice-Hall, Inc., 1963.

KELLOGG, RHODA. *Analyzing Children's Art.* New York: National Press, 1969.

LERNER, MORRIS. *Practical Pediatric Dermatology.* St. Louis: C. V. Mosby, 1961.

NATHAN, PETER. *The Nervous System.* Philadelphia: J. B. Lippincott Company, 1969.

NELSON, WALDO E. *Textbook of Pediatrics.* Philadelphia: W. B. Saunders Company, 1969.

PFEIFFER, CARL C. *Mental and Elemental Nutrients.* New Canaan, Conn.: Keats Publishing, Inc., 1976.

PRICE, WESTON A. *Nutrition and Physical Degeneration.* La Mesa, Calif.: Price-Pottenger Nutrition Foundation, 1970.

SHELDON, JOHN M., ROBERT G. LOVELL, and KENNETH P. MATTHEWS. *A Manual of Clinical Allergy.* Philadelphia: W. B. Saunders Company, 1967.

SHELDON, WILLIAM. *Varieties of Temperament.* New York: Harper Bros., 1942.

SMITH, LENDON H. *The Children's Doctor.* Englewood Cliffs, N.J.: Prentice-Hall, Inc., 1969.

———. *Feed Your Kids Right.* New York: McGraw-Hill Book Company, 1979.

———. *Improving Your Child's Behavior Chemistry.* Englewood Cliffs, N.J.: Prentice-Hall, Inc., 1976.

———. *New Wives' Tales: Conversations with Parents About Today's Pediatrics.* Englewood Cliffs, N.J.: Prentice-Hall, Inc., 1974.

INDEX